NINTH EDITION

DYNAMIC PHYSICAL EDUCATION FOR SECONDARY SCHOOL STUDENTS

TIMOTHY A. BRUSSEAU
UNIVERSITY OF UTAH

HEATHER ERWIN
UNIVERSITY OF KENTUCKY

PAUL W. DARST
ARIZONA STATE UNIVERSITY

ROBERT P. PANGRAZI
ARIZONA STATE UNIVERSITY

HUMAN KINETICS

Library of Congress Cataloging-in-Publication Data

Names: Brusseau, Timothy A., Jr. author. | Erwin, Heather, 1979- author. | Darst, Paul W., author. | Pangrazi, Robert P., author.
Title: Dynamic physical education for secondary school students / Timothy A. Brusseau, University of Utah, Heather Erwin, University of Kentucky, Paul W. Darst, Arizona State University, Robert P. Pangrazi, Arizona State University.
Description: Ninth edition. | Champaign, IL : Human Kinetics, [2021] | "This book is a revised edition of Dynamic Physical Education for Secondary School Students, eighth edition, published in 2015 by Pearson Education, Inc" -- T.p. verso. | Includes bibliographical references and index.
Identifiers: LCCN 2020011611 (print) | LCCN 2020011612 (ebook) | ISBN 9781492591092 (paperback) | ISBN 9781492591108 (epub) | ISBN 9781492591115 (pdf)
Classification: LCC GV365 .P36 2021 (print) | LCC GV365 (ebook) | DDC 613.7071/2--dc23
LC record available at https://lccn.loc.gov/2020011611
LC ebook record available at https://lccn.loc.gov/202001161

ISBN: 978-1-4925-9109-2 (paperback)
ISBN: 978-1-7182-0025-8 (loose-leaf)

The web addresses cited in this text were current as of February 2020, unless otherwise noted.

Acquisitions Editor: Scott Wikgren; **Developmental Editor:** Jacqueline Eaton Blakley; **Managing Editor:** Anna Lan Seaman; **Copyeditor:** Bob Replinger; **Indexer:** Michael Ferreira; **Permissions Manager:** Dalene Reeder; **Graphic Designer:** Sean Roosevelt; **Cover Designer:** Keri Evans; **Cover Design Specialist:** Susan Rothermel Allen; **Photograph (cover):** kali9 / Getty Images; **Photographs (interior):** © Human Kinetics, unless otherwise noted on the Photo Credits page; **Photo Asset Manager:** Laura Fitch; **Photo Production Manager:** Jason Allen; **Senior Art Manager:** Kelly Hendren; **Illustrations:** © Human Kinetics, unless otherwise noted; **Production:** Walsworth

We thank the STEAM Academy in Lexington, Kentucky, for assistance in providing the location for the photo shoot for this book.

Printed in the United States of America   10 9 8 7 6 5 4 3 2

The paper in this book was manufactured using responsible forestry methods.

Human Kinetics
1607 N. Market Street
Champaign, IL 61820
USA

United States and International
Website: **US.HumanKinetics.com**
Email: info@hkusa.com
Phone: 800-747-4457

Canada
Website: **Canada.HumanKinetics.com**
Email: info@hkcanada.com

Tell us what you think!
Human Kinetics would love to hear what we can do to improve the customer experience. Use this QR code to take our brief survey.

E7809 (paperback) / E8170 (loose-leaf)

To my wife, Megan, for the constant love and support. To my children, Cooper and Adalyn, who inspire and motivate me every day.

—Timothy A. Brusseau

To my family: Aaron, your excitement for *Dynamic Physical Education for Secondary School Students* is energizing, and I am grateful for your support. Libby, Emily, Faith, and Hope, I love watching you grow into beautiful young women and find physical activities you each enjoy.

—Heather Erwin

To my wife, Charlene; my son, Seth; my daughter, Jessica; and my five grandchildren, Callie, Kenna, Hayden, Raegan, and Kylee. Fitness and physical activity are a defining part of each of their lives. I am most appreciative of having their continuing love and support and being included in their many athletic and dance endeavors. Quality physical education has been at the center of our lives for the past 50 years. Although it is changing in appearance and presentation, it is still one of the most important aspects of education. Thanks, too, to the multitude of students who have enhanced our lives.

—Paul W. Darst

To my wife, Deb, whom I love and respect. She is not only a valued professional colleague but also a special friend and companion who has enriched my life. I regard Deb as a silent author who has contributed much to this textbook.

—Robert P. Pangrazi

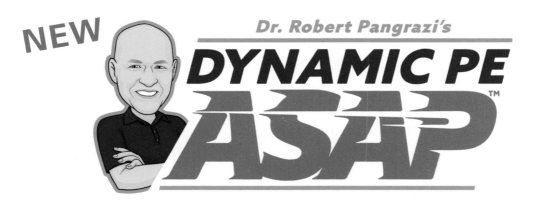

NEW — Dr. Robert Pangrazi's

DYNAMIC PE ASAP™

Create FREE PE Lessons in Seconds!

With the cooperation of two outstanding companies, Human Kinetics and Gopher Sport, we are offering a free online curriculum guide that complements *Dynamic Physical Education for Secondary School Students, Ninth Edition.* It is located at DynamicPEASAP.com, and it's fast, effective, and free! The lessons and activities provided cover grades K-8. Therefore, you will select the "5-8" section to find the lessons and activities directly related to content covered in *Dynamic Physical Education for Secondary School Students, Ninth Edition.* Using this site will help you learn the process of building lessons, a curriculum, and a yearly plan for middle school physical education. The process you learn will also prepare you for creating a high school program.

Visit DynamicPEASAP.com for FREE lesson plans today!

DPE ASAP offers the flexibility and depth you need to design a curriculum that meets your local needs.

DPE ASAP is an Internet-based curriculum that is broad in scope, yet easy to manage, modify, and organize.

DPE ASAP is based on the evidence-based, field-tested textbook *Dynamic Physical Education for Elementary School Children*, which has sold more than a million copies. It is also closely affiliated with *Dynamic Physical Education for Secondary School Students, Ninth Edition.*

Easily take lessons with you on the go! Dynamic PE ASAP now features more ways to use your unique lessons. Download and print your favorite lesson plans on 5" x 8" activity cards or view them on any device.

Scan to visit
DynamicPEASAP.com

Creating lesson plans has never been easier!

 ## Browse Lessons

Step 1: Easily filter and browse lessons based on your specific interests! Choose from hundreds of options for grades K-8 that include Introductory Activities, Fitness Development, Lesson Focuses, and Closing Activities.

 ## Add the Lessons You Like

Step 2: Once you've found the activities that meet your needs for each class, build your complete lesson by simply dragging and dropping the four components of a complete lesson plan to the designated fields.

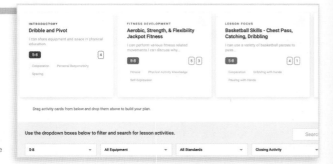

 **Introductory Activity**
Instant activities that physiologically prepare students for activity and the upcoming lesson.

 Fitness Development
Familiarize students with physical fitness principles and fitness-related activities.

 Lesson Focus
Teach physical skills and movements that are aligned with SHAPE standards and specific instructional objectives.

 Closing Activity
Games or cooperative activities that help students apply skills learned during the Lesson Focus.

 ## Save Lessons

Step 3: Once you have your completed lesson plan, save it and name it! Whether you build just one, or plan your entire year, your lesson plans will be saved and stored for you to use as desired.

> Also available to you is the Dynamic PE Yearly Plan, which has 36 weeks of preconfigured lesson plans for grades 5-8. There are enough plans to last you the entire year!

 ## Download, Print, and Go

Step 4: Quickly download and print (or just download to use electronically) your lesson plan, and you're ready to go!
It's that easy!

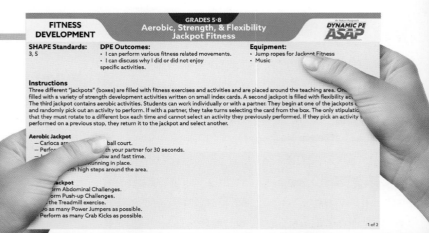

Visit DynamicPEASAP.com to start building your FREE lessons today!

What's in a Lesson Plan?

A yearly curriculum offers a roadmap to success. Without adequate planning it is difficult to know your ultimate goals (SHAPE standards) and your student expectations (DPE outcomes). In addition to standards and outcomes, DPE ASAP lessons are organized by grade level with equipment and keywords listed. These are important, but the real core of instruction is the activities. Instructional activities are listed in order of difficulty to help teachers meet the developmental needs of all students. Teaching hints explain how to organize your lesson and are based on the advice of experienced and successful teachers.

Each lesson falls into one of four lesson parts:
- Introductory Activity
- Fitness Development
- Lesson Focus
- Closing Activity

DPE ASAP outcomes list specific behaviors you should expect your students to learn.

Each lesson contains enough activities for a week of instruction.

It is not expected that all activities will be taught. It is best to teach a few activities well rather than many activities in a cursory manner.

Activities and skills are presented in progression of less to more challenging.

Basketball Skills - Chest Pass, Catching, Dribbling

LESSON FOCUS

Outcomes:

I can use a variety of basketball passes to pass to a moving partner.
can dribble and pass to a partner.

Instructions:

Skills
Practice the following skills:
1. Chest (or Two-Hand) Pass
   For the chest, or two-hand, pass, one foot is ahead of the other, with the knees flexed slightly. The ball is released at chest level, with the fingers spread on each side of the ball. The elbows remain close to the body, and the ball is released by extending the arms and snapping the wrists as one foot moves toward the receiver.
2. Catching
   Receiving the ball is a most important fundamental skill. Many turnovers involve failure to handle a pass properly. The receiver should move toward the pass with the fingers spread and relaxed, reaching for the ball with elbows bent and wrists relaxed. The hands should give as the ball comes in.
3. Dribbling
   Dribbling is used to advance the ball, break for a basket, or maneuver out of a difficult situation. The dribbler's knees and trunk should be slightly flexed, with hands and eyes forward. The fingertips propel the ball with the hand cupped and relaxed. There is little arm motion. Students tend to slap at the ball rather than push it. The dribbling hand should be alternated.
4. Shooting - One-Hand (set) Push Shot
   The one-hand push shot is used as a set shot for young children. The ball is held at shoulder-eye level in the supporting hand with the shooting hand slightly below center and behind the ball. As the shot begins, the supporting (non-shooting) hand remains in contact as long as possible. The shooting hand then takes over with fingertip control, and the ball rolls off the center three fingers. The hand and wrist follow through, finishing in a flexed position. Vision is focused on the hoop during the shot. Proper technique should be emphasized rather than accuracy.

Drills
Passing and Catching Drills
1. Slide Circle Drill
   In the slide circle drill, a circle of four to six players slides around a person in the center. The center person passes to and receives from the sliding players. After the ball has gone around the circle twice, another player takes the center position.

Add to Lesson Plan

Print Lesson

Print on Index Cards

View Assessment

Grade Level:
5-8

Equipment:
Junior Basketballs
8.25" Coated-Foam Balls

Standards:
1 4

Keyword
Cooperation
Dribbling with hands
Passing with Hands

There are many ways to view lessons. They can be printed on 8.5" x 11" paper or 5" x 8" cards. If desired, they can be uploaded to your mobile phone or iPad as a PDF file.

Three distinct sets of lesson plans by grade level are offered.

The amount and type of equipment, music, and instructional signs needed for the lesson are listed.

SHAPE national standards are listed for each lesson.

Video

Video Training

Dr. Pangrazi walks us through using the Dynamic PE ASAP website. He also shares helpful tips for implementing the lessons into your program.

Activity Videos

The Dynamic PE ASAP digital curriculum now features more than 100 free lesson plan videos. Learn how to teach curriculum lessons from trained PE professionals.

Dynamic PE ASAP Yearly Plan

The yearly plan lists 36 weeks of lesson plans for three distinct grade levels: K-2, 3-4, and 5-8. The majority of activities for younger children (K-2) are individual in nature and center on learning movement concepts and cooperative activities. Lessons for 3-4 are focused on helping youngsters refine fundamental skills and learn visual-tactile skills. Emphasis is placed on giving students the opportunity to explore, experiment, and create activities without fear. Students in grades 5-8 begin a shift toward learning specialized skills and sport activities. Students learn team play through cooperative sport lead-up activities. Adequate time is set aside for the rhythmic program and gymnastics-type activities.

[5-8] Week 17 + Save to Your Plans	● Dribble and Pivot	● Partner Aerobic Fitness & Resistance Exercises	● Basketball Skills - Chest Pass, Catching, Dribbling	● Flag Dribble; Captain Basketball; Sideline Basketball
[5-8] Week 18 + Save to Your Plans	● Barker's Hoopla	● Partner Aerobic Fitness & Resistance Exercises	● Basketball Skills - Defending, Lay-up, Jump shot	● Twenty-One; Lane Basketball; One-Goal Basketball
[5-8] Week 19 + Save to Your Plans	● Run, Stop and Pivot	● Exercises to Music	● Throwing Skills	● In the Prison; Center Target Throw; Target Ball Throw
[5-8] Week 20 + Save to Your Plans	● Agility Run	● Exercises to Music	● Cooperative Game Skills	● Lifeboats; Moving Together; Group Juggling; Stranded; Centipede
[5-8] Week 21 + Save to Your Plans	● Rubber Band	● Aerobic, Strength, & Flexibility Jackpot Fitness	● Hockey Skills - Controlled Dribble, Front Field, Forehand Pass, Face-off, Goalkeeping	● Lane Hockey; Goalkeeper Hockey; Sideline Hockey

Six types of assessment instruments used throughout Dynamic PE ASAP

Over 130 different assessment instruments that cover ASAP lesson plans

1. **Teacher Questioning** is an excellent strategy to probe student understanding and provide time for student reflection.

2. **Teacher Checklists** are designed to help teachers efficiently observe students' performance.

3. **Self-Assessments** are great formative assessment tools that give students the chance to take ownership of their learning.

4. **Peer Assessments** let students showcase their learning in multiple ways.

5. **Written Exit Slips** are designed for efficiency and reflection.

6. **Bike Rack** assessments are an efficient strategy for assessing students' understanding.

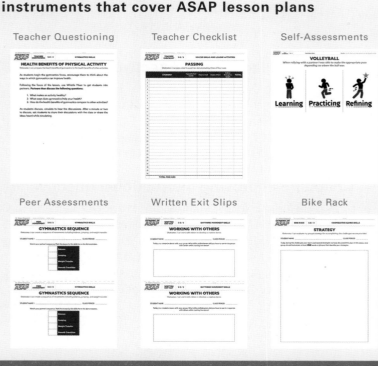

Teacher Questioning Teacher Checklist Self-Assessments

Peer Assessments Written Exit Slips Bike Rack

CONTENTS

PART III   DEVELOPING AND ADMINISTRATING A TOTAL PROGRAM

PART IV | **IMPLEMENTING INSTRUCTIONAL ACTIVITIES**

PREFACE

For more than 30 years *Dynamic Physical Education for Secondary School Students* (*DPE*) has been the go-to resource for preparing future secondary physical educators. The leadership of Dr. Paul Darst and Dr. Robert Pangrazi led this text to be one of the most widely used and influential secondary physical education texts. Over the previous eight editions under their leadership, countless teachers were guided to become great secondary physical education teachers. The ninth edition of this book marks a change in leadership. Dr. Timothy Brusseau and Dr. Heather Erwin, who had previously worked on the eighth edition as coauthors, have now taken the helm as the lead authors. They will maintain the principles that *DPE* was built upon while continuing to move the textbook and the field into the future. The textbook will stretch users' thinking, provide contemporary perspectives, examine pertinent literature, include teacher-tested activities, and exude a passion for physical education—just as it has for over 30 years.

DPE emphasizes the skill development, activity promotion, and physical fitness behaviors that are the foundation of physical literacy. *DPE* advocates instructional practices designed to create a learning environment where students are free to experiment, learn, and experience physical activity in a positive climate. *DPE* goes beyond physical education classes by promoting physical activity throughout the school day and beyond. For years, *DPE* has stood out for its inclusion of a vast array of instructional activities that help teachers in training see theory in practice. No text on the market offers preservice and in-service teachers a greater variety of evidence-based activities and strategies designed to help them develop curriculum that meets the SHAPE America standards defining quality physical education. The ninth edition of *DPE* includes numerous updates and changes:

- *Chapter realignment:* For the ninth edition, the chapters have been realigned slightly to add space for two new chapters (chapter 11, Supporting and Advocating for Physical Education, and chapter 12, Comprehensive School Physical Activity Programs). This change allowed us to bring together content about secondary physical education and the importance of physical activity as well as the importance of technology in chapter 1. Similarly, the previous chapters on improving instruction and systematic observation have been combined.

- *Advocacy:* Our programs are constantly in danger of being minimized or eliminated. A new chapter has been added that highlights the importance of advocating for our physical education programs along with strategies that teachers can use to promote and improve their programs.

- *Comprehensive school physical activity programs* (*CSPAP*): Increasingly, physical educators are being asked to infuse physical activity throughout the school day. We have added a standalone chapter that discusses the CSPAP components and strategies for coordinated and comprehensive physical activity efforts.

General Organization of the Text

Part I (Designing an Effective Physical Education Program) includes chapters 1 through 3. Chapter 1 offers the background information on secondary physical education, the importance of physical activity for adolescents, and the importance of technology. Chapter 2 provides an overview of the most common curricular approaches used in secondary schools. Chapter 3 provides a guide as well as strategies for developing a curriculum that will work best for each individual teacher.

Part II (Teaching Students in an Effective Physical Education Program) includes chapters 4 through 9. Chapter 4 discusses the importance of preparing and planning a high-quality physical education lesson. Chapter 5 provides the tools and resources needed to improve instruction as well as ways to evaluate the effectiveness of instruction. Chapter 6 provides an overview of a variety of teaching styles that move from teacher-centered approaches to student-centered styles. Class management and discipline often dictate whether teachers will succeed or fail, and chapter 7 offers practical information for successfully teaching adolescents in an activity setting. Chapter 8 offers strategies for assessing student performance and provides many practical examples. Chapter 9 shows how to adapt and modify activities to ensure inclusion and purpose for all students in physical education classes.

Part III (Developing and Administrating a Total Program) includes chapters 10 through 13 and focuses on successful implementation of a physical education program, including such topics as safety issues and liability concerns (chapter 10), the importance of advocating for our programs (chapter 11), understanding the importance of implementing physical activity throughout the school day and ways to develop a comprehensive school physical activity program (chapter 12), as well as ways to implement intramural programs (chapter 13).

Part IV (Implementing Instructional Activities) includes chapters 14 through 20 and is designed to provide strategies, ideas, and examples of a variety of activities and units. Chapters on introductory activities, physical fitness, healthy lifestyles, cooperative and nontraditional activities, sports, lifetime activities, and outdoor and adventure activities are included.

Instructor Resources

The ninth edition includes access to an integrated and comprehensive set of instructional tools for chapters 1 through 13. The instructor guide provides chapter takeaways, learning objectives, lab activities, and a cooperative learning project. The test package offers true–false and multiple-choice questions for these chapters. Using the questions supplied in the test bank, instructors can create tests, edit questions, and add their own material. The presentation package offers PowerPoint lecture outlines with key figures and tables from the book.

PREPARATION FOR PASSING THE EDTPA

The edTPA is a performance-based, subject-specific assessment and support system to emphasize, measure, and support the skills and knowledge that all teachers need from day 1 in the classroom. It is currently used by more than 600 teacher preparation programs in 41 states and Washington DC, and many states require that preservice physical educators pass the edTPA physical education assessment in order to become certified to teach in K-12 schools. To learn if the edTPA is being used in your state visit https://edtpa.aacte.org/state-policy.

Stanford University faculty and staff at the Stanford Center for Assessment, Learning, and Equity (SCALE) developed edTPA. The edTPA website (http://edtpa.com/) describes the edTPA assessment process this way:

Aspiring teachers must prepare a portfolio of materials during their student teaching clinical experience. edTPA requires aspiring teachers to demonstrate readiness to teach through lesson plans designed to support their students' strengths and needs; engage real students in ambitious learning; analyze whether their students are learning, and adjust their instruction to become more effective. Teacher candidates submit unedited video recordings of themselves at work in a real classroom as part of a portfolio that is scored by highly trained educators. edTPA builds on decades of teacher performance assessment development and research regarding teaching skills and practices that improve student learning.

The three edTPA tasks you will have to complete are the following:
- Planning for instruction and assessment
- Instructing and engaging students in learning
- Assessing student learning

Dynamic Physical Education for Secondary School Students provides the foundational content you need to successfully complete all three tasks and score high on the edTPA:

- **Planning for instruction and assessment:** Chapter 4, Planning for Effective Instruction, provides an overview of planning for instruction and assessment as well as very specific examples and teaching tips.

- **Instructing and engaging students in learning:** This book advocates instructional practices designed to create a learning environment where students are free to experiment, learn, and experience physical activity in a positive climate. Best teaching practices are addressed throughout the book, notably in chapters 5 (Improving Instructional Effectiveness), 6 (Teaching Styles), 7 (Management), 9 (Including Students With Disabilities), and 10 (Safety and Liability).

- **Assessing student learning:** Chapter 8, Assessment, Evaluation, Grading, and Program Accountability, goes into great depth about effective assessment practices.

PHYSICAL EDUCATION EDTPA ONLINE PREPARATION GUIDE

In addition to the foundational content found in this book, additional help in preparing for the edTPA is provided in the Physical Education edTPA Online Preparation Guide, created by Rebekah A. Johnson and Nicholas Brummitt. More information on this product can be found here: https://us.HumanKinetics .com/products/physical-education-edtpa-online-preparation-guide

PHOTO CREDITS

ACKNOWLEDGMENTS

We appreciate Human Kinetics for their partnership in preparing this edition. They have been a tremendous asset to the development of and changes made to this new edition. We thank Scott Wikgren, who has supported and guided us through the transition to Human Kinetics. We also appreciate the attention to detail and great editing given to this text by Jackie Blakley. We also thank the many members of the HK teams who have supported this effort behind the scenes.

We are thankful for physical education teacher Jordan Manley, principal Tina Stevenson, and the physical education students at STEAM Academy in Lexington, Kentucky, for allowing us to take updated photos that will be an exciting addition to this new edition.

We are also grateful for the many physical education teachers and teacher educators who have field-tested the ideas and concepts presented in our text. Their efforts and feedback have been essential for the continued development of this book.

Finally, we are forever indebted to Dr. Paul Darst and Dr. Robert Pangrazi, who pioneered *Dynamic Physical Education for Secondary School Students*, for their decades of work. They have continued to mentor and support us as we move this ninth edition forward, and we are forever thankful for their trust in us!

Physical Education in the Secondary School

Physical education is a phase of the general educational program that focuses on movement experiences that contribute to the total growth and development of each student. Program objectives provide the framework and direction to the physical education curriculum. Systematic and properly taught physical education can help achieve the outcomes set by national content standards, such as movement competence including skills and knowledge; participation in physical activity and maintenance of physical fitness; exhibition of personal and social behavior that respects self and others; and recognition of the value of physical activity for health, enjoyment, challenge, self-expression, and social interaction. Modern programs of physical education have been influenced by cultural and educational factors, and many issues influence physical education programs. Quality programs include essential components and specific characteristics.

Learning Objectives

- ► Describe why people have misconceptions about physical education.
- ► Define physical education and describe how it functions as part of the secondary school experience.
- ► List program objectives and recognize the distinctive contributions of physical education.
- ► Cite the content standards of secondary physical education.
- ► Explain how a variety of societal influences and federal mandates have affected secondary school physical education.
- ► Describe various trends and issues in secondary physical education.
- ► Describe the educational reasons for including physical education as part of the school experience.
- ► Identify essential components of a quality physical education program.
- ► Describe the characteristics of successful physical education programs.
- ► Discuss the Common Core Standards and describe how they can influence physical education

Physical education can be a positive and exciting experience for secondary students. A quality program can offer the opportunity to choose between activities such as mountain bicycling, skating with in-line skates, golf, rock climbing, tennis, racquetball, group activities on a ropes course, and wilderness survival. Some high schools offer elective choices, including sailing, scuba diving, martial arts, disc games, pickleball, spikeball, eclipse ball, and water aerobics. Modern fitness centers with indoor climbing walls are becoming more common, providing access to a variety of machines and equipment for working on the various components of health-related physical fitness. Creative teachers are designing two- or three-week minicourses as well as semester-long, in-depth units to meet student needs and desires. New program offerings include adventure and wilderness courses that teach caving, rock climbing, stream fishing, and backpacking as part of the physical education program. Middle schools are offering a wide variety of units—including cardio kickboxing, step aerobics, walking activities using pedometers, modified team handball, initiative challenges, ropes course activities, modified lacrosse, disc skills, bicycling, and orienteering—allowing students to explore and find activities they enjoy. Many of the physical activities are at times being integrated with academic concepts from math, science, writing, literacy, and geography.

Many programs are emphasizing a more positive and inclusive atmosphere. Strict dress codes have been relaxed to provide students with more choices. Instructional procedures include learning stations in which students work on different tasks at different ability levels. Teachers move around the gymnasium providing information and correcting, encouraging, and praising students. Students have more input about the type of activities they would like to see offered. Physical fitness activities include innovative visual materials and music; choices may include work with large and small exercise balls; fitness scavenger hunts; rope jumping; circuit training; partner resistance activities; use of stationary bicycles, rowing machines, and stair-climbing machines; and participation in orienteering or geocaching courses with compass or GPS activities and use of math skills involving bearings and angles. These activities are arranged and presented so that all students can find personal satisfaction and success. Students at all ability levels are provided with challenging activities that encourage them to expand their physical limits, achieve a level of personal success, and develop confidence.

So is this how the public perceives physical education today? What is physical education? Ask this question, and an infinite number of answers will result. People have varied images of the physical education environment. Some envision a class in which students dress in a required uniform and exercise in straight lines under the watchful eye of a regimental instructor. Accompanying this image is a negative atmosphere where running laps and exercise are used as punishment for dress code infractions or misbehavior. Others might view physical education as a subject to be avoided because of crowded classes, smelly locker rooms, forced showers, and insufficient time to change clothes. Athletically inclined participants often remember physical education as a time for playing sports daily with little or no instruction.

These memories of physical education create a public perception package that might be described as follows: Students are hurried into their gym clothes only to wait at attention for dress inspection. Next, never-changing group calisthenics and stretching are followed by a lap around the track. Students then choose up sides and play the traditional team sport or game of the day (e.g., flag football, basketball, softball, or volleyball). The final activity is hurrying to get ready to go back to class within four minutes. Curriculum variety, student input, activity choices, coed activities, and individualized instruction are seldom part of the program that most people remember.

This negative perception has contributed to a diminishment of the importance of physical education in the total school curriculum, even though physically active forms of sport and play can have a positive effect on students. Even more unfortunate, unsatisfactory physical education classes still exist in many schools across the country. In these negative programs, adolescents do not experience the quality physical education that could significantly improve their health and well-being (Pangrazi & Beighle, 2013).

Clearly, the term *physical education* implies widely differing experiences to the public. It is easy to see why many people have misunderstood physical education. Programs vary significantly from place to place and situation to situation. Knowledge, attitudes, and behaviors toward physical activity are strongly influenced by the type of physical education program that students experience. Consequently, in developing an effective physical education program, teachers must have a clear understanding of what physical education is and what it should be doing in school settings.

What Is Physical Education?

Physical education is a learning process that focuses on knowledge, attitudes, and behaviors relative to physical activity. It is an educational endeavor through schools that can be formal or informal. Physical education is the passing of information, attitudes, and skills from one person to another. It might include a mother teaching her son or daughter how to play golf or a player receiving information from the coach of the youth soccer team. It can be a family walking together with pedometers and keeping track of their steps or a mother explaining pacing to her children during a 10K run. It can be a youth explaining the rules of football to his grandfather or a wife teaching her husband how to play racquetball. It is a group of seventh graders learning to play badminton in a middle school, or high school students learning the concepts of health-related fitness in a classroom setting. Physical education is the passing of information, attitudes, and skills from one person to another.

Physical education is an important component of the overall school program that contributes, primarily through physical activity experiences, to the total growth and development of all students. Physical education programs make four unique contributions to the lives of students. The first is the achievement of daily physical activity. The second is the achievement of a personalized level of physical fitness. Third is the development of competency in a variety of physical skills to ensure successful functioning in physical activities that students can use for the rest of their lives. The fourth contribution requires that students acquire requisite knowledge for living an active and healthy lifestyle. If these contributions are not accomplished in physical education classes, they will not be realized elsewhere in the school curriculum. Physical education instructors have a responsibility to develop and teach a systematically organized curriculum for kindergarten through grade 12 that favorably influences all students and enhances their physical activity habits. Students deserve a thoughtful program of physical education that contributes to their quality of life and an active lifestyle. The transmission of knowledge, skills, and attitudes toward this end is physical education.

Rationale for Physical Education

Quality physical education is certainly a need in schools. The Youth Risk Behavior Surveillance System (YRBSS) is a nationwide survey conducted by the Centers for Disease Control and Prevention (CDC, 2017). The 2017 survey showed that only 47% of youth were active at least 60 minutes a day on five or more of the past seven days. To compound the lack of physical activity, students in grades 11 and 12 are rarely required to take physical education classes. The number of youths who attended daily high school physical education classes according to

Positive physical education experiences can encourage students to become physically active adults.

the YRBSS survey is only 30%. Additionally, adolescents continue to have high levels of overweight and obesity (Abarca-Gomez et al., 2017), and studies show that adolescents who are overweight are more likely to be overweight as adults (Simmonds, Llewellyn, Owen, & Woolacott, 2016). The push for academic performance is clearly surging, while concern for the health of students is lagging.

The national health goals for 2020 (U.S. Department of Health and Human Services [USDHHS], 2010) are designed to increase daily levels of physical activity. Many of the goals directly target schools or programs that take place within the school setting. These goals emphasize reducing inactivity and increasing moderate to vigorous physical activity. One 30-minute physical education class can provide 2,000 or more steps (nearly a mile) of moderate to vigorous physical activity for students (Morgan, 2004). In addition, physical education programs can be part of the solution to the bigger problem, by teaching youth how to live an active and healthy lifestyle. Currently, many studies offer a strong rationale for increasing the amount of physical education contact offered to students:

- The school environment discourages physical activity. Students are asked to sit most of the day and walk between classes, which results in decreased energy expenditure. A physical education class can offer up to 2,000 or more steps of moderate to vigorous physical activity to counteract the effects of an inactive day (Morgan, Pangrazi, & Beighle, 2003). This period of activity can make a substantial contribution to the daily energy expenditure of students, particularly those who are inactive. For example, for students who average 8,000 steps a day, a quality physical education class could increase their number of steps by 20%, a substantial increase in physical activity.

- A positive experience in physical education classes can encourage young people to be active as adults. Children and adolescents who had positive physical education experiences are more likely to have greater physical activity intention and attitude as adults (Ladwig, Vazou, & Ekkekakis, 2018). Similarly, negative physical education experiences are linked to more sedentary time as an adult (Ladwig et al., 2018). The high school years are usually the last contact that students have with physical education. Their opinion of physical education will primarily be based on the type of experience they received.

- The percentage of overweight youth has more than tripled in the past 30 years (Skinner, Ravanbakht, Skelton, Perrin, & Armstrong, 2018). Studies show that adolescent weight is a good predictor of adult obesity (Suchindran et al., 2010). The chance that childhood overweight will persist into adulthood increases from 20% at age four to 80% by adolescence (Guo & Chumlea, 1999). Considering that a quality program encourages active behavior, it makes sense to have in place a program that helps young people understand the importance of proper weight management and an active lifestyle.

- A quality physical education program educates young people physically but does not detract from the academic performance of the school. An argument often made is that spending time on physical education will lower the academic performance of students because they have less time to study and learn. To the contrary, studies have shown that students who spend time in physical education classes do equally well or better in academic classes (Trost & van der Mars, 2010). Donnelly and colleagues (2016) in their meta-analysis show that numerous cross-sectional and observational studies have positively linked physical activity with academic achievement.

- Physical education gives students the skills they need to be active as adults. One commodity that youth have, in contrast to adults, is the time to practice and learn new skills. Few adults learn an entirely new set of physical skills. Often, they practice and enhance skills they have learned in childhood. Considering that many adults like to participate in activities that require skill (e.g., golf, tennis, racquetball, and so on), learning such skills during their school years makes it more likely they will feel able and competent to participate in later life.

- Physical activity (which most often occurs in physical education classes) provides immediate and short-term health benefits for youth (Poitras et al., 2016). For overweight students, increased physical activity results in a reduction of the percentage of body fat. Additionally, increased activity reduces blood pressure and improves the blood lipid profile for high-health-risk students. Finally, evidence shows that weight-bearing activities performed during the school years offer bone mineral density benefits that carry over into adulthood.

- Active youth tend to become active adults. Telama and colleagues (2014) looked at retrospective and longitudinal tracking studies and concluded that the results "indicate that physical activity and sport participation in childhood and adolescence represent a significant prediction for physical activity in adulthood." Their work has shown that physically active lifestyle starts to develop very early in childhood and that the stability of physical activity is moderate or high along the life course from youth to adulthood. This finding highlights the concerns we should have for youth being in an inactive school environment.

Major Outcomes for Physical Education

Two words often used in education are *outcomes* and *standards*. Many use the terms interchangeably, but in this text they have different meanings. **Outcomes** are defined here as the knowledge and skills that students should attain by the end of each unit. In physical education, the two major outcomes that should override everything else are physical activity and health, particularly healthy eating habits. In other words, all the activities and content of a physical education program are targeted to improve health and increase the activity levels of students. Additionally, these outcomes are reached through behavior-based activities so that students live what they learn in school throughout life. If a physical education program can increase the amount of moderate to vigorous physical activity students achieve and improve their eating habits, more than likely the issue of being overweight in our society can be stemmed.

It makes sense to monitor and evaluate the success of a physical education program in terms of physical activity and healthy behaviors because all students can achieve those behaviors, regardless of genetic limitations and ability levels. All students can learn to live an active lifestyle and increase the amount of activity they perform daily. Physical educators now have pedometers and other tracking devices available that monitor total daily activity and the amount of moderate to vigorous physical activity that students accomplish. Teachers can assign activity homework that can be monitored and logged into notebooks and online programs. In terms of healthy eating habits, schools and physical education programs can take a much more active role in helping students learn how to fuel their bodies. Eating to live rather than living to eat is an important distinction that students

must learn. Physical educators can spearhead efforts to improve the quality of food offered in school cafeterias, improve the quality of brown-bag lunches that students carry to school, and monitor the types of celebratory foods offered to students. In addition, the current push to offer healthy drinks and snacks in vending machines has not resulted in reduced funds for schools as once feared. Instead, students learn to choose from a healthy assortment of attractive and healthy snacks.

Physical Education Content Standards

Content standards dictate the curriculum and the skills, knowledge, and behavior that will be taught to students. They are the framework of a program; they determine the focus and direction of instruction. Standards specify what students should know and be able to perform, with the purpose of reaching the activity and health outcomes. Physical education teaches skills and behaviors taught nowhere else in the school curriculum. When these standards are not accomplished in physical education classes, students leave school without skills, knowledge, and attitudes related to an active lifestyle.

The Society for Health and Physical Educators (SHAPE) of America has identified a set of standards that give direction to physical education (SHAPE America, 2013):

Standard 1: The physically literate individual demonstrates competency in a variety of motor skills and movement patterns.

Standard 2: The physically literate individual applies knowledge of concepts, principles, strategies and tactics related to movement and performance.

Standard 3: The physically literate individual demonstrates the knowledge and skills to achieve and maintain a health-enhancing level of physical activity and fitness.

Standard 4: The physically literate individual exhibits responsible personal and social behavior that respects self and others.

Standard 5: The physically literate individual recognizes the value of physical activity for health, enjoyment, challenge, self-expression and/or social interaction.

The standards are supported with grade-level outcomes (SHAPE America, 2014). Student expectations are delineated for each standard and show what students should know and be able to do at the end of each grade-level range. Examples of sample student performance outcomes are included to give teachers ideas about how their students should be progressing toward the achievement of each standard.

The standards not only give direction to instruction but also form the framework for assessment and accountability in the program. SHAPE resources also offer an assessment series with a wide range of strategies for assessing progress toward the standards, including teacher observations, written tests, student logs, student projects, student journals, class projects, and portfolios. The teacher can modify and select assessment tools that are meaningful in his or her setting. The following sections show how the Dynamic Physical Education for Secondary School Students program addresses the National Standards for Physical Education.

Standard 1

The physically literate individual demonstrates competency in a variety of motor skills and movement patterns.

The secondary school years are an opportune time to teach motor skills because students have the time and the predisposition to learn. People tend to repeat activities they do well or find rewarding; success is a great motivator. If students improve their volleyball bumps, disc backhand throws, or tennis serves, chances are great that they will repeat the activity and incorporate it into their lifestyles. Skill development does not occur overnight or in a three-week unit. Students should be counseled about how to find opportunities for developing physical skills outside the school program. Teachers provide a support system for students as their skills improve, and the positive benefits of physical activity begin to appear. Students change their attitudes toward physical activity when personal skill levels improve. Students expect instant success, and teachers can help them learn that physical skill development is not easy and demands sustained, continuous effort. The role of teachers is to help students find individual levels of success—success that is unique to each person.

The range of skills presented in physical education should be unlimited. Because students vary in genetic endowment and interest, they should have an opportunity to explore and learn about their abilities in many types of physical skills. The hierarchy of skill development progresses from fundamental motor skills to specialized skills. Components of motor skill development and movement competence follow.

Fundamental Motor Skills

Fundamental motor skills are the utilitarian skills that people use to enhance the quality of life. The designation *fundamental skills* is used because these skills are basic to a fully functioning person. These skills help students to function in the environment around them. These skills are divided into three categories: locomotor, nonlocomotor, and manipulative. Students should learn most of these skills during the elementary school years.

- **Locomotor skills** are used to move the body from one place to another or to project the body upward, as in jumping and hopping. These skills also include walking, running, skipping, leaping, and galloping.
- **Nonlocomotor skills** are performed in place, without appreciable spatial movement. They include bending, stretching, pushing and pulling, raising and lowering, twisting and turning, shaking, bouncing, circling, and so on.
- **Manipulative skills** are developed through object handling. This manipulation of objects leads to eye–hand and eye–foot coordination, which are particularly important for tracking items in space. Manipulative skills form the important basis for many game skills and lifetime activities. Propulsion (throwing, striking, kicking), receipt (catching), rebounding or redirection of objects (such as a volleyball) are basic to this set of skills.

Rhythmic Movement Skills

People who excel in movement activities possess a strong sense of rhythmic ability. **Rhythmic movement** involves motion that possesses regularity and a predictable pattern. The aptitude to move rhythmically is basic to skill performance in all areas. A rhythmic program that includes aerobic dance, folk and square dancing, rope jumping, and rhythmic gymnastics offers a set of experiences that help attain this objective.

Specialized Motor Skills

Specialized skills are used in various sports, games, and other areas of physical education, including adventure activities, apparatus activities, tumbling, cooperative activities, swimming, dance, and so on. When developing specialized skills such as tennis strokes, racquetball serves, or softball fielding techniques, progression is attained through planned instruction and drills. These skills have critical points of technique, and proper teaching emphasizes correct performance. In most cases, students do not learn these skills well until the middle and high school years.

Rope jumping is a great way to develop students' rhythmic movement skills.

Standard 2

The physically literate individual applies knowledge of concepts, principles, strategies and tactics related to movement and performance.

A physical education program should provide students with a wide range of knowledge about many areas. A knowledge component is intertwined with all objectives. Indeed, accomplishing any outcome is difficult if students lack a certain amount of knowledge. For example, getting students to enjoy tennis without understanding rules, strategies, and etiquette is difficult, and most people will not incorporate an aerobic activity into their lifestyle without understanding the possible health-related benefits.

Students need to learn about the classification of **movement concepts**, which includes body awareness, space awareness, qualities of movement, and relationships Learning only the fundamental skills is not enough; students need to perform these skills in a variety of settings. For example, students are asked to run in different directions, at different levels, and along different pathways. They can learn to move slowly or quickly or to make a series of strong movements. **Movement themes** form the foundation of movement experiences necessary for developing specific fundamental skills. Through this process, students develop an increased awareness and understanding of the body as a vehicle for movement and for the

acquisition of a personal vocabulary of movement skills. These skills are usually taught in elementary and middle school years. They are used in the secondary school years without instruction and practice; it is usually assumed they have been learned in the earlier grades.

The school years should be the years of opportunity—the opportunity to explore and experience many different types of physical activity. Students should be able to find physical activities that provide personal satisfaction and success. The curriculum should be expansive rather than restrictive. It should allow students to gain a better understanding of their strengths and limitations and to establish the types of activities they prefer and dislike. Related to this experience is the opportunity to learn basic concepts of movement and physical activity. Students should leave school knowing about center of gravity, force, leverage, stability, and other factors related to efficient movement. Learning basic principles and concepts of physical activity, especially with reference to how physical activity contributes to good health and wellness, is important in this knowledge objective. Understanding the genetic diversity among people, such as body physiques, muscle fibers, cardiorespiratory endurance, and motor coordination, is requisite for helping students evaluate their physical capabilities. Learning how to assess personal fitness and activity levels, how to plan activity levels, and how to make informed decisions about physical activity and fitness are all important objectives in this domain.

Related to understanding principles of human performance is knowing how to participate safely in activities. The school has both a legal and moral obligation to provide a safe environment. Safety must be actively taught, and activities must be conducted in a safe environment. Instructional procedures in activity must include safety factors, and active supervision is necessary to guide students in safe participation. Students must leave school with an understanding of safety principles of human movement.

Standard 3

> The physically literate individual demonstrates the knowledge and skills to achieve and maintain a health-enhancing level of physical activity and fitness.

An important objective of a secondary school physical education program is to help students incorporate physical activity into their lifestyles. Meeting this goal requires that curriculum, instruction, and teachers have a positive effect on students' knowledge, attitudes, and skill behaviors relative to physical activities. A successful physical education program is not measured by the current level of knowledge, the physical fitness level, or the physical skills of students, nor is it measured by the number of participants on the varsity athletic teams. Certainly, success is not evaluated by the number of victories that the football or basketball teams accumulate. The ultimate measure of success is the number of students who participate in daily physical activities such as exercise, sports, dance, and outdoor adventure activities throughout their lives.

Several basic considerations apply to lifetime activity. Sallis (1994) classifies the factors that influence people to be active in four categories: psychological, social, physical–environmental, and biological. Physical education programs should foster those factors, often referred to as the determinants of active learning.

Psychological determinants are among the most powerful. For example, students must derive enjoyment through activity so that they will seek further participation. To this end, students must become proficient in a variety of motor skills. Most adults will not participate in activities unless they have an adequate level of perceived competence. Because learning new motor skills takes a great deal of time and repetition, everyday life often prohibits busy adults from developing a level of skill competence to ensure play without embarrassment. Students also need a rational basis for play. This can be established through activity orientations that can be transferred to other situations. Such activities should include a variety of games suitable for small groups and sport activities adapted to local situations.

Social influences include factors such as family and peer role models, encouragement from significant others, and opportunities to participate in activity with others in one's social group. *Physical–environmental factors* include adequate programs and facilities, satisfactory equipment and supplies, safe outdoor environments, and available opportunities near home and at school. Included are adequate school opportunities in physical education, intramural sports, and after-school recreation and sports programs. *Biological factors* include age, gender, ethnic, and socioeconomic status (Sallis, 1994).

Without proper planning and systematic arrangement of the learning environment, the probability of developing positive student attitudes and physically active lifestyles declines significantly. Secondary curriculum plans and instructional strategies should be concerned with developing learning environments that help students enjoy physical activities for a lifetime.

Physical educators provide experiences for students that lead to successful encounters with exercise and regular physical activity. Therefore, the physical education curriculum should focus on regular physical activity that results in a fitness level that motivation and heredity allow, which in turn can lead to improved health-related physical fitness (cardiorespiratory efficiency, flexibility, body fat reduction, and muscular strength and endurance). Recent physical fitness test batteries focus on the development of criterion-related health standards associated with reduced health risk rather than skill-related fitness based on normative standards (Welk & Meredith, 2010).

Students need to experience activities that demonstrate the benefits of physical fitness firsthand. Student participation in activity choices and the opportunity to offer input about the fitness program help create a personalized program. Learning how to develop and arrange suitable fitness routines that positively influence health is an important higher-order objective. Physical fitness development is like physical skill development in that it requires time, energy, and self-discipline. Students need to be aware of the factors that influence fitness development. Eating habits, types of activities, heredity, and frequency of activity are just a few of the factors that students must learn.

Allotting a portion of each class to fitness activities helps students understand what is necessary for fitness enhancement. Learning about fitness is much more than absorbing facts; students need the participation experience to make fitness activities a habit. A positive experience in fitness activities can help students develop attitudes that ensure active adult lifestyles. Programs are not successful if students leave school with a dislike for physical activity. Establishing a desire in students to maintain fitness and wellness throughout their adult years is the most important outcome.

Standard 4

> The physically literate individual exhibits responsible personal and social behavior that respects self and others.

Responsible behavior involves behaving in a manner that does not negatively affect others. Hellison (2011) and others have developed methodology for teaching responsible behavior. (See chapter 7 for a more detailed discussion of this methodology.) It is generally accepted that if responsible behavior is to be learned, it must be taught through experiences in which such behavior is reinforced on a regular basis. Accepting consequences for one's behavior is learned and needs to be valued and reinforced by responsible adults. Responsible behavior occurs in a hierarchy of behavior, ranging from acting irresponsibly to caring and behaving in a responsible manner. Physical education classes are an excellent setting for teaching responsibility because most behavior is highly visible. Some young people in a competitive setting may react openly in an irresponsible fashion, offering instructors a "teachable moment" to discuss such unacceptable behavior. Additionally, students must learn to win and lose in an acceptable manner and assume responsibility for their performances. Accepting the consequences of one's behavior is a lesson that arises regularly in a cooperative or competitive environment.

Cooperation precedes the development of competition, which makes it an important behavior to teach in physical education settings. Without cooperation, competitive games cannot be played. The nature of competitive games demands cooperation, fair play, and "sportspersonship," and when these are not present, the joy of participation is lost. Cooperative games teach students that all teammates are needed to reach group goals.

Physical activity environments provide several unique opportunities for students to experience and develop social–emotional skills. Getting along with other people, being part of a team, accepting an official's judgment, losing the final game of a tournament, dealing with peers who have varying levels of ability, or changing clothes in a crowded locker room are just a few of the many experiences that may occur in a physical education class. These experiences are important for students. Physical educators have a responsibility to help guide and direct students in understanding these various social–emotional behaviors.

All students need to understand and internalize the merits of participation, cooperation, competition, and tolerance. Good citizenship and fair play help define a desirable social atmosphere. A teacher who listens, shows empathy, and offers guidance can help students differentiate between acceptable and unacceptable ways of dealing with others and expressing feelings. Students need to develop an awareness of how they interact with others and how the quality of their behavior influences others' responses to them. If students do not receive feedback about negative behavior from teachers and peers, they may not realize that the behavior is inappropriate. Establishing reasonable limits of appropriate student behavior followed by consistent enforcement of those limits will help students understand the parameters of acceptable behavior.

Teachers help students develop positive attitudes toward learning by teaching an understanding of various student ability levels, the role of winning and losing, and the value of trying to succeed. Positive and concerned instruction has a powerful effect on students' attitudes and self-concepts. A positive teacher communicates to students that they are likable, capable, and contributing individuals. Teachers must understand students, but students should also understand themselves because self-understanding has a powerful influence on human behavior. The self-concept that students develop is vital to the learning process. If students believe that they belong, that they are important people, and that their successes outweigh their failures, they gain momentum toward developing a desirable self-concept. Encouraging students to provide positive feedback to each other will help students feel positive about their efforts.

The ability to move with grace, confidence, and ease helps students perceive themselves in a positive manner. Achieving self-satisfying levels of skill competency and fitness can also make students feel confident and assured. The self-concept is related to perceived physical skill competence. If students perceive themselves as competent in a physical activity setting, they will want to participate in physical activity outside the school environment. On the other hand, if they feel incompetent, they will avoid activity at all costs to maintain their self-esteem and avoid embarrassment.

Standard 5

> The physically literate individual recognizes the value of physical activity for health, enjoyment, challenge, self-expression and/or social interaction.

This standard focuses on the development of students' awareness of the wide variety of benefits that they can obtain from leading a physically active life. The benefits can take many forms, and people can perceive them differently. Students need to know about the variety of benefits and be able to look at all the options involved with different types of physical activity and the way in which they relate to their personal interests. They need to know how to make thoughtful decisions about which activities improve health and wellness and which are fun. Some students will select activities because of the challenge or the opportunity for self-expression. Many activity opportunities are available for a lifetime of regular physical activity, and a quality program will help students discover the activities that meet their needs. As students develop this understanding of all the benefits of physical activity participation, they will pursue activities that are meaningful to them.

All standards are reprinted by permission from SHAPE America, National Standards and Grade-Level Outcomes for K–12 Physical Education (Champaign, IL: Human Kinetics, 2014).

Perspectives Influencing Physical Education

Although physical education programs vary widely across the United States, most endorse similar outcomes. Programs are greatly influenced by current social and professional perspectives. Most curricula are based on an assortment of goals and objectives emanating from a wide variety of sources. Nevertheless, some schools orient their programs more closely to one perspective than another. Therefore, an understanding of these perspectives will help the reader better understand how curricula reflect the social needs of a culture.

Social–Historical Perspective

European gymnastics and highly organized and disciplined calisthenics programs dominated early physical education in the United States. Many of the early leaders were European immigrants, primarily from Germany and Sweden, who brought these formal programs with them and implemented them first in colleges and then in the public schools. These systems included formal and structured exercises centered on development of the body. Some have called this an education of the physical focus.

In the early 1900s, a major shift in perspective began to occur. As education in general altered its perspective based on the teachings of John Dewey and others, physical education shifted as well. Two of Dewey's cardinal aims of education stressed the promotion of health and a worthy use of leisure time. People became interested in using sports and games to foster these two aims. The school curriculum became a logical place to include these sports and games. Jesse F. Williams, whose text (1927) was published in numerous editions, was one of several leaders who did much to change the perspective of American physical education at this time. Williams and others championed democratic ideals and the concepts of sportspersonship and teamwork. Team sports began to be emphasized in physical education. This focus is called the "education through the physical" approach. This perspective did not negate the importance of physical fitness and "education of the physical," but it did place strong emphasis on social development through physical education. This perspective was perpetuated by followers of these early leaders and continues to have currency in the secondary physical education field.

Cultural–Sports Perspective

Sports have become a diversion not only for millions of Americans who are participants but also for millions of American spectators (Eitzen & Sage, 1986). Youth sports are now highly organized and have high participant rates. Collegiate and professional sports have become big business. Title IX of the Education Amendments Act of 1972 was enacted to provide greater access for girls and women in sports. With the shift from more formal gymnastics to more "American" activities such as football, basketball, and softball, sports became central to the programs of physical education. Because sports are part of American culture, the development and appreciation of sports skills were logically accepted as a part of American education. This perspective accounts for the emphasis on sports in the expanded curriculum, which includes interscholastic and intramural programs.

Public Health Perspective

A renewed emphasis on physical fitness occurred in the 1950s, caused by the publication of the Kraus-Weber tests comparing fitness levels of American and European students on strength and flexibility. The public became concerned about the comparative weakness of U.S.

students. In response to this concern, President Dwight Eisenhower established the President's Council on Physical Fitness and Sports, an agency that promotes physical fitness not only for students but also for citizens of all ages. This action was the beginning of a fitness boom that has continued to this day. In recent years, increasingly more evidence indicates that the lack of regular physical activity among adults is a primary risk factor for heart disease and a major contributor to other diseases as well.

Healthy People 2000: National Health Promotion and Disease Objectives (U.S. Public Health Service, 1990) was released by the government and had the goal to improve the health of all Americans. Many of the target goals were directed toward improving the health status of American youth. All the objectives in the physical activity area emphasized increasing the amount of time students participate in light to moderate activity. Based on this evidence, several public health experts called for the use of physical education as a public health tool (Sallis & McKenzie, 1991). They suggested that implementation of programs designed to promote lifetime physical activity in the school would reap important public health benefits, including reduced morbidity and mortality from hypokinetic conditions such as heart disease, back pain, obesity, diabetes, high blood pressure, and cancer. The public health perspective has had considerable influence on curriculum and instruction in physical education. This perspective gave impetus to the recommendation within *Healthy People 2000* that physical education in schools be increased by the year 2000.

The release of *Physical Activity and Health: A Report of the Surgeon General* (USDHHS, 1996) documented many health benefits achieved through moderate and regular activity. The report showed that people of all ages, both male and female, benefit from regular physical activity. Never had a body of research been compiled to show the strong need for activity and fitness in the lives of young people. Activity programs are a requisite for healthy young bodies and minds. Yet despite the strong emphasis the report placed on regular and daily activity, many physical education programs continue to emphasize physical fitness goals instead of lifestyle physical activity goals.

Because of the surgeon general's report promoting physical activity, the United States now sets national goals. The latest version is set forth in *Healthy People*

Physical education programs should promote lifetime physical activity to improve students' personal health as well as public health.

2020: National Health Promotion and Disease Objectives (U.S. Public Health Service, 2010). This document again continued to focus on physical activity goals that would increase the years of healthy life and eliminate health disparities. These major goals are supported with enabling goals concerned with promoting healthy behaviors, protecting health, achieving access to quality health care, and strengthening community prevention. The objectives are grouped into several focus areas similar to those described in *Healthy People 2010*. New focus areas in this document include disability, people with low income, race and ethnicity, chronic diseases, and public health infrastructure.

Issues Affecting Physical Education Programs

Several trends and related issues affect the development of secondary school physical education programs. Some of the factors considered when developing a program are discussed in the following section.

Growth and Development of Adolescents

Adolescence is a time of rapid growth and development. Much variation exists in the actual onset of adolescence and entry into adulthood. For example, CDC defines adolescence as occurring between ages 12 and 19 in their operational definitions for *Healthy People 2020* (2010). During this period, the body matures physically and sexually.

Genetic makeup at birth generally controls growth patterns. Although unhealthy parents or poor dietary practices can have a negative effect on proper growth and development, the focus in this section is on normal maturation common to most young people. Maturing adolescents follow a general growth pattern, but each person's timing is unique. Some students are advanced physically for their chronological age, whereas others are slow maturers. Only when aberration from the norm is excessive should teachers and parents become concerned.

Early maturation tends to improve the opportunity for success in physical activities. Early maturing students of both sexes are generally heavier and taller for their age than average- or late-maturing students. Overweight youth are often more mature for their age than their normal-weight peers. Early maturing young people also have larger amounts of muscle and bone tissue because of their larger body size. But the early maturer also carries a greater percentage of body weight as fat tissue (Malina, Bouchard, & Bar-Or, 2004). Late-maturing youth usually catch up to early maturers in height but not in weight. In addition, an early maturing student in elementary school will also be an early maturer in secondary school. Generally, early maturing males have mesomorphic physiques, and early maturing females are characterized by endomorph. These differences in body size and composition probably account for male–female performance differences in activities that require strength and power. Young people who mature early are often better athletes because they show success and receive many opportunities to practice skills. Late maturers are often left behind because they are not capable of succeeding at complex skills. Thus, they are not as successful in group activities. When these slowly developing students reach maturity, their lack of practice opportunities limits their ability to catch up with peers. Females often reach their growth spurt first, meaning that they are often taller and heavier during the sixth and seventh grades. Males catch up and often grow larger and stronger. Physical education teachers must consider these growth patterns when designing activities and planning groups or teams.

TEACHING TIP

When growth increases in large amounts, a person's ability to learn motor skills decreases. Because the growth of boys and girls occurs at different times and rates, different strategies for instruction should be used. The middle school years are a critical time for teachers to understand how the great variation in growth and development affects physical performance.

Students who might have been early maturers may become discouraged because their peers are improving more than they are. On the other hand, the early maturers may make the late maturers feel inept in performing physical tasks. These years require sensitive and caring teachers to help students understand how growth and development patterns affect their performance.

Boys continue to grow rapidly throughout high school. This swift development often reduces their capacity to learn and perform motor skills. On the other hand, the growth of girls has slowed by seventh or eighth grade, improving their readiness to learn new skills. Focus on learning motor skills should be minimized during periods of rapid growth. During this time emphasis should be placed on creating a positive learning environment and facilitating the learning of correct movement patterns (as contrasted to a focus on skill outcomes) until growth slows.

This rapid growth spurt brings adolescents a new body. The head is about 90% of adult size by age six, so as youth enter adolescence, they become less top heavy (see figure 1.1). They must adapt to a lower center of gravity as they grow "into their head," and their arms and legs increase in length in proportion to their trunk. In addition, muscle fiber differentiation occurs, meaning that adolescents now have a combination of slow-twitch (aerobic) and fast-twitch (anaerobic) muscle fibers. This change means they may no longer excel at certain types of activities as their muscle physiology changes. Elementary-school-aged children do not have muscle fiber differentiation, so those who excel at anaerobic activities also excel at aerobic activities. Muscle fiber differentiation occurs during the adolescent growth spurt; students who end up with more slow-twitch fibers tend to do better at aerobic activities, whereas those who have a higher proportion of fast-twitch fibers perform better in anaerobic activities. A broad-based middle

school program should offer students a chance to find their new areas of physical competency.

The motor performance of males is related to early maturity; more mature boys usually perform better on motor tasks (Malina, Bouchard, & Bar-Or, 2004). For females, however, motor performance appears to be less related to physiological maturity. Because many sports require size and strength, male early maturers have a strong advantage in athletic endeavors. This circumstance points out the need to design a physical education curriculum to meet the needs of both early and late maturers. Include units of instruction that emphasize activities relying less on strength and size and more on aerobic capacity, agility, balance, and coordination. Instruction that forces students to learn at the same rate or participate in activities with other students regardless of skill level negatively affects the entire group. This practice slows down gifted students and frustrates less able students. Teachers often expect students to perform the same activity at the same time, regardless of maturation. Students do not mature at the same rate and are therefore not at similar levels of readiness to learn. If physical education is intended for all students, the curriculum must offer successful experiences for all participants regardless of personal ability.

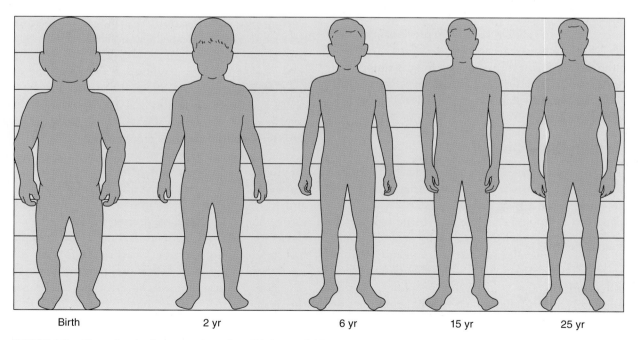

Birth   2 yr   6 yr   15 yr   25 yr

FIGURE 1.1   Changing body proportions from birth to adulthood.

TEACHING TIP

You cannot always gear your instruction to meet the needs of all students. Should you teach at a level to challenge gifted students or to allow less able students to find success? Activity should be adjusted to the needs of the less able students because this may be their last opportunity to learn skills and leave school feeling positive about physical activity. Keep in mind that gifted students have many opportunities to practice their skills outside physical education, such as in recreation leagues, youth sport teams, and private clubs. But students who lack competency and confidence have few opportunities. Physical education teachers should ensure that these students find success and the joy of movement in class situations.

Students going through all these developmental changes need a teacher who can help them find and develop new physical competencies. Because these students have a different body than they had in elementary school, they need to relearn and practice skills they were taught previously. Secondary school physical educators often criticize students and elementary physical education teachers because the students arrive in middle school with a general lack of competency in motor skills. But this circumstance usually occurs because maturity changes a student's ability to perform previously learned skills. Middle school teachers must be adept at reteaching the basic skills of throwing, catching, striking, and kicking. With effective skill instruction, the middle school years are a time when students learn what their true abilities are.

Common Core

The Common Core Standards provide instructional guidance with a consistent, clear understanding of what students are expected to learn. The standards are designed to be robust and relevant to the real world. They reflect the knowledge and skills that our youth need for success in college and in their careers (National Governors Association, 2013). The standards address reading, writing, and math. Many people expect that science and social studies standards will be on the way soon. Forty-one states have adopted the standards. What does this mean for physical education? Many states are requiring all teachers, regardless of their discipline (including physical education), to address math

and literacy (reading and writing) in their classrooms. Teachers must document how they are addressing each component. Most physical educators already infuse many of the concepts relevant to these standards daily even if they do not realize it. For example, many games and physical activities include a discussion on angles of shooting or angles of passing. Most PE teachers use statistics or percentages during class activities. Within the literacy standards at the secondary school level, PE teachers include many concepts in numerous areas of their program. Teachers need to learn and document these concepts for each day's lesson within the various units in the curriculum.

State and Local Physical Education Requirements

Most state departments of education set some type of requirement for physical education. Policies differ dramatically from state to state. Some require a certain number of minutes per week for each grade level, whereas others specify a number of days per week. Several states do not have any physical education requirement. Each school district usually sets requirements designed to fit within the requirements defined by the state department of education. Consequently, district policies can vary dramatically and still be within state guidelines. As an example, Arizona (which has standards and recommendations by grade level) has no requirement at the state level for physical education. Most Arizona high schools have a one-year physical education requirement, others have a two- or three-year requirement, and some offer only an elective physical education program. The state requirement significantly affects the curriculum, the students, and the teachers. Physical educators have always been involved to ensure that physical education is a basic part of the school district's requirements.

Many school districts continue to allow substitutions for physical education credit. Most notable is the substitution of varsity athletics, cheerleading, marching band, and ROTC training programs for physical education credit. Some districts have created physical education classes for specific athletic teams such as soccer, basketball, football, and so forth. Coaches of the teams then teach these classes, even though they may not be physical educators. Physical educators have discussed and debated this issue for many years. There are two sides to the debate, and physical educators should think about this issue and have an opinion for their administrators and school board. Physical education should be designed around standards, not athletics or extracurriculars. These other programs are valuable and can be a rewarding experience for students, but they are different from physical education and its goals.

Designing local requirements can often be a positive practice for physical education programs because doing so lends stability and credibility at the district level. Some districts have developed requirements that facilitate a selective or elective type of curriculum. This process involves specifying requirements by activity category such as team sports, lifetime sports, gymnastics, aquatics, recreational activities, and dance. For example, students might be required to complete 12 activities in one year. The requirement might be that three of the activities are team sports, three are lifetime sports, and one each is selected from the areas of dance, aquatics, and gymnastics. The remaining activity choices would be left to the student. This procedure gives students choice within a requirement and ensures that students will receive a variety of activities as well as the opportunity to choose according to their interests. Students have choice but not total freedom, so a balanced curricular approach is ensured.

Increases in Overweight and Obese Students

Body composition refers to the varying amounts of muscle, bone, and fat within the body. More than half of the fat stored in the body is located in a layer just below the skin. A number of methods can be used to measure body fat, from underwater weighing to BMI. Recently, Burns et al. (2013) published research showing that methods such as waist-to-height ratio, two-site skinfolds, and a handheld bioelectric impedance body fat analyzer were better measures than BMI for analyzing body composition. But because BMI is a more common measure, it is often the tool of choice for teachers. BMI is a relationship between weight and height associated with body fat and health risk. The equation is BMI = body weight in kilograms divided by height in meters squared, or BMI = weight (lb) divided by height (in.) and divided again by height (in.) multiplied by 703. BMI has replaced skinfolds as a measure because it is less invasive. People can calculate their own BMI by weighing and measuring themselves. Many BMI calculators available online make it simple to compute.

Obesity is defined as a BMI equal to or above the 95th percentile for age and sex. Data gathered for the 2017 YRBSS showed that 14.8% of high school students were obese. The percentage of obese students was 10.6 in 1999. Over 17 years, the proportion of students who were obese increased slowly by 4%. Although signs indicated that the upward trend in obesity among high school students is slowing down, many youths are still overweight. This increase is occurring at all ages and shows the need to increase the amount of activity youth receive in and out of the school environment.

Inactivity and overweight issues are closely linked. Lack of physical activity is common among both normal-weight and overweight young people. Only about 28% of high school students met recommended levels of physical activity (USDHHS, 2012). Physical education classes need to teach overweight students how to increase their daily physical activity and develop an active lifestyle. Students need to develop positive feelings about the role of physical activity in weight management strategies. Rather than push overweight youths to solve their problems through increased and mandated exercise, a better approach is to promote physical activity in a positive fashion. If the treatment is unsuccessful, students may view it as another failure in trying to manage their weight and be strongly opposed to future activity programs.

Adults often say, "Don't worry about excessive weight; it will come off when the student reaches adolescence." The opposite, however, is usually true. If a youth's parents are both overweight, he or she has an 80% chance of being overweight. Most overweight preadolescents grow into overweight adults. There are no easy answers, and to solve such a complex problem as weight management, physical educators need to involve parents, nutritionists, counselors, nurses, and physicians in the process.

The advantage of using physical activity to treat weight problems is that it increases energy expenditure. In contrast to rigid diets, exercise minimizes the loss of lean body mass and stimulates fat loss. Physical activity is inexpensive, easy to do in a variety of situations, and often a positive social experience.

Coeducational Classes

Title IX of the Educational Amendments Act of 1972 has had a significant effect on most secondary school physical education programs. The law is based on the principle that school activities and programs are of equal value and importance for male and female students. Students should not be denied access to participation in school activities based on gender. This law has stirred up much debate and controversy. School districts, state departments of education, and the judicial system continue to study interpretations and details.

Legal ramifications mandate equal access to physical education activities for both boys and girls. Separate classes for males and females have been reduced in most schools. This trend does not imply that students of both genders must wrestle together, share locker facilities, or have the same activity interests, but it does mean that, for example, males can participate in a dance class and females can elect a strength-training class when they have interest in those areas. In principle, the law also means that the most qualified person provides the instruction, regardless of gender.

The law allows schools to group students by ability, even if the result is groups consisting of primarily one gender. The law also allows teachers to segregate the sexes during a game or competitive aspect of contact sports such as wrestling, basketball, football, ice hockey, and others. Teachers must also ensure that grading standards and procedures are not having an adverse effect on one gender group, a specified regulation of Title IX. Standards must be fair to both sexes.

Amid all the controversy, the focus should be on examining the objectives of the physical education program and developing an environment that will meet the requirements of Title IX. The challenges are a small price to pay in exchange for mitigating inequities in opportunities for learning and participation in sports and physical education. Law or no law, physical education is important to all students, regardless of gender. Coeducational programs offer clear advantages in the areas of social development, activity offerings, and instructional quality. Teachers should be responsible for all students in their classes, regardless of ability or gender.

Students With Special Needs

Public Law (PL) 94-142, the Education of All Handicapped Children Act, was signed in 1975 by President Gerald Ford. This law ensures that all young people with disabilities receive an appropriate public education that serves their unique needs. A 1990 amendment, PL 101-476 (also known as IDEA—Individuals with Disabilities Education Act), continues with the objective of providing students with the least restrictive environment in the school setting. Autism and traumatic brain injury have been added to the list of handicapping conditions that should receive the least restrictive environment. IDEA provides that an individual transition plan be developed no later than age 16 as a component of the individualized education program (IEP) process. Rehabilitation and social work services are included as related services.

The law has compelled physical educators to develop specialized classes and programs for many students with disabilities. Other students are mainstreamed into the regular physical education program as part of the least restrictive environment advocated by PL 94-142. School districts are required to hire qualified instructors for

Students of every ability level deserve quality physical education.

these programs as well as to encourage current teachers to develop skills for providing meaningful experiences for mainstreamed children with disabilities. Physical education has been specified as an important part of the disabled student's curricula or IEP. The IEP contains extensive information covering the student's present status, program objectives, learning activities, and evaluation procedures.

The law can create challenges for physical educators in planning, organizing, managing, and evaluating daily and yearly programs for students with disabilities. In most situations, the teacher must establish learning environments concurrently for students with and without disabilities. Regardless of the law, the issue is a moral necessity. All students deserve physical education experiences regardless of their abilities.

Conceptual Physical Fitness Programs

A program that started at the college level and has filtered down to many secondary schools, including the middle school, is called the conceptual approach. An example of the conceptual approach for secondary high schools is the text *Fitness for Life* by Corbin and Le Masurier (2014). This approach has been called a lecture–laboratory method. Students spend time receiving information in a lecture situation and then try out or test the information on themselves or on peers in a laboratory setting. Emphasis is placed on information, appraisal procedures, and program planning. Students are expected to understand the how, what, and why of physical activity, physical fitness, and exercise. They learn to use diagnostic tests in areas such as cardiorespiratory endurance, muscular strength and endurance, flexibility, body composition, and motor ability. Corbin, LeMasurier, and Lambdin (2018) have developed a fitness for life model for middle school that is currently available and in use with many school districts.

A variety of conceptual programs have been field-tested in various situations. In some schools, concepts make up the entire physical education program, whereas in other programs, the concepts may be only a portion of the requirement such as a semester class or six-week unit. Several books are available with lesson sequences and other instructional materials such as slide–tape lectures, scripts, review questions, tests, handouts, overhead transparencies, and laboratory experiments.

The conceptual approach is currently popular for several reasons. First, many believe an academic approach focused on knowledge and cognitive growth instead of on physical skill is a more respectable educational endeavor. Others believe that when student knowledge increases, attitudes and behaviors also change, causing students to integrate physical activity into their lifestyles. This phenomenon is not proved. Increasing a person's knowledge does not ensure a change in behavior, and students must experience physical activity as well as understand it conceptually. Conceptual learning is an important part of a physical education program, but physical skill development must also receive strong emphasis.

Interdisciplinary Courses

In some secondary schools, physical education is combined with other disciplines, such as health, biology, geology, and geography. In these programs, students have opportunities to learn about subjects such as drugs, alcohol, diseases, safety, first aid, rock formations, and environmental concerns. Emphasis is placed on combining physical skill development with knowledge. For example, students can learn about the flora and fauna of an area while concurrently learning camping and backpacking skills. This approach is the basic thesis of many outdoor education programs in which several disciplines are integrated to teach students about the outdoors.

This approach also balances the acquisition of knowledge and physical skill development, and it offers interesting opportunities for students and teachers. Teachers can take advantage of geographical locations, various learning environments, and the interests of students living in these areas. The physical education teacher can team-teach with teachers from other subject areas such as biology, zoology, or geography. In this way, many interesting learning experiences can be developed. A downside of this approach is that the time available for physical skill development is usually reduced in favor of building more knowledge, thus reducing the opportunity to become competent in physical skills.

Off-Campus and Online Physical Education

Off-campus physical education programs give students an opportunity to earn credit for advanced study or off-campus courses not available in the basic curricula. Students are offered the opportunity to earn credit for off-campus study involving surfing, ice skating, horseback riding, bowling, golf, and other disciplines. These programs are available to students after they have completed basic requirements on campus. Some type of monitoring and weekly check-in procedure is arranged in which the student, parent, and teacher agree to a contract. Many of these programs also contain a fitness component requiring that students show some evidence of maintenance or improvement in fitness (e.g., body composition or cardiorespiratory endurance).

A common model, currently used in Florida and Minnesota, involves offering personal fitness classes to students in an online and unstructured environment. Students can sign up for the class, receive instruction from videos and class materials, and do their workouts at home or in other settings. The class has no walls, no whistles, and no teachers on-site. Instead, students design their fitness programs based on personal needs and desires. One of the requirements is that students keep a log of their daily activity with a record of exercises and activities they complete. Students can record their progress in a personal log or online. Jan Braaten, curriculum coordinator for physical education and health for the Minneapolis Public Schools (MPS), explained why her district began offering online physical education classes: "Things have changed in the 21st century in many ways, and one change is the wide variety of options and lifestyles for our students." In the Minneapolis courses, students are asked to perform 30 minutes of vigorous activity three days a week. Students record the type of activity they did, their heart rate, and their perceived exertion. The students in these online courses must have their log signed off by a parent, coach, trainer, or other adult. The Florida program is slightly different in that students record their activity on the web and can interact with a number of sources, including the instructor, who will give advice and answer student questions throughout the day by email or phone.

These online programs offer possibilities for advanced study and can add an exciting dimension to the curricula. Students often develop self-management skills and become self-motivated because they select activities that appeal to them and are primarily responsible for what they learn from the experience. Both program leaders admit that cheating is possible. Most students, however, view such programs as a privilege and usually respond in a mature manner. The bottom line is that if students learn to direct their own physical activity experiences without adult supervision, they are a step closer to a lifetime of activity and better health.

Instruction in Community Facilities

Another trend that can be positive for school programs is the use of community facilities. This approach allows schools to use community bowling alleys, golf courses, ski slopes, and skating rinks to enhance the physical education program. Many schools bus students to a bowling alley or golf course once a week. Sometimes schools provide transportation and participation funds; in other cases, students pay the expenses. Funding can also be provided through car washes, candy sales, and raffles. Programs and procedures are limited only by a teacher's ingenuity and creative direction.

Community facilities can add a valuable dimension to secondary programs. Physical educators can broaden their areas of competency or find other professionals who have requisite expertise. A noted physical educator once asked a physical education teacher who taught at a school situated near a beautiful lake, "Do you teach swimming, boating, and sailing here?" "No," replied the teacher, "we don't have the facilities." Finding a way to use community resources for the betterment of students is surely possible. Qualified personnel from the community often want to share their expertise.

Private Sports Instruction

Opportunities for sports and fitness instruction in the private sector continue to expand rapidly. These programs are responsive to the demands of consumers. Indoor climbing walls, YMCA basketball, gymnastics clubs, soccer leagues, Pop Warner football, motocross bicycle racing, Little League Baseball, and racket clubs are a few examples of programs available to students. Students receive in-depth instruction, practice with adequate equipment, have many competitive opportunities, and receive trophies, T-shirts, and similar rewards. Private instruction programs must meet the demands of consumers or lose their clientele. Often, such programs use quality equipment, the newest techniques, highly skilled instructors, and excellent teachers. Many of these instructional programs offer strong competition for physical education programs because of their ability to provide personalized instruction.

Private-sector instructional programs can create challenges for school-based physical education programs. The first challenge is that private instruction creates a wide range of backgrounds, experiences, and abilities among students who are participating in school physical education. Students from middle- and upper-class families may have a wealth of experience in sports such as tennis, golf, soccer, and gymnastics, whereas students from lower-income families might not be able to afford private instruction. Another problem is the difficulty of developing a gymnastics unit that is meaningful to eighth-grade students who have had five years of intensive training at a private sports academy. This same point can be illustrated by comparing students involved in a soccer league for several years with students who have never played the game. Teachers face a hard challenge when trying to motivate students with such diverse backgrounds.

A second concern relates to public opinion. As opportunities in the private sector increase, public support for the school physical education curricula may decrease. Some people currently believe that secondary school physical education programs can be eliminated because adequate opportunities are available in the private sector. "Let students learn physical activities outside the school setting so that more time and money are available for academic subjects" is a common viewpoint. An opposing viewpoint argues that private instruction opportunities are available only to the upper-middle class and that lower socioeconomic groups will have limited opportunities. Physical educators need to find ways to use the specialized private-sector opportunities to enhance the physical education experience for all students in their programs. There are ways to take students to these opportunities and bring these programs to the schools. The trend toward private instruction is continuing to grow, and the possibility is strong that the private sports industry will become a serious competitor of school programs. Physical educators face the challenge of developing quality programs that provide meaningful learning experiences for all students regardless of background.

Technology

In a society saturated in technology, physical educators must use technology to enhance student learning experiences and better prepare them for the future. But the use of technology does not come without some controversy. One side suggests that technology can be used in physical education to boost curiosity about learning and link students to the world. It can be used as a means of motivating students to engage in more physical activity for health. The other side suggests that technology is the antithesis of physical education in that it often encourages sedentary behavior. Although this proposition may be true, teachers need to use technology to their advantage with the purpose of teaching students to be active for life.

Technology is ever-changing, and new gadgets become available all the time. Thus, quality teachers are looking to use it to assist in every aspect of their careers including planning, teaching, assessing, and continuing their lifelong learning experience. In doing this, a variety of technological resources are required, such as cameras, tablets, apps, and social media. This approach may require more funding and professional development to keep teachers up to date. For planning, teachers may use versatile calendars, the Internet, and social media. For teaching, they may create signs and task cards with graphic programs; show videos, pictures, or other materials with a projector; use apps for management and instructional ideas; search the Internet for guidance; and use social media as a means for promoting their program. Regarding assessment, tablets and smartphones can be convenient ways of entering and storing data. Videos and class polling apps are other ways to collect data and begin making decisions. Sounds systems coupled with apps and websites that offer music are effective ways to motivate students to move. Other technology gadgets that may entice youth to move include pedometers, fitness trackers (such as Fitbits and Apple Watches), digital badges, gamification strategies, and quick response (QR) codes. Overall, technology can be an excellent way to enhance student experiences in physical education and connect them to the real world.

Equipment, Facilities, and Class Size

A continuing and growing problem that physical educators at all levels face is inadequate equipment, limited facilities, and increased class sizes. For some reason, many administrators believe that physical education classes can be larger in number of students and yet be managed with less equipment than an academic class. They fail to realize that learning to dribble a basketball is impossible without having access to a basketball on a regular basis. Students become frustrated and bored when standing in line waiting for a turn to dribble the ball. Teachers have a difficult situation with 50 students on six tennis courts. Economic conditions make these problems difficult, and physical educators must strive to get a fair share of the budget and contribute to fundraising ideas. Many schools are doing multiple fundraising projects to combat this problem. Physical educators need to get involved and contribute to this endeavor. Students are not asked to learn to read and write without books, paper, and pencils. Physical education is just as important as other discipline areas and should receive an equal share of the budget dollar and have similar class sizes for the most part. Many secondary programs are increasing their health club type activities with large group classes on activities such as kickboxing, yoga, aerobics, and so forth.

Legal Liability

Many lawsuits appearing in various aspects of society concern physical educators. Teachers are not immune to liability lawsuits, as evidenced by an increasing number of cases involving parents and students suing teachers, administrators, and school boards. This situation is unnerving when teachers attempt new activities or use new teaching techniques that involve any type of risk. Many teachers and administrators have become extremely cautious and conservative about activities that contain an element of risk, yet often many of these activities are safer than those traditionally included in the curriculum. Teachers may refuse to offer new activities for fear of a lawsuit. Ultimately, students become the victims in this process because programs become limited in scope.

Teachers certainly need to acquire adequate knowledge about safety and instructional procedures before implementing a new activity. They must understand legal ramifications when developing a broad and balanced curriculum. With proper information and careful planning, the instructional risks of various activities can be minimized. If sound policies and procedures are followed daily, teachers should not worry about legal liability.

Teaching and Coaching Conflicts

The public often has a difficult time separating the physical education program from the athletic program. The athletic program is concerned with recruiting, coaching, and administering teams that will compete against other school teams. These goals are significantly different from the goals of the secondary school physical education program, yet athletics and physical education are often linked because the programs share facilities, equipment, fields, and teachers.

In addition, pressure often comes from the local community to produce winning teams. Pressure to develop outstanding physical education programs is not nearly as strong, and the visibility of the two programs is markedly different. This conflict creates a difficult situation for the physical education teacher who is also a coach. The coach may support the concept of an outstanding curriculum but may not find enough time and energy to do both, causing physical education to take a backseat. This problem has no simple solution. Many physical education teachers want to work in both programs. The pressure to produce winners is apparent, and the individual instructor will determine the quality of the physical education program that is implemented. Many people do excellent work in both areas, but doing so is not easy.

Essential Components of a Quality Program

Physical education teachers need to know the essential components of a quality physical education program. In other words, what critical elements should be included to ensure that young people receive a quality physical education experience? The following components interlock to form a comprehensive physical education program that will be valued by parents, teachers, and students. Each of the components is described briefly in this section. In-depth coverage is offered in the referenced chapters under each point. Figure 1.2 identifies eight essential components of a quality program.

- *A quality physical education program is organized around national content standards that offer direction and continuity to instruction and evaluation.* These standards are defined by several competencies that young people are expected to accomplish. They are measurable so that both teachers and students know when progress has been made. Previously in this chapter, you read about a comprehensive set of physical education content standards. Chapter 8 offers several assessment strategies for checking to see whether you and your students are meeting the standards.

- *A quality program is student-centered and based on the developmental urges, characteristics, and interests of students.* Students learn best when the skills and activities they must learn match their physical and emotional development. Including activities in the program because they match the competencies of the teacher is not a criterion. Teachers must teach new activities outside their comfort zone if they are going to present a comprehensive program. A quality program focuses on the successes of students so that they are motivated to continue. Developing a positive set of behaviors toward physical activity is a key goal of physical education. Chapter 5 discusses essential elements of teaching and how to reinforce students in a positive way during learning situations.

- *Quality physical education makes physical activity and motor-skill development the core of the program.* Physical education is the only place in the total school curriculum where instruction is focused on teaching motor skills. It is a unique discipline that focuses on physical activity to ensure the physical development of students. The program

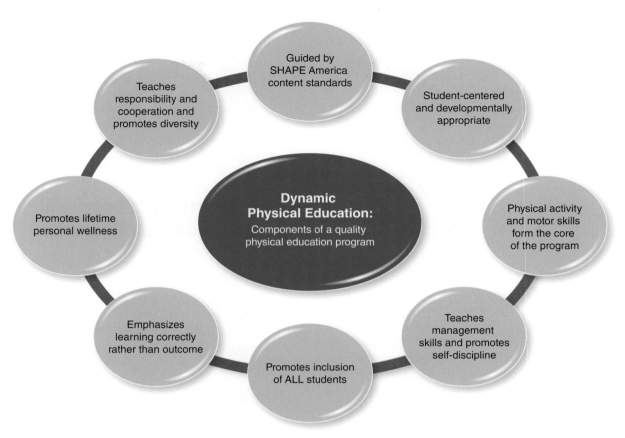

FIGURE 1.2 Essential components of a quality program.

Reprinted from R.P. Pangrazi and A. Beighle, *Dynamic Physical Education for Elementary School Children,* 19th ed. (Champaign, IL: Human Kinetics, 2019), 3.

must focus on skill development and quality physical activity. A quality program also follows the national standards. Teacher candidates should demonstrate personal competence in motor-skill performance for a variety of activities. Teachers should also achieve and maintain a health-enhancing level of fitness not only for themselves but also with their students. The teachers should also be able to demonstrate performance concepts as they relate to skillful movement.

- *Physical education programs teach management skills and self-discipline.* Physical education teachers are usually evaluated based on how students in their classes behave. Administrators and parents look to see that students are on task and receiving many opportunities to learn new skills. When a class is well managed and students work with self-discipline, the experience compares well to classroom instruction, bringing credibility to the program. Chapter 7 offers many different methods for teaching management skills and promoting self-discipline.

- *Quality programs emphasize inclusion of all students.* Instruction is designed for students who need help the most, those with fewer skills, and students with disabilities. Students who are skilled and blessed with innate ability have many opportunities to learn. They have the confidence to take private lessons, join clubs, and play in after-school sport programs. Unskilled youth or children with disabilities may lack confidence and often are unable to help themselves. Physical education is often one of the few opportunities that many young people will have to learn skills in a caring and positive environment. Instructional progressions designed to help young people whose ability places them in the lower 70% of the class ensure a positive experience for all. Students who are not naturally gifted must feel successful if they are expected to enjoy and value physical activity. See chapter 9 for teaching youth who have disabilities and modifying activities so that all children can be successful.

- *In a quality physical education setting, instruction focuses on the process of learning skills rather than the product or outcome of the skill performance.* When young people are learning new motor skills, performing the skill correctly is more important than the outcome of the skill. Young learners need to understand proper techniques first and then focus on the product of the skill performance. This approach means teaching a young person to catch a softball properly rather than worrying about how many he or she catches or misses. Chapter 4 offers strategies for optimizing skill learning. Chapter 8 helps explain when to focus on the process or product evaluation of motor skills.

- *A quality physical education program teaches lifetime activities that students can use to promote their health and personal wellness.* Quality physical education programs prepare young people to participate in activities they can perform when they become adults. If a program is restricted to team sports, the program will be of little value to most adults. Participation in sport activities declines rapidly with age. Less than 5% of adults above age 30 report playing a team sport (USDHHS, 1996). By far, walking is the most frequently reported activity in adulthood. Other activities such as stretching exercises, bicycling, strength development exercises, jogging, swimming, and aerobics are also popular with adults. Quality physical education looks to the future and offers activities that young participants can enjoy over the years and use as adults. Chapter 15 offers information about the importance of teaching lifetime physical activity skills in a physical education setting. Chapter 16 offers instructional strategies for teaching health and wellness.

- *Quality physical education teaches cooperative and responsibility skills and helps students develop sensitivity to diversity and gender issues.* Cooperative skills precede competitive skills. Students must agree to follow rules in order to enjoy group activities. Most fights and physical violence in schools occur when young people are in a physical activity setting. Physical education is an effective laboratory for learning to behave responsibly because behavior is highly observable to others. Situations in physical activity give rise to the need to resolve conflicts in a peaceful manner. Students need to learn about similarities and differences

between cultures. Competitive activities such as the Olympics often bring cultures together and offer students the opportunity to see different cultures compete with respect and dignity. Coeducational activities help students understand how activities cut across gender and stereotypes. The occurrence of gender differences in physical activities is an excellent time to point out that individuals differ regardless of race or gender.

Characteristics of Successful Physical Education Programs

A quality physical education program can be designed and implemented in many ways. As discussed earlier, several factors influence physical education programs. A wide spectrum of possibilities makes the accomplishment of a quality program possible. The following are characteristics often found in successful programs regardless of the model or design of the curriculum.

A Positive Learning Environment Exists

The instructor is the most important factor in the learning environment. Regardless of the teaching method or curriculum design, a perceptive, analytical teacher is paramount to student learning. An effective teacher creates a teaching–learning atmosphere that is both positive and caring. Instructional procedures are planned carefully so that students experience immediate success. The instructor keeps her or his reactions to student failure minimal and momentary. Instruction focuses feedback and reactions on positive student behaviors rather than uses a "correction complex" that responds only to students' mistakes. Effective teachers realize they must take an active role in the teaching–learning process by demonstrating, participating, encouraging, giving feedback, and hustling. Teachers who incorporate physical activities into their lifestyles influence students significantly.

Competent teachers use positive methods to discipline, teach, and motivate. Students are taught to enjoy physical education instead of learning to avoid the environment. Running and exercise are not used as a form of punishment. Students are rewarded for competitive efforts even if their team happens to lose on a given day. Teachers use students' first names and interact with all students daily. Students are offered a degree of choice and freedom in the learning process to increase student motivation.

Research on teaching provides information about ways that effective teachers influence the teaching–learning process (Siedentop and Tannehill, 2000). Modeling behavior is an effective strategy for influencing specific types of student behavior. Guidelines concerning how to model have long been available. Students want to see models of people who have incorporated physical activity in their lifestyles. Teachers can discuss their exercise habits with students and allow students to see them participating in and enjoying physical activity. Influential teachers are aware of the powerful effect that their behavior has on students and use modeling to help students develop healthy activity habits.

Enthusiasm is another behavior that promotes a positive environment. Evidence shows that this difficult-to-define behavior is a teaching skill associated with student learning. Teachers need to display their love of and excitement for physical activity and their joy in teaching. Expecting students to perform well is another critical factor in developing a positive atmosphere for teaching. If students are expected to be unmotivated and troublesome, then the possibility is strong that those behaviors will occur. If students are expected to learn and work hard, then the chance is better that they will perform at a higher level.

Physical educators need to look carefully at the effects of policies and procedures used in programs. If procedures discourage students from being active, they should be reevaluated. If dress codes and grading procedures are causing students to develop avoidance behaviors, acceptable alternatives must be developed. The overall atmosphere of the physical education environment has a strong influence on students and on their attitude toward physical activity. When students leave the physical education environment, they should have a good feeling about physical activity and a desire to return for more.

Student Choice Is Offered

The elective approach to physical education curricula refers to allowing student choice for an optional or elective year of physical education or allowing students to select among several activity options during each activity interval. For example, students can select tennis, weight training, or soccer during the first three-week unit, and racquetball, archery, or flag football during the second three weeks, and so on. The choice can occur not only during the optional class but also during a required class. The choice process starts in some schools as early as middle school, whereas in others it does not begin until high school. This type of program gives students an opportunity to choose activities of personal interest to them and to avoid activities in which they have little interest. Surveys have shown that some students would not elect to take an extra class of physical education because they wanted to avoid one or two specific units of activity, such as swimming, gymnastics, or wrestling. These students would sacrifice an entire year of physical education to avoid certain activities. To circumvent this behavior, curriculum planners design elective programs so that students can choose from a number of activities.

Another advantage of the elective approach is that students will be more motivated when they have influenced the selection of learning activities (Prusak, Treasure, Darst, & Pangrazi, 2004). Fewer problems occur in the areas of participation and discipline. Having more students involved in the program can also mean more support for teachers, equipment, and facilities. Flexibility in class size is yet another advantage. Certain activities can easily accommodate more students, depending on the equipment and facilities. For example, golf and tennis might have smaller classes than soccer and flag football.

Finally, considering these advantages, many teachers are motivated and enthusiastic about teaching in this type of program. An elective program can improve the motivational level of both students and teachers. Any educational practice that can affect the teaching–learning environment should be considered when developing programs in secondary school physical education. Problems do have to be worked out concerning grades, registration procedures, teaching attitudes, and class-roll procedures. But several solutions are available to a teaching staff that believes in the advantages of the approach.

Elective programs can provide a positive influence. Several secondary school physical education programs that have converted to elective programs have experienced an increase in number of students. Teachers point out that an elective program offers advantages such as increased student participation, enthusiasm, and motivation as well as increased enthusiasm and motivation of teachers. Students in 10th grade and above should be able to select all their physical activities and not be forced into activities they dislike or are not interested in learning. Students in middle school might be restricted to choosing from categories of activities such as team sports, lifetime sports, fitness activities, dance, aquatics, and adventure activities to ensure a measure of breadth in activity experiences. If possible, they should be permitted to choose from several activities in each category. In the fitness area, for example, they might choose aerobic dance, weight training, or jogging. In the lifetime sport area, the choices might be tennis, golf, or bowling.

A Wide Variety of Activities Are Available

The variety of physical activities available to consumers continues to expand. New and exciting activities such as Spin Jammer Discs, waveboards, in-line skates, cardio kick boxing, yoga and Pilates, medicine and stability balls, body bars, pedometer walking activities, step aerobics, cooperative games, and rock climbing are included in programs across the country. A broad-based program increases the possibility that all students will find an enjoyable physical activity. Physical education programs should offer as many activities as possible. A balance among team sports, lifestyle sports, dance, aquatics, outdoor activities, and physical-conditioning activities should be a major program goal. The following categories illustrate the wide range of activities that can be incorporated into an exemplary program.

Lifestyle Sports and Activities

This area of activities in the secondary school physical education curriculum continues to grow and evolve. These sports and activities are primarily individual or dual activities that can be used for a lifetime as opposed to team sports that are difficult to continue after the school years. These activities are easily incorporated into a person's lifestyle. Today, lifestyle sports and activities have become tremendously popular and have been expanded to include a host of activities such as walking, disc activities, racquetball, sand volleyball, and even lunchtime basketball. The expanded offering of lifestyle activities has provided many participation opportunities for students and adults who are not interested in traditional team sports. Secondary school physical education programs are better able to serve all students when a wide variety of lifestyle sports and activities are offered. Different students are successful and motivated with different activities.

Outdoor and Adventure Activities

Another category of activity that has continually gained popularity in the past 30 years is the outdoor adventure or wilderness sports. Backpacking, rock climbing, various ropes course activities, orienteering, and mountain bicycling are just a few of the activities in this category. These activities are like the lifestyle sports or activities and are primarily individual or dual activities that people can enjoy over a lifetime. The emphasis is on risk and excitement in using the earth's natural environments such as snow, water, mountains, ice, rivers, and wilderness areas. Exploration, travel, and adventure are important elements in these activities. To train students in outdoor adventure skills, many schools are developing on-campus facilities such as climbing walls, ropes courses, and orienteering sites as well as using nearby community environments such as ski slopes, parks, rivers, and mountains. These activities emphasize competition with oneself and the environment in contrast to competition with other people. This feature is attractive for many students. They can also enjoy outdoor adventure activities with family and friends during expanded leisure hours, providing an opportunity to get away from the city and experience the natural environment in a time of vanishing wilderness areas.

Health-Related Physical Activities

Aerobic rhythmic exercise, aerobic kickboxing, walking activities, step aerobics, jogging, weight training, and weight-control classes are extremely popular with secondary students and adults. Modern fitness centers are being built in high schools and shared with community partners after school hours. Many schools now offer a variety of classes—such as step aerobics, Pilates method, exercise balls, CrossFit exercise and competition, and aerobics—that emphasize topics such as nutrition, weight maintenance, coronary heart disease, flexibility, strength, and endurance. Human Kinetics, the Cooper Institute, and SHAPE America joined forces to create the American Fitness Alliance, with updated materials including the FitnessGram/ActivityGram K–12 program (Welk & Meredith, 2010), which includes an updated fitness education program that focuses on increasing activity in everyday activities. Accompanying the FitnessGram is a program called the ActivityGram that emphasizes monitoring and recording the amount of moderate physical activity accumulated each day for three days. The program prints out a view of the student's activity patterns after all the data have been entered.

Novel or Modified Team Sports

Finally, the development of novel or modified team sports is continuing in many schools. Activities such as eclipse ball, pickleball, spikeball, modified team handball, Ultimate, floor hockey, speed-a-way, broomball, flickerball, angleball, modified lacrosse, and pillow polo are some of the newer and novel team sports variations that are popular in various areas of the country. Some of these are new activities, whereas others are modifications of existing sports. They add another positive dimension to programs because of the increased variety and opportunities for success with certain types of students.

New team sport activities provide many interesting and exciting challenges for both students and instructors.

Physical education programs should offer a variety of activities, including aerobic activities.

In teaching almost any activity, problems may exist with safety, liability, competent instruction, equipment, and teachers' comfort zones, but the advantages of offering new team sports are well worth the encountered problems. A wide variety of activities should enhance the objective of developing in all students a positive attitude toward a lifetime of physical activity.

Students Receive In-Depth Instruction

Some high schools offer varying levels of instruction, such as beginning and intermediate classes. Some schools use the classifications beginning, team, and recreational. Three-week units are now offered for beginning basketball, team basketball, and recreational basketball. The beginning class covers dribbling, passing, pivoting, rebounding, and so forth, whereas the team class includes such areas as offensive strategy, zone defenses, and techniques on beating a half-court trap. The final recreational class allows opportunity for team play and tournaments. Students can take three units in a progressive, systematic procedure. An advantage of this approach is that teachers can do a better job of instruction because classes are more homogeneous in motivation and ability. Students usually feel more comfortable in a group in which similar attitudes and abilities prevail.

In grades 10 through 12, programs should offer intermediate and advanced levels of instruction. Students at these developmental levels choose one or two activities in which they want to excel. Advanced instruction is different from a free-play recreational situation commonly found in many programs. Depth refers to organized instruction rather than simply increasing the amount of participation time. Physical educators must move away from the notion that physical education programs should focus only on beginning levels. Many students do not participate in intramural sports, sport clubs, athletics, or outside-school programs; therefore, the physical education program may be their only opportunity to receive in-depth instruction. A high level of skill development usually increases a person's tendency to repeat and enjoy an activity.

The length of activity units has shortened over the past decade, especially at the middle school level. In quality programs, six- to nine-week units are becoming obsolete. In most middle school programs, two- to three-week units are the norm. These shorter units enable physical educators to expand the breadth of their programs and give students an introduction to a wider variety of activities. Some people question this trend because of the reduction in depth of instruction, but students can choose to develop depth in an activity in the high school years. Short units also reduce boredom and frustration, which are common problems among middle school students. With increased program breadth, educators have a better opportunity to provide students with some type of physical activity that they can enjoy and continue to use.

Depth in an activity is made available in high school curricula by allowing students to choose a semester-long unit. This specialized approach is part of an elective or optional program instead of a required program. Semester-long classes give students a chance to gain in-depth skill in an activity of their choice after they complete the required program. Many schools offer semester- or year-long units focusing on popular activities such as fitness center classes, cardio combinations, lifetime racket sports, and weight training. The middle school program provides breadth of activity, whereas the high school program gives students the opportunity to develop a high level of skill competency.

Diagnostic and Counseling Practices Are Evident

Students in middle school need guidance and counseling to direct them toward activities that match their interests and physical abilities. Teachers can help students understand their physical strengths and shortcomings and the possibilities for alleviating problems. Teachers must collect data and interpret it for students and parents. Obese and overweight students, for example, might be channeled into activities in which they can find success and feel competent. Students with strong upper bodies might be encouraged to try activities that involve strength. Activity counseling can help students make wise decisions about activities that are well suited to their abilities and will help them address problem areas.

High school students also need to learn about the benefits of physical activity and the types of activities available. They can use counseling in several other areas, such as behavioral self-modification techniques to aid them in the change and maintenance of activity habits. Students should understand environmental factors and obstacles that work against their attempts to participate in physical activities. Employment parameters, marriage, children, and climate are factors that affect activity lifestyles. Learning to keep records, set goals, and establish reinforcement procedures can help students with their activity habits. Another important area of activity counseling deals with changing interests and activities of people as they grow older. Many adults have been conditioned to think that physical activity is only for the young. This attitude needs to change considering the revelation that people at all age levels derive numerous benefits from being active. Fitness and play activities are important regardless of age.

Some secondary schools have designed a series of compulsory units that require students to assess their physical abilities and make decisions about physical activities that offer them success and remediate weaknesses. A counseling program helps channel students into physical education activities that can enhance their strengths and alleviate weaknesses. The testing and counseling procedures should be set up in a systematic, organized fashion. A physical education advisor should be assigned to each student to guide her or him through the process of making sound decisions about the future. Counseling students combined with implementing the previously described elective program is an effective way to fuse students' interests with their physical abilities. This model provides a blend of information about physical activity and gives students experiences in improving physical skills and physical fitness. Students should leave the program with approach tendencies for physical activity instead of avoidance behaviors.

All School Physical Activity Programs Are Integrated and Organized

Activity programs such as sport clubs, intramural sports, in-school activity programs (before school, noon hour, and after school), and interscholastic athletics can help students improve their skills and become more proficient. Such programs also provide opportunities for young people to meet others with similar interests. A variety of important qualities can be experienced through these programs (e.g., teamwork, dedication, perseverance, deferred rewards, and loyalty). These qualities should be nurtured in today's youth.

School physical activity programs could include community youth sports, YMCA activities, parks and recreation activities, private sport programs such as soccer or swimming, as well as basic physical activity programs for students at the schools. Physical educators should contribute to the leadership aspects of physical activity programs that augment physical education. Strong leadership ensures the quality of these programs and guards against possible abuses. Many teacher education programs across the country (for example, Arizona State University) are encouraging and providing coursework and internships for undergraduate and graduate students on how to run school physical activity programs before, during, and after school when facilities and equipment are available and are not being used at the school. Unqualified leaders with inappropriate program goals can lead to a discouraging experience for young, immature students. Programs must be developed with the idea of fostering a love of physical activity in students (rather than promoting escape or avoidance behaviors). Physical educators should help parents, other teachers, and adults organize these programs with the proper goals in mind. School wide physical activity promotion is often recognized as a comprehensive school physical activity program (see chapter 12).

LEARNING AIDS

STUDY STIMULATORS AND REVIEW QUESTIONS

1. Describe the public's general perception of physical education.
2. Explain the unique contribution of physical education to the lives of students.
3. What is the role of the national standards for physical education?
4. Explain why physical education is an excellent environment for teaching students about responsible behavior.
5. How would you use the public health perspective to defend physical education as a subject in the schools?
6. Describe four essential components of a quality physical education program.
7. Explain the limitations of a curriculum dominated by team sports.
8. List and discuss strategies teachers can use to develop positive attitudes toward physical activity in their students.
9. Explain how the SHAPE America standards should influence quality physical education programs across the country.
10. Discuss the Common Core Standards and how they might affect secondary physical education.
11. What growth and maturation components should be considered when teaching secondary physical education?
12. Describe five characteristics of successful physical education programs.
13. Discuss the role of physical education teachers as it relates to their involvement in the leadership of the various physical activity programs (intramurals, lunchtime activities, before-school and after-school open gym, sport physical activity clubs, staff programs, and athletics) at the school where they are teaching.

WEBSITES

SHAPE America

www.shapeamerica.org

American Heart Association

www.americanheart.org

Centers for Disease Control and Prevention

www.cdc.gov

Fitness for Life

www.fitnessforlife.org

FitnessGram/ActivityGram

www.fitnessgram.net

Human Kinetics

www.humankinetics.com

REFERENCES AND SUGGESTED READINGS

Abarca-Gómez, L., Abdeen, Z.A., Hamid, Z.A., Abu-Rmeileh, N.M., Acosta-Cazares, B., Acuin, C., . . . ,& Agyemang, C. (2017). Worldwide trends in body-mass index, underweight, overweight, and obesity from 1975 to 2016: A pooled analysis of 2416 population-based measurement studies in 128.9 million children, adolescents, and adults. *The Lancet, 390*(10113), 2627–2642.

Burns, R., Hannon, J.C., Brusseau, T.A., Shultz, B., & Eisenman, P. (2013). Indices of abdominal adiposity and cardiorespiratory fitness test performance in middle-school students. *Journal of Obesity.* doi:10.1155/2013/912460

Centers for Disease Control and Prevention. (2017). High school YRBS: United States 2017 results. Retrieved from https://nccd.cdc.gov/Youthonline/App/Results.aspx?.

Corbin, C., & Le Masurier, G. (2014). *Fitness for life* (6th ed.). Champaign, IL: Human Kinetics.

Corbin, C., Le Masurier, G.C., & Lambdin, D.D. (2018). *Fitness for life middle school* (2nd ed.). Champaign, IL: Human Kinetics.

Corbin, C., & Pangrazi, R. (2004). *Physical activity for children: A statement of guidelines for children ages 5–12*. Reston, VA: NASPE.

Corbin, C.B., Pangrazi, R.P., & Welk, G. (1994). Toward an understanding of appropriate physical activity levels for youth. *Physical Activity and Fitness Research Digest*, 2(2), 1–8.

Donnelly, J.E., Hillman, C.H., Castelli, D., Etnier, J.L., Lee, S., Tomporowski, P., . . . , & Szabo-Reed, A.N. (2016). Physical activity, fitness, cognitive function, and academic achievement in children: A systematic review. *Medicine and Science in Sports and Exercise*, 48(6), 1197.

Eitzen, D.S., & Sage, G. (1986). *Sociology of North American sport*. Dubuque, IA: W.C. Brown.

Guo, S.S., & Chumlea, W.C. (1999). Tracking of body mass index in children in relation to overweight in adulthood. *American Journal of Clinical Nutrition*, 70, 145S–148S.

Hellison, D. (2011). *Teaching responsibility through physical activity* (3rd ed.). Champaign, IL: Human Kinetics.

Ladwig, M.A., Vazou, S., & Ekkekakis, P. (2018). "My best memory is when I was done with it": PE memories are associated with adult sedentary behavior. *Translational Journal of the American College of Sports Medicine*, 3(16), 119–129.

Malina, R.M., Bouchard, C., & Bar-Or, O. (2004). *Growth, maturation, and physical activity*. Champaign, IL: Human Kinetics.

Morgan, C. (2004). *A longitudinal study of the relationships between physical activity, body mass index, and physical self-perception in youth*. Unpublished dissertation, Arizona State University.

Morgan, C.F., Pangrazi, R.P., & Beighle, A. (2003). Using pedometers to promote physical activity in physical education. *Journal of Physical Education Recreation and Dance*, 74(7), 33–38.

National Governors Association. (2013). Common core state standards initiative: Preparing America's students for college and career. Retrieved from www.corestandards.org.

Pangrazi, R.P., & Beighle, A. (2013). Dynamic physical education for elementary school children (17th ed.). San Francisco, CA: Benjamin Cummings.

Poitras, V.J., Gray, C.E., Borghese, M.M., Carson, V., Chaput, J.P., Janssen, I., . . . , & Sampson, M. (2016). Systematic review of the relationships between objectively measured physical activity and health indicators in school-aged children and youth. *Applied Physiology, Nutrition, and Metabolism*, 41(6), S197–S239.

Prusak, K., Treasure, D., Darst, P., & Pangrazi. (2004). The effects of choice on the motivation of adolescent girls in physical education. *Journal of Teaching in Physical Education*, 23(1), 19–29.

Sallis, J.F. (1994). Influences on physical activity of children, adolescents, and adults or determinants of active learning. *Physical Activity and Fitness Research Digest*, 1(7), 1–8.

Sallis, J.F., & McKenzie, T.L. (1991). Physical education's role in public health. *Research Quarterly for Exercise and Sport*, 62, 124–137.

SHAPE America. (2013). *National standards for K–12 physical education*. SHAPE America, Reston, VA.

SHAPE America. (2014). *National standards and grade-level outcomes for K–12 physical education*. Champaign, IL: Human Kinetics.

Siedentop, D., & Tannehill, D. (2000). Developing teaching skills in physical education (4th ed.). Mountain View, CA: Mayfield.

Simmonds, M., Llewellyn, A., Owen, C.G., & Woolacott, N. (2016). Predicting adult obesity from childhood obesity: A systematic review and meta analysis. *Obesity reviews*, 17(2), 95–107.

Skinner, A.C., Ravanbakht, S.N., Skelton, J.A., Perrin, E.M., & Armstrong, S.C. (2018). Prevalence of obesity and severe obesity in US children, 1999–2016. *Pediatrics*, 141(3), e20173459.

Suchindran, C., North, K.E., Popkin, B.M., & Gordon-Larsen, P. (2010). Association of adolescent obesity with risk of severe obesity in adulthood. *Journal of the American Medical Association*, 304(18), 2042–2047.

Telama, R., Yang, X., Leskinen, E., Kankaanpaa, A., Hirvensalo, M., Tammelin, T., & Raitakari, O.T. (2014). Tracking of physical activity from early childhood through youth into adulthood. *Medicine and Science in Sports and Exercise*, 46(5), 955–962.

Trost, S.G., & van der Mars, H. (2010). Why we should not cut P.E. *Educational Leadership*, December 2009/January 2010, 60–65.

U.S. Department of Health and Human Services. (1996). Physical activity and health: A report of the surgeon general. Atlanta, GA: U.S. Department of Health and Human Services, Centers for Disease Control and Prevention, National Center for Chronic Disease Prevention and Health Promotion.

U.S. Department of Health and Human Services. (2002). Prevalence of overweight among children and adolescents: United States, 1999. Atlanta, GA: Centers for Disease Control and Prevention, National Center for Health Statistics.

U.S. Department of Health and Human Services. (2010). Healthy people 2020: National health promotion and disease objectives. Washington, DC: U.S. Government Printing Office.

U.S. Department of Health and Human Services (2012). Physical activity guidelines for Americans midcourse report: Strategies to increase physical activity among youth. Washington, DC: U.S. Department of Health and Human Services.

U.S. Public Health Service. (1990). *Healthy people 2000: National health promotion and disease objectives*. Washington, DC: U.S. Government Printing Office.

Welk, G., & Meredith, M.D. (Eds.). (2010). *FitnessGram and ActivityGram test administration manual, updated* (4th ed.). Champaign, IL: Human Kinetics.

Williams, J.F. (1927). *The principles of physical education*. Philadelphia, PA: W.B. Saunders.

Curriculum Approaches

Chapter 2 focuses on the process of writing the physical education curriculum. Allied to this purpose is an analysis of the characteristics and strengths of the various approaches to curriculum writing.

Learning Objectives

- ► Describe curriculum approaches and explain the various ways that physical educators use them.
- ► List and discuss commonly used organizing centers in secondary school physical education.
- ► List and describe the popular categories of activities commonly used in the approach known as promoting physical activity and skill development.
- ► Discuss the advantages and disadvantages of the popular promoting physical activity and skill development approach.
- ► Discuss the problems and advantages of implementing an outdoor adventure activity approach in a high school.
- ► Describe the pros and cons of a sport education approach for secondary school physical education.
- ► Explain the characteristics of a knowledge concepts curriculum approach.
- ► Describe the games classification, problem classification, and tactical complexity associated with the tactical games approach.
- ► Understand how fitness education can be integrated into a knowledge concepts curriculum approach.
- ► List the different levels of social development in Hellison's teaching (taking) personal and social responsibility approach.

Curriculum approaches are built on a set of beliefs and goals that evolve from a theoretical framework or value base. These approaches provide the basis for organizing objectives and content, structuring and sequencing activities, and evaluating the curriculum plan. The scope and sequence of activities for the instructional program evolve from the curriculum approach (see chapter 3). Approaches provide interrelationships between content and the instructional process. An understanding of popular curriculum approaches and how they can be adapted to unique situations facilitates the development process.

TEACHING TIP

A common misconception is that teachers should only use one curriculum approach. But remember that the seven common approaches identified in this chapter can be interchangeable depending on the expertise of the teacher, facilities and equipment available, characteristics of the students and community, and so on. The key, regardless of approach, is promoting student learning and helping them achieve national, state, and local standards and grade-level outcomes.

When building a quality physical education curriculum, different approaches can be used:

1. A curriculum approach functioning in another school can be incorporated into a new setting. The program can be accepted in total with only minor changes for local school or community preferences.

2. Adaptation of an existing curriculum approach to meet the local interests, preferences, and school priorities is a second alternative. The existing approach is modified by incorporating local interests, preferences, and school philosophies into a restructured program.

3. A new approach is constructed, coordinating ideas from many sources to form a unified program. This difficult and time-consuming challenge requires a breadth of experience and clear understanding of the curriculum process.

Formal curricula should be centered on national or state standards and are usually organized around a major theme, often called an **organizing center**. The most common organizing centers for physical education curricula are the following:

- Physical skills involved in various movement forms, sports, and physical activities; commonly included units are basketball, tennis, volleyball, weight training, walking, and jogging.
- Both health-related (e.g., cardiorespiratory endurance, muscular strength and endurance, flexibility, and body composition) and skill-related fitness (e.g., agility, speed, power, and so on) and skills such as goal setting and program planning to improve both health-related and skill-related fitness.
- Health and wellness knowledge and activities involving stress management, nutrition, weight control, substance abuse, personal safety, physical fitness, environmental awareness, and behavioral self-control.
- Movement themes such as propelling, catching, striking, and balancing.
- Student motives such as appearance, health, and achievement.
- Developing a tactical understanding of game play.
- Disciplinary knowledge from such areas as biomechanics, motor learning, exercise physiology, and sport philosophy.
- Social development themes, such as competition, emotional control, sportspersonship, and cooperation.

Promoting Skill Development and Physical Activity Approach

The most used curriculum approach at the secondary level is a broad-based multiple activity approach that focuses on promoting physical activity and developing physical skills with students. A variety of activities are included from several categories. These include fitness activities such as strength training; sport units including tennis, basketball, softball, aquatics, and dance; and nontraditional activities like disc golf and eclipse ball. This system uses units of physical activity or sport as the basic core of the curriculum. These skills and activities provide the content of the model and the structure or format of the curriculum. Units vary in length from two weeks to one full school year, depending on program philosophy and the school level of the student. Middle schools usually offer shorter units that ensure variety and introduction to skills, whereas high schools have longer units with an in-depth focus on activities. Included activities change depending on the desires of society and needs and interests of the students. Most often, activities are classified in the following categories:

- Team sports: basketball, volleyball, flag football, softball, and soccer
- Lifetime sports: golf, tennis, bowling, archery, and racquetball
- Dance: folk, line, social, modern, and country swing
- Fitness activities: jogging or walking, aerobics, weight training, CrossFit, yoga, Pilates, exercise balls, and cardio kickboxing
- Recreational games: horseshoes, shuffleboard, and table tennis
- Outdoor adventure activities: cycling, rock climbing, skiing, and orienteering
- Aquatics: swimming, diving, skin and scuba diving, and water sports
- Nontraditional activities: disc golf, modified sports or games (i.e., touch rugby), eclipse ball, throtons, Spin Jammer Discs, martial arts, cooperative activities, and new games

This type of curriculum is usually arranged with a balance of activities from those categories. But a possible approach is to concentrate the focus on one or more categories of activity such as the outdoor adventure activities or fitness activities. In most cases, activities are included based on mediating factors such as student interest, teacher interest and expertise, community interest, class size, facilities, equipment, and climate. Activities in the curriculum generally follow the preferences of society, usually with a significant time lag. The arrival of the "new" units and skills in physical education curricula—such as cardio kickboxing, CrossFit, in-line skating, mountain biking—are usually indicative of the desires of the people whom the program serves. Instructors must stay aware of student activity interests and trends of society to update the curriculum.

This approach is popular because it allows diversity and flexibility in meeting the changing interests and desires of today's students. To attract students to this program, a variety of current and popular activities with "cool new equipment" need to be offered. Because students have different competencies and interests, most want to be able to participate in activities related to their personal abilities. Offering a wide range of instructional units makes the program more appealing to the entire student body.

This approach provides the opportunity for students to explore, experiment, and experience a variety of physical skills and physical activities. The approach also provides the potential for in-depth units that help students gain enough experience and skill competency for adult participation. Students have many opportunities to learn lifetime skills and compete with others, the environment, or against themselves in various units.

Curriculum experts have begun to suggest that middle school programs should prepare students for a wide range of activities (Rink, 2014) and should provide opportunity for exploring numerous physical activity possibilities (Graham, Holt/Hale, & Parker, 2013) and ensure success (SHAPE America, 2009b). Furthermore, high school physical education should provide an opportunity to develop an expertise in several activities that may provide a lifetime of physical activity opportunities (SHAPE America, 2009a, Graham, Holt/Hale, & Parker, 2013).

To meet these recommendations, we suggest short units for middle school students and long units for high school students because of their interests and developmental characteristics. Middle school students going through puberty, a rapid growth spurt, or a period of slow motor development need successful experiences with a wide variety of activities. At a time when students find it difficult to tolerate failure, longer units can lock students into a frustrating or boring experience for a long time. Variety and novelty in a success-oriented atmosphere are important motivational keys for this age group. Short units of instruction are usually presented in middle school so that students can experience many activities and learn about their areas of personal interest and competency. The flow of the curriculum from middle school to high school goes from short units to long units—from searching for areas of competency to consumer-driven choices for achieving high levels of interest and success.

Students can find success in short units when emphasis is on exploring and learning about personal strengths and weaknesses. Finally, because most students are still trying to identify their strengths and weaknesses, the middle school years may be the last opportunity they will have to experience a wide variety of activities. Nontraditional (activities that are new or different from the established norm) units of instruction (see chapter 17) can offer variety and help maintain student interest. The middle school years should not be a time of specialization and refinement but rather a time of exploration and discovery.

Learning environments can be productive when units are changed often. Students and teachers are excited when a new activity begins. Long units can turn into a prolonged class tournament without variety and structured skill work. Some students, usually unskilled, may think they are placed in tournament play and forced into highly competitive situations without the opportunity to develop an adequate skill level. This approach only adds to the frustration for less skilled students. Finally, some teachers advocate long units to minimize their preparation duties and requisite instructional competency. Teaching fewer units requires less planning and knowledge. This rationale is difficult to accept if the needs and interests of all students are kept in focus.

Choice in the Approach

Instruction in a promoting physical activity and skill development curriculum proceeds from introductory lessons to advanced and specialized courses. Students are more often grouped by grade level than by ability or developmental level. In most situations, students proceed through a sequence of required physical activities throughout the school year in middle school and continue to an elective program in high school.

The choice concept can be used in several ways with units of any length and with any type of organizational schedule in the skills-based curriculum. This strategy in the curriculum can increase the level of motivation of both students and teachers and help create a more positive learning environment. Allowing for choice offers the following advantages:

- Increased student motivation and enthusiasm and a desire to take more physical education because of a higher interest level
- Fewer problems with dressing, participation, and management and discipline
- Better use of teaching expertise and the development of specialists
- Improved instruction over time
- Increased teacher motivation and enthusiasm

This trend of incorporating choice into the curriculum, which started at the college level and filtered down to high school and middle school programs, allows students a degree of choice for activities in the program. Classes are open to both genders, and the gender composition of the class will depend on personal interests in the activities. Using this approach, male and female teachers work together and decide who is better qualified to teach a specific activity. Each teacher develops two or three specialties and teaches those specialties to different classes of students, rather than teaching all activities to the same students.

Many schools are on a nine-week grading schedule. Students could choose physical education units at the beginning of each semester. An example of this design with three teachers has been used in mixed-gender classes that allow males and females to select all activities. If more than three teachers are available, students can make choices from a broader selection. The following is an example of alternating four- and five-week units in a mixed-gender curriculum with choices for students:

First Nine Weeks:
- Eclipse ball or volleyball, yoga or Pilates, or soccer (four weeks)
- Flag football, archery, or tennis (five weeks)

Second Nine Weeks:
- Pickleball, badminton, or lacrosse (four weeks)
- Basketball, team handball, or field hockey (five weeks)

Third Nine Weeks:
- Aerobics, speed-a-way, or bowling (four weeks)
- Cardio kickboxing, orienteering, or line dancing (five weeks)

Fourth Nine Weeks:
- Circuit training, track and field, or flag football (four weeks)
- Swimming, disc games, cardio kickboxing, or physioballs (five weeks)

Some schools vary this approach by developing requirements by activity categories to ensure that breadth across categories is provided. For example, students take a certain number of team sports, lifetime sports, physical fitness activities, dance units, aquatics, or recreational activities. This concept is referred to as a choice within a requirement. Depending on the number of units offered, students are required to take a specified number of units from each category. For example, if the program offers 24 three-week units over a two-year period, the requirements might include the following:

- One unit of *Fitness for Life: Middle School* concepts (Corbin, LeMasurier, & Lambdin, 2018)
- Two units of aquatics
- Two units of dance

- Four units of physical fitness
- Five units of lifetime sports
- Five units of team sports
- Five units of elective activities

Consideration of Proficiency Levels in the Approach

Many high schools are attempting to offer different proficiency levels for various activities. This approach implies sections for beginning, intermediate, and advanced levels of instruction for the most popular activities. Grouping students by ability and experience can offer efficient teaching and learning situations for teachers and students. Students may be more comfortable with others near their ability level. Students can skip a level if they are proficient at the earlier level. Teachers can provide more specialized and in-depth instruction when students are similar in experience and ability with the activity. The following are descriptions that can be used for different levels of instruction:

- Beginning level: introductory units for the development of the basic skills and knowledge of the activity
- Intermediate level: more advanced skills and knowledge about the activity and the team concepts of the team sports
- Advanced level: advanced units that allow the students to continue pursuing higher skill levels, examine tactical strategies, and focus more on competitive or challenging activities

Suggested Middle School Curriculum for Promoting Skill Development and Physical Activity

The daily lesson plan format for this approach in the middle school should include an introductory or warm-up activity (6%–10% of class time), a physical fitness routine (23%–27% of class time), and a lesson focus and game segment (50%–66% of class time). This format should be consistent and an outgrowth of the elementary physical education program. A consistent instructional format within each class provides teachers and students with an important measure of stability and routine. Each of the three areas in the lesson plan should be planned out for the year so that all activities will be covered. If activities are not planned, teachers will find that they forgot to include certain activities or that they

do not have enough activities for the remainder of the year. In addition, trying to design a scope and sequence is impossible if activities are not in a written format. How does a teacher modify the curriculum when the activities presented cannot be recalled?

Introductory Activities

The introductory activity occupies three to five minutes of the total lesson format. The purpose of this segment is to prepare students physiologically for strenuous activity. An allied purpose is to ready students psychologically for activity. Students usually take a few minutes to become emotionally involved in activity after a day of sitting in classes. The introductory activity requires minimal organization and demands large-muscle movement. It may be an integral part of the fitness routine or can be a separate entity. In either case, the introductory activity should raise the heart rate, warm up the body, and stretch the muscles in anticipation of the fitness development activity. Traditional static stretching should be used not for warm-ups but for cooling down or flexibility-specific training. Teachers should change the introductory activity each week to add variety to the warm-up procedure. The sixth-, seventh-, and eighth-grade students can perform similar introductory activities. Figure 2.1 shows a recommended yearly sequence (36 weeks). An in-depth discussion of introductory activities is found in chapter 14.

Fitness Routines

The fitness routines use 10 to 15 minutes of the lesson, and their primary purpose is the development of physical fitness and positive attitudes toward lifetime activity and fitness. Fitness routines should offer total fitness development to the students. In other words, an attempt should be made to develop and enhance major components of (health-related) fitness—especially flexibility, muscular strength and endurance, body composition, and cardiorespiratory endurance. The activities should be demanding, progressive in nature, and useful after graduation and into the future. Students must experience a wide variety of fitness routines so that they can learn to select methods acceptable to them for a lifetime. They should leave school with an understanding that they can develop and maintain an active lifestyle in many ways and that the responsibility for doing so lies with them.

Students in middle school should stay with the same routine for two weeks to get a good feel for a routine over a 10-day period. Minor changes and variations can be used with each routine to provide success, variety, and a challenge for all the students. Variations for

Week	Introductory activity	Week	Introductory activity
1.	Move and freeze	18.	Form running
2.	Basic movements (walk, slide, carioca, step-hop)	19.	Jumping and plyometric drills
3.	Fugitive tag with a variety of movements	20.	Fastest tag variations
4.	Walk, trot, sprint	21.	Seat rolls and wave drill
5.	Basic movement (pivots, slide and pivot, carioca and pivot)	22.	Standing high fives
6.	Run, stop, and pivot	23.	Loose caboose
7.	Flag grab with a variety of movements	24.	Spider tag variations
8.	Marking variations	25.	Leaping Lena
9.	Move and change directions	26.	Rooster hop
10.	Quick hands with beanbags	27.	Move, change directions, and freeze
11.	Flash drills	28.	Triangle and one
12.	Partner over and under	29.	Making variations
13.	Throw and catch on the move	30.	Power-walk variations—add 'em up
14.	Clothespin tag variations	31.	Throwing and catching variations on the move
15.	File running variations	32.	Follow the leader
16.	Quickness drills	33.	Triangle and two
17.	Movements with high fives	34.	Wave drill variations
		35.	Blob tag
		36.	Ball Activities

FIGURE 2.1 Yearly sequence of introductory activities for middle school students.

each routine are discussed in chapter 15. Success in the fitness routines will help motivate students and serve as a basis for future skill development in the lessons. Students need to experience and learn that fitness is individual and relative to their genetic and trainability background. Teachers need to remind students that through continued efforts in the fitness area, all students can be successful. The FitnessGram (Cooper Institute, 2017) can be used to educate and monitor students in the fitness area. A fitness report and ActivityGram can be used for self-testing, goal setting, and communication with parents. A printout graphically reveals the student's fitness profile and identifies the student as being in the healthy fitness zone, needs improvement–some risk zone, or needs improvement–high risk zone for each of the five components of health-related fitness. The profile can be a positive part of the fitness segment of the class and a good way to involve students and parents by collecting information, entering it in the computer, and analyzing it for future use. Fitness self-testing should not take a lot of class time, and it maintains the purpose of teaching students skills that they can use for a lifetime.

Fitness routines recommended for the middle school are shown in figure 2.2. An in-depth discussion with samples and variations is included in chapter 15.

Week	Fitness routines
1–2	Teacher–leader activities
3–4	Stretching and form running
5–6	Four corner fitness
7–8	Partner race track fitness
9–10	Exercise to music
11–12	Jump bands fitness
13–14	Circuit training fitness
15–16	Step aerobics
17–18	Jump and jog fitness
19–20	Monopoly fitness
21–22	Power-walking variations
23–24	Partner resistance and aerobic fitness
25–26	Long jump-rope fitness
27–28	Fortune cookie fitness
29–30	Squad leader fitness
31–32	Cardio kickboxing
33–34	Jump-rope fitness
35–36	Group fitness scavenger hunt

FIGURE 2.2 Yearly sequence of fitness routines for middle school students.

Lesson Focus and Game

The lesson focus and game should last 25 to 35 minutes, depending on the length of the period. This segment is the instructional part of the lesson and emphasizes skill development, cognitive learning, and enhancement of the affective domain. This phase of the lesson contains skills to be taught, drills, and lead-up activities necessary for skill practice, all of which culminate in games and tournaments. The length of activity units in the lesson focus should be short, in the range of two to three weeks if the classes meet daily. Two-week units are recommended with a daily format. Three-week units can be a combination of two activities, such as football and Ultimate. The combination-type unit allows daily alternation of the two activities. This combination can be an effective way to keep all students involved; if they do not like football, they can always look forward to Ultimate the next day.

 TEACHING TIP

Combination-type units are especially effective when the games share similar tactical strategies. For example, concepts related to creating space and defending are similar in many invasion team games (e.g., football and Ultimate, or soccer and team handball).

Middle school students should have some choice as to which units they take. They should be required to take at least one unit from each of the following categories: team sports, lifetime sports, nontraditional activities, rhythms, and aquatics (if possible). Physical fitness routines should be required in all units of instruction on a daily basis. Teachers should decide which activities in their program fit the various categories. The category requirement ensures a measure of breadth for each student in the program. Students should not be allowed to repeat the same unit because the emphasis of the model is to ensure that students explore and receive a breadth of activities.

Students should have the opportunity to learn the fundamentals of personal fitness and physical activity before they leave the middle school in case the high school they attend does not have a physical education requirement. Each student will thus have five required categories of activity. Students then choose the remaining units in any category in which they have an interest.

They can take advanced-level units after meeting their basic requirements.

The specific activity units offered should be determined through a student interest survey (see chapter 3; figure 3.7). This approach offers the physical education staff insight into units that are attractive to students. Activity units must accomplish national and state standards and be updated from year to year, depending on the interests of the students and the opinions of the staff. This approach should provide a balance of activities from the required categories.

A school with four physical education teachers might offer the curriculum design shown in figure 2.3. During the first unit of each semester, students would make their eight choices based on the required categories and their personal interests. At that time, students would be reminded to select activities based on their interests and curriculum requirements, rather than on the teacher or on who else is in the class. Student interests and course requirements should determine the composition of the class. The first unit of the semester is a required unit that focuses on an introduction to the program and a discussion and practice of all rules, routines, and policies.

Previous learning is considered in the sequence of the horizontal or yearly curriculum. Activities that use common skills can be placed later in the year (e.g., team handball, speed-a-way, and floor hockey can build on basketball, volleyball, and soccer). Within the vertical arrangement, the seventh grade should build on the sixth grade in terms of skills, cognitive learning, and lead-up games. The eighth-grade curriculum should then build on the seventh grade. Increased knowledge, more in-depth strategies, and higher skill levels are the focus of the eighth grade. Because of scheduling problems, some schools must put seventh- and eighth-grade students together in the same class. This situation is unfortunate because of the wide range of developmental levels of students in these two grades. Principles of individualized instruction, discussed in chapters 4 and 5, can help individual physical skill development instruction within these classes. Teachers always face many different physical skill levels within their classes no matter what the organizational scheme. Teachers must be aware of the developmental differences and provide a variety of learning activities for different levels within each unit.

This curriculum approach for middle school students can be implemented effectively with a variety of adaptations depending on the number of students and teachers, the school requirements, the teaching facilities, the equipment available, the school schedule, and other environmental factors discussed in chapter 1. This

Week	Lesson focus choices
First semester (weeks 1–18)	
1–2	Introduction and orientation to physical education
3–4	Swimming, volleyball, eclipse ball, disc games, or flag football
5–6	Swimming, tennis, badminton, or soccer
7–8	Weight training, tennis, basketball, or lacrosse
9–10	Gymnastics, badminton, soccer, or disc games
11–12	Aerobics, basketball, field hockey, or lacrosse
13–14	Orienteering, basketball, team handball, or wrestling
15–16	Jogging, yoga, speed-a-way, or aerobics
17–18	Modern dance, step aerobics, team handball, or golf
Second semester (weeks 19–36)	
19–20	Dance: folk, square, line and country; aerobics and cardio kickboxing; weight training; or cooperative activities
21–22	Orienteering, speed-a-way, weight training, or new games
23–24	Disc games, basketball, soccer, or volleyball
25–26	Gymnastics, badminton, tennis, or field hockey
27–28	Track and field, softball, volleyball, or physical conditioning
29–30	Modern dance, self-defense, lacrosse, or disc games
31–32	Track and field, walking activities, team handball, or new games
33–34	Swimming, modern dance, recreational games, or flag football variations
35–36	Swimming, speed-a-way, group team building, or team handball

FIGURE 2.3   Middle school lesson focus sequence for a four-person physical education department.

framework serves as the basis for the Dynamic Secondary School Physical Education curriculum approach used in many middle schools across the country.

Suggested Grade 9 Curriculum for Promoting Skill Development and Physical Activity

The ninth-grade year is often the last required class of physical education in many schools. Consequently, ninth graders need to leave with positive attitudes toward physical activity, a desire to return for additional physical education classes, and a desire to pursue a lifetime of physical activity.

Ninth graders are usually in a transition from middle school to senior high school. Some districts put the 9th graders with 7th and 8th graders, but most districts place them with 10th-, 11th-, and 12th-grade students. Both arrangements have advantages and disadvantages, and decisions are usually based on such factors as historical arrangements, class size, building space, and projected district growth. The 9th-grade curriculum design usually resembles that of the other grades with which the students are grouped. The requirements, schedules, length of units, types of activities, amount of choice, and other factors are usually the same as the middle school programs. A major difference is that the 9th-grade units tends to be longer than the middle school units. Some schools also allow ninth graders to take longer, specialized units in a few popular activities such as dance or weight training. Different proficiency levels may also be available for some 9th graders (e.g., beginning, intermediate, and advanced units).

The grade 9 curriculum design for physical education should be especially attractive to students because it may be their last organized physical activity experience. Making a curriculum attractive does not mean compromising educational objectives. The curricula must be designed with specific, valuable objectives in mind, and students should not be allowed to make all their curricular decisions in any situation.

A curriculum approach can be made both attractive and educationally sound by incorporating several factors. First, students should have some activity choices for each unit. At this grade level, they need continued opportunities to explore different activities. Second, the arrangement should incorporate organized self-testing, personal counseling, and a wellness orientation to give students additional information for making decisions about physical activity and their lifestyles. Third, the choices of activity should include a wide variety of different categories of physical activity, especially new and popular units such as in-line skating, mountain biking, cross-country skiing, rock climbing, disc games, walking, cardiorespiratory machines, weight training, physioballs, and cardio kickboxing. Fourth, the program should lead students into more depth in their selected activities so that they can develop a higher skill level. This goal can be met by having different proficiency levels, such as beginning, intermediate, and advanced sections, or at least the opportunity to repeat favorite units. Finally, efforts should be made to develop a positive learning environment so that students will enjoy the process and have a desire to return for additional learning during the remainder of their high school years.

Classes should meet daily, and units should be two to three weeks in length. Ninth graders should be required to take units from the following categories:

- Two units of *Fitness for Life* (Corbin & Le Masurier, 2014) and wellness concepts
- One unit of team sports
- One unit of lifetime sports
- One unit of rhythms
- One unit of aquatics (if possible)
- One unit of novel activities or adventure activities
- Five units of electives from any category

This requirement ensures a measure of breadth by category. The electives can be used for greater depth in an activity or for additional breadth, depending on the interests of the student. Ninth graders should be able to repeat a unit or take an intermediate-level class as part of their electives. Because students at this age have started to narrow their activity interests, they should be able to start specializing in their favorite activities. Their developmental level will allow them to improve faster than the sixth, seventh, or eighth graders in the motor skills area. Students who take two three-week units of the same activity should demonstrate visible improvement in skill-level development.

TEACHING TIP

Consider requiring junior varsity and varsity student athletes to choose activities outside their sport. They will gain greater breadth in their experiences and provide other students additional learning opportunities in those sports.

Introductory Activities

A short introductory or warm-up activity (three to five minutes) is useful to prepare students for the physical fitness routine (see chapter 15). These activities should be attractive and challenging with lots of variety. Low organization and large-muscle activities that get students moving quickly should dominate this segment of the lesson. An example is the popular high-five activity in which football, baseball, and basketball teammates slap hands together overhead or down low after performing some feat of excellence. Ninth graders can be challenged to warm up by alternating various locomotor movements (walking, jogging, sliding, and doing carioca) with giving classmates a high five, a low five, or a medium five. Music can be programmed with 15-second intervals on and off to change the movements of the students. Another example is to have student partners give each other a high five after a 90-, 180-, 270-, or a 360-degree turn and jump to the right or left. These activities are good ways to prepare students for the vigorous fitness routines in a novel and interesting manner.

The introductory activity should be changed at least every week. There are many ways to add variety and challenge with each weekly introductory activity. The yearly sequence suggested for middle school students can serve as the basis for the ninth graders. The ninth-grade sequence should be developed with additional examples from chapter 14. For added interest, modified or new warm-up activities can be created, depending on the season, the type of fitness routine that follows (strength, endurance, or flexibility focus), or the type of lesson focus activity that follows (basketball, golf, or tennis). The yearly sequence of introductory activities for ninth graders shown in figure 2.4 is suggested.

Fitness Routines

A vigorous and demanding physical fitness routine (10 to 15 minutes) should follow the introductory segment

Week	Activity	Week	Activity
1.	Basic movements (walk, slide, carioca, triple jump)	18.	Jumping and plyometric drills
2.	Stretching and flexibility exercises	19.	Fastest tag variations
3.	Form running variations	20.	Seat rolls and wave drill
4.	Basic sport movement (pivots, slide and pivot, carioca, run backward)	21.	Standing high fives with a turn
		22.	Loose caboose variations
5.	Fugitive tag variations	23.	Spider tag variations
6.	Flag grab with a variety of movements	24.	Flexibility challenges
7.	Marking variations	25.	Quarter eagle footwork
8.	Move and change directions	26.	Move, change directions, and freeze
9.	Quick hands with throtons	27.	Triangle and one
10.	Flash drills	28.	Making variations
11.	Jog and stretch variations	29.	Power-walk variations
12.	Throw and catch on the move	30.	Throwing and catching variations on the move
13.	Clothespin tag variations	31.	Blob tag variations
14.	File running variations	32.	Triangle and two
15.	Quickness drills	33.	Wave drill variations
16	Movements with high fives	34.	Student choice
17.	Form running	35.	Student choice
		36.	Student choice

FIGURE 2.4   Yearly sequence of introductory activities for ninth graders.

of the lesson. A different routine every three weeks gives students a final chance to explore many different fitness activities. Emphasis should be placed on imparting knowledge to students so that they understand which activities affect various parameters of fitness. Students need to be taught and encouraged to make decisions relative to physical fitness and their personal fitness routine choices. Students should self-test their fitness level at least once a year with the FitnessGram system (Cooper Institute, 2017) and be educated on the various components of health-related fitness. Teachers need to ensure that students understand the role that genetics and training factors play in the results of fitness testing (see chapters 1 and 15 for evidence) and make sure that students understand the importance of regular activity relative to the results of the fitness test.

The three-week physical fitness routines in figure 2.5 are suggested for the ninth-grade curriculum. Instructors should carefully explain and demonstrate progression and overload principles to the students. Within each of the three-week routines, teachers should vary the activities as much as possible to provide variety, success, and a challenge for all students.

Week	Activity
1–3	Teacher–leader activities and form running
4–6	Weight training stations
7–9	Partner race track fitness
10–12	Step aerobics
13–15	Exercise machines
16–18	Circuit training stations
19–21	Jump and jog fitness
22–24	Fitness scavenger hunt
25–27	Power-walk variations
28–30	Cardio kickboxing fitness
31–33	Partner jump-rope activities
34–36	Fortune cookie fitness or Monopoly fitness

FIGURE 2.5   Yearly sequence of fitness routines for ninth graders.

Lesson Focus and Games

Results of a student interest survey combined with the opinions of teachers can be used to determine the activity units offered during the lesson focus segment (25 to 35 minutes). Classes should meet daily, and the units should be three weeks long. When feasible, the curriculum should be extended into the community to use nearby facilities, such as disc golf courses, local climbing gyms, golf ranges, bowling alleys, ski slopes, and rivers or lakes. Community resources can become an important part of the program in terms of both facilities and instructional personnel. Schools must work in concert with private sport and recreation groups in the community. Students need to be socialized into the activities available in the local community.

Physical skills can be taught and monitored with performance objectives written for each unit. Programmed practice sheets can also be added to structure skill work during the lesson focus. Examples are provided in chapters 18 through 20. A strong knowledge component should also be incorporated into all units. A written test or other cognitive assessments should be given every nine weeks after completing three units. Students should be given reading assignments, written work for portfolios, and outside-of-class projects to enhance their attitudes toward physical activity. Ideas for student assessment are included in chapter 8.

Instructors must take care to organize the curriculum activities horizontally throughout the year and ensure vertical articulation with the eighth-grade program. Opportunities should be available to increase skill levels and knowledge of activities included in previous years. The sequence of activity units in figure 2.6 is suggested for a ninth-grade curriculum with six teachers. The first unit of each semester is required for all students. It should consist of a fitness for life concepts class (see the section Fitness Education Approach in this chapter). The remaining units are choices for the students based on the category requirements and the students' interests. Students must meet the category requirement, and then the remaining units are electives.

Suggested Grades 10 Through 12 Curriculum for Promoting Skill Development and Physical Activity

At these grade levels, students continue to narrow their range of interests in many areas, including physical activity. Students are capable and should be allowed to choose the physical activities they want to pursue. By 10th grade, the program should be totally elective and participant driven. This is not the time to force students into activity settings that are of no interest to them. It is a time to promote student independence and choice. Students should decide what activities to take under the structure and guidance of a well-developed physical education elective approach.

Classes should meet daily and last six to nine weeks, depending on the school schedule. Student interest should guide units offered and class composition. These longer units allow in-depth instruction and the development of a high level of skill competency. High school

Week	Lesson focus options
First semester (weeks 1–18)	
1–3	Fitness for life concepts (required: six sections) (Corbin & Lindsey, 2007)
4–6	Swimming 1 and 2, novel activities (eclipse ball), dance 1, badminton, or soccer
7–9	Swimming 1 and 2, volleyball, dance 1 and 2, or fitness walking
10–12	Dance 1 and 2, disc games, speed-a-way, team handball, or volleyball
13–15	Dance 2, tennis, basketball, field hockey, novel activities (eclipse ball), or combatives
16–18	Aerobic and weight training 1 and 2, tennis, golf, badminton, or lacrosse
Second semester (weeks 19–36)	
19–21	Fitness for life concepts (required: six sections) (Corbin & Lindsey, 2007)
22–24	Soccer, basketball, tennis, weight training, orienteering, or field hockey
25–27	Gymnastics, basketball 2, disc games, lacrosse, speed-a-way, or tennis
28–30	Dance 2, volleyball, recreational games, softball 1 and 2, or weight training
31–33	Soccer, team handball, dance 1 and 2, weight training, or new games
34–36	Swimming 1 and 2, disc games 1 and 2, or orienteering games 1 and 2

FIGURE 2.6 Ninth-grade lesson focus sequence for a six-person physical education department.

students can persist at tasks for a longer period and can benefit from the long units of instruction. After six to nine weeks of instruction, students should have enough skill and knowledge so that the reinforcing aspects of the activity will motivate them to continue outside the school environment. The curriculum should emphasize a health club or fitness center approach of lifetime or lifestyle-type activities usually available in a community health club or elsewhere in the community. This approach could include such activities as walking, jogging, step aerobics, yoga, Pilates, cardio kickboxing, CrossFit, physioballs, body bars, medicine balls, swimming, tennis, racquetball, weight training, bicycling, hiking, and so on. The program should also offer as many proficiency levels of instruction as possible to accommodate different students' abilities.

Students switch lesson focus activities only after a minimum of six to nine weeks of instruction and practice. They can repeat a lesson focus unit at a higher skill level if it is offered, or they can take different units for another six to nine weeks. Facilities, student interest, and faculty expertise will determine which activities are taught each period. Community facilities and programs should be used as much as possible within the existing parameters available for funds, travel arrangements, and legal liability. Students can go into the community for units, or the community programs can be brought to the schools. The community facilities might include swimming pools, fitness centers, rock-climbing gyms, hiking or cycling trails, martial arts centers, orienteering sites, ski slopes, bowling alleys, golf ranges, or canoeing areas.

The fitness portion of the lesson (15 to 20 minutes) should also be elective in nature. It could be organized in several ways. One format would have each available teacher coordinating a different fitness activity at a different teaching site. Specific activities might include stretching, weightlifting, walking and jogging variations, step aerobics, high-intensity interval training, box aerobics, and rope jumping. Students could pursue their preferences on certain days of the week and then switch to different activities on alternate days. The only requirement is that students must maintain a balance of cardiorespiratory activities and muscular strength or flexibility activities. Students could switch instructors and activities depending on their needs and interests. After the fitness portion of the lesson, students and teachers move on to their selected lesson focus unit. This approach allows students to select the type and variety of fitness activity they desire, as long as they maintain the balance described earlier. Teachers would work out details for switching from activity to activity and keeping track of student attendance.

A school that has six teachers available per period and appropriate facilities could offer the following fitness stations:

- Stretching and brisk walking
- Slow jogging and interval training
- Aerobic dance (beginning level)
- Aerobic dance or cardio kickboxing (intermediate level)
- Weight training (beginning and intermediate)
- Yoga or Pilates exercise and work with physioballs or medicine balls

If facilities are limited and certain fitness activities are extremely popular (weight training or aerobic dance), then a rotation schedule might allow students whose last names start with letters A through M to participate on Monday and Wednesday, while N through Z would participate on Tuesday and Thursday. In any of these formats, teachers must solve potential problems with attendance and rotation procedures for students who might ride a bus to a ski slope or walk to a local bowling alley. At times some students would have to miss the fitness portion of the lesson because of the logistics of the situation.

Figure 2.7 is an example of a yearly lesson focus sequence for a high school promoting a physical activity and skill development program with a health club focus that has six teachers available. Teachers can become specialists in certain popular activities that students elect each year. The quality of instruction should be at the highest possible level. Activities in the program will change as often as students desire. Communities with strong interests in specific activities (golf, tennis, sailing, skiing, horseback riding, hockey, rock climbing, lacrosse, and so on) will dictate the activity choices of students. The schools will then be cooperating with the private sector by preparing students for lifestyle activities available in the surrounding community. The physical education profession can no longer afford to offer programs that show little or no concern for student preference.

Articulation in Promoting Skill Development and Physical Activity

The approach presented here is carefully articulated from elementary school through high school. It is built on the popular elementary (K–6) physical education model in *Dynamic Physical Education for Elementary School Children* (Pangrazi & Beighle, 2020). It follows the same daily format and uses arrangements of learning activities appropriate for the developmental levels of students. The entire K–12 sequence emphasizes skill development, individual success, a process focus, regular physical activity, exploration, guidance, self-monitoring, knowledge, and a lifetime of physical activity. The components of this model are shown in figure 2.8. This model provides school districts with a sound, progressively arranged physical education curriculum that has been field-tested by the authors in many districts. Various options have been used depending on the specific factors involved. The model is built on educational theory and research as well as on practical environmental factors that influence learning environments. By giving students many successful encounters with physical activity, they will leave school with a positive approach toward learning in general and physical activities in particular.

Outdoor Adventure Activities Approach

Another variation of the promoting physical activity and skill development approach is the outdoor adventure activities approach. This approach has a focus on communication, cooperation, trust, and group problem solving that usually consists of structured experiences or obstacles (e.g., a high-ropes course). Outdoor education occurs in the natural environment where students must work together to overcome hazards that may include weather, wildlife, or difficult terrain (Lund, 2015). The outdoor adventure approach centers on personal and group development and attempts to minimize competition as well as winning and losing. Popular activities in this approach are cycling, orienteering, backpacking, skin or scuba diving, canoeing, cross-country skiing, downhill skiing, caving, rock climbing or rappelling, group initiatives, and ropes course activities. Some schools include a limited number of short units (either elective or required) of outdoor adventure activities as part of the program, whereas others offer an entire semester course of activities. Most often, high schools offer a yearlong elective course designed with a variety of outdoor adventure pursuits. The program might include a yearlong elective wilderness adventure class in the physical education program that includes instruction and field trips for rock climbing, rappelling, caving, beginning and advanced backpacking, and day hikes. Usually, the focus of these programs is on the development of basic skills requisite for participation in these

Week	Elective class offerings
1–9	Fitness for life concepts (Corbin & Lindsey, 2007)
	Tennis
	Golf
	Dance
10–18	Racquetball
	Volleyball or eclipse ball
	Fitness center activities
	Rock climbing
	Disc games
	Soccer
19–27	Bowling
	Bicycling
	Badminton
	Fitness center activities
	Orienteering
	Basketball
28–36	Fitness center activities
	Dance
	Water sports and activities
	Tennis
	Racquetball
	Hiking and camping

FIGURE 2.7 Grades 10 through 12 lesson focus sequence for a six-person physical education department.

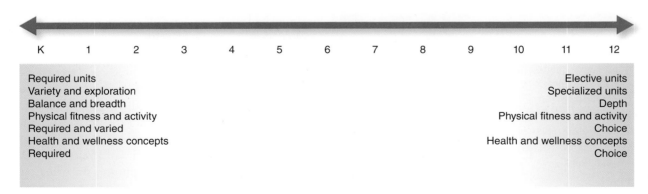

FIGURE 2.8 K–12 curriculum components.

activities. Another approach is to offer group initiative and cooperative activities that help students learn group and individual problem-solving skills under stressful situations. Many of these activities (especially those that may pose some emotional or physical challenges or risk) can be intimidating to students. Where potential risk increases, it is essential to challenge by choice. For example, a student may have anxiety about climbing to the top of a high-ropes activity. This approach does not permit a student to opt out of participating, but an alternative adventure activity should be available for that student.

Adding outdoor adventure activities to the program creates significant change for teachers, students, administrators, and parents. Many of the activities must be done off campus. For example, rock-climbing areas, wooded or desert locations, caves, rivers, and lakes can be used. Establishing a nearby off-campus environment with various outdoor facilities can provide a variety of teaching areas for these activities. The units can culminate with an off-campus trip during the school day or as an after-school or weekend trip with parents involved. The trips give students an opportunity to learn and experience activities that are different from regular school offerings. After-school, weekend, and vacation times are often used for these classes.

Safety and liability problems related to these activities require special safety and insurance arrangements. Many administrators and parents show little concern about injuries related to athletic programs such as football, wrestling, and gymnastics, but they are extremely cautious about implementing adventure activities that appear risky. Most of the activities require funding for specialized equipment such as compasses, climbing ropes, and camping gear. Teachers must show evidence of having proper qualifications because of the expertise required for high-risk activities.

TEACHING TIP

Start small by choosing an activity that may be considered lower risk (e.g., snow shoeing or hiking) and easier to implement (e.g., can be done on campus) to demonstrate the feasibility of outdoor activities. Often these activities, when done properly, will show parents and administrators the benefits, which will allow your program to gradually expand the offerings of these activities.

With the difficulties inherent in outdoor adventure activities, why take the time to do the extra work? Because, in most cases, secondary students are highly motivated and enthusiastic about the activities. Their interest may be heightened for many reasons. Some students enjoy the novelty of the activities; others like the risk and excitement, the challenge of the environment, or the opportunity to make decisions. Still others like the social opportunities that arise without competition between people. Some are attracted to the lifetime participation emphasis and the opportunities that exist within the community. The activities offer the opportunity to travel, explore new areas, and enjoy competition with an environment of wind, water, snow, mountains, and woods. These activities satisfy the objectives of physical education and make it worth the extra effort. Many of the activities that take place in natural settings will easily allow the implementation of academic content related to geology, ecology, and other life sciences and provides a natural opportunity for the physical education teacher to collaborate with teachers in other content areas.

Physical educators continually need to dispel the following four myths that often block the introduction of outdoor pursuits into the physical education curriculum (originally identified by Parker & Steen, 1988).

1. The school must be located near major outdoor areas or state parks.
2. The teacher must have advanced skill levels in outdoor activities.
3. Concerns about safety, legal liability, and insurance present insurmountable obstacles.
4. The cost of outdoor pursuits is prohibitive for schools.

Schools and physical educators can overcome these problems in several ways. By starting small and being creative and innovative, much can be accomplished. Many of the activities are easy to implement and can be started on campus with a limited budget. With proper training and supervision, students can experience a safe and rewarding experience with outdoor activities.

Some schools have offered an elective outdoor adventure curriculum with two different levels. The first level is an introductory course that gives students an opportunity to enjoy and learn about the local outdoor areas. Students learn the fundamental skills of backpacking, fishing, hunting, camping, and wilderness first aid. Field trips are set up during the school day, after school, and over weekends. Students make choices on which and how many field trips they are going to take. Examples of activities and trips that have been used in Phoenix, Arizona, include hiking along a river or stream, fishing and camping in the high desert, participating in desert awareness activities at the Arizona-Sonora Desert Museum in Tucson, learning trap or skeet shooting and gun safety at a shooting range, hunting pheasants at a local hunting club, shooting arrows at an archery range, and learning basic horsemanship skills at a local horse stable.

Another more advanced and demanding course could include skills in rock climbing, backpacking, caving, orienteering, and skiing. Students in Vermont could select field trips from the following choices: hiking the Long Trail, backpacking up to Mt. Mansfield, orienteering in the Green Mountains, rock climbing at Wheeler Mountain, exploring at Nickwackett Cave, cross-country skiing in Bolton Valley, downhill skiing at Stowe. These classes could be elective and meet daily to work on the skills involved and prepare for the various field trips. Students may have to pay a special class fee for travel expenses and extra equipment (see figure 2.9).

Austin O'Brien High School in Calgary, Alberta, Canada, has offered a variety of outdoor adventure-type activities as part of their curricular offerings. Students select units on canoeing, sailing, kayaking, basic rock climbing, orienteering, outdoor survival, wilderness camping, backpacking, and cross-country skiing. A senior-level elective physical education class includes the yearly sequence of activities, including outdoor adventure activities and several popular lifetime activities:

1. Learn-to-sail program—Lake Wabamun
2. Wallyball
3. Bicycle mechanics course and Elk Island Tour
4. Curling
5. Archery
6. Rifle target shooting (trap and skeet)
7. Camping and hiking program
8. Cross-country skiing
9. Tennis
10. Social dance
11. Badminton
12. Racquetball
13. Bowling
14. Downhill skiing
15. Volleyball and pickleball
16. Coaching certification level-1 theory

Sport Education Approach

The sport education curriculum was developed to promote a positive sport experience for all students regardless of their ability (Siedentop, Hastie, & van der Mars, 2020; Bulger, Mohr, Rairigh, & Townsend, 2007). The curriculum includes a combination of physical education, intramural sports, and interscholastic athletics. It allows students, regardless of ability, to experience the positive values of sports in a manner similar to involvement in an interscholastic sports program. The goal of the sport education approach is to help students experience such qualities as working to reach deferred goals, teamwork, loyalty, commitment, perseverance, dedication, and concern for other people. The approach emphasizes the importance of teams, leagues, seasons, championships, coaches, practice, player involvement, formal records, statistics, and competitive balance. These characteristics are usually emphasized in sport programs but not in a physical education program. This model gives all students a chance to experience a quality competitive sports program that is organized and supervised by an unbiased physical educator who will protect the important values of sports. Students learn to compete and be good competitors. A desired outcome is that students become competent, literate, and enthusiastic sports participants who want to play sports at local, national, and international levels.

The model uses the following six characteristics that make the sport education approach different from more traditional approaches to physical education.

1. Sport education involves seasons rather than units.
2. Students quickly become members of teams (affiliation).
3. The model includes a formal schedule of competition.
4. There is usually a major culminating event.
5. Records are kept and publicized.
6. Festivity is included to provide excitement, meaning, and a social element.

Each season begins with instruction and development of team strategies according to the teams' strengths and weaknesses. The teacher helps organize the class into teams and elect a student captain; he or she then instructs team members about skill development. Teams take the initiative to organize practice, decide on players' positions, and determine strategies for playing other teams.

Outdoor Adventure Schedule

Date(s)	Day(s)	Activity	Destination	Depart	Return approx.	Fee	Comments	Types of trans.
Sept. 19	Friday	Day hike	Wet Beaver Creek—Sedona	7 a.m.	5 p.m.	Paid	Bring a swimming suit and old tennis shoes. Do not forget water and your lunch.	SB
Sept. 27–28	Sat.–Sun.	Fishing or camping trip	Payson area	8 a.m.	8 p.m.	$20	Great place to fish and swim—may need license.	CV
Oct. 7	Tuesday	Desert awareness	Arizona-Sonora Desert Museum—Tucson	8 a.m.	5 p.m.	Paid	This is the best desert museum in the Southwest.	SB
Oct. 24	Friday	Gun safety	Black Canyon Range	8 a.m.	2 p.m.	Paid	Bring your own shells—adults needed.	SB
Oct. 25	Saturday	Trap or skeet competition	Black Canyon Range	8 a.m.	2 p.m.	$10	Includes two rounds of shooting and prizes. Bring your own shells.	SV
Nov. 15	Saturday	Pheasant hunt	Salt Cedar Preserve	7 a.m.	2 p.m.	$15	Bring own gun and shells—must have adult with each student—you keep pheasants you shoot.	CV
Nov. 26	Wednesday	Field archery	Black Canyon Range	8 a.m.	2 p.m.	Paid	Compound bows OK—adults needed. Wear tennis shoes.	SB
Dec. 9	Tuesday	Horsemanship	Pointe Stables	8 a.m.	1 p.m.	Paid	Wear jeans and tennis shoes or boots.	SB
Dec. 12	Friday	Horsemanship	Pointe Stables	6 p.m.	10 p.m.	Paid	All parents are invited and needed for potluck under the stars—guests of students are welcome.	None
Jan. 31	Saturday	Downhill skiing	Flagstaff	6 a.m.	8 p.m.	Varies	Rent boots, skis, and poles in Phoenix.	CB
Feb. 7	Saturday	Cross-country skiing	Flagstaff	6 a.m.	6 p.m.	Paid	Bring gloves, hat, change of clothes—overdress.	CV
March 6	Friday	Rock climbing	South Mountain Park	8 a.m.	5 p.m.	Paid	Bring chocolate chip cookies for instructor.	SB
March 28	Saturday	Rock climbing	McDowell Mts.	6 a.m.	6 p.m.	Paid	Bring chocolate chip cookies for instructor.	SV
April 4–5	Sat.–Sun.	Caving or day hike	Tucson Area	6 a.m.	8 p.m.	$25	Bring change of clothes and plastic bag.	CV
April 16	Thurs.	Map and compass	North Mountain Park	8 a.m.	2 p.m.	Paid	Bring water, lunch, hat, sunglasses, notebook, ruler, and pencil.	SB
April 25	Saturday	Day hike	Superstitions	6 a.m.	5 p.m.	Paid	Bring water, hat, sunglasses, and lunch.	SB
May 8	Friday	Day hike	Mt. Humphreys	5 a.m.	9 p.m.	Paid	Bring warm clothing, rain gear, lunch, water, and hat.	SB
May 14–18	Thurs.–Mon.	Backpacking trip	North Rim—Grand Canyon	4 p.m.	4 p.m.	$30	Advanced hike—30 miles—qualifying hike will be Thurs., May 7, 6 p.m., Squaw Peak Park.	CV

*SB = School bus, CB = Commercial bus, SV = School van, CV = Commercial van.
REMINDER! Unless someone takes your place, there will be no refunds on nonpaid field trips for any reason. Nonpaid field trips are limited in number. Participants will be selected by physical conditioning or class grade point average.

FIGURE 2.9 Course sequence for an outdoor adventure program.

Students assume more responsibility as the program evolves and they begin to understand its goals.

The program can be implemented in several ways, depending on the situation and the comfort zone of the teacher. It might be accomplished in a single class, with one teacher and one class. It could involve several classes that meet during the same period of the day. It could also be implemented with classes that meet during different periods of the day, with competition scheduled at a common time. Another implementation style involves practice during the regular class period followed by competition outside class.

Depending on student interests, available facilities, and school schedules, different activities can be selected for the program. Traditional team sports and individual sports such as basketball, volleyball, flag football, soccer, softball, badminton, or track and field can be selected. The sports could be modified into activities such as three-person volleyball, three-person basketball, or over-the-line softball. Lifetime sports such as tennis, bowling, or golf are popular choices. Other less common possibilities include Ultimate, cycling, orienteering, speed-a-way, team handball, floor or field hockey, and modified lacrosse.

If several teachers are working together, students have several choices for leagues that are of interest to them. The leagues vary in length from 3 to 4 weeks to 9 to 10 weeks depending on student interest, facilities, and the school schedule. Students can participate in approximately 5 to 12 leagues in a year of physical education. The seasonal schedule for a school could adhere to grading periods. For example, six- or nine-week grading periods could drive seasons for the leagues (see figure 2.10).

When preparing for a sport education season, addressing the following points is important:

1. Select your sport.
2. Identify number of students in class.
3. Describe your space and equipment needed.
4. Determine the length of the season and number of lessons.
5. Choose a method of team selection.
6. How will you decide team names? What are some acceptable team names?
7. Identify team roles.
8. Identify nonplaying (duty) team roles.
9. What instruction will you give for duty team roles?
10. Are there any specialist roles?
11. Develop an overview of the season (preseason, regular season, postseason, culminating event).

Season Sport Education Schedule

Season	Team sports	Individual sports
Autumn	Flag football Cross country	Tennis Archery Table tennis
Early winter	Volleyball Soccer	Fencing Bowling Badminton Racquetball
Late winter	Basketball Swimming	Fencing Bowling Racquetball Riflery
Spring	Baseball Softball Track and field	Badminton Golf Archery

FIGURE 2.10   Season sport education schedule.

Reprinted by permission from D. Siedentop, P.A. Hastie, and H. van der Mars, *Complete Guide to Sport Education,* 2nd ed. (Champaign, IL: Human Kinetics, 2011), 17.

12. Develop content for the season. What on-the-ball and off-the-ball skills will you teach (direct instruction)?
13. What tactics and strategies will you teach?
14. How will you facilitate team practices during guided practice?
15. What awards will you give?
16. How will you create festivity in the season?
17. What activities will contribute to earning points toward the championship? Fair play, roles, duty team, wins, or others? Identify point values that are appropriate to each element.
18. How will you assess learning in this unit?

All leagues include aspects of sports (Bulger, Mohr, Rairigh, & Townsend, 2007; Siedentop, Hastie, & van der Mars, 2020). Leagues and rules of competition can be modified to ensure that students are successful. For example, volleyball and basketball leagues could have choices for three-on-three competition in addition to the five-on-five format. There could be a boys' league, a girls' league, and a mixed-gender league. Participation is required of all students, and developmentally appropriate competition that is equitable is implemented. Students handle all roles in the units, including playing, scorekeeping, and refereeing. Students may have additional duty roles within their team including coach, fitness specialist, publicist, and journalist. A specific sport may also have specialist roles including timekeeper, statistician, judge, starter, and spotter. The teacher's role is to ensure that the sport environment is safe and that students learn the values of fair play and equal competition as well as the skills, rules, and etiquette of the sport. Students are involved as coaches and instructors for their teams. Students select uniforms, team names, starting lineups, substitution patterns, and practice arrangements and times. Records are kept and posted in public areas, and awards are given for a variety of student accomplishments in addition to winning games or matches. Research on this model has revealed that many students enjoy this approach because they believe that they have more opportunities for socializing and having fun (Hastie, de Ojeda, & Luquin, 2011). Many students point out the development of leadership skills, and other students express an increased sense of belonging and trust with peers in the model. The following example uses three-person teams in a volleyball league setting.

TEACHING TIP

Because of the many roles that students may have in sport education, the model works well for extremely large classes or when adequate equipment is not available.

Three-Person Volleyball

This model is for a middle or junior high school setting in which two teachers share classes that total 50 to 70 students. Students play three-person volleyball with a junior-size volleyball, a 7-foot (2.1 m) net, and a 15-by-40-foot (4.6 by 12.2 m) court.

The class meets four days per week, and the volleyball season is designed for eight weeks, or a total of 32 sessions. With 64 students, this class has two volleyball leagues. One league is for skilled players, and the other is for less-skilled players. (Note that other legitimate ways can be used to divide students for competition.)

The first week is devoted to practice and instruction. Four students of varying levels of skill are selected to assist the teachers in assigning students to teams. After three days of observation, the students are assigned to teams, four students to each team. The teams are then assigned to two leagues of eight teams each. On the

fourth day of class, students begin to receive instruction and practice as a team. One teacher takes administrative responsibility for each league.

During the second week, the students have two practice days and two scrimmage days. Scrimmage days allow teachers to make sure that students understand rules and to teach refereeing as a skill. During the third week, double round-robin league play begins for each league; there are two match days and two practice days. From the third through the seventh weeks, students have three match days and one practice day per week. During the eighth week, the championship tournament is held, involving all 16 teams.

During match days, students participate in a warm-up period followed by a timed match; the duration of the match is determined by the length of the teaching period, for example, 22 minutes. All matches start and stop at the same time. A signal is given every 5 minutes for substitutions. Students referee their own games, done by those students not playing at the moment. Referees also keep score. The winner of each match is the team with the most points at the final time signal. Standings can be kept in terms of total points scored or win–loss records (or some combination of the two). The teachers observe games and make notes for individual players and teams about skills and strategies to be worked on at subsequent practice sessions. Team captains are responsible for seeing that a certain portion of practice session is devoted to those notes. In other practice sessions, all teams and players practice certain skills and strategies as directed by the teachers.

Students get to choose a name for their team and adopt a uniform (as long as it meets the standards set by the teachers for physical education clothing). Each Monday, the league standings are posted along with other items concerning the league. If team play in any league is unequal, the teachers and the four student representatives can, at the end of the first round of play, make personnel changes in teams to equalize competition for the second round.

Tactical Games Approach

The tactical games approach (sometimes referred to teaching games for understanding, or TGfU) to teaching (Mitchell, Oslin, & Griffin, 2013) is designed to promote interest in learning games, the understanding of game play, and the ability to play games. It is based on a sequence of developmentally appropriate gamelike learning activities that focus on tactical problems for students to solve first cognitively and then perform through skill execution. The basic assumption that drives the model is that students learn best if they understand what to do before they understand how to do it.

Most physical education curricula involve game teaching and participation, but the tactical aspects of game play are rarely taught. Even when they are taught, tactics are not often connected with game skills. Many teachers teach skill in a static setting or nonauthentic experience, so students rarely respond appropriately to various scenarios during game play. The development of tactical awareness or the ability to identify a tactical problem and respond correctly during a game is essential to success in game play. This approach emphasizes decision making and understanding the application of skills within a game context.

The tactical approach includes a games classification system, specific tactical and subtactical problems, and levels of tactical complexity. The games classification system identifies games into four distinct categories, each of which have similar tactical characteristics. Each category of games encourages a transfer of learning within that group. The four games categories are invasion, net or wall, target, and striking or fielding. Invasion games, for example, share a common goal of invading an opponent's territory with the hope of scoring on their goal. Figure 2.11 illustrates the game classification system.

Each set of games has important tactical problems that are essential to solve to be successful in that activity. Figure 2.12 illustrates the tactical problems associated with team handball and badminton. To match the

Invasion Games	Net or Wall Games	Target Games	Striking or Fielding Games
Basketball	Badminton	Golf	Softball
Soccer	Tennis	Archery	Baseball
Team handball	Pickleball	Bowling	Cricket
Ultimate	Racquetball	Billiards	
Lacrosse	Volleyball		
Flag football			
Floor hockey			
Rugby			

FIGURE 2.11 Tactical games classification system.

Invasion Games

	Tactical problem	Subtactical problems
Team handball	Scoring	• Maintaining possession of ball • Attacking the goal • Creating space in attack • Using attack in space
	Preventing scoring	• Defending space • Defending the goal • Winning the ball
	Restarting play	Penalty shot
Badminton	Offense	• Creating space on opponent's side of net • Winning the point • Attacking with a partner (doubles)
	Defense	• Defending space on own side of net • Defending against attack • Defending as a pair (doubles)

FIGURE 2.12 Sample problem classification.

tactical problem with students' development level, an examination of the tactical complexity is essential. Some tactical problems can be either too complex for novel students or too simple for more advanced performers. For example, a novice student may understand that dribbling and passing are essential to maintain possession of the ball to attack the goal but may have difficulty comprehending the need to time a run to avoid an offsides trap. Tactical problems are presented when developmentally appropriate.

A sample tactical games lesson starts with an initial game. For example, students participate in a four-versus-four Ultimate game with a focus on maintaining possession. A series of questions would follow that leads students to discover essential aspects of maintaining possession and lead to the practice tasks that will follow. A few sample questions with responses follow:

Teacher: *What was the purpose of that game?*
Student: *To keep possession as long as possible.*
Teacher: *What did you do to make this possible?*
Student: *Pass the disc.*
Teacher: *Absolutely. What else did you have to do?*
Student: *We had to get open to catch the pass.*
Teacher: *How did you do this?*
Student: *We made fakes and cuts to create an opening.*
Teacher: *How many teams had success getting open and maintaining possession?*
Students: *Very few teams had success.*
Teacher: *OK, today we are going to practice creating space and getting open to receive a pass from our teammate.*

These questions set up the formal practice tasks for that day's lesson. The questions lead students to discover what they need to do to be successful during the practice tasks and ultimately during game play. A sample practice task may be a three-versus-one passing activity that requires the offensive players to create space and get open with one defender. This task may be extended by adding a second defender. The lesson is completed by having students participate in game play that reinforces the skills and tactics practiced throughout the lesson.

Knowledge Concepts Approach

In a knowledge concepts approach, more emphasis is placed on knowledge and cognitive understanding of the various subdisciplines of physical education and kinesiology. Students learn the how and the why of physical activity through involvement in problem-solving experiments. Less emphasis is placed on doing activities in

this scheme. Students still spend time with activities in the gym and on playing fields, but they also spend time in a classroom with lectures, PowerPoint presentations, study guides, worksheets, and videos like those that a classroom teacher prepares in a more academic subject. Time is set aside for laboratories designed to help students discover important conceptual knowledge. Figures 2.13 through 2.16 show examples of worksheets that assist in this process. Knowledge objectives become an important concern in this approach. The rules, strategy, knowledge concepts, and history of a sport or physical activity are discussed throughout each unit. Some experts believe that school physical education will survive only if it becomes more academically oriented (Buck, Lund, Harrison, & Blakemore, 2007). The argument is for more academic rigor in our physical education curricula.

Several variations for implementing concepts into a curriculum are possible: (1) integrate the concepts into regular activity-based units; (2) include several separate units on concepts to supplement activity-based units; and (3) teach concepts only on special occasions, such as rainy days or shortened periods. Some argue that a curriculum based on concepts is easier to defend to a school board. Other educators believe that knowledge-based discussions divert too much time from promoting activity and physical skill development. Balancing these areas of emphasis is important because instructional time for knowledge and skill is limited. If one area is emphasized, then another area must be reduced or eliminated. Knowledge concepts are important, but if the increased emphasis reduces time available for physical skill development and physical activity time, these important objectives may be slighted. Knowing about physical activities is different from experiencing them. If students are going to incorporate activities into their lifestyles, they need an opportunity to gain knowledge and develop competency in several physical activities.

Fitness Education Approach

The fitness education idea is most consistent with the public health perspective of physical education and is an example of a knowledge concepts approach. This idea has gained popularity in many universities, colleges, and high schools (Corbin & Le Masurier, 2014). The model focuses on imparting physical fitness concepts to students. The theory is that at some point in a student's education, a course should be devoted to the knowledge concepts related to the physical education objectives: The student is active, has knowledge, values regular activity, and is fit (see chapter 1). Evidence suggests that

BASKETBALL DRIBBLING

Name _____ Date _____

Dribbling skill in basketball can be observed in two ways. One way is to look at the process of performing the skill. This approach involves looking at the mechanics of performing the skill during the process. How efficient was the performer in using his or her body to perform the skill? The second way to observe is to look at the results or the product of the performance. How fast did the student dribble to half-court and back? How fast did he or she dribble around the cones?

Use the following checklist and practice with a classmate. Watch him or her dribble a basketball and check each component of the skill listed.

1. Head is up and looking at the defenders.   Yes _____   No _____

2. Fingertips are used to control the ball.   Yes _____   No _____

3. Knees are bent and center of gravity is low.   Yes _____   No _____

4. Nondribbling hand protects the ball.   Yes _____   No _____

5. Height of the dribble is below the waist.   Yes _____   No _____

After each dribbling trial, explain to your partner how you evaluated each segment of the skill. Repeat the process so that each of you has an opportunity to work on all elements of the dribbling skill. After working on the checklist of skill components, move on to dribbling around a set of cones to see how fast you can dribble in and out of the cones. Use a stopwatch to record the time of each trial.

6. How did it feel to make corrections on your partner's dribbling skill?

7. How did your partner feel about being corrected on the elements?

8. Can you explain the difference between the process and product of a physical skill?

9. Do you think that this activity helped you to understand and improve your dribbling skill?

FIGURE 2.13 Practicing, observing, and evaluating basketball dribbling worksheet.

ORIENTEERING SKILLS

Name _____ Date _____

1. Stand on the 50-yard line of the football field. Find north and write down what you are facing.

2. Stand at the east field-goal pole. Find 40 degrees and write down what you are facing.

3. Start at the east 20-yard line. Take 20 paces west. What yard line are you standing on?

4. Shoot a bearing at the baseball batting cage from the west 40-yard line. What angle are you standing at?

5. Start at the trash can in front of the bleachers. Take 15 paces east. Where are you standing?

6. Stand at the east end zone of the football field. What is directly south of you?

7. Stand at the drinking fountain. Take 10 paces north. Where are you standing?

8. Face 40 degrees, walk 40 paces. Add 120 degrees, walk 40 paces. Add 120 degrees, walk 40 paces. What shape am I?

9. Face 360 degrees and then walk 20 paces. Turn to 90 degrees and then walk 20 paces. Turn to 180 degrees and then walk 20 paces. Turn to 270 degrees and then walk 20 paces. What shape am I?

10. Turn to 120 degrees and then walk 30 paces. Turn to 240 degrees and then walk 30 paces. Turn to 360 degrees and then walk 30 paces. What shape am I?

11. Stand under the football scoreboard facing east. Shoot a bearing at the closest corner of the bleachers. What is your bearing?

FIGURE 2.14 Orienteering skills practice worksheet.

Reprinted by permission from Jessica Richardson, Smith Junior High School, Mesa, Arizona.

VOLLEYBALL SERVE

Name _____ Date _____

Practice several overhand and underhand volleyball serves. Try putting different types of spins on both serves. Complete the following questions:

1. Where do you have to contact the ball to make it spin to the right?

2. Where do you have to contact the ball to make it spin to the left?

3. Can you serve the volleyball with backspin toward you?

4. Can you serve the volleyball with topspin away from you?

5. Can you serve the volleyball with no spin?

6. Explain where you must strike the volleyball in order to get the proper spin as described in questions 3, 4, and 5.

7. Describe the flight of the volleyball with the spins described in questions 3, 4, and 5.

8. How can these different spins affect your ability as a volleyball player?

9. Relate this concept of spin to baseball, softball, racquetball, tennis, or basketball and give a specific example of the use of spin in these activities.

10. What conclusion can you make about the use of force in creating spin on an object?

FIGURE 2.15   Problem-solving questions for volleyball serve.

JUMP BANDS

Name _____ Date _____

Partner _____

Group members _____

_____

_____

Place a check beside each skill that your partner is successful in performing.

My partner can move the jump bands to the rhythm of the music. _____

My partner can move to the single foot pattern of in, in, out, out on one side _____ or both sides _____ of the jump bands.

My partner can move to the double foot pattern of in, in, out, out. _____

My partner can dance from one side of the jump bands to the other using one of the methods taught. _____

Answer the following questions.

1. Why are jump bands considered an excellent cardiorespiratory endurance activity?

2. Why is it critical to work together when using the jump bands in class?

3. How could the jump bands be used as part of a fitness circuit in class?

FIGURE 2.16 Jump bands worksheet.

Reprinted by permission from Char Darst, Mesa Public Schools, Mesa, AZ.

fitness education courses promote knowledge, improve attitudes about activity, and affect lifestyle activity patterns later in life (SHAPE America, 2020).

The two most popular fitness education approaches are the fitness for life approach (Corbin & Le Masurier, 2014) and the physical best approach (SHAPE America, 2020). Physical best and fitness for life complement one another well because they are both based on the HELP philosophy, which specifies the goal of promoting health for everyone with a focus on lifetime activity of a personal needs. Both physical best and fitness for life offer training session for course instructors allowing for specialist certification in fitness education. This approach to physical education and fitness development places instructional emphasis on lecture, laboratory experiments, and exercise programs for use in adult-

hood. Lessons help students learn facts about fitness and physical activity so that they can be good consumers, program planners, and problem solvers. Students participate in both classroom activities and gymnasium or outdoor fitness activities. They receive experiences with self-testing procedures to establish a fitness profile. A variety of fitness activities and routines are taught that students can do individually or in groups for a lifetime of regular activity. The fitness for life program answers the following questions:

- Why is physical activity important to every person?
- How should physical activity take place?
- What forms of physical activity are available?

The objectives for this approach are arranged in a hierarchical order called the stairway to lifetime fitness (see figure 2.17). The rationale is that if students climb the lifetime fitness stairway, they will be more likely to be active throughout life. Information and activities are provided on several topics, including cardiorespiratory fitness, strength, endurance, flexibility, fat control, skill-related fitness, correct ways to exercise, and planning an exercise program. Students learn to diagnose and solve personal fitness problems. They have opportunities to develop exercise programs to remediate health concerns.

Several options are available for incorporating fitness for life into a school curriculum. Common alternatives are to offer a one- or two-semester program using the fitness for life model. Some schools combine teaching knowledge concepts with participation in a modern school fitness center equipped with the latest fitness machines and technology. Gilbert High School, in Gilbert, Arizona, offers an elective "supercircuit" class using a fitness circuit developed by the Universal Company in Iowa. Students work out on the supercircuit every other day and participate in lifetime sports such as tennis, golf, and racquetball during other days. Students take a fitness for life section of the class one or two days per week.

Many states and school districts have adopted a requirement or a recommendation for a fitness concepts-type course to address many of the state standards for physical education. For example, fitness for life is required for all students in the state of Utah and is a graduation requirement for all students in the Minneapolis Public Schools. In addition, several provinces in Canada and the Department of Defense Dependent Schools worldwide have added such a requirement or recommendation. A wide variety of curriculum and instructional materials are available to teachers such as books for students, lesson plans for teachers, worksheets and study guides, vocabulary cards, activity cards, PowerPoint presentations, review questions, laboratory experiments, and test materials (Corbin & Le Masurier, 2014). The recommended content for a high school fitness for life class is shown in figure 2.18. More recently, a middle school version of the curriculum was created (Corbin, Le Masurier, & Lambdin, 2018). Both approaches are based on two days per week in the classroom and three days per week in an activity setting. Students learn the concepts of healthy activity and apply these concepts by designing fitness activities and self-assessing personal fitness. This program is compatible with the FitnessGram/ActivityGram (Cooper Institute, 2017) and the physical best materials from SHAPE America (2020). The newest edition has web icons that direct students to a variety of Internet sites from the Fitness for Life site (www.fitnessforlife.org).

Another similar knowledge concept approach to secondary curriculum focuses on the components of human health (see chapter 16 for a variety of health and wellness activities). The model is more comprehensive than the fitness concepts approach. Units of instruction in health and wellness include stress management, alcohol and drug abuse, nutrition, weight control, physical fitness, coping skills, personal safety, environmental awareness, behavioral self-control, and problem-solving skills related to those specific topics. Many view health and

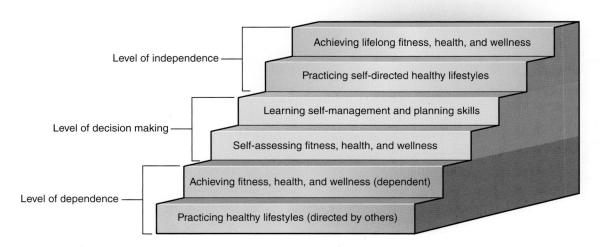

FIGURE 2.17 The stairway to lifetime fitness, health, and wellness.

Reprinted with permission from C. B. Corbin and G Le Masurier, *Fitness for Life*, 6th ed. (Champaign, IL: Human Kinetics, 2014), 32.

Discussion Topics

Table of contents	Self-management or group discussion
Fitness and wellness for all	Learning to self-assess
Safe and smart physical activity	Building self-confidence
Benefits of physical activity	Reducing risk factors
How much is enough?	Choosing good activities
Learning self-management skills	Setting goals
Lifestyle physical activity and positive attitudes	Building positive attitudes
Cardiorespiratory fitness	Learning to self-monitor
Active aerobics and recreation	Finding social support
Active sports and skill-related fitness	Building performance skills
Flexibility	Building intrinsic motivation
Muscle fitness: basic principle and strength	Preventing relapse
Muscle fitness: endurance and general information	Managing time
Body composition	Improving physical self-perceptions
Choosing nutritious food	Saying "no"
Making consumer choices	Learning to think critically
A wellness perspective	Thinking "success"
Stress management	Controlling competitive stress
Personal program planning	Overcoming barriers

Activity-Based Topics

Table of contents	Self-management	Activity
Starter program	Exercise basics	Skill- or health-related fitness
Fitness games	FitnessGram 1	Safe exercise
Cooperative games	Healthy back test	Back-exercise circuit
Line exercise	Posture	Circuit workout
Fitness trail	FitnessGram 2	Elastic-band circuit
School stepping	Walking test	Walking for wellness
Aerobic dance	Step test and mile run	Cardiorespiratory fitness
Step aerobics	FitnessGram 3	Jogging principles
Orienteering	Skill-related fitness	The sports star program
Jump and stretch routine	Arm, leg, and trunk flex	Flexibility circuit
Partner resistance exercises	Modified one rep max or grip strength	Weight training
Homemade weights	Muscular endurance	Endurance circuit
Exercise circuit	Skinfolds and height and weight charts	Muscular fitness exercises
Jollyball	Body measurements	Cooperative aerobics
Rhythmical exercise	Body composition, flex, strength	Isometric exercise circuit
Cooper's aerobics	Cardio and muscular endurance	Health and fitness club
Disc golf	Signs of stress	Relaxation exercises
Exercising at home	Evaluating your personal program	Performing your plan

FIGURE 2.18 Contents of a fitness for life class.

Data from D. Dale, K. McConnell, and C. B. Corbin, *Fitness for Life Lesson Plans,* 6th ed. (Champaign, IL: Human Kinetics, 2004).

wellness as an important area that should be an ongoing part of the educational process throughout life. This preventive approach expands the fitness concepts approach. To maintain health and wellness, students need requisite information and skills. Advocates of this program point to numerous health problems that abound in our society. A healthy lifestyle for all students is the major objective of this model. Both the health and wellness and the fitness education models focus primarily on knowledge. People who advocate these models find the emphasis on knowledge to be an advantage because it adds credibility to a program. The downside is that the increase in time spent on lecture and analysis reduces the time available for learning physical skills and promoting physical activity. Students not only need information but also need successful encounters with physical activity and time to practice and perform physical skills. Determining exactly how much time should be spent on knowledge acquisition and how much should be spent on physical skill development is difficult. Schools using a concepts approach offer a balance of physical activity and knowledge concepts. For example, a common approach is to offer several units on health activities (including fitness) to supplement or complement physical activities units.

Personal and Social Responsibility Approach

Hellison (2011) developed a set of ideas and a curriculum approach that focus on enhancing social competence, self-control, responsible behavior, and concern for others within the physical education class environment. Emphasis on fitness and the development of sports skills and knowledge is reduced to accomplish the primary goal of personal and social competence. Sports and physical activities are used as a means of accomplishing personal and social goals. The basic philosophy of the personal and social development approach is that personal and social problems in society have created situations that require schools to offer this type of focus. Professionals subscribing to this approach believe that many students are disruptive and difficult to manage, making it the school's responsibility to provide better personal and social development training. This approach has been field-tested with underserved or at-risk youth and general student populations over a 30-year period. The approach has been used in many different forms and with different terms for the various levels of responsibility.

In one variation of this approach, students proceed through six developmental levels of social competence.

Different students enter at different levels and proceed upward through the steps. Students are encouraged to rate themselves on each of the levels and compare their ratings with their teacher's ratings (see figure 2.19). Discussion between the teacher and students examines perceptions of how students are progressing. The following are examples of levels of personal and social development:

- Level 0: Irresponsibility. Students do not participate and are unmotivated and undisciplined. They interrupt and intimidate other students and teachers. They make excuses and blame others for their behavior. Teachers find it difficult to manage or accomplish much with these students.

- Level 1: Self-control. Students at the self-control level can control themselves without the direct supervision of the teacher and do not infringe on the rights of other students or the teacher. They can begin to participate in class activities and enhance their learning.

- Level 2: Involvement. Level 2 involves student self-control and desired involvement with the subject matter of fitness, skills, and games. Students are enthusiastically involved in the program without constant prompting or supervision of the teacher.

- Level 3: Self-responsibility. Students at level 3 begin to identify their interests and start to make choices within the parameters of the program. Motivation and responsibility are characteristics of these students. They start to take more responsibility and explore options for their lives outside the program. This stage represents a start of their own identity.

- Level 4: Caring. The caring stage has students moving outside themselves and showing concern for other students and the teacher. Students are cooperative and helpful and show a genuine interest in the lives of others. They have a real concern about the world around them.

- Level 5: Going beyond. The highest level is characterized by student leadership and additional responsibility for program decisions. Students get involved with the teacher on decisions that will affect all students in the program. Students become coworkers with teachers.

This model can be implemented in various ways depending on the specifics of the school situation and the type of students. Hellison (2011) suggests an option that uses a day-to-day consistency with the following five parts to the lesson:

SOCIAL DEVELOPMENT

Definition of Ratings			Name		Teacher	
			Date	Rating	Rating	Comments
0	**Little self-control**					
	Not involved					
	Uses put-downs					
	Irresponsible					
	Disruptive					
1	**Under control, not involved**					
	Not participating					
	Not prepared					
	Nonproductive					
2	**Under control, involved when teacher directed**					
	Frequently off task					
	Needs prompting					
	Needs frequent reminders					
3	**Self-responsibility**					
	Works independently					
	Self-motivated					
	Positive attitude					
4	**Caring**					
	Cares about others					
	Involved with others					
	Sensitive to needs of others					
5	**Going beyond**					
	Displays leadership					
	Assumes more responsibility					
	Helps instructor					

FIGURE 2.19 Social development checklist.

1. Counseling time for connecting with students
2. An awareness talk about the responsibility levels
3. The physical activity lesson with integrated personal and social discussions
4. A group meeting for students' opinions
5. Reflection time to self-evaluate personal and social responsibility for the day (see figures 2.20 and 2.21)

Examples of strategies available to the teacher for implementing personal and social responsibility are teacher talk, modeling, reinforcement, self-reflection, reflection-in-action (snap judgment based on previous experiences), student sharing, sport court (small group

of students making a decision for the class), the talking bench (where two students go to work out a problem), journal writing by students, student checklists, student achievement records, and behavior contracts between the student and the teacher. Many specific strategies have been used and are available to the teacher for each of the social development levels (0–5). For example, rubrics for assessment of students can be developed to provide students with feedback or to grade them on their personal and social responsibility in physical education classes (see figure 2.22). Refer to chapter 8 for a discussion on developing rubrics. Finally, figure 2.23 is a form that could be used with student personal development plans in level 3 (self-responsibility).

SELF-RESPONSIBILITY

Name _____ Date _____

My Self-Control

____ I did no name calling.

____ If I got mad, I tried to exert self-control.

____ I didn't interrupt when someone else was talking.

____ My self-control was not that good today.

My Involvement

____ I listened to all directions.

____ I tried all activities.

____ I worked even when I didn't feel like it.

My Self-Responsibility

____ I followed all directions.

____ I did not blame others.

____ I was responsible for myself.

My Caring

____ I helped someone today in or out of class.

____ I said something positive to someone today.

____ I did not help anyone at all.

Comments:

FIGURE 2.20 Self-responsibility checklist.

SELF-EVALUATION

Name _____ Date _____

Self-Control
How well did you control your temper and language today?   0 1 2

Effort
How hard did you try today?   0 1 2

Self-Coaching
Did you have a self-improvement or basketball goal and work on it today?   0 1 2

Coaching
Did you help others, do some positive coaching, or help make this
a good experience for everyone today?   0 1 2

Outside the Gym

Self-control?   0 1 2

Effort?   0 1 2

Goal setting?   0 1 2

Helping others?   0 1 2

One comment about yourself today:

FIGURE 2.21 Self-evaluation form.

Adapted by permission from D.R. Hellison, *Teaching Personal and Social Responsibility Through Physical Activity,* 3rd ed. (Champaign, IL: Human Kinetics, 2011), 60.

RESPONSIBILITY

Student _____ Date _____

	Consistently	Sporadically	Seldom	Never
Contributes to own well-being:				
Effort and self-motivation	___	___	___	___
Independence	___	___	___	___
Goal setting	___	___	___	___
Contributes to others' well-being:				
Respect	___	___	___	___
Helping	___	___	___	___
Leadership	___	___	___	___

FIGURE 2.22 Rubric for assessment of personal and social responsibility.

Adapted by permission from D.R. Hellison, *Teaching Personal and Social Responsibility Through Physical Activity,* 3rd ed. (Champaign, IL: Human Kinetics, 2011), 166.

MY PERSONAL PLAN

Name _____ Date _____

1. Fitness: Choose at least one.

My flexibility goal is _____.

My strength goal is _____.

My aerobic goal is _____.

Today in fitness I did _____.

2. Motor skills: Choose at least one skill from one activity.

My basketball goal is _____.

My volleyball goal is _____.

My soccer goal is _____.

My _____ goal is _____.

Today in motor skill development I did _____.

3. Choose one.

The creativity or expressive activity I did was _____.

I spent my "pal time" with _____ doing _____.

The stress management activity I did today was _____.

The self-defense activity I did today was _____.

4. During my level III time,

My respect for others was	___ Good	___ OK	___ Not OK
My effort was	___ High	___ Medium	___ Low
My plan was	___ My own	___ Somewhat my own	___ Not my own
My self-discipline in carrying out my plan was	___ Good	___ Fair	___ Poor
I helped someone else.	___ Yes	___ A little	___ No

FIGURE 2.23 My personal plan.

Adapted by permission from D.R. Hellison, *Teaching Personal and Social Responsibility Through Physical Activity,* 3rd ed. (Champaign, IL: Human Kinetics, 2011), 79.

LEARNING AIDS

STUDY STIMULATORS AND REVIEW QUESTIONS

1. List and explain the common organizing centers for physical education curricula.
2. Why is it better to have shorter units for the middle school and longer units for the high school?
3. What are the advantages of offering choices to students in the physical education curriculum?
4. Discuss the unique features of the promoting physical activity and skill development approach widely used today.
5. How does the promoting physical activity and skill development approach change from middle school to high school?
6. How does the tactical approach differ from the skill development approach?
7. List examples of culminating events in an outdoor adventure curriculum approach.
8. What is the fundamental goal of the sport education approach?
9. Briefly describe and explain the stairway to lifetime fitness.
10. What tends to be the dilemma for teachers who wish to emphasize the teaching of both knowledge concepts and physical skills?
11. Provide the underlying rationale for the personal and social responsibility curriculum.

WEBSITES

Action for Healthy Kids

www.actionforhealthykids.org

American Hiking Society

www.americanhiking.org

Fitness for Life

www.fitnessforlife.org

Physical Education Teaching and Curriculum Information

www.pecentral.org
www.pheamerica.org

Project Adventure

www.pa.org

REFERENCES AND SUGGESTED READINGS

Buck, M.M., Lund, J.L., Harrison, J.M., & Blakemore Cook, C.L. (2007). *Instructional strategies for secondary school physical education* (6th ed.). Boston. MA: McGraw-Hill.

Bulger, S.M., Mohr, D.J., Rairigh, R.M., & Townsend, J.S. (2007). *Sport education seasons.* Champaign, IL: Human Kinetics.

Casten, C. (2015). *Lesson plans for dynamic physical education for secondary school students* (4th ed.). San Francisco, CA: Pearson/Benjamin Cummings.

Cooper Institute. (2017). *FitnessGram test administration manual* (5th ed.). Champaign, IL: Human Kinetics.

Corbin, C., LeMasurier, G., & Lambdin, D. (2018). *Fitness for life: Middle school* (2nd ed.). Champaign, IL: Human Kinetics.

Corbin, C., & Le Masurier, G. (2014). *Fitness for life* (6th ed.). Champaign, IL: Human Kinetics.

Corbin, C., & Lindsey, R. (2007). *Human kinetics fitness for life.* (updated 5th ed.). Champaign. IL: Human Kinetics.

Graham, G., Holt/Hale, S.A., & Parker, M. (2013). *Children moving: A reflective approach to teaching physical education* (9th ed.). New York, NY: McGraw-Hill.

Hastie, P.A., de Ojeda, D.M., & Luquin, A.C. (2011). A review of research on sport education: 2004 to the present. *Physical Education and Sport Pedagogy, 16,* 103–132.

Hellison, D.R. (2011). *Teaching responsibility through physical activity* (3rd ed.). Champaign, IL: Human Kinetics.

Lund, J. (2015). Standards-based physical education curriculum development (3rd ed.). Boston, MA: Jones and Bartlett.

McConnell, K., Corbin, C. B., & Dale, D. (2004). *Fitness for life teachers resources and materials* [computer software]. Champaign, IL: Human Kinetics.

Mitchell, A.A., Oslin, J.L., & Griffin, L.L. (2013). *Teaching sports concepts and skills: A tactical games approach* (3rd ed.). Champaign, IL: Human Kinetics.

National Governors Association. (2019). *Common Core State Standards initiative: Preparing America's students for college & career.* www.corestandards.org.

Pangrazi, R.P., & Beighle, A. (2020). *Dynamic physical education for elementary school children* (19th ed.). Champaign, IL: Human Kinetics.

Parker, M., & Steen, T. (1988). Outdoor pursuits and physical education: Making the connection. *Newsletter of the Council on Outdoor Education, 30*(1), 4.

Rink, J.E. (2014). *Teaching physical education for learning* (7th ed.). Boston, MA: McGraw-Hill.

SHAPE America. (2009a). *Appropriate instructional practice guidelines for high school physical education* (3rd ed.). Reston, VA: Author.

SHAPE America. (2009b). *Appropriate instructional practice guidelines for middle school physical education* (3rd ed.). Reston, VA: Author.

SHAPE America. (2011). *Physical best activity guide: Middle and high school levels* (3rd ed.). Champaign, IL: Human Kinetics.

SHAPE America. (2020). Conkle, J. (Ed.). (2020). *Physical best teacher's guide: Physical education for lifelong fitness* (4th ed.). Champaign, IL: Human Kinetics.

Siedentop, D., & Hastie, P., & van der Mars, H.(2004). *Complete guide to sport education.* Champaign, IL: Human Kinetics.

Steps in Developing an Effective Curriculum

3

A written curriculum gives direction to an instructional program. This chapter offers a systematic approach for planning and designing a comprehensive curriculum, with suggested formats for organization and evaluation. The concepts of scope, sequence, breadth, depth, and balance help ensure that the curriculum will meet the needs of all students. The chapter also provides a discussion on the importance and advantages of articulating the curriculum from kindergarten through 12th grade.

Learning Objectives

► Discuss the common value orientations in physical education curriculum approaches.
► List and discuss the steps of curriculum construction.
► Describe the issues that must be considered in developing a philosophy and conceptual framework.
► Describe various environmental factors that must be considered when developing a physical education curriculum.
► Analyze the content standards that should guide curriculum development.
► Explain how to write the parts of student-centered objectives.
► Discuss the goals of adults and students regarding physical education activities.
► Explain the physical, social, emotional, and intellectual differences between middle and senior high school students.
► Discuss scope, sequence, breadth, depth, and balance as they relate to curriculum construction.
► Give several examples of how curriculum can be evaluated.
► Explain the advantages of an articulated K through 12 curriculum.

The **physical education curriculum** is a framework of student-centered physical activities that promotes physical activity and skill development. A curriculum is a delivery system that gives sequence and direction to learning experiences. Curriculum is based on a theoretical framework in addition to local, state, and national standards already established. Oftentimes, curriculum is based on the values of a teacher or group of teachers. Teachers have a defined set of personal and professional beliefs that guide what they believe should be included in the curriculum (see figure 3.1). A department of physical educators will generate a curriculum that reflects a number of different value sets or **value orientations**. For example, curricula often contain different activities and outcomes because multiple teachers have advocated for including the activities they think most important. The final curriculum may include a wide variety of units such as lifetime activities, sports skills, fitness, social skills, and so on even though teachers may not agree on the need for all the inclusions. They may also be integrated together, such that fitness may be included within a sports skills unit and social skills may be highlighted within a lifetime activities unit.

When developing or revising an existing curriculum, all teachers on the staff must have the opportunity to state their personal values and preferences. Most of the issues that occur when teachers hesitate to follow the curriculum are related to the belief that they had no say about what was included in the curriculum. Three major components dictate the content of the curriculum: the subject matter to be learned, the students for whom the curriculum is being developed, and the society that has established the schools. Physical educators who place highest priority on subject matter mastery include an emphasis on sports, dance, outdoor adventure activities, physical fitness activities, and aquatic activities. The curriculum emphasizes learning skills and gaining knowledge because students must learn the subject matter so that they can continue active participation for a lifetime. In contrast, instructors who favor a student-centered approach value activities that develop the individual student. They emphasize helping students find activities that are personally meaningful. Other physical educators see student autonomy and self-direction as the most important goals. They focus instruction and curricula on lifetime sport skills and nontraditional activities—such as cooperative games, trust-building procedures, and group activities—in an attempt to foster problem-solving and interpersonal skills.

Usually, most curricula in the secondary schools are put together by committee and therefore reflect several value sets. Teacher's values influence their curricular decisions, so discussing personal beliefs is helpful in develop-

Value orientations	Outcomes	Learning domain focus
Disciplinary mastery	Emphasis is placed on motor skill acquisition, skill and discipline knowledge (e.g., biomechanics, exercise physiology), and skill performance.	Psychomotor and cognitive
Learning process	Emphasis is placed on using new knowledge and developing problem-solving skills.	Psychomotor and cognitive
Self-actualization	Emphasis is placed on developing self-direction and taking personal responsibility for learning. Students learn about themselves.	Affective
Ecological integration	Emphasis is placed on the learning process and discovering needs and interests as students develop and interact with the world around them.	Affective
Social reconstruction and social responsibility	Emphasis is placed on developing prosocial behaviors.	Affective

FIGURE 3.1 Value orientations provide direction in developing a curriculum.
Based on Ennis (1992).

VALUE SET

Just what is a *value set* and how does it influence curriculum development? Many of you teach as you were taught. You leave high school thinking you want to teach like your teachers taught you. This idea is your value set at graduation. You have not experienced teaching and other teachers, so your beliefs and values about what physical education should be are based on your personal experience. When you enter junior year of college and start taking classes on teaching, you soon find that many of the things you believe about teaching are now being challenged. This circumstance is an example of value sets colliding. Professors and other teachers may believe differently than we do. You take all your classes and head out to do your student teaching. All the things you learned in college now form a new value set that you take to your student teaching experience. Immediately, you find that your master teacher does not have the same value set as you. How are you going to handle it when you are told to teach something or discipline in a way you do not believe is right? Value sets will conflict in some situations. How you handle these situations will have a lot to do with how you ultimately feel about teaching and getting along with others. Back to curriculum development: If you are part of larger physical education faculty group, as you develop and write a curriculum, you will quickly learn the value sets of others. To create a successful curriculum, compromise will be needed.

ing clarity between curriculum and instructional goals. By finding shared values, a staff can present lessons that reflect common goals and objectives. Before accepting a teaching position, ask the following questions about the curriculum at a prospective school:

- Will the school curriculum express a point of view about the subject matter that I can accept and support?
- Does the school curriculum express a point of view about student learning that I share?
- Does the school curriculum express a point of view that is consistent with mine about the school's role in accomplishing social or cultural goals?
- Can I implement instructional strategies that I value using the school's model?

Designing a Quality Curriculum

Quality physical education programs are guided by quality curriculum. Developing an effective curriculum is critical for equipping students with the appropriate knowledge, skills, and confidence to be physically active throughout their life. The steps that follow (see figure 3.2) offer a sequential approach for constructing a meaningful, well-planned curriculum. The first four steps are designed to establish a framework that guides selection of activities for the curriculum. These steps ensure that the activities

selected are based on how well they contribute to content standards; otherwise a curriculum has little direction, a situation similar to building a house without blueprints.

Step 1: Develop a Guiding Philosophy

Defining a philosophy that reflects the beliefs that guide the developmental process is the initial step in curriculum design. Answering questions about your beliefs such as the following can clarify and guide your physical education curriculum.

1. What are your personal and professional beliefs about physical education?
2. What do you think is the primary purpose of secondary-level physical education?
3. What do you think is the physical educator's role in achieving the outcomes of her or his personal and professional beliefs about physical education?
4. What do you want your students to have accomplished upon completion of your curriculum?

A philosophical statement defines how physical education fits into the total school curriculum and what it will accomplish for each student. Differentiated instruction within a curriculum will allow teachers to meet the needs of individual students based on their ability. The following is an example of a philosophical platform for physical education.

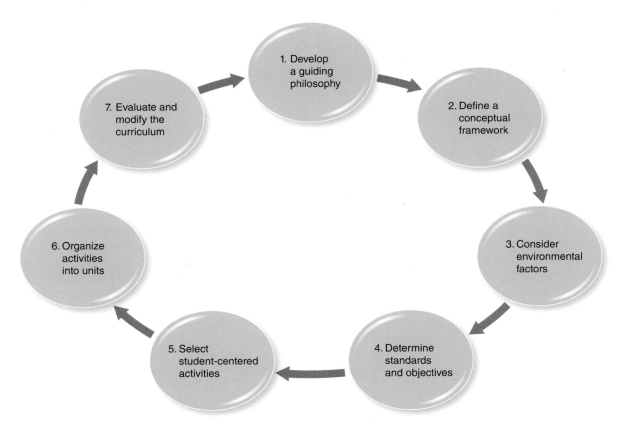

FIGURE 3.2 Steps for designing a quality curriculum.

Physical education is that portion of the student's overall education that is accomplished through physical activity, that is, the process of educating the entire person: the body and the mind. Physical education is responsible for developing the body through instruction predominantly focused on physical activity and skill development. A quality physical education program uniquely contributes to the development of students in the following ways:

- Develop personal activity and fitness behaviors. Students experience a large variety of activities as they develop an understanding of their personal strengths and weaknesses. Knowledge is a component needed to develop activity and fitness behaviors. Many adults have plenty of knowledge related to the need for fitness and activity but do not practice what they know. Engaging in physical activity that leads to personal health is a habit that students can learn during the middle and high school years. Physical education at this level may be the last opportunity for many students to learn personal activity skills as they enter adulthood. Students must learn personal physical activity behaviors and fitness through regular participation in daily physical activity.

- Learn motor skills that can be used for recreational activity throughout life. Movement competency is rooted in developing a broad base of motor skills. Focus instruction on learning motor skills in a positive and nurturing environment that assures students of the joy of activity as opposed to the fear of making mistakes. Personal competency in a wide variety of skills gives students the tools they need to lead an active and rewarding life.

- Develop an understanding of the concepts related to active and healthy behaviors. Being active without understanding the need for being active and healthy is not enough. Moving efficiently requires understanding anatomical and mechanical principles of skill performance. Physical education instruction integrates knowledge about physical activity and skill performance so that students learn how to maintain personal fitness.

Step 2: Define a Conceptual Framework

A conceptual framework is a series of statements that characterize the desired curriculum. These concepts establish the criteria used to select activities and experiences included in the curriculum. The framework not only directs the activities but also reflects beliefs about education and the learner. Following are some conceptual statements that define a student-centered, developmental curriculum.

- Curriculum goals and objectives are appropriate for all students. This statement implies a balanced curriculum that covers fundamental skills, sport skills, games, fitness, rhythms and dance, gymnastics, and lifetime activities. Emphasis is placed on developing a broad physical activity foundation for all students.

- Activities in the curriculum are selected based on their potential to help students reach content standards. Middle and high school students benefit from physical experiences that provide experimentation, exploration, practice, and decision making with many movement possibilities. Inclusion of activities in the curriculum is based not on teacher or student preferences but on how they contribute to student progress toward content standards.

- The curriculum helps students develop lifelong physical activity habits and understand basic fitness concepts. A curriculum guides student experiences so that they graduate with active lifestyle habits. A meaningful curriculum helps students understand that physical activity and fitness are personal in nature, need to be maintained throughout life, and contribute to better health. Fitness is an important component of the curriculum that provides students with opportunities to participate in fitness activities that are varied, positive, and educational.

- The curriculum includes activities that enhance cognitive and affective learning. Students are whole beings and need to do more than just practice skills. They must understand skill performance principles and develop cognitive learning related to physical activities. Affective development, the learning of cooperative and social skills, is fostered through group activities that include all students regardless of their widely varying skills and abilities.

- The curriculum provides experiences that allow all students to succeed and feel satisfaction. Quality programs focus on emphasizing success and minimizing failure. Activities that encourage self-improvement, participation, and cooperation enhance the development of positive self-concepts. Physical education instruction focuses on developing a learning environment that supports all students.

- The curriculum is planned and based on an educational environment consistent with other academic areas in the school. Physical education teachers need the same working conditions as other teachers in the school setting. Class sizes like those of other classroom teachers (20 to 35 students) and an assigned teaching area (e.g., gym space, outdoor fields, or exercise rooms) are needed for physical education instruction. Enough equipment for maximum activity and participation implies one piece of individual equipment for each student and ample apparatuses to limit lines while waiting for a turn. A consistent program ensures maximum opportunity for learning and retention. Because many schools are increasing the number of students in physical education, teachers find it difficult to maintain quality of instruction.

- Activities in the curriculum are presented in an educationally sound sequence. Progression is the center of learning, and the curriculum should reflect progression vertically (between grade and developmental levels) and horizontally (within each level and within each activity). Sequencing is developmentally appropriate and moves from simple to more complex, both vertically and horizontally.

- The curriculum includes an appropriate means of assessing student progress. Student assessment includes health-related fitness, skill development and application, cognitive learning, and attitude development toward physical activity. Assessment should enhance the effectiveness of the program and help teachers communicate learning outcomes, individualize instruction, communicate with students and parents, and identify students with special needs.

Step 3: Consider Environmental Factors

Environmental factors are conditions within the community and school district that limit or extend the content of the yearly curriculum. Examples of environmental factors include the cultural makeup and interests of the community, the amount and type of equipment, and budget size. Other factors, such as administrator support, can affect the type of scheduling or amount of required physical education. Although environmental factors need to be examined carefully, they should not circumvent and limit curriculum scope and sequence. These factors should give direction to the curriculum development process. A well-designed curriculum provides a goal, direction, and destination for the future, a map to instructional success. Environmental factors can be used to enhance the creativity and scope of the curriculum.

Following are specific examples of environmental factors that may limit the development of a quality curriculum. Although these factors can sometimes be limiting, they can be handled creatively to ensure an effective curriculum. Think big; develop a comprehensive and ideal curriculum that is as varied, broad, and creative as possible. Seek to expand and develop the curriculum beyond these limiting factors.

School Administrators

School administrators' support has a significant influence on the curriculum. Program goals must be communicated clearly to administrators. Administrators may have misconceptions about physical education and its contribution to students' overall education. They are more likely to support a program built on sound educational principles that are documented and evaluated. School administrators' support yields positive dividends over time. They have the power to influence situations and implement strategies. Areas where administrative support is necessary include the following:

- Determining the number of staff members and class size
- Hiring staff to fill specific departmental needs
- Constructing or developing facilities and teaching areas (e.g., racquetball courts, weight rooms, exercise trails, or swimming pools)
- Purchasing equipment and teaching aids (e.g., golf clubs, jump bands, in-line skates, medicine balls, body bars, physioballs, or jump ropes)
- Supporting innovative ideas or new activities (e.g., a pilot unit on orienteering, an off-campus

cross-country skiing lesson, or a team-teaching presentation of a golf unit)
- Maintaining existing teaching stations (e.g., watering the fields, cleaning the gymnasium, or repairing weight machines)
- Supporting professional development with in-service workshops, professional conferences, and current literature
- Providing useful and meaningful feedback to teachers on their teaching performance (e.g., collecting data on management time, productive time, active learning time, or behavior patterns)

The Community: People and Climate

Occupations, religions, educational levels, cultural values, and physical activity habits within the community are factors that might affect curriculum development. Parents have a strong influence on children's activity interests and habits. Geographical location and climate of the area are also important factors for consideration. Terrain (mountains, deserts, plains, and so on) and weather particular to each area influence people's activity interests. Hot or cold climates markedly influence what activities are included in the curriculum and at what time of the year activities should be scheduled.

Facilities and Equipment

Available teaching facilities dictate activity offerings. Facilities include on-campus as well as neighboring community off-campus areas (e.g., swimming pool, park, fitness facilities). One piece of good condition equipment per child is necessary if students are to learn at an optimum rate. School funds or special funds raised by students through selective programs can be used to purchase equipment. School maintenance departments or industrial arts programs can be asked to construct some equipment. Students can also be asked to bring equipment, such as in-line skates, soccer balls, and basketballs. Establishing community use of equipment outside school hours is crucial.

Laws and Requirements

Laws, regulations, and requirements at the national, state, and local levels may restrict or direct a curriculum. Programs must conform to these laws. Examples of two federal legislation acts affecting physical education programs are the **Individuals with Disabilities Education Act (IDEA) of 2004** (U.S. Department of Education, 2005) and **Title IX of the Educational Amendments**

Act of 1972. IDEA defines physical education as a necessary component of special education for student ages 3 through 21. Title IX enforces equal opportunities for both sexes. Individual states may have various laws that affect physical education programming.

Scheduling

School time schedules or organizational patterns have an effect on curriculum development. Consideration of how many times per week classes meet, how long class periods are, and who teaches the classes are important factors in the development of curriculum. Many scheduling alternatives exist: 9-week quarters, 12-week trimesters, 18-week semesters, and year-long. Regardless of the various parameters, most secondary schools put together a scheduling committee consisting of administrators, teachers, parents, and students to develop a workable schedule for all parties.

The two basic types of schedules are the traditional schedule and the flexible, or block, schedule. The traditional plan divides the school day into five or six equal periods. Each class, such as math, science, and physical education, meets for the same length of time on each day of the school week. Traditional schedules (see figure 3.3) offer some advantages over others; it is easier to set up, more economical, and easier to administer. Students are in the same class at the same time each day, providing a stable routine for students, teachers, and administrators.

Flexible, or block, schedules (see figure 3.4) provide a varying length of time for classes depending on the nature of the subject matter and the type of instruction given. Block schedules offer periods almost two times longer than a traditional schedule. Seventy to 90 minutes is a common length for a block schedule. A block schedule allows physical education students time to travel to alternative locations (e.g., a local ski slope, a rock-climbing center, a disc golf course). Schools use different flexible schedules to meet the needs of students and teachers involved. One popular block schedule is the four-by-four format in which students take only four classes each semester, usually two 90-minute classes in the morning and two in the afternoon. Another variation is the alternating block plan in which students go to four classes one day and four different classes the next day. This schedule rotates every day and gives students eight classes for the year. A flexible, or block, schedule provides more time for skill development, the option of grouping students for different types of instruction (large or small groups), or the use of limited and specific types of equipment. These longer periods offer an opportunity to teach two focus sessions per lesson. For example, the teacher could teach an introductory activity, a fitness activity, a focus or game, and then another focus or game. This approach allows two units to be taught simultaneously. Some physical education teachers believe that that block schedules improve learning in their classes.

Budget and Funding

Budget and funding procedures differ among school districts, but the physical education department chairperson is usually involved in developing and submitting the budget. Understanding the funding procedures and planning an aggressive strategy for obtaining an adequate budget is a necessity for a quality program. Physical edu-

Period	Time	Monday	Tuesday	Wednesday	Thursday	Friday
Homeroom	8:00–8:15					→
1	8:15–9:10	Math				→
2	9:15–10:10	English				→
3	10:15–11:10	Biology				→
Lunch	11:15–11:45					→
Study hall	11:45–12:15					→
4	12:15–1:10	Physical education				→
5	1:15–2:10	History				→
6	2:15–3:10	Home economics				→

FIGURE 3.3 Example of a traditional schedule.

Block	Time	Semester 1	Semester 2
1	8:00–9:30	Math	History
2	9:35–11:05	Physical education	Computers
	11:05–11:30	Lunch	Lunch
3	11:35–1:05	Biology	Geography
4	1:10–2:40	English 1	English 2

FIGURE 3.4 Example of a four-by-four block schedule.

cators should seek parity with other school departments in terms of class size and equipment. Student learning in physical education is dependent on appropriate amounts and quality of necessary equipment.

In addition to the basic departmental budget, funds are available through outside sources. Sometimes the athletic and physical education departments can share equipment. With tight budgets, this approach is an effective way to cut costs. Various community and parent groups, such as the Lions or Rotary Club, may help with short-term funding for special facility or equipment needs such as a weight room, racquetball courts, or tennis rackets. Some schools allow departments to have special fund-raising campaigns involving students and faculty. Car washes, candy sales, and admission to special sports demonstrations are useful projects for generating funds. Additionally, some schools charge a minimal fee for those enrolled in physical education. Some states offer tax incentives for contributions to school programs. The best programs are not always the ones with the most funding, but adequate funding is necessary to produce a quality curriculum.

Step 4: Determine Standards and Objectives

Content standards determine the direction of the program as directed by the state, district, or individual school. Such standards provide fixed goals for learning and determine what students should know and be able to do when they complete their schooling. Student progress is determined by how students compare to the fixed standards rather than how they compare with other students. Content standards determine what criteria will be used to select instructional activities for the curriculum. The SHAPE America (SHAPE America, 2013) standards should be reviewed carefully—in addition to state and local standards—and should guide the depth and breadth of standards-based curriculum in middle and high school.

After content standards have been defined, student-centered objectives are written. **Student objectives** dictate the specific learning outcomes that students will achieve by participating in activities throughout the school year. Student-focused learning objectives are

 TEACHING TIP

When you get involved in choosing or writing a curriculum, you will start to consider many activities and units you want to teach. Often, there will be teachers in your group who have a counter to every idea proposed. They will say things like, "We can't do that here because we lack facilities" or "Our students wouldn't like that activity." That negative and counterproductive approach to designing a curriculum means that constructive change will never occur. A better approach is to think of all the activities you would like to offer students regardless of whether you have the instructional expertise, facilities and equipment, or money. Then plans can be made about how to phase in many of these activities over time. More physical education programs have been lost or dropped because they continued to offer the "same old things" while ignoring the interests of parents and students. Administrators are not likely to support a program that has parents complaining that nothing is offered in PE for their son or daughter. Dream and think about what could be.

usually written in behavioral terms. Behavioral objectives contain four key characteristics that can be remembered with the ABCD acronym: (1) *A* for actor, or student, (2) *B* for a behavior that is observable and measurable, (3) *C* for the conditions or environment where the behavior should occur, and (4) *D* for degree or criterion for success that can be measured. Objectives are written for all three of the learning domains: psychomotor, cognitive, and affective. A description of each domain follows.

1. Psychomotor domain. This domain is the primary focus of instruction for physical educators. The seven levels in psychomotor domain taxonomy are movement vocabulary, movement of body parts, locomotor movements, movement implements and objects, patterns of movement, movement with others, and movement problem solving. This graduated list progresses in line with the developmental level of learners. Students learn the vocabulary of movement before proceeding to simple body-part movements and then on to more complex sport skills. They learn more complex movements so that they can participate in activities with others and solve personal movement dilemmas.

2. Cognitive domain. The cognitive domain includes six major areas: knowledge, understanding, application, analysis, synthesis, and evaluation. The focus of the cognitive domain for physical education is knowing rules and strategies, health information, safety, and so on

and being able to understand and apply such knowledge. As students mature, they learn to analyze activities, develop personalized exercise routines (synthesis), and evaluate their fitness and activity levels.

3. Affective domain. The affective domain deals with feelings, attitudes, and values. The major categories of learning in this area are receiving, responding, valuing, organizing, and characterizing. The affective domain changes more slowly than the psychomotor and cognitive domains. How teachers treat students and the feelings that students develop toward physical education are ultimately more important than the knowledge and skills developed in physical education programs.

Behavioral objectives must represent students' developmental needs. When teachers write objectives with the students in mind, they ensure that motor skills, physical activity, and fitness assessments are age and developmentally appropriate. Student learning objectives represent levels of learning within each learning domain. Six levels of learning have been identified (see figure 3.5; Bloom, 1956; Anderson, Krathwohl, & Bloom, 2001). They range from simple recall or recognition of facts at the lowest level to more complex and abstract learning such as evaluation. Figure 3.6 provides examples of behavioral objectives within each of the domains and levels of learning.

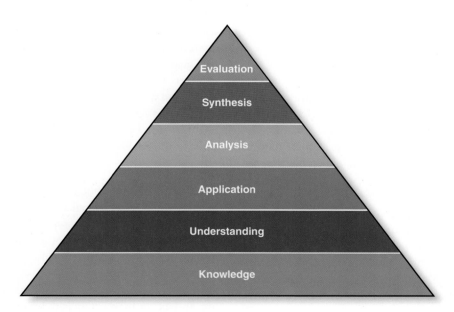

FIGURE 3.5 Bloom's six levels of learning.

Psychomotor Domain

1. Move efficiently using a variety of locomotor skills, such as walking, sliding, carioca, running, and backward running.
2. Use the proper technique to throw a disc accurately to an established target.
3. Knock down three bowling pins using correct stance and approach.
4. Use strategies to get into open space during a modified game.

Cognitive Domain

1. Understand how warm-up and cool-down periods prevent injuries.
2. Analyze bowling movements to improve accuracy and consistency in knocking down specific arrangements of pins.
3. Use principles of rhythm and beat to design an activity performance in small groups.

Affective Domain

1. Show empathy for the concerns and limitations of peers.
2. Demonstrate a willingness to participate with diverse peers regardless of disabilities.
3. Use teamwork to incorporate syncopation and fluid beats in a small-group performance.

FIGURE 3.6 Examples of behavioral objectives within learning domains.

Step 5: Select Student-Centered Activities

When selecting activities for a student-centered curriculum, a clear understanding of students is required. The task of designing a program that flows with students rather than runs contrary to their desires, characteristics, and interests requires a clear view of their nature. Gathering activities for instruction makes little sense if they are not developmentally appropriate or do not appeal to students. The major criterion to follow when selecting activities for the curriculum is "Do the activities contribute to content standards and student-centered objectives?" This approach contrasts with selecting activities because they are fun or are the teacher's favorite. Some teachers do not include activities in the curriculum if they lack confidence or believe that they are incompetent regarding the activity (such as rhythms). Activities

should be included because they contribute to student achievement of content standards, not because they are easy for a teacher to present. Teachers are responsible for developing requisite instructional competency and learning to teach new activities so that students experience and learn all requisite physical skills.

Breadth of content refers to the variety of content to be covered, and depth means that students will develop competence and mastery. Depending on the selected curriculum models, as many activities as possible that contribute to content standards and goals should be gathered in the planning stage. The greater the number of activities considered, the more varied and imaginative the final program will be. Emphasis is placed on brainstorming, creating, and innovating without restriction. Later steps will offer an opportunity to remove inappropriate activities.

Desires of Parents and Students

Years ago, people banded together and decided to set aside land and build schools because they wanted their children to acquire certain information, attitudes, and skills in a systematic manner from professionally prepared teachers. These parents had certain ambitions for their youth. Even though society has changed dramatically and much new information has been discovered, parents and students still have several desires that may influence physical education curriculum planners.

Desire to Be Healthy

All of us want to feel good, and parents expect schools to contribute to their children's health and well-being. Physical education is a crucial tool by which schools can help students develop knowledge and skills that will enable them to make health-enhancing choices. Scientific evidence and personal experiences overwhelmingly support the contributions of physical fitness to overall health and well-being, and the physical education curriculum meets parents' and students' desires for enhanced health to the extent that it equips students to increase activity and make healthy lifetime choices.

Desire to Play

Play has been frequently discussed as an important behavior that permeates all cultures in a variety of forms. Sports, dance, and various types of physical activity are serious forms of play. Many other forms of play, including music, drama, and art, are also important in society. Indeed, play is as important to most people as work, and an enjoyable play life is as valuable as a productive work life. In fact, to many, play is the most important aspect of their lives. It is what they would call "paradise" or "the good life." They look forward to a round of golf, a jog along a canal, or a backpacking trip in the mountains. Physical education can make a significant contribution to this universal desire to play.

Desire for Knowledge

Humans continue to search for knowledge in all areas. People are curious about the world around them. Physical education has an extensive body of knowledge that comes from the various subfields, including exercise physiology, kinesiology, motor learning, sport psychology, and sport sociology.

Desire for Success, Approval, and Satisfaction

People tend to repeat activities that provide them with success. They also tend to avoid activities in which they are not successful. Various types of success usually lead to recognition, approval, or self-satisfaction. People participate in activities in which they are successful because feelings of success lead to satisfaction and happiness. Physical activities are in this category and thus make a significant contribution to a person's life. Many students find that physical education makes them feel incompetent and unsuccessful, quite the opposite of what is suggested here. Quality physical education can help students experience success, and indeed it should.

Desire for Social and Emotional Competence

Most people are concerned about how other people feel about them. People want to be accepted, respected, and liked. Adults want their children to develop acceptable social and emotional skills so that they can enjoy life. Schools are the major social agency in our culture.

Information is imparted in the school setting regarding dating, mental health, sex education, nutrition, and many other important areas. Physical education offers unique opportunities in this social–emotional area because of the nature and arrangement of its subject matter. Competitive situations (involving winning, losing, and accepting referee decisions) and coeducational activities (with emphasis on movement skills) provide a rich source of social and emotional experiences for youth. For some students, physical education offers some of the worst social and emotional experiences of their entire time in school. Physical education teachers can have a tremendous effect on students in these areas.

Desire to Compete

Most societies are competitive. Indeed, competition is present in almost all aspects of our culture. People learn to compete at an early age, and many employers believe that the best competitors are the most successful workers in the business world. Adults want their children to be competitors and winners. In many youth sport leagues, children at an early age compete for league championships, trophies, and adult approval. Some people believe this early competitive experience is beneficial for young people, but others question these assumptions and practices. Regardless of the stand taken, most societies are competitive. The competitive nature of sports and physical activity requires physical educators to take a stand on competition. Physical education programs can have a strong influence on young people and their ability to compete.

Desire for Risk, Adventure, and Excitement

Perhaps because of increased urbanization, mechanization, and impersonal, fast-paced lifestyles, many people are turning to high-risk adventurous activities for fun. Physical activities such as rock climbing, skiing, white-water canoeing, and backpacking are increasing in popularity because they give people an opportunity to do something new, risky, and exciting. The physical education curriculum can provide many experiences to satisfy this desire.

Desire for Rhythmic Expression

Most people enjoy listening to and moving to music. Many forms of rhythmic activity have been popular in a wide variety of cultures throughout history. These activities can include many forms of dance, such as folk, hip-hop, and aerobic dancing, as well as sport movements, such as jumping rope, running hurdles, or exercising to music. Rhythms can be both enjoyable and motivational. A variety of rhythmic activities are an important part of a physical education curriculum.

Desire for Creative Expression

People look for ways to express their autonomy and individuality. Clothes and hairstyles are popular ways to reveal oneself to the world. Play and leisure time is another opportunity for self-expression. The work world often puts limits on individuality, causing people to channel their creative and individual desires into play or leisure pursuits. Physical activities provide numerous possibilities for creative outlets structured by the rules that govern the activities. In basketball, students enjoy trying to develop acrobatic shots or creative drives to the basket, passes, and assists. In gymnastics, the opportunity to develop a creative routine to music or to perfect new moves may be challenging. New plays and defenses are created in football. The challenges are unlimited, and the opportunities for creative expression appeal to students.

Rhythmic activities are an important part of a physical education curriculum.

Physical education curricula should be planned carefully to help satisfy this desire.

Developmental Levels and Characteristics of Students

Besides the desires of parents and students, the developmental levels and characteristics of students should also be examined. Characteristics are typical or distinctive features of students that represent a given developmental or age level. As students grow and develop, certain characteristics appear and disappear. Within a specific age range, most students exhibit similar characteristics, although some will be at the extreme ends of the normal curve regarding developmental levels. Students will vary in height, weight, social abilities, and in many other areas at each chronological age.

Developmental characteristics are often defined by **chronological age**. The problem with this approach is that four or five different **developmental age** levels may exist within a given chronological age range (e.g., seventh grade may contain students who have developmental ages ranging from 10 to 14 years old). Most schools, however, group students by chronological age rather than developmental level because of administrative ease. Physical education teachers must be aware of the wide range of developmental levels that exist at a given grade level. These developmental differences affect physical abilities and performance in physical activities.

Student characteristics are categorized into physical, social, emotional, and intellectual areas. Curriculum planners carefully consider all areas because physical education programs contribute to all four. Some physical educators mistakenly believe that their program contributes only to the physical area, but students do not learn physical activities in a vacuum; they are also involved mentally, socially, and emotionally. **Physical characteristics** encompass defining traits or features about the body. These are visually apparent but provide no other knowledge about the person. **Intellectual characteristics** have to do with using the mind or intellect. In this case, it relates to using the mind or intellect to be physically active. **Social characteristics** are the type of person someone is in society. Finally, **emotional characteristics** are a person's ability to deal with challenges and bounce back from them and not necessarily how they respond in a given moment. The characteristics of students are important to understand when determining the types of activities, the length of units, the amount of student choice, and the content to be emphasized. In addition, pay special attention to the unique developmental influence of the middle school period.

Middle school students' characteristics are different from those of senior high students, and their developmental levels should be considered separately. Sorting out characteristics by each of the four categories (physical, social, emotional, and intellectual) is difficult. In the following discussion of middle and high school student development, two areas will be highlighted: the physical and a combination of the social, emotional, and intellectual.

Middle school curriculum is an important link in the total school curriculum. Plenty of data supports the importance of physical education. Middle school years represent the first time that students are able to make personal decisions about what they like and dislike. Decisions made are often irreversible and last a lifetime. Middle school is a time when students may choose to avoid physical activity whenever possible. Teachers and administrators understand that this time is difficult for most young people, so they need to keep students turned on to activity through a well-organized and expertly taught program. Finding a curriculum designed expressly for the adolescent student is often difficult. Curricula for middle school students may be a watered-down high school program or an extension of the elementary school curriculum. Neither program suits adolescents; they need a program designed to meet traits and characteristics that are unique to their stage of development.

Middle school can be a challenging and difficult time for students. Many students are confused by their rapidly changing physical appearance and the transition from childhood into adulthood. Never again will young people have to experience as many personal changes as they do during middle school. They will make many important decisions during this period about their careers and life goals. The challenges that students experience can also be frustrating and demanding, as well as rewarding, for physical edition teachers. Students at this level want to be independent but still desire the security of authority. This puzzle places teachers in a situation where they are consistently challenged and questioned but ae expected to exert direction when necessary. Physical education can play a significant role in these students' lives.

Tables 3.1 and 3.2 examine the physical and social, emotional, and intellectual characteristics of middle and high school students, including some of the broader implications of various traits.

Consider the Activity Interests of Students

Program planners should examine students' interest in activities being offered. A teacher's comfort zone can be narrow and limit curriculum development. This circumstance often leads to a lack of content variety, which may cause students to develop escape or avoidance behaviors in physical education. Students may like physical activity but dislike the content activities presented or the methods of instruction. Effective teachers learn to expand their teaching repertoire of activities and methods to meet students' interests better.

When the activity interests of students are not considered, students try to avoid taking physical education, especially at the high school level, where the program should be consumer driven. For example, teachers at a particular school may try offering units on lifetime activities such as golf, bowling, and archery and then find that only a few students register because of the lack of interest or the expense of the activities. In another example, if all the units in the curriculum are required during an optional year of physical education, some students may avoid the entire year because they do not wish to take one or two of the specific units. In other words, a student may avoid an entire year because of one or two compulsory activities. At a minimum, the high school program should offer students four or five activity choices. High school is not the time to force students into activities in which they have little or no interest.

Surveys or checklists can be used to gather data about student activity interests. Surveys completed in the spring can be used to determine the curricular offerings for the following fall and spring semesters. The survey can be administered every other year to all demographic groups within the schools (i.e., boys, girls, athletes, nonathletes, various racial groups, and various grade levels). As many students as possible should be surveyed to ensure the collection of valid information. Ideally, the survey can be administered in a class or homeroom period (math, science, or English) so that all students have the opportunity to respond. Complete an analysis of student interests using separate categories by age, sex, or racial group.

When designing a survey instrument include all possible physical activities that contribute to content standards. Student surveys should not be restricted by environmental restrictions (e.g., lack of a pool, racquetball courts, ski slopes, or various types of equipment for specific activities). Most communities have nearby golf driving ranges, racket clubs, bowling alleys, pools, ski slopes, or wooded areas that can be used for the school program. Data collected from surveys can be used to support the need for expanding physical facilities. If student interest is evident, administrators may be convinced that facilities and equipment, course offerings, or new teachers should be added to the physical education program.

An example of an interest survey is shown in figure 3.7. Survey instruments can be revised every other year to include new activity trends. Professional and popu-

TABLE 3.1 Physical and Other Characteristics of Middle School Students

Characteristic	Implications
I. Physical development	
Rapid and uneven growth: Middle school students go through a rapid and uneven growth spurt. Girls enter this spurt about 18 months earlier than boys and are usually taller and more mature early in this period.	• Girls become stronger, faster, and larger than boys. • Size and skill influence performance in activities. • Physical activities should be designed to support variations in student developmental levels. • Insecurities arise based on different developmental levels between boys and girls. • Teachers should educate students about developmental differences. • Students should be educated about the influence of their size and developmental levels relative to their participation in physical activities.
Decreased effectiveness to learn motor skill: The range of motor ability levels increases among students, and the skill level differences of students become increasingly apparent. Awkwardness, poor coordination, low strength, and low endurance are common during rapid growth spurts.	• Teaching motor skills is difficult during this time. • Students often fear failure and embarrassment. • Students avoid learning new skills because of fears. • Selected activities should ensure initial success. • Center of gravity and perception influence success in activities requiring balance and body coordination.
Changes in physical traits: Boys become stronger and gain endurance. Females often gain an advantage over boys in the areas of balance and flexibility. Posture is sometimes a problem with young people. Ossification of the bones is usually not complete.	• Teachers should discuss the differences and effect of body types. • Focus discussions on the importance of posture and lifetime fitness. • Help students select activities that are well suited to their build and physique. • Avoid heavy physical contact sports because of incomplete bone ossification. • Students learn to participate with others of differing ability.
II. Social, emotional, and intellectual development	
Independence and peer groups: Students have a strong need for independence. Peer groups provide the standards for behavior and represent independence.	• Provide situations that allow students to make decisions. • Students learn consequences of their decisions and behaviors. • Offer opportunities for leaderships and decision-making skills. • Participation in games and sport activities fosters an understanding of rules in maintaining an acceptable learning environment for all students.
Emotional instability: Moods change quickly; students are often angry, fearful, and easily upset.	• Teachers should be even-tempered and unruffled by students' mood changes. • Teachers should display patience and give direction without making excessive demands. • Teachers should model desirable behavior and avoid using double standards.
Social awareness: Students are interested in improving themselves, especially in the physical area. Strong concerns about size and abilities are common. Grooming, clothes, and appearance become important. Social activities become important, and dances, movies, parties, and athletic events serve as social meeting places.	• Discuss physiological changes and their implications. • Allow student expression without ridicule or embarrassment. • Encourage self-expression. • Develop activities that provide students with opportunities to learn proper social behaviors.

Characteristic	Implications
II. Social, emotional, and intellectual development	
Intellectual development: Intellectual development continues throughout this period. Students can concentrate longer, are able to understand more complex concepts, and are better able to follow directions. An interest in the "why" of physical activity occurs. Students begin to make decisions about areas in which they want to specialize. A strong interest in risk, excitement, and adventure is common.	• Explain why certain activities are being taught. • Help students become familiar with their physical abilities so that they can make thoughtful activity choices. • Thoroughly cover safety procedures so that students understand the consequences of their choices.

TABLE 3.2 Physical and Other Characteristics of High School Students

Characteristic	Implications
I. Physical development	
Increased motor ability and coordination: Most students have finished their growth spurt and are approaching physical maturity. Bone growth and the ossification process are complete for most students. Motor ability and coordination improve quicker during this period.	• This period is an excellent time to improve motor skills and learn new skills. • Instructional progressions move at a much faster rate.
Modification of physical traits: Strength, endurance, and speed continue to increase. Boys surpass girls in height and weight. Boys continue to develop muscularity, whereas most girls level off in this area.	• Help students understand the effect of physical differences on skill performance. • Guide students toward activities they will be able to participate in successfully by matching their physical strengths. • Develop sensitivity toward participating with people of differing abilities.
II. Social, emotional, and intellectual development	
Social awareness: Social activities such as going to dances, parties, athletic events, and clubs dominate the lives of high school students. Peer groups are important and help provide behavioral standards in areas such as dress, grooming, and interests. Peer groups teach students group loyalty yet independence from adults. Students continue to be concerned about size, strength, and physical ability, but they show more interest in cosmetic fitness than health-related fitness.	• Provide students with choice of activities. • Students should have input on dress requirements, time for dressing in and out, and course requirements. • Students should be able to express their opinions and ideas. • Activities such as personal fitness (e.g., Pilates, weightlifting, aerobics) are attractive to students.
Emotional development: Most students have completed the puberty cycle and are comfortable with their bodies and the direction of their lives. Mood swings occur less frequently, and students seem to be more stable emotionally. Problems with fighting, extreme competitiveness, and arguing over issues start to diminish.	• Students need additional experiences with emotional control. • Teachers should model appropriate behaviors and emotional control.
Intellectual development: Students are approaching their intellectual potential. Their memories and their abilities to reason, concentrate, imagine, and think conceptually have improved and continue to develop. They have a large base of knowledge and experience. Students express strong concern about security, attention, affection, self-worth, and intellectual improvement. They continue to focus their interests more narrowly and tend to specialize in activities in which they perceive themselves to be competent.	• Focus on the why of physical education and the objectives of the program. • Allow student choice of activities they want to learn. • Use longer units to ensure in-depth instruction. • Emphasize cognitive concepts and improving physical skills. • Students practice decision making to help transformation to the realities of the world. • Teachers should impart information, attitudes, and skills.

PHYSICAL ACTIVITY INTEREST

Name _____

Grade _____ Age _____ Sex _____

Athletic team _____

Instructions: Which of the following physical activities or sports would you be most interested in taking as a course in the physical education program? Please list your top five choices on the lines provided. Place a number 1 in front of your highest choice, a number 2 in front of your next choice, and so on, until you reach choice number 5. Remember to make only five choices.

Aquatic Activities
____ Lifesaving, water safety
____ Skin and scuba diving
____ Surfing
____ Swimming, diving
____ Water sports (polo, volleyball, basketball, and so on)

Individual Activities
____ Archery
____ Badminton
____ Fencing
____ Disc sports
____ Golf
____ Gymnastics
____ Handball
____ Racquetball
____ Recreational games (bowling, horseshoes, shuffleboard, and so on)
____ Roller skating
____ Skateboarding
____ Squash
____ Tennis
____ Track and field

Physical Conditioning Activities
____ Aerobic dance
____ Body conditioning, weight control
____ Cardio kickboxing
____ Martial arts (judo, karate, kendo, and so on)
____ Medicine balls
____ Physioballs
____ Pilates
____ Walking activities
____ Weight training
____ Yoga

Outdoor Adventure Activities
____ Backpacking
____ Canoeing, kayaking
____ Cycling (bicycling)
____ Fishing
____ Horseback riding
____ Hunting
____ Ice-skating
____ Orienteering
____ Outdoor survival
____ Rock climbing
____ Sailing
____ Skiing (cross-country)
____ Skiing (downhill)
____ Snowshoeing

Rhythmic Activities
____ Ballet
____ Country swing dance
____ Disco
____ Folk and square dance
____ Jazz dance
____ Modern dance
____ Social dance

Team Activities
____ Baseball
____ Basketball
____ Eclipse ball
____ Field hockey
____ Flag football
____ Ice hockey
____ Lacrosse
____ Soccer
____ Softball
____ Speedball or speed-a-way
____ Team handball
____ Volleyball
____ Wrestling

Directions for the teacher: Remind students to select only five choices, using the numbers 1 through 5 on the lines beside the activities. When analyzing the data, transposing numbers 1 and 5 and numbers 2 and 4 can be helpful. In other words, a 1 becomes a 5, and a 5 becomes a 1. A 2 is worth 4, and a 4 worth 2. The numbers are added for each activity. The activities with the most points are the most popular, and those with the least points are the least popular.

FIGURE 3.7 A physical activity interest survey.

lar literature help provide information about the new activity patterns and habits. Interests in the community can be determined by looking at recreation programs offered through the Y (YMCA), the parks and recreation department, private clubs, community leagues, and corporations. Facilities available, such as bowling alleys, golf courses, ski slopes, health clubs, and swimming pools, provide additional information about interests in the community.

Step 6: Organize Activities Into Units

A yearly plan is developed after appropriate activities have been selected. The purpose of a written curriculum is to ensure that all activities are scheduled and taught. Activities are most often organized into units and then broken down into weekly plans. Weekly plans have three major advantages. First, a comprehensive lesson plan for the week can be developed and divided into the appropriate number of days in the school calendar. Instructional pacing of the content allows students to move along the path of learning at an optimal rate. What cannot be covered one day is taught in the next lesson. Second, less orientation instruction is needed after the first day. Safety factors, teaching hints, and key points need only a brief review each day, and equipment needs are similar from day to day. Third, progression and learning sequences are evident; both teacher and students can see progress.

Determine Length of Activity Units

Activity units can vary in length from two days to a semester. For example, a unit could be a two-day miniunit on juggling or combatives, a two-week unit on disc activities, or a semester-long course on weight training or dance. Developmental levels and interests of students affect the length of a unit, as does the school schedule and the number of days per week that a class meets. The number of class meetings per week is a key factor in deciding the length of a unit. A three-week unit that meets daily offers 15 sessions, whereas a three-week unit that meets twice a week allows only six sessions. Although both are three-week units, the difference in the amount of actual class time for instruction is significant.

Figure 3.8 is an example of an arrangement using short one-, two-, and three-week units (breadth) that offer students 12 to 18 different activities during the year:

Weeks	Activity
1–3	Cooperative activities, group team building, or rhythmic activities
4–6	Modified rugby or soccer
7–9	Pickleball or racquetball
10–12	Volleyball or eclipse ball
13–15	Social dance or aerobic variations
16–18	Recreational games or team handball
19–21	Badminton or fishing
22–24	Tumbling or basketball
25–27	Disc games or floor hockey
28–30	Speed-a-way or flickerball
31–33	Disc golf or golf
34–36	Orienteering or new games

FIGURE 3.8 Yearly plan with one- or two-week activity units.

Each unit starts with basic skills and strategies and progresses to a point where instruction and skill practice is necessary because students cannot perform adequately. Starting each unit with the easiest activity ensures success and review for all students. Instructional sequences for each day are built on the preceding lesson.

Check the Scope, Sequence, and Balance of the Curriculum

An important step in creating a quality program is to review and monitor the scope, sequence, and balance of the curriculum, in addition to its breadth and depth. These concepts are the foundation of a quality curriculum.

Scope is the yearly curriculum content. Monitoring the scope of the curriculum ensures that the desired content of the program will be covered in a systematic and accountable manner each year. In middle school physical education, the scope of the curriculum is broad; many activities are presented to ensure that a breadth of activities is included. Student interest wanes if units are too long. Also, middle school physical education is designed to help students learn about and explore all the available types of physical activity. In high school, fewer in-depth activities are generally offered, but students may choose longer activity units that help them increase their skills more dramatically. Figure 3.9 shows an example of a nine-week plan with a four-part lesson for seventh graders that focuses on breadth with 18 to 20 units in the curriculum. Figure 3.10 shows a sample scope and sequence chart for a K-12 curriculum; note that in this chart, different units and skills are introduced[I], reviewed and reinforced[R], and taken to proficiency[P] at the indicated grade levels.

Balance ensures that all objectives in the program receive adequate coverage. When reviewing the scope and sequence of the curriculum, checking balance avoids skewing toward one area. To ensure balance, major areas of emphasis are determined based on program objectives. These areas can be allotted a percentage of program time based on the characteristics and interests of students. This determination reveals to administrators, teachers, and parents the direction and emphasis of the program. All areas have a proportionate share of instructional time,

and the percentage of time allotted to each area reflects the needs and characteristics.

Common categories of activities emphasized are team sports, lifetime activities, physical conditioning or fitness activities, dance activities, gymnastics activities, aquatic activities, and adventure activities. Ensure that all students have experience with a variety of activities selected from as many categories as possible in the middle school setting. Too often, the curriculum is heavily tipped toward team sports because of class size, facilities, equipment, or the instructor's lack of interest or ability in other areas. An unbalanced curriculum is not appropriate for students interested in activity categories not offered. For example, some students enjoy disc sports, orienteering, dance, or skin diving but do not enjoy football, basketball, wrestling, or volleyball. If the curriculum is unbalanced, these students will not have access to potentially fulfilling activities. Teachers must make every effort to offer a balanced program.

Unit number	Introductory	Fitness	Lesson focus	Game
1	Move and freeze	Orientation	Orientation	Simple games
2	Basic movements	Teacher leader	Soccer skills	Lead-up soccer games
3	Walk, trot, jog	Stretching	Soccer skills	soccer game
4	Fugitive tag variations	Form running	Football skills	Lead-up football games
5	Pivot variations	Racetrack fitness	Football skills or throton	Small-sided football games
6	Flag grab	Aerobic fitness and partner resistance	Group team building	Rock–paper–scissors
7	Marking	Walking activities	Pedometer activities	Pedometer game
8	Run, stop, and pivot	Circuit training	Volleyball skills	Lead-up volleyball games
9	Flag grab variations	Astronaut drills	Volleyball skills or eclipse ball	Small-sided volleyball games
10	Marking variations	Jump rope continuity	Rope-jumping skills	Chicken baseball
11	Move and change directions	Squad leader	Floor hockey	Lead-up hockey games
12	Quick hands	Step aerobics	Floor hockey or roller hockey	Small-sided hockey games
13	Partner over and around	Dyna-bands	Team handball	Lead-up team handball games

FIGURE 3.9 A yearly curriculum plan for seventh graders.

(continued)

Unit number	Introductory	Fitness	Lesson focus	Game
14	Flash drills	Cardio choice	Team handball	Small-sided team handball games
15	Agility drills	Jump and jog	Tennis skills	Lead-up tennis games
16	Moving throw and catch	Fortune cookie	Tennis skills	Eclipse ball variations
17	Clothespin tag	Scavenger hunt	Basketball skills	Lead-up basketball games
18	File running	Basketball circuit	Basketball skills	Small-sided basketball games
19	Moving high fives	Monopoly fitness	Rhythms	Dances
20	Jumping and plyometrics	Squad leader variations with task cards	Rhythms	Dances
21	Fastest tag variations	Kickboxing aerobics	New games	New game activities
22	Standing high fives	Novel walking activities	Track and field	Running relays
23	Loose caboose	Pacer run	Track and field	Running relays
24	Leaping Lena or rooster hop	Long jump rope fitness	Gymnastics	Pyramid building
25	Move and change directions	Scavenger hunt	Disc skills or Spin Jammers	Ultimate
26	Triangle and one	Circuit training with a jog	Softball skills	Disc softball
27	Spider tag variations	Yoga or Pilates	Softball skills	Over-the-line softball
28	Marking variations	Walking activities	Golf skills	Golf skills
29	Blob tag	Cardio choice or medicine balls	Badminton skills	Lead-up badminton games
30	Quarter eagle agility	Disc fitness	Badminton skills	Badminton games
31	Triangle and two	Scavenger hunt	Orienteering skills	Orienteering meet
32	Power-walk variations	Rope jumping and partner resistance	Flickerball skills	Flickerball game
33	Move and perform a stretch	Cardio choice or physioballs	Speed-a-way	Speed-a-way game
34	Tag games	Monopoly fitness	Juggling skills	Partner juggling
35	Fitness self-testing	Fitness self-testing	Fitness self-testing	Fitness self-testing
36	Teacher choice	Teacher choice	Cageball games	Relays or tag games

FIGURE 3.9 *(continued)*

	Preschool	Elementary	Middle	Senior	K	1	2	3	4	5	6	7	8	9	10	11	12
Archery																	
1. History															I	I	R
2. Safety, rules, strategy															I	I	R
3. Equipment															I	I	R
4. Shooting															I	I	R
Badminton															**I**	**I**	**R**
1. History															I	I	R
2. Safety, rules, strategy			I	P					I	R					R	R	R
3. Equipment			I	P					I	R					R	R	R
4. Skills			I	P					I	R					R	R	R
a. *Grip*			I	P					I	R					R	R	R
b. *Serves*			I	P					I	R					R	R	R
c. *Strokes*			I	P					I	R					R	R	R
Bowling																	
1. History												I	R				
2. Safety, rules, strategy			I	R								I	R				
3. Equipment			I	R								I	R				
4. Skills			I	R								I	R				
a. *Grip*			I	R								I	R				
b. *Approach*			I	R								I	R				
c. *Delivery*			I	R								I	R				
Cross-Country Skiing																	
1. History															I	I	R
2. Safety, rules, strategy			I	R											I	I	R
3. Equipment			I	R											I	I	R
4. Skills			I	R											I	I	R
a. *Kick glide*			I	R											I	I	R
b. *Stop*			I	R											I	I	R
c. *Turns*			I	R											I	I	R

I = Introduce: initial instruction of psychomotor, cognitive, and affective skills that are explained, demonstrated, and practiced.

R = Review and reinforce: continued instruction of skill-level improvement and increased knowledge of techniques.

P = Proficiency: the attainment of an individual's maximum skill level through instruction and practice.

FIGURE 3.10 An example of a scope and sequence chart for a K through 12 curriculum.

(continued)

	Preschool	Elementary	Middle	Senior	K	1	2	3	4	5	6	7	8	9	10	11	12
d. Poling			I	R											I	I	R
e. Climb			I	R											I	I	R
Curling																	
1. History															I	I	R
2. Safety, rules, strategy															I	I	R
3. Equipment															I	I	R
4. Skills															I	I	R
a. Deliver															I	I	R
b. Sweeping															I	I	R
Golf																	
1. History															I	I	R
2. Safety— Rules—Strat- egy															I	I	R
3. Equipment															I	I	R
4. Skills															I	I	R
a. Grip															I	I	R
b. Full swings															I	I	R
c. Approach shots															I	I	R
d. Putting															I	I	R

I = Introduce: initial instruction of psychomotor, cognitive, and affective skills that are explained, demonstrated, and practiced.

R = Review and reinforce: continued instruction of skill-level improvement and increased knowledge of techniques.

P = Proficiency: the attainment of an individual's maximum skill level through instruction and practice.

FIGURE 3.10 *(continued)*

Based on information from LaCrosse, WI, Public Schools.

Skillful curriculum planners arrange activities in the program to influence the habits of students regarding physical activity, rhythms, and sports areas. Initially, students not interested in physical activity may have to be encouraged to try such activities. All students need to find activities for personal enjoyment and health. Physical education programs can take a leadership role in trying to shape activity preferences that students can use after graduation.

Team sports dominate most secondary school curriculums. Many physical educators claim that these activities are the most popular with students and are the most economical in terms of facilities and equipment. Often, they are popular with vocal students who are skilled, whereas less skilled students may be intimidated and afraid to admit they do not like team sports. Another claim suggests that team sports are more economical to offer (in terms of required equipment). This point may be true if teachers use limited pieces of equipment, resulting in the majority of students standing rather than practicing skills in a semi-individualized manner in which every student has a piece of equipment. When developing the curriculum, educators need to consider activities that students will engage in beyond the high school years. According to the Physical Activity Council's annual study tracking sports, fitness, and recreation participation in the United States, adults ages 20 and older report the highest participation rates in fitness activities, outdoor activities, and individual activities, respectively (Physical Activity Council, 2018). Team sports, racket sports, water activities, and winter sports showed the lowest participation rates as people age. Why not include activities that students might engage in for a lifetime?

More teachers now include a variety of lifetime activities such as walking, jogging, hiking, step aerobics, kickboxing, Pilates, yoga, weight training, racquetball, pickleball, tennis, badminton, bowling, and golf. These activities have more carryover value for later life because they do not require several teammates for participation. Successful programs develop a balance of team sports, lifetime sports, physical fitness, gymnastics, dance, aquatics, and currently popular activities. Curricula that offer an activity balance have a higher potential for positively affecting all students within the school.

Step 7: Evaluate and Modify the Curriculum

Regular evaluation is an important step in ensuring that physical education programs are effective and in alignment with national, state, or district standards. What makes a quality physical education program? Until recently, physical educators had limited access to tools that assess the quality of physical education curricula. The **Physical Education Curriculum Analysis Tool** (PECAT; Centers for Disease Control and Prevention, 2019) was developed to assist in the development and enhancement of programs for the purpose of influencing school-aged students' physical activity behaviors. PECAT is designed to analyze curricula content and student assessment. It can

- assesses how closely physical education curricula align with national standards for physical education;
- analyzes outcomes, content, and assessment components of a curriculum that correspond to national standards for physical education for three grade levels: K–5, 6–8, and 9–12;
- helps school districts or individual schools identify changes needed in locally developed curricula; and
- helps school districts or individual schools use the PECAT to develop a physical education curriculum.

Revisions can be made with existing curriculum or provide a focus for what should be included when writing a new curriculum.

Several sources can supply evaluative data: pupils, teachers, consultants, parents, and administrators. Achievement test scores can supply hard data to compare preassessments and postassessments with those of other programs. Subjective assessments might include likes and dislikes, value judgments, problem areas, and needed adjustments. The evaluation schedule can include a limited area for assessment, or assessment can be broadened to cover the entire program such as PECAT (see figure 3.11). Modification of possible program deficiencies is based on sound educational philosophy and valid and reliable assessment and evaluation tools. Identifying weaknesses and determining causes are important steps in developing physical education programs that provide students with opportunities to develop lifetime physical activity habits.

A pilot or trial project can help teachers and students transition from the old to the new. One school in the district might be chosen to develop and implement a pilot physical education program. Pilot programs provide quality instruction and services to ensure student success. In some cases, the experimental program might be implemented with only one class in a school. Enthusiastic, skilled direction is necessary for such projects. Pilot programs can be analyzed and results used to refine and adjust areas before an entire program is implemented throughout the school system.

An Articulated Curriculum: Grades K Through 12

Often, physical education curricula are developed in parts. There is usually a curriculum for the elementary school level, one for middle school, and another for the high school. Each curriculum is written and organized independently of the others. A districtwide K through 12 plan that considers all the steps mentioned is seldom developed. In many cases, elementary physical education specialists do not know middle and high school physical education teachers, let alone understand the curriculum taught at each level. Teachers might operate autonomously, without concern for or knowledge of what teachers do at other levels. This practice leads to a fragmented program that shows little articulation between levels. Time, energy, and learning of activities may be wasted, duplicated, or omitted when a K through 12 curriculum is not vertically articulated.

Curriculum planners need to understand the effect that these curriculum steps have on students in terms

High-quality physical education teaches students the knowledge, skills, and confidence to be physically active for a lifetime.

Appropriate actions must be taken in four main areas to ensure a high-quality physical education program:

- curriculum,
- policies and environment,
- instruction, and
- student assessment.

Policy and environmental actions that support high quality physical education require the following:

- adequate instructional time (at least 150 minutes per week for elementary school students and 225 minutes per week for middle and high school students),
- qualified physical education specialists to teach all classes,
- reasonable class sizes, and
- proper equipment and facilities.

Instructional strategies that support high quality physical education emphasize the following:

- the need for inclusion of all students,
- adaptations for students with disabilities,
- opportunities to be physically active most of class time,
- well-designed lessons,
- out-of-school assignments to support learning, and
- not using physical activity as punishment.

Regular student assessment within a high-quality physical education program features the following:

- the appropriate use of physical activity and fitness assessment tools,
- ongoing opportunities for students to conduct self-assessments and practice self-monitoring of physical activity,
- communication with students and parents about assessment results, and
- clarity concerning the elements used for determining a grading or student proficiency system.

FIGURE 3.11 The PECAT definition of high-quality physical education.

Reprinted from Centers for Disease Control and Prevention (2015).

of overall program objectives. An articulated curriculum with consistent policies and procedures on instruction, management, discipline, grading, student choices, dress codes, and so forth affects students in a positive manner and improves participation in the program. For example, a teacher who does not look carefully at the scope, sequence, and balance of the curriculum may repeat or omit important aspects of the program. A well-developed K through 12 curriculum plan provides fitness activities, lifetime sports, rhythmic activities, gymnastics, and outdoor adventure activities as well as team sports. An articulated physical education program should also consider after-school opportunities for students such as activity clubs, intramural sports, and athletic programs.

An articulated quality physical education curriculum can lead students into these after-school opportunities. Consider these curriculum steps and elements when policies, procedures, yearly plans, daily plans, and other aspects of dealing with students are formulated. Specific suggestions are made throughout this text with respect to each of these program steps.

Elementary School Program

Elementary school physical education programs emphasizes expanding the activity experiences of students. Although children entering kindergarten generally have similar skills, elementary school curricula strive to offer a wider variety of activities to ensure that students can experience success. In addition, a wide variety of activities ensures that students are involved in short units of instruction that minimize long bouts of failure. If units are short, students who do not like a certain activity or feel like failures know they will not have to continue the activity for an extended time. In addition, the variety of short units ensures that all students will find some activity they enjoy, increasing their opportunity to experience success.

Middle School Program

In middle school, program variety continues with short units that assure students that they will not have to endure an activity they dislike for long. A balanced curriculum places equal emphasis on all activities in the curriculum consistent with program objectives and goals. Activities are included if they meet the needs and interests of all learners and contribute to program standards. For example, a design that offers only four or five team sports during the year does not meet the needs of students who do not like team sports, are uninterested in the sports offered, or prefer individual activities.

Another important consideration in developing middle school curriculum is the matter of sequence. Organized correctly, sequence ensures that students receive instruction in a progressive manner from kindergarten to graduation. They learn skills and knowledge in a sequential manner, so previous material taught contributes to current learning. An example of a lack of sequence is teaching students basketball skills in the first grade and continuing to teach these same skills until students leave school. It would be unthinkable to give children a calculus book in first grade, ask them to repeat the material for 12 years, and then assume they have learned calculus through repetition.

Sequence in the middle school years ensures that units of instruction are organized and designed expressly for that level. Emphasis on strategy and advanced skill should be minimized because students at that age enter a rapid growth curve that reduces their ability to learn motor skills. Middle school is the time to concentrate on skill development. Asking students to concentrate on both skill performance and strategy reduces the odds they will learn either. As an example, think back to the initial stages of learning to drive a car. Concentrating on the fine motor skills involved in driving while thinking about the rules of the road is difficult. After driving skills are overlearned, people begin to consider doing many other things at the same time (e.g., putting on makeup and talking on a cell phone). Frustration and fear can be the result of this type of overload. Until a skill is overlearned, concentration should be on skill performance, not strategy. When the

skills become overlearned, students can concentrate on the cognitive aspect of sport strategy. Most middle school students have not overlearned skills, so strategy should be a minor part of instruction.

When developing scope and sequence for middle school students, designing a sequence that is perfect for everyone is difficult. Students are grouped (whether by grade, age, or developmental level), and every group is characterized by a range of differences. To expect students to follow a predetermined sequence is unrealistic. Effective teachers modify the sequence depending on the capabilities of the student. The best teaching is one on one, in which activities and instruction are in line with student ability level. Regardless, scope and sequence are important because they lend general direction to instruction.

High School Program

High school physical education curricula vary greatly from state to state and from large urban schools with six to eight physical education teachers to the small rural schools with one or two teachers. Local school districts have the ultimate responsibility for developing a program that meets state guidelines. State requirements are different, and some school districts allow a number of substitutions for physical education. Some districts have a four-year requirement, but others have no requirements at all. Another district may have a three-year requirement but allow substitutions such as cheerleading, athletics, orchestra, and band to fulfill the requirement. The variations and possibilities are endless. Nevertheless, the high school program should build on the middle school program.

At the high school level, quality programs come in many sizes and shapes. A small high school in upstate New York, a large urban high school in eastern Pennsylvania, or a medium-sized high school in central Arizona can all have quality programs within their existing frameworks. Some programs will have more students, more teachers, more facilities, and better equipment. Requirements, schedules, and administrative support may be quite different in each situation. Quality programs are not, however, a function of large facilities, abundant equipment, extensive physical education requirements, numerous teachers, or small class sizes. Outstanding high school programs are developed by a group of hardworking, dedicated professionals who are doing their best with given resources. Strong leadership and purpose are found in successful programs. A continual effort must be made to improve programs and to change those aspects that are detrimental to accomplishing goals. A sense of excitement and enthusiasm must be found within the program. Curriculum developers can work positively within the existing framework to change existing parameters that cause difficulties.

The high school years offer opportunities to polish and improve their ultimate product: young adults who are productive members of society. To ensure that the physical education program contributes to this long-term objective, educators need to understand the growth and development of students and the implications that these characteristics have on designing a well-planned curriculum. A quality experience for the entire K through 12 sequence emphasizes individual success, physical fitness, exploration, guidance and counseling, self-testing, monitoring, physical skill development, requisite knowledge, wellness concepts, choice, and preparation for a lifetime of physical activity. The high school curriculum should build vertically on the middle school curriculum and the middle school curriculum build on the elementary curriculum.

CASE STUDY

Advocating for Your Physical Education Program

"If it's to be, it's up to me!" This aphorism is the harsh reality for many physical educators when promoting their programs in this day and age. Budget cuts, time constraints, and academic pressures often curb the amount of time, resources, and energy devoted to physical education programs in schools today. Knowing that this was the case in his school district, Mr. Conn, physical education teacher at Warrensville High School, decided to be proactive in advocating for his physical education program. In his efforts, his most important step was ensuring that his physical education program was of the highest quality. After all, why would an administrator or the public support him if he offered inefficient lessons that the students did not enjoy? The next step he took was to make his administration look good. When he received accolades for participation in outside programs (e.g., Active and Healthy Schools, Alliance for a Healthier Generation's Healthy Schools) or going above and beyond, he always gave credit to his amazing administration and colleagues for their support. By doing so, he believed that they would be more open-minded when he approached them with ideas.

After Mr. Conn established that he offered a quality physical education program and earned respect from his administration, he began reaching out to the public through media outlets. He sent physical education news-letters to parents through email. He offered open-gym opportunities for students who arrived early to school. In collaboration with the instructional technology teacher, he created school-wide competitions for students to create and record themselves leading five-minute movement breaks. These videos were streamed through the school public address system during passing periods. He contacted the local newspaper crew to inform them of family and community nights that he hosted. He collaborated with the local YMCA to provide free Pilates and yoga classes for staff after school for six weeks. Finally, he worked with two other physical educators in the district to host a 5K walk–run to earn money for his school physical education program. He was able to fund a paved walking track on school property.

Other tips that Mr. Conn deemed important for garnering support for his program include the following:

- Demonstrating to his administration that he exhibited excellent behavior management by rarely, if ever, sending students to the office. Principals and other administrators appreciate this practice, and it instills confidence in the teacher's ability to control students in their classroom.

- Starting small. The student-created movement breaks began as assignments for students in one of his physical education classes. They became a hit, and he eventually opened the invitation to all students in the school to enter the contest, if they chose.

- Involving staff and community members. Mr. Conn understood the demands placed on teachers and other staff in the school. Thus, he wanted to give back in some way and show them how much they were valued. Providing a means for them to relieve stress was an effective way to get his colleagues on board with his physical activity promotion plan.

- Raising money. With budget cuts, physical education often suffers repercussions. Equipment breaks, and replacing it is not cheap. One effective way to replenish supplies is to conduct fund-raisers and host events to gain resources.

Mr. Conn is obviously a seasoned teacher who understands how to advocate for his program. If you start advocating when your teaching position is on the chopping block, it is often too late, so being proactive is rec-ommended. What other ideas can you provide to advocate for your physical education program? How much time and what resources might be necessary to get those ideas in place?

LEARNING AIDS

STUDY STIMULATORS AND REVIEW QUESTIONS

1. Explain the role of a teacher's value orientation when developing a curriculum.
2. List and explain three environmental factors that will influence the scope and general focus of a curriculum.
3. Explain the focus of the affective learning domain.
4. What are the central components of a behavioral objective?
5. List and briefly explain two societal influences that should be considered when designing a curriculum.
6. Discuss the implication of students' rapid and often uneven growth patterns for physical education teachers.
7. Compared with middle school students, why do high school students generally have less difficulty learning new skills?
8. Explain what is meant by the scope of a curriculum.
9. Discuss the importance of periodically evaluating the curriculum.

WEBSITES

Physical Education Teaching and Curriculum Information

www.cdc.gov/healthyschools/pecat/index.htm
www.pecentral.org
www.shapeamerica.org/publications/resources/teachingtools/teachertoolbox/curriculum.aspx

McREL International

www.mcrel.org

REFERENCES AND SUGGESTED READINGS

Anderson, L.W., Krathwohl, D.R., & Bloom, B.S. (2001). *A taxonomy for learning, teaching, and assessing: A revision of Bloom's taxonomy of educational objectives*. London, United Kingdom: Longman.

Bloom, B. (1956). *Taxonomy of educational objectives, handbook I: Cognitive domain*. New York, NY: McKay.

Buck, M.M., Lund, J.L., Harrison, J.M., & Blakemore Cook, C.L. (2007). *Instructional strategies for secondary physical education* (6th ed.). Boston, MA: McGraw-Hill.

Centers for Disease Control and Prevention. (2015). CDC healthy schools: High quality physical education. Retrieved from https://cdc.gov/healthyschools/pecat/highquality.htm.

Centers for Disease Control and Prevention. (2019). *Physical Education Curriculum Analysis Tool*. Atlanta, GA: Centers for Disease Control and Prevention, US Dept of Health and Human Services.

Ennis, C.D. (1992). Curriculum theory as practiced: Case studies of operationalized value orientations. *Journal of Teaching in Physical Education, 11*, 358–375.

Himberg, C., Hutchinson, G.E., & Roussell, J.M. (2003). *Teaching secondary physical education preparing adolescents to be active for life*. Champaign, IL: Human Kinetics.

Kelly, L., & Melograno, V.J. (2004). *Developing the physical education curriculum: An achievement-based approach*. Champaign, IL: Human Kinetics.

Lund, J., & Tannehill, D. (2009). *Standards-based physical education curriculum development* (2nd ed.). Boston, MA: Jones and Bartlett.

Metzler, M.W. (2011). *Instructional models for physical education* (3rd ed.). Scottsdale, AZ: Holcomb, Hathaway.

Physical Activity Council. (2018). *2018 participation report: The Physical Activity Council's annual study tracking sports, fitness, and recreation participation in the US*.

Rink, J. (2014). *Teaching physical education for learning* (7th ed). Boston, MA: McGraw-Hill.

SHAPE America. (2013). *National standards for K–12 physical education*. Reston, VA: Author.

Siedentop, D., & van der Mars, H. (2012). *Introduction to physical education, fitness, and sport* (8th ed.). Boston, MA: McGraw-Hill Education.

U.S. Department of Education. (June 21, 2005). *Individuals with Disabilities Education Act Amendments of 2004*. Vol. 70, Number 118, 34 CFR, 300. Washington, D.C.

Planning for Effective Instruction

4

Policies and procedures need to be defined before planning for instruction. Such procedures give direction to the program and offer the framework for planning quality lessons for students. Preinstructional decisions must be considered part of planning a lesson that considers space, equipment, and a safe environment. Various stages of planning ensure quality instruction. In addition, the components of a multipart lesson plan ensure that students receive a balanced approach to instruction. After a lesson has been presented, reflection is a necessary component of quality instruction.

Learning Objectives

▶ Write and define policies and procedures that will guide your physical education program.

▶ Describe the role of planning in preparing for quality instruction.

▶ Understand how arousal influences skill learning.

▶ Give meaningful skill feedback.

▶ Identify the characteristics of effective practice sessions.

▶ List preinstructional decisions that must occur before the actual delivery of the lesson, including use of space, equipment, time, and pace.

▶ Articulate how students can become involved in developing the learning experience.

▶ Describe ways in which learning in the affective domain can be enhanced.

▶ Discuss the various parts of a meaningful unit plan.

▶ Understand the rationale for the three components of a lesson and describe the characteristics of each.

▶ Analyze and reflect on completed lesson plans.

Develop Departmental Policies

Physical education teachers should create a student and parent handbook, based on policies approved by their school and district administrators. It should be brief, clear, and succinct and sent to all students, parents, and administrators, either in hard copy or electronically. Discuss the information in the letter with the class and ask students to discuss it with their parents. Ask students to have their parents read the guidelines, sign an approval form, and return it within one or two days (see figure 4.1). Students and parents often have misconceptions about the nature of physical education, and clarifying all aspects of the program limits future problems.

A quality physical education program requires that policies and procedures be determined, communicated, and applied consistently to all students. To ensure consistency in the program, all members of the physical education department need to be in general agreement on several issues. These policies and procedures guide not only the staff but also students and parents. A set of written guidelines should be presented to students on the first day of school and reinforced continually throughout the year. An excellent curriculum is not effective without a well-developed set of policies and procedures and an ongoing revision process.

Topics that might be included in your physical education handbook are the following:

- Attendance and participation
- Excuses and makeup procedures
- Equipment
- Grading procedures

Attendance and Participation Policies

If students enjoy physical education, fewer problems will arise with attendance and participation. The overall curriculum and instructional procedures will have a greater effect on students' attendance and participation than will policies and procedures. Some teachers spend so much time and energy on the latter concerns that they lose sight of the importance of curriculum and instruction. Students are more enthusiastic about physical education if a quality curriculum and an effective instructional program exists.

Nevertheless, structure and guidelines are always a trademark of a quality program. Policies need to be in place for attendance, participation, and excuses from class. A system that allows students to earn positive

---

POLICIES AND PROCEDURES

Dear Parents or Guardians:

This booklet contains the policies and procedures of the physical education department. We would like you to carefully read and discuss the program regulations with your son or daughter. These policies and procedures are important for making the learning environment a pleasant experience for all students.

We desire to have all students leave physical education classes with a positive attitude and the urge to be physically active throughout their lifetime. If you have any questions about the curriculum or the policies and procedures of the department, please call me at 555-4724.

Please sign the slip at the bottom of the sheet and have your child return it to school.

Thank you.

Sincerely,

_____

Physical education teacher

- -

We have read the booklet and understand the policies and procedures.

Parent or guardian _____   Student _____

Date _____

FIGURE 4.1 Sample letter to parents regarding policies and procedures.

reinforcements (e.g., points, activity time, privileges) for attending and participating is an effective strategy. Too often, a negative, or "chop," system is used in which students lose points or privileges or receive lower grades for inappropriate behavior. This approach creates a negative environment, whereas the positive approach has the opposite effect. Students can be awarded 1 point per day for attendance, 1 point for dressing, and points for participating, rather than having points be subtracted for not attending and participating. Of course, participation would need to be outlined and clearly defined to students upfront.

All medical excuses and notes from parents should be presented to the school nurse at the beginning of the school day rather than during class time. As a health professional, the nurse is knowledgeable about medical problems that require special attention. If a question arises about participation, the nurse should make a final decision and send it to the physical education teacher. A form can be developed to facilitate this communication (see figure 4.2). If students cannot participate for three consecutive days, most schools recommend that they visit a physician. A physician's report form (see figure 4.3) can be sent to the student's doctor. This type of form helps improve communication between the school nurse, the physician, and the physical educator. Students need to understand that they do not receive credit for physical education if they cannot participate in class sessions. Students who have minor problems, such as tiredness, a sore throat, a headache, or cramps, should be handled on an individual basis. Some students can participate with modifications, whereas others cannot. If confusion arises about excuses related to minor illness, students should be allowed to see the school nurse.

Teachers must become knowledgeable about the backgrounds and personalities of their students. A policy that treats all students the same is usually misdirected. Religious beliefs relative to participating on various holidays or holy days often result in students asking to be excused. Such circumstances should be handled individually through the school administration. Students should be directed to a guidance counselor or administrator about their preferences and beliefs.

Students also have bad days, headaches, cramps, family problems, and other concerns that affect their daily performance. Sometimes students need a little extra encouragement to participate; at other times, they may need the day off. Teachers need to know their students so that they have some basis for judging individual situations. In contrast, some teachers believe that students are not giving full effort or not fulfilling their responsibility as students if they do not want to participate on a given day. Initially, students should be given the benefit of the doubt because they may indeed have a problem. If the same student continues to have participation problems, contact the parents or apply some alternative procedures such as accommodations to meet her or his abilities to take part in class or ways for the student to experience the activity in a different environment.

Develop a policy for tardiness. Start each class at a precise time, and let students know exactly what time class begins. Excessive tardiness should be integrated into the makeup policies and procedures for grades.

SCHOOL NURSE EXCUSE

Student _____ Date _____

Please excuse the above-named student from physical education class for the following day(s):

_____

The reason the student is excused is _____

_____

_____.

Thank you,

_____

School nurse

FIGURE 4.2 Sample school nurse excuse form.

PHYSICIAN'S REPORT FORM

Date _____

Dear Dr. _____

The following student, _____, has requested that he or she be excused from physical education activities. We request your help in designing a program that is appropriate for this student's physical condition. Our program offers a wide variety of physical activities. Please complete the following information to assist us in developing an appropriate, personalized program.

Thank you for your time.

Sincerely,

_____

Physical education department head

- -

Type of illness, injury, or handicap _____

Restrictions _____

Activities to be avoided _____

Duration of restriction _____

Other important information _____

_____

Physician's name _____

Address _____ Phone _____

Signature _____ Date _____

Please send form to: Person _____

School _____

Address _____

FIGURE 4.3 Sample physician's report form.

TEACHING TIP

Developing departmental policies is important because they communicate to others (parents, administrators, teachers, as well as students) your clear expectations for student behavior and participation. But a word of caution: Sometimes teachers take the easy way out by rigidly standing behind policies or procedures without considering *why* an exception might be the best choice. Occasionally making an exception to rules can be an effective way of communicating to students that you care about them and can understand all the circumstances in each situation. So, be thoughtful, not inflexible. Students deserve your full consideration, and you should always listen carefully before deciding on how and when to enforce policies.

Class Makeup Procedures

Most teachers give students the right to make up missed classes because of excused absences. Try to focus the makeup work on missed activities. Attending another physical education class is an option. Possibilities for makeup work can focus on performance activities, knowledge activities, or spectator activities. Options for these will be described a bit later. Depending on the objectives of the lessons missed, some activities will be more valuable than others. Ideally, the makeup assignment would be active in nature; thus, we present performance activity examples first. The following are examples that can be used in each area.

TEACHING TIP

Assigning makeup work is important because it conveys to students the message that missing class means missing important material. When you assign makeup assignments, avoid associations that might connote busywork or, worse, punishment. A makeup assignment should be presented as a learning opportunity that will benefit the student. Both the teacher and the student can have a positive experience if the makeup assignment is determined by collaboration after discussing the circumstances.

Makeup Work: Performance Activities

Students who have missed performance activities might be asked to participate in any of the following activities and to write a one-page analysis (form provided):

- Run a mile for time or walk or jog for 15 minutes.
- Run a parcourse.
- Ride a bike for 30 minutes.
- Attend an aerobics class.
- Lift weights for 30 minutes.
- Play 18 holes of disc golf.
- Play one set of tennis.
- Play two games of racquetball.
- Play 18 holes of regular golf.
- Engage in a workout at a health club.
- Create a how-to video addressing five skills necessary for participating in the current physical education unit.
- Choose an activity (approved by instructor).

These activities outside class should not be an athletic practice or event in which the student is already participating. The form in figure 4.4 can be used for the analysis of the performance.

Makeup Work: Knowledge Activities

The following are examples of activities that could be offered to students who missed a knowledge activity. Students complete one of the following assignments and turn it in to the instructor:

- Read an article in the sports section of the newspaper and write a one-page analysis (form provided).
- Read an article in any sports magazine and write a one-page analysis (form provided).

PERFORMANCE ANALYSIS

Name _____ Date _____

Event _____

Opponents _____

Final score _____

Type of offense and defense of each team:

How the scoring occurred:

Strengths and weaknesses of each team:

Your reactions to the event:

Parent or guardian signature _____

FIGURE 4.4 Performance analysis form.

- Read a short biographical sketch about a noted sports figure and write a one-page analysis (form provided).
- Create a show video showing 15 terms or skills used in the current physical education unit.
- Write strategies based on the current unit that help make it more enjoyable to engage in (form provided).
- Create a podcast listing and explaining 10 rules for the current physical education unit.
- Choose a project (with teacher approval).

- The form shown in figure 4.5 can be used for student reports on these knowledge activities.

Makeup Work: Spectator Activities

Students observe one of the following events and write a one-page analysis (form provided). Events can take place at the middle or senior high school, community college, college, or professional level. Students, however, should be encouraged to make up classes by engaging in physical activity rather than being a spectator. Figure 4.6 is an analysis sheet that can be used for reporting spectator activities.

STUDENT REPORT

Name _____ Date _____

Publication _____

Author _____

Major idea in the material:

Your opinion of the material:

What are the benefits of this material to you?

Parent or guardian signature _____

FIGURE 4.5 Knowledge analysis form.

SPECTATOR ANALYSIS

Name _____

Event _____

Date and location _____

Opponents _____

Final score _____

Type of offense and defense of each team:

How the scoring occurred:

Strengths and weaknesses of each team:

Your reactions to the event:

Parent or guardian signature _____

FIGURE 4.6 Spectator analysis form.

Equipment

Proper types of equipment in adequate amounts are necessary for quality programs. Students cannot learn physical skills without proper equipment. Physical education departments need basketballs, tennis rackets, and discs, just as math and reading departments need books, paper, and pencils. In many instances, physical education departments are asked to get along without proper amounts of equipment. A class of 35 students needs more than 5 basketballs, 6 volleyballs, or 10 tennis rackets. Administrators need to be informed that physical education is more than one or two games of a specific activity.

Equipment Purchasing

An adequate budget is necessary for purchasing equipment for the physical education program. The physical education budget needs to be separate from the athletic budget because sharing equipment is an issue.

Equipment priorities should be based on student interest surveys and the number of students who will use the equipment. If certain activities are offered more frequently than others, equipment for these should be a higher priority. The quality and price of equipment should be studied carefully before making a purchase. Equipment orders will go out on bid. If the order does not contain clear specifications, cheap and poorly made equipment may be the result. Check with other schools to see what experiences they have had with specific equipment. The cheapest price is not always the best deal. Durability and longevity are especially important. Write a justification that includes desired specifications so that the buyer understands the importance of meeting your needs. Understand that buyers will accept the lowest price if there are no specifications, leaving you with equipment that may be unsatisfactory.

Using a multiyear approach for buying expensive equipment is useful for negotiating with budget committees or school boards when a large amount of capital is necessary for equipment. If several thousand dollars are needed to add equipment for a new activity, implementing the activity in phases over a period of years may be possible. Student interest and willingness to bring in personal equipment for particular activities is also an effective strategy for gaining administrative support. Depending on the resources your students have available, offering a cycling unit with each student bringing a bicycle or offering golf classes with students bringing their clubs is an effective strategy for generating student and administrative interest in new activities. It is possible to request companies to donate gently used equipment if they are willing (or are looking for a tax write-off). A word of caution, however: If you find ways of creating new units without district support, you may never receive funding in the future. Administrators may assume that you can always solve the funding issues.

Another source of equipment involves the physical education staff, the maintenance department, or the industrial arts classes. Starting blocks, relay batons, soccer goals, team handball goals, and jump ropes are examples of equipment that can be constructed. Take care to ensure that all safety specifications have been met. Several books and articles describe how to make homemade equipment (Pangrazi & Beighle, 2020).

Physical education equipment can also be purchased jointly with other schools, city parks and recreation departments, and the athletic department. Many districts, for example, jointly purchase free weights and weight machines for the use of athletes, physical education classes, and adult community education programs. Joint purchases are an excellent way to share costs and

---

TEACHING TIP

Homemade equipment is usually a last resort and should be used only with the approval of the administration. We do not advocate making your own equipment for the following reasons:

1. Self-constructed equipment is usually lower quality, is not up to code, and may convey to administrators the message that you do not need quality commercial equipment.

2. Companies that manufacture standard equipment assume liability if it is not constructed properly. So, if you build your own equipment, you may be held liable for any injuries that occur while using it.

Young students with limited skills need quality equipment. Often, used and old equipment is handed down to the physical education program. A high-quality physical education program should provide high-quality equipment for students.

involve the entire community. This method can be used for purchasing tennis, racquetball, badminton, volleyball, softball, basketball, and aerobic dance equipment. Fund-raising for equipment has also become popular. Many programs are available to help teachers and parents do fund-raising for physical education equipment. See chapter 11 for more information on fund-raising and advocating for your program.

Storage, Distribution, and Maintenance of Equipment

An accurate equipment inventory should be completed at the beginning and the end of each school year. Records kept year to year help determine the needs of the department and facilitate the purchasing process. Documenting the type and amount of equipment lost each year provides information for improving security and distribution procedures.

A storage area that is easily accessible to all teachers is desirable. The storage area should be close to the teaching area (e.g., the gym, fields, and courts). Picking up and returning equipment to an area far from where you teach is inconvenient. The storage area should be designed with labeled shelves, bins, and containers for all pieces of equipment. All teachers, student leaders, and students who have access to the area need to cooperate fully in keeping the area clean and orderly. Becoming disorganized is likely when many people are sharing equipment. Transporting equipment to and from the teaching areas requires that a variety of ball bags, equipment carts, and portable ball carts are available. These items will reduce the amount of class time expended on equipment transport. Students can be given responsibilities for the movement of equipment if they are trained properly.

Develop a system for using equipment that is not designated on the yearly curriculum. A sign-up and checkout list can be posted in the storage area along with the yearly sequence of activities. See figure 4.7 for an example equipment checkout list. The department head or equipment coordinator is notified if any changes are made in the schedule regarding equipment. This practice prevents the problem of teachers not having necessary equipment for their classes. Equipment should not be loaned to outside groups without following designated procedures. If equipment is shared or loaned to other groups, the items must be marked or identified with some regulation code to prevent losses or mix-ups with equipment from other sources.

These decisions are all part of the ongoing process of implementing a quality physical education curriculum.

EQUIPMENT CHECKOUT

Name	Equipment	Quantity	Date borrowed	Date returned

FIGURE 4.7 Sample equipment checkout record.

Equipment is part of a program's lifeblood. Without adequate equipment, the effectiveness of the teaching and learning environment is reduced because students without equipment become bored, unmotivated, and troublesome for the teacher. How can students learn to dribble, pass, and shoot a basketball when they stand in line and take turns sharing a ball with five or six other students? The goal of a program should be to provide every student with a piece of equipment. Productive learning time can thus be greatly enhanced.

Grading Procedures

Grading is an important part of the policies and procedures described in the department handbook and should be determined and discussed with students during the first week of classes. Teachers within the department should generally agree on the components and application of grading guidelines. If one teacher grades differently from the others, students will soon communicate among themselves about the aberration. Parents should also be made fully aware about how their children will be graded. Evaluation and grading recommendations are discussed in detail in chapter 8.

Factors Influencing Preinstructional Decisions

As a teacher, you may be presented with a variety of different teaching situations. When making preinstructional decisions, it is important to examine what you have in terms of student numbers, ages or grade levels, genders, skill level, experience, and any special needs. Additionally, each state, district, and school may have different graduation requirements for physical education.

Class Size

Class size plays a critical role in your preinstructional decisions, and teachers must plan accordingly to maintain quality instruction. In many states class size has been bumped up to 40 students or more, whereas previously class size was maintained at 30 students. What instructional decisions need to be made to accommodate these numbers regarding equipment, space, safety, and assessment?

Class Composition

Class composition has continued to change over the years. Many states and school districts require classes to integrate boys and girls together. Mixed-gender classes may pose some issues for locker room supervision if students choose to change clothes, because of the gender of the teacher. Some administrators handle this situation by requiring the door to the locker room to remain open, and students can use bathroom stalls or shower spaces for changing privacy. The teacher can then hear what is going on in the area and intervene if necessary. If certain students are known to have issues being together when unsupervised, the teacher can arrange for them to enter the locker room at different times. Additionally, another school employee of the appropriate gender can be required to monitor the locker room at the beginning and end of class. Classes may also include a variety of grade levels (sixth graders, seventh graders, and eighth graders are significantly different in their development, interests, and skill levels). These differences need to be addressed and planned for daily.

Physical Education Requirements

States and districts have different credit requirements for physical education. Requirements might be six weeks, nine weeks, one semester, two semesters, or two years. Middle and high school graduation requirements may differ as well. Does ninth grade reside at the junior high, and is it considered a credit requirement for graduation? Some high schools either require or allow band, ROTC, and athletics to fulfill the physical education requirement. We oppose this substitution model because these programs neither meet the national standards (SHAPE America, 2013), nor do they constitute quality physical education instruction. These alternative substitution activities neither include instruction on lifetime physical activity, nor do they prepare students to become and maintain practices of healthy adults. Participation on a basketball team may improve a student's movement competency in that particular sport and address some positive outcomes of the affective domain such as cooperation and enjoyment of activity, but basketball is a narrow curriculum that does not expose students to activities and concepts that are balanced and push them to be active for a lifetime.

Making Preinstructional Decisions

Preinstructional decisions are basic to the success of a lesson. They are rather mundane, which causes many teachers to forget to plan for them. But they are as important as planning the content of the lesson. In fact, if this phase of the lesson is not carefully considered, effective presentation of the content may be impossible.

Determine the Instructional Format

How students are grouped for instruction is a decision that is made early in the lesson-planning process. More than one arrangement can be used in a single lesson. The objectives and nature of the instructional experiences, as well as the space and equipment available, determine the type of grouping. Teachers use three basic schemes, with numerous variations and subdivisions.

Large-Group Instruction

Large-group instruction demands that all students respond to the same challenge, whether as individuals, partners, or members of a group. This format allows the teacher to conduct the class in a guided progression. The single-challenge format is convenient for group instruction and demonstration because all students are involved in similar activities. Pacing is a problem with no easy solution, considering that effective instruction must be personalized to meet each student's needs. Student differences are recognized, yet the assumption is made that a central core of activity is acceptable for students of the same age.

Small-Group or Station Instruction

In the small-group (or station) format, the class is divided into two or more groups, each working on a different skill or activity. Some system of rotation is provided, and the students change from one activity to another. Dividing a class into groups for station teaching is valuable at times, particularly when supplies and apparatuses are limited. Use procedures outlined in chapter 7 for management ideas and suggestions (e.g., toe to toe for partners, whistle mixer for groups). This arrangement can save time in providing apparatus experiences because after the circuit is set, little change in apparatuses is needed. The participants are changed, not the apparatuses. Some system of rotation is instituted, with changes either by signal or at will. Sometimes all stations are visited during a single class session, and in other cases, students make only a few station changes per session.

Class control and guidance may be a problem with the small-group format, because stopping the class to provide instruction and guidance is not practical. Posting written and visual guidelines at each station can help students be more self-directed. The instructions should include rearranging the station before moving on to the next. These measures reduce the need for the teacher to divide his or her efforts over several stations. If a station has a safety hazard (e.g., rope climbing), the teacher may wish to devote more attention there.

Individual Skill Instruction

In the individual skill format, students select their skills from a variety of choices and rotate to new skills after they have mastered the skill. They can get equipment themselves or choose from pieces provided. The most effective format has students working independently on skills at a comfortable rate. In addition, students can select a variety of skills and activities based on their competency.

Determine the Use of Space

A common error is to take a class to a large practice area, give students a task to accomplish, and fail to define or limit the space in which the task should be performed. The class spreads out in an area so large that communicating and managing the class is impossible. The type of skills practiced and the ability of the teacher to control the class dictate the size of the space. Delineating a small area for participation makes it easier to control a class because students can see and hear better. As students become more responsive, the size of the area can be enlarged. Regardless of the size of the space, delineate the practice area. An easy way is to set up cones around the perimeter of the area. Chalk lines, evenly spaced equipment, or natural boundaries can also serve as restraining lines. Starting the lesson by having the class jog within the delineated area is an excellent way to communicate to students the boundaries for participation.

A factor affecting the size of the practice area is the amount of instruction needed. When students are learning a closed skill (only one way to perform or respond) and need constant feedback and redirection, they should stay near the instructor. Establish a smaller area where students move for instruction and then return to the larger area for practice.

Available space is often divided into smaller areas to maximize student participation. An example is a volleyball game in which only 12 students can play on one available court. In most cases, a more effective approach is to divide the area into two smaller courts to facilitate participation by a greater number of students.

A related consideration when partitioning space is safety. If the playing areas are too close together, players from one area might run into players in the other area. For example, an Ultimate setting is unsafe if a player on one field can run into another play area while attempting to catch the disc.

Determine the Use of Equipment

Inventorying equipment on a regular basis ensures that teachers know exactly what equipment is available and in

Teachers should check inventory regularly to ensure a supply of working equipment.

working condition. The amount of equipment available influences the structure of the lesson. For example, if only 16 rackets are available for a class of 30, some type of sharing or station work will be necessary. Alternatively, multiple activities could be run concurrently.

How much equipment is enough? If equipment is for individual use, such as rackets, hockey sticks, and balls, one should be available for each student. If equipment is for group use, such as mats or parachutes, enough should be available to limit waiting lines to no more than four students. Too often, teachers use minimal equipment because they teach the way they have been taught. For example, a teacher is teaching volleyball and has plenty of volleyballs. Rather than have students practice individually against the wall or with a partner, the students are divided into two long lines, and only one or two balls are used. Most of the time is spent waiting in line rather than practicing. Another reason for not using an adequate amount of equipment is that teachers get tired of moving it in and out so they organize activities that take one or two balls.

If the program lacks equipment, be cautious about accepting limited equipment without expressing concern because many administrators believe that physical educators are always capable of "making do." Communicate with your educational leader regularly and explain the importance of equipment for effective instruction. Ask parent–teacher groups to help with fund-raising to purchase necessary equipment. When teachers settle for less, they usually get less.

TEACHING TIP

How can you get by with a dearth of equipment? The most common solution is to teach using the small-group format. This method implies dividing students into stations where each group has enough equipment. For example, in a softball unit, some students practice fielding, others are batting, others are making the double play, and so on. Another approach is to divide the class in half and allow one group to work on one activity while the other is involved in an unrelated activity. For instance, because of a shortage of rackets, one-half of the class is involved in practice while the other half plays half-court basketball. This approach is less educationally sound and increases the demands made on the instructor.

Another solution is to use the peer review approach. While one student practices the activity, a peer offers feedback and evaluation. The two share the equipment and take turns in practice and evaluation. The final approach is to establish stations to allow students to practice different skills at each teaching area.

The initial setup of equipment depends on the focus of the lesson. For example, the height of the basket can be reduced to emphasize correct shooting form. The height of the volleyball net can be lowered to allow more success. Nets can be placed at different heights to allow different types of practice. Equipment and apparatuses can be modified to best suit the needs of the learner. Nothing is sacred about a 10-foot (3.05 m) basket or a regulation-sized ball. If modifying the equipment improves the quality of learning, do it.

Determine the Use of Time and Pace

Several decisions related to time need to be made before instruction. How time allotted for a lesson is used influences instructional outcomes. The amount of time allowed for fitness and skill development has a bearing on what is accomplished in a physical education program. For example, if a teacher decides to use 10 additional minutes per lesson for fitness development, the result will be an increase of nearly 30 hours of time devoted to physical fitness during the school year. The multipart lesson comes into play here. Mentally divide the total lesson time into four parts. It has been suggested that 6 to 10% of class time be devoted to the introductory activity, 23 to 27% to fitness, 50 to 66% to the lesson focus, and 16 to 23% to the game portion of the lesson (Pangrazi & Beighle, 2020). In a secondary lesson, the focus and game portion of the lesson are often combined, but the focus should still incorporate skill practice, not just a game.

The pace of a lesson is related to time. Skillful teachers know when to terminate practice sessions and move on to new activities. Students become bored and begin to display off-task behaviors if practice sessions are excessively long. Knowing when to refocus on a different task is important. In most cases, erring on the short side is better than allowing practice to continue to the point of fatigue and boredom. A rule of thumb is to refocus or change the task when five or more students go off task. If extending the length of the practice session is necessary, try the following:

1. *Refocus the class.* Ask the class to observe another student's performance or explain the importance of the skill and the way in which it will help their game-time performance.

2. *Refine or extend the task.* Stop the class and ask them to improve their technique by focusing on a phase of their performance. Try challenging them with a more difficult variation. This approach redefines the challenge and is a more difficult variation of the skill they were practicing.

3. *Stop and evaluate.* Stop the class and take time to evaluate performance. Students can work with a partner and check for key points. Emphasis is placed on evaluating and correcting performance. Practice resumes after a few minutes of evaluation.

Pacing is affected by who directs the lesson: teacher or student. When the teacher directs the pace, the instructor controls timing, and students are expected to perform the task at the same time. Determining whether a presentation should be teacher or student paced depends on the type of skill being taught. If the skill is closed in nature, teacher pacing appears to be most effective. Teacher pacing can be accompanied by verbal cues and modeled behavior. It is effective for learning new skills because cues and visual imagery help learners develop a conception of the pattern to be performed. Student pacing allows learning to progress at different rates. It is effective when open skills (variety of correct responses) are being learned and a variety of responses are preferred or encouraged.

Determine the Use of Instructional Devices

Instructional devices include a variety of materials, equipment, or people—any of which supplement, clarify, or improve certain instructional procedures. These devices can be used to present information, stimulate different senses, provide information feedback, restrict movements, control practice time, or aid in evaluation and motivation. The devices may be simple, such as targets taped on the wall or cones to dribble around in basketball, or they may be more sophisticated, such as video clips, cameras, or ball machines for tennis. Technological devices are often utilized in physical education to enhance student learning and practice opportunities. As long as this is their purpose, they can be a positive asset to the physical education program. A variety of apps may supplement instruction in the form of watching how-to videos, recording student performance for self-evaluation, providing timed musical increments, and dividing students into teams. Again, if these applications emphasize learning and do not detract from the teaching environment, they are definitely encouraged for teacher and student use.

Instructional devices help impart more information and improve the motivational aspects of the class. Because most public school environments have a large student-to-teacher ratio, finding enough time for each student is difficult. A number of challenging and success-oriented activities can be developed using instructional devices. The following are examples:

- In basketball, tape targets on a wall for various types of passes. Use a stopwatch to time students dribbling through a course of boundary cones. Pictures, diagrams, and handouts can provide students with graphic information about various skills and rules.

- In volleyball, hoops, jump ropes, or tape on the floor can be used as targets for setting, bumping, or serving. Extend a rope across the top of the net to help students hit serves above or beneath the rope to ensure height, accuracy, or velocity. Videotapes are available to provide instruction for various volleyball skills.

- In tennis, use empty ball cans as targets when working on serves. A tennis ball suspended on a small rope that can be adjusted up or down on a basketball hoop teaches students the feel of extending the arm for serves and overhead shots. A list of performance objectives for partners can give direction to a tennis class.

- In track and field, a student leader can run a station on low hurdles by timing heats and providing corrective feedback. A string stretched between two chairs can help students practice jumping for height in the long jump. Laminated diagrams of the release angle of the shot put combined with a discussion can give students important information.

- In badminton, targets can be placed in various sections of the court. Suspend shuttlecocks on a light rope to practice overhand shots. A rope suspended on high-jump standards will force students to get the proper height on clear shots.

- In flag football, a punting station can use a goal post for height and accuracy, boundary corners for placement accuracy, and a stopwatch for hang time. A swinging tire or a hoop suspended from a tree or goalpost can be used for passing accuracy, and boundary cones can be used for passing distance. Whiteboards, magnetic boards, and tablets are useful for diagramming plays and defensive strategy. Student leaders can supervise each station, record the completion of various skills, and provide corrective feedback for each student.

A creative teacher uses instructional devices in many ways. These devices certainly do not replace the teacher but can supplement the teaching and learning environment. Effective teachers continually try to add devices that motivate students, provide more feedback, or increase practice attempts. Teachers with a limited budget can create instructional devices with such basic components as a roll of tape, several ropes, string, and hoops. An extensive budget does not always produce the best learning environment. Students seem to enjoy

4

Spotting can help to make the physical education environment safer.

the challenge related to practicing with various types of instructional devices.

Create a Safe Environment

A safe environment is a prerequisite for effective teaching. Safety results from behaviors taught by the teacher. "Safety first and everything else second" should be the motto of every teacher. A teacher can be removed from the teaching profession if accidents occur because of faulty planning and lack of foresight. More than half of the injuries in schools occur in physical education classes; if they result from poor planning and preparation, a teacher may be found liable and responsible for such injuries (see chapter 10).

 TEACHING TIP

If you do not think that safety is important, check to see what activities have been eliminated from a school's physical education curriculum. All it takes to get an activity eliminated is a few student injuries. Two or three injuries will probably result in the elimination of a given activity. If you want the leeway required to try new and innovative activities, make sure you show your administrators or supervisors the safety precautions that will be implemented.

Teachers are expected to foresee the possibility of hazardous situations that result in student injury. Safety inspections should be conducted at regular intervals (see chapter 10). Equipment and apparatus that have not been used for some time should be inspected. Rules are only the beginning with students; safe and sensible behavior needs to be taught and practiced. For example, if students are in a tumbling unit, they must receive instruction and practice in developing proper methods for absorbing momentum and force. It may be necessary to practice safety, such as by taking turns, spotting, and using the apparatus as directed.

An important way to ensure safety is to write curricular activities in proper progression. Injuries are avoided if students perform only those activities for which they are prepared. A written curriculum will reassure a safety committee or court of law that proper sequencing of activities was used. In addition, proper progression of activities generates a feeling of confidence in students because they believe they have the necessary background to perform adequately.

Teach Each Student as a Whole Person

When planning learning experiences, consider that people are whole beings. They do not learn a new skill in the psychomotor domain without developing some allied cognitive and affective outcomes. For example, if people are taught a new soccer drill, they will wonder why they need to learn it. They are integrating the activity cognitively into their total selves. At the same time, they are developing a related feeling about the skill (e.g., "I'm good at this drill," or "I'm never going to use this.").

Teachers can enhance the effectiveness of instruction by integrating educational goals in all domains. Tell students why they are learning new skills or performing them in a certain fashion. Learning in the cognitive area may involve knowing when to use a certain skill or how to correct errors in an activity. It involves decision making based on facts and information gathered from various sources. Cognitive development emphasizes helping students understand why they are doing something, rather than just telling them to do something.

The performing arts (physical education, music, and drama) offer many opportunities for affective domain development. They have many occasions to learn personal responsibility, share, express feelings, set personal goals, and function independently. Working as a team, learning to be subordinate to a leader, and being a leader are skills that can be taught. Teach the whole person. It is discouraging to hear teachers say, "My job is just to teach physical skills. I'm not going to get involved in developing attitudes. That's someone else's job." Physical educators have an excellent opportunity to develop positive attitudes and values. The battle may be won but the war lost if teachers produce graduates with good skill development and negative attitudes toward physical activity and participation.

Instructional effectiveness can be enriched by encouraging students to improve their techniques or try to remedy problems they are having in skill performance. Offer students opportunities to help each other diagnose and improve techniques. Strategies for game situations can be developed through group discussions and planning. The point is to enrich and enhance learning situations so that students understand why they are being asked to learn in a specified manner. A golden rule does not have to be taught in every lesson, but little is learned if teachers fail to offer rationale and justification to accompany their skill presentation.

Integrating humor into your instructional approach has become a popular topic in recent years (Barney & Christenson, 2013). A wide variety of research has been conducted regarding humor in educational settings (Banas, Dunbar, Rodriguez, & Liu, 2011). Humor adds a positive tone to your class environment and enhances your instructional effectiveness. It can get students interested in the class activities and help them recall concepts taught in class (Barney & Christenson, 2013). Students relate to a teacher who incorporates humor into their daily instruction. Humor can be planned for and inserted into your lesson plans. Effective incorporation of humor in your instruction should bring about a feeling of amusement and laughter. Humor should be devoid of sarcasm or ethnic remarks. A conscious effort should be made not to offend students because of the broad base of various cultures within a typical school environment. Be yourself and know your audience.

Teach for Cognitive Development

Involving students in organizing the content and implementation of the lesson can enhance cognitive development. This idea is not to suggest that students decide what, when, and how learning will take place, but rather that they are involved in improving the structure of the learning tasks. The following are some of the advantages to involving the learner in the instructional process:

- Learners usually select experiences within their abilities and skill levels.

- When learners help make a decision, they accept some of the responsibility for learning. Blaming others for failure is easy if the learner is not involved in some of the decisions. Personal involvement means accepting the responsibility to make decisions and ensuring that such decisions are implemented.

- Most people feel better about an environment in which they have input and control. Self-concepts can be enhanced when learners help determine their destiny.

- When lessons fail because incorrect decisions were made, the learner shoulders some of the blame. This approach helps develop decision-making skills that focus on personal responsibility.

Decision making and involvement in the learning process are learned. Students need the opportunity to make decisions and be placed in a situation where they realize the effect of their decisions. The opportunity to make incorrect as well as correct decisions is an important part of the learning process. No decision making is involved when the teacher accepts and approves only the correct decisions. Soon, students begin to choose not to make decisions at all rather than risk making an incorrect choice.

Responsibility is learned when students are allowed to make decisions that affect their own and others' futures. Decision making in school teaches students to learn from their mistakes at a time when the consequences are not as severe if they make a poor choice. Responsibility training involves allowing learners to make decisions after considering the alternatives. Allowing students to make choices should be done gradually by using some of the following strategies.

1. *Limit the number of choices.* This approach allows students some control over the ultimate outcome of the situation but offers them a chance to help decide how the outcome will be reached. This

---

TEACHING TIP

An example of adding humor and academic learning in a middle school physical education class could be to tell your class that they are going to do some running and play cross-country kickball today, as did the Hopi Indians of northeastern Arizona. The only difference is that for today's class they are going to run barefoot (without shoes) like the Hopis regularly did. Although the Hopis had to run around and through cacti and thorny bushes, you will give them a break and let them run on the track and the football field. You can talk about an Olympic medal winner in 1908 and 1912, Hopi Indian Louis Tewanima, who set an American record for the 10-kilometer run of 32:06.6 in the Olympics. The record stood for 52 years before it was broken. After talking about the Hopis and their love of running, you can tell your class that you were just teasing about running barefoot in class today and add a big smile. You could also integrate some math problems into the class by talking about the Mesa, Arizona, 10K Turkey Trot on Thanksgiving morning. Ask the class to figure out how many yards a 10K covers and how many laps on your track would equal a 10K. You could also give them some extra credit for running in the 10K and some extra points for beating the Mesa man who runs in the turkey costume in 45 minutes every year. Students could also come to class dressed like a turkey on a certain day close to Thanksgiving for fun and to earn some extra points.

idea may prudent when learners have had little opportunity for decision making in the past. New teachers often have little understanding about their students and may want to select this method until they are more familiar with the class.

2. *Let students modify activities.* If used effectively, this strategy allows learners to adapt the activity to suit their individual skill levels. Involving them in this process can reduce student complaints that "It is too hard to do" or "I'm bored." The student has the responsibility to personalize the task. Options allowed might be to change the rules, the equipment, the number of players on a team, or the type of ball or racket. Some examples are the following:

- Using a slower-moving family ball rather than a handball.
- Increasing the number of players in a volleyball game.
- Lowering the basket in a basketball unit.
- Decreasing the length of a distance run or the height of hurdles.

3. *Offer open-ended tasks.* This approach allows students the most latitude for deciding the content of the lesson. In this situation, they are given a task and take on the responsibility to solve it. The teacher decides the educational end, and students decide the means. As students become adept at using this approach, they can develop several alternatives. This is similar to problem solving or guided discovery teaching style. The following are examples:

- "Develop a game that requires four passes before a shot at the goal."
- "Develop a floor exercise routine that contains a forward roll, backward roll, and cartwheel."
- "How many games can you and your partner create with one ball and one racket?"

This problem-solving approach has no predetermined answer (see chapter 6). The technique is effective in helping students apply principles they have learned previously to new situations. Ultimately, they solve the problem through a movement response guided by cognitive involvement.

TEACHING TIP

Be sure to consider the academic content that you can reinforce in your instruction. Your district and state academic standards that can be reinforced could include math, science, language arts, and writing. An example might be to have students write and discuss a health concept related to fitness each day. You could grade these and return them to students.

Design physical education experiences that help students feel good about physical activity.

Enhance the Affective Domain

How each student feels about physical education has an effect on his or her level of motivation to be active throughout life. Little is gained if students participate in a class yet leave hating it. It is possible to design experiences that develop positive attitudes and values. When developing a lesson plan, evaluate its effect on the attitudes of students. Will the planned lesson result in a positive experience for students? Few people develop positive feelings after participating in an activity when they were embarrassed or failed. Ponder some of the following situations and the attitudes that might result:

- Think of a situation in which the teacher asks everyone to run a mile (1.6 km). Overweight students are slowest and run for the longest time, while the rest of the class waits for them to finish. These students cannot change the outcome of the run even if they wanted to. Failure and belittlement occur every day. It is a small wonder they come to dislike running and exercise.

- How might students feel when they are asked to perform in front of the rest of the class even though they are unskilled? For example, a student is asked to dribble a soccer ball through a set of cones for a timed performance. The added stress probably results in a poorer-than-usual response. They may not want to play soccer anymore.

- What feelings do students have when they are asked to be the goalkeeper in a soccer game and are unable to prevent anyone from scoring? Might they do everything possible to avoid playing soccer in the future?

Students need to know that teachers care about their feelings and want to avoid placing them in embarrassing situations. Sometimes, teachers have the idea that caring for students indicates weakness. Seldom is this the case. Teachers can be firm and demanding as long as they are fair and considerate. To knowingly place students in an embarrassing situation is never justified.

Students form attitudes and values based largely on how teachers and peers treat them. When enhancing the affective domain, how a teacher teaches is more important than what she or he teaches. Students want to be acknowledged as human beings with needs and concerns. They want to be treated in a courteous and nonderogatory manner. If teachers avoid trying to empathize with students, they teach without concern for students' feelings. Often, the best way to discover how students feel is to ask them. The majority will be honest.

If a teacher can accept student input, the result is an atmosphere that produces positive attitudes and values.

Plan for Optimal Skill Learning

A major objective of physical education is to teach physical skill techniques. Students want to be physically educated. If they go to a math class, they expect to learn math. Students deserve an educational experience rather than a recreational one, when playing rather than learning is the goal. When developing a lesson plan, the following points help form the underlying foundation of the planning effort.

TEACHING TIP

Stop class often to introduce a new strategy or to refine the correct technique for a specific skill. For example, during a round robin tournament, games need to be stopped to reinforce the level of play by addressing strategy and skill refinement and reinforcement. Take advantage of these teachable moments.

Know the Purpose of the Lesson

The lesson should be designed to improve the skill performance of students so that they are able to meet program standards. What is the purpose of the total program, the unit, and the lesson plan? If the lesson presentation does not contribute to learning and improving skills, it probably is a recreational approach rather than an educational lesson. Lessons should contribute to positive lifestyle changes that carry over to adulthood. Knowing program standards, desired outcomes (SHAPE America, 2013), and the way in which instruction contributes to those outcomes gives direction to the program.

Include Instruction as Part of Every Lesson

Instruction is an observable action. Many methods can be used to accomplish instructional outcomes, but all the methods demand instruction. Instruction can take many forms, such as working individually with students, evaluating a student's progress on a mastery learning packet, developing task cards, or conducting group instruction. Regardless of the method used, instruction must be a regular and consistent part of each lesson. Physical education must go beyond the recreational aspects of activity and be instructive in nature. A major problem with a recreational approach is that "the rich get richer and the poor get poorer." For example, if the teacher "rolls out the ball" and leaves students on their own for basketball games, skilled players will handle the ball most of the time and dominate less skilled players. Unskilled students may feel pressure during competitive situations and find it difficult to think about technique and proper performance when they are concentrating on strategy and not making mistakes.

Integrate the Lesson With Past and Future Instruction

A sound secondary school physical education program should build on the foundation built by the elementary school physical education experience. Many school districts lack adequate communication between elementary and secondary program organizers. Each section may act autonomously, without regard for what is taught in other grades. Secondary curriculum planners should consider elementary school program goals, activities, and teaching procedures. The transition from elementary to secondary programs is smoother if learning activities and teaching procedures progress with continuity. High school teachers who know the previous experiences of students in elementary and middle school programs can present instruction that is not repetitious or too difficult because of lack of previous experience in the activity. This progression is referred to as scaffolding.

Well-planned lessons reflect a progression of activities between lessons. Skill development activities taught throughout a unit ensure that practice opportunities are sequential and regular. An unacceptable but common approach is to bunch all instruction into the first day or two of a unit. This approach makes it difficult for unskilled students to develop motor skills because little instruction and opportunity for skill feedback and correction occurs after the start of the unit.

The philosophy of the teacher determines whether a plan is in place for effective instruction. Do you believe that young people must learn on their own and that students are solely responsible for learning? Or do you believe that student and teacher share the responsibility of learning in an environment where both are determined to reach educational outcomes? A teacher's plan for skill development strongly affects student learning. If instructors fail to assume responsibility for teaching and refining skills, who will?

If their students are to learn physical skills, teachers need to understand a few basic principles of motor learning. Teaching motor skills is not difficult when teachers understand the basic tenets of proper performance techniques.

Understand Arousal

Arousal is the level of excitement that stress produces (Schmidt & Lee, 2011). The level of arousal can have either a positive or negative effect on performance of motor skills. The key to using arousal is to find the amount that is just right. Too little arousal creates little interest in learning among youth. On the other hand, too much arousal fills youth with stress and anxiety, resulting in a decrease in motor performance. The more complex the skill is, the more that arousal can disrupt learning. On the other hand, if a skill is simple, such as running, a greater amount of arousal can be tolerated without causing a reduction in skill performance. Optimally, youth should be aroused to a level at which they are excited, confident, and positive about participation.

Competition affects the arousal level of students. When competition is introduced in the early stages of skill learning, stress and anxiety reduce the performer's ability to learn. On the other hand, when competition is introduced after a skill has been overlearned, performance can improve. A skill is overlearned when a person can perform it without having to think about technique. Because many middle and high school youths have not overlearned skills, teachers should avoid highly competitive situations when teaching skills. For example, assume that the objective is to practice basketball dribbling. Students are placed in squads to run a relay requiring that they dribble to the opposite end of the gym, shoot a basket, and return. The first squad to finish is the winner. Instead of concentrating on dribbling form, students focus on winning the relay. They are overaroused and determined to run as quickly as possible. They dribble poorly (if at all), the balls fly out of control, and the teacher is dismayed by the result. In this case, the competitive situation overexcited those who had not yet learned dribbling skills.

Give Meaningful Skill Feedback

Feedback is important in the teaching process because it helps the instructor to know what is being learned, what should be avoided, and how the performance can be modified. Skill feedback is any kind of information about a movement performance. The two types of skill feedback are intrinsic and extrinsic. Intrinsic feedback is internal and inherent to the performance of the skill. It travels through the senses such as vision, hearing, touch, and smell. Extrinsic feedback is external and comes from an outside source such as a teacher, a videotape, or a stopwatch. Feedback from the instructor should be encouraging (or constructive), frequent, public (so that all students benefit), and contingent on performance or effort. Feedback, regardless of whether it is intrinsic or extrinsic, can be general or specific. General feedback consists of broad statements regarding the skill such as, "Great job!" or "Thanks for following instructions!" Specific feedback provides much more detail regarding the behavior or skill performance. An example is, "You did an excellent job following through on that pass. I can tell because the ball went right where your fingers are pointing." Knowledge of results and knowledge of performance are discussed in the following section. These are two classifications of feedback that teachers can provide, depending on the situation.

TEACHING TIP

Meaningful feedback can be instructional, and those instructional cues can also be used to assess a specific skill. Fronske (2012, p. 176) has a cue, a why, and common errors for each component of a skill. An example for throwing a football might be include grip, throwing action, stance and leg action, release point, and follow-through action.

Knowledge of Results

Knowledge of results is extrinsic feedback given after a skill has been performed. It involves information about the skill outcome so that students know whether their attempts were successful (or not). Knowledge of results provides information about an incorrect or unsuccessful performance. Learners need feedback about outcomes

4

Feedback should be specific and positive.

so that they can adjust the practice trials that follow. This type of feedback need not be negative; instead, it should be a statement of fact telling whether the skill performance resulted in a successful outcome. Often, feedback is not needed because the task outcome is obvious, such as making a basket or jumping a rope.

Knowledge of results originates externally from a teacher, peer, or successful performance of a skill, that is, making a basket or scoring a goal. Most often, teachers deliver external feedback to improve skill performance. Knowledge of results is critical in the early stages of learning motor skills. After performers start to master a skill, they can analyze their performance and develop a personal system of internal feedback rather than depend on knowledge of results from a teacher or peer.

TEACHING TIP

A public reinforcement to a specific student affects multiple students within hearing range. A public reinforcement to a student might be about a student's behavior or it might include a reminder to complete the skill with a follow-through. Those students in the surrounding area will also be affected by the teacher's reinforcement to that specific student.

Knowledge of Performance

This type of feedback is like knowledge of results in that it is verbal, extrinsic in nature, and occurs after the performance. Knowledge of results focuses on the outcome (product) of a skill, whereas **knowledge of performance** relates to the process (mechanics) of the skill performance. When using this type of feedback, refer to specific components of the learner's performance. For example, say, "I like the way you kept your chin on your chest during the forward roll," or "That's the way to step toward the target with your left foot when throwing."

Knowledge of performance can increase a student's level of motivation because it provides feedback about improvement. Frustration often sets in when a student finds it difficult to discern improvement. Feedback provides a lift and a rededication to continued practice. Knowledge of performance is a strong reinforcer, particularly when an instructor mentions something performed correctly. This feedback motivates young people to repeat the same pattern, ultimately resulting in improved performance. The most important aspect

of this feedback is that it provides information for future patterns of skill performance.

Make performance feedback short, content filled, and concise. Explain exactly what was correct or incorrect (e.g., "That was excellent body rotation."). Concentrate on one key point to avoid confusion. Imagine a performer who is told, "Step with the left foot, rotate the trunk, lead with the elbow, and snap the wrist on your next throw!" Excessive feedback confuses anyone trying to improve a skill.

When working with students new to a skill, focus on knowledge of performance. Knowledge of results focuses solely on the skill outcome and does not consider whether the skill was performed correctly. An unskilled youth who makes a lucky basket might believe that she or he performed the task correctly even though the technical points of the throw were performed incorrectly. The goal of physical education is to teach correct performance of skills; less emphasis is placed on the outcome of the skill performance. In contrast, in the competitive world of athletics, more emphasis is placed on product (results) than on the process (technique).

TEACHING TIP

A final point about knowledge of performance is to allow time for performers to internalize feedback. Often, teachers give a student feedback and then ask him or her to try it again. The student may make the same mistake because he or she did not have time to internalize the feedback. In addition, the instructor may make the student tense and reduce the effectiveness of the attempt. Offer knowledge of performance feedback and move to another participant. Observe how students perform following your feedback. Follow up on your feedback later. This approach allows students a chance to relax, internalize the feedback, and modify future practice attempts.

Provide Effective Practice Sessions

Practice is a key part of learning motor skills. But having the opportunity to practice is not enough; students must practice with emphasis on quality of their mechanics (practicing correctly). This section explains how to design practice sessions that optimize motor skill learning.

Focus Practice on Process

Practice can be focused in two directions—product or process. Product-based practice places emphasis on the desired outcome of skill performance. For example, when teaching the forehand, reinforcement is offered only when the student hits the ball for a win. This leads to a product–process conflict. Process-based practice, however, has the teacher encouraging students to perform the skill correctly with little emphasis on the outcome. Students who think the teacher is interested only in the product may not concentrate on proper technique. Overemphasis on product or skill outcome decreases a student's willingness to take risks and learn new ways of performing a skill. Focus practice on correct skill technique when youth are in the learning and practice phase of skill development.

Use Mental Practice Techniques

Mental practice involves thinking about the successful performance of a motor skill in a quiet, relaxed environment. The experience involves thinking about the activity and its related sounds, colors, and other sensations. Students visualize themselves doing the activity successfully and at regular speed. They should avoid creating images of failure (Schmidt & Lee, 2011). Mental practice stimulates performers to think about and review the activity they are to practice. Some experience or familiarity with the skill is needed before the performer can derive value from mental practice. Mental practice is used in combination with regular practice, not in place of it. Before performing the task, prompt students to mentally review the critical factors and sequencing of the act.

Offer Variable Skill Practice

Motor tasks are usually grouped into classes of tasks. For example, throwing is a collection of a class of movements. Throwing a ball in a sport can be performed in many ways, such as at different speeds, different trajectories, and varying distances. Even though throwing tasks are all different, the variations have fundamental similarities. Movements in a class usually involve the same body parts using a similar rhythm, but they are performed with many variations. These differences create the need for variable practice in a variable setting.

Practice sessions should include a variety of skills in a movement class with a variety of situations and parameters in which the skill is performed. If a skill to be learned involves one fixed way of performing it (a "closed" skill), such as serving a tennis ball or bowling, variability is much less important. Most skills, however, are "open," and responses are somewhat unpredictable. Therefore,

variability in practice is important (e.g., catching a ball moving at different speeds and from different angles). Motor skills should be practiced under a variety of conditions so that students can respond to a variety of novel situations.

Design Comprehensive Unit Plans

Units of instruction offer a method for organizing and presenting activities over a stipulated period. Without units, offering scope and sequence for various instructional activities throughout the year is difficult. Units vary in length depending on the age and ability of students and the design of the curriculum. Most units focus on physical activity or movement forms, such as team sports, lifetime sports, dance, or physical fitness.

When unit plans are developed, a variety of sources should be reviewed to ensure that the unit is comprehensive. Units of instruction usually reflect a range of activities gathered from materials produced by experts. Another advantage of unit plans is that they give teachers a plan for how instruction should proceed. This approach prevents fragmentation. An instructor with a coherent unit plan does not teach from day to day and hope that everything will somehow fit together by the end of the unit.

TEACHING TIP

Planning is your roadmap to success. How can you know what to teach if you do not know where you are going? The unit plan shows you when you are going to teach necessary skills and activities. The lesson plan then shows how you will accomplish the unit plan each day. Make your lessons meaningful to you and others. Many administrators believe that a lesson plan is effective and useful only when others (such as substitute teachers) can read and implement it.

There are many ways to write and organize units of instruction. Most plans contain the following elements, even though they may have different titles or be listed in a different order.

Objectives or Standards for the Unit

Objectives should be written before organizing the activities and experiences. The objectives state what the students are expected to know on completion of the unit. Make students aware of what they are expected to learn. Objectives are usually listed for the three learning domains. For example, what cognitive understandings should students have, and will they be tested in these areas? What are the social and emotional concepts that students should develop through participation in this unit? Finally, what skills, techniques, and game strategies should students learn on completion of the unit?

Many districts are now asking that teachers include the state or national standards for physical education (SHAPE America, 2013) into the unit and lesson plans. The standards give direction to the entire physical education program and help clarify what students should learn.

Skills and Activities

This section is the instructional core of the unit and is organized according to unit objectives. Specific skills to be developed, activities to facilitate skill development, lead-up games to be taught, and culminating experiences are listed in this section. Scope and sequence are also integrated into this section to ensure a meaningful presentation. Proper sequencing of activities makes lessons instructionally sound and safer. Students and teachers may list the learning experiences as desirable student outcomes to ensure simple translation.

Instructional Procedures

Instructional procedures determine how activities will be presented to ensure the maximum amount of learning. Points included are instructional techniques, transitions, observations on the efficient use of equipment, necessary safety procedures, and teaching formations.

Equipment, Facilities, and Instructional Devices

Listing equipment and facilities needed for instruction makes it easy to see what is available and whether other teachers are using these items or facilities for a unit being taught concurrently. If facilities or equipment need to be prepared before the start of the lesson (e.g., lowering goals or inflating or deflating balls), this task should be listed on the lesson plan.

Culminating Activities

This section identifies how the unit will be concluded. A tournament between selected teams, an intraschool contest, or a school demonstration play day could be implemented. In any case, the unit should finish with an activity that is enjoyable to students and leaves them with a positive feeling toward the unit of instruction.

Evaluation

The final section outlines how student progress is monitored. The instructor can carry out monitoring, or students can be given guidelines for self-evaluation. Written tests can be administered to evaluate the knowledge gained through instruction. Skill tests can be used to assess the level of performance and skill development. An attitude inventory can measure the effect of the unit on the affective area of learning.

Another phase of evaluation involves asking students to comment on the unit and its method of presentation. This critique should be done in writing (anonymously) rather than orally because some student comments may anger or belittle the teacher. Student evaluations offer direction for modifying the unit and making it more effective in the future.

Suggested Weekly (Block Plan or Curriculum Map) Schedule

The purpose of a block plan or curriculum map is to distribute the activities of the unit into weekly segments. This approach gives the teacher a sense of timing and an indication of what to teach and when. A block plan or curriculum map alleviates problems such as insufficient time to teach the desired activities or insufficient activities to fill up the time frame. It eases the burden of writing lesson plans because the material to be taught is identified and sequenced into a meaningful time frame. Daily lesson plans are developed by following the outline of the block plan or curriculum map. Figure 4.8 is an example of a block plan or curriculum map for a unit on racquetball.

Bibliography and Resources

The bibliography contains materials used by students and teacher. Students are given a list of materials they can peruse if they desire more information. Location of materials should be identified. Teachers may have a separate list and collection of resources they use for instruction. For example, pamphlets on nutrition or physical fitness, available films, bulletin board materials, and textbooks could be included in the resource section.

The following outline is an example of a skeleton structure for designing unit plans.

I. **Title and grade level**
II. **Analysis and description of setting**
   A. Previous experiences and exposure to activity
   B. Limiting factors: class size, class organization, mixed grades, facilities and equipment, period of day class meets
   C. Rationale for including the activity

Introduction	Review	Review	Review	Review
What is racquetball? Grips—ready position Forehand stroke Backhand stroke Class procedures Practice bounce and hit Rule of the day	Grip, forehand, backhand Equipment **Teach** Serves—drive, Z lob **Activities** Serves—practice Bounce and hit Rule of the day	Serves, rules **Teach** Back-wall shots Hinders **Activities** Back-wall practice Serve practice Rule of the day	Forehand, backhand **Teach** Court position Kill shots **Activities** Performance objectives or short game Rule of the day	Back-wall shots **Teach** Ceiling shots Passing shots **Activities** Ceiling games 1, 2, or 3 shots
Review Problem rules Serve strategy Court coverage **Activities** Accuracy drills Drive serve Lob serve Backhand Backhand games 1 or 2 shots	**Teach** Cutthroat Doubles **Activities** Performance objectives 8-ball rally Rotation workup	**Review** Problem areas **Activities** Performance objectives 5 and out Ceiling games	**Review** Rules **Activities** Performance objectives Regular game Cutthroat or doubles	**Review** Kill shots **Activities** Rotation workup
Activities Performance objectives Backhand games Regular game Tournament games	**Review** Rules, strategy, shots, serves **Activities** Performance objectives Tournament games	**Written exam** **Activities** Performance objectives Tournament games	**Activities** Performance objectives Tournament games Cutthroat or doubles	**Final performance objectives** **Review course objectives** Final games Return exam

FIGURE 4.8 Example of racquetball block plan.

III. Objectives
A. General unit objectives (SHAPE America, 2013), which include four parts (refer to chapter 3 for more information):
  1. Actor
  2. Behavior
  3. Condition
  4. Degree (ABCD)
B. Specific objectives
  1. Psychomotor (physical performance skills)
  2. Cognitive (knowledge, rules, and strategies)
  3. Affective (attitudes and values)

IV. Organization
A. Time (length of unit)
B. Space available
C. Equipment and supplies
D. Basic grouping of students
E. Number of groups

V. Content
A. Introduction of the activity
B. Rules
C. Skills (diagram all drills)
D. Activities and lead-up games
E. Skills tests
F. Written tests
G. Block plan for entire unit
H. Grading procedures

VI. References and resources

Create Quality Lesson Plans

The importance of lesson planning cannot be overemphasized. Instructors at the middle and high school level are, at times, criticized for their lack of planning. A cycle of not planning often begins early in a teacher's career when student teachers observe master teachers doing little, if any, planning. The emphasis placed on developing meaningful lesson and unit plans in professional preparation courses appears unnecessary when a master teacher teaches without the aid of thoughtful planning. The beginning teacher is unable to judge the effectiveness of the master teacher because of a lack of perspective and experience. The master teacher has taught the material for many years and has evolved a method of presentation through trial and error. Presenting a lesson without planning may be possible, but the quality of any lesson can be improved through research, preparation, and a well-sequenced plan.

Planning helps teachers present quality instruction and maintain meaningful interaction with students. Teachers, regardless of experience and ability, have many things to remember while teaching. When presenting a lesson, situations occur that are impossible to predict. For example, dealing with discipline problems; modifying lessons spontaneously; relating to students by name; offering praise, feedback, and reinforcement; and developing an awareness of teaching behavior patterns need to be done regularly. If the content of the lesson is planned, written, and readily available, greater emphasis can be placed on other equally important phases of teaching.

When planning a lesson, the skills and abilities of students need to be considered if success is going to be an integral part of the presentation. This understanding results in activities that are challenging but not threatening. Remember that an activity is challenging or threatening based on the student's perception, not the instructor's. An activity is challenging if the learner believes it is difficult but achievable. It is threatening if the learner perceives it to be impossible. The same drill could be challenging to some students and threatening to others. Trying to sort out how students perceive various activities makes teaching a difficult task.

Regular success is necessary if students are expected to enjoy an activity for a lifetime. An instructor can force students to do just about anything within the educational setting. If forced into activities that result in frequent failure, students will probably learn to dislike or avoid them in the future. To give students lifetime skills and attitudes, monitor and adjust lessons regularly. Maintain sensitivity to the learner's perceptions and feelings, and teach with concern for each student as an individual.

Lesson planning is unique to each teacher. The competency of the individual in various activities will determine the depth of the lesson plan. A teacher who has little experience with a unit will need to do more research and reading. When a teacher is unfamiliar with a unit and still refuses to plan, the quality of instruction is compromised. Solid planning helps overcome a lack of competency and demonstrates the willingness to change and learn new skills and knowledge. Planning increases the effectiveness of the instructor. Regardless of the content, consider the following points when planning a lesson:

- Learning physical skills takes practice and repetition. Each lesson should be organized to maximize the amount of meaningful participation and to minimize the amount of teacher verbalization and off-task student behavior.

- Practice combined with instruction and meaningful feedback ensures skill development. Instructional sequences and procedures that increase the amount of feedback in a lesson are part of the written lesson plan. Key points to be learned may require regular and specific feedback to ensure that correct learning patterns occur.

- Lesson plans allow for differing ability levels of the students. Build a range of activities into each lesson plan so that students can progress at varying rates, depending on their levels of skill. List the activities in progression to simplify presentation and enhance learning.

- Needed equipment should be listed in the lesson plan. This record prevents the problem of being in the middle of a lesson only to find that you lack what you need to conduct the lesson. The initial placement of equipment and the way in which it is distributed and put away are tasks that are planned before teaching.

- Time needed for management activities can be minimized with planning. List whether students are to be in small groups or partnered, the type of formation required, and the way that those procedures will be implemented.

- Outcomes of the lesson should be listed. The outcomes of the lesson are easier to reach when both the instructor and students know where they are going. Outcomes can be written in brief form and stated clearly so that students know what they are expected to learn.

- Because lesson plans are personal, they can be written in code. All information need not be written out in longhand. For example, many teachers write their lesson plans on 4-by-6-inch (10 by 15 cm) cards, which can be carried easily and used with minimal distraction. The card contents reflect the instructor's thoughts and planning, which have occurred before the actual teaching session.

- Time should be estimated for various activities needed in the lesson. For example, the amount of time for roll call, a warm-up activity, fitness development, and the lesson's focus should be estimated. The time schedule need not be inflexible, but it should be followed closely enough so that planned activities are taught.

- Planning is an important phase of teaching. Few teachers instruct for more than four to five hours per day. If an eight-hour day is expected of other workers, instructors should use some of their remaining work time for planning. Consider a comparison with coaching. All successful coaches spend a great deal of time planning, observing film, and constructing game plans. The game may not last more than an hour or two, but many hours of planning take place before the contest. Teachers of physical education should recognize the need to spend time each day planning for four to five hours of teaching. The results of a well-planned lesson are rewarding to both students and the teacher.

- Successful experiences should be planned for students. The plan should include enough challenge to motivate and enough variety to maintain interest. A balance of safety and challenge is required in the school setting.

Major Instructional Components of the Lesson

A daily lesson plan format provides teachers and students with a measure of stability. A consistent daily instructional format offers routine and structure. Lesson plans offer a systematic approach to teaching. When planning a lesson, the skills and abilities of students need to be considered if success is going to be an integral part of the presentation. This understanding results in drills and activities that are challenging but not threatening. In effect, because the least gifted students may find difficulty in learning, the best approach is usually to gear instruction to the ability level of such students. Students can become discouraged when they find tasks too difficult to learn. The amount of time spent on different parts of the lesson can be predetermined. Most lesson plans cover three or four parts: a warm-up activity, a fitness component, and the lesson focus or game.

Introductory (Warm-Up) Activity

The **introductory (warm-up) activity** occupies 6 to 10% of the total lesson. The purpose is to prepare students for activity. Students require a few minutes to become emotionally involved in the activity after sitting in classes. Introductory activities (see chapter 14) require minimal organization and place demands on large-muscle movement. The activities may be an integral part of the fitness routine or a separate entity. In either case, the introductory activity is used to raise the heart rate, warm up the body, and stretch the muscles in anticipation of a fitness development activity. Teachers can change the introductory activity each week to add variety to the warm-up procedure.

Fitness Development Activity

Fitness activities take 23 to 27% of the lesson and focus on the development of physical fitness. Instruction centers on developing major components of fitness, especially flexibility, muscular strength and endurance, body composition, and cardiorespiratory endurance. A wide variety of fitness routines are offered so that students can learn to select methods acceptable to them in adulthood. Graduating from school knowing many ways to develop and maintain physical fitness is a program objective that will allow students to select lifetime fitness activities. A successful experience in fitness activities is motivating and creates positive attitudes. An in-depth discussion of physical fitness and examples of routines are found in chapter 15.

Lesson Focus and Game or Closing Activity

The **lesson focus and game activity** make up 50 to 66% of the lesson depending on the length of the period. This segment is the instructional part of the lesson, which emphasizes skill development, cognitive learning, and enhancement of the affective domain. This phase of the lesson contains skills to be taught, drills, and lead-up activities, all of which culminate in games and tournaments.

In elementary schools, games are often played at the end of the lesson so that students leave with a positive feeling about physical activity. These games are often unrelated to the lesson focus activity because students often desire a new and exciting activity to renew their enthusiasm. As students mature into the middle and high school years, the game or closing activity is often an extension of the lesson focus. For example, in a badminton unit, the culminating activity might be a king of the court tournament. Students engage in the game of badminton using the skills taught throughout the unit. On the other hand, if students show they are ready for a new activity, introducing a cooperative or competitive game activity is often beneficial. Note that the length of time dedicated to the lesson focus and game depend on the length of the class period. Longer class periods lend themselves to longer focus and game portions of the lessons. Some teachers elect to incorporate two versions of the lesson focus to prevent boredom and to address more content throughout the year.

TEACHING TIP

When planning your game activity be sure to consider planning small-sided games rather than one large game. This method allows maximum participation and opportunities for all students to respond. For example, multiple small-sided games of flag football can be going on at the same time, allowing more students to practice skills within the game setting. Opportunities to respond correspond to how many times students get to touch the ball or perform specific skills taught during the lesson focus.

Content of the Lesson Plan

Lesson plans should include a variety of components. Specifically, it is important to list student outcomes or objectives for the particular lesson, instructional activities that will be included, and teaching and organization hints that plan out the transitions. Depending on the administrator, additional components may be required.

Expected Student Outcomes

Before the lesson, establish what students are expected to experience, learn, and perform. List curriculum objectives to give direction to instruction. With careful planning of expected student outcomes, teachers can offer a wide variety of experiences throughout the school year to help students develop in all domains—psychomotor, cognitive, and affective.

Instructional Activities

Specific skills and activities to be taught need to be listed in the lesson plan, and they need to reflect the expected student outcomes. These items are listed in proper progression to ensure that instruction builds on previously learned skills. Progression helps ensure that activities are presented in a safe manner. The skills and related activities need not be written out in detail. Write enough to permit easy comprehension of the activities when teaching.

Teaching and Organization Hints

A list of instructional procedures can help teachers conceptualize before the lesson the details that need to be prepared, including organization of the equipment,

formations to use, key points of instruction to share with students, and the specific feedback used. New instructional procedures can be recorded after a lesson and maintained for the next time the lesson is taught.

Reflect on the Completed Lesson

Teaching is a full-time job. Teachers who excel and influence the lives of their students put a great deal of time and energy into their teaching. Obviously, all who teach physical education work hard to accomplish goals. But people can always identify a truly outstanding teacher who seems to get students to perform at a high level. One of the elements that is obvious among great teachers is their level of caring and thinking. They spend a great deal of time thinking about the lessons they have presented to find new and better ways to get students to respond. This process is often referred to as reflection—the act of sitting back and asking the question, "How could I have done that better so that students would learn more?"

Many things make teaching difficult (e.g., accommodating the weather, having to teach outside, having a limited amount of equipment, not knowing how certain students will respond to your discipline techniques). There are no simple answers to be found. What works one time may not work the next. Some teachers like to put in an 8:00 a.m. to 3:00 p.m. day, and you better not be in their way when the clock strikes three. These teachers teach the same way and the same thing year after year. Some say that these teachers have been teaching for 20 years and have 1 year of experience. That approach is the opposite of reflecting and trying to improve.

Quality teachers find time to reflect on all the factors related to their lessons. Most teachers admit that their first lesson of the week is not as polished and effective as one taught near the end of the week. A lesson taught during the first period of the week does not include all the finer points learned through trial and error. Instruction improves when teachers reflect on why some things worked and others did not. Leave time at the end of the day to reflect and note ways in which you can improve the lesson. Try keeping a portfolio related to inspiration and insight you uncover during the reflection process. Write down personal growth indicators and situations that offer evidence you are growing professionally. Continue to reflect and see it as a dynamic and ongoing process. Examine figure 4.9 for a list of questions that aid the reflection process. Add other questions that are specific and related to your professional growth.

Planning

- Did I prepare ahead of time? Mental preparation before a lesson ensures that continuity occurs in a lesson.
- Did I understand the "whys" of my lesson?
- Knowing why you are teaching something will give you greater strength and conviction in your presentation.
- Did I state my instructional goals for the lesson? Students are more focused if they know what they are supposed to learn.
- Did I plan the lesson so that students can participate safely, such as by creating safe areas for running with no slippery spots, broken glass, or objects to run into and by setting aside adequate room for striking activities?

Equipment

- Was my equipment arranged before class? Proper equipment placement reduces management time and allows more time for instruction and practice.
- Did I use enough equipment to keep all students involved and assured of maximum practice opportunities?
- Did I notify the principal about equipment that needs to be repaired or replaced? On a regular basis, do I record areas where equipment is lacking or insufficient in quantity? Do I inform the principal of these shortcomings?
- Did I select equipment that is appropriate for the developmental level of the students (e.g., proper size and types of balls, basketball hoop height, hand implements)?

Methodology

- Did I constantly move and reposition myself during the lesson? Moving allows you to be close to more students so that you can reinforce and help them. It usually reduces behavior problems.
- Did I teach with enthusiasm and energy? Energy and zest rub off on students.
- Did I try to show just as much energy for the last class of the day as I did for the first class of the day? Did I work just as hard on Friday as I did on Monday?
- Did I keep students moving during lesson transitions? Did I plan my transitions carefully so that little time was needed to proceed to the next part of the lesson?

Instruction

- Was I alert for children who were having trouble performing the activities and needed some personal help? Youngsters want to receive relevant but subtle help.
- Did I praise youngsters who made an effort or improved? Saying something positive to children increases their desire to perform at a higher level.
- Did I give enough attention to the personalization and creativity of each student? Everybody feels unique and different and wants to deal with learning tasks in a personal manner.
- Did I teach for quality of movement or just offer a large quantity of activities to keep students on task? Repetition is a necessary part of learning new skills.

Discipline and management

- Did I teach students to be responsible for their learning and personal behavior? Students need to learn responsibility and self-direction skills.
- Did I evaluate how I handled discipline and management problems? Did I preserve the self-esteem of my students during behavior correction episodes? Did I yell out my corrective feedback for the entire class to hear? What are some ways I could have handled situations better?
- Did I make positive calls home to reinforce students who are really trying and working hard?

Assessment

- Did I bring closure to my lesson? This practice gives feedback about the effectiveness of instruction. It also allows students a chance to reflect on what they have learned. Did I ask for answers in a way that allows me to check quickly that all students understand?
- Did I evaluate the usefulness of the activities I presented? Did I make changes as quickly as possible to ensure that my lessons were improving and becoming better at meeting the needs of my students?
- Did I communicate with teachers and the principal about things that need to be improved or better understood? Did I leave my office and meet other teachers on a regular basis for the sake of goodwill and program support?

FIGURE 4.9 Questions to aid the reflection process.

LEARNING AIDS

STUDY STIMULATORS AND REVIEW QUESTIONS

1. Explain why students should not be allowed to get physical education credit for band or athletics.
2. Discuss the difference between knowledge of results and knowledge of performance by using an example involving volleyball or any other sport activity.
3. Describe a process you might use for storing equipment for your physical education program.
4. When designing a unit plan, identify the components you will include and describe how you will determine each.
5. What is the rationale for embedding a culminating activity at the end of lessons and units?
6. Other than purchasing new equipment, what are two effective strategies that programs can employ to increase the amount of equipment available for instruction?
7. What benefits are there to having students share in some of the decision-making processes?
8. Provide an example of a makeup assignment in fitness that includes a knowledge, performance, and spectator task.
9. How are lower-skilled students shortchanged when most of the instruction is limited to the first two days of a unit?

WEBSITES

Unit and Lesson Planning

www.pecentral.org
www.pheamerica.org
www.masterteacher.com

REFERENCES AND SUGGESTED READINGS

Banas, J.A., Dunbar N., Rodriguez D., & Liu, S. (2011.) A review of humor in educational settings: Four decades of research. *Communication Education, 60*, 115–144.

Barney, D., & Christenson, R. (2013). Using humor in physical education. *Strategies, 26*(2), 19–22.

Barreiros, J., Figueiredo, T., & Godinho, M. (2007). The contextual interference effect in applied settings. *European Physical Education Review, 3*(2), 195–208.

Buck, M.M., Lund, J.L., Harrison, J.M., & Blakemore Cook, C.L. (2007). *Instructional strategies for secondary physical education* (6th ed.). Boston, MA: McGraw-Hill.

Casten, C.M. (2012). *Lesson plans for dynamic physical education for secondary school students* (7th ed.). San Francisco, CA: Pearson Benjamin Cummings.

Fronske, H. (2012). *Teaching cues for sport skills for secondary school students* (5th ed.). Boston, MA: Benjamin Cummings.

Goode, S., & Magill, R.A. (1986). The contextual interference effects in learning three badminton serves. *Research Quarterly for Exercise and Sport, 57*, 308–314.

Greenberg, J.D., & LoBianco, J.L. (2020) *Organization and administration of physical education.* Champaign, IL: Human Kinetics.

Kelly, L.E., & Melograno, V.J. (2004). *Designing the physical education curriculum: An achievement-based approach.* Champaign, IL: Human Kinetics.

Pangrazi, R.P., & Beighle, A. (2020). *Dynamic physical education for elementary school children* (19th ed.). Champaign, IL: Human Kinetics.

Rink, J.E. (2009). *Teaching physical education for learning* (6th ed.). Boston, MA: McGraw-Hill.

Schmidt, R.A., & Lee, T. (2011). *Motor control and learning* (5th ed.). Champaign, IL: Human Kinetics.

SHAPE America—Society of Health and Physical Educators. (2013). *National standards for K–12 physical education.* Reston, VA: Author.

Siedentop, D., & Tannehill, D. (2000). *Developing teaching skills in physical education* (4th ed.). Mountain View, CA: Mayfield.

Skinner, M.E., & Fowler, R.E. (2010). All joking aside: Five reasons to use humor in the classroom. *Education Digest, 76*(2), 19-21.

Wuest, D.A., & Fisette, J. (2012). *Foundations of physical education, exercise science, and sport* (17th ed.). Boston, MA: McGraw-Hill.

Improving Instructional Effectiveness

5

This chapter presents effective methods for becoming an active teacher who is aware of student needs. Quality instruction requires effective communication between teacher and student that can be enhanced by using instructional cues, demonstrating, modeling, and providing meaningful feedback. Often overlooked, however, is the importance of establishing a quality relationship with students, exemplified by mutual respect. An important part of teaching is understanding the personal needs of students, which includes teaching for diversity and understanding gender differences. Teaching is a skill that can be improved by using a systematic, data-based approach in an ongoing manner. Teachers can identify areas that need to be modified and improved and develop a system of self-evaluation to improve the instructional process. Areas that teachers can evaluate include practice time for students, instructional and management time of teachers, student performance, instructional feedback, and active supervision by the teacher. As the Common Core Standards are being implemented around the nation, many districts and states are moving toward a common, valid, reliable rubrics-based evaluation for improving instruction.

Learning Objectives

► Identify various ways to stay connected with students, including using active supervision and maintaining the flow of the lesson.
► Speak effectively to a class using proper techniques.
► Understand procedures needed to develop effective instructional cues.
► Cite various ways to enhance the clarity of communication between the teacher and the learner.
► Effectively use instructional cues to facilitate student learning.
► Describe demonstration and modeling skills that facilitate an environment conducive to learning.
► Articulate strategies and techniques used to supply students with meaningful feedback regarding performance.
► Teach effectively for diversity and gender differences.
► Explain the advantages of self-evaluation concerning instruction in physical education.
► Describe the use of the specific systematic observation methods.
► Define specific teacher and student behaviors that are part of an ongoing evaluation scheme.
► Set up a systematic observation plan for analyzing a specific teaching or student behavior.
► Complete a self-evaluation and set future goals for instructional improvement.

Effective teachers create a learning environment in which students want to learn their physical potential and receive personal and equitable treatment. Such an environment is created by a sensitive and caring teacher who fosters learning in all students. Teachers do not treat all students alike, because all students are different. Often, students know they are unique, and each would like to be treated as a special individual. The challenge is to gain a better understanding of which techniques and strategies are most effective for each student.

The main purpose of this chapter is to help teachers develop a repertoire of teaching skills to meet the needs of all students in a class, not only the most talented or motivated. Many teachers gravitate toward students who want to learn, but only the best teachers can reach students who do not particularly like the subject matter. This is the challenge: Teach, and reach, all students regardless of their intrinsic desire to learn. The skills of garnering student interest, listening to students' needs and desires, communicating effectively, and caring for students are conducive to establishing positive relationships with them and to fostering their openness to trying new activities and potentially finding activities they will enjoy for a lifetime increases.

Defining Effective Instruction

Effective instruction is a broad and general term that can be defined many ways. Simply put, it is best char-acterized by what students learn through contact with a teacher. The goal of an instructor is to teach new skills, refine previously learned skills, change attitudes, and leave students with a positive feeling about what they have learned. If students do not learn, effective instruction has not occurred. Some physical education teachers think they are successful if they teach students all the key points of skill performance. If, despite the presentation of key points, students do not perform differently than they did before the skill analysis, instruction was ineffective.

A common saying in education is "Students learn when teachers teach." This statement is probably true if teachers are effective in their teaching methods. On the other hand, learning is not guaranteed. Teaching effectively demands that positive changes in behavior occur. The changes may be attitudinal (affective), skill oriented (psychomotor), or knowledge (cognitive) based. Regardless of the learning domain affected, learning occurs and teaching is effective only when measurable changes result. This goal speaks to the need for systematic evaluation of instruction.

Demonstrate a Caring Attitude Toward Students

The communication techniques that a teacher uses go a long way in determining how students feel toward them. Teachers who take a positive approach to communication with students and establish a warm, caring

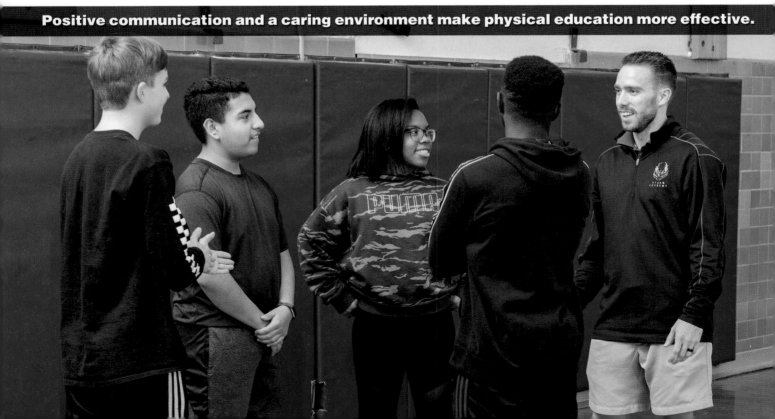

Positive communication and a caring environment make physical education more effective.

environment are effective. A positive approach to student motivation is recommended because it has long-term effects on both students and teachers. Teaching and learning are more enjoyable when students and instructors look forward to participating in a positive environment. The positive approach enhances the overall motivation of both teachers and students.

Students often judge the quality of a teacher on attributes unrelated to the teacher's knowledge of subject matter. The teacher's style of presentation can influence how students feel about physical education. Students eventually tune out teachers who shout commands, speak like drill sergeants, appear disengaged from the material they are teaching, or repeat certain phrases (nagging). Students want to understand and be understood. The following points are behaviors that will help students feel that you care about them.

1. *Speak about the behavior of students, not about their personal character.* The following is an example of speaking about a student's *behavior*: "Talking when I am talking is unacceptable behavior." Such feedback identifies behavior that can be improved on and avoids questioning the self-worth of the student. This approach helps students feel you are interested in helping rather than belittling them. In contrast, saying something like, "Why do you always have to act like a fool?" reflects on the student's *character* and undermines his or her self-esteem. The question is also nonspecific, making it difficult for the student to determine what behavior concerns you. Identify the specific misbehavior followed by the type of behavior that should be displayed.

2. *Put yourself in the student's shoes.* How would you feel if someone embarrassed you in front of a class? How do you feel when you are inept and trying to learn a new skill? These and other emotions often make listening difficult for youths, and the long-term ramifications are a student's lack of respect for the teacher. What conditions are necessary to make it easy for you to accept constructive feedback? Excessive feedback may stress a student and cause a reduction in performance. Offer feedback in small doses. If you are going to suggest ways to improve performance, do so on a personal basis and leave the student to practice without scrutiny. To ask students to change and then stand over them until they do so may cause resentment and internal pressure.

3. *Identify your feelings toward students.* At times,

teachers send mixed messages to students. They may be unhappy with students because of situations unrelated to class performance yet unwilling to discuss the real issues. Instead, they respond with unkind feedback about skill performance. Their negative feelings are transferred to the students regarding their performance in class. This was not the teacher's intent but the result of pent-up feelings over an unrelated issue. Students perceive negativity from a teacher. Take responsibility for communicating how you feel (albeit negative), but make sure you direct it toward the undesirable behavior, not the student as a person.

4. *Accentuate the positive.* When phrasing the instructional points of a lesson, stress the positive. For example, tell students, "Make a sharp cut," rather than say, "Don't round off your cut." An easy way to emphasize the "why" of an activity is to say, "Do this because. . . ." If students can perform the movement patterns in several different and acceptable ways, be explicit. Show students various ways and discuss reasons for the differences. Students like to know the correct technique, even if it is beyond their sphere of accomplishment. Explain only enough, however, to get the activity successfully underway.

5. *Optimize speech patterns.* Avoid sermonizing at the least provocation. Excessive reliance on certain words and phrases, such as "OK," "All right," and the irritating "You know" are unappealing to students. Many adolescents focus on repetitive speech patterns rather than listen to what the teacher is expressing. Acquire a broad vocabulary of effective phrases for indicating approval and good effort and vary verbal patterns. Multiple documents show ways to reinforce students in a positive manner.

6. *Conduct cognitive discussions in the classroom.* Whenever possible, lengthy discussions should be held in the classroom (as opposed to the gymnasium or fields or courts) for reasons of comfort and student expectations. Students expect to move in the activity area, whereas they have learned to sit and interact cognitively in the classroom. Rules can be explained, procedures and responsibilities outlined, and formations illustrated on the chalkboard. If discussions will last longer than one or two minutes, place students in a comfortable setting and use instructional aids such as multimedia presentations, handouts, and video.

7. *Treat all responses to questions with dignity.* Respect students' responses and opinions and avoid humiliating a student who gives a wrong answer. Pass over inappropriate answers by directing attention to more appropriate responses. Or, tell students that they have offered a good answer, but that the question is not the right one. Remind them to save the answer and then go back to the students when the answer is correct for another question. Refrain from injecting opinion into the instructional question-and-answer process. At the end of the discussion, summarizing important points may be valuable.

Develop Effective Listening Skills

For most teachers, listening skills are more difficult to learn than speaking skills. Instructors learn to impart knowledge to students and have practiced speaking for years. Many students view teachers as people who teach but do not care about their point of view. Poor communication usually results from a breakdown in listening rather than speaking. There is a lot of truth in the adage "People were given two ears and one mouth so they could listen twice as much as they speak." The following activities will help you become a more effective listener.

1. *Be an active listener.* Effective listeners convince the speaker that they are interested in what is being said. They do this largely through non-verbal behavior such as maintaining eye contact, nodding the head in agreement, using facial expressions, and moving toward the speaker. Active listening shows students that their ideas and thoughts count and that they have some input into their destiny.

2. *Determine what the student is really trying to say.* Many students are not capable of clearly expressing their feelings, particularly if they have deep concerns. The words expressed may not clearly signal what the student is feeling. For example, a teenager may say, "I hate PE." In most cases, students do not hate all phases of physical education; rather, something more immediate may be the problem. An effective response might be, "You sound upset; are you having a problem you want to discuss?" Asking about feelings makes students feel important and gives them an opportunity to clarify their concerns. It also prevents the teacher from internalizing a student's emotion

and responding in a heated manner, such as, "I don't care whether you like it or not; get with it!"

3. *Paraphrase what the student said.* Paraphrasing is restating what was said to you, including the feelings detected, in your own words. For example, the teacher might respond, "Do I hear you saying that you are frustrated and bored with this activity?" If the paraphrasing is correct, the student feels validated and understood. If the interpretation is incorrect, the student has an opportunity to restate the problem. In addition, paraphrasing offers the teacher an opportunity to understand clearly how students perceive various situations.

4. *Allow students to tell you how they feel.* Teachers who listen to students learn about their feelings. Let students know you will listen. If you are an effective listener, you may hear things that are not positive. For example, students may tell you honestly which activities they enjoy and which they do not. They may tell you how you made them feel when you criticized them. This type of communication is constructive only if you can accept it objectively and not be threatened by the feedback. Such feedback can be helpful in improving instruction. Even though the criticism of the program or procedures may not be valid, it offers opportunity for program and instructional improvement. Perhaps providing students the opportunity to complete a questionnaire in which they indicate activities they enjoy will help the teacher select units for the curriculum and show the students that their opinions are valued. For a variety of reasons, however, not all activities they want will be included. A word of caution: If you find it difficult to accept such communication, telling students that you prefer not to hear about it is probably best. Avoid such interaction with students if it affects your confidence or starts a confrontation.

5. *Avoid situations that undermine effective communication.* Certain types of verbal interaction convince students that the teacher is unwilling to listen. The following are some common examples:

   • *Preaching or moralizing.* This type is often manifested by telling students, "You should know better than that!" Students make mistakes because they are immature and learning how to behave. A big part of learning is making mistakes and knowing how to avoid doing so in the future. Teachers who expect such mistakes are not shocked by student misbehavior and are able to deal with it in a rational manner.

- *Threatening.* Threats are often used to control students. They are usually ultimatums given to students to terminate undesirable behavior, even though the teacher knows they will be impossible to implement. For example, the threat "If you do not stop that, I'm going to kick you out of class" is difficult to enforce. Most teachers are not able to expel students. If students hear enough idle threats, they soon learn to ignore and mock the teacher. As a reminder, it is not a threat if you are able to stop the misbehavior.

- *Ordering and commanding.* If teachers appear to be bossy, students begin to think they are nothing more than pawns to be moved around the area. Try to develop patterns of communication that ask students to carry out tasks. Courtesy and politeness are requisites for effective teacher–student relationships. Consider allowing students to work with peers, for example, as opposed to always forming groups for them. In addition, if teachers want to be treated with respect, they need to treat others similarly.

- *Interrogating.* When a problem occurs, such as a fight between students, a common approach is to try to determine who started the fight rather than deal with the feelings of the combatants. Little is gained by trying to identify who started it. Students usually shirk the blame and suggest that the altercation was not their fault. A much better solution is to begin by acknowledging feelings: "You know that fighting is not accepted in my class; you must have been very angry to place yourself in this predicament." This statement allows students to talk about their feelings rather than place the blame on the other person. It also tells them that even when they do something wrong, the teacher cares about them.

- *Refusing to listen.* This technique usually manifests itself by saying, "Let's talk about it some other time." In some situations, this response is necessary. But if it is always the case, students will begin to avoid interaction with the instructor. If the student needs to

In a positive learning environment, students feel safe and accepted.

discuss something important during class, the teacher should try to get the remaining students involved in an activity and talk with that student individually. If the situation requires a lengthier conversation, the teacher should show the student that he or she cares by finding a time to meet with the student outside of class.

- *Labeling.* In this situation, the teacher tells students, "Stop acting like fools," or "You're behaving like a bunch of animals." These responses are not only degrading but also dehumanize students. In most cases, labeling is done because teachers think it will improve performance, but it is usually destructive and leaves a student with a negative feeling about the teacher.

- *Sarcasm.* This kind of expression is frequently used as humor in day-to-day interactions among peers. Within the classroom, sarcasm is often misunderstood and can create hard feelings between the teacher and students. If the listener must ask, "What did he or she mean by that?" the message was not understood as intended. A better approach is to respond to students in a caring and respectful manner. Sarcasm does not create the positive learning environment needed for students to feel safe and accepted.

TEACHING TIP

If you are going to earn the respect of students, you will have to develop a relationship with them. Listening to them and responding in a caring manner is what it takes to earn respect. Why would students respect a teacher who only prodded and pushed them without concern for their feelings?

If you want students to talk with you openly, remember to listen without judging the student. Too often, we try to teach a lesson when a student merely wants to talk. Trust is the foundation of respect—if students trust you, they will treat you with care because you are an important person in their life. Effective teaching is all about relationships. You are able to teach students when they choose to cooperate and respect you.

Maintain Student Interest

A component of effective teaching is a learning environment that facilitates student learning and maintains interest. Environmental and instructional planning ensure that students have an opportunity to learn skills in a positive setting. Active teacher supervision and instructional flow help students feel as though the teacher is competent and aware of the learning environment.

Use Active Supervision

Observation of class performance is critical to ensuring that students stay on task and practice activities correctly. This undertaking requires *active* supervision of students—that is, taking a position where eye contact can be maintained with all students. In other words, the teacher should keep his or her back to the wall. **Proximity** is helpful to consider when teaching. It describes a teacher's nearness to his or her students during a lesson. Students tend to stay on task if they know that someone is watching. Therefore, teachers should stay out of the center of the area, but they often ignore this guidance. They place students in a circle and then stand in the center of the formation. This positioning makes it impossible to see all students and difficult for students facing the back of the teacher to hear. Because students cannot hear and the teacher has little eye contact with half of the class, control of the class is easily lost.

Some teachers assume they must move to the same location in the teaching area when giving instructions because students listen only when they are on or near this spot. This assumption is not only incorrect but also can result in negative consequences. Students who choose to exhibit deviant or off-task behavior usually move away from the instructor. If the teacher's movement patterns are predictable, deviant students move farthest from the teacher in a position that is difficult to observe. In addition, the teacher may never move into certain areas, causing some students to believe that the teacher does not care about them. Active supervision requires the instructor to move around the perimeter of the area. Another reason for moving in an unpredictable manner is to keep students on task. For example, when using several teaching stations, some teachers move from station to station in the same order consistently. Students may perform the tasks while the teacher is watching but move off task as soon as the teacher moves to the next station. Here is the bottom line: Move in a random fashion so that students cannot anticipate where you will be next.

Active supervision requires movement and effective observation. If you develop and implement a plan for reaching all students, they believe you are concerned about them, eliciting a more positive rapport. In addition, you should place yourself in an optimum position to observe skill performance. For example, if you are observing kicking, stand to the side rather than behind the student. When observing performances, you need to decide how long to stay with a single group or student. If you get too involved with one student, the rest of the class may move off task. On the other hand, if contacts are short and terse, the student may not benefit from the interaction. Learn to pace **instructional feedback** by giving one or two pointers and moving to another student.

Develop a Plan for Active Supervision

Beginning teachers often look at students but do not see. When teachers do not have a plan for actively supervising behavior, they usually are unable to recall whether students exhibited desired behaviors. To keep all students on task, teachers need a plan for monitoring this behavior. A practical plan might be to scan the class from left to right at regular intervals and observe the number of students performing the assigned task. When teaching a class of 25 to 35 students, scanning an entire class usually takes four to six seconds. If done faster, internalizing the results of the scan is difficult. Several variables can be evaluated through systematic observation, such as students responding to a start or stop signal (response latency), key points of skill performance, adherence to safety procedures, and on-task performance.

An active supervision plan should include where to stand for observation, how long to stay with each student, and how to move through the instructional area. One approach to ensure that all students receive personal contact is to check off the names of students addressed during the lesson. This task can be done immediately after the lesson with a roll sheet or later if the lesson is recorded. Often, teachers find they do not make regular contact with certain students and make excessive contact with others. This practice leads to feelings of favoritism or some students' concern that the teacher does not like or care about them. Interacting with all students in a single physical education lesson is difficult, but in a one- or two-week period, all students should receive feedback and positive attention.

Teacher movement should be planned because it affects supervisory effectiveness. To facilitate learning to move, divide the teaching area into four equal parts and set a goal of moving into each area a certain number of times. Give instructions and reinforcement from all quadrants.

Maintain the Flow of the Lesson

An important phase of effective instruction is pacing the lesson to keep students interested in learning, yet not frustrated or bored. The following points offer ways to improve the flow of a lesson and maintain student motivation to reach desired goals.

Minimize Verbalization and Increase Activity

Teachers can easily become engrossed in instruction and lose sight of student interest. Students enter class expecting to be involved in activity. If a teacher spends 5 minutes on attendance followed by 5 or 10 minutes of lecture, students lose interest and motivation. Move the class first and give instructions later. This method gets students warmed up and ready to relax while listening. As a rule, if instruction is going to take longer than a minute, break it into several short sessions. Alternating instruction with application of the information will help keep students on task. The following are suggestions for effective instruction:

1. *Focus instruction on one or two key points.* Students cannot easily remember a series of instructions. Telling them too many points related to skill performance leaves them baffled, frustrated, or clueless. In a series of points, most learners remember the first and last point. Emphasizing one or two key points makes it easier for students to focus their concentration.

2. *Refrain from lengthy skill descriptions.* When instructions last longer than 30 to 60 seconds, students become listless because they cannot remember all the input. Develop a pattern of short, concise presentations, alternated with practice sessions. Short practice sessions offer an opportunity to refocus on key points of a skill many times.

3. *Present information in its most basic, easy-to-understand form.* If a class does not understand the presentation, you have failed, not your students. The best way to know whether the students understand is to have them show you, as opposed to asking if everyone understands.

4. *Separate management and instructional episodes.* Consider a common approach often used to present a new game: "In this game, we will break into groups of five. Each group will get a ball and form a small circle. On the command 'Go,' the game will start. Here is how you play the game . . ." A lengthy discussion of game rules

Move the class first and give instructions later.

and conduct follows. Because the instructions are long, students usually forget what they were asked to do earlier. Or they think about whom they want in their group rather than the game rules. A better approach is to move the class into game formation (management) and then discuss the activity to be learned (instruction). This method serves two purposes: (1) It reduces the length of the episode, and (2) it makes it easier for students to conceptualize how the game is played.

Maintain the Focus and Pace of Instruction

Teachers can easily become derailed when an unanticipated event occurs in class. Lesson plans are designed to guide the instruction toward desired objectives. When teachers constantly allow students to sidetrack them and get them to talk about subjects unrelated to instructional outcomes, goals may not be reached. Some students intentionally try to move teachers away from the tasks at hand so that they can participate in activities they

 TEACHING TIP

What are signs that you are losing control of a class or they are losing interest in the lesson? Students always tip off the teacher with their off-task behavior. One sign that you need to refocus your lesson is a rapid increase in unacceptable behavior. For example, students may chat with friends, stand around and agitate others, talk about how they hate this activity, or clown around. These behaviors are clear signs that it is time to refocus or change to another activity.

Often, the easiest way to refocus is have the class stop what they are doing, put down their equipment and move around the area. Move and freeze them a couple of times and then play a simple game for a minute or two (see chapter 14). Always remember that the pace of the lesson is your responsibility. If the lesson is not going well, stop and refocus. Do not be stubborn and say something like, "We're going to do this activity whether you like it or not." That sort of remark is a way of telling them you do not care about how they feel.

prefer. Effective teachers maintain their momentum toward objectives, yet they are able to show interest in student ideas. Sometimes teachers may choose to deviate from planned objectives to take advantage of a teachable moment. But this tactic should be the exception, not the rule. Students know that the teacher is responsible for guiding the content of the lesson, and they expect it.

Effective lessons flow in a consistent manner when they are well planned. Many **transitions** occur during a lesson: organizing students into groups, changing from one part of the lesson to another, and issuing and putting away equipment. Transitions are an integral part of effective instruction. An excessively long transition interrupts instructional momentum, possibly causing students to lose interest. Try to minimize time spent on transitions, which, in turn, leaves more time for practice and instruction.

Pace of instruction affects the flow of the lesson (Siedentop & Tannehill, 2000). How often should a teacher break into practice sessions to clarify a point or refocus instruction? Usually, a natural break occurs in practice episodes when students become bored or fatigued and begin to move off task. This is a signal for the teacher to refocus on the same goal or introduce a new one. If most of the students are not performing correctly after an instructional episode, freeze them, restate the situation, and get them back into practice quickly.

Communicate Effectively With Your Class

Many words can be spoken, but little is accomplished if students do not understand what has been said. Communication implies more than words; it assumes that understanding has occurred. The following points can enhance the effectiveness of instruction:

1. *Develop a stimulating speaking style.* You do not need to be an outstanding speaker, but you do have to be interesting and exciting. Show students you care about the material you expect them to learn. The chance for effective communication improves if students want to listen to a teacher. Use your voice effectively: Alter the intensity, raise and lower the pitch, and change the speed of delivery. Smile! Use nonverbal behavior to emphasize important points. In addition, keep discussions short and to the point so that students are willing to stop what they are doing and listen.

2. *Use a teaser to create interest.* If a concept is somewhat difficult to comprehend, set the stage by briefly describing what is to follow and why it is important. A teaser is a sentence or two that makes learning the forthcoming information seem important. The teaser usually tips off students that something important to them will follow. This tactic gets students ready to listen so that they do not miss the first part of the discussion. Use current events to set the stage, such as offensive or defensive strategies applied during the school's recent basketball tournament.

3. *Build on previous learning experiences.* Whenever possible, try to tie the discussion to previous skills and knowledge that students have mastered. An effective method is to show students how a skill is similar (or dissimilar) to one learned earlier. Transfer of learning can be optimized if students understand the relationship to their previous experiences. Using the inquiry teaching style (see chapter 6) can help students link past experiences to upcoming activities. Using questions based on this teaching strategy can also provide opportunities for teachers to check for student understanding.

4. *Present the material in proper progression.* Teach skills in the sequence in which they will be performed. An exception may be when a teacher wants to focus on a critical step first and then build around it. For example, in dance, a teacher may teach step patterns and then put them together to complete the dance. In most cases, however, the progression should mimic the sequence of performance. Students assume that the order of activities is the correct progression.

5. *Model correct and incorrect examples.* Most adolescents learn physical skills quicker by observing rather than listening. This approach mandates modeling desirable and incorrect examples. For example, some students will comprehend quicker if they are shown the correct way to pivot and one or two examples of incorrect pivoting. Often, teachers talk students through all skills and movements. When possible, you should combine instruction with demonstration. Demonstrate each skill in the playing area where students will practice (i.e., on the tennis court, in the pool, on the track, and so on).

6. *Check for understanding.* Monitor student understanding through active responses to assess instructional clarity. Having students respond

with an observable behavior or asking an open-ended question allows the teacher to monitor effective communication. For example, you might say, "Show me the triple-threat position," or "See how many times you can serve the ball cross court."

7. *Separate management and instructional episodes.* Much emphasis has been placed on maintaining short episodes of instruction and focusing on cues that are easily understood. Here is a special point of attention: Teachers often unsuccessfully combine management activities with instructional activities. For example, during a presentation of a new game, the teacher says the following: "In this game, we will break into groups of five. Each group will get a ball and form a small circle. On the command 'Go,' the game will start. Here is how you play the game." At this point, a lengthy discussion of game rules and conduct is given. By this time, most students have forgotten the management behavior stated. Instead, use this approach. First, move the class into the game formation: "When I say, 'Go,' break into groups of five and form a small circle. One person needs to grab a tennis ball. . . . Go." Then discuss the activity: "Begin by tossing the ball underhand to someone across from you. Form a pattern in your circle. Go." This approach serves two purposes: It reduces the length of the instructional episode,

and it helps the class conceptualize how the game is played. In addition, by forming groups first, students are no longer thinking about whom they want for partners when they are listening to the rules. Teach students one thing at a time. Remember to manage first and instruct second.

Use Nonverbal Communication

Using nonverbal communication is an important way to tell students about their behavior. Nonverbal communication is effective because students often perceive it as more meaningful than words. For example, beginning teachers often have a difficult time making their feelings align with their body language. They may be pleased with student performance yet portray a less-than-pleased message (e.g., frowning or placing hands on hips). Another common example occurs when teachers want to assert themselves and gain control of a class. They often place their hands in their pockets, stand in a slouched position, and back away from the class. This nonverbal behavior signals anything but assertiveness and gives students mixed messages.

Nonverbal behavior can be used to praise a class, including thrusting of a finger into the air to signify number 1, giving a thumbs-up or a high five, shaking hands, and so on. Nonverbal behavior can also be negative, including placing hands on the hips, holding a finger to the lips, frowning, and staring. In any case,

Nonverbal communication is an effective way to tell students about their behavior.

effective use of nonverbal behavior can increase the validity and strength of verbal communication.

When using nonverbal communication, consider the customs and mores of different cultures. The teacher must learn how students respond to different types of gestures. For example, Hmong and Laotian adolescents may be touched on the head only by parents and close relatives. A teacher who pats a student on the head for approval is interfering with the student's spiritual nature. The OK sign (touching thumb and forefinger) is an indication of approval in the United States, but in several Asian cultures, it is a zero, indicating that the student is not performing properly. In many South American countries, the OK sign carries a sexual connotation. Teachers new to an area should ask for advice when expressing approval to students from other cultures.

To make nonverbal behavior convincing, teachers can watch their behavior and then practice necessary modifications. An effective method is to practice in front of a mirror and display different emotions. Another is to work with someone who does not know you well. If this person can identify the emotions demonstrated by the nonverbal behavior, it will likely be effective in a teaching situation. Recording yourself is an effective tool for self-analysis. Analyze yourself to see how you look when teaching under stress, disciplining a student, or praising a class.

Demonstrate and Model Skills

Most students learn faster if they see a demonstration of a skill or technique. The adage "A picture is worth a thousand words" holds true in physical education. Demonstrations can illustrate variety or depth of movement, show something unique or different, point out items of technique or approach, illustrate acceptable styles, and show progress. Another important reason for demonstrating is to help develop credibility with students. For example, many students may question whether a skill can be performed until they see the teacher or another student do it. Secondary school students are notorious for their "show me" attitude; a demonstration can show that the skill is in their range of abilities.

Teacher Demonstration

Be sure the class can see and hear the performance. Demonstrate the performance in the correct location; for example, if the triple-threat position for basketball is performed, the demonstration should take place in the appropriate location at a basket. When explaining technique, highlight key points of performance. Show the proper starting position and verbalize the instructions from that point on or provide a more complete, point-by-point demonstration. Terminology should be clear and include the use of visual words, such as "tabletop," "belly button to the target," or "flat platform." Techniques should be demonstrated within the student's skill level. The more complex a skill is, the more demonstration is needed. Questions can be raised during the demonstration, but avoid allowing the question-and-answer period to take up too much time. Effectiveness of teacher demonstration depends on a combination of visual cues, proper location, and clarity of verbal instruction.

Student Demonstration

Student demonstration is an effective teaching technique because it interjects the students' ideas into the lesson. Using students to demonstrate provides their classmates with the opportunity to see one of their own performing the skill. Involving students also demonstrates accountability of the task.

As students practice and move, the class can be stopped for a demonstration. Rarely is it acceptable to pick out a student and ask him or her to demonstrate in front of the class without first asking the student if he or she wants to demonstrate. A safe way to avoid embarrassing a student is to check his or her performance while the class is engaged in activity. If the demonstration is unsatisfactory, you can decide to ask another student to demonstrate. If partner or small-group work is undertaken, the same principle applies.

If You Cannot Demonstrate

Because of physical and skill limitations, some teachers cannot demonstrate. Few teachers can perform all physical activities, so you should not think that you must be an expert at every activity. Even a skilled teacher needs to devise a backup plan when he or she is unable to offer an effective demonstration. Through reading, study, and analysis of movement, teachers can develop an understanding and knowledge of the activities. Even if performing the activity is impossible, study and understand how the activity is done. Telling your students you cannot perform the skill to perfection is OK. This admission shows them not only that they do not need to excel at every skill but also that you are human. Other options are to use video clips or teaching signs to supplement instruction or ask a student (who is known to be able to perform the skill correctly) to demonstrate if she or he feels comfortable doing so.

Facilitate Learning With Instructional Cues

Instructional cues are words that quickly and efficiently communicate to the learner proper technique and performance of skills or movement tasks. When learning skills, young people need a clear understanding of critical skill points. Students often understand mentally how to perform a skill before successful application. Cues provide students a clear mental and physical understanding of performance stages.

Motor learning and cognitive understanding of a skill must be developed simultaneously. Sometimes, teachers carefully plan skill and movement activities but fail to plan

Short cues should help the student focus on one phase of a skill.

for the instructional cues to be used during skill practice. The result may be that students do not clearly understand technique and points of performance. When developing instructional cues, consider the following points.

Use Accurate Cues

If the cue is going to help the learner perform a skill correctly, it must be precise and accurate. It needs to lead the learner in the proper direction and be part of a comprehensive package of cues. All instructors must teach activities they know little about. Few, if any, teachers know everything about all activities. Textbooks and media aids are available for reference. These resources delineate the key points of the skill (Fronske, 2012; Fronske & Wilson, 2002). Other options include asking other teachers who have specific knowledge or videotaping an activity and analyzing points of performance that give students the most difficulty. In any case, cues are developed through study, practice, and experience. Even a beginning teacher needs to possess ample learning cues for teaching preliminary experiences.

Use Short, Descriptive Cues

Sometimes teachers use cues that are more comprehensive and lengthier than necessary. Many teachers teach as they were taught in high school. They remember a class in which the teacher told them everything they needed to know at the start of the unit and let them practice without instruction for the rest of the period. This approach assumes that students can comprehend a long list of instructions and correctly apply them to skills. If this is not the case, students spend the rest of the unit performing skills incorrectly. An incorrect motor pattern practiced for a long period is difficult to correct later.

To avoid confusing and overwhelming the learner, choose three or four cues for each lesson. The cues should be short and contain keywords. They should help the learner focus on one phase of skill during practice. Integrating several small movement patterns into one explicit cue reduces the number of cues needed and their length. For example, when teaching batting, a cue might be "Squish the bug." The purpose of this cue would be to rotate the hips and complete the follow-through. Other examples of hitting cues follow:

- "Step toward the target."
- "Keep your elbows away from your body."
- "Shift weight from the rear to front foot."

One way to examine the effectiveness of the cues is to see if they communicate the entire skill. Have all the critical points of batting been covered, or is the skill done incorrectly in certain phases? In most skills, the performance can be broken into three parts: preparing to perform, performing the skill, and following through. Focus cues on one phase at a time because it is difficult for students to remember more. Descriptive words are most effective with adolescents, particularly if they have an exciting sound. Examples of this are "Snap your wrists," "Twist the upper body during the follow-through," and "Explode off the starting line." In other situations, make the voice influence the effectiveness of the cue. For example, if a skill is to be done smoothly and gently, the teacher can speak in a soft tone and ask students to "let the movement floooooow" or to "move smooooothly across the floor." Cues are most effective when voice inflections, body language, and action words are used to signal the desired behavior.

Integrate Cues

Integrate cues to combine parts of a skill and use words that focus on the skill as a whole. These cues depend on prior cues used during the presentation of a skill and assume that concepts delineated in earlier phases of instruction were correctly understood. Examples of integrating cues might be the following:

- "Step, rotate, throw."
- "Run, jump, and forward roll."
- "Stride, swing, follow through."

Integrated cues are a set of action words that help students sequence and time parts of a skill. These cues are reminders of the proper sequence of skills and the mental images of the performance. Depending on the rhythm of the presentation, the cues can signal the speed and tempo of the skill performance. In addition, they can serve as a specialized language that allows the student and teacher to communicate effectively.

Use Effective Instructional Feedback

Effective teachers use instructional feedback to promote student learning. Used properly, it can enhance a student's self-image, improve the focus of performance, result in individualized instruction, increase the rate of on-task behavior, and improve understanding. Proper feedback can affect skill performance or the results of skill performance. The following points offer direction for improving the quality of feedback used in the instructional setting.

Know When to Use Positive, Corrective, and Negative Feedback

Most teachers use corrective feedback to alter student performance. In most cases, unless a teacher focuses totally on mistakes and failures, negative feedback (e.g., "That was a lousy throw.") is seldom used. Instead, corrective feedback is used to redirect the incorrect part of the performance (or related behavior). Students usually expect this, but if corrective feedback is the only type offered, students begin to perceive it as negative. The danger of overusing corrective feedback is that it creates a climate where students worry about making errors for fear the instructor will embarrass or belittle them. In addition, excessive correction may cause students to think that no matter what they do correctly, the teacher never sees the positive aspect of their efforts.

Focus on the positive points of student performance. This approach creates a positive atmosphere in which students are willing to accept a challenge and risk error or failure. Teachers who use positive feedback usually feel better about their students because they look for strengths in performance and use them as a foundation for skill improvement. Many physical education instructors rely heavily on corrective feedback, leading to the observation that they have a correction complex. Corrective statements are appropriate if the learning environment has a balance of positive and corrective feedback. Using a positive, corrective, positive pattern is known as the sandwich approach. Siedentop and Tannehill (2000) recommend that an educational environment have a three-to-one or four-to-one ratio of positive feedback to corrective feedback. A higher ratio of positive feedback enhances the overall positive atmosphere of the class. Because the use of corrective feedback comes easily for most teachers, focus on increasing the amount of positive feedback used.

Understand Different Types of Information Feedback

Information feedback is given when students have completed a skill attempt. Feedback on the result of skill attempts is obvious in many activities, such golf swings, basketball shots, or baseball swings. Feedback is inherent in the activity, and students immediately know the results of the skill attempt. Feedback on the form or process of skill behavior is, however, difficult to attain. Feedback can easily be tied to the instructional cues developed for each skill performance. Using feedback that integrates skill cues provides students with useful information on how well they are performing a skill.

Plan carefully for information feedback delivered in classes. You need to determine the specific skill behaviors you are trying to foster. The feedback should be prescriptive in nature so that it helps eradicate errors. You can use various ways to tell students they are performing at an acceptable level. Feedback statements can be general, specific, verbal, or nonverbal. Including a student's first name with the feedback is a meaningful way to help students realize that the teacher is aware and sincere about their skill development. The following are some examples of different types of feedback:

Corrective or Prescriptive

- "Get the shot-put angle up to 42 degrees."
- "Bend your knees more and uncoil."
- "Adjust your grip by spreading your fingers."
- "Accelerate through the ball."
- "Keep your wrists stiff and start the action with your shoulders."
- "Transfer your weight as you contact the ball."

Positive General

- "Good job."
- "Way to go."
- "Nice defense."
- "All right, Jim."
- "Very nice hustle."
- "Interesting question, Mary."
- "OK, class."

Positive Specific

- "Good angle of release."
- "Perfect timing on the outlet pass."
- "Way to hit the soft spot in the 1-3-1 zone."
- "Great job looking off the under coverage."
- "That's the way to vary your serves. It keeps them off balance."
- "Karen, good job keeping your head down."

Nonverbal positive or corrective actions might include the following:

- Smiling
- Thumbs up or down
- Pat on the back
- Clapping the hands
- Facial gestures
- Shaking the fist

Plan a variety of feedback options, including statements that use first names, specific positive information, and nonverbal messages. Variety is necessary to avoid satiation and redundancy. Feedback should be directed at key points of the specific skill and appropriate to the student's age and developmental level.

Give Feedback to All Class Members

Teachers have many students in class and must decide on the length of feedback episodes and the number of students to contact. The skill being taught may be a factor. For example, if students will learn the skill quickly, movement from student to student will ensure that no major dysfunctions are occurring. This ongoing approach allows contact with many students during the lesson. In addition, the students stay on task because they know that the teacher is moving and watching the class regularly. The drawback to this approach is that it offers little opportunity for in-depth feedback. If skills are complex and refinement is a goal, taking more time to observe students is more effective. The teacher must watch a student long enough to offer highly specific and information-loaded feedback. The result is high-quality feedback to fewer students. One way to foster this type of feedback is to have students perform activities in stations. The teacher can monitor all students yet provide individual or small-group feedback at one particular station.

TEACHING TIP

Feedback establishes the flavor of your class. Think about it—if most of the feedback you deliver throughout the day is corrective, will students want to listen to you? A positive comment can keep students on task, increase their confidence, and make them want to be around you.

Most students prefer feedback delivered to them on a one-to-one basis. Even if the feedback is positive, many students are embarrassed when feedback is delivered in front of others, who may tease them later. The bottom line is that both positive and corrective feedback should be delivered personally. Consequently, you do not have time to stand around and watch your class. Move around and interact with as many students as possible.

Avoid Scrutiny After Feedback

When giving feedback to students, avoid scrutiny of the student at the completion of your input. Students become tense if a teacher tells them how to perform a skill correctly and then watches to see if they do it exactly as instructed. Students are willing to try new ways of performing if they are allowed to practice without being closely observed by the teacher or class. In short, observe carefully, offer feedback, move to another student, and recheck progress later.

Use Peer Feedback to Increase Quality Performance

Secondary students can enhance their understanding of skill performance if they are given opportunities to serve as peer coaches (e.g., reciprocal teaching). Using peer coaches can address the large class sizes frequently seen in physical education. For example, have students work in groups of three. One person serves as the coach and focuses on a second student's skill performance, while the third person is the support player passing the ball or rebounding. During the skill performance, the peer coach focuses on the cues previously highlighted during the instructional part of the lesson and shares feedback on the strengths and weaknesses of the skill performance. Students rotate through the positions. Feedback can be both oral and written and focuses on the key points of the specific skill. Figure 5.1 shows a sample form that can be used to collect peer feedback.

Know When to Use Group or Individual Feedback

In school settings, much feedback is group oriented. The most common method is to freeze the class and offer

5

PEER FEEDBACK

Passer _____ Coach _____

Practice task: Three people—one passer, one shooter, one coach

The passer passes four balls from the top of the key by using either a bounce pass or chest pass; the coach provides the passer with feedback based on the critical elements and cues listed below. Rotate roles after four passes.

Goal: Effective layups using the correct form

Layup
Essential elements:
(Reverse for left- or right-hand layup)

1. Carry the ball with the left hand in front and under the ball.
2. Place the right hand on top and slightly behind.
3. Carry the ball to shoulder and head height as the left foot pushes off.
4. Lift the body with the right knee.
5. Direct the ball to the backboard with the right hand.
6. Place the ball against the backboard rather than throw it.
7. Follow through with the palm of the right hand high in the direction of the backboard.

Cues:
- Scoop.
- Lift (right or left leg).
- Flick to target (square on backboard).

Things my partner did well:

Things for my partner to focus on to improve the layup:

FIGURE 5.1 Example of a peer feedback form to increase quality performance.

feedback to all students. This method is the fastest, but it allows the most room for misinterpretation. Some students may not understand the feedback, whereas others may not listen because it does not seem relevant to them. Directing feedback (positive only) to a student so that the rest of the class can hear it can be effective. Feedback can thereby ripple through the class, triggering other students to pay attention to something specific they are practicing at the time. An example would be to say, "Sarah is hitting the tennis ball at its peak when she serves." Even when it is positive, be sure that feedback does not embarrass the student for whom it is intended.

In addition, feedback should focus on the desired task. For example, if students are asked to catch a batted ball in front of their body, the issue becomes clouded if the teacher offers feedback on the quality of the return throw. If catching is the focus, feedback should be on catching so that students continue to concentrate on that skill. An example of feedback in this setting would be to say, "Watch the way Michelle keeps her body in front of the ball when catching ground balls." As a final clarification, students do not need to watch other students to accomplish the desired outcome. In fact, it is effective only if the performer can show the skill correctly. If this approach is used exclusively, less skilled (or shy) performers will seldom have an opportunity to receive feedback from the class. Just as effective is telling the class how well a student is doing and then moving on, for example, by saying, "Mike always keeps his head up when dribbling."

Offer feedback to students as soon as possible after the performance. Allow opportunity for immediate practice so that students can apply the information. Little is gained and much is lost if students are told how to improve and then leave class without opportunity for practice. Few, if any, students will remember the suggestions for the next time. If the end of class is approaching, limit feedback and work on situations that can be practiced immediately. Other problems can be solved at the next class.

Consider the Personal Needs of Students

If teaching involved only presenting physical activities to students, the endeavor would be simple. The uniqueness of each student in a large class is a factor that makes teaching both complex and challenging. This section focuses on ways to make instruction meaningful and personal. Teachers who make each student feel important affect the lives of their students. Empowering students to take responsibility for their learning can be accomplished through positive interactions and acknowledgment of effort and improvement. Understanding the diversity of classes, allowing students to make educational decisions, and encouraging student creativity are some of the ways to make a lesson feel as if it was specifically designed for each student.

Teach for Diversity and Equity

Multicultural education allows all students to reach their potential regardless of the diversity among learners. Four major variables of diversity influence how teachers and students think and learn: race and ethnicity, gender, social class, and ability. Multicultural education creates an educational environment in which students from a variety of backgrounds and experience come together to experience educational equality (Manning & Baruth, 2009). Multicultural education emphasizes the contributions of various groups that make up our country and focuses on how to learn rather than on what to learn.

Current trends in growth in the United States are causing changes in classrooms. Children previously excluded from classes because of language, race, economics, and abilities are now learning together. Teaching now requires a pluralistic mindset and the ability to communicate across cultures. Educators have the responsibility to teach children to live comfortably and to prosper in this diverse and changing world. Students should celebrate their own cultures while learning to integrate into the diversity of the world. For most students, classroom interaction between teachers and students is the major part of multicultural education they will receive. Teachers can do several things to teach and value diversity.

1. Help students learn about the similarities and differences between cultures.

2. Encourage students to understand that people from similar cultures share common values, customs, and beliefs.

3. Make children aware of acts of discrimination and teach them ways to deal with inequity and prejudice.

4. Help youngsters develop pride in their family's culture.

5. Teach youngsters ways to communicate effectively with other students who are different from them.

6. Instill respect for all people regardless of race and ethnicity, gender, social class, and ability.

7. Help students understand that people learn differently.

8. Teach students strategies for dealing effectively with diverse skill levels and creating equitable experiences.

How teachers perceive students strongly influences student performance. Teachers who effectively teach for diversity hold high expectations for all students, including children and youth from ethnic minorities. Teachers tend to have lower expectations for ethnic minority youth (van den Bergh, Denessen, Hornstra, Voeten, & Holland, 2010). These low expectations occur in interpersonal interactions and in placing students in opportunities for enrichment and personal growth. At-risk youth need a rich curriculum that provides the necessary support for success.

Teachers must know and educate themselves so that they better understand the needs of all students. Diversity implies differences within and between cultures. By learning about other cultures, teachers can work with students with greater understanding of the experiences that each student has endured. When working with different cultures, the focus should be on understanding the culture and the individuals. This practice contrasts with learning about a culture and then stereotyping its members as all the same. Teachers need to gather information about cultures that are different from their own. Teachers almost always teach like they have been taught and often with inadequate knowledge about other cultures. Fuller (2001) offers several questions to answer when working with a group or culture different from one's own.

1. *What is their history?* Certainly, few teachers can become experts in the history of all cultures they teach. But they can recognize and be familiar with major events and important names within the culture.

2. *What are their important cultural values?* Different cultures interact with and discipline students in different ways. Ask parents and students how they work with children and what values are particularly important in their households.

3. *Who are influential individuals in their group?* Students identify with local people who are held in high esteem in their community. Teachers who are aware of these important people will have insight into their students by the role models they admire.

4. *What are their major religious beliefs?* Often, many values of children in a community area are driven by religious beliefs. Teachers should keep this in mind as they plan their curriculum.

5. *What are their important political beliefs?* Important political issues are often discussed at home. By trying to learn about these issues, teachers show they are interested in how their students live in their communities.

6. *What political, religious, and social days do they celebrate?* Students discuss these important days and expect teachers to understand why they celebrate them. Talking about these days with students creates goodwill and makes students feel as if their cultures are valued.

Another way to facilitate student diversity during group instruction is to vary teaching presentations. Students learn through a variety of styles. Some learn by listening, others by watching, and many others through firsthand, kinesthetic experiences. Group instruction through problem-solving (or cooperative), reciprocal (or peer), and guided discovery strategies can be used to facilitate a better understanding of diversity. Each strategy focuses on clear interactions between small groups of students to answer a question, solve a problem, or achieve a goal. Providing opportunities for students to engage in a mix of individual and interactive classroom tasks can deepen understanding of people from diverse backgrounds. Group problem solving can develop skills such as teamwork, collaboration, and a basic understanding of diverse backgrounds. Some students learn easily through auditory methods, whereas others learn better using visual means. Cooperative learning (see chapter 6) offers students the opportunity to work together toward common goals and to feel positive about the contributions of each of the members of the group. Appreciation of diversity can also be increased through discussion sessions. Using small groups or small-sided teams provides a larger number of students the opportunity to offer individual perspectives, allowing a greater array of diverse points of view. When students are involved in decision making and leadership opportunities followed by facilitated discussions, increased attention and participation in the learning process occur. The following teaching tips can help increase instructional effectiveness in a diverse setting:

- At the start of the school year (and at regular intervals thereafter), speak about the importance of individuality and respecting differences.

- When using group activities, encourage students to work with different classmates each time. Students need to get to know other students to appreciate their differences.

5

- Be aware of how you speak about different groups of students. Do you refer to all students the same way? Do you address boys and girls differently? Develop a consistent style for addressing all students regardless of their differences.

- Encourage all students to participate in discussions. Avoid allowing students from certain groups to dominate interaction. Use a random method of picking students so that all have an equal chance of contributing.

- Treat all students with respect and expect students to treat each other with dignity. Intervene if a student or group of students is dominating.

- When a difficult situation arises over an issue with undertones of diversity, take a time-out and ask students to think about their thoughts and ideas. Allow all parties time to collect their thoughts and plan a response.

- Make sure to write evaluations and grades in gender-neutral or gender-inclusive terms.

- Invite guests who represent diversity in gender, race, and ethnicity to present new activities to class, even if they are not speaking about multicultural or diversity issues.

- When students make comments that are sexist or racist, ask them to restate their ideas in a way that is not offensive to others. Teach students that it is all right to express one's opinion but not in an inflammatory manner.

- Rotate leaders when using groups. Give all students the opportunity to learn leadership skills.

- Developing a classroom environment free from inequity in diverse settings requires planning. Figure 5.2 provides you some practice in thinking about and developing specific strategies to address issues of diversity in a fair and equitable manner.

EQUITABLE LEARNING ENVIRONMENT

Instructions: Respond to the following questions and develop an inclusive list of strategies.

1. **Do I have a plan to handle negative comments based on race, gender, sexual orientation, skill abilities, or ethnic diversity?**

   Write down any comments you have heard and list possible strategies for addressing these comments that will ensure the development of a positive learning environment.

2. **Do I systematically select students to demonstrate, speak, or lead?**

   List the type of strategies you would use to ensure that all students have opportunities to interact with other students, demonstrate, express their opinions, and serve as a captain or squad leader.

3. **Do I use equitable language, pictures, activities, and instructional tools?**

   List the terms you can use to address students; develop task cards, bulletin boards, and study guides; and check selected activities for skill or gender biases.

4. **Will my interactions with students be rated as inclusive, neutral, and equitable?**

   Make audio or video recordings of your verbal interactions with students and colleagues for equity and diversity.

5. **Do I ensure that all students have an opportunity to be selected and work with different individuals on a regular basis?**

   Develop strategies that ensure that all students have several opportunities to be selected; rotate partners, teams, and individuals selected to demonstrate or lead in a way that is equitable and not based on stereotypes or gender bias.

6. **Do my teaching style, strategies, and teaching content present opportunities for all students to learn and participate equitably?**

   Identify strategies that will assess your teaching styles based on student success across diverse student populations.

FIGURE 5.2 Sample worksheet for developing an equitable learning environment in diverse settings.

Avoid Gender and Racial Biases

Teachers play a large role in how children learn to behave. Adults model gender-specific behaviors for children and youngsters who, in turn, copy the behavior. Research shows that teachers tend to treat boys and girls differently (Banks & McGee Banks, 2010). For example, teachers pay more attention to boys and give boys more encouragement. Teachers give more praise for achievement to boys and call on girls less often than they call on boys. Teachers also respond to inappropriate behavior from boys and girls in different ways. Aggression is tolerated more in boys than in girls, although disruptive talking is tolerated more in girls than in boys. Boys are reprimanded more than girls, and teachers use more physical means of disciplining boys.

The expectations that a teacher has for boys and girls strongly influence how the teacher interacts with them. These expectations are frequently based on stereotypes and social expectations. For example, teachers expect boys to be more active, more precocious, and not as good academically. As a result, they pay closer attention to them, and when they do well, they are more likely to get positive attention. Girls, on the other hand, are expected to be more reserved and to do well academically, so they tend to be overlooked when they are doing what they are supposed to do. When girls misbehave, teachers see this behavior as an aberration and are more negative to the female than they might be to the male. This pitfall is common among teachers, yet unacceptable. Overcoming these biases takes a concerted effort. Some teachers believe that girls are not able to perform physically at a level like boys, even though research shows otherwise. Particularly in elementary school, differences in strength, endurance, and physical skills are minimal. Teachers may harbor gender beliefs and expectations that directly or indirectly affect their interactions with boys and girls as well as their expectations of appropriate and inappropriate behaviors. When teachers become aware of how specific behaviors can affect students and address them in a positive and equitable manner, they can develop an effective physical education environment that helps all youngsters find success. Using the following teaching behaviors minimizes stereotyping by gender:

- Reinforce the performances of all students regardless of gender.
- Provide activities that are developmentally appropriate and allow all students to find success.
- Design programs that ensure success in coeducational experiences. Boys and girls can challenge each other to higher levels if the atmosphere is positive.

- Do not use and do not accept students' stereotypical comments such as, "You throw like a girl."
- Include activities in the curriculum that cut across typical gender stereotypes, such as rhythms are for girls and football is for boys.
- Arrange activities so the more aggressive and skilled students do not dominate. Little is learned if students are taught to be submissive or play down their abilities. Modifications may be required for certain lead-up games or activities. For instance, all students on a team must pass the ball before that team can score a point.
- Arrange practice sessions so that all students receive equal amounts of practice and opportunity to participate. Practice sessions should not give more practice opportunities to the skilled while the unskilled stand aside and observe.
- Expect that boys and girls will perform as well as they can. Teacher expectations communicate much about a student's ability level. Students view themselves through the eyes of their teacher.

Few professionals question the need for trying to improve instructional effectiveness. Most teachers want to be respected for their ability to impart knowledge and change behavior patterns of their students. University classes in teacher education strive to impart teaching skills to students. Those students who become effective instructors have one thing in common: They are motivated to improve and excel. Being motivated, however, is not enough. Motivation without proper teaching skills leaves teachers in a predicament. They want to change and grow but do not know what needs to be changed and learned. Therefore, a systematic approach for evaluating instruction is advocated so that teachers can assess when they are improving or need to improve.

Improving Teaching Skills

Teaching is learned just like any other skill. If you want to learn to play racquetball, you practice racquetball. Most people who have learned sport skills have followed the process of setting goals, diagnosing their problems, prescribing methods for improving, and evaluating their progress. This approach is needed to improve teaching skills as well. To learn to teach, a cyclical process must occur: teach, analyze the results, prescribe changes, and evaluate progress made. Listening, reading, and observing are not enough. Active participation in teaching is necessary.

The second part of improving teaching skills requires that teachers do more than teach. Many teachers have taught the same thing for years without changing. They have not incorporated new skills and ideas into their teaching methods. These teachers have become stagnant and unchanging. What if athletes never tried to change or use newly discovered techniques? Quite likely they would not remain competitive. When teachers fail to update their techniques, the public may believe they do not care about being effective.

Quality practice and improvement go hand in hand. Teachers need to evaluate their performances so that they know whether they are improving or becoming stagnant. Ask teachers you know whether they are better teachers this year as compared with last year. If they say yes, ask them to prove it. If they cannot give you anything more than a belief that they are better, you probably have found teachers who have never used the process of systematic instructional improvement.

Need for Goals and Feedback

Teachers need goals aimed at improving their teaching effectiveness. Establishing goals and not evaluating them is like driving down a highway without a map. How can you know when you have reached your goals if you do not establish some method of evaluation? Goals and feedback need to be developed concurrently. An objective way of evaluating whether teachers have improved is needed. The solution is feedback: information gathered for the purpose of modifying future responses.

Feedback about teaching can be used to guide improvement in instructional methods. Assume you have a goal of improving volleyball skills. For comparative purposes, you want to try teaching the volleyball set using a reciprocal teaching method for instruction. You allow half the class to teach a friend the set, while you teach the other half using a teacher-centered, direct style of instruction. After a week of practice, you evaluate the performance level of the volleyball set. Comparing the reciprocal style with the direct style generates feedback about the effectiveness of the method.

This example illustrates goal setting and data gathering related to instructional outcomes. Learning to collect meaningful data about teaching is necessary for improvement.

Need for Systematic Evaluation

Instruction has most often been evaluated using inexact and insensitive methods such as intuition, checklists, rating scales, and observation. Over time, these methods have proved to be relatively ineffective for improving the quality of instruction. The use of intuition relies on the expertise of a supervisor who observes the instructor, recommends changes, and reinforces the result. Improvement is difficult to identify because the evaluation process offers little or no quantification. The supervisor may forget what the quality of the first lesson was compared with the present teaching episode. In this situation, evaluating whether improvement has occurred is next to impossible.

Checklists and rating scales are used as evaluation tools and give the appearance of an objective, quantified method (see figure 5.3). Rating scales, however, can be unreliable and become more so when the number of rating points is increased. Scales and checklists are open to a wide spread of interpretation, depending on who is performing the evaluation. Most evaluations that use checklists and rating scales are subject to the impressions and opinions of the evaluator.

This lack of objectivity indicates the need for a systematic method of observing teaching effectiveness that focuses on observable and measurable behaviors by both the teacher and the student. Siedentop and Tannehill (2000) have developed several systematic methods for teacher evaluation and research. These techniques have led to increased educational research about pedagogy. The methods we are discussing are systematic in nature and feasible for self-evaluation of instructional effectiveness.

Methods described here use systematic observation for self-improvement. Lacy (2011) offers a variety of additional ideas for using systematic observation for self-improvement as a beginning or novice teacher. If the reader chooses to conduct research projects or studies and to look at this area more in depth, in addition to the Lacy text (2011), *Developing Teaching Skills in Physical Education* (Siedentop & Tannehill, 2000) is an excellent resource. This current chapter shows how systematic evaluation can be implemented in a typical school setting primarily in the simplest format.

Evaluating Effective Teaching

What should be evaluated in the teaching process? Three major areas can be observed and evaluated. The first is teacher behavior, which includes evaluation of areas such as teacher movement, instruction presentation, the praise-to-criticism ratio, use of first names, and the length of instructional and management episodes. Focus is on the performance of skills managed by the

RATING SCALE

Student _____ Activity _____ Grade _____

	5	4	3	2	1	Comments
1. Use of language						
2. Quality of voice						
3. Personal appearance						
4. Class management						
5. Presentation and teaching techniques						
6. Professional poise						
7. Enthusiasm, interest						
8. Adaptability, foresight						
9. Adequate activity						
10. Knowledge of subject						
11. Appropriate use of student help						
12. Demonstration (if any)						
13. Progression (if applicable)						
14. General organization						

General Evaluation

   5–superior

   4–above average

   3–average

   2–below average

   poor

Evaluating teacher _____

Date _____

FIGURE 5.3 Example of a rating scale.

teacher. The responsibility for performing behaviors in this category rests solely with the teacher.

The second category of observable behavior is student behavior. Examples of student behavior are the rate of deviant behavior, the amount of time that students stay on task, the number of students on task, the number of practice trials that students receive, and the amount of time that students are engaged in physical activity. These variables can be evaluated through direct observation; they link to student learning more closely than teacher behavior variables. Note that these behaviors are process

oriented; emphasis is placed on increasing or decreasing the occurrence of student behavior rather than measuring the actual performance of a skill.

The third category is student skill performance, knowledge, and attitudes toward physical activity and physical education. This category focuses primarily on the product of learning. How students learned is not the issue; *if* they learned is the concern. On the surface, this category seems to many teachers the only important evaluative area. Either students learn the skill or they do not. If they learn the skill, teachers have taught.

But things are not always so simple. Students may have learned the skills but leave physical education with a negative attitude toward activity. What would be gained if students learned skills they never wanted to use again? What about unskilled students? Can they ever find success in physical education classes?

The best evaluation system includes behavior from all three categories. Looking at teaching behavior is important. Evaluating how students respond in a class setting is also necessary. If both teachers and students are demonstrating effective behavior patterns, the evaluation of skill performance is appropriate. All three areas are interrelated, and all three need to be evaluated.

Systematically Observing to Improve Quality of Instruction

Each teacher has different strengths and weaknesses and different concerns for improvement. The approach used for systematic observation directed at self-improvement varies greatly from teacher to teacher. Instructors decide which variables they want to evaluate and determine the best way to record and monitor the data. Evaluating one area at a time is usually best. Trying to record more than one variable at a time may be frustrating and confusing. It may also confound the picture by making it difficult to decide how to change the teaching behavior in question.

After deciding which behavior needs to be changed, a plan for meaningful evaluation is developed. Identifying the behavior that affects the desired educational outcome is necessary, as is deciding which method of observation to use. A coding form is developed to facilitate recording the data. Coding sheets should be specific to each situation and suited to the teacher. Areas on the sheet can provide for recording the teacher, the date, the focus and content of the lesson, the grade level and competency of the students, the duration of the lesson, and a short description of the evaluation procedure. The sheets should be consistent for each type of behavior so that the instructor can compare progress throughout the year. Examples will be provided throughout the remainder of the chapter.

Deciding what behavior to record depends on the instructor's situation. For example, can students who are not participating gather the data? Can another teacher easily gather the data? Can the data be gathered from an audio recording, or is video necessary? Is the instructor willing to let others gather the information, or does the teacher want to keep the data confidential? These and other questions determine what areas the teacher is willing to evaluate. In most cases, the teacher

is least threatened by self-evaluation techniques and more willing to change when outside authorities do not require it. Another advantage of self-evaluation is that teaching behavior changes least when outside observers are not present. Self-evaluation techniques can better reveal actual patterns exhibited in day-to-day teaching.

At this time, what do you see as the advantages of using systematic observation compared with using traditional methods of evaluating teaching? How well do you understand these procedures? How can these procedures help you develop as a teacher or coach?

Instructional and Management Time

The educational process requires that teachers instruct. The roll-out-the-ball approach is nothing more than leisure-time activity in a school setting. Instructors need to know the amount of instruction they offer students. Instructional time refers to initial demonstrations, cues, and explanations to get students started on an activity. This time deals directly with physical education content.

Find a meaningful balance between instruction and practice. An observer can tally the number of instructional episodes and the length of each episode occurring in a daily class. Later, the average length of instruction as well as the proportion of the lesson used for instruction can be evaluated. Instructional episodes should be short and frequent with an attempt made to limit episodes to 45 seconds or less.

Effective teachers efficiently manage students. Management time is the time during which no instruction or practice is taking place. Management occurs when students are moved into various formations, when equipment is gathered or put away, and when directions are given about these tasks. It also includes taking roll, keeping records, recording fitness scores, and changing clothes.

Understanding the amount of time used for class management, and the length and number of episodes, is useful. The number of episodes and the length of each can be recorded by an observer. These data are useful for analyzing how much lesson time is devoted to the area of management. A high percentage of management time can indicate an inefficient organizational scheme or students' slow response to explanations.

How to Determine Instructional and Management Time

1. Use a simple form like figure 5.4.
2. Have a colleague or a nonparticipating student start the stopwatch every time an instructional

episode begins and stop the watch when instruction ends. Record the episode on the form, clear the watch, and be ready to time the next instructional episode. An alternative method is to record the lesson and listen to or watch the recording at the end of the day. Establish a criterion for identifying the difference between instructional and management episodes.

3. Total the amount of time spent on instruction.

4. Find the percentage of lesson time devoted to instruction by dividing the time spent on instruction by the length of the lesson. The average length of an instructional episode can be determined by dividing the total instructional time by the number of instructional episodes.

Practice and Activity Time

To learn physical skills, students must be involved in meaningful physical activity. Physical education programs deal with a finite amount of scheduled time per week. Learning is related to the amount of time that students are involved in productive, on-task activity. In a well-regarded school district, the average amount of activity time per 50-minute period was only 9 to 12 minutes. Evidence shows that teachers can significantly increase the amount of activity time for students. This component of physical education classes has been studied in many ways and with many different instruments (McKenzie, 2005).

To evaluate activity or practice time, a student or fellow teacher can observe a lesson and time the intervals when students are practicing skills. The goal is to increase the amount of time that students perform meaningful practice. A teacher could increase the amount of practice time by using more or different equipment, selecting drills that require a minimum of standing in line, or streamlining the amount of verbal instruction. Teachers can use many methods to increase and improve activity time and practice time depending on the unit and the teaching environment.

TEACHING TIP

A good rule to follow is that effective instruction does not take place without effective management. When you evaluate your teaching and think that you are not as effective as you would like to be, you might want to ask yourself a series of questions. Do I know all my students' names and use them in my instruction on a daily basis? Am I using a consistent start and stop signal? Are my directions clear and concise? Am I stuck in one area of the teaching arena, or am I moving efficiently throughout each quadrant? Is my feedback more negative than positive? Is my feedback more general rather than specific? Each of these questions can be observed and measured by one of the systematic evaluation tools discussed in this chapter. Try several of the tools and see how you fare. Set yourself a goal for the future and try to improve every day.

INSTRUCTIONAL AND MANAGEMENT TIME

Teacher _____ Date _____ Grade and period _____

School _____ Activity _____

Activity: 50% or more of students engaged in movement activity or practice

Management, organization, or instruction: time when fewer than 50% of students are moving

Instructions: Write start time and stop time of observation period. Start the stopwatch for activity. Stop during management, organization, or instruction. Repeat for the duration of the lesson.

Start time _____

Stop time _____

Total class time (in minutes) _____

Total activity time (in minutes) _____

Divide total activity time by total class time (percentage) _____

Remarks:

FIGURE 5.4 Sample form for instructional and management time.

Instructional Feedback

The feedback that teachers offer to students influences instructional effectiveness. Instructors can analyze their interaction patterns and set meaningful goals for improvement. Few teachers enter the profession with the ability to communicate with clarity. The process of changing communication behaviors can create discomfort and concern but will ultimately pay rewarding dividends. Evaluation in the following areas can create improvement in feedback delivery.

Praise and Criticism

When students are involved in activity, teachers deliver feedback dealing with student performance. This feedback can be positive and constructive, or negative and critical. Measuring the occurrences of praise and criticism is easy. The occurrences can be tallied and evaluated at the end of the day. Calculate the number of instances and the ratio of positive-to-negative comments. Using these data, begin to set goals for increasing the number of comments per minute and modifying the ratio of positive-to-negative comments. A teacher can expect to average one to two comments per minute with a positive-to-negative ratio of three or four to one.

General Versus Specific Feedback

Feedback given to students can be specific or general. Comments like "Good job," "Way to go," and "Cut that out" are general in nature. General feedback can be either negative or positive and does not specify the behavior being reinforced. In contrast, specific feedback identifies the student by name, mentions the behavior being reinforced, and can be accompanied by a valuing statement.

TEACHING TIP

An example of using specific feedback correctly might be to say, "Ron, excellent job of keeping your elbows straight and your thumbs turned down on that forearm pass. Near perfect form." Notice the student name, the behavior being reinforced, and the valuing statement. Hilda Fronske's popular text (2012) includes instructional cues for a variety of sport skills. Teachers can teach the skills using these cues and then use the same language for providing specific feedback.

To evaluate this area, teachers can tally the number of instances of general and specific feedback. The type of feedback—negative or positive—can also be counted. Using first names personalizes the feedback and directs it to the right person. Total the number of times that first names are used. The number of valuing statements can also be monitored. Divide the totals in all the categories by the length of the lesson (in minutes) to render a rate per minute. Figure 5.5 is an example of a form that can be used to tally the feedback behaviors described in this section.

Positive feedback should be specific whenever possible so that students know exactly what it was they did well. An instructor might say, "Your throw to second base was exactly where it should have been!" This type of feedback creates a positive feeling in a class. Sometimes, however, teachers use this type of feedback to such an extent that it becomes a habitual form of communication (e.g., "Good job, nice serve."). These comments do not identify specific desirable behavior, and students may ignore them. In addition, an undesirable behavior may be reinforced when feedback is general.

Corrective Instructional Feedback

Effective teachers coach students to higher levels of performance by giving performers meaningful corrective feedback. Corrective feedback focuses on improving the performance of the participant. Teachers should ignore poor performances if students are already aware of them. Corrective instructional feedback is specific whenever possible so that performers know what it is they must correct. An example of corrective instructional feedback might be to say, "Your throw to second base was too far to the left of the base! Try to throw the ball directly over the base." This type of feedback tells the student what was incorrect about the skill attempt and how the skill should be performed.

Nonverbal Feedback

Much performance feedback can be given nonverbally. This from of feedback is certainly meaningful to students and may be more effective than verbal forms of communication. Examples of nonverbal feedback that could occur after a desired performance are a pat on the back, a wink, a smile, a nod of the head, the thumbs-up sign, and clapping the hands. Nonverbal feedback can also be negative: frowning, shaking the head in disapproval, walking away from a student, or laughing at a poor performance.

Tallying the number of positive and negative nonverbal behaviors exhibited by a teacher is possible. A student

INSTRUCTIONAL FEEDBACK

Teacher _____ Observer _____

Class _____ Grade _____ Date and time _____

Lesson focus _____ Comments _____

Starting time _____ End time _____ Length of lesson _____

Interactions unrelated to skill performance	+							
	−							
General instructional feedback	+							
	−							
Specific positive instructional feedback								
Corrective instructional feedback								
First names								
Nonverbal feedback	+							
	−							

Ratio + to −, nonskill related _____

Ratio + to −, skill related _____

FIGURE 5.5 Sample form for tallying feedback behaviors.

or another instructor can do the tallying. Students may be better at evaluating the instructor in this domain because they are aware of what each of the instructor's mannerisms means.

Active Supervision and Student Contact

Contact and active supervision are important in maintaining students' involvement with learning tasks (van der Mars, Vogler, Darst, & Cusimano, 1994). Contact means moving among and offering personalized information feedback to the students. To evaluate student contact, count the number of times that an instructor interacts with a student. This type of feedback differs from total class interaction and demands that the instructor have keen insight into each student's behavior and needs.

Related to this area is teacher movement and supervision. Instructors often have an area in the gymnasium where they feel comfortable teaching. Before instruction begins, the teacher moves back to this area. The teacher's

movement pattern causes students to drift to different areas, depending on their feeling about the activity or the instructor. Students who like the instructor will usually move closer, whereas students who dislike the teacher or are uneasy about the activity may move away from the teacher or to an area where they are less visible. In this configuration, competent performers are near the instructor and students who are deviant or less competent move away and become difficult to observe.

Another measure is the amount of time that a teacher stays in a quadrant. Teachers should try to spend the same amount of time in each teaching quadrant. The length of time can be recorded on the form in relationship to where the teacher stands. At the end of the lesson, analyze the amount of time spent in each quadrant. Recording can be difficult if the teacher is an active mover and does not stay in the same quadrant for long.

Another suggested technique is to code the type of teacher behavior that occurs each time the instructor moves into a new quadrant. For example, an "M" might signify management activity, an "I" might indicate instructional activity with the entire class, and a "P" might stand for practice time interactions with individual students. This tally reveals the number of these three types of instructor interactions with students and the location of the teacher when conducting the different types of interactions.

How to Quantify Active Supervision and Student Contact

1. Develop a coding form like the one in figure 5.6.
2. Ask a nonparticipating student or a colleague to record the lesson so that you can evaluate it later.
3. Evaluate the data by calculating the number of moves per lesson and the number of moves that involved instruction, management, and practice interactions.

You should now see how these beginning techniques and forms can help teachers self-analyze their teaching situations. For example, a kickboxing teacher using the health club model can look at the students in his or her class and determine how many use the proper form for jabs and kicks during the lesson focus. These techniques can be used with both large and small classes. These techniques are valuable to teachers from middle school through high school. All teachers should look critically

TEACHER MOVEMENT

Teacher Danny Marcello Observer Ken Coyle

Class 5th period Grade 9 Date and time 3/17, 1:05

Lesson focus Volleyball Comments

Starting time 1:15 End time 2:01 Length of lesson 46 min

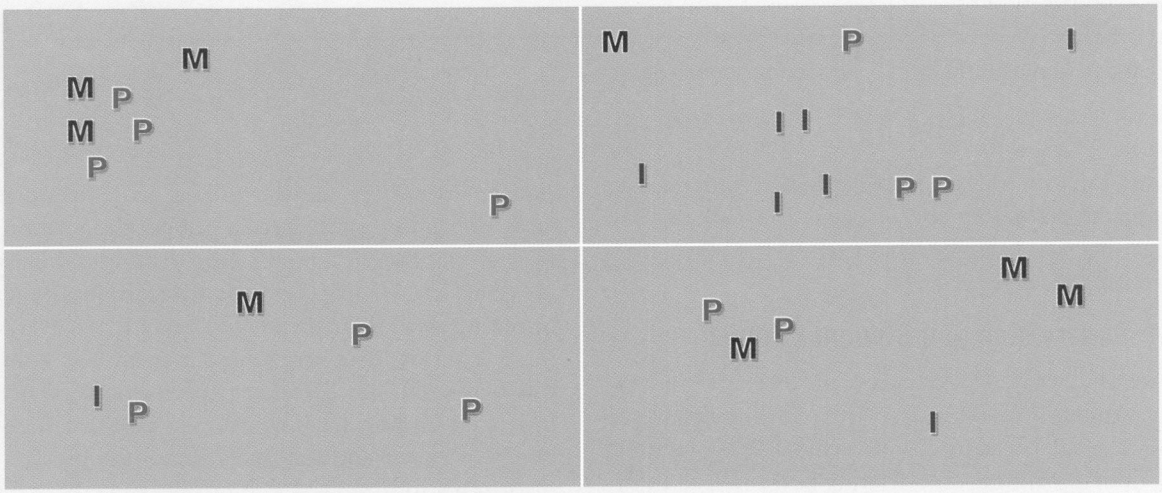

M = management activity, I = instructional activity, P = practice time.

Total number of moves 28

Number of moves (I) 8 (M) 8 (P) 12

Average number of moves per min. 6

FIGURE 5.6 Sample form for recording active supervision and student contact.

at their teaching techniques and the way they organize their classes. They can then practice seeing how students are doing with the skills. There are many ways to improve the learning environment for all participants.

A Popular Rubric for Evaluating Teachers in All Subject Areas

Many districts and states have moved to Charlotte Danielson's rubric-based teacher evaluation for all subject areas based on her text *Enhancing Professional Practice: A Framework for Teaching, 2nd edition* (2007). Many principals, physical education directors, athletic directors, and assistant principals have been trained in using the rubrics in her text that measure the four domains to evaluate their teachers. The domains include planning and preparation, the classroom environment, instruction, and professional responsibilities. The rubrics provide four levels of performance and are labeled unsatisfactory, basic, proficient, and distinguished.

Using this evaluation requires the administrators to script each teacher's lesson. This information is then entered into a computer program to determine the level of performance under each category. These rubrics have now become popular for assessment.

Most people consider good teaching to be good teaching regardless of subject matter. As you look at the rubrics of Charlotte Danielson, planning and preparation is critical for teacher effectiveness regardless of your area of expertise, whether math, science, English, or physical education. Classroom environment, instruction, and professional responsibilities are inherent to high-quality learning environments. Most people would agree that these four domains cross all subject areas. As a future professional, what do you think?

5

LEARNING AIDS

STUDY STIMULATORS AND REVIEW QUESTIONS

1. Describe the types of behaviors that teachers exhibit when they actively supervise their students.
2. Discuss the importance of developing a plan for actively supervising students.
3. Discuss the strategies available to teachers to manage the need to individualize instruction.
4. List and briefly explain four ways in which good teacher-to-student communication can be undermined.
5. Discuss the importance of teachers matching their nonverbal expressions with their words.
6. What are the problems of overusing corrective feedback?
7. Discuss the teacher's dilemma between attending to all students and providing in-depth feedback to individual students.
8. Discuss the influence of teachers' perceptions regarding cultural and ethnic differences on their ability to be successful at teaching diverse groups of students.
9. Discuss the stages involved in the systematic process of improving your teaching skills.
10. Why do the authors advocate that teachers engage in self-evaluation as opposed to assessment only by a principal?

WEBSITES

Teacher Effectiveness

www.inclusiveeducation.ca
www.shapeamerica.org/events/upload/20-Indicators-Brochure-WEB-003-2.pdf

Assessment Ideas

www.pecentral.org/assessment/assessment.html
www.ascd.org

Physical Education General Information and Assessment Ideas

www.pecentral.org
www.pelinks4u.org/index.htm

SHAPE America: Teacher's Toolbox

www.shapeamerica.org/publications/resources/teachingtools/teachertoolbox/Teachers_Toolbox.aspx

REFERENCES AND SUGGESTED READINGS

Banks, J.A. (2009). *Teaching strategies for ethnic studies* (8th ed.). Boston, MA: Allyn & Bacon.

Banks, J.A., & McGee Banks, C.A., Eds. (2010). *Multicultural education issues and perspectives* (7th ed.). Hoboken, NJ: Wiley.

Bennett, C.L. (2011). *Comprehensive multicultural education: Theory and practice* (7th ed.). Boston, MA: Allyn & Bacon.

Buck, M.M., Lund, J.L., Harrison, J.M., & Blakemore Cook, C.L. (2007). *Instructional strategies for secondary physical education* (6th ed.). Boston, MA: McGraw-Hill.

Cushner, K.H. (2006). *Human diversity in action: Developing multicultural competencies for the classroom* (3rd ed.). Boston, MA: McGraw-Hill.

Danielson, C. (2007). *Enhancing professional practice: A framework for teaching* (2nd ed.). Alexandria, VA: ASCD.

Darst, P.W., Zakrajsek, D.B., & Mancini, V.H. (Eds.). (1989). *Analyzing physical education and sport instruction* (2nd ed.). Champaign, IL: Human Kinetics.

Fronske, H. (2012). *Teaching cues for sport skills for secondary school students* (5th ed.). Boston, MA: Benjamin Cummings Pearson.

Fronske, H., & Wilson, R. (2002). *Teaching cues for basic sport skills for elementary and middle school students.* San Francisco, CA: Benjamin Cummings.

Fuller, M.L. (2001). Multicultural concerns and classroom management. In C.A. Grant & M.L. Gomez. *Campus and classroom: Making schooling multicultural* (pp. 109–134). Upper Saddle River, NJ: Prentice Hall.

Koppelman, K., & Goodhart, L. (2008). *Understanding human differences: Multicultural education for a diverse America* (2nd ed). Boston, MA: Allyn & Bacon.

Lacy, A (2011). *Measurement and evaluation in physical education and exercise science* (6th ed.). San Francisco, CA: Benjamin Cummins.

Lacy, A., & Darst, P. (1989). The Arizona State University Observation Instrument (ASUOI). In P.W. Darst, D.B. Zakrajsek, & V.H. Mancini (Eds.), *Analyzing physical education and sport instruction* (2nd ed., pp. 369–377). Champaign, IL: Human Kinetics.

Manning, M.L., & Baruth, L.G. (2009). *Multicultural education of children and adolescents* (5th ed.). Boston, MA: Allyn & Bacon.

McKenzie, T.L. (2005). *System for Observing Fitness Instruction Time (SOFIT) procedures manual.* Unpublished manuscript, San Diego State University.

Pang, V.O. (2005). *Multicultural education: A caring-centered, reflective approach* (2nd ed.). Boston. MA: McGraw-Hill.

Pangrazi, R.P. (2010). *Dynamic physical education for elementary school children* (16th ed.). San Francisco, CA: Benjamin Cummings.

Rink, J.E. (2010). *Teaching physical education for learning* (6th ed.). Boston. MA: McGraw-Hill.

Schmidt, R.A., & Wrisberg, C. (2008). *Motor learning and performance* (4th ed.). Champaign, IL: Human Kinetics.

Siedentop, D., & Tannehill, D. (2000). *Developing teaching skills in physical education* (4th ed.). Mountain View, CA: Mayfield.

Tiedt, P.L., & Tiedt, I.M. (2010). *Multicultural teaching: A handbook of activities, information, and resources* (8th ed.). Boston, MA: Allyn & Bacon.

van den Bergh, L., Denessen, E., Hornstra, L., Voeten, M., & Holland, R.W. (2010). The implicit prejudiced attitudes of teachers: Relations to teacher expectations and the ethnic achievement gap. *American Educational Research Journal, 47,* 497–527.

van der Mars, H. (2007). Instructional analysis forms. Unpublished materials. Arizona State University-Polytechnic, Mesa, Arizona.

van der Mars, H., Vogler, W., Darst, P., & Cusimano, B. (1994). Active supervision patterns of physical education teachers and their relationship with student behavior. *Journal of Teaching in Physical Education, 14*(1), 99–112.

Wardle, F., & Cruz-Janzen, M.I. (2004). *Meeting the needs of multiethnic and multiracial children in schools.* Boston, MA: Allyn & Bacon.

Welk, G. (2002). *Physical activity assessments for health-related research.* Champaign, IL: Human Kinetics.

Teaching Styles

The purpose of this chapter is to explore the variety of instructional styles that exist and how they can be used to enhance instruction. No one style is best for all situations. Each style has advantages that will be effective depending on the type of students, specific activities, and desired objectives. The teaching styles covered in this chapter include the direct style, task (station) style, mastery learning style, individualized style, cooperative learning style, and inquiry style. Mounting evidence from research on teacher effectiveness indicates that many teaching styles can be effective if certain characteristics are present in the teaching situation.

Learning Objectives

▶ Discuss the specific areas where an instructional style provides direction for the teacher.
▶ Plan and teach an appropriate secondary school physical education lesson using each teaching style discussed.
▶ Describe the advantages and disadvantages of each teaching style.
▶ Give examples that illustrate when a particular teaching style should be used.
▶ Discuss the reasons why a physical education teacher should be able to use a variety of instructional strategies.

A teaching style is an instructional strategy used to organize the educational environment. Using a particular style of teaching provides direction for presenting information, organizing practice, providing feedback, keeping students engaged in appropriate behavior, and monitoring progress toward selected goals or objectives. Teaching styles are defined in terms of the teacher's planning and setup of the environment, the teacher's approach during the lesson, the students' responsibilities during the lesson, and expected student learning outcomes.

Various teaching styles and models have been used successfully in secondary school physical education classes (Mosston & Ashworth, 2008; Metzler, 2011; Rink, 2014; Siedentop & Tannehill, 2000).

No single teaching style is universally the best. Professionals label and categorize styles in many ways. Many of the labels overlap and can be confusing to the beginning teacher. Even though educators endorse their favorite approach, evidence does not suggest that one style is more effective than another. Being able to teach with a repertoire of styles that can be used with different objectives, students, activities, facilities, and equipment is the mark of a master teacher. In addition, a teacher may decide to combine various styles during one unit or even one lesson (see the section Sport Education Approach in chapter 2). Making the most appropriate choice of teaching styles is a crucial decision that should be given much thought. The following variables must be considered to select an appropriate style:

- Specific student learning outcomes based on state and district standards, as well as daily objectives of the lesson, such as physical skills, physical fitness, knowledge, and social behaviors
- The nature of the activities involved such as tennis, weight training, swimming, or fencing
- The nature of students, including individual characteristics, interests, developmental level, motivation, and background

- The total number of students in the class
- The equipment and facilities available such as tennis rackets and courts
- The abilities, skills, and comfort zone of the teacher

Instructional effectiveness is enhanced by the selection and implementation of various teaching styles. Both teachers and students maintain interest and enthusiasm when a variety of styles are used. Too often, a single favorite teaching style becomes the norm. The use of a different teaching style in a particular setting may improve the learning environment for students and teachers. A new or modified teaching style is not a panacea for all the ills of every school environment or setting, and a teaching style is not selected without considering all variables. Different styles do, however, offer advantages in certain situations. A teacher who has developed a quality instructional program can keep the program exciting by implementing various teaching styles.

Teachers can use combinations of styles in a lesson or unit plan; they do not have to adopt just one style at a time. Mosston's continuum of teaching styles (Mosston & Ashworth, 2008) identifies a teacher-centered approach at one end of the spectrum and a student-centered approach at the other. A continuum of teaching styles based on the degree of teacher control exercised in a lesson is shown in figure 6.1. Although the continuum appears to work in a linear direction, in which the teacher controls learning at one end and the student at the other, each of the teaching styles is designed to enhance the learning of all students. A lesson using a particular teaching style or one that uses multiple styles must have student learning outcomes as its end product. Remember that students are the key participants and recipients of each style.

Direct instruction, as a teaching style, is probably the most common approach used in the secondary schools. It

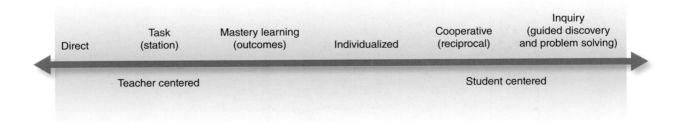

FIGURE 6.1 Continuum of teaching styles.

is teacher centered and can be effective, depending on the learning outcomes to be accomplished and the manner of its implementation. The task style of instruction involves selecting and arranging tasks for students to practice in specific learning areas called stations. Students usually rotate through each learning area in small groups and work on the preselected tasks. The mastery learning style takes terminal target skills and divides them into progressive subskills. Individualized styles of teaching use learning packets, resource centers, and self-paced learning activities. Cooperative learning places students in groups with common goals. Students depend on one another to achieve group goals. The inquiry model of instruction focuses on the process of instruction rather than the product of instruction. Students are placed in situations where they must inquire, speculate, reflect, analyze, and discover. Guided discovery is an inquiry style of instruction in which the teacher leads students to discover one planned solution to a given problem. Problem solving is another inquiry style. With this style, students move to the discovery of multiple correct answers to a problem.

Direct Instruction Style

The **direct instruction style** is looked on with disfavor by some teachers because they identify it with Mosston and Ashworth's (2008) command style, in which all actions performed by students are commanded by a teacher signal or demonstration. The direct teaching style, however, has more flexibility and variations than the command style. The direct teaching style, like any other type of instruction, can be effective or ineffective depending on how it is used and administered. It is effective for teaching beginning levels of physical skills and fitness activities such as aerobic routines and martial arts. When activities present an inherent hazard or danger, such as fencing, archery, or rock climbing, instruction needs to be well organized and activities highly supervised. The teacher is responsible for directing all learning outcomes and facilitating the timing and selection within each lesson. Students are given little freedom until they understand the hazards and demonstrate responsibility. The direct style may also be effective in situations where student discipline is a problem. Because the teacher controls student activities, this style offers greater control and class management. For a beginning teacher with new students, large classes, or high rates of inappropriate student behavior, the direct style is an excellent choice until he or she becomes more familiar with the classes.

When using this teaching style, the teacher provides instruction to either the entire class or small groups, guiding the pace and direction of the class. Direct instruction is followed by guided practice so that errors can be corrected. Guided practice is then followed by independent practice that is supervised by an actively involved teacher. Students spend most of class time engaged in appropriate subject matter. Specific learning outcomes are communicated to students, and much time is devoted to practice while the teacher actively supervises and provides frequent feedback. Even though instruction is direct, it should be conducted in a positive and supportive manner.

A common model of direct teaching begins with the teacher explaining and demonstrating skills to be developed. Students are organized into partners, small groups, or squads for practice. As students practice, the teacher moves around the area, correcting errors, praising, encouraging, and asking questions. On the signal to stop, students gather around the teacher for evaluative comments and a redirection toward another skill. The teacher serves as the major demonstrator, lecturer, motivator, organizer, disciplinarian, director, and error corrector.

A direct teaching style emphasizes instruction in a controlled class environment that ensures safety. Although the teacher is in direct control of the learning outcomes and pace of the activities, emphasis is placed on minimizing the amount of time students passively watch, listen to a lecture or demonstration, or wait in line. Learning for all students must be an impending result of the direct teaching style. Students need to be active, participate at a high level of success, and experience a variety of practice opportunities that support learning outcomes. Higher-skilled and lower-skilled students are hindered when learning activities are too easy and unchallenging or too difficult, resulting in repeated failure. Teachers need to offer enough options to cover various ability levels. Direct instruction provides limited opportunities for student choice, social interaction, and self-pacing.

Task (Station) Style

Student skill levels differ widely in physical education classes. This range of ability must be addressed if students are to achieve a high level of success. To offer opportunities for success, the **task (station) style** of teaching provides students with challenging yet appropriate tasks. When teachers encounter large classes, the task style provides multiple activity areas and addresses the problem of minimal equipment and supplies.

Task-style teaching focuses on arranging and presenting learning tasks at several learning areas or stations. Students rotate between learning stations to work on assigned tasks. At each station, students have several tasks to learn and practice. They work on the tasks without specific teacher directions. Preset time intervals controlled by the teacher or music can signal students to move from one station to another. For example, students may be given five minutes to work at stations that have four or five predetermined tasks. A cue (music stopping) or signal (whistle) to rotate to a new station is given after time has elapsed. An option is to allow students to pace themselves and monitor their progress. Providing students with task sheets containing a series of activities and variations based on difficulty is a means of developing ownership of learning. Students complete the tasks selected and continue to another station.

This style offers more freedom compared with the direct approach because students work individually on the tasks. Student accountability and ownership of learning can be developed through the task style. Worksheets, content development, and peer coaching can be integrated at each station (see figure 6.2).

Some teachers are uncomfortable with the task style because it appears to offer less order and control compared with direct instruction. Visually, the task style appears more chaotic because students are engaging in a variety of activities at the same time. With proper planning, organization, and supervision, however, teachers can effectively order and manage the environment. In fact, a well-organized lesson relieves the teacher of some organizational duties during in-class participation. Task-style teaching is motivating to students because of the variety and levels of learning tasks. Having multiple tasks representing low to high levels of challenges at each station provides opportunities for students to select activities that match their comfort zones. Middle and high school students enjoy opportunities to select activities and demonstrate learning to others. Students have opportunities to be responsible for learning. They

---

BASEBALL OR SOFTBALL SKILL STATION

1. Fielding Ground Balls

a. One partner rolls or hits, and the other fields the ball. They switch after the allotted time. Distance increases as the fielder becomes highly successful.

b. The hitting partner also assesses the fielder based on the critical elements listed below and uses the cues to assist the partner.

Critical Elements

a. Position the feet so that the body is centered toward the incoming ball.

b. Lower the hips to position the glove to the ground.

c. Focus the eyes on the ball and place the throwing hand over the mitt and in position to trap the incoming ball.

d. Extend the arm with the mitt and follow (with the eyes) the ball into the mitt.

Cues for Feedback

a. Center the ball.

b. Keep hips down.

c. Watch the ball into your hand.

Partner Assessment

1. Where were most of the mistakes made?

2. What area needs to improve?

3. What can you do to help your partner improve?

FIGURE 6.2 Example of a task-style worksheet for baseball or softball skill stations.

(continued)

2. Leading Off and Stealing a Base

    a. One player acts as the pitcher, while the other takes a lead from first base. The base runner must "read" the pitcher to get a good start. The pitcher watches the runner to assess performance based on the critical elements listed below. Feedback is given using the specified cues. Switch positions after the allotted time.

Critical Elements

    a. Begin in a comfortable ready position with the feet shoulder-width apart and both knees bent. Place hands out in front of the chest with the arms slightly bent.

    b. First, swing the arms. Swing the left arm toward the desired base and pump back the right arm.

    c. Simultaneously plant the left foot and thrust the right foot forward.

    d. Keep the body low and the knees bent while initiating the first explosive movements toward the base.

Cues for Feedback

    a. Bend the knees; keep the feet wide.

    b. Explode toward the other base, out not up.

    c. Drive forward using the arms.

Partner Assessment

    1. Were the knees bent?

    2. Did your partner stay loose and in a ready position?

    3. Did your partner swing his or her arms and stay low through the first steps of stealing (explode)?

    4. Give suggestions for two specific areas.

3. Throwing to a Target (Second to First)

    a. Two players practice throwing from a second-base position to first base. Distance is extended after five successfully completed throws.

    b. A third player begins the task by throwing a grounder from home plate to the second-base person, throwing to the first-base side. After five successful completions players rotate from first base, to home plate, to second base.

Critical Elements

    a. Gather the ball as in the fielding task. Pivot and step with the nondominant foot toward the target and aim at the desired target.

    b. Extend the arm, releasing the ball.

    c. After releasing the ball, follow through by allowing the arm to swing freely.

Cues for Feedback

    a. Gather.

    b. Step.

    c. Extend.

    d. Follow through.

Partner Assessment

    1. Did he or she step toward the target?

    2. Was the throw on the line?

    3. Did he or she follow through?

    4. Where did most of the throws end up and why?

FIGURE 6.2 *(continued)*

often need time to adjust to the increased freedom, flexibility, and opportunities to make decisions, but the result is better self-management skills. The task style is flexible in terms of its use across the curriculum. This style can be used for aspects of skill development, fitness engagement, social interactions, and cognitive learning. Design, planning, and implementation of appropriate task stations are the only aspects that limit the use of this style.

This instructional style allows teachers to move off center stage and away from being the central figure in the instructional process because students assume more responsibility. Teachers become agents of feedback and facilitate learning by visiting various learning stations and interacting with students who need help with tasks. Predetermined cues become the focus of the feedback

and interactions. Less time is spent directing and managing the entire group, and more time is focused on learning. This approach does require preparation time to plan and design tasks that meet the needs of all students. Tasks must be designed that provide all students with a high level of success and accountability. During the lesson, teachers may need to use strong supervision and active movement skills to facilitate on-task behavior and learning at all the stations. Teachers who stand in one spot or move in ways that keep them from seeing all their students may encourage off-task behavior. Adequate facilities, equipment, and instructional devices are necessary to keep students productive and working on appropriate tasks. Consider the following guidelines when selecting, writing, and presenting tasks for secondary school physical education classes:

Dribbling Tasks (What to Do)

1. Standing—right and left hand—25 times
2. Half speed—right and left hand—baseline to midcourt
3. Full speed—right and left hand—baseline to midcourt
4. Around the cones—25 seconds

Dribbling Cues (How to Do)

Fingertips
Lower center of gravity
Opposite hand in front
Eyes on opponents

Ballhandling (What to Do)

1. Around head—left and right—5 times each
2. Around waist—left and right—5 times each
3. Around each leg—left and right—5 times each
4. Figure eight around legs—10 times
5. Hand switch between legs—10 times
6. Bounce between legs and switch—10 times

Jump Shots (What to Do)

1. 3 feet (1 m) away—right angle, center, left angle
2. 9 feet (3 m) away—right angle, center, left angle
3. 15 feet (5 m) away—right angle, center, left angle
4. 20 feet (6 m) away—right angle, center, left angle
5. Follow-through

Jump-Shot Cues (How to Do)

Straight-up jump
Wrist position
Elbow position
Slight backspin on ball

Passing Skills (What to Do)

Strike the target from 8 feet (2.5 m), 10 feet (3 m), 12 feet (4 m), 15 feet (5 m)

1. Chest—10 times
2. Bounce—10 times
3. Overhead—10 times
4. One hand overhead (baseball)—10 times

Passing Cues (How to Do)

Use your peripheral vision—do not telegraph
Step toward target
Transfer your weight to the front foot
Aim for the numbers

FIGURE 6.3 Sample basketball tasks.

- Select tasks that cover the basic skills of an activity.
- Select tasks that provide students with success and challenge. Tasks should be designed for the appropriate ability range of the students. High-skilled students should be challenged, and the low-skilled students should be successful.
- Avoid tasks that demand excessive risk and possible injury.
- Post task cards on the wall or strap them to boundary cones. An alternative is to give students a copy of the tasks on a sheet of paper that they carry from station to station. Task sheets can be maintained by students and taken home for practice after school.
- Write the tasks so that they are easy to comprehend. Use keywords or phrases that students have learned previously. Effective task descriptions using words explain what to do and how to do it (see figure 6.3). It is helpful if you can add photos or drawings of correct skill execution to the sheet with the descriptions. Perform regular visual checks to see if students understand the tasks and are able to practice unsupervised. In situations where there are reading or language barriers, pictures or symbols can clarify the tasks that students are to perform.
- Incorporate a combination of instructional devices that add feedback, variety, and challenge to the environment. Examples of such devices include targets, cones, hoops, ropes, and stopwatches.
- Include individual or peer assessment sheets to increase accountability and student learning (see figure 6.4).

6

PEER FEEDBACK

Passer _____ Coach _____

Practice task: Three people—one passer, one shooter, one coach

The passer passes four balls from the top of the key using either a bounce pass or a chest pass. The coach provides the passer with feedback. Rotate roles after four passes.

Goal: Effective layups using the correct form

Layup
Essential elements:
(Reverse for left- or right-hand layup)

1. Carry the ball with the left hand in front and under the ball.
2. Place the right hand on top and slightly behind.
3. Carry the ball to shoulder and head height as the left foot pushes off.
4. Lift the body with the right knee.
5. Direct the ball to the backboard with the right hand.
6. Place the ball against backboard rather than throw it.
7. Follow through with the palm of the right hand high in the direction of the backboard.

Cues
- Scoop.
- Lift (right or left leg).
- Flick to target (square on backboard).

Things my partner did well:

Things for my partner to focus on to help improve the layup:

FIGURE 6.4 Sample peer assessment basketball layup.

Task-style instruction allows students to work alone, with a partner, or in a small group. Partner or reciprocal groups are useful with large classes, limited amounts of equipment, and with activities in which a partner is needed to time, count, record, or analyze the skill work. For example, one student can dribble through a set of cones while the other is timing and recording. In a group of three students, one student might bump a volleyball against the wall while another analyzes the form with a checklist and the third records the performance. Being able to work on tasks with a partner or friend is a form of cooperative learning. To allow students to find success and challenge, arrange tasks by offering a progressive arrangement of experiences, from simple to complex. Allow students to progress at their own speed through the activities, challenging themselves by choice. As they build a backlog of success, make learning activities more challenging.

Consider an example of this instructional approach using learning stations for soccer: The soccer field practice area is arranged with four learning stations and learning outcomes written on a card at each station. Students spend three to five minutes working on the activities designed to achieve the outcomes at each station. Upon completion, they rotate to the next station. Station activities are arranged so that students experience success quickly and frequently at first and then are challenged by later tasks. Student learning outcomes can be changed daily or repeated, depending on the how the class progresses. Points earned through successful completion of the learning outcomes can be used to signal a degree of competency in the area.

Mastery Learning (Outcomes-Based) Style

Mastery learning (outcomes-based) style is an instructional strategy that breaks down a complex skill (terminal outcome) into a series of smaller and progressive subskills. The assumption is that when students learn the subskills, the desired terminal outcome is reached. Each of the subskills becomes the focus of learning. Subskills are usually written as objectives that must be mastered to achieve the target outcome. Subskills must be mastered at a high level of success (usually 80 to 90% correct) and contain all the critical elements, as determined by the cues, before students attempt more complicated tasks (see figure 6.5).

Complexity of the skill determines the number of subskills. If mastery is not achieved, corrective activities

are offered so that students have the opportunity to learn from alternative materials, peer tutoring, or any type of learning activity that meets personal preferences. For an in-depth discussion of mastery learning, see Lawrence, Lawrence, and Samek (2006).

Mastery learning as an instructional strategy is useful in several ways. First, students move at an individualized pace and master preliminary skills needed for the desired learning outcome. This style is well suited for students who may require extra time and practice on certain skills. It also provides homework, when necessary, enabling students to work during their spare time on areas needing improvement. Mastery learning can be outlined as follows:

1. The target skill or outcome is divided into sequenced, progressive units.

2. Prerequisite competency is evaluated.

3. Performance objectives for each of the successive learning units are established.

4. The performer can do informal progress testing to determine readiness for more formal testing by the teacher or a peer (see figure 6.6).

5. When a student has determined readiness, testing by the teacher determines pass or fail for a particular subskill. A student who passes the task moves up to the next learning outcome.

6. If the student is unable to pass the subskill, practice continues, incorporating alternative or corrective measures designed by both the teacher and student.

A mastery learning breakdown for soccer skills follows. Proficiency with the skill and the ability to use the skills successfully in a modified soccer game are target outcomes. Accomplishing the outcomes ensures that students have a basic level of competency in dribbling, trapping, kicking, heading, and making throw-ins.

Dribbling Tasks

1. Dribble the soccer ball under control 20 yards (m) three consecutive times, keeping the ball within a running stride with each foot touch.

2. Dribble the soccer ball under control against a shadow defender 30 yards (m) while jogging or running.

3. With a partner, pass the soccer ball back and forth under control while in a running motion for 50 yards (m) two consecutive times. Maintain control by keeping the ball between your knee

MASTERY LEARNING OUTCOMES-BASED

Hockey

Slap Shot Practice

- Work in pairs to develop skill (must receive the pass from your partner) after you know how to perform a slap shot correctly. Practice the slap shot, focusing on the cues and checking that you are performing the shot according to the cues listed later.

- Each performer must have proficiency in the skill before he or she moves on to the higher-level assessments listed later.

- Each of you takes turns being the coach or teacher, and the performer suggests to you when he or she is ready to move to the next level based on success rate of both the skill performance and the outcome of the performance.

- If the performer does not complete each level of the assessment at the minimum standard, she or he must stay with that level and continue to practice until criteria are successfully met.

Slap Shot Assessment (Use Spots to Mark the Appropriate Distances)

- From 6 feet (1.8 m) away, right angle, center, left angle, three out of four times, receive pass from partner, and shoot between cones.

- From 12 feet (4 m) away, right, center, and left, four out of six times, receive pass from partner.

Cues: One hand high, one hand low, elbow at right angle (on take back), puck low and fast—extend to waist

FIGURE 6.5 Sample mastery learning outcomes-based worksheet for hockey.

TENNIS READINESS

	Yes	No	Percentage correct
Ready position			
Hips to net	1 2 3 4 5 6 7 8 9 10	1 2 3 4 5 6 7 8 9 10	
Racket between belly button and chest	1 2 3 4 5 6 7 8 9 10	1 2 3 4 5 6 7 8 9 10	
Medium body posture	1 2 3 4 5 6 7 8 9 10	1 2 3 4 5 6 7 8 9 10	
Execution			
Racket taken back	1 2 3 4 5 6 7 8 9 10	1 2 3 4 5 6 7 8 9 10	
Feet to the ball	1 2 3 4 5 6 7 8 9 10	1 2 3 4 5 6 7 8 9 10	
Swing low to high	1 2 3 4 5 6 7 8 9 10	1 2 3 4 5 6 7 8 9 10	
Follow-through			
Finishes by shoulder	1 2 3 4 5 6 7 8 9 10	1 2 3 4 5 6 7 8 9 10	
Return to ready position	1 2 3 4 5 6 7 8 9 10	1 2 3 4 5 6 7 8 9 10	

FIGURE 6.6 Sample readiness checklist for performing a tennis forehand.

and the ground and using no more than three foot touches before you pass.

Trapping Tasks

1. An advanced player can trap the soccer ball successfully when it is rolled by a partner from 10 yards (m) away four of five times, using the instep method with the right and then the left foot and using no more than two foot touches to control the ball.

2. With a partner tossing the ball, trap four of five shots using the chest method.

Kicking Tasks

1. Pass the ball to a partner who is standing 10 yards (m) away five consecutive times using the right and left side of the foot after trapping and controlling the ball from your partner using no more than three foot touches; the ball remains below the knee.

2. Repeat using the instep kick. Loft the ball to your partner; the ball should be above the knee as it travels.

3. Against a shadow defender and from a partner pass, kick four of five shots that enter the goal in the air from 20 yards (m) using an instep kick from both the right, left, and middle of the goal.

Heading and Throw-In Tasks

1. From a partner toss, head three consecutive balls in the air at a height of at least 10 feet (3 m) in a soft arch.

2. Beginning with a partner toss, head six consecutive balls back and forth with a partner, resulting in a soft arch to the ball.

3. Make four of five throw-ins from out-of-bounds into a hoop placed 15 yards (m) away; keep your back foot on the ground.

Designing Mastery Learning Units of Instruction

The first step in designing any type of mastery learning unit is deciding what students are to learn. This procedure is called content analysis (Siedentop & Tannehill, 2000)—a technique for determining all aspects important to student learning outcomes. There are two types of content analysis. First is *procedural analysis*, which is simply creating a list of all the subskills that must be performed for an event to be considered successful. Students can work on these subskills in any order, and the order

of the subskills has no effect on a student's ability to complete the overall task. This list can be thought of as a to-do list without priority for any of the components. A procedural analysis of a social dance unit might look like the following:

1. Procedure for asking a partner to dance:
   Hello, my name is _____. May I have this dance?

2. Procedure for accepting an invitation to dance:
   Thank you. My name is _____, and I would like to have this dance with you.

3. Escorting dance partners to and from the dance floor
   - Asking
   - Extending or accepting elbow
   - Bow and curtsy

4. Dance steps
   - Fox-trot
   - Waltz
   - Swing
   - Tango
   - Cha-cha

5. Participating in a social dance:
   Filling out a dance card

Although this list looks like it follows a progression, none of the tasks are relevant to learning the next one, and students can learn and work on any task independent of the others. In contrast to this approach is another type of content analysis called *hierarchical analysis*. In this type of analysis, teachers produce a sequential chain of events that define a skill or event. This type of analysis often is used in describing the learning components of a physical skill because the components must be learned in the proper order. A hierarchical analysis of spiking a volleyball might look like the following:

1. Preliminary movements
   - Knees are bent, and feet are slightly staggered.
   - Eyes track the ball from the setter.
   - Beginning movements start from 8 to 10 feet (2 to 3 m) behind the net, approaching from an angle.
   - Body is aligned with the ball so that no adjustments need to be made in the air; body is square to the net.

2. Backswing and recovery
   - Directional step with the opposite foot is taken to the ball.
   - Hitting side foot is swung even with the guidance foot.
   - Body is gathered to jump with bent knees.
   - Arms start in front and are swung behind the body in extended position.

3. Force-producing movements
   - Heels are planted, and the jump is generated off both feet, straight up, with extension of the hips, knees, and ankles.
   - Arms are swung forward and extended upward.
   - Striking arm is cocked with the elbow higher than the shoulder.
   - Elbow is extended, and the wrist is flexed to contact the ball downward.

4. Critical instant
   - Contact of the ball occurs between the heel and lower palm of the hand.
   - Ball is contacted slightly above center.
   - Contact with the ball is slightly above the head in front of the contact shoulder.
   - Contact with the fingers is over the top of the ball.

5. Follow-through
   - Contact arm moves through the ball from the shoulder.
   - Wrist snaps after contact, and the arm continues to the opposite hip.
   - Player lands on the toes with the feet shoulder-width apart.
   - Knees bend to absorb impact and maintain balance.

This list provides teachers and students with a learning progression that is ordered and followed for optimal learning. Performing these types of analyses on all aspects of the target outcome is crucial for matching student learning outcomes with students' developmental levels for optimal student success. Teachers have the autonomy to decide what their definition of success is and which subskills students must master. Determining how the subskills must be performed to reach the student learning outcomes based on an appropriate match between subskill and students' developmental levels is required.

Teachers should review references to determine how to do it if they lack sufficient knowledge about certain aspects of the content.

Another way to use mastery learning is to develop units of instruction. Such instructional units have been used successfully in secondary schools for many activities, including badminton, volleyball, soccer, tennis, racquetball, aquatics, and gymnastics. Middle and high school students are gradually given opportunities to make decisions and control their practice behaviors. This type of instruction is effective with physical activities that require the development of individual skills (e.g., volleyball passes, forehands, backhands).

The following steps define the process for developing instructional units for mastery learning:

1. Define the specific tasks or behaviors in observable, measurable terms (e.g., volleyball passes, badminton clears, tennis serves, and soccer kicks).

2. Clearly specify the final learning outcomes for the end of the unit and final goals such as performing two successful forearm passes during game play.

3. Develop a monitoring and assessment system. Skill rubrics provide a clear understanding of how skills will be assessed and when mastery is achieved (see figure 6.7). In addition to teacher assessment, peer assessment and self-assessment should be encouraged.

4. Develop meaningful learning outcomes that consider the various parameters of successful performance. These aspects include speed, strength, endurance, accuracy, and consistency. For example, have students hit serves between the net and a rope strung 10 feet (3 m) higher than the net. The serves must land in bounds and 10 feet (3 m) or less from the back line. This requirement ensures both speed and accuracy. Combinations can also be developed in similar sequences as those performed in game play.

5. Arrange performances in a progressive sequence so that students can experience success quickly and frequently. As students build a backlog of success, the tasks will become more difficult and challenging.

A volleyball mastery unit appropriate for high school students is shown in figure 6.7. All students must accomplish the core objectives, but they can choose from optional objectives. Figure 6.8 is for a flag football unit that can be implemented with middle school students. It

6

VOLLEYBALL

Core Objectives

Forearm Pass (Bump)

1. Bump 12 consecutive forearm passes against the wall at a height of at least 10 feet (3 m).
2. Bump 12 consecutive forearm passes into the air at a height of at least 10 feet (3 m).
3. Bump 10 consecutive forearm passes over the net with the instructor or a classmate.

Overhead Set Pass

1. Hit 15 consecutive set passes against the wall at a height of at least 10 feet (3 m).
2. Hit 15 consecutive set passes into the air at a height of at least 10 feet (3 m).
3. Hit 12 consecutive set passes over the net with the instructor or a classmate.

Serves

1. Hit three consecutive underhand serves into the right half of the court.
2. Hit three of four underhand serves into the left half of the court.
3. Hit three consecutive overhand serves inbounds.

Attendance and Participation

1. Be dressed and ready to participate at 8 a.m.
2. Participate in 15 games.
3. Score 90% or better on a rules, strategies, and techniques test (two attempts only).

Optional Objectives

1. Standing 2 feet (60 cm) from the back line, bump three of five forearm passes into an 8-foot (2.5 m) circle surrounding the setter's position. The height must be at least 10 feet (3 m), and the instructor or a classmate must throw the ball.
2. Bump three of five forearm passes over the net at a height of at least 12 feet (4 m) that land inbounds and not more than 8 feet (2.5 m) from the backline.
3. Standing in the setter's position, hit three consecutive overhead sets at least 10 feet (3 m) high that land in a 5-foot (1.5 m) circle where the spiker would be located. The instructor or a classmate throws the ball.
4. Hit three of five overhead passes over the net at least 12 feet (4 m) high that land inbounds and not more than 8 feet (2.5 m) from the backline.
5. Standing in the setter's position, hit three of five back sets at least 10 feet (3 m) high that land in a 5-foot (1.5 m) circle where the spiker would be located. The instructor or a classmate throws the ball.
6. Volley 12 consecutive times over the net with the instructor or a classmate by alternating forearm passes and overhead passes.
7. Alternate forearm passes and overhead passes in the air at a height of 10 feet (3 m) or more for 12 consecutive times.
8. Spike three of four sets inbounds from an on-hand position (three-step approach, jump, extended arm, hand contact).
9. Spike three of five sets inbounds from an off-hand position.
10. Recover three consecutive balls from the net. Recoveries must be playable (8 feet [2.5 m] high in the playing area).
11. Hit three consecutive overhand serves into the right half of the court.
12. Hit three of four overhand serves into the left half of the court.
13. Hit three of five overhand serves under a rope 15 feet (5 m) high that land in the back half of the court.
14. Officiate at least three games, using proper calls and signals.
15. Coach a team for the class tournament. Plan strategy, substitution, and scheduling.
16. Devise and carry out a research project that deals with volleyball. Check with the instructor for ideas.

FIGURE 6.7 Sample volleyball mastery unit for high school.

FLAG FOOTBALL

Core Objectives

Passing Tasks

1. Throw 10 passes to the chest area of a partner standing 10 yards (m) away.
2. Throw three of four consecutive passes beyond a target distance of 20 yards (m).
3. Throwing five passes, knock over three targets from a distance of 10 yards (m).
4. Throw four of six passes through a tire from a distance of 10 yards (m).

Centering Tasks

1. With a partner 5 yards (m) away, execute 10 over-the-head snaps to the chest area, using correct holding, proper rotation, and follow-through techniques.
2. Facing the opposite direction from a partner, 5 yards (m) away, execute a proper center stance with feet well spread and toes pointed straight ahead, knees bent, and two hands on the ball. Snap the ball back through the legs 10 consecutive times.
3. Perform the previous task but move back 10 yards (m).
4. Center snap four of six times through a tire 5 yards (m) away.

Punting Tasks

1. With a partner 5 yards (m) away, execute 10 over-the-head snaps to the chest area, using correct holding, proper rotation, and follow-through techniques.
2. Facing the opposite direction from a partner, 5 yards (m) away, execute a proper center stance with feet well spread and toes pointed straight ahead, knees bent, and two hands on the ball. Snap the ball back through the legs 10 consecutive times.
3. Perform the previous task but move back 10 yards (m).
4. Center snap four of six times through a tire 5 yards (m) away.

Catching Tasks

1. With a partner centering the ball from 10 yards (m) away, punt the football using proper technique to another set of partners 15 yards (m) away three consecutive times.
2. Perform the previous task but at a distance of 20 yards (m).
3. Punt the ball three consecutive times within the boundary lines of the field and beyond a distance of 20 yards (m).
4. Punt the ball three consecutive times with a hang time of two and a half seconds or better (use stopwatch).

Attendance and Participation

1. Be ready to participate in football activities five minutes after the last bell rings each day.
2. Use proper locker-room behavior (will be discussed or posted) at all times.
3. Score at least 90% on a written test (two attempts only).

Optional Objectives

1. Attend two football games (flag or regular) during the grading period.
2. Throw three of four passes through a tire from a distance of 10 yards (m).
3. Throw three of four passes through a tire from a distance of 15 yards (m).
4. Throw three of four passes through a moving tire from a distance of 10 yards (m).
5. Throw three of four passes through a moving tire from a distance of 15 yards (m).
6. Catch two passes in a game.
7. Intercept a pass in a game.
8. Write a one-page report on a fiction or nonfiction book related to the topic of football.

FIGURE 6.8 Sample flag football mastery unit for middle school.

follows the same format as the volleyball unit, including core and optional performance objectives.

In chapters 15 through 20, several mastery learning units are provided. These units are general in their orientation, and objectives may be modified depending on contexts. Objectives may be too difficult for some students and too easy for others. All students should find success and challenge with some of the objectives.

Performance objectives listed focus primarily on physical skills rather than tactical or cognitive activities. Teachers may want a specific combination of tactical or cognitive and physical skills to be built into the unit. For example, the unit could provide a balance of learning outcomes related to teamwork, participation, physical skills, and cognitive activities. Mastery learning style provides teachers and students the flexibility of choice and allows opportunities to select activities that match students' developmental level.

Using Mastery Learning Units of Instruction

When using mastery learning units, students need to understand the learning outcomes, performance activities, and the importance of self-direction. Units are given to students so that they can explain them to their parents, work on the objectives at home in their free time, or keep records of their performance at school. Students must respect how involvement in this strategy is different from other instructional strategies. Some students take longer to adapt and become comfortable with this instructional format. Students may need experience controlling the pace of their learning. Promote their success by actively monitoring student progress, developing personal and peer assessments, facilitating the pace of the learning experience, and designing activities that demonstrate student progress. Explain and demonstrate expected outcomes to students in the learning areas where they will be practicing. Arrange the gymnasium or playing field with learning areas for specific objectives, such as the passing area, shooting area, or ballhandling area.

A rotational scheme can be incorporated using small groups placed at learning stations. Depending on class size, multiple stations supporting the same learning outcomes may be needed to prevent overcrowding and allow students continued control of their learning and practice pace. An alternative is to allow students to rotate to any learning area they need to practice. Use a variety of grouping patterns (individual, partners, or small groups) based on available facilities, equipment,

objectives, and student choice. Consider the amount of freedom, flexibility, and choice that students can handle and yet be productive. The best approach is to start with less freedom and then gradually increase choices and options as students get used to self-selection and monitoring their learning.

Successful completion of learning outcomes can be monitored by the teacher, peers, or individually. Depending on the class size and number of outcomes, the teacher may be able to do all the monitoring. Otherwise, a combination of procedures is recommended. Student involvement in the monitoring process enhances their understanding of learning expectations and increases their level of personal responsibility. Students can use a performance chart to monitor learning outcomes at each practice station or carry a master list from station to station. Another approach is to develop a performance sheet for each student that combines teacher and peer monitoring (see figure 6.9). Peers monitor easy-to-interpret outcomes, whereas the teacher monitors more difficult ones. A third method allows students to monitor their progress privately in attaining specified learning outcomes (see figure 6.10). Experiment with several monitoring approaches depending on the activity, the number of learning outcomes, the students' abilities, the size of the class, and the available equipment and facilities.

Individualized Style

Learning packages that incorporate a learning laboratory or resource center are used in the **individualized style**. An example of a learning center is shown in figure 6.11. Individualized style is based on student-centered learning through an individualized curriculum, which is most useful when there are vast skill or ability differences among students. Students select the level of proficiency they want to pursue and proceed at their desired rate of learning. Learning packets with objectives, study guides, learning activities, and assessment procedures are developed as independent study guides. Students work independently on objectives, view videos and slides, work on tablets, look at smart board materials, read books and articles, and prepare for the assessment procedure. Assessment usually progresses from self to peers and finally to the teacher. This approach requires that teachers develop learning materials and procedures for supervising the distribution and return of those materials.

BEGINNING RACQUETBALL

Instructor checked	Class member checked	
		1. Stand approximately 6 feet (1.8 m) from the back wall and in the center of the court. Bounce the ball against the sidewall and hit three of four shots below the white line with a forehand shot.
		2. Perform objective 1 but hit three of five balls with the backhand shot.
		3. Hit three of five power serves that land within 2 feet (60 cm) of the sidewall and are otherwise legal.
		4. Hit three of four lob serves within approximately 3 feet (1 m) of the sidewall that do not bounce out from the back wall more than 8 feet (2.5 m).
		5. Stand approximately 6 feet (1.8 m) from the back wall, bounce the ball against the back wall, and hit three of four shots below the white line on the front wall with a forehand shot.
		6. Perform objective 5 but hit three of five balls with the backhand shot.
		7. Hit three of four diagonal, or Z, serves that hit the front, side, floor, and opposite side, in that order. (The ball may hit but need not hit the backwall for the serve to be effective.)
		8. Hit three of four scotch serves, or scotch toss, serves that hit the front, side, floor, back, and side, in that order. This serve is like the Z serve in execution, except that the ball hits the back wall after bouncing on the floor.
		9. Return three of four serves hit to you by the instructor. (One of each of the following will be used: power, lob, diagonal, and scotch.)
		10. Execute three of four attempts at three-hit drill. (Instructor will explain in detail.)
		11. Execute three of four attempts at four-hit drill. (Instructor will explain in detail.)
		12. Hit three of five ceiling shots with a forehand shot. The ball will be thrown or hit by the instructor and must be returned to the ceiling, front wall, and floor, in that order.

Note: Entry into ladder tournament is contingent on completion of any 8 of the 12 objectives. To receive a grade of A for the class, you must exhibit proficiency in all 12 objectives.

Objectives 1 through 8 may be checked by a class member, but the instructor may spot-check any objectives at his or her discretion.

Objectives 9 through 12 will be checked by the instructor. Performance objectives may be tested in courts 1 and 4.

FIGURE 6.9 Sample performance sheet for racquetball.

SNORKELING

Use of Face Mask

Mark the date that each performance objective is met.

_____ 1. Adjust face mask strap to your head size.

_____ 2. Apply saliva to face mask—rub all around face plate; do not rinse (fog preventive).

_____ 3. Vertical tilt: Fill mask with water and hold to face without strap. In chest-deep water, go under in vertical position and by tilting head backward, away from chest, push against upper edge of mask and exhale gently. Completely clear mask in three of five attempts.

_____ 4. Horizontal roll: Fill mask with water and hold to face without strap. While in a horizontal position, roll onto left shoulder, push gently with right hand against side of mask, and exhale gently. Completely clear mask in three of five attempts.

_____ 5. Repeat objective 3 with strap around back of head.

_____ 6. Repeat objective 4 with strap around back of head.

_____ 7. In 6 feet (1.8 m) of water, submerge to bottom of pool by pinching nostrils and gently exhaling into mask until you feel your ears equalize. Successfully equalize pressure in four of five attempts.

_____ 8. Repeat objective 7 in 9 feet (3 m) of water.

_____ 9. Repeat objective 3 in deep water.

_____ 10. Repeat objective 4 in deep water.

_____ 11. Throw mask into shallow water, submerge, and put on mask. Complete vertical tilt clear in one breath, in four of five attempts.

_____ 12. Throw mask into shallow water, submerge, and put on mask. Complete horizontal roll clear in one breath, in four of five attempts.

_____ 13. Repeat objective 11 in 6 feet (1.8 m) of water.

_____ 14. Repeat objective 11 in 9 feet (3 m) of water.

_____ 15. Repeat objective 12 in 6 feet (1.8 m) of water.

_____ 16. Repeat objective 12 in 9 feet (3 m) of water.

FIGURE 6.10   Sample self-assessment for snorkeling.

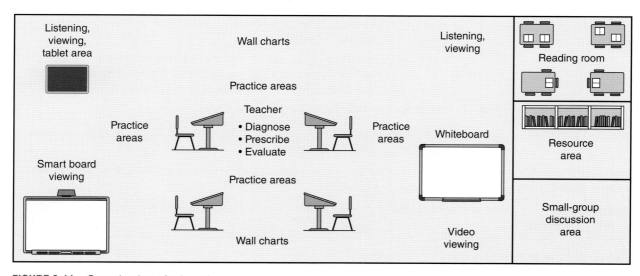

FIGURE 6.11   Organization of a learning center.

Reprinted from R. P. Pangrazi and A. Beighle, *Dynamic Physical Education for Elementary School Children*, 17th ed. (Pearson Education, 2012), 41). By permission of R.P. Pangrazi.

Problems to be solved when using the individualized approach include the following:

- Performance outcomes are time consuming to write and require constant revision.
- A monitoring and assessment system that is efficient and reliable yet streamlined needs to be developed.
- Instructional devices are necessary to provide variety and feedback, but they increase the setup and takedown time of each class for the teacher.
- Teachers and students may need practice time to get used to the contract format. Changing to an individualized format will require time for adjustment.

Teaching using the individualized style follows five basic steps:

1. Diagnosis. Preassessment is done to determine the student's current level of cognitive knowledge and psychomotor skill.
2. Prescription. Individual students begin at a level related to their performance on the initial assessment.
3. Development. All students receive a learning package that guides them toward successful completion of the predetermined criterion level. Students proceed to the next learning level after successful completion of the preceding level.
4. Evaluation. Each student receives a final evaluation by a peer or the teacher after completing the steps in the learning package. Evaluation includes both cognitive and psychomotor skills.
5. Reinforcement. As students complete the learning packages, accomplishments are recorded. New packages are prescribed, and teaching is given for key points of the material.

Individualized instruction offers the following advantages:

- Students, parents, and administrators know exactly what is expected of students and what they accomplish.
- Self-direction enhances the motivational level of most students.
- Students at most competency levels find success and challenge with objectives.
- Students progress through the learning outcomes at their own rate.

- Students can choose and sequence learning activities.
- Students have some choice concerning the grouping arrangement of skill practice (e.g., alone, with a partner, or in a small group).
- Students accept a large degree of responsibility for learning.
- Teachers have more freedom to give individual attention and offer feedback.

Metzler (2011) highlights a version of individualized instruction that is called personalized system for instruction. This style allows students to progress as fast as they can or as slowly as they need to, meaning that students move through tasks at an individual pace of learning. The style requires significant planning by the teacher because she or he must provide each student with management information, task presentations, task structures, learning activities with performance criteria, and assessments. This information is typically presented by a workbook, website, or tablet. Students follow the workbook as closely as possible, and the teacher provides only clarification or supplemental information not in the workbook. Students progress individually through a series of learning tasks. At the start of each new lesson, students pick up where they left off the previous class period. The teacher primarily needs to be aware of which tasks students will be attempting each day to ensure that the appropriate equipment is provided. The personalized system of instruction encourages independent learning while freeing up the teacher to work with students who need extra instruction or assistance.

Cooperative Learning

Cooperative learning places students in groups to work together toward common goals using problem-based learning. Through cooperative learning activities, students achieve outcomes that are beneficial in solving predetermined problems through group interaction and participation. Student work is arranged so that they depend on one another to achieve group goals but are also individually accountable (Johnson, Johnson, & Holubec, 2009). When cooperative strategies are used appropriately in diverse settings, students develop a better understanding of how their peers' skill levels differ from their own. Social gains develop in the areas of communication, compromise, and acceptance of diverse ideas. Learning outcomes are achieved through group interactions including participation through different roles such as performer, observer, recorder, or evaluator. Physical educators can facilitate growth in social, cognitive, and psychomotor areas by using cooperative learning formats.

Teachers who want to foster constructive relationships among students and improve skills and knowledge use cooperative learning strategies. Emphasis is placed on group outcomes rather than on individual outcomes. Students are placed in groups or teams and are given an opportunity to work together to solve problems in a team approach. Groups are usually heterogeneous (i.e., containing a mix of skill level, knowledge, race, and gender). Small teams of two to five students participate to attain the goal. The focus is on working together with peers rather than competing against them. Students learn that the problems cannot be solved without the cooperation of their peers. All members of the group must reach established goals, and success is determined when members work with each other to complete their assignments through cooperation and participation. Before implementation, the teacher develops content to be learned and social interaction criteria expected within each team. Selected content allows students to develop and apply appropriate and successful solutions through application and refinement (trial and error). Problem-based learning provides opportunities for members of each team to develop, select, and implement a variety of strategies for solving each problem.

The following roles can be assigned to group members:

- A performer who does the skills or tasks
- A recorder who keeps track of statistics, trials, or key points made by the group

- A coach who provides feedback to the performer or times practice trials
- A presenter who communicates key points to the rest of the class
- A motivator who encourages and provides positive feedback to all group members

Students should switch roles often, and stated group tasks should be organized so they proceed from simple to complex. Teachers observe and facilitate team member participation so that all members contribute. Selected content activities require the knowledge and effort of all group members. Although each member may contribute based on personal strengths and abilities, if one student is allowed to dominate and direct the team, other members may think that their contributions are not necessary to complete the task. Students must understand that all members of the team are needed, even if their involvement varies. Students can be provided with personal and team assessments that highlight expectations while a team member is attaining the selected tasks (see figure 6.12), and they can convey those expectations to team members and provide the teacher with levels of contribution made by each team member. Cooperative learning tasks can include cognitive or psychomotor skills.

The following are examples of class activities that can be used with the cooperative learning style:

- Make teams responsible for developing a warm-up or physical fitness routine appropriate for a specific sport (e.g., rugby, water polo). Each member of the team can focus on a different component of fitness as he or she addresses

SELF EVALUATION: COOPERATIVE LEARNING ACTIVITY

Using a check mark, rate the following expectations based on your involvement today.

	Always	Sometimes	Never
Listened when others offered ideas.			
Accepted others' ideas without disagreement or questioning.			
Congratulated team members' efforts.			
My teammates would agree I was a team player.			
Give examples that support why you rated yourself as you did for each category.			

FIGURE 6.12 Sample self-evaluation for team member expectations in a cooperative learning activity.

the sport or activity (e.g., flexibility, abdominal strength, cardiorespiratory efficiency, or upper-body strength).

- Ask each member of a team to be responsible for teaching others a skill that is a part of a sport unit and a specific offense or defense. For example, in floor hockey, team members teach dribbling, passing, slap shots, setting a pick, using a give-and-go, or playing a defensive position.

- Teams develop a dance that includes a variety of dance steps or skills. Each member of the team is responsible for incorporating the specific skills into the routine. Ask each dance team to teach other teams their routines.

- Set up a class tournament in a sport unit such as volleyball. Each team is responsible for some aspect of the tournament such as creating tournament brackets, producing media guides, training and assessing scorekeepers and game officials, reporting each team's statistics, announcing game play-by-plays, and analyzing team strategy for offense or defense. Roles are switched on a regular basis.

- Students develop a small group stunt or routine and then teach another team the same stunt during a tumbling unit. Another example is to have an "expert" from each team get together with "experts" from other teams for a short clinic on a particular stunt. These experts then return to their teams and teach the stunt.

- Team members modify or redesign a sport or activity to make it more inclusive or success oriented, allowing more team members to participate and succeed. Using a larger ball, more bounces, a lower net, and a larger goal are examples of game modifications.

- Teams work with a study sheet that focuses on three to five key elements of a skill, such as serving in volleyball or tennis. Teams design several drills that emphasize each of the key points of the skill. Examples of student roles are drill planner, director of the drill, coach for the skill points, and recorder of the attempts and successful trials.

Student learning is enhanced when team members depend on their peers for both individual and team success. Students can develop many of the behaviors and leadership skills needed to create a positive learning environment. Cooperative learning also reflects the social behaviors and patterns expected of people in the working environment. As students learn to solve problems as members of a team, they can develop an appreciation for the benefits of shared successes. The adage "Two heads are better than one" reflects the added knowledge potential available to solve a task.

Reciprocal Teaching Style

Reciprocal teaching style (Mosston & Ashworth, 2008) is a form of cooperative learning because several students are involved with different roles such as a doer, retriever, and observer. The primary difference between the two styles is that in reciprocal teaching, all students do not necessarily walk away with the same learned outcomes. Students have more freedom to work at their own level and receive appropriate feedback on their performance rather than on a group performance. Figures 6.13 and 6.14 are examples of reciprocal style sheets that can be used with badminton and soccer. Doers are the performers, and observers are watching and providing feedback to the doers. Retrievers are returning the balls for more trials. Tossers are helping with the setup of the drill.

Metzler (2011) uses the term *peer teaching* as a form of reciprocal or cooperative learning. The general premise is that in many situations the teacher cannot realistically teach all students. The style is intended to be used for small portions of the instructional process when students need additional instruction and the teacher is unable to observe or instruct all students directly because of the large number of students in a class. The peer teaching style requires a student to be assigned the role of tutor while another student remains the learner. The students switch roles to make sure that they receive equal instruction and physical activity. Peer teaching is not just telling a student to go teach another student. Metzler (2011) identifies nine training requirements necessary for students to implement the peer teaching style:

1. Clarification of the learning objectives
2. Expectations of tutors (what they should and should not know)
3. Task presentation and check for understanding
4. Task structure and check for understanding
5. How to communicate errors to learners
6. How to provide praise appropriately
7. How to practice safely
8. How to assess mastery or task completion
9. Knowing when to ask questions of the teacher

BADMINTON RECIPROCAL STYLE

Name (doer) _____ Date _____

Name (observer) _____

Badminton Forehand Clear Shot

This task is to be done in groups of three: doer, hitter, and observer.

The hitter: Hit a high and deep service to the doer.

The doer: Practice the forehand clear shot 10 times.

The observer: Assess the doer's form by comparing her or his performance to the established criteria (following). Provide specific feedback on what the doer has done well and what needs improvement.

Forehand Clear Shot Criteria

1. Ready position with feet and shoulders parallel to the net.
2. Hold the racket slightly to the backhand side and bend the knees slightly.
3. Contact the shuttlecock as high as possible and in front of the body.
4. The racket face should be tilted upward, and the shuttlecock should clear the opponent's racket and land close to the back line.

FIGURE 6.13 Sample reciprocal style worksheet for badminton forehand overhead clear.

Reprints from Teaching Physical Education Fourth Edition are used with permission from Dr. Sara Ashworth, Director of the Spectrum Institute. Free Digital Download of, Teaching Physical Education First Online Edition, 2008, Available at: www.spectrumofteachingstyles.org

SOCCER RECIPROCAL STYLE

Name (doer) _____ Date _____

Name (observer) _____

Soccer Instep Pass

Get into groups of three: two doers and an observer.

The doers: Practice the instep pass 10 times at a distance of 10 yards (m).

The observer: Assess the doers' form by comparing their performance to the established criteria (following). Provide specific feedback on what the doers have done well and what needs improvement.

Soccer Instep Pass Criteria

1. Plant the nonkicking foot alongside the ball with the foot pointing in the desired direction of the kick.
2. Contact the ball with the inside portion of the foot.
3. Shift the body weight forward after the kick.
4. Follow through toward the target (partner).

FIGURE 6.14 Sample reciprocal style worksheet for soccer instep pass.

Reprints from Teaching Physical Education Fourth Edition are used with permission from Dr. Sara Ashworth, Director of the Spectrum Institute. Free Digital Download of, Teaching Physical Education First Online Edition, 2008, Available at: www.spectrumofteachingstyles.org

Inquiry Style

The **inquiry style** is process oriented, rather than product oriented. A student's experience during the process is considered more important than the outcome or solution. Students experience learning situations that require them to inquire, speculate, reflect, analyze, and discover. They are cognitively active in this type of instruction. Teachers guide and direct students—rather than commanding or telling—thus allowing students to discover their own answers and solutions.

Teachers are responsible for stimulating student curiosity about the subject matter. A combination of questions, problems, examples, and learning activities leads students toward one or more solutions. This is called the "Ask, don't tell, principle." The steps follow a sequence and are arranged logically so that students can move from one step to the next after a certain amount of thinking. Each step should be neither too large nor too small to prevent students from becoming frustrated or bored. An open instructional environment is one that allows students opportunities to communicate openly and feel comfortable experimenting and inquiring without fear of failure.

Some educators believe inquiry methods of instruction should play a more prominent role in educational methodology (Mosston & Ashworth, 2008). They posit that students need opportunities to inquire, solve problems, and discover, instead of primarily experiencing approaches that emphasize listening, absorbing, and complying. Arguments have been made to expand the focus of physical education methodology to include the inquiry style. Proponents of this style believe that it enhances students' ability to think, improves creativity, creates a better understanding of the subject matter, enhances self-concept, and develops lifelong learning patterns. Students develop ownership of the answers and solutions. Students who actively engage in solving the problem are more likely to remember later. Some educators argue that students who do not experience inquiry methods may become dormant, unchallenged, and unused.

Inquiry is used when students have a basic understanding of sports and games. Teachers can use this style to help students understand when to apply certain skills. What to do when they do not have the ball, where to be to receive a pass, and how to split the defense are just a few examples of tactics that teachers can use to develop areas of critical thinking necessary to be successful in game play. If students do not have basic understanding and application of motor skills, the inquiry style may not be appropriate.

After students acquire these skills, inquiry helps foster higher level thinking skills such as application, integration, refinement, and other examples of critical thinking. Application and best practice can frequently be discovered using inquiry related to problem solving. Most beginning teachers are practiced in telling students information rather than fostering critical thinking. This complex skill needs time and training to develop and should be considered when choosing these styles. Depending on the situation, these methods offer advantages when learning about cognitive issues. The inquiry style offers teachers another teaching tool in their repertoire of skills. The inquiry style in physical education is generally characterized by two approaches: guided discovery (or convergent) and problem solving (or divergent) (Mosston & Ashworth, 2008).

Guided Discovery (Convergent) Style

Teachers using the **guided discovery (convergent) style** lead students through a series of preplanned tasks to guide students toward a specific solution (convergent) or an effective solution (divergent). Activities are designed so that students reach the answer desired by the teacher. Guided discovery can be used to help students discover knowledge about some of the following:

- Court coverage strategies that prevent scoring in tennis, badminton, racquetball, and handball
- Effective angles of release for distance throwing with the shot put, discus, football, and softball
- Batting stance and foot pattern alterations for hitting the baseball or softball to the open space in various fields or through the gaps in the infield
- Specific offensive strategies for scoring in the key depending on the defenders and the type of defense
- Dribbling techniques in soccer used to fake out a defender and advance the ball down the field
- When to use a give-and-go in certain situations to advance the ball in a game of team handball
- A person's center of gravity and the role of momentum role in performing activities in gymnastics such as the balance beam or the side horse

The learning environment can be arranged in many ways for these activities. Give students an activity that asks them to solve a problem, ask a series of questions, and then have students participate in several learning activities based on their answers. After allowing students to practice using their solutions and strategies, hold a

6

brief discussion to see if they have grasped the application of the strategies. The following are examples of learning activities:

- In basketball, students analyze and determine the best offensive solution when a defender is playing tight defense. Often, the best solution is to fake a shot and then drive to the basket. If the defender is playing off the offensive player, she or he should shoot the ball. Students should have the opportunity to practice defense playing both tight and off the ball as well as the opportunity to reverse roles and play offense. This gives them a chance to discover different solutions.

- In soccer, students can experiment with long and short passes with defenders in certain positions. Long, high passes are necessary to get the ball over a defender, whereas quick, short passes that stay on the ground prevent the defender from intercepting the ball and are easier for a teammate to receive and trap.

- In the shot put and discus throws, students might experiment with various release angles to see how they affect the flight and distance of the throws. The objective is to discover the best angle of release for maximum distance.

Problem-Solving (Divergent) Style

The second inquiry approach is the **problem-solving (divergent) style**. Rather than converge on one solution, students move through a series of experiences and attempt to devise as many acceptable solutions to the problem as possible. Many times, these activities are posed in terms of a student challenge in which teachers give students an opportunity to solve problems or activities in different ways. Assessment of learning takes place through demonstration. Encourage students to be creative and develop unique solutions while analyzing the pros and cons of each solution. This style is useful for discussions and assignments dealing with values, social issues, wellness concepts, and controversial topics related to sport and physical education. Honesty in sport, cooperation with teammates, competition, violence in sport, amateur versus professional sports, athletes' use of performance-enhancing drugs, and arguing with officials are examples of topics that can be researched, explored, discussed, and debated in a physical education class.

Wellness is an area that lends itself to the problem-solving approach. Many approaches and methods can be used to maintain good health. Students can learn to solve their personal fitness problems with physical activity programs that are personalized to meet their needs. Problem-solving approaches are also useful in resolving the issues of proper diet and weight control. Stress reduction, alcohol and drug abuse, and tobacco use are areas that can be addressed effectively with problem-solving techniques.

When using this style, the teacher is responsible for creating an open environment in which students are encouraged to explore all aspects of these controversial topics. Books, articles, movies, interviews, questions, and discussions are possibilities for accumulating and sharing information. Students are encouraged to gather information and weigh all alternatives before making a decision. A teacher's opinion does not carry more weight or emphasis than student opinion. An effective strategy for starting the problem-solving process involves using a "trigger story."

Problem-solving approaches are useful when physical skills can be performed or developed in more than one way. Students are allowed to experiment briefly with these skills to determine which approach is most effective. In this example, an individualized style and a divergent style would work nicely in combination. In many cases, a skill can be adapted for certain situations. Some examples are the batting stance in baseball, golf grips and swing, putting grip and stroke, starts for sprints, high-jumping technique, and training methods for distance running. A problem-solving style can also be used to develop routines for gymnastics, including different ways to correctly perform on pieces of apparatus. Students can experiment with different ways to mount the equipment, make various turns or swings, travel across the equipment, and perform dismounts. In team sports, students design offenses that work against a particular defense and defenses that work against a specific offensive strategy. A basketball defender can experiment with options against a taller or quicker player. Students can also determine their options against opponents in various individual sports. In racquetball, several serves can be used to counter an opponent's strong forehand or extreme quickness. If a lob serve does not work, maybe a power serve or Z serve will be more effective.

Teaching Styles and Student Learning

Teaching styles were developed to produce student learning. Teachers may lose sight of why things need to be taught in a certain manner, and information about the various teaching styles may seem overlapping and confusing. Although space and equipment may be limited,

STORIES TO PROMPT STUDENT DISCUSSION USING CRITICAL THINKING

- You and your partner are involved in a tightly contested golf match with another pair of students. Your partner hits his drive into the woods. While you are getting ready for your second shot, you turn and see your partner kick his ball out of the woods into an area that offers a clear shot to the green. The kick was not visible to either of your opponents. What would you do in this situation?

- You are playing on a Pop Warner football team. During the game, you make an aggressive yet legal tackle on your opponent's best running back. The running back receives a leg injury as a result and must be carried off the field. Your teammates cheer and praise you for injuring the star player. Your coach also praises you when you come off the field. What should you do?

- At a bicycle motocross race, you hear a father criticizing his five-year-old daughter for losing the championship race. The daughter is crying. You hear the father say to the mother, "She has to learn to compete. That's what life's all about." How do you react?

- You are coaching a freshman volleyball team. The game is close, and everyone is excited. The mother of a member of your team is being obnoxious. She yells mean things at players on both teams, at the coaches, and at the officials. During a time-out, the referee comes over and says, "Can't you do something about her?" What would you do?

- Your team is warming up when the referee walks in. Everybody recognizes him. He refereed the last game that you lost because he called a foul every time you moved. A member of your team says loudly, "Not him again!" What would you say?

- Right after the fourth game of the season, which your team just lost by four points, you are walking out of the locker room when you hear a parent say to a player on your team, "Boy, did you embarrass me tonight. You were terrible!" How would you react in this situation?

6

a teaching style should be selected because it enables the development of an environment better suited for learning. Teachers are encouraged to remember the following when it comes to teaching styles and student learning:

- One style does not cover all situations. All styles offer various strengths and obstacles in a physical education setting. The list for choosing a style at the beginning of the chapter should be regularly reviewed to ensure that the correct style is used for the situation.

- A combination of styles can be an effective way to reach more students. When choosing a teaching style, the teacher does not need to choose just one and design the entire experience of the lesson around it. Using different styles for different parts of a lesson or unit may provide students with better learning opportunities.

- Student diversity is an issue that faces every teacher, and the use of various teaching styles may appeal to a diverse group of students. Student diversity includes ethnicity, socioeconomics, language, gender, ability, and learning styles. With this amount of diversity, one teacher may not be able to meet the demands of all students. Using different teaching styles and having students take on some of the instructional roles may allow diversity issues to be met. Certain styles are better suited for different learning styles, language skills, and so on. Using a variety of styles may increase the chance of reaching more students.

- A teacher's abilities should be considered when choosing a style. Teachers often choose a style because literature states that it would be effective in a specific situation. If it works for the teacher, that is the style of choice, but if the teacher feels uncomfortable, the lesson will suffer regardless of the style used. The best approach is to use each style in small doses until students recognize that the teacher is confident and comfortable. The teacher's confidence in using the style may be the most important element in being successful with it.

A Framework for Using Multiple Teaching Styles

Middle and high school students should be moving from teacher-dependent learning toward independent learning styles. Providing students with multiple opportunities to understand how to be successful in physical movement can support progress toward such independence. Multiple teaching styles encourage students to make decisions and solve problems. In *Teaching Sport Concepts and Skills,* authors Mitchell, Oslin, and Griffin (2013) developed a student-centered approach to learning game play. This framework builds on the use of a modified game approach using guided discovery and inquiry styles to develop tactical understanding and skill development. Within this framework, teachers are encouraged to be facilitators of learning and focus activities using a discovery-based approach. Each step of the framework is shown in figure 6.15.

Step 1 of the framework is the application of a modified game in which students play and discover the solution to a task that allows the best strategy to surface. The solution could be understanding specific skills or using a specific strategy. An example of a modified game of three-on-three basketball would be discovering how to score multiple times from inside the basketball key and below the last hash mark. Each game is developed with specific rule modifications that help focus students' play toward discovering the correct solution (as predetermined by the teacher). Using this problem, the rules state that players may not dribble the basketball, all passes must be either chest or bounce passes, players may not hold the ball for more than three seconds, all shots must be made inside the key and below the last hash mark (block), and defenders cannot reach in.

Step 2 of the framework is then completed after students have had an opportunity to play the game (step 1). Questions are used to guide the students toward the correct responses. For instance, a teacher may ask students the following questions: "How was your team able to score from inside the key?" "How did you try to get ahold of the ball?" "How did you help your teammates get the ball?" "What was the best way to shoot the ball from inside the key?" Focusing on a specific skill should lead students to identify that a basketball layup is the most effective shot to use from inside the key. If the teacher's goal focused on a specific strategy, the questions would lead students toward identifying setting screens or using a give-and-go.

After students clearly understand which skill or strategy allows successful accomplishment of the problem defined in step 1, they move on to practice either the

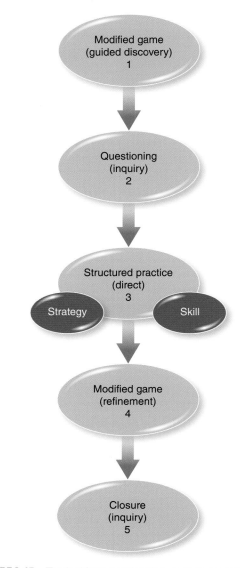

FIGURE 6.15 Tactical framework using multiple teaching styles.

skill or strategy in a gamelike situation (step 3). For instance, if the solution was to get team players open, then practice would focus on the give-and-go. Each team would select one side of the basket, one player would be placed at the top of the key with the ball, one player would be on the wing, and the third member would be a defender on the point player only (levels of defense start from a shadow level and progress to competitive as players improve). The point passes the ball to the wing and then cuts to the basket to receive the ball and attempt a layup (with no dribble). Key phrases such as *scoop*, *lift*, and *flick* can be used to focus on the layup technique. If the focus is the give-and-go, phrases can include *fake*, *cut*, and *target hand*.

Active engagement is the key to learning and refining a task. Step 4 has players returning to a modified game to reapply the skill or strategy after practice. By playing the game after practice, students should have a better understanding of which skill to use, when to use it, and why. During closure, teachers can use inquiry to affirm that students understood and were able to apply the solutions they developed and practiced.

Students are actively engaged in this multiple-stage process that applies multiple teaching styles. Steps 1 and 2 apply forms of guided discovery-based learning (divergent and convergent), whereas steps 3 (direct instruction) and 4 (application and integration of what was learned in step 3) engage learners in understanding and refinement of skills or strategies through active learning. Students can apply previously learned skills and knowledge to solve the problem designed for step 1. Students are actively engaged in each stage, and the teacher facilitates student learning. This example shows how teachers "ask and don't tell" and illustrates indirect instructional practices. Students can understand why certain skills and strategies are used in certain situations, and the new content, skills, and knowledge have meaning. Applying multiple teaching styles within a specific framework based on TGfU can enhance students' long-term understanding and retention.

Dynamic Instruction: Elements Common to All Styles

Regardless of the teaching style used, an effective learning environment can be identified by a set of instructional behaviors that occur regularly. These behaviors do not describe a specific method or style and provide significant room for individual approaches to teaching content. The focus is less on what the teacher does and more on what students are doing. For example, any style of teaching that produces high rates of student engagement and positive attitudes toward the subject matter is considered an effective learning environment. Evidence from teacher effectiveness research (Siedentop & Tannehill, 2000) indicates that regardless of the teacher's instructional style, an educational environment is most effective when the following elements are present:

- Students are engaged in appropriate learning activities for a large percentage of class time.
- Effective teachers use class time wisely, wasting little time on noninstructional activities such as taking attendance, dressing, checking lunch tickets, or taking yearbook photos.
- Teachers plan carefully and insist on appropriate learning activities that deal with the subject matter.

- Effective teachers make sure that students use class time to receive information and practice skills.
- The learning atmosphere is success oriented with a positive, caring climate.
- Teachers support appropriate social and organizational behavior.
- Students are given clear objectives and receive high rates of information feedback from the teacher and the environment.
- Class activities are arranged so that students spend large amounts of time on the required objectives.
- Activities are meaningful and are clearly tied to the class objectives.
- Positive and corrective feedback are available from the teacher.
- Peers and instructional devices are used to provide feedback.
- Student progress is monitored regularly, and students are held accountable for learning in physical education.
- Records are kept relative to various objectives.
- Students know exactly what is expected of them and how the expectations are tied to the accountability system.
- Students are rewarded for small steps of progress made toward larger goals.
- Effective teachers are efficient managers of students. Students move from one learning activity to another smoothly and without wasting time.
- Time-saving procedures are planned and implemented efficiently.
- Students spend little time waiting during class transitions.
- Equipment is organized to facilitate smooth transitions.
- Attendance procedures, starting and stopping procedures, and instructional procedures are all tightly organized with little wasted time.
- Students spend a limited amount of time waiting in line or participating in other unproductive behaviors.
- Effective environments are characterized by high rates of time engaged in subject matter.
- Physical education is activity based, and students spend class time doing the activity, not waiting for an opportunity.

- Teachers are organized with high but realistic expectations for student achievement.
- Structured learning activities challenge students.
- Teachers expect students to learn and hold them accountable for their progress.

- Teachers are enthusiastic about what they are doing and are actively involved in the instructional process.
- Active involvement means active supervision, enthusiasm, and high interaction rates with students.

LEARNING AIDS

STUDY STIMULATORS AND REVIEW QUESTIONS

1. Discuss the various factors that should be considered when choosing a teaching style.
2. Explain why problem solving is not a good approach to teaching rock climbing.
3. Provide an overview of what teachers need to do from a planning perspective to use the task style of teaching.
4. Discuss the attractive features of mastery learning.
5. What is the focus of a teacher's monitoring effort when using mastery learning?
6. Explain the various roles of students in the cooperative learning style.
7. Discuss the various criticisms that have been voiced about inquiry styles of teaching.
8. Develop a short "trigger story" with a focus on ethical behavior in sport.
9. Why should a teacher develop a large repertoire of teaching styles?
10. Discuss the dynamic instruction elements common to all styles.

WEBSITES

Physical Education Teaching and Curriculum Information

www.pecentral.com
www.pheamerica.org

McREL International

www.mcrel.org

Spectrum of Teaching Styles

www.spectrumofteachingstyles.org

REFERENCES AND SUGGESTED READINGS

Casten, C.M. (2015). *Lesson plans for dynamic physical education for secondary students* (8th ed.). San Francisco, CA: Pearson Benjamin Cummings.

Johnson, D.W., Johnson, R.T., & Holubec, E J. (2009). *Circles of learning: Cooperation in the classroom* (4th ed.). Edina, MN: Interaction.

Lawrence, C.M., Lawrence, G., & Samek, L.S. (2006). *Organizing classrooms for small-group instruction: Learning for mastery.* Lanham, MD: Rowman & Littlefield.

Metzler, M.W. (2011). *Instructional models for physical education* (3rd ed.). Scottsdale, AZ: Holcomb Hathaway.

Mitchell, S.A., Oslin, J.L., & Griffin L.L. (2013). *Teaching sport concepts and skills: A tactical games approach* (3rd ed.). Champaign, IL: Human Kinetics.

Mosston, M., & Ashworth, S. (2008). *Teaching physical education* (1st online ed.). www.spectrumofteachingstyles.org

Pangrazi, R.P. (2013). *Dynamic physical education for elementary school children* (17th ed.). San Francisco, CA: Benjamin Cummings.

Rink, J.E. (2014). *Teaching physical education for learning* (7th ed.). Boston, MA: McGraw Hill.

Siedentop, D., & Tannehill, D. (2000). *Developing teaching skills in physical education* (4th ed.). Mountain View, CA: Mayfield.

Management

7

This chapter covers many ways of teaching class organization skills through physical activity. Emphasis is on a positive and constructive approach to moving students quickly into instructional settings. Teaching and expecting responsible behavior are important parts of effective class management, and students should know what acceptable behavior is and how to resolve conflict in a nonphysical manner. Preventing behavior problems is always more effective than dealing with problems after they occur. Organizing an environment that offers a behavior management component helps students become good citizens. In this chapter you will learn how to maintain and increase desirable behavior while at the same time decreasing undesirable behavior. We will also explore how to implement behavioral correction techniques when all else fails. Several strategies are offered, from reprimands to behavior contracts.

Learning Objectives

▶ Manage a class by delivering instruction efficiently and moving students into instructional settings quickly.

▶ Teach students responsible behavior by using responsibility development techniques and conflict resolution.

▶ Create a behavior plan and establish rules and consequences to minimize behavior problems.

▶ Increase desirable behavior by using social reinforcers effectively.

▶ Decrease undesirable behavior by designing a behavioral response plan. The range of teacher behaviors includes reprimands, removal of positive consequences, and behavior games.

▶ Avoid the use of criticism when interacting with students.

▶ Know when to resort to punishment (rarely) to stifle undesirable behavior.

It is often said, "If you can't manage, you can't teach." This assertion suggests that appropriate management skills are a prerequisite to effective teaching. **Management** refers in this chapter to techniques and strategies for moving, organizing, and grouping students for instructional purposes and developing appropriate behavior during class. Effective management results in reduced discipline problems and enhanced opportunities for students to develop individual responsibility, independence, and personal motivation. **Discipline** in this text is defined as dealing with unacceptable behavior and behavior that disrupts the flow and continuity of teaching and learning. Management minimizes discipline problems by building a framework that positively influences students in an efficient and self-directed manner. Management strategies also involve modifying and maintaining desirable behavior as well as decreasing undesirable behavior.

Successful teachers effectively manage student behavior. Management skills may vary among teachers in emphasis and focus, but collectively they characterize quality teaching. Effective teachers make three assumptions: (1) teaching is a profession, (2) students are in school to learn, and (3) the teacher's responsibility is to facilitate student learning. These assumptions indicate that instructors will teach a range of students, including those who readily accept instruction and those who do not. Competent teachers maintain faith in students who have not yet found success and expect them to do so eventually. The majority of students in a class are relatively easy to teach, but a great teacher can bring about appreciable gains among low-aptitude and indifferent students.

Strive for a Well-Managed Class

A well-managed class has the teacher and students assuming dual responsibility for reaching targeted learning goals. This accomplishment requires presentations and instructional strategies to match students' development levels. Effective class management and organizational skills create an environment that provides students with opportunities to learn free from discord. Effective teachers have the ability, skills, and strategies to prevent problems before they occur and create a learning environment where little time is spent dealing with off-task behavior.

A teacher's behavior and personal conduct does not occur in a vacuum. Students reflect the personality, outlook, ideals, and expectations of their teacher. Teachers should examine and reflect on their personal habits and attitudes to see if their behaviors could negatively influence students. Effective teachers model the behavior expected of their students. They move quickly if the request is that students hustle. They listen carefully to students and perform required tasks and fitness activities from time to time. Modeling desired behavior strongly influences students. The phrase "Your actions speak louder than your words" is true because students often make judgments about teachers based on their nonverbal behaviors. Too often, physical education teachers model nonactive behaviors. Students view them as authoritative figures carrying a clipboard, using a whistle, and ordering students to do things they themselves are unwilling to do.

Effective instruction and management can help students become more capable and self-sufficient, offering experience to promote success and develop a positive self-concept. Teachers who have clear expectations for learning and behavior develop classes that function with little wasted time or disruptions. Lessons run smoothly and are characterized by instructional routines that students expect and follow. A productive class setting is work oriented and on task, yet relaxed and pleasant. The next section shows how to organize and move a class quickly and effectively.

Use Effective Class Organization Strategies

Successful teachers quickly organize students for instruction. To move and organize students efficiently, teachers must understand various techniques and strategies and secure student acceptance of those techniques. If a class is poorly managed, the result is a lesson with excessive time spent on tasks that are not learning oriented. Students appreciate an organized and efficient learning environment that allows a maximum amount of class time to be devoted to learning and practicing skills and game play.

Management techniques can be seen as skills that students need to practice and learn. Viewing class management strategies in this light makes it easier to understand that students need time to develop classroom management skills. Just as students need time to improve physical skills, they need repeated practice of management routines. Simple statements can be a constructive way to remind students of expected behavior; for instance, the teacher may say, "It appears we have forgotten how to freeze quickly. Let's practice." Regardless of the educational setting, effective teachers have students practice management skills to reach expected behavior outcomes.

Start and Stop a Class Consistently

Starting and stopping activity during a class ensures that valuable time will be spent learning and practicing, not waiting or performing off-task behaviors. This tool is important for keeping youth safe during physical education class. Effective teachers select start and stop signals that ensure that students respond in a timely fashion. To stop a class, teachers must pick a consistent signal that all students can easily hear. The signal can be almost anything, as long as it always means the same thing: "Freeze!" A basketball lesson may produce a high level of noise as compared with yoga and may need a loud signal such as a whistle.

TEACHING TIP

Although a whistle does not always need to be used, a quality whistle is an essential tool of any physical education teacher. A whistle allows a teacher to get instant attention from her or his students. It provides a loud signal that all can hear in a noisy gymnasium or a large open space or field. A whistle can help get students' attention when a potential safety issue arises. and over a long career it will save the vocal muscles of the physical education teacher. Stop your class with a whistle and start it with a voice command to encourage listening skills.

Music can also be an effective stop signal during quieter activities. For instance, when the music stops, students know they are to stop and listen. Stop signals are important because they may have to be used for safety purposes (e.g., a student injury). Including a visual signal, such as raising the hand overhead, with the audio signal is effective because some students may not hear the audio signal if they are engrossed in activity or are hearing impaired. Avoid confusion by using a start signal different from the stop signal. Voice signals can frequently be used to start the class. Reinforcement of students' responses to start and stop signals ensures that students know classroom expectations and are held accountable. If students do not respond to the signal to stop, take time to practice the procedure and reinforce students when they perform management behavior properly. Often, skill performance is reinforced regularly, but correct management behavior is not. Behavior that is not reinforced will not be performed often.

Teachers can reasonably expect 100% compliance when asking students to stop. If some students stop and listen to directions and others do not, accountability is lost. Students quickly begin to wonder why they must stop but other students do not. Scanning the class to see if all students are stopped and ready to respond to the next set of directions provides teachers with needed information, confirming that all students are prepared to listen, that the stop signal is clear, and that students know what is expected of them. Teachers who settle for less than full attention will soon have a class that ignores stop signals. Students must be held accountable for responding appropriately to an instructor's expectations.

Many variables affect the rate and speed of response of a class. The nature of the activity, the students' motivational level, their feelings about the teacher, the time of day, and the weather are a few examples. Teachers control only some of these variables. A positive, success-oriented atmosphere helps decrease response time. Positive teacher reactions focused on appropriate student managerial behaviors are effective. Examples of such responses include the following:

- "Way to go class—everyone is prepared and ready to go in four minutes."
- "Carmen, great hustle back to your home base."
- "Thank you for getting quiet so quickly."
- "Look at group 1 line up quickly."
- "Hey, I'm impressed how quickly you all got in position."
- "Way to stop on the whistle; thank you."

Distributing and Retrieving Equipment Effectively

In physical education today, every student ideally has a piece of equipment for practice and skill development. Acceptable teaching practices ensure that students spend limited time waiting for a turn to practice and perform expected skills. Having a specific routine for placement of equipment during instruction can reduce off-task behavior and lack of attention. Placing the equipment in a home position avoids the problem of students' striking one another with the equipment, dropping it, or practicing activities when they should be listening (see figure 7.1). To prevent students from playing with the equipment when it is placed on the floor, ask them to put down the equipment and take a large step away from it. For example, hockey sticks are placed on the floor, basketballs are placed between the feet, and jump ropes are folded in half and placed behind the neck.

7

FIGURE 7.1 Home position for equipment during instructional periods.

TEACHING TIP

Require students to set equipment down gently and quietly. This practice will eliminate loud disruptive noise when 40 floor hockey sticks are slammed to the ground and help to minimize damage to rackets or other equipment. This management skill needs to be practiced as needed.

Distribution of numerous pieces of equipment in large classes can reduce the amount of time that students must develop and understand skills and cause more time to be spent in noninstruction. Therefore, equipment should be distributed to students as quickly as possible, yet in a safe manner. When students must wait for a piece of equipment, time is wasted and behavior problems occur. A common practice is to assign leaders to get the equipment for their squads, but that routine often results in many students waiting. A better and faster method is to have the equipment placed around the perimeter of the practice area (see figure 7.2).

Following clear instructions and a predetermined signal, students acquire a piece of equipment, take it to their personal space, and begin practicing an assigned task. This approach takes advantage of the natural urge to try the equipment and reinforces students who procure equipment quickly. Students put away equipment using the same routine. Placing equipment in the middle of the area in one container and telling students to "run and get a ball" creates an unsafe situation as well as wastes valuable time. Regardless of the method used to distribute equipment, clearly state what students are to do with the equipment after they take it to their personal space. If safety is not an issue, get students engaged immediately. Asking students to hold the equipment until everybody is ready may reinforce students who lag behind. Having students start practicing immediately can act as a prompt to those students who are slow responders.

TEACHING TIP

Use hoops or long jump ropes in various locations around the gym to house balls. This system eliminates the need for all students to use one ball rack or ball bag and minimizes wait time for retrieving and returning equipment.

FIGURE 7.2 Placement of equipment around the perimeter of the activity area saves time distributing equipment.

Alternate Instruction and Practice Episodes

Students' lack of interest during the teacher's instruction frequently occurs when the instruction is delivered as a long, involved technical monologue. Little learning occurs when students do not listen or have forgotten most of the information. Information regarding skill performance often includes a list of items to complete. Because people usually remember the first and the last point, most students are able to integrate and concentrate on only one or two points following the instructional episode. Instructions should be specific and rarely last longer than 30 to 45 seconds. Deliver instructions in small doses, focusing on one or two points at a time. An effective approach is to alternate short instructional episodes with periods of activity. Have students model what was just emphasized, such as how to hold the racket, stand in ready position, or follow through. Minimizing the amount of content per instructional episode allows them to focus clearly on stated goals and attain better understanding. This suggestion does not mean that information should not be delivered to students, but the tell-it-all-at-the-start style should be replaced by integrated instruction: input, practice, and feedback.

New units of instruction can be introduced using an interactive instructional period involving questions, modeling, and short periods of practice. Infusing alternative or novel instructional tools (including signs and short video clips) may help to motivate or keep students engaged. Beginning with 30 minutes of instruction on the first day followed by student practice or play results in limited understanding of the new content. Engage students through activity and build interest and understanding.

TEACHING TIP

Many youths today are visual learners. When introducing new material or spending time in instruction, an effective approach is to combine any verbal instruction with illustrations such as physical demonstrations, posters or signs, or video clips. Many teachers make the mistake of spending time explaining a skill and following it with a demonstration. If possible, combine the instruction and demonstration or illustration so that students are hearing and seeing it at the same time.

Middle and high school students are eager to move and, as a result, may not hear all the instructional information. An effective strategy is to manage first before giving instructions. If students are to be in groups of two or a small team, divide them quickly using the "when before what" technique. This technique is also effective to get students ready for skill practice or game play. Tell students when to perform before stating what. For example, say, "When I say, 'Start,' I'd like you to get a partner . . ." or, "When I say, 'Go!' I want you to jog over, get a volleyball, and practice volleying against the wall." When you have finished giving necessary instructions, students start on the word "Go." Because the keyword is not given until all directions have been issued, students must be attentive.

Expedite Instructional Transitions

Instructional transitions involve a change in instructional focus that, in turn, demands a reorganization of the class. Discipline problems frequently occur during transitions, often because disorganization creates time to stand around and visit with peers while students wait for the next task. Instructional momentum diminishes, and teachers often become frustrated when students must be redirected. Students will also stray off task when the activity lasts longer than is desirable. Transitions can add to the pace of the lesson when they result in effective flow of instruction. Transitions are planned episodes and should be written and thought out in a manner similar to instructional content.

TEACHING TIP

When possible, minimize reorganization for the sole purpose of giving new direction or minimal instruction. If students are well managed, many of these small bouts of direction or instruction may be done from a distance.

Errors in instructional planning can cause students to finish early and go off task waiting to see what is next. Activities need to support choice and allow students to guide themselves in learning new tasks. Specifying the number of repetitions offers an end in sight; some students will finish early, whereas others may talk and move at a slow pace. Any time the number of repetitions is stipulated, completion time will vary among students. Here is an example: Instructions are given to students to practice

chipping 20 golf balls. Obviously, the speed at which students will carry out this task will differ. A better approach is to give students an amount of time to complete the task. When time is up, instruction moves on to the next task. This approach is like station teaching in which students work for a specified time. This method has the side effect of teaching students to maximize the amount of practice they get in a certain amount of time. Certainly, this is a lesson that students can use throughout life to make the most of their time. Another option is to have additional tasks for students to complete when they finish early. But students may view this approach negatively if they perceive that they must do more than others because they were efficient in completing the previous task. Repetition and refinement determine the amount of skill learning that takes place, so doing more repetitions is better.

Group Students Effectively

Physical education requires moving students into small groups and instructional formations on a regular basis. Simple techniques can be used to accomplish this task in rapid fashion. For example, using a technique such as toe to toe teaches students to find partners quickly. The goal of this activity is to get toe to toe with a partner as quickly as possible. Other challenges may include having students find someone their approximate height or touch fists with a partner. Students without a partner go to the center of the teaching area (marked by a cone or spot and called the friendship spot) and find someone else without a partner. Students therefore have a designated spot to locate a partner as opposed to feeling unwanted and running around the area searching for (or avoiding) a partner. Emphasis is placed on finding a partner within two giant steps rather than looking for a favorite friend or snubbing someone. When students are asked to find a partner, they frequently stay near a friend; if a different mix is needed, then have students find a different partner each time toe to toe is called.

TEACHING TIP

When a few students are left without a partner or group, the teacher can expedite the process by defining the remaining groups or creating an odd-numbered group. This method often saves valuable time and minimizes the chances that someone will be intentionally left out by their classmates.

Many activities require the class to be divided in half for skill practice. An efficient way to achieve this is to have students get toe to toe with a partner. One partner then takes a knee while the other remains standing. Those standing are asked to go to one side of the area, while those kneeling move to the other side. This strategy divides partners into opposing sides and can address the problem that may arise when friends select each other. A quick game of rock–paper–scissors can be used to designate which person in a pair will get equipment, go to a specific side, or be captain.

Another technique that is effective when the goal is to place students quickly into small groups is to signal (with whistle blasts or loud hand claps) a certain number of times. Students form groups that correspond to the number of signals and sit down to signify that they have the correct number in their group. Students who cannot find a group in their immediate vicinity go to the center of the area and find the needed number of members. The use of hand signals (e.g., three fingers) to show the size of the desired group can be an effective way to signal the class to move into small groups.

After entering the facility, students also can be given a piece of paper or a token with a number or color. While the music is playing, they exchange the paper with several different people. When the music stops, they must find the person or people in the class with the same number or color. This technique can be used to select partners or teams. Using hoops of various colors can be another fun and effective approach to creating small groups. As in musical chairs, when the music stops, students quickly place a foot into the closest hoop with other people to form the designated number (e.g., groups of three, four, or five). All students must find a hoop and place one foot inside, but the number cannot go above the designated number. Hoops can be color coded, and the red hoop will join a blue hoop, green will join yellow, and purple will join white.

Many teachers use phone apps that randomly create teams or groups ahead of time. For example, after teachers specify how many groups are needed, the app makes a list of teams with students' names listed. Teachers can easily post different groups each day on the gym wall, so students will know what team or group they are in and which color jersey (or other item) they need to wear. Various selection criteria may also be used to ensure an equal number of boys and girls or even skill level.

When different techniques are used frequently to form groups, students accept this system as a regularly occurring routine and know that they will be expected to work with a variety of people for short periods. Stu-dents learn that working with a variety of classmates provides opportunities to work with people they might not otherwise get to know. This practice can contribute to a positive learning environment.

TEACHING TIP

Getting into groups or teams is a common transition during which valuable participation time is lost. Regardless of the grouping technique, teachers must practice with students regularly until the class becomes proficient.

Use Groups to Expedite Class Organization

Some teachers find that placing students into groups helps them manage a class effectively. These groups or teams offer a place for students to assemble, a way to group students into prearranged teams of equal ability, and a method to expedite learning students' names.

Home Base and Station Teaching

Creating a home base is a way of using groups to facilitate the management of students in a variety of educational settings. Groups also help to expedite taking role by instantly knowing that someone is missing. Place several marking spots around the area that corresponds to the number of groups. On the command "Home base," group leaders move to the nearest marking spot, and their respective squad members line up behind them. After students learn this basic skill, it can be used to facilitate instruction. For example, before the start of the lesson, station teaching signs and a marking spot are put out around the perimeter of the area. Students complete the initial parts of the lesson. When instruction at the stations is about to start, the teacher calls out, "Home base," and group leaders hustle to a marking spot at each of the stations. The result is a rapid transition; a group of students at each station is ready to begin. This activity can also be used to split the class in half by placing an equal number of marking spots in each half of the area.

Guidelines for Forming Groups

The following are guidelines for using group formation to maximize teaching effectiveness.

1. Avoid selecting groups in a manner that embarrasses a student who might be chosen last. In all cases, avoid using an auction approach in which student leaders look over the group and visibly pick those whom they favor. Computer programs are excellent for randomly selecting.

2. Establish a designated location where students are to assemble. On signal, students move to the designated area, with group leaders in front and the rest of the group behind.

3. Use groups to provide opportunities for leadership and following among peers by appointing group leaders. Examples of leadership activities are moving groups to a specified location, leading groups through exercises or introductory activities, and appointing group members to certain positions in activities. Rotate leaders every two to three weeks so that all students have an opportunity to lead.

TEACHING TIP

Consider predetermining the composition of groups. Having equal representation of ability levels in each group may be important. Groups can also be used to separate certain students so that they do not have the opportunity to disrupt the class. To ensure that students get to work with all students in the class, change group members on a regular basis. In most cases, an even number of groups should be formed so that the class can be broken quickly into multiple teams for games or activities.

Learn Students' Names

Learning the names of students not only personalizes instruction but also facilitates the management of students. Praise, feedback, and correction go unheeded when the teacher addresses a student by saying, "Hey, you!" Develop a system that helps expedite learning student names. One approach is to memorize three or four names per class period. Use a note card to help recognize each student by name at the start and throughout the period. At the end of the period, identify the students again. After memorizing the first set of names, the teacher can learn a new set. At the start of class when the meeting occurs, the names learned previously can be reviewed and new students identified. Teachers can

tell students they are trying to learn their names. Asking students to say their name before performing a skill or answering a question can help teachers learn their names. After learning students' names, teachers can use the student's name before instructional questions or skill performance feedback (e.g., "Rudy, it's your turn to try it.").

Another effective way to learn names is to take a photograph of each class in squads and identify students by keying names to the picture. Many school computer systems now have student names with photos in attendance programs. Teachers can use this tool to learn names or use it as a cheat sheet if they forget a name. Identification is easier with students in squads because they will be in the same location. Before the start of each class period, teachers can continue to learn student names by identifying a few students' names already learned and a few that still need to be learned. Setting personal goals based on calculating the percentage of students whose names have been learned each period ensures that teachers are accomplishing this effective management technique.

Establish Class Procedures and Expectations

Students enjoy the sense of security that comes from knowing what to do from the time they enter the instructional area until they leave. Several procedures need to be handled routinely. The following are situations that arise often and need to be planned for ahead of time.

Motivating Students to Prepare for Activity Quickly

If required or given the option, students must change into activity clothes in locker rooms located some distance from where attendance will be taken. A rather slow and unorganized start can be the result. Students also dress at different rates and enter the activity area at different times. Inappropriate activity can occur when the students who have dressed quickly are waiting for slower students to arrive. This dressing time difference also means that students are in two different and separate places, both of which require supervision. Fights, robbery, and other malicious activity often takes place in locker rooms. How a lesson starts often determines how a lesson finishes (good start means a good finish). A positive approach is to allow students who dress quickly to participate in activities they enjoy until the entire class is assembled. Therefore, students have a reason to change quickly because they know they will have time to participate in activities they enjoy. Allow students to select things they like to do from a list of safe activities (e.g., shooting baskets, juggling objects, passing and catching discs). Developing an award system for individuals or squads is another effective way to expedite the dressing process. Free time points are awarded each time individuals or all group members are ready to participate by a specific time. When positive reinforcement is provided, the responsibility for getting students ready can shift from the teacher to students.

TEACHING TIP

Many major issues can occur in the locker room. For example, fighting, bullying, and stealing are more common in the locker room than in the gymnasium. The locker room must always be adequately supervised. When possible, students should not be allowed to reenter the locker room during class time to eliminate potential issues.

Dealing With Nonparticipation

Identifying students who are not participating in the lesson should be done in a consistent and efficient manner. The teacher must determine why the nonparticipation is taking place to help eliminate future episodes. A routine that addresses this issue is effective when the decision for nonparticipation is made by someone (nurse or classroom teacher) other than the physical education teacher before students arrive at the lesson area. If a school nurse is not available, a written policy approved by the school administrator should be in place to prevent the physical education teacher from encouraging students to participate when they are not supposed to do so. A note from the school nurse listing the student's name, health problem, and reason that he or she must sit out or take part in modified activities should be presented to the physical education teacher. This information is accepted at face value, thus relieving the teacher from having to question students to determine what the problem is and what the solution should be. Because most teachers are not health agents, they are not qualified to determine whether a health problem should disqualify a student from participation. A student with a note from home or a physician should never be allowed to return to participation without parental permission. Nonparticipation because the student lacks a uniform should be avoided if possible. Teachers can have extra clothes and shoes for students who forget their clothes. Students who will not be participating for any reason should be provided an alternative assignment or responsibility. For example, a student with an injury may be able to keep statistics or even referee. Other students who are nonparticipants may be given an alternative assignment. Alternative assignments (see figure 7.3) may include a written report, peer assessment, or similar activity and should be related to physical education content when possible.

Taking Attendance

Attendance is a daily routine that could lead to boredom among students. While waiting to participate they may begin to socialize or get involved in horseplay, resulting in a class getting off to a noisy and disorganized start. An effective method for taking attendance each day helps reduce time spent in management of behavior problems. An effective technique is to use group leaders. Each leader reports any absentees to the teacher orally or by

NONPARTICIPATION ALTERNATIVE ASSIGNMENT

Write a three-page, double-spaced, printed paper (no handwritten papers accepted), including all the following elements:

1. Research and describe the history of soccer beginning with the Chinese and Roman empires.
2. Discuss how soccer has evolved over time and what its effect has been in the United States.
3. Choose one current, well-known soccer player (male or female) and write a brief biography of this person.
4. Finally, include a description of some of your personal experiences playing soccer either competitively or recreationally. If you have not previously played soccer, describe another activity that you have participated in competitively or recreationally.

FIGURE 7.3 Sample alternative assignment for nonparticipation worksheet.

filling out an attendance sheet. Another approach is to paint numbers on the floor and assign each student a number. A teacher or a student leader can quickly glance through the numbers and record any absentees. Posting a sign-in sheet for attendance, which students quickly initial, can also be effective. Another approach is to check attendance while students are beginning the first class activity. Regardless of the method used, the technique should save time and foster student self-management qualities. Many tablets and smart phones provide a tool for instantly entering attendance information. The use of technology can often expedite this task and reduce required paperwork between class periods.

Closing a Lesson

A regular routine for closing the lesson is beneficial. Closure provides opportunities to check student understanding of the day's lesson, review material for the next day, or record achieved outcomes. For example, ask the class to identify verbally (or demonstrate physically) the key points of a skill learned during class, give the results of games being played, or discuss new ideas learned during a strategy session. Closure can also be used to prepare students for the next lesson, by saying, for example, "Tomorrow we will apply the skills you learned today in a game setting." It is also a good time to have discussions related to quality efforts and willingness to work independently. Closure may be done while students are lined up at the door, in scattered formation, or while grouped in a semicircle. Time must be provided for closure related to the instructional content as well as a procedure for students to leave the teaching area.

Teach Responsible Student Behavior

Physical education should be a positive experience for all students. To experience the benefits of physical education, students must accept that they are mutually responsible for contributing to a positive learning environment. Increased emphasis on teaching responsible behavior to students has been placed with teachers. A basic premise for learning responsible behavior is that it must be planned, taught, and reinforced. Responsible behavior takes time and practice to learn, much like any other skill. Don Hellison (2011) developed strategies and programs for teaching responsibility to older students. Hellison suggests that there is a hierarchy of responsible behavior. The focus in this section is on the idea that students can learn different levels of respon-

sible behavior. Teaching responsible behavior described here involves five levels of behavior. Each is defined in the following text, accompanied by examples of typical student behavior at each level. One point to note is some teachers take issue with identifying a level as 0. If that is a problem, renumber the levels (1 through 5, with 1 being the lowest level), letter them a through e, or create your own category names. The important point is the process of learning to participate at a higher level of responsibility.

Level 0: Irresponsibility

Level 0 students are unmotivated and undisciplined. Their behavior includes discrediting other students' involvement and interrupting, intimidating, manipulating, and verbally or physically abusing other students and perhaps the teacher. Behavior examples include the following:

- At home: blaming brothers or sisters for problems, lying to parents
- During free time: calling other students names, laughing at others
- In physical education: talking to friends when the teacher is giving instructions, pushing and shoving when selecting equipment

Level 1: Respect

Students at this level do not participate in the day's activity or show much mastery or improvement. These students control their behavior enough so that they do not interfere with the other students' right to learn and the teacher's right to teach. Behavior examples include the following:

- At home: keeping self from hitting a brother or sister even though angry
- During free time: not getting angry at others because they did something to upset them
- In physical education: waiting until an appropriate time to talk with friends, having control and not letting behavior of others bother them

Level 2: Participation

These students show self-control and are involved in the subject matter or activity. Behavior examples include the following:

- At home: helping with chores around the house
- During free time: visiting with friends, participating in a game

- In physical education: listening and performing an activity, trying an activity even if it is not a favorite, participating in an activity without complaining

Level 3: Self-Direction

Level 3 students take responsibility for their choices and for linking these choices to their own identities. They can work without direct supervision, eventually taking responsibility for their intentions and actions. Behavior examples include the following:

- At home: cleaning up without being asked
- During free time: taking the initiative to involve others in activities
- In physical education: following directions, practicing a skill without being told, trying new activities without prompting

Level 4: Caring

Students behaving at this level are motivated to extend their sense of responsible behavior by cooperating, giving support, showing concern, and helping. Behavior examples include the following:

- At home: helping take care of a younger brother or sister or a pet
- During free time: asking students who they do not know or who feel left out to join them in play
- In physical education: helping someone who is having trouble, helping a new student feel welcome, working with all students, showing that all people are worthwhile

Responsible behavior is taught using several strategies. Posting the levels of responsibility in the teaching area provides a continuous reminder (see figure 7.4). Each level of behavior must be explained and acceptable behaviors identified. Middle and high school students can actively engage in this process. Including students in the process of identifying what is and is not acceptable behavior is often valuable. When students are involved in the process, they often maintain a greater awareness of their behavior because they helped create the list of what is appropriate. Teachers can provide opportunities for their students to identify examples in their own lives that can be shared with small peer groups and a list of acceptable behaviors developed and posted for levels 2, 3, and 4. After students have received an introduction to responsible behavior, reinforcement of desired behavior and redirection

of inappropriate behavior can begin. A two-pronged approach is used: (1) catch students using responsible behavior and reinforce them; and (2) redirect students behaving at level 0 by asking, "At what level are you performing, and what level would be more acceptable?" An example is the following discussion between teacher and student when a student is behaving at level 0. The teacher has an open dialogue with the student in a nonconfrontational and nonadversarial manner.

Teacher: *Tyler, it looked like you were making fun of someone.*
Student: *I wasn't making fun of anyone!*
Teacher: *Maybe you don't see it that way. But if you were making fun, what level of behavior would it be?*
Student: *Zero?*
Teacher: *Yes. Is that really the way you want to be with other students?*
Student: *Not really.*
Teacher: *If you were at level 0, why do you think it would be good to move to a higher level?*
Student: *Maybe moving to up a level shows you have good self-control even if someone else makes you mad or if you don't like that person.*

Teacher feedback forms the core of the responsibility approach, but many strategies can be used to increase responsible behavior in the instructional setting, such as the following:

- *Model desirable behavior.* Interact frequently with students to encourage responsible behavior. Students do not care how much a teacher knows until they know how much a teacher cares. Youths should be treated with dignity and respect, and teachers should follow through with responsible actions and words. In return, teachers should expect students to treat teachers and others with dignity and respect.

- *Use reinforcement.* Give students specific feedback about the quality of their behavior. If corrective feedback is given, make sure it identifies the desired level of behavior. When reinforcing desirable behavior, be specific in identifying why the behavior is desirable and conveying that such acts are appreciated. In some cases, identify a student as a "super citizen" or make a positive phone call home to recognize special behaviors or efforts.

- *Allow student sharing.* Offer student opportunities to give their opinions about responsible behavior. Students' feelings and perceptions are important.

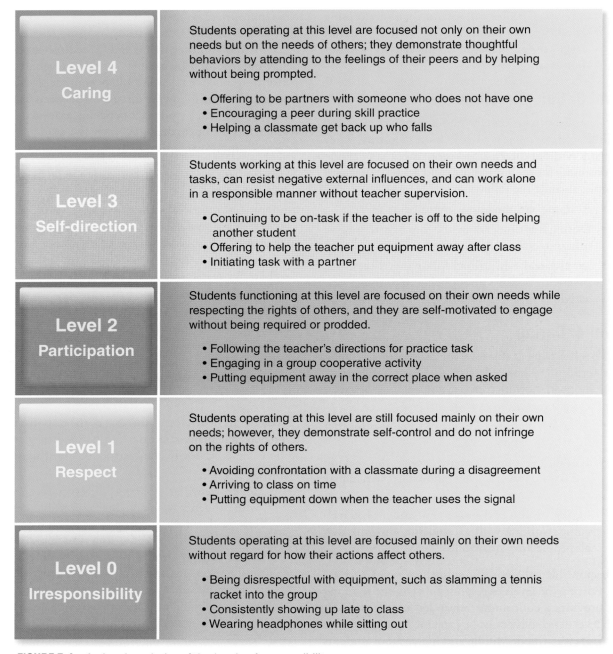

Level 4
Caring

Students operating at this level are focused not only on their own needs but on the needs of others; they demonstrate thoughtful behaviors by attending to the feelings of their peers and by helping without being prompted.

- Offering to be partners with someone who does not have one
- Encouraging a peer during skill practice
- Helping a classmate get back up who falls

Level 3
Self-direction

Students working at this level are focused on their own needs and tasks, can resist negative external influences, and can work alone in a responsible manner without teacher supervision.

- Continuing to be on-task if the teacher is off to the side helping another student
- Offering to help the teacher put equipment away after class
- Initiating task with a partner

Level 2
Participation

Students functioning at this level are focused on their own needs while respecting the rights of others, and they are self-motivated to engage without being required or prodded.

- Following the teacher's directions for practice task
- Engaging in a group cooperative activity
- Putting equipment away in the correct place when asked

Level 1
Respect

Students operating at this level are still focused mainly on their own needs; however, they demonstrate self-control and do not infringe on the rights of others.

- Avoiding confrontation with a classmate during a disagreement
- Arriving to class on time
- Putting equipment down when the teacher uses the signal

Level 0
Irresponsibility

Students operating at this level are focused mainly on their own needs without regard for how their actions affect others.

- Being disrespectful with equipment, such as slamming a tennis racket into the group
- Consistently showing up late to class
- Wearing headphones while sitting out

FIGURE 7.4 A visual reminder of the levels of responsibility.

Students can identify ways to encourage higher levels of responsible behavior. They can also brainstorm to identify consequences of high- and low-level behavior. Another practice is to ask students to give examples of responsible behavior at different levels. Allow time for students to share how they feel when someone uses a high- or low-level behavior around them.

- *Encourage goal setting.* Help students set goals for the responsible behavior they want to exhibit. Do this at the start of a lesson by asking students to tell a partner the level of behavior they want to use today. At the end of the lesson, partners evaluate each other to see if the behavior was exhibited. Examples of behaviors are listening, hustling, following directions, taking turns, and complimenting others.

- *Offer opportunities for responsibility.* Give students responsibility in a class setting. Being a group leader, team captain, referee, scorekeeper, rule maker, or dispute arbitrator encourages students to exhibit high-level behavior. Because responsible positions affect other students, effective leaders must behave responsibly.

- *Allow student choice.* Realize that responsible behavior is best learned when students make choices. The natural consequences of self-selected choices are often the best teachers. Students can make choices about games they choose to play, fitness activities they select, and friends they choose. Discussing how to make meaningful choices (see chapter 16) is an important phase of learning to make responsible choices.

Resolve Conflicts

Conflict between students can result in aggression and violence. Almost 30% of youth in the United States (or over 7.1 million) are estimated to have been bullied at school (Robers, Zhang, & Truman, 2012). Studies exploring bullying in physical education have found that 11% of youth have been physically bullied, 14% verbally bullied, and 13% socially bullied in physical education class (Hurley & Mandigo, 2010). Furthermore, those who were bullied would often avoid physical education in the future (Hurley & Mandigo, 2010; O'Connor & Graber, 2014). Sadly, adults often provide mixed information regarding bullying and ignore nonphysical instances of bullying during physical education (O'Connor & Graber, 2014). Nobody wants to create a world where the strong dominate and the weak live in fear and submission. Conflict is a part of daily life, and students must understand that they need to deal with conflict in an effective manner. Students can learn ways to respect others' opinions and feelings while maintaining their own worth and dignity.

TEACHING TIP

The National Education Association website includes many resources that can help teachers address bullying in schools and promote a safe learning environment. See "10 Steps to Stop and Prevent Bullying" at http://nea.org/home/72595.htm.

TEACHING TIP

As social media and technology continue to evolve, cyber bullying has become increasingly rampant. Recent research has suggested that up to 18% of youth have been cyber bullied (Hinduja & Patchin, 2018). Teachers need to be aware of the evolving methods used to bully or pick on others.

7

There are several ways to solve conflicts, but the most common methods identified involve three types of behavior—dominating, appeasing, and cooperating. Students who use the dominating style are often unsure about their standing in the group. They want things to be done their way but are afraid others will reject them. They often lack confidence and try hard to get others to accept their way of doing things. Youth who are appeasers lack confidence but want others to accept them. They do not like conflict and are willing to suppress their feelings to placate others.

Neither the dominating nor the appeasing approach is effective for solving conflicts in the long run. No one likes to be dominated or placed in the position of having to appease others. Conflict resolution can help students learn to solve conflicts in a peaceful manner with no apparent losers. A cooperative approach to solving problems can build positive feelings between students and lead to better group cohesiveness. The following are steps typically followed to resolve conflicts. If youth are experienced at conflict resolution, they may be able to carry out the steps without instructor intervention.

1. *Stop the aggressive behavior immediately.* Separate students in conflict immediately and give them an opportunity to cool down. A predesignated cool-down area is an excellent place to send students to relax and calm down.

2. *Gather data about what happened and define the problem.* Find out what happened, who was involved, and how each person feels about the conflict. Open the discussion with a feeling-oriented statement such as, "You must have really been angry to get involved in a fight." This allows students to talk about their emotions and the incident.

3. *Brainstorm possible solutions.* Keep in mind that brainstorming is a nonjudgmental process in which all solutions are accepted regardless of

their perceived value. Encourage the students to think of as many options as possible by asking open-ended questions, such as, "How could we solve this problem?" and "What other ways could we deal with this?"

4. *Test the ideas generated through brainstorming.* Ask a question such as, "What solutions might work best?" Help students understand the implications of the solutions and the way in which the solutions can be implemented. Accept solutions that may differ from your way of solving the problem.

5. *Help implement the plan.* Walk students through the solution so that they develop a perception of the approach. Guide them through the steps by asking, "Who goes first?" or "Who will take the next step?" As the solution is implemented, a change may need to be made, which can be agreed on by the involved students.

6. *Evaluate the approach.* Observe to see that the plan is accomplishing the desired outcome. Encourage students to change the plan if necessary.

The conflict resolution process takes practice and time. Teachers who take time to develop students' conflict resolution skills live with the knowledge that they are teaching students to solve problems without violence or excessive emotion. An objective approach to resolution is needed. Facilitating the conflict resolution process demands certain teacher behaviors including empathetic listening to both parties, exploring both sides of the problem, and helping students believe that the process was equitable. Blame is not assessed in this process. Placing blame encourages defensive student behaviors. Students must trust that the process will be fair and objective and that they will receive fair treatment if they deal with the issue cooperatively.

Implement a Proactive Behavior Management Approach

Many class management and discipline problems can be prevented through anticipation and planning. Anticipating the types of problems that might occur and having a plan for dealing with them provide the backdrop for developing effective strategies. Developing a plan of attack for dealing with problems offers a sense of confidence and peace of mind. Phase 1 of an effective behavior management plan is beginning the year on a proactive and positive note. Developing a comprehensive behavior

A cooperative approach to solving problems can build positive feelings between students and lead to better group cohesiveness.

management approach is a systematic way to deal with problems that affect all teachers and are generally ranked as the most serious concerns of teachers and parents.

Create a Behavior Plan for Yourself

The adage "Know thyself" is never more important than when having to manage a class of students. The one thing to assume is that management and discipline skills will be needed regardless of what age or type of class is being taught. How a teacher responds to misbehavior will make a huge difference in how students respond to him or her.

Here are some key points to consider in reflecting on your management plans:

- How will you respond when misbehavior occurs? Will you be threatened, angry, sad, or unmoved?
- What types of behaviors might set you off or anger you?
- How will you control your emotions?
- How do you usually behave and respond to students when you are angry or stressed?

Generally, a teacher communicates to students in three ways when various types of misbehavior occur: passively, aggressively, or assertively.

Passive Communication

A passive teacher hopes to make all students happy. Passive means trying to avoid all conflict and please others. Directly or indirectly, the passive teacher is constantly saying, "Like me; appreciate what I do for you." Many passive teachers want to be perfect so that everybody will like them. They hope that students will behave perfectly. When students go off task, Mr. or Ms. Passive becomes upset and angry. A common pattern is for the passive teacher to let behavior slide until she or he cannot take it anymore. Then the teacher loses composure and lashes out at the class in anger. When the anger subsides, Mr. Passive wants to make up again and restarts the cycle of letting things go and then blowing up.

Passive teachers often turn over their power to students, particularly the least cooperative students. For example, they will say things like, "We are not going to start until everyone is listening!" Interpreted concretely, students may hear, "This is great. We don't have to start until we are finished with our conversation." Passive teachers also ignore unacceptable behavior and hope it will disappear. Ignoring seldom causes behavior to disappear; rather, such behavior often becomes worse over time. Passive teachers often make threats but never

follow through with them. For example, a teacher might say, "If you do that one more time, I am going to call your parents." When no follow-through occurs or it is impossible to follow through, the words are empty and meaningless and students soon learn to disrespect the teacher. Another common trait of a passive teacher is to ask questions that will result in information that is meaningless. For example, the teacher might ask, "What did you do that for?" or "Why are you doing this?" or "Don't you know better than that?" These questions do not elicit useful information, and the teacher's frustration level is elevated because of students' "I don't know" responses.

Aggressive Communication

An aggressive teacher wants to overpower others by coming on strong. Aggressive instructors believe that communication is a competition, and they must win at all costs whenever it occurs. A common trait with aggressive communicators is that they use the word "you" all the time. Statements containing "you" keep students feeling defensive and attacked. Examples include, "You never listen to me; you are always the one in trouble; you are the problem here; you are always talking." Aggressive responders often have all the answers and express others' viewpoints (which are often wrong). For example, they may say, "You think that because you did that in your other class, you can do it in my class." No one knows what another is thinking, and communicating this way serves no purpose.

Aggressive communicators often use the words "always" and "never." These words are labeling words. They make students feel as if they are bad people who always behave in certain ways or never do anything right. Words that generalize and label create communication problems and can result in alienation rather than respect. Aggressive communicators often see students as personally attacking them and focus on labeling the other person rather than dealing with the behavior. Often, they do not reveal how they feel about things and are unwilling to express their own thoughts and feelings. If students never know how a teacher feels, they are unlikely to develop much empathy for their instructor. A good rule is this: Any statement about the other person rather than telling her or him how you feel will give your communication an attacking and aggressive flavor.

Assertive Communication

An assertive teacher does not beg, plead, or threaten. Instead, the approach is straightforward and focused on feelings and expectations. An assertive person is not afraid to say what he or she wants and does not worry about what others will think of him or her. A teacher who wants to be liked is quite concerned about what students think of him or her. An assertive teacher wants what is best for students and does not worry about what they think. Assertiveness comes across to students as a no-nonsense approach that needs to be carried out. It is clear, direct, and concrete. It requires little interpretation to carry out. For example, an assertive teacher might say to a student who has been talking out of turn, "It bothers me when you talk while I am talking." The teacher is expressing her or his feelings and making the unacceptable behavior clear. Following that statement with an assertive statement that expresses the desired behavior, such as, "That is your second warning; I'd like you to stop immediately," is clear but not angry. Emotion is not part of an assertive response because emotion turns assertion into aggressiveness.

An excellent way to make messages more assertive is to make them using the word "I" instead of "you." Talking about personal feelings and emotions will make the messages sound more reasonable and firm. For example, the teacher might say, "When you are playing with your equipment while I am talking, it bothers me and makes me forget what I planned on saying. Please leave your equipment alone when I talk." Such messages identify the behavior that is disruptive or annoying, state how the teacher feels, and direct the student to behave in a proper manner.

A key element to managing students effectively is being aware of the influence of certain behaviors when disciplining students. Teachers can become angry when they feel threatened or when students seriously misbehave, and some teachers may behave in a tyrannical manner. A teacher's behavior plan is a reminder of how to behave when student misbehavior occurs:

1. *Maintain your composure.* Students do not know your trigger points unless you reveal them. If you lose your temper students may lose respect for you and regard you as an ineffective teacher.

2. *Acknowledge your feelings when student misbehavior occurs.* Do you feel angry, threatened, challenged, or fearful? How do you typically respond when a student defies you? Know and understand yourself.

3. *Design a plan for when difficult feelings arise.* When you feel anxiety building because of student misbehavior, use a calming approach such as counting to 10 or taking five deep breaths before responding. You can also choose to avoid dealing with the student misbehavior until you have your emotions under control.

4. *Know your options for dealing with the challenging behavior.* Talking meaningfully with students is best done after class if it is going to take more than a few seconds. Options to use when you have only limited time include discreetly warning the student, removing the student from class, or sending another student for help if a situation is severe or escalating.

Assertive communication is clear, direct, and concrete.

Determine Rules and Procedures for the School Year

Rules are an expected part of the school environment. Most teachers want students to be respectful to them and other students. Expecting students to behave is not unreasonable. If teachers cannot manage students, teachers cannot teach. In fact, many school administrators judge teacher effectiveness by how well they manage students. Managing students is a necessary and important part of teaching; in fact, it is a requisite to the delivery of content. When creating rules, select general categories rather than specific behavior. For example, the rule "Respect your peers" includes many things, from not physically abusing others to not swearing. Post rules in the teaching area where all students can easily read them. General rules for a physical education classroom might include the following:

- *Stop, look, and listen.* This rule means stopping on signal, looking at the instructor, and listening for instructions.
- *Take care of equipment.* This rule includes caring for, distributing, gathering, and using equipment properly.
- *Respect the rights of others.* This rule includes behavior such as not bothering others, respecting their equipment, and not fighting and arguing.

Limit the number of rules to three to five. Establishing more rules makes it difficult for students to remember all the details and makes the teacher appear excessively strict. Student may also become rule specific. A student may choose to chew gum in the gym room because the school rule is "No gum chewing in the halls or classrooms." When students become rule specific, they often fail to think about right and wrong and follow only stipulated rules. Rules are guidelines for desired behavior rather than negative statements telling students what they cannot do. Consider the following points when designing rules:

- Select major categories of behavior rather than a multitude of specific rules.
- Identify observable behavior. This makes it easy to determine whether a person is following a rule and does not involve subjective judgment.
- Make rules reasonable for the age level of students. The best rules are those that cut across all ages and situations.
- Try to limit the number of rules to three to five.

- State rules briefly and positively. Writing a rule that covers all situations and conditions is impossible. Make the rule brief yet broad. An important part of teaching is to get students to think about the ethical implications of the rule rather than seeing it as someone telling them what they cannot do.
- Consider including students in the rule development process. Doing so will empower them and may help in accountability.

Communicate the Consequences of Misbehavior

When rules are broken, students must learn to accept the consequences of their behaviors. A sign of a mature student is the willingness to accept the consequences of improper behavior. Immature students argue, try to place the blame on others, or refuse to accept the need for such rules. List and post the consequences of misbehavior in a prominent place in the teaching area. Discuss the rules with students to ensure they understand and see the necessity of having behavior guidelines. Be sure to apply rules and consequences consistently to ensure that no students are punished excessively or unfairly. For example, a teacher who likes some students more than others may inadvertently punish students differently for the same misbehavior. Students then believe that the teacher is unfair. Giving students a say in the development of rules and consequences helps them create an environment in which they feel some sense of ownership. When consequences have been mutually agreed on, teachers have no need to feel upset, disappointed, or angry when students are held accountable for breaking the class rules. This process reduces anger and guilt so that both teacher and students feel better about each other.

Consequences for Unacceptable Behavior

First Misbehavior

1. Warn the student quietly on a personal basis.
2. Use a gentle reminder to refocus the student.

Second Misbehavior

1. Quietly ask the student to go to the time-out area until he or she is ready to participate properly.
2. Specify an amount of time or tell the student to remain there until you give him or her permission to return.

Third Misbehavior

1. Send the student to time-out for the remainder of the period and inform her or him that non-participation will result in a loss of points. If the behavior continues, the student should lose free-time privileges.

2. Identify a single behavior that needs to be changed, improved, or strengthened. Do not pick more than one behavior because it will make it much more difficult to monitor change and may decrease the student's chance for success.

3. Identify a behavior that will be substituted for the behavior to be modified.

4. Determine what positively reinforces the student. Have a discussion with the student to learn what is reinforcing.

5. Decide whether a negative reinforcer (see the following section) is needed to give momentum to the change process.

6. Develop a plan for getting the desired behavior to occur. This plan will generate a behavior that can be reinforced and used to replace the undesirable behavior.

7. Put the plan into effect and set a time frame for evaluation of the plan. Decide what modifications are needed to make the plan more effective. This modification may demand a different set or schedule of reinforcers or negative consequences. If an entirely different plan is needed (because the behavior has not decreased or changed), make such changes and proceed.

8. Continue evaluating and modifying the plan.

Implement Your Management Plan

Several things can be done during the first few weeks of teaching to ensure that classes begin successfully. During this time, communicate expectations in a positive manner that leaves students with a good first impression. A meaningful start leaves students feeling confident and excited about the experience. Consider the following points.

Develop Awareness and the Ability to Coprocess

Teachers must be aware of what is going on in their classes if they are going to be effective managers. Some beginning teachers do not even see students misbehaving or going off task. Two common traits of effective classroom managers are "with-it-ness" and "overlappingness." With-it-ness is the ability to be aware of what is going on in class regard-less of what you are doing or teaching. Overlappingness is the ability to process many things at once in an effective manner. What this means is that teachers must do many things at once. Teaching is not a profession for those who have a single goal in mind and tend to be able to concentrate on only one thing at a time. Rather, teachers must see how students are behaving regardless of what they are teaching. "Spinning many plates at one time" is a descriptive catchphrase for an effective teacher.

Be a Leader, Not a Friend

Students want a teacher who is a knowledgeable, personable leader. They are not looking for a friend; in fact, most students feel uncomfortable if they perceive that a teacher wants to be one of them. This notion can be especially difficult for new teachers who are often close in age to high school students. Teachers should communicate to students what they will learn during the semester but not be part of their personal discussions. Teachers should maintain a comfortable distance between themselves and students. This is not to say that teachers should not be friendly and caring; being concerned about students is important, but the concern must be expressed in a professional manner. Being a leader means knowing that the teacher's charge is to direct a class and be responsible for what is learned and how it is presented. Student input is important, but ultimately the teacher is responsible for leading a class to desired objectives.

Communicate High Standards

Students respond to expectations. If students are expected to perform at high levels, most of them will strive to do so. A common but accurate expression is, "You get what you ask for." If students are expected to perform to the best of their abilities, they probably will do so. On the other hand, if teachers act as if they do not care whether students try to achieve to the best of their abilities, some will do as little as possible.

Use Activities That Involve the Entire Class

To minimize class management problems, select instructional activities that keep the entire group involved in simultaneous activity. As rapport is developed with a class, different styles of teaching and class organization can be used. Using a more direct style of teaching (see chapter 6) in the first few weeks of teaching is usually better. This strategy allows a teacher to view the entire class and see how students respond to the educational setting. Less directed teaching styles and varied organizational schemes are usually implemented after class management skills have been developed and students have shown the ability to work independently. Station teaching, peer teaching, and other approaches are more effective when the teacher and students feel mutual respect.

TEACHING TIP

Whenever possible, avoid having students sitting out or waiting to participate. Everyone may not be able to play at the same time. If this is the case, teachers may have nonparticipating students referee, keep score, peer assess, or do some other activity to help minimize potential management issues.

Give Positive Group Feedback

Positive feedback delivered to a class develops group morale and points the class toward common goals. Classes should learn to view themselves as units that work together and are rewarded when they meet group goals. Students must work within groups as adults, so learning about group cooperation and pride in accomplishment helps ensure a smoothly running class and prepares them for adulthood.

Discipline Individually and Avoid Group Negative Feedback

When negative feedback is delivered, it should be done privately and personally to individual students. Few people want to have negative comments delivered globally for others to hear. In addition, never punish all students for the behavior of a few who misbehave. This approach leads to resentment and contrary results. If the entire group is criticized, the teacher is likely to lose the respect and admiration of students who were behaving properly.

TEACHING TIP

When negative or corrective feedback is warranted, use the sandwich approach if possible. This approach requires the teacher to provide positive feedback first, give the negative or corrective message next, and conclude with another positive feedback. For example, a teacher might state, "I really like how you are always calling for the ball, but I would like to see you give your teammates an opportunity as well. Keep up the great hustle."

Classes should learn to view themselves as units that work together and are rewarded when they meet group goals.

Avoid Counterproductive Feedback

Some verbal types of interactions work in the short term but cause long-term negative consequences. The following types of feedback often work immediately but cause greater problems over time. If students grow resentful, they will become deviant when the teacher is not around.

- *Preaching or moralizing.* A common example of moralizing is telling students, "You should know better than that!" If they actually knew better, they might not have behaved in an unacceptable manner in the first place. Students make mistakes because they are inexperienced and learning as they go. Part of learning is making mistakes. Correct mistakes in a quiet and caring manner.

- *Threatening.* Threats are ultimatums intended to terminate undesirable behavior, even though you know you cannot carry them out. For example, "If you don't stop that, I'm going to kick you out of class," sounds tough but is usually impossible to enforce. If students hear numerous idle threats, they will start to tune out and their respect will wane.

- *Ordering and commanding.* If teachers sound too bossy, students begin to feel as if they are nothing more than pawns to be moved around. Ask students firmly but respectfully to carry out tasks. Courtesy and politeness are requisites for effective teacher–student relationships.

- *Interrogating.* When a problem occurs (e.g., an argument between students), an initial reaction is to try to figure out who started the argument rather than deal with the feelings of the students. Little is gained by trying to determine who started it. Try calmly saying, "You know loud arguing is not acceptable behavior in my class. You must have been very angry to place yourself in this situation." This response encourages students to talk about their feelings rather than place blame on others. It also communicates a caring and concerned attitude toward students even when they misbehave.

- *Refusing to listen.* This response commonly manifests itself when the teacher says, "Let's talk about it some other time." At times, such as during instruction, this response is necessary. But if you always refuse to listen, students will avoid interaction and believe you do not care.

- *Labeling.* Labeling is characterized by telling students, "Stop acting like babies" or "You're behaving like a bunch of loonies." On a personal level, this may sound more like, "You're always the problem in this class." This statement is degrading and dehumanizing to students. Often, labeling is done with the intent of improving performance, but it is usually destructive and leaves students with negative feelings.

Give Clear and Specific Instructions

Students may misbehave because they do not understand the instructions. Keep directions targeted and brief and use the following guidelines:

- Give instructions and then proceed immediately with the activity.

- Monitor the group to see whether most students do not perform correctly. If more than half of your students appear unsure or confused, stop the class and reinstruct.

- If students are focused and listening, yet they are still confused when it is time to participate, monitor and adjust.

Maintain and Promote Acceptable Behavior

Managing student behavior is an ongoing task. A class of students is really a group of individuals, each of whom must be uniquely treated and understood. Some teachers question the importance of instructional discipline. Teaching discipline allows students to learn effectively without encroaching on the rights of others.

Most students choose to cooperate and participate positively in the educational setting. In fact, learners are largely responsible for allowing the teacher to teach. Students who chooses not to cooperate cannot be taught. Effective management of behavior means maintaining an environment in which all students have the opportunity to learn. The teacher is responsible for fashioning a learning environment where all students learn and feel comfortable. Students who choose to be disruptive and off task infringe on the rights of students who choose to cooperate. If a teacher must spend a great deal of energy working with students who are disorderly, students who want to learn are shortchanged.

This section provides a plan for modifying and maintaining desired student behavior. The overall approach is two pronged and straightforward: (1) increase levels of desired behavior, and (2) eliminate or reduce undesirable behavior by focusing on a positive and constructive approach that teaches students responsible behavior.

Increase Desired Behavior

Behavior that is followed by appropriate positive reinforcement will occur more often in the future. This principle is a key for increasing desired behavior. The strength of this simple principle is that it focuses on positive and desired educational outcomes. A critical component of increasing desired behavior through reinforcement is that such behavior must occur. For example, if a student often makes negative comments about peers, addressing this issue may be a difficult and slow process because reinforcement can only be given when a student makes a positive comment. Arranging the environment is often necessary to stimulate the behavior to be reinforced. Some suggested ideas discussed in detail later in the chapter are to use the Premack principle, use behavioral contracts, use failure-proof activities, and prompt students for the desired behavior. Key points for increasing desired behaviors lie in deciding what to use as reinforcers, selecting those that effectively reinforce individuals, and properly using the reinforcers.

Social Reinforcers

With secondary school students, it is best to use social reinforcers to increase desired behavior. Teachers and parents most often use this class of reinforcers such as praise, physical contact, and facial expressions to acknowledge desirable and acceptable behavior. The following are examples of reinforcers that can be used with students in a physical education setting:

Words of Praise

Great job	Nice going
Exactly right	I really like that job
Perfect arm placement	That's the best one yet
Way to go	Nice hustle

Physical Expressions

Smiling	Nodding
Clenched fist overhead	Clapping
Thumbs-up	

Physical Contact

Handshake	High five
Fist bump	

7

Social reinforcers increase desired behavior.

An early step is to identify the social reinforcers that students of different ages find acceptable in the school setting. As students mature, they become much less willing to accept certain types of reinforcers. Picking out individual students for praise in front of peers may embarrass them or make them feel uncomfortable. With such students, the best approach is to deliver praise on a personal basis whenever possible to avoid any negative spin. Some students may not want to be touched even to the point of receiving a high five, and those of the opposite sex may interpret a hug or pat on the back incorrectly. If unsure of how students will react, ask the school administrator or other experienced teachers to define the social reinforcers that are acceptable and to which students respond positively.

Effective use of social reinforcers requires giving praise and making positive statements. Many teachers feel uncomfortable when learning to administer positive reinforcement to students because such behavior feels inauthentic. A common complaint from teachers learning how to reinforce is, "This is not who I am; students will know I am a fake." Any change in communication patterns feels uncomfortable at first. Trying new ways of communicating with a class requires a period of adjustment. New patterns of praise and reinforcement often feel contrived and insincere. (Fortunately, students do not know the difference because they do not know who you really are.) You cannot avoid discomfort if you want to improve your teaching effectiveness. Teachers unwilling to experience this initial period of uneasiness will not improve. Assuming that patterns of speech learned during youth and into college are naturally suited for teaching is false. Teachers are made, not born, and success is reached through hard work and dedication. If practiced regularly, new behavioral patterns become a natural part of a teacher's interactions in a short time.

Praise is most effective when it identifies and reinforces specific behavior. This type of praise contrasts with general statements, such as, "Good job" or "You are an excellent performer." General and nonspecific statements do not communicate to students what they did well, leaving them to guess what you had in mind. A student who guesses incorrectly may think that he or she is being reinforced for a behavior deemed unacceptable. To improve the specificity and effectiveness of feedback, describe the exact behavior to be reinforced. At the same time, do not make feedback judgmental in nature. Describing behavior identifies the specifics of performance and makes no judgment about the individual. Judging the person, however, is general and often criticizes the individual instead of the desired behavior.

Compare the following:

- *Describing*: "I saw your throw, Eric; your follow-through was just right."
- *Judging*: "That's a good try, but I think you can do better the next time."

In the first example, Eric is identified by name, and a specific behavior he performed is reinforced. In the second situation, the student cannot identify what is good and comes away with an empty feeling. In most cases, if a question can be asked about delivered praise or criticism (e.g., what was good, or how can it be performed at a higher level), the feedback is open to misinterpretation. To increase desired behavior, verbally or physically describe what makes the performance effective, good, or noteworthy. This type of description reinforces the student and communicates to the rest of the class the performance expected by the instructor.

Extrinsic Reinforcers

Social reinforcers are by far the best method when trying to change or maintain student behavior. But at times the teacher's ability to reinforce behavior intrinsically is seriously compromised. For example, a new or substitute teacher has not established a relationship with students. Students must value and respect a teacher before social reinforcers become meaningful and filled with value to students. In this case, extrinsic reinforcers may have to be used. For example, free time that allows students to participate in their choice of activities can be used as reinforcement. One of the best ways to identify activities that students want to do is to ask them. Administer a quick informal poll of two or three choices. When students get to vote and choose an activity that is reinforcing to them, the entire class usually accepts it. Free time usually ranks highest among middle and high school students' preferences. Some examples of activities that might be used to reinforce a class are free time to practice a skill, the opportunity to play a game, the chance to act as a teacher's aide, the chance to be a teacher in a cross-aged tutoring situation, and the opportunity to be a team captain. Prudent use of free time as a reinforcement can get students to participate in a self-selected activity.

Access to novelty activities, competitive games, and class tournaments can be used as reinforcers. Disc games such as golf, baseball, and Ultimate are recreational activities that may be highly desirable for some classes. By analyzing the likes and dislikes of students, teachers can develop a set of activity reinforcers that work.

Premack Principle

Teachers often unknowingly use the Premack principle (Premack, 1965) to increase desired behavior. The principle states that when a high-frequency behavior (preferred) is contingent on completion of a lower-frequency behavior (less desirable), the lower-frequency behavior is likely to occur more often. This theory implies that when the less desirable behavior is completed, a more desirable behavior is allowed. An activity that students enjoy is used to increase the occurrence of an activity that students are reticent to perform.

Learning activities can be planned using the Premack principle, sometimes referred to as Grandma's law or "Eat your spinach; then you may have dessert." Teachers can arrange the environment so that students must spend a certain amount of time completing a certain number of attempts at a less popular activity before they can gain access to a preferred activity. For example, seventh-grade students would have to complete the nine skill objectives described below before being allowed to participate in a three-on-three class tournament; objectives focused on skill development demand practice and are less favorable activities, whereas the three-on-three tournament is the favored activity.

Dribbling

1. Dribble the ball several times consecutively with control against a lukewarm defender.
2. Advance the ball walking toward the basket while dribbling the ball with control.
3. Advance the ball running forward toward the basket from half-court while dribbling the ball with control.

Passing (With a Partner)

4. Make accurate chest passes to a partner cutting toward the basket from a wing position.
5. Make accurate bounce passes to a partner cutting toward the basket from a wing position.
6. Make accurate overhead passes to a partner cutting to the basket from a low-post position.

Shooting

7. Make consistent layups from the preferred side using a three-step approach.
8. Make consistent set shots from inside the key using appropriate base, elbow, extension, and follow-through.
9. Make consistent set shots from the perimeter of the key using appropriate base, elbow, extension,

and follow-through.

If possible, select reinforcing activities related to the physical education class setting. In some situations, when student motivation and interest are low, teachers may choose to use reinforcements outside the physical education area. These rewards might include enjoying free time, talking with peers, or going to a sporting event. Such rewards are harder to defend educationally but may be necessary in extreme situations.

Extrinsic Reinforcers: A Word of Caution

The question here is whether to use extrinsic reinforcers on a regular basis with students to shape their behavior. Consider the example in which the physical education teacher gives points that lead to a special day of free activity. Students in this setting earn points when they wear the proper uniform, get to class on time, and behave properly. An increase in desirable behavior resulting from a reward given when a specified number of points are earned is the goal. This strategy suggests that students will choose to perform the desired behavior because they want to earn points and ultimately receive the reward. But if students find themselves in a setting where points are not assigned, they may be less motivated to behave in a desirable manner. Students may see little payoff to behaving properly because they do not receive any reward for their behavior. Their level of internal motivation and self-discipline may decline. Evidence suggests that overuse of extrinsic rewards can decrease a student's intrinsic motivation (Blankenship, 2008). Limiting the use of extrinsic reinforcers to situations where social reinforcers are ineffective is recommended. Extrinsic reinforcers should be removed as soon as possible so that students' motivation levels are based on personal satisfaction as a result of accomplishment. Nothing is more rewarding to most students than accomplishing a goal they did not think possible. Learning does not get any better than when students are motivated to perform for their own personal reason, resulting in true intrinsic motivation.

Prompt Desired Behavior

Prompts are used to remind students to perform desired behavior. They encourage the development of new patterns of behavior. Students can be prompted in several ways in the physical education setting. The most common are the following:

1. *Modeling.* A desired behavior is modeled by the teacher or another student, and the expectation

Model the behavior you want from your students.

is that students will respond in similar fashion. For example, placing a piece of equipment on the floor when stopping the class will remind the class to do likewise. Modeling is an effective prompt for desired behavior because students often emulate a teacher they respect.

2. *Verbal cues.* This common method of prompting involves using words such as "hustle" and "keep going". Students are reminded of desired behavior. Usually, verbal cues are used to maintain the pace of the lesson, increase the intensity of the performance, or motivate students to stay on task.

3. *Nonverbal cues.* Many physical cues are given through body language to communicate concepts such as "hustle," "move over here," "great performance," "quiet down," and so on. When teaching skills, nonverbal physical cues can prompt students by moving them into proper position, helping them through the correct pattern, or placing body parts in proper alignment.

Prompts are often most effective when a teacher combines modeling, verbal cues, and nonverbal cues together. Prompts should not be used to the point where students will not perform without them. Prompts should be removed so that behavior becomes self-motivated. This process, called fading, involves gradual removal of the prompt. Use prompts at opportune times to increase the occurrence of desired behavior. Prompts should be unobtrusive and used to stimulate the behavior.

For example, when students are not staying on task, a teacher could give students a long lecture (longer than 30 seconds often becomes a lecture) about the importance of staying on task. This approach, however, is time consuming and overreactionary. It is not suited to repetitive use and is ineffective in the long run. Select a cue that is short, concise, and closely linked to the desired skill.

TEACHING TIP

Be sure that the prompt identifies the desired task. For example, if the teacher prompts the class by saying, "Hustle," but does not link it to the desired behavior, confusion may be the result. Some students may think that the prompt means to perform the skill as fast as possible; others may think they should stop what they are doing and hustle to the teacher. Link the prompt to the desired behavior in a consistent manner to ensure that students clearly understand the meaning of your prompt.

Shape Desired Behavior

Shaping techniques can be used to build new and desired behavior. When desired behavior does not exist, shaping—which uses extinction and reinforcement—is used to create new behavior. Shaping tends to be slow and inefficient and is used only if prompting is not possible. Two principles form the foundation for shaping behavior.

1. *Differential reinforcement is used to increase the incidence of desired behavior.* Responses that reach a predetermined criterion are reinforced, whereas behaviors that do not meet the criterion are ignored (extinction). An example of this principle involves asking a class to put their equipment down quickly. Students should put the equipment on the floor within 5 seconds; using differential reinforcement, reinforce the students whenever they meet the 5-second criterion and ignore their performance when it takes longer than 5 seconds.

2. *The criterion that must be reached for reinforcement to occur is increased.* In this step, a shift is made gradually toward the desired goal. For example, if the desired behavior is for the class to become quiet within 5 seconds after a signal has been given, it might be necessary to start with a 12-second interval. Why the longer interval? In all likelihood, expecting that an inattentive class will quiet down quickly is not reasonable. If a 5-second interval is selected initially, students will likely be frustrated by the lack of success. In addition, this stringent standard of behavior will not be achieved often, resulting in few opportunities to reinforce the class. This may result in a situation in which both the teacher and the class think they have failed. To avoid this possibility of failure, gradually move toward the desired terminal behavior. In this case, start with 12 seconds until the class performs as desired. Next, shift to a 10-second interval and ask the class to perform to this new standard. The process is gradually repeated until the terminal behavior is reached.

Decrease Unacceptable Behavior

Society is based on personal freedom hinged to self-discipline. People have freedom as long as they do not encroach on the rights of others. In similar fashion, students can enjoy freedom if their behavior is consistent with educational objectives and does not prevent other students from learning. Discipline teaches students what behaviors are appropriate in the teaching and learning situation. Discipline is used when attempts to increase desirable behavior have failed.

Know Your Options for Dealing With Unacceptable Behavior

One of the more important things for a teacher to know is what options are available when students behave in an unacceptable manner. What is acceptable and unacceptable in dealing with a student who has misbehaved? A surprising issue for most beginning teachers is that they have many options for stopping student misbehavior. Check with administrators and fellow teachers to see what they use or accept for dealing with student misbehavior. Then decide the order in which to administer those behavior response steps. What follow are some general steps that most school districts allow when dealing with inappropriate behavior. Each of these steps is described in detail later. The first three steps assume that the student can work with the teacher, and the last three steps are based on needing outside help to rectify the situation. Teachers should always try to handle the discipline first before involving parents or administrators. Suspending students ultimately does not solve the problem between teacher and student.

1. *Ignore or gently reprimand the behavior.* Minor disruptive behavior can often be ignored. Alternatively, use the following to get students to behave in acceptable ways:

   - Look in the direction of the student to terminate the behavior.
   - Use a quiet reprimand to get the student back on task.
   - Use a quiet warning delivered personally and not within earshot of other students.
   - Use proximity control by ignoring the behavior but moving to a position near the student or students who are off task.

   If a student behavior is ignored, it may continue and cause the teacher to lose patience. The teacher may then behave in a way that actually reinforces the misbehaving student. The caution here is to make sure that the behavior can be ignored over time or to use the least forceful reprimand.

2. *Give a time-out.* The purpose of this step is to remind the student in a gentle and unobtrusive manner. Strategies for time-outs are described in more detail later.

7

3. *Remove the student from the activity.* This step occurs for behavior that occurred earlier but has not stopped as requested.

- The student is asked to leave class and sit on the side somewhat out of sight from the rest of the class.
- This step is used when the behavior occurs a number of times or has escalated in seriousness.

4. *Make a phone call home.* This approach is taken when the misbehavior occurs a number of times and the previous steps are not effective. Phoning parents or guardians is a step that must be carefully considered. Many parents do not want to hear negative reports and may believe that the school has the responsibility to handle their youngster. Depending on how the parents react, this step could backfire. For example, a parent may severely punish the youngster, causing the student to blame the teacher for the punishment received at home and to take it out on the teacher. Behavior might get worse rather than better. Before calling parents, talk to administrators and other teachers to find out whether calling home will be an effective approach.

5. *Send student to the principal.* This step must be thought about carefully before being invoked. As a result of sending students to the principal, it may appear that the teacher is not capable of dealing with student behavior. When a student is sent to the principal's office, the principal may have a brief discussion with the student but internally think that the teacher is the problem. Because administrators are not emotionally involved, they may not view a student's misbehavior in the same way that the teacher does, resulting in little being accomplished. If this approach is used, consider the following:

- Communicate to the principal ahead of time about what is going on in class and describe the misbehavior.
- Another approach is to call the office and tell the principal's secretary what has happened. This call will help the principal get tuned in to the problem and will make it difficult for the student to say that nothing happened.

6. *Suspend or reassign the student.* Student suspension from school is not possible in some states and school districts. Suspension is a serious issue, but it may actually give a student who

dislikes school exactly what he or she wants. A more effective approach is in-school suspension, which takes away all the free time that the student has. Removing the student from a familiar environment separates her or him from a setting that is filled with a number of reinforcers and issues that get in the way of learning. A student who has an obvious conflict with the teacher can also be reassigned to another teacher's class. Suspension is a complex method for dealing with misbehaving students because it involves parents, other teachers, other school administrators, and legal ramifications. Preventing behavior from escalating must be done at earlier levels in the sequence of discipline alternatives.

Identify Acceptable and Unacceptable Behavior

An important step in behavior control is to decide exactly which behaviors are acceptable and which are unacceptable in the learning environment. These can be listed in a handout and discussed with students at the beginning of the year. The list should be posted in the locker room and in the gymnasium and sent to parents and administrators. How teachers react to student behavior plays a powerful role in managing student behavior and establishing a positive learning environment. Teachers should have a personal plan in place for responding to different types of misbehavior. Determine specific student behaviors that will be praised, reprimanded, or ignored. Each teacher should develop a list of specific student behaviors and accompanying reactions. An instructor's list might look like this:

Behavior to Praise

- Listening
- Following directions
- Hustling
- Being on time
- Dressing properly

Behavior to Reprimand

- Arguing
- Embarrassing others
- Interrupting others
- Going off task
- Talking during instructions

Behavior to Ignore

- Talking out
- Raising a hand
- Snapping fingers
- Showing off
- Constantly asking questions

Negative student behavior is often reinforced by the teacher and the peer group. For example, assume that a student misbehaves and the teacher publicly reprimands the student. The friends of the student laugh at the situation. Unfortunately, peer laughter is reinforcing to this student, and the behavior occurs more often in the future. When an undesirable behavior is not seriously distracting, selectively ignoring it and showing a positive reaction to a simultaneously occurring appropriate behavior is effective. If necessary, explain to the students that they also should ignore the student's inappropriate behavior. In this way, the misbehaving student does not receive attention from either the teacher or peers.

 TEACHING TIP

Inappropriate behavior is often a way for a student to get attention. When possible, look for an appropriate behavior from that student and praise it. This tactic may help the student realize that the teacher also notices appropriate behavior.

Use Behavior Correction Techniques

Behavior correction techniques can be used to decrease undesirable behavior after positive reinforcement has failed. Using positive reinforcement to increase desired behavior is done with the hope that it will replace negative behavior. A rule of thumb to follow before correcting behavior is to reinforce the desired behavior twice. For example, suppose that a student keeps talking while other students are listening properly. Reinforce the students who are behaving correctly. Often, the misbehaving student will emulate those being reinforced in order to receive similar positive feedback. If that approach fails, the use of corrective feedback is warranted. See figure 7.5 for a checklist of the main points found in this discussion.

Corrective Feedback (Reprimands)

Corrective feedback should be specific and have a clear meaning. Timing is important, and the corrective statement is most effective when issued as near to the misbehavior as possible. Just as positive reinforcement should be delivered immediately following the desired behavior, so should negative consequences. Negative consequences can be anything the student does not want or need as long as the rights or dignity of the student are not violated. Just as teachers need to know what reinforces students, they need to know what a negative experience is for students who misbehave.

Behavior correction is designed to teach students how to behave properly rather than to punish them. No punitive measures should be involved. Focus on natural consequences that occur when students behave improperly. When students are disciplined, they can respond in a negative manner, causing class disruption. The following steps help prevent teacher–student conflict in front of the class.

1. *Do not reprimand the student publicly.* Putting down a student in front of the class is never productive and can stir up resentment toward the teacher. Assign the class a task to perform to free up 10 to 20 seconds to talk with the student privately. Simple and quick reengagement in the activity they just completed keeps the class engaged as the situation is discussed with the misbehaving student.

2. *Isolate the student during the discipline session.* Discipline a student where others cannot hear what you are saying. The problem is a private matter between the teacher and the student. Often, a couple of students may misbehave together. Separate them and deal with their behavior individually.

3. *Address the behavior, not the person.* Ask that the behavior be stopped rather than telling a student, "You are always causing problems in this class." Avoid general and negative statements related to the personality of the student.

4. *State the position once; repeat it once if the student does not understand.* Do not argue or try to prove a point. Take no more than 10 to 15 seconds to tell the student what unacceptable behavior occurred and describe the acceptable behavior. For example, say, "Luis, you were talking while I was talking; I need you to listen when I am

CORRECTIVE FEEDBACK

❏ Make a positive statement to the class.

❏ Use proximity—move to the area of deviancy.

❏ Get the entire class involved in a physical activity (preferably moving around the area or using a piece of equipment). The class should be unaware that a warning is being delivered.

❏ Quietly, individually, and unemotionally deliver the statement redirecting the student (warning).

___ State the behavior that needs to change (the student is OK, but the behavior needs to change).

___ State how to correct the behavior.

___ Avoid visual confrontation with the student.

___ Move away.

___ Never touch the student.

❏ Say something positive to another student or to the class to help you refocus on the positive things going on in class.

❏ Give the student a chance to change the behavior.

___ Go back to the student to reinforce progress toward the desired behavior.

___ Remember that shaping the correct behavior will take time.

___ Reinforce even small steps in the right direction.

FIGURE 7.5 Checklist for delivering corrective feedback.

explaining things." If the discussion continues for more than 10 seconds, the rest of the class may start to lose control, and the correction turns into a lecture.

5. *Walk away after conveying the desired behavior.* Eyeballing students after they have been reprimanded is confrontational. To get back on track, positively reinforce one or two other students.

6. *Never threaten or bully the student.* These actions build resentment and may cause greater problems later. Do not be sarcastic. Instead, state clearly what you want from the student in terms of acceptable behavior.

7. *Avoid touching the student when correcting behavior.* Even positive intentions can send mixed messages. Some students do not want to be touched and will aggressively pull away and make a scene in front of the class.

8. *Reinforce acceptable behavior.* Be vigilant in looking for the desired behavior because reinforcing such behavior will cause it to occur more often in the future.

Removal of Positive Consequences

Parents often use this approach, so many students are already familiar with it. The basic approach is to remove something positive from the student when misbehavior occurs. For example, students give up some of their free time because of misbehavior. They lose points related to a grade. They are not allowed to participate in an activity that is exciting to them. For removal of positive consequences to be effective, make sure that students really want to participate in the removal activity. Keeping a student out of a game will not work if the student does not like the game. A few key principles should be followed when using this technique:

• Make sure that the magnitude of the removal fits the crime. In other words, students who commit a minor infraction should not have in-school suspension for a week.

• Be consistent in removal among all students and with the same students. Students believe that teachers are unfair if they are more severe with one student than another. In addition, a student penalized for a specific misbehavior should receive the same penalty for a later repetition.

- Make sure that students understand the consequences of their misbehavior before the penalties are implemented. This step avoids applying penalties in an emotional, unthinking manner. If students know what the consequences will be, they are making the choice to accept the consequences when they choose to misbehave.

- At times, charting a student's misbehavior is helpful to learn whether the frequency is decreasing.

- Regardless of the method used, if the behavior is not decreasing or is increasing, change methods until a decrease in frequency occurs.

Time-Out

In time-out, students are removed from a positive (reinforcing) situation. A time-out is like the penalty box in an ice hockey game. If a student is behaving inappropriately, he or she is asked privately to go to the time-out area. The area should be far enough away from the class to avoid the ridicule of peers but close enough to be within the supervision of the teacher. The area can be specifically designated in the gymnasium, or it can be an area in an outside field, such as under a tree, on a bench, or in a baseball dugout.

Being placed in time-out should communicate to students that they have disrupted the class and must be removed so that the rest of the class can participate as desired. Students can also use the time-out area as a cooling-off spot that they can move to voluntarily if they are angry, embarrassed, or frustrated. If students have been placed in the time-out area for fighting or arguing, they should be placed at opposite ends of the area so that the behavior does not escalate. In addition, it can be mandated that they stay in their own half of the gymnasium until the next meeting of the class. This practice prevents the possibility of continued animosity.

Time-out does not stifle misbehavior if the student receives reinforcement for being there. Time-out means receiving no reinforcement. If class is a negative experience for students, taking them out of class is not a punishment and may be a reward. Class must be enjoyable and reinforcing to students, and having a student sit out of class may result in an experience that is reinforcing to him or her. For example, the student who is sent to the office gets to avoid activity while visiting with friends who come into the office. Notoriety can be achieved among peers for surviving the office experience and being able to tell others, "It doesn't matter one bit what that teacher does to me." Do not put students in time-out and then let them sit on the side of the gymnasium, watching peers participate. For some students being a spectator is more reinforcing than participating in class activities. One of the ways to avoid this problem is to penalize students for nonparticipation (when they are in time-out). They lose credit for that day, so being in time-out will affect the grade they earn in class. Many teachers also provide an assignment that requires the student to reflect on why she or he is in time-out and how her or his behavior needs to change in the future (see figure 7.6). Placing a student in time-out can be effective when used appropriately. Time-outs are to be used infrequently and seen as a punishment that should be equal for all students. If time-out consequences are ineffective, calling the parents for a conference with the principal and teacher may be an effective last measure. Student participation in educational endeavors should be seen as a privilege, and those who choose to disrupt the learning of others ultimately lose their privileges. This process attempts to teach students that they are not bigger than the system—that rules pertain to all.

Implement a Behavior Change Plan

Changing behavior is a slow process. Teachers want to change behavior quickly and on the spot. At times, they make incorrect decisions because they do not have time to think out an effective solution. In-class misbehavior can be temporarily stopped, but it may often go unchanged for the future. Understand that change will require action that must be planned and repeated several times. The following steps can be used to develop a plan for changing behavior.

Create Behavior Contracts

A behavior contract is a written statement specifying certain student behaviors that must occur to earn certain rewards or privileges. Students and teachers sign the contract generated after a private conference to decide on the appropriate behaviors and rewards. Letting the students make some decisions about the contract is often useful.

TEACHING TIP

Private conferences should be done in a location where other students or teachers can see the interaction. A closed-door private conference may allow the student to make false accusations or create larger problems.

TIME-OUT ASSIGNMENT

Name _____ Grade _____ Date and time assigned _____

Fill in the blanks in your own words and using complete sentences.

Think carefully about your responses.

1. What was I doing wrong?

2. What should I have been doing instead?

3. What can I specifically do to improve my behavior in PE class?

FIGURE 7.6   Sample time-out assignment.

Behavior contracts may be a successful strategy for students with difficult behavior problems. Make every attempt to use rewards that occur naturally in physical education class (such as disc play, fitness games, and small-sided sport games). In some cases, however, different types of rewards may have to be used. For example, a student who is interested only in music or motorcycles could be allowed to spend some time reading, writing about, or discussing one of these topics. As behavior improves and the student's attitude becomes more positive, the rewards are switched to physical education activities. A contract is gradually phased out over time as the student gains control of his or her behavior and demonstrates the ability to participate in a regular class environment.

Contracts can be written for a small group of students or for an entire class with similar problems, but teachers must be careful about setting up a reward system for too many students. Separate systems can become too complex or time consuming to supervise properly. Contracts are best used with a limited number of students. An example of a behavior contract that can be used with an individual, a small group, or an entire class of students is shown in figure 7.7.

Deal With Severe Misbehavior

At times, corrective behavior techniques do not work. Many strategies may have been tried with a student with little success. At this time, teachers must go beyond their own resources. As a note of caution, all the previous techniques have assumed that a teacher is working individually to solve the problem. This approach is the first and best solution. Sending the student to the office and asking someone else to solve the problem is easier but it does not solve the problem between the student and the teacher. The steps listed here assume that all other avenues have been tried and were unsuccessful.

Most secondary schools have some type of disciplinary referral form for severe problems. The form is used to keep an accurate record of behavioral problems and is a part of the communication process among students, teachers, parents, administrators, and counselors. Referral forms (see figure 7.8) are effective tools for documenting student behavior. One disadvantage is that the approach is time consuming. But there are few shortcuts to a well-disciplined class. The following is a four-step approach for dealing with behavior that is difficult and continuous.

BEHAVIOR CONTRACT

	Points
1. Class Preparation	
a. Attendance	1
b. On time	1
c. Properly dressed	1
2. Social Behavior	
a. Showering	1
b. Lack of inappropriate behaviors	5
	___
Cursing	
Fighting	9 points per day
Disrupting	(36 points per week)

During Friday's class, points may be exchanged for time in aerobics, weight training, disc games, or basketball.

I agree to these conditions.

_____

Student

_____

Teacher

FIGURE 7.7   Sample behavior contract.

- *Step 1*. Initiate an informal, private conference between the teacher and student, focusing on the behavioral aberration. An agreement should be reached regarding the consequences of future behavior.

- *Step 2*. Check with other teachers and administrators to see if a telephone call to the parents will help the situation. As discussed earlier, it might not, depending on the situation. The nature of the call home should be to find solutions for the existing problem. Focus the conversation on soliciting help and advice rather than denouncing their youngster. Alienating the parents may make it even more difficult to deal with the student. During the phone discussion, ask the parents if they would like to participate in a conference with their youngster, the school counselor, and yourself.

- *Step 3*. Schedule a conference with the teacher, parents (if they are willing), student, and principal or counselor to discuss the problem and develop a plan for changing the behavior. A written copy of the plan should be distributed to all involved.

- *Step 4*. If necessary, use severe disciplinary actions, such as the following:

  - *Loss of privileges*: Privilege losses could include access to the cafeteria (lunch detention), clubs, athletics, or dances. Parents are notified in writing about the procedures used.

  - *In-school suspension*: Students are sent to a designated area with a supervisor who enforces strict rules and guidelines for schoolwork.

  - *Short- and long-term suspensions from school*: Suspension from school could be for 1 to 10 days, depending on the severity of the behavior and the student's history. Strict policies and procedures are arranged and followed carefully to ensure due process. Parents must be notified in writing about the steps that have been followed.

STUDENT REFERRAL

Student _____ Referring teacher _____ Grade ____ Date _____ Time _____

Location (circle all that apply):

Classroom	Cafeteria	Gymnasium	Bus zone	Restroom
Hallway	Library	Parking lot	Field trip	Other

Problem behavior (circle all that apply):

Abusive or inappropriate language	Bullying	Physical contact	Defiance or disrespect	Disruption
Dress code	Technology violation	Tardiness	Cussing or inappropriate language	Fighting
Insubordination	Harassment	Bullying	Truancy	Forgery or theft
Lying or cheating	Tobacco, alcohol, or drugs	Vandalism	Weapons	Other

Possible motivation:

_____

_____

_____

Others involved (circle all that apply):

None   Peers   Staff   Teacher   Substitute teacher   Other

Administrative decision (circle all that apply):

Time in office   Loss of privilege   Conference with student   Detention

Press conference   In-school suspension   Out-of-school suspension

Comments:

_____

_____

FIGURE 7.8 Sample student referral form.

- *Expulsion*: The final step used in extremely severe instances is expulsion. The principal initiates the action with a letter to the student and parents. An official action from the board of education may be required to expel a student. Due process and appeal procedures must be used and made available to the student.

Use Criticism Cautiously

Criticism must be used with caution and judgment. Criticism is often used with the belief that it will improve the performance of students. Scolding and criticism are often the behavior control tools of choice because they give the impression that the results are effective and immediate. Usually, misbehavior stops, and it is assumed the situation has been rectified. Unfortunately, this is not always the case. Criticism and punishment lend a negative air to the instructional environment and have a negative effect on both student and teacher. The old saying "It hurts me more than you" often applies. Many teachers feel uncomfortable when they must criticize or punish students. They feel as though they cannot handle students and that the class is incorrigible. This feeling of incompetence leads to a destructive cycle whereby students feel negative about the instructor and the instructor feels negative about the class. Overall, this is one of the most debilitating effects of criticism and punishment.

TEACHING TIP

When criticism or punishment is required, a valuable practice is to follow up with the student to make sure that he or she understands why the action was taken and how the teacher and student can move forward to ensure a successful relationship.

As mentioned earlier, another negative aspect of criticism is that it does not offer a solution. In a landmark study by Thomas, Becker, and Armstrong (1968), a teacher was asked to stop praising a class. Off-task behavior increased from 8.7% to nearly 26%. When the teacher was asked to increase criticism from 5 times in 20 minutes to 16 times in 20 minutes, more off-task behavior occurred. On some days, the percentage of off-task behavior increased to more than 50%. The point is that when attention is given to off-task behavior and no praise is offered for on-task accomplishment, off-task behavior increases dramatically. Criticism shows results (students respond to the request of the criticism), but students do not change. Students are reinforced (they receive attention from the teacher) for their off-task behavior. In addition, because their on-task behavior is not praised, it decreases, resulting in the opposite of what is desired.

Make Punishment a Last Resort

A difficult question is whether punishment should be used in an educational setting. Punishment can have negative side effects because fear is the primary motivator. Consider the long-term need for punishment.

If the long-term effects of using punishment are more beneficial than not using it, it is unethical not to use punishment. In other words, if a student is going to be in a worse situation because punishment was not used to deter self-destructive behavior, it is wrong not to use it. Punishing a student may be necessary for protection from self-inflicted harm (e.g., using a certain apparatus without supervision). Punishment may be needed to teach students not to hurt others or bully. Punishment in these situations can cause discomfort to the teacher and student in the short run, but it may allow the student to participate successfully in society later.

Most situations in the educational setting do not require punishment because they are not as severe as those described previously. A major reason for not using punishment is that it can have undesirable side effects. When students are punished, they learn to avoid the source of punishment. They must be more covert in their actions. They spend time finding ways to be devious without being caught. Instead of encouraging students to discuss problems with teachers and parents, punishment teaches them to avoid those individuals for fear of being punished. Another side effect is that punishment teaches students to be aggressive toward others. Students who have been physically or emotionally punished by parents act in similar fashion to others. The result is a student who is secretive and aggressive with others—certainly undesirable traits. Finally, if punishment is used to stop certain behavior, as soon as the punishment stops, the behavior will return. Thus, little has been learned, and the punishment has just led to short-term change.

If it is necessary to use punishment, remember the following points:

1. *Be consistent and make the punishment fit the crime.* Students quickly lose respect for a teacher who treats others with favoritism. They view the teacher as unfair if punishment is extreme or unfair. Peers quickly side with the student who is treated unfairly, causing a class morale problem for the instructor.

2. *Offer a warning signal (as discussed previously).* This practice may prevent excessive use of punishment because students often behave after receiving a warning. In addition, they probably view the teacher as caring and fair.

3. *Do not threaten students.* Offer only one warning. Threats have little effect on students and make them think that you cannot handle the class. One warning gives students the feeling you are not looking to punish them and are fair. Follow

through; do not challenge or threaten students and then fail to deal with the behavior.

4. *Follow the misbehavior with the punishment as soon as possible.* Punishment is much less effective and more often viewed as unfair when it is delayed.

5. *Punish softly and calmly.* Do not seek revenge or be vindictive. If you expect responsible behavior from students, make sure you reprimand and punish in a responsible manner. Soft reprimands are more effective than loud ones.

In addition, try to avoid having negative feelings about a student and internalizing student misbehavior. Being punitive when handling deviant behavior destroys any chance for a worthwhile relationship. Misbehavior should be handled in a manner that contributes to the development of responsible, confident students who understand that people who function effectively in society must adjust to certain limits. Forget about past bouts of deviant behavior and approach the student in a positive fashion at the start of each class. If this is not done, students are labeled, making behavioral change more difficult. Students may also learn to live up to the teacher's negative expectations.

TEACHING TIP

Avoid labeling students with other school personnel or giving too much credence to a label given by another teacher. You should make your own judgments and give all students a fresh start when they come to your class.

If punishment is used, make sure that only those students who misbehaved are punished. Punishing an entire class for the deviant behavior of a few students is unfair and may trigger undesirable side effects. Students become hostile toward those who caused the loss of privileges, and this peer hostility lowers the level of positive social interaction with the deviants.

Know the Legal Consequences of Expulsion

If serious problems occur, discuss the problems with administration. Deviant behavior is often part of a larger, more severe problem that is troubling a student. A cooperative approach may provide an effective solution. A group meeting involving parents, classroom teacher, principal, counselor, and physical education specialist may open avenues that encourage understanding and increase productive behavior.

Legal concerns involving the student's rights in disciplinary areas are an essential consideration. Although minor infractions may be handled routinely, expulsion and other substantial punishments can be imposed on students only after due process. Student rights issues are complicated, and most school systems have established guidelines and procedures for dealing with students who have been removed from the class or school setting. Students should be removed from class only if they are disruptive to the point of interfering with the learning experiences of other students and if all other means of altering behavior have failed. Sending a student out of class is a last resort and means that both teacher and student have failed.

LEARNING AIDS

STUDY STIMULATORS AND REVIEW QUESTIONS

1. Explain how effective class management and discipline are related.
2. Discuss how the teaching of management skills is like the teaching of physical skills.
3. What is an appropriate strategy to use if students do not respond to a signal to stop?
4. Design a motivating strategy aimed at encouraging students to prepare for activity quickly and enter the gym.
5. Briefly describe Hellison's hierarchy of responsible behavior.
6. Why should class rules be stated in more general terms?
7. List and explain the negative consequences of teacher comments that students interpret as preaching or threatening.

8. Briefly explain and give a practical teaching application of the Premack principle.
9. List and explain two essential characteristics of effective praise.
10. Why should prompts be gradually faded out?
11. Provide three examples of the strategy called removal of positive consequences.
12. Explain the negative consequences of using verbal criticism.
13. Identify steps for minimizing bullying.

WEBSITES

Classroom Management
www.inclusiveeducation.ca
www.teachingmatters.com

The Master Teacher
www.disciplinehelp.com

PE Central: Climate
www.pecentral.org/climate

Lorenz Educational Press
www.teachinglearning.com

REFERENCES AND SUGGESTED READINGS
Bailey, B.A. (2001). *Conscious discipline.* Oviedo, FL: Loving Guidance.

Blankenship, B.T. (2008). *The psychology of teaching physical education: From theory to practice.* Scottsdale, AZ: Holcomb Hathaway.

Hellison, D. (2011). *Teaching responsibility through physical activity* (3rd ed.). Champaign, IL: Human Kinetics.

Hinduja, S., & Patchin, J. W. (2018). Cyberbullying research summary: Cyberbullying and suicide. Retrieved from http://www. cyberbullying. us/myspace_youth_research. pdf.

Hurley, V., & Mandigo, J. (2010). Bullying in physical education: Its prevalence and impact on the intention to continue secondary school physical education. *Revue phénEPS/PHENex Journal, 2*(3).

National Education Association. (2013). 10 steps to stop and prevent bullying. Retrieved from www.nea.org/home/51629.htm.

O'Connor, J.A., & Graber, K.C. (2014). Sixth-grade physical education: An acculturation of bullying and fear. *Research Quarterly for Exercise and Sport, 85*(3), 398–408.

Premack, D. (1965). Reinforcement theory. In D. Levine (Ed.), *Nebraska symposium on motivation.* Lincoln, NE: University of Nebraska Press.

Robers, S., Zhang, J., and Truman, J. (2012). *Indicators of school crime and safety: 2011* (NCES 2012-002/NCJ 236021). Washington, DC: National Center for Education Statistics, U.S. Department of Education, and Bureau of Justice Statistics, Office of Justice Programs, U.S. Department of Justice.

Thomas, D.R., Becker, W.C., & Armstrong, M. (1968). Production and elimination of disruptive classroom behavior by systematically varying teachers' behavior. *Journal of Applied Behavior Analysis, 1*, 35–45.

Assessment, Evaluation, Grading, and Program Accountability

This chapter offers a broad overview of practical and appropriate assessment, evaluation, and grading techniques for secondary physical education. The psychomotor (physical), cognitive (knowledge), and affective (social) learning domains are targeted. Sample evaluation assessments for physical skills, cognitive knowledge, and affective behavior are offered. These tools include scoring rubrics, checklists, rating scales, personal interviews, and self-evaluation logs. Grading is always a difficult issue, and the task for physical education teachers can be daunting because philosophical differences exist. Both sides of the grading issues are presented in this chapter so that teachers can see the varying viewpoints that must be considered.

Learning Objectives

- ► Explain the differences between assessment, evaluation, and grading.
- ► Administer a physical skills assessment to a class of secondary school students in physical education.
- ► Know how to assess performance outcomes using a variety of instruments including rubrics, student self-evaluations, and anecdotal record sheets.
- ► Devise a cognitive assessment for secondary school students on specific units.
- ► Create a study guide and related exam for students.
- ► Discuss issues related to assessment, evaluation, and grading, including educational objectives versus administrative tasks, process versus product, improvement versus potential, and pass–fail versus letter grades.
- ► Explain the pros and cons of specific methods of grading in physical education.
- ► Develop a grading scheme in line with stated objectives for secondary school physical education.

Assessment, evaluation, and grading are important components for teachers to implement into their teaching process. Regardless of how teachers choose to integrate these processes, the emphasis on accountability continues to place more importance on this area. These issues become vital for justifying physical education programs, providing valuable performance feedback to students, and showing teachers their areas of strength and growth. National, state, and district standards are becoming the norm, and many physical education programs are required to infuse core content from math, science, and literacy within the physical education class. No longer are school boards willing to support a program that does not document its effect on students. Teachers must demonstrate that each student meets specific learning outcomes specified by content standards. Student learning, achievement of content, assessment, and grading can be means of accountability that inform parents and the public about how well their child's school is achieving. Similarly, students are much less willing to accept a grade in physical education if it is not objective in nature and grounded on principles like those in other academic areas.

Assessment, evaluation, and grading are three different entities that are often used interchangeably. **Assessment** is defined as the measurement or collection of information regarding student performance of skills, knowledge, and attitudes taught in physical education classes. Student assessment should answer the question "What does this student know how to do?" or "What can this student do?" From an instructional perspective, results from the assessment should answer the question "What does the student need to learn next?" **Evaluation** is defined as the process of using the assessment information to make a judgment about student performance. Based on the assessment data, does the student meet the intended objective? **Grading** is a composite score that incorporates the information and data gathered through the assessment and evaluation process. Used together, assessment, evaluation, and grading offer students a view of how they are performing in different areas under the physical education umbrella. For example, a student might earn high marks in Ultimate and basketball skills but lower marks in yoga or orienteering. Or a student may earn high scores on physical assessments but not on affective assessments. A grade is assigned as a composite score for all the areas measured in physical education; to some degree, it is an average report of all data gathered through the process of assessment and evaluation.

Assessment of Student Performance

Student assessment, defined as the collection of information about student performance, has always been a tough area for teachers, particularly in physical education, to tackle. Because physical education addresses the whole child, we need ways to assess for all three learning domains as opposed to one in most other subject areas. Traditionally, assessment in physical education has been directed at functions of compliance (e.g., dressing, participation, attendance), not on components that reflect student learning (Lund & Kirk, 2020). Even when performance is considered, assessment is often done in ways that are artificial in nature and do not represent student achievement.

Two types of assessments are conducted in physical education: **formal assessment**—assessment with the intent to affect grading procedures, and **informal assessment**—assessment conducted to obtain knowledge about student performance but not for use in the determination of grades. Most physical educators use informal assessment. Although physical educators tend to perform numerous daily informal assessments, this information cannot be used to evaluate or grade students.

Within the field of physical education, assessment is an area of varying difficulty. Classes are frequently larger than those in traditional classroom settings, students have various skill abilities, content is derived from multiple content areas, and formal protocol are often not established to collect student work and develop permanent records such as standardized testing results used in mathematics and literature. Assessment and evaluation procedures and protocols in physical education are left to individual teachers and departments, even if state standards provide the content to be covered at each grade level in predetermined areas. Given multiple obstacles, teachers face the challenge of developing and implementing assessment techniques and strategies that are authentic representations of what students have learned and can do. The key to conducting effective assessments is to make them efficient so that they not only provide information about student performance but also do not take away valuable practice and activity time for the students during physical education lessons. The following sections are designed to give teachers the framework and tools to perform more meaningful, efficient, and accurate student assessments.

Psychomotor Assessments

Physical skill development is a primary purpose of physical education. Cognitive and affective development can be addressed in other areas of the curriculum, but physical skill development occurs only through an effective physical education program. Physical skills can be divided into three subsets: The first set relates to the ability to perform specific sport or activity skills such as those found in badminton, rugby, and team handball.

The second set of skills contains health-related fitness components, which incorporate cardiorespiratory endurance, muscular endurance, muscular strength, flexibility, and body composition. The third set assesses student physical activity levels (during and beyond the physical education classroom).

Specific Sport Skills and Activity Skills Tests

In many core subjects, standardized testing is frequently used to communicate levels of student learning outcomes. In physical education, a wide number of formal

tests have been designed to evaluate sport skills objectively. These tests are usually carefully designed and score high in validity and reliability. Most assessments have norms available so that teachers can compare the performance of their students with a larger number of students who have been tested. Other assessments can be personalized to assess the process of performing a skill based on the cues provided by the teacher. Figure 8.1 is an example of a volleyball underhand or overhand serving skills test, which focuses on the process of performing the skill instead of the outcome. This skills test rubric is meant to be used as a peer assessment and can be used with all different types of skills. Simply replace the cues from volleyball with the cues for the skill being assessed.

This section is not meant to be comprehensive but rather to give a few examples of the types of objective assessments available to physical education teachers. Two excellent textbooks that contain a wide variety of tests

8

VOLLEYBALL UNDERHAND OR OVERHAND SERVES

Name (doer) _____ Date _____

Name (observer) _____

Directions: Practice the skills below with a partner. Take turns observing and performing. When observing, help your partner by providing feedback according to the criteria below. Check off your partner's technique after each set of five trials (serves).

When you both have finished all sets for all the skills, turn in your task sheets.

Skill	Technique criteria	Write got it (GI) or needs practice (NP)
Underhand serve	Opposite leg forward, both knees slightly bent	
	Ball held in nondominant hand at waist height	
	Dominant hand long backswing, strike below midline	
	Contact ball with heel of dominant hand	
	Follow-through with arm in straight line	
Overhand serve	Legs staggered with opposite foot forward	
	Toss is approximately 2 to 3 ft (60 to 90 cm) high	
	Hitting hand back by ear	
	Quick swing and reach with hitting hand	
	Little follow-through, "pop and stop"	

FIGURE 8.1 Sample sport skill assessment.

are *Measurement and Evaluation in Physical Education and Exercise Science* (Lacy & Williams, 2018) and *Performance-Based Assessment for Middle and High School Physical Education* (Lund & Kirk, 2020).

Bear in mind that many formal assessments evaluate components of specific sport skills in isolation and do not evaluate actual performance in game situations. An actual performance assessment would be called an **authentic assessment**, which determines how successful a student is in the application of skills in a gamelike setting. One recent form of authentic assessment for physical educators is PE•Metrics (SHAPE America, 2019), which is a standards-based assessment package for cognitive, physical, and affective skills in a physical activity setting. The tools have been tested for reliability and validity with physical educators and K through 12 students from schools across the country. In particular, the assessments for standard 1 are designed to measure student performance in a real setting.

Unfortunately, skill application complexity can limit such testing, so teachers may find them unacceptable in the instructional setting. Another drawback is that some tests require a large number of trained personnel for administration, which may not be feasible in large secondary classes. Regardless of these restrictions, an effective teacher will arrange his or her instructional environment to include both formal and authentic skill assessments and evaluation. Students should know that learning is an integral part of physical education. Assessment should answer these questions: "What does this student know how to do?" and "What can this student do?"

Dynamic PE ASAP Assessments

Dynamic PE ASAP assessments are outcome-based tools created to assess student progress toward competency for Dynamic Physical Education (DPE) outcomes. The DPE outcomes, although derived from SHAPE America's grade-level outcomes, are written specifically for this curriculum. Thus, the assessments are developed specifically for this curriculum. Assessments have been created for grade 5 through 8 students at the Dynamic PE ASAP website (DynamicPEASAP.com).

Disc Throw

Partners practice throwing the disc back and forth using a peer assessment method. Figure 8.2 is a form that students use to rate each other.

Changing Speed—Soccer

Students dribble a soccer ball and change speed while they try to demonstrate at least three of four cues. Figure 8.3 is a form that students use to rate themselves.

	Dr. Robert Pangrazi's DYNAMIC PE ASAP	*Assessment Method* PEER ASSESSMENT	*Grade / Level* 5-6 / 3	*Lesson* MANIPULATIVE SKILLS USING DISCS

DISC THROW

Outcome: I can throw a disc to a partner demonstrating 3 of 4 cues.

STUDENT NAME 1 _____ CLASS PERIOD _____

Observe your partner demonstrating the following skills.
For each cue, rate your partner as: L = Learning , P = Practicing, R = Refining:

	Same Side
	Thumb on Top
	Curl It
	Let It Fly

FIGURE 8.2 Sample peer assessment.

Reprinted by permission from R.P. Pangrazi, *Dynamic PE ASAP* (Owatonna, MN: Gopher Sport).

FIGURE 8.3 Sample self-assessment.

Reprinted by permission from R.P. Pangrazi, *Dynamic PE ASAP* (Owatonna, MN: Gopher Sport).

Health-Related Fitness Assessments

Physical fitness testing has occurred for decades in physical education. Some experts make an argument for placing less emphasis on fitness testing and more on activity evaluation (Pangrazi & Beighle, 2013). As long as it is used for appropriate purposes, assessing student fitness can be useful. Currently, the FitnessGram physical fitness assessment program (Welk & Blair, 2008) is the most popular health-related fitness test being used and is the test recommended by SHAPE America. The Presidential Youth Fitness Program (PYFP) has adopted it as part of their program, which strives to take the emphasis off the test and focus on the process and promotion of health-related fitness. Each test item has been checked for validity and reliability. The FitnessGram assessment program offers a choice of protocols for all the health-related fitness components: aerobic capacity, muscular endurance, muscular strength, flexibility, and body composition. Physical education teachers can select assessments most appropriate for their students and develop a customized test battery. The top priority of the FitnessGram program is personal fitness self-testing. Students are taught to evaluate themselves and interpret their test results.

In collaboration with PYFP, the FitnessGram program results help teach students about the importance of physical activity for good health. Students are not compared with one another but are given personal feedback about their fitness and whether it meets the minimum standard for good health. If this objective is met, students can test themselves and plan personal programs throughout life (Corbin & Pangrazi, 2008). Test results are acknowledged and commended in the FitnessGram program, but the program places its highest priority on the development and reinforcement of health-related behaviors that are attainable by all students. Behavior programs recognize participants for completion of exercise logs, achievement of specific and personalized goals, and fulfillment of a contractual agreement (with a responsible adult). A helpful text for understanding fitness and activity topics is *Fitness for Life* (Corbin, & LeMasurier, 2018).

FitnessGram Test Items

The suggested test items in the FitnessGram (Cooper Institute, 2017) are briefly described here. Other test items are included in the manual to give teachers a choice of designing a different test battery. See the Websites section at the end of this chapter for information on how to obtain a comprehensive test administration manual, related materials, and software.

Aerobic Capacity

The Progressive Aerobic Cardiovascular Endurance Run (PACER) test is an excellent alternative to the mile (1.6 km) run; it involves a 20-meter shuttle run (a 15-meter PACER is also included for elementary settings) and can be performed indoors (see figure 8.4). The PACER test is progressive, starting at a level that allows all students to be successful and gradually increasing in difficulty. The objective of the PACER is to run back and forth across the 20- or 15-meter distance within a specified time limit that gradually decreases. The 20- or 15-meter distance is not intimidating to young participants (compared with the mile run) and teaches students to pace themselves rather than run all out and fatigue rapidly.

Body Composition

Body composition is evaluated using percent body fat, which is calculated by measuring the triceps and calf skinfolds, or the body mass index (BMI), calculated using height and weight. It can also be measured using bioelectrical impedance analysis (BIA; Kahlil, Mohktar, & Ibrahim, 2014). Several hand-held devices to measure BIA are available to assist with efficient measurement of this component for students (see figure 8.5).

FIGURE 8.4   PACER test.

FIGURE 8.5   Bioelectrical impedance analysis (BIA) device.

Muscular Strength (Abdominal)

The curl-up test uses a cadence (one curl-up every three seconds) with a maximum limit of 75. Students lie in a supine position with the knees bent at a 140-degree angle. The hands are placed flat on the mat alongside the hips. The objective is to sit up and gradually move the fingers down the mat a specified distance (see figure 8.6).

Muscular Strength (Upper Body)

The push-up test is done to a cadence (one every three seconds) and is an excellent substitute for the pull-up. A successful push-up is counted when the arms are bent to a 90-degree angle (see figure 8.7). This item allows many more students to experience success as compared with the pull-up and flexed-arm hang. Other alternative test items to the push-up are the modified pull-up, the pull-up, and the flexed-arm hang.

FIGURE 8.6   Curl-up test.

FIGURE 8.7   Push-up test.

Muscular Strength and Flexibility (Trunk Extensor)

The trunk lift test is done from a facedown position (see figure 8.8). This test involves lifting the upper body 6 to 12 inches (15 to 30 cm) off the floor using the muscles of the back. The position must be held until the measurement can be made.

Flexibility

The back-saver sit-and-reach (see figure 8.9) is like the traditional sit-and-reach test except that it is performed with one leg flexed to avoid encouraging students to hyperextend. Measurement is made on both the right and left legs.

FIGURE 8.8   Trunk lift test.

FIGURE 8.9   Back-saver sit-and-reach test.

Criterion-Referenced Health Standards

A major reason for doing health-related fitness evaluations is to provide students, teachers, and parents with information about good health. The FitnessGram program (Cooper Institute, 2017) uses criterion-referenced health standards that represent good health instead of traditional percentile rankings. In other words, all students have an opportunity to achieve the standards. These standards represent a level of fitness that offers some degree of protection against diseases resulting from sedentary living. The FitnessGram program uses an approach that classifies fitness performance into two categories: needs improvement and healthy fitness zone (HFZ). All students are encouraged to score within the HFZ, but scoring beyond the healthy fitness zone offers little advantage (see figure 8.10). Thus, to save time during physical education lessons, teachers should consider stopping the PACER test, curl-up cadence, and push-up cadence after the student has achieved the HFZ.

Criterion-referenced health standards do not compare students against each other the way that percentile rankings do. Instead, the focus is on personal fitness and minimizing possible health problems by trying to score within the HFZ. Criterion-referenced health standards for aerobic fitness are based on an early study by Blair and colleagues (1989). A significant decrease in risk of all-cause mortality occurred when people were active enough to avoid classification in the bottom 20% of the population. The risk level continues to decrease as fitness levels increase but not significantly when compared with moving out of the least active group. The aerobic performance minimums (mile [1.6 km] run or PACER) for the FitnessGram HFZ require achieving a fitness level above the least-active portion (bottom 20%) of the population.

Effective Uses of Fitness Tests

Fitness tests are designed to evaluate and educate students about the status of their physical fitness. Despite continued research and improvement, fitness tests have limitations and usually show low validity (that is, they do not measure what they purport to measure). Bear in mind that the results of fitness evaluation are often flawed or inaccurate. Therefore, how the tests are used becomes an important issue. The three major ways to use fitness tests are (1) to teach personal self-testing, (2) to establish personal best fitness performances, and (3) to evaluate institutional fitness goals. The personal self-testing program is most strongly advocated in the physical education program. It can be done in the least amount of time, is educational, and can be done frequently. In addition, little instructional time is lost, and students learn how to evaluate their fitness, a skill that will serve them for a lifetime.

Personal Self-Testing

The personal fitness self-testing approach is student centered, concerned with the process of fitness testing, and emphasizes learning to self-evaluate. When using this technique, students can work individually or find a friend with whom they would like to self-test. With a partner, they evaluate each other and develop their own fitness profiles. The goal is to learn the process of fitness testing so that they will be able to evaluate their health status during adulthood. Students are asked to do their best, but the teacher does not interfere in the process. Fitness results are the property of the student and are not posted or shared with other students. Self-testing is an educational endeavor; it also allows for more frequent evaluation because it can be done quickly, privately, and informally. A considerable amount of practice is needed

	Aerobic capacity PACER,* one-mile (1.6 km) run and walk test	Percent body fat	Body mass index	Curl-up number completed	Trunk lift inches (cm)	90-degree push-up number completed	Modified pull-up number completed	Back-saver sit-and-reach** inches (cm)	Shoulder stretch
Girl 14	≥39.4*	14.0–28.5	15.9–22.8	>18	9–12 (23–30)	>7	>4	10 (25)	Healthy fitness zone = touching fingertips together behind the back on both right and left sides
Boy 14	≥42.5*	7.1–21.3	16.1–22.1	≥24	9–12 (23–30)	≥14	≥9	8 (20)	

*Either the one-mile walk/run or the PACER test can be selected for aerobic capacity.
**Test scored yes or no; must reach this distance on each side to achieve the HFZ.

FIGURE 8.10 Healthy fitness zones (HFZ) for a 14-year-old girl and boy.

to self-test effectively, so students should have multiple opportunities to practice. In addition, teachers must help students interpret the results. Students who fall below the healthy fitness zone (HFZ) should be assisted in developing a program of improvement. Students who reach the HFZ should be taught how to determine goals for fitness within the zone and how to maintain that level of fitness.

Figure 8.11 is an example of a self-evaluation form that students can use. It contains a column to check off whether the minimum criterion-referenced health standard for each test item has been met. The purpose of recording the data is to help students learn to evaluate themselves without others having to view or know about it. As a final note, it is acceptable for some students to choose not to be tested on a certain item because they fear embarrassment or failure. Being tested and embarrassed is worse than not being tested at all.

Institutional Evaluation

The institutional evaluation program involves examining the fitness levels of students to see if the institution (school) is reaching its desired objectives. Institutional objectives are closely tied to the physical education curriculum. If the curriculum taught to students is adequate and the goals is meaningful, most students should be able to reach institutional goals. A common approach for institutional goal setting is to establish a percentage of the student body that must meet or exceed criterion-referenced health standards for a fitness test. If the percentage is below established institutional standards, the curriculum may need to be modified to meet the objective.

PERSONAL FITNESS

Name _____ Age _____ Grade _____ Room _____

	Score	HFZ*
Body composition		
Calf (leg) skinfold		
Triceps (arm) skinfold	+	
Total (leg and arm)	=	
Cardiorespiratory endurance		
PACER		
Abdominal strength		
Curl-ups		
Upper-body strength		
Push-ups		
Back strength		
Trunk lift		
Lower back flexibility		
Sit-and-reach	L R	
Upper-body flexibility		
Shoulder stretch	L R	

*HFZ means you have scored in the healthy fitness zone, which means that you have achieved or passed the minimum fitness standard required for good health and minimal health risk. Regardless of whether you passed all the tests, you must maintain an active lifestyle for good health. Try to accomplish at least 60 minutes of activity every day.

You do not have to share the results of your personal fitness record. It is for your information and should help you determine your health status. Ask your teacher if you need ideas for increasing your physical activity level.

Students are learning the process of evaluating their fitness. The scores recorded may not be accurate.

FIGURE 8.11 Sample personal fitness record.

Because this type of testing affects teachers and curriculum offerings, it is done in a formal and standardized manner. Each test item is reviewed separately because objectives may be reached for some, but not all, of the items. To avoid testing all students every year, some districts evaluate only during entry-level years (e.g., the seventh and ninth grades). This approach minimizes the amount of formal testing that students must endure during their school career. See the section Program Accountability for more information on how to use these data.

Physical Activity Assessment

One major measure of teacher effectiveness in physical education is student physical activity levels. *Healthy People 2010* (United States Department of Health and Human Services, 2000) recommends that students be active at least 50% of the time during physical education lessons. But this outcome is rarely assessed, nor is it reported as an accountability measure of teacher or program effectiveness. Thus, one logical outcome of student performance is physical activity levels both during physical education and beyond the school day. Accurate instruments are available for measuring physical activity. One cost-effective and efficient method is pedometers (Beighle, Pangrazi, & Vincent, 2001). They can measure the number of steps, activity time, and calories burned, among others. Pedometers can be considered a school supply item for students, and teachers can require students to buy one. Class sets can be purchased with the physical education budget. Money from fund-raisers can go toward pedometers as well. Data from pedometers can be used for several accountability purposes. First, rubrics with step requirements can be implemented in physical education. These step counts (or activity times) can be translated into a grade. Second, the teacher can use the physical activity data to support his or her physical education program by demonstrating how much physical activity students accumulate during class. Third, the teacher can implement personalized plans using pedometers. The students can gather baseline physical activity during physical education and beyond and develop strategies for increasing or maintaining their physical activity levels. Specific protocols are available for collecting accountability data with pedometers (see Pangrazi & Beighle, 2013). Four days of pedometer data are needed to establish a baseline activity level. After this number has been established, physical activity goals can be set for classes or individual students.

Students can also report physical activity levels with physical activity logs. One means for reporting these data is ActivityGram, in which students recall their physical activity for three days. Activity is reported for 30-minute blocks of time between 7 a.m. and 11 p.m. Information related to the type, intensity, and length of activity is included. A new module in which students enter step counts or activity time from pedometers has been added to the FitnessGram web-based software. Other physical activity self-report instruments are available for student and teacher use as well. The children's physical activity research group at the University of South Carolina has a three-day physical activity recall available on their website (see the Websites section at the end of this chapter). PE Central has a "log it" program that encourages students to be active. This program can be conducted by the physical educator, or students can complete this on their own. Additional means for measuring student physical activity include accelerometers, heart rate monitors, and direct observation. Uses for these techniques can be found in Welk (2002).

Cognitive Assessment

Cognitive assessment is an integral part of evaluating the whole child. A combination of all three learning domains (cognitive, psychomotor, and affective) influence students' desire to participate in movement activities, and all three should be incorporated into the assessment process. Traditional evaluation of content knowledge through written tests has been viewed in a controversial light. Students may think that learning skills is enough and that they should not have to take written exams in physical education. Some parents are offended when their children receive a low grade because of poor performance on written tests. Teachers have often been unwilling to administer written tests in physical education because of the amount of time that such testing takes from skill practice. Regardless of these issues, knowledge is involved in the application of all motor skills. A person must know rules, regulations, and proper etiquette to participate fairly and enjoyably with others. Proper skill performance is knowledge based, and skill improvement will not occur if the person does not know proper skill technique. To minimize concern, teachers need to explain to students and parents why cognitive achievement is as important in physical education as it is in any other academic area.

Evaluating the cognitive domain through alternative assessment can be done efficiently and authentically. Physical education should always be focused on maximizing activity and ensuring that students learn physical skills; in addition, they need to know the "whys" of physical movement. Cognitive assessment of physical education content does not have to be an endeavor that occurs only in the physical education classroom. Physical educators can collaborate with teachers in other content areas to integrate concepts into multiple subjects and to measure requisite knowledge. Examples include analysis of exercise heart-rate zones in math class, biomechanical effect on sport skills in physics, and nutritional analysis and its effect on calorie consumption in aerobic sports. Additionally, students can be required to complete cognitive assessments outside physical education class. Including the cognitive component as part of a total program indicates that effective skill learning requires knowledge.

Assessing knowledge of the rules, strategy, and history of a sport or activity can be accomplished through alternative and more authentic unique techniques. For example, students can, individually or in small groups, develop a crossword puzzle based on the rules of a specific sport. These crossword puzzles are then exchanged with classmates to be completed and used to document cognitive understanding. Students can demonstrate their understanding of rules by performing referee duties during game and tournament play. Accuracy of decisions and calls can be determined by a peer assessment. Both alternative methods of assessment represent cognitive understanding in an authentic setting.

Application of fitness formulas, concepts, and principles (e.g., exercise heart rate, overload, FITT) and development of personal exercise programs can be documented through completion of fitness portfolios. Students complete fitness assessments, create personalized fitness plans based on areas for improvement, and maintain records of their participation in such activities. They may track activity scores (e.g., with a pedometer) to support their outcomes. Fitness portfolios can be an authentic representation of knowledge and application.

Regardless of the cognitive assessments used, teachers must match the developmental levels of the students at the different grade levels. When developing written test questions using multiple choice, true–false, completion, or essay options, teachers can use a combination to meet student abilities. When using essay questions, remember that grading time will increase, as compared with multiple choice or true–false questions. Figure 8.12 is an example of a test that might be administered to first-year students at the completion of a unit on racquetball.

When designing written tests, observing a few key points can make the examinations more effective.

1. Group different types of questions by format. True–false, multiple choice, and matching questions should be in separate sections.

2. Place all instructions on the test. Specific instructions for different types of questions should precede each section.

3. Place the test items in increasing order of difficulty. Students may give up on the exam if the first question or two is high in difficulty.

4. Ensure that the exam does not have an obvious pattern, such as alternating true–false items or keywords that tip off the answer (e.g., using *always* or *never* in true–false questions).

5. Carefully monitor the exam. Students will think that the instructor is unfair if cheating or sharing answers is easy. Also, when monitoring the exam, teachers can listen to student questions. Similar questions about similar items often tip off an instructor to a poorly designed or written item.

Another approach to check cognitive outcomes is to give students a study guide. The study guide should contain knowledge that students need to participate successfully in a unit of instruction. Figure 8.13 is an example of a rugby study guide and exam developed for entry-level high school students. It contains the basic formations, terminology, and rules necessary to participate in a touch rugby unit.

Affective Assessment

Standard 5 of the SHAPE America national standards for physical education states that "the physically literate individual recognizes the value of physical activity for health, enjoyment, challenge, self-expression, and/or social interaction" (SHAPE America, 2013). There is a clear relationship between participation and value, enjoyment, and social interaction. Traditional assessments such as attendance, dressing out, and written tests give little support to students' affective growth and development. Assessment in the affective domain supports the positive effect that physical education has on students' feelings toward movement. Few educators measure the effect that their program and instruction have on this important area. Usually, teachers agree about what to do for students in the affective learning domain. Most teachers want to do the following:

RACQUETBALL EXAM

Name _____ Date _____

I. In the blanks below, fill in the name of the area of the court designated by each letter. (10 points)

A _____ line
B _____ line
C _____
D _____ court
E _____ court

II. In the following diagrams, draw an arrow to indicate the path that the ball is most likely to follow. None of these shots has hit the floor. The (X) indicates the point of origin of the shot. (6 points)

III. In the spaces at the left, place a (+) if the statement is true; place a (0) if the statement is false. (60 points)

____ 1. A game consists of 15 points.

____ 2. Only the server may score a point.

____ 3. The server may either bounce the ball before serving or hit it straight out of his or her hand.

____ 4. Only one foot needs to be in the service zone when serving.

____ 5. In doubles, the partner with the better left hand usually plays the left side.

____ 6. The choice for the right to serve is decided by the toss of a coin, and the side winning the toss starts the first and third games.

____ 7. If a player swings and misses on the serve, he or she is given only one more chance.

____ 8. A legal serve must bounce in the backcourt on a fly or after touching one sidewall.

FIGURE 8.12 Sample cognitive assessment for racquetball.

(continued)

____ 9. In doubles, only one person serves in the first and second service. After that, both players on each team serve.

____ 10. A player is out if he or she is hit with his or her own shot on the fly, but it is a hinder if his or her own shot hits him or her on one bounce.

____ 11. It is common courtesy to alternate serves to each court, but in tournament play, there is no such rule.

____ 12. The more walls that a shot hits, the deader the rebound will be.

____ 13. When playing a lane shot, hitting the ball underhand is usually best.

____ 14. Using the sidewall is a good tactic when using the lob serve.

____ 15. The kill shot should be attempted when the ball is chest high.

____ 16. The most advantageous court position is just behind the short line.

____ 17. Letting a waist-high shot bounce off the back wall is often wise because it can be returned from a lower height.

____ 18. In doubles, a player may call a hinder when he or she is obstructed from hitting the ball by his or her partner.

____ 19. In doubles, the server's partner must lean against the sidewall until the ball passes the service line.

____ 20. The ball should be contacted at the junction between the fingers and the palm.

IV. In the spaces at the left, place the letter of the answer that best completes the statement. (24 points)

____ 1. Which of the following is *not* a serve?
   a. scotch-toss serve
   b. ceiling serve
   c. power serve
   d. Z serve

____ 2. All the following points concerning body position for hitting the kill shot are correct *except*
   a. bend at the knees and waist
   b. weight transfer is from the front foot to the rear foot
   c. contact should be at shin level or lower
   d. the forearm should be parallel to the floor

____ 3. All the following are "shorts" *except*
   a. hitting the sidewall and then the front wall
   b. hitting the front wall and then having the ball bounce in front of the short line
   c. hitting the front wall and then the two sidewalls
   d. hitting the front wall and then the ceiling

____ 4. All the following statements concerning receiving the serve are true *except*
   a. the receiver must be behind the short line while the ball is being served
   b. the receiver may return the service on either the volley or the first bounce
   c. a short may be returned if so desired
   d. the receiver does not have the option of returning the service on a foot fault

____ 5. How many bounces are permitted on the serve?
   a. 2
   b. 3
   c. 4
   d. unlimited amount

FIGURE 8.12 *(continued)*

RUGBY STUDY GUIDE AND EXAM

The following is information you are expected to know when the written exam is given at the end of the week. We will discuss any questions you have before the exam.

Rugby is a game played by two teams of 15 players who are allowed to carry, kick, and throw the ball. Players attempt to score points by placing the ball over the opponents' goal line (a try) or by kicking the ball over the crossbar (a goal).

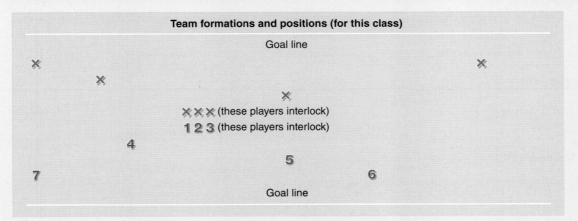

Team formations and positions (for this class)

Names of players by position: 1 = prop forward, 2 = hooker, 3 = prop forward, 4 = scrum halfback, 5 = center, 6 = wing (strong side), 7 = wing (weak side)

Terminology

Try (touchdown)—4 points. When the ball is touched down in the opponents' end zone.

Conversion (extra point)—2 points. Attempted kick after the try is scored. The ball is kicked from any distance beyond 10 yards and directly out from where the ball was touched down.

Penalty goal—3 points. This follows an infraction of the rules and is kicked from the point of infraction or anywhere behind it. It may be placekicked or drop-kicked over the bar of the goalpost.

Drop goal—3 points. This is a dropkick that is taken at any time while the game is in progress. The ball must go over the bar.

Lineout. Formed by the two teams of the scrum forwards in opposing lines wherever the ball goes into "touch" (out of bounds); both teams jump to try to obtain possession, and then the ball is thrown between them by the wing.

Scrum. Forwards bind together against each other while the scrum half throws or rolls the ball directly between the two rows. Both sides try to gain possession by "hooking" the ball back with their feet so that the backs start a running movement.

Rules

1. Seven players make up a team.
2. Match begins with a kickoff, which must travel at least 10 yards (m).
3. Play is continual and is stopped only when the ball is out of bounds (like soccer).
4. When the player with the ball is tagged, that player must stop, place the ball on the ground, and quickly line up in position.
5. Three players (on each team) will form a scrummage by the two forwards and the hooker. These players will interlock. This group of three players is called the pack.
6. As the pack forms a scrum, the other players remain behind them.

FIGURE 8.13 Sample study guide and exam for rugby.

(continued)

7. The scrum should be steady until the ball is put in by the scrum half of the nonoffending team. If the ball runs straight through the scrum, it must be put in again.

8. The three front players must not raise a foot until the ball touches the ground. These players cannot handle the ball.

9. The scrum half is expected to pick up the ball smartly and pass it sharply back to the next person in line. Following this, a series of backward laterals occurs, each pass made just before the ball carrier is tagged.

10. A ruck occurs when one or more players from each team close around the ball when it is on the ground between them. Players must be on their feet and must bind with at least one arm around a teammate.

11. A maul occurs when one or more players from each team close around a player who is carrying the ball.

Rugby Test

20-point unit test

Name _____ Date _____

Multiple Choice

1. In the game of rugby played in class, each team has _____ players.

    a. 10
    b. 7
    c. 22
    d. 14

2. The game begins with a kickoff, which must travel at least _____ yards (m).

    a. 40
    b. 30
    c. 20
    d. 10

3. Play is continual and is only stopped when

    a. a player calls, "Time-out"
    b. the ball is out of bounds
    c. a player falls down
    d. the ball is kicked

4. A _____ is formed by the two teams' forwards and hookers in opposing lines wherever the ball goes into "touch" (out of bounds); both teams jump to try to obtain possession as the ball is thrown in bounds.

    a. conversion
    b. scrum
    c. lineout
    d. ruck

5. In class, when the player with the ball is _____, that player must stop, place the ball on the ground, and quickly line up into position.

    a. scared
    b. tackled
    c. tagged with either hand
    d. tagged with both hands

FIGURE 8.13 *(continued)*

Matching

1. Known as the pack _____

2. Puts the ball in and takes it out _____

3. Must not raise a foot until the ball touches the ground _____

4. Fastest-running player or players on the team _____

5. Players who will interlock _____

Positions

a. two forwards and hooker

b. scrum halfback

c. center and two wings

True–False

___ 1. A 98-pound (44 kg) player will most likely play the position of a prop forward.

___ 2. A try is scored as soon as the player carrying the ball crosses the opponents' end zone.

___ 3. A player can pass the ball forward, sideways, and backward.

___ 4. Rugby is a team sport played at many colleges that may offer scholarships to both male and female students.

___ 5. A 280-pound (127 kg) player will most likely play the position of a wing.

FIGURE 8.13 *(continued)*

8

1. *Develop positive attitudes toward physical activity.* If students learn physical skills but develop a negative feeling about activity, they likely will not participate when left on their own. Feeling positive about one's ability and competency in physical activities will increase the possibility of participation.

2. *Enhance a positive self-concept.* Students will most likely be viewed positively by their peers when they learn to perform physical skills appropriately. Self-concept is reinforced through feedback from others. When teachers and peers respond positively, students learn that they are worthy.

3. *Develop proper social skills.* Students need to learn to play fair and with proper respect for others. The opportunity to cooperate and compete with peers offers students a chance to learn what personal behavior is acceptable and unacceptable. Because most behavior in physical education is visible to others, feedback about proper social behavior is effective and immediate.

4. Behavioral attitudes can be informally monitored with a checklist like the one in figure 8.14. This instrument is informal and relates specific behaviors to attitude. Teachers often view a good attitude as one in which the student does what the teacher tells her or him to do. This approach deals more with behavior than attitude toward physical education or physical activity. If such a tool is used, it offers the advantage of listing specific criteria. At times, teachers tell a student that he or she has a bad attitude but do not define why he or she is being chastised. A checklist defines what behavior is expected and helps prevent teachers from making snap judgments about attitudes.

Several instruments are available for measuring attitudes and values. A few examples are offered here. For a review of a wide variety of instruments, see the text by Lacy and Williams (2018). Such instruments have been evaluated over time and are somewhat more accurate in evaluating long-term attitudes and values. Regardless of the instrument used, teachers should use caution; personality traits change and are difficult to measure.

Using Affective Assessment

Assessing the affective development of students is important information that can be used to develop a physical education program that will have positive long-term effects. Caution must be issued when evaluating a student's emotional side. Adolescence is a time filled with great change, and students are often viewed as moody, self-absorbed, confrontational, and even as know-it-alls. This changing and emotional time will not always provide objective affective results that can be incorporated into an overall evaluation score. Yet assessing how students feel about physical education and ensuring that students engage in positive experiences that help build self-esteem and self-confidence is criti-

ATTITUDE

Assign 0 to 5 points during each observation with 5 being the highest score. Several observations should be made during the semester to reveal consistency and improvement.

Student _____ Date _____ Lesson focus _____

1. Tries all activities	0	1	2	3	4	5
2. Is on time	0	1	2	3	4	5
3. Consistently gives a maximum effort	0	1	2	3	4	5
4. Shows concern for others	0	1	2	3	4	5
5. Listens to and applies criticism	0	1	2	3	4	5
6. Shows enthusiasm	0	1	2	3	4	5
7. Participates with all students	0	1	2	3	4	5
8. Shares ideas with teacher and class	0	1	2	3	4	5
9. Demonstrates leadership	0	1	2	3	4	5
10. Volunteers to help others	0	1	2	3	4	5

FIGURE 8.14 Sample affective assessment.

cal. Help them feel as though their opinions are valued. Students' perceptions can be used to address changes in content or instructional delivery. No assessment tool is better than gathering attitudes and beliefs from the students themselves.

Types of Assessments

Assessment in physical education is often difficult because of the nature of the subject matter. A perfect and correct performance rarely occurs. Even outstanding athletes who have practiced for years make performance errors. But student performance can be assessed in a way that allows a continuum of performance levels between good and poor. Assessment of student performance is an important issue that can be accomplished in many ways. Assessment can become more than an end product that results in an evaluation of good or poor; it can be used as an integral part of student learning and understanding. Assessment can and should be used as a tool to guide the instructional process and develop in-depth student understanding.

What students are to learn is directed by national, state, or content-specific standards. These standards serve as a guide to what can be expected on completion. Expectations and outcomes are clarified with standards, but whether the learning outcomes based on these standards are achieved is difficult to know without input derived from alternative and authentic assessment. When authentic assessment is used, teachers can state that students know and do what is stated in the standards. Information collected from alternative and authentic assessment makes it clear what students have learned. Standards direct the learning, giving it a framework; objectives are more immediate outcomes and can be developed to focus on the progressive nature of learning as well as outcomes. Student learning objectives are written so that both the teacher and students know what they can do at the end of the course or on completion of the lesson. Results from student assessments also provide information to teachers about whether their teaching practices are effective.

How do teachers help students engage in meaningful assessment? This question drives the principles of using assessment as a tool to assess student skill level and understanding and to involve the student with outcomes-based learning. Meaningful information should result from systematic and ongoing assessments that involve all three learning domains: psychomotor, cognitive, and affective. Assessment can occur throughout multiple levels of learning, including knowledge, comprehension, application, analysis, synthesis, and evaluation.

Traditionally, assessment in physical education has been accomplished informally, often done on the spot when a teacher corrects or reinforces a student's performance. Visual monitoring or observation of students' performance has also been accepted as a form of assessment. Teachers visually scan to see if students are successfully accomplishing specific tasks. Informal assessment typically produces no documented evidence to show students or parents that objectives have been attained; thus, these types of assessment should be converted to formal assessments to provide accountability for program success.

Standards-based content highlights what students should know and be able to do at the end of specific grade levels (SHAPE America, 2013). Standards provide guidelines for teachers and departments to communicate and give direction to physical education. With the introduction of physical education content standards, more formal yet alternative assessments are becoming popular because teachers are expected to assess and report student progress toward program standards (Chepko & Arnold, 2000). Although similar to alternative assessment, authentic assessment is another aspect to assessing student performance. Authentic assessment is defined as measuring student performance in a real-world application of knowledge or skills. Unlike many of the skills tests listed in the previous section, authentic assessment allows students to perform in a normal setting rather than a contrived testing environment. What good is performing a skill well if a student is not able to perform it when it counts? Student outcomes on a written rules test mean little if they cannot be applied appropriately during game play. By assessing students during normal participation, a teacher ensures that the assessment reflects actual knowledge or ability. In all the following examples of assessment instruments, ensuring that each has at least some authentic components is relatively easy. Examples of conditions that represent authentic assessment include the following:

- Adherence to rules during play
- Strategy formulation and execution
- Skill selection and application during play
- Performance of physical skills under gamelike or competitive situations
- Self-monitoring for performance indicators of activity involvement, fitness, and appropriate social engagement

Rubrics

A rubric is one means to evaluate a specific outcome. Rubrics can be used to objectively judge student performance. Effective rubrics focus on specific learning outcomes or objectives that students are expected to achieve. Criteria are established to ensure that scores are assigned consistently for each level of attainment. Rubrics can be used to assess product, process, and progress. A product-oriented rubric refers to the product, such as how many times a basket is made or a pamphlet or brochure promoting a physical activity club. When a rubric is used as a process assessment, information is shared with the student and becomes an excellent tool to self-diagnose both strengths and weaknesses and develop a practice plan (see figure 8.15). A progress rubric demonstrates how much students have improved. This type of rubric requires multiple assessments.

Students are provided with the rubric before assessment so that they understand how they will be assessed and held accountable. The scoring system and the criteria assigned each level must be objective and attainable and answer a basic question common to most assessments: "Does the student consistently meet the stated criteria required for completion of the course requirement?" Figure 8.16 is an example of an outcomes-based product rubric for grading a weight-training class.

Figure 8.17 is an example of a bowling rubric using video analysis. In this case, students work together in groups of three and analyze their own and their peers' skill performance. Each performer receives the average of three scores, her or his own score and the scores of two peers.

Checklists

Checklists are a type of rubric in which the criterion is scored as a yes-or-no rating (Lund & Kirk, 2020). A checklist sheet can be used to evaluate skill development or successful application of skills in an authentic setting. For example, teachers select the types of skills they believe that a student should learn in a basketball unit, and the checklist allows them to indicate whether the student exhibits the criteria. No judgement regarding the quality of the characteristic or criteria is made.

Checklists are useful for reporting progress to students, parents, and administrators as well for identifying students in need of special help. Using a class list with skills displayed across the top of the sheet is a common method used for recording class progress. If grading is based on the number of activities that students master, the checklist can deliver this information. Checklists

Levels of learning	Punting within a limited time	Punting to a partner	Punting at angles
Professional	• Watches the ball and not the partner. • Only two steps are taken before the ball is punted.	• Eyes are on the ball. • Distance is adjusted to location of receiving partner; partner does not move more than 10 feet (3 m). • The step-hop technique is used.	• Eyes are on the ball. • Leg angle extends toward the intended target. • Ball is within 15 feet (5 m) of the target.
Collegiate	• Eyes are on the ball. • Three or more steps are taken.	• Eyes are on the ball. • Distance is adjusted to location of receiving partner; partner moves no more than 15 feet (5 m). • The step-hop technique is used.	• Eyes are on the ball. • Leg angle extends toward the intended target. • Ball is within 20 feet (6 m) of the target.
Varsity	• Eyes are taken off the ball. • Three or more steps are taken.	• Eyes are on the ball. • Distance is adjusted to location of receiving partner; partner moves no more than 20 feet (5 m). • The step-hop technique is not used.	• Eyes are taken off the ball. • Leg angle extends toward the intended target. • Ball is not catchable.
Junior varsity	• Eyes are taken off the ball. • Ball is dropped. • Ball is not kicked.	• Eyes are taken off the ball. • Ball is not catchable for partner. • The step-hop technique is not used.	• Eyes are taken off the ball. • Leg angle does not extend toward the intended target. • Ball is not catchable.

FIGURE 8.15 Sample high school process rubric for punting.

WEIGHT-TRAINING CLASS

Name _____ Date _____

Outstanding

A. Participates in weight-training activities over and above class requirements

B. Expresses positive views toward safety in the weight room

C. Participates in three intramural or extramural weight-training competitions

D. Gives examples of proper techniques for five basic lifts

E. Leads by example in the weight room by taking turns and encouraging peers

F. Can self-analyze each lift and explain what part of the body is being developed

G. Records all lifts by weight and repetitions into log

FIGURE 8.16 Sample product rubric for a weight-training class.

(continued)

Satisfactory

A. Participates in all class requirement activities

B. Shows concern for safety but is not overt about safe practices

C. Participates in two intramural or extramural weight-training competitions

D Usually, but not always, able to demonstrate proper technique for five basic lifts

E. Displays primary interest in self-development rather than helping others

F. Usually knows what body part each lift develops

G. Usually records all lifts by weight and repetitions into log

Needs Improvement

A. Does not always complete class requirement activities

B. Usually shows concern for safety but at times lifts using unsafe practices

C. Participates in one intramural or extramural weight-training competition

D. Often not able to demonstrate proper techniques when a new lift is introduced

F. Rarely knows what body part is developed by a lift

G. Often fails to record all lifts by weight and repetitions into log

Unsatisfactory

A. Demonstrates spotty record of completing class requirement activities

B. Considers safety a low priority and needs correction regularly

C. Does not participate in intramural or extramural weight-training competition

D. Fails to use proper techniques when lifting

E. Often fails to allow peers to work in and share weights

F. Displays unorganized total weight program

G. Does not maintain a log of lifts by weight and repetition

FIGURE 8.16 (continued)

BOWLING

Name (doer) _____ Name (observer) _____

This assignment requires you to evaluate yourself using video analysis. Over the next three weeks, have one of the members of the group record you while you are performing the following skills. You must be recorded at least twice doing the same skills. Make sure that everyone in your group has been recorded performing all the skills listed below. Evaluate your video at home or at school. Then give your video to each of the members in your group and ask them to evaluate it. When you have completed all the skills, turn in the tape (label it with your name) and your evaluation sheet.

Approach	Always 2 points	Usually 1 point	Rarely 0 points
Push away on first step			
Push away: out and down—elbow straight			
Backswing: straight—in line with boards			
Steps: smooth, gliding, even rhythm			
Steps: increase in length and speed			
Slide on left foot			

FIGURE 8.17 Sample progress rubric for bowling.

(continued)

Approach	Always 2 points	Usually 1 point	Rarely 0 points
Release			
Shoulders: parallel to foul line			
Shoulders: level			
Upper body: inclined forward			
Left foot: in line with boards			
Weight balanced on left foot			
Thumb in 12 o'clock position			
Ball first strikes alley 18 inches (45 cm) in front of left foot			
Follow-through: straight and to shoulder height			
Aim			
Approach: straight, in line with boards			
Release: proper dot to dots at foul line			
Crosses proper dart			
Where does ball strike pins? (e.g., 1–3, 1, 3, 1–2)			
Scoring: total points accumulated in each area above			
Self-evaluation:	Approach	Release	Aim
Trial 1			
Trial 2			
Peer 1 evaluation of me	Approach	Release	Aim
Trial 1			
Trial 2			
Peer 2 evaluation of me	Approach	Release	Aim
Trial 1			
Trial 2			

Total score:

Write a short evaluation about how you will improve your bowling skills based on your evaluation of your bowling form.

FIGURE 8.17 (continued)

are usually most effective when skills are listed in the sequence in which they should be learned. In this way, the teacher can gear the teaching process to diagnosed needs. To avoid disrupting the learning process, teachers can record student progress informally while students are practicing. Figure 8.18 is an example of a pass–fail task checklist used in softball. In this example, students work with a partner and are responsible for evaluating each other. When a task is evaluated, the form is dated, scored, and initialed.

SOFTBALL PEER ASSESSMENT

Name _____ Date _____

Work with a partner. Each of you has a task sheet and is responsible for evaluating each other. You will have to find other peers to complete some of the tasks. Record the date the task was tried and whether it was successfully accomplished (yes or no). Then initial the sheet.

Date	Score	Initials	Description of task
			Stand 45 feet (14 m) from a partner who is inside a hoop and complete five consecutive underhand pitches to that person without causing him or her to move outside the hoop.
			Stand 60 feet (18 m) from a partner who is inside a hoop and complete five overhand throws to that person without forcing him or her to move more than 1 foot (30 cm) outside the hoop.
			Demonstrate the proper stance, windup, and delivery of the windmill pitch.
			From a designated area of the outfield, situated 150 feet (45 m) for boys or 100 feet (30 m) for girls away, throw the softball through the air directly to a 10-foot-wide (3 m wide) circle chalked in front of home plate. To count, the throw must bounce only once before landing or going through the circle. Make three of five throws.
			Display pitching skills by striking out three or more batters or by allowing no more than five base hits in an actual game.
			Using the correct fielding stance, cleanly field five consecutive ground balls or fly balls hit by partner.
			Play a game of pepper with a group of no more than six players, demonstrating good bat control, eye–hand coordination, and fielding skills.
			Play a game of 500 with no more than five players and demonstrate skills in catching flies and line drives and in fielding ground balls.
			Using a batting tee, hit five consecutive softballs, on the fly or on the ground, past the 80-foot (25 m) semicircle line marked off in chalk.
			Execute proper bunting form and ability by dumping three of five attempts into designated bunting areas along the first or third baselines.
			In an actual game, make two or more base hits.
Bonus requirements (You may substitute the following for tasks above you did not accomplish.)			
			Make a diagram of an official softball diamond on poster board. Illustrate proper field dimensions.
			On a piece of paper, show how batting average and earned run average are computed.
			Umpire a game for three or more innings.
			Keep accurate score in an official score book for three or more innings.

FIGURE 8.18 Sample peer assessment task checklist for softball.

Point System Rubrics

Point system rubrics are similar to checklists, but they assign points for different criteria on the list. No judgement is made on the quality of the performance. Points are awarded if the student demonstrates the criteria. One way that this type of checklist is advantageous is that the teacher can add up the points earned and convert the total to a grade. Additionally, more emphasis can be placed on certain criteria (Lund & Kirk, 2020).

Figure 8.19 is an example of a volleyball skills point system rubric. In this situation, a partner observes and completes the assessment. Points are earned by completing tasks. At the end of the unit, a grade is assigned based on the number of points accumulated. If the accuracy of evaluation is of concern, students can be spot-checked on different skills. In most cases, the strength of a checklist is that it gives direction to instruction. Students know what is expected of them and how they will be evaluated.

Rating Scales

Another type of rubric is a rating scale, or analytic rubric. Teachers can use rating scales to evaluate the performance of a class of students. Rating scales list the tasks that students need to complete. To some degree, these tasks form the outcomes for the unit. Figure 8.20 is an example of a teacher rating scale for team handball. Rating can be done on a scale ranging from three to infinity levels but ideally should have no more than six levels. When grading using A through F, six levels could be used with one level per letter and the sixth level meaning no response. Ideally, four levels are recommended for the most reliability. Using an even number of levels also forces the score to lean toward either competent or noncompetent. In any case with rating scales, the most points are awarded for a task completed successfully. Required tasks should be

VOLLEYBALL

Work with a partner. See the course syllabus for the days when you should evaluate the following skills. If you successfully pass the skill, have your partner verify your performance by dating and initialing this sheet. When finished, calculate the total number of points you have earned.

Name _____ Date _____

Skill to be tested	Points possible	Date passed	Partner's initials
Wall sets: Set the ball 12 to 15 inches (30 to 40 cm) above a 10-foot (3 m) line against the wall 25 times (try to make them consecutive).	5		
Quick hands sets: Set the ball 12 to 15 inches (30 to 40 cm) above hands in the air or against the wall for 30 seconds.	5		
Partner sets: Do 25 sets with your partner 15 feet (5 m) away (try to make them consecutive).	10		
Hoop sets: Set 10 balls into a hoop 12 feet (4 m) away from a partner-tossed ball from a right angle to the net or wall.	15		
Wall bumps: Bump the ball above a 10-foot (3 m) line against the wall 25 times (try to make them consecutive).	5		
Partner bumps: Do 25 bumps with a partner 15 feet (5 m) away (try to make them consecutive).	10		
Hoop bumps: Bump 10 balls into a hoop 12 feet (4 m) away from a partner-tossed ball. The ball should be tossed at a 30- to 45-degree angle to the net.	15		
Overhand serves: Make 10 successful overhand serves.	10		
Wall spikes: Do 10 consecutive floor-to-wall spikes.	5		
Four-step approach: Perform five dry approaches.	5		
Spikes: Do five successful spikes.	10		
Blocking fundamentals: Perform five static jumps and five crossover step jumps to the right and left.	5		
Total score:			

FIGURE 8.19 Sample point system rubric for volleyball.

TEAM HANDBALL

Students will be rated on the following team handball skills. The following rating scale will be used for evaluation purposes.

1 = Student is unable to complete the task.

2 = Student usually does not complete the task successfully.

3 = Student usually completes the task successfully.

4 = Student always completes the task successfully.

Names of students

Skill task											
Dribble the ball with the right hand (standing position) 10 consecutive times.											
Same as previous task but with the left hand.											
Dribble the ball with the right hand (moving forward) from the centerline to the goal line without losing the dribble.											
Same as previous task but with the left hand.											
Pass the ball to a partner standing 3 meters away with a two-handed chest pass to the chest area (between chin and waist) 8 of 10 times.											
Pass the ball to a partner standing 3 meters away with a two-handed bounce pass to the waist area 8 of 10 times.											
Pass the ball to a partner standing 3 meters away with a 2-handed overhead pass to the chest area 8 of 10 times.											
Pass the ball to a partner standing 3 meters away with a one-handed overhead pass to the chest area 8 of 10 times.											
While running from the centerline, alternately pass a two-handed chest and bounce pass that can be caught by a partner running at a parallel distance of 4 meters with three of four passes hitting the partner in the hands.											
While standing 7 meters from the goal, hit three of five goals.											
Defend three of five attempted shots taken by a partner from 7 meters.											
Dribble the ball with the right hand (moving forward) from the centerline to the goal area without losing the dribble. Jump up and make a goal three of five times.											
From 6 meters, hit a target five consecutive times with the following passes: roller, hook, jump, shovel, one-handed shoulder, sidearm, and behind-the-back.											
From 9 meters away, hit two of five goals.											
From 9 meters away, defend four of five goal shots.											
Dribble through a set of six cones in 25 seconds.											

FIGURE 8.20 Sample rating scale for team handball.

posted in the teaching area so that students know what skills they are expected to learn and how they will be evaluated. In a longer unit of instruction, ratings can be done at the end of each week. Using students' peers to assist in the assessment process can be a valuable method. Large class numbers can prevent in-depth assessment from being completed in a timely manner, but by developing peer assessment tasks, teachers are relieved of being the sole individual determining students' level of success. Peer assessment can also increase communication and observation skills and add to a student's understanding of effective skill performance. Time can be used more effectively when peers assist in the assessment process.

Student Self-Evaluation

Developing personal ownership for success is an important goal during middle and high school years. Teaching students how to assess their own performances can be useful in helping them develop independence as well as providing a component of the grading system. Goal setting is a common approach used to assist students in developing strategies for attaining success and assessing their performance. For self-assessment to be valid and reliable, students must be taught how to assess themselves and be given multiple opportunities to practice. Even though instructional time will be spent teaching and practicing self-assessment, meaningful information and knowledge can be developed. Teachers who use this approach also assess and evaluate these students. The final grade will be a composite of student and teacher assessments and evaluation.

Logs

The process involved in reporting physical activity or skill practice can be shown through student logs. Logs require students to document the activities, identified by the teacher, in which they partake. Additional information such as the date, length of time, location of the activity, and others involved can also be noted. As with nutritional logs, students can demonstrate their progress toward meeting the objectives set by the teacher. Scoring rubrics can be established by the teacher to serve as an evaluation.

Figure 8.21 is an example of a weekly physical activity log. Students are expected to monitor and record their accumulated physical activities outside the school day. Goals can be set for how much activity they should accumulate. In this case, the goal is 60 minutes of moderate or vigorous physical activity per day. This log could also be used for extra credit or homework so that students could augment their in-class grade by participating in physical activities outside school.

Journals

Student journals measure their depth of knowledge of physical education concepts and their process for understanding how the concepts relate to activity or skill levels. The affective domain can be assessed using journals if the prompting questions are worded appropriately. Using *why* and *how* can help teachers gain deeper understanding about student learning and feelings toward physical education and physical activity. Writing prompts should be multifaceted to garner more information from the students. Yes-or-no questions do little to gain rich data from students.

Teachers must be willing to read journal entries if they are assigned so that students will take the assignment seriously. Responding to student statements can help with future journal entries as well. Be open to student responses. When establishing a rubric for journal writing, teachers should grade on completion, length of entry, and addressing the topics requested. Teachers should be aware that if honest responses to questions are desired, grading on the student's philosophy is not necessary and can often turn students off from writing their true feelings in a journal entry. Journals are excellent means for discovering students' affective dispositions toward the class.

Personalized Plans

Another variation of the self-evaluation approach is to allow students to develop goals they want to achieve based on specific standards and outcomes. Democratically, the class decides how students will accomplish these outcomes. Students are also responsible for completing the assessment materials to ensure that the specified learning outcomes are achieved. At the end of the instructional session, both students and the teacher evaluate the progress made and the final grade.

Some teachers add a third phase to the self-evaluation process by having students evaluate each other, resulting in a three-pronged evaluation scheme: teacher, student peer, and self-evaluation. One of the strongest reasons given for using this approach is that it makes students feel more involved in the educational process. Students are more likely to believe that the grading system is fair when it manifests itself through teacher, peer, and self-evaluation. This approach also encourages transfer of learning from PE to real-world situations. Figure

SELF-EVALUATION: WEEKLY PHYSICAL ACTIVITY

Your assignment is to keep track of the physical activity you do when you are not in school. Although you should try to accumulate at least 60 minutes of physical activity each day to maintain good health, 30 minutes is acceptable. If you are active each day, you will not only look better but also be healthier and have more energy.

Name _____

Activities done this week	Amount of time (minutes)						
	M	Tu	W	Th	F	Sa	Su
Walking							
Jogging							
Bicycle riding							
Rope jumping							
Playing or practicing a team sport with friends							
In-line skating							
Playing disc games							
Hiking							
Practicing martial arts							
Practicing cheerleading skills							
Swimming or playing a water sport							
Playing or practicing tennis							
Playing or practicing golf							
Playing or practicing racquetball							
Going to a health club for a workout							
Other activities (list below)							

Number of days I was active for at least 60 minutes: _____

Number of days I was active for at least 30 minutes: _____

Number of days I was not active for at least 30 minutes: _____

Grading: You will receive 5 points for each day you are active for at least 30 minutes. If you are active for at least 60 minutes, you will receive 10 points for that day. If you are active for more than 30 minutes at least five of the seven days, you will receive a bonus of 30 points.

My weekly score: _____ points

FIGURE 8.21 Sample self-evaluation of weekly physical activity log.

8.22 shows an example of a module from a self-paced notebook that students must complete during a unit in the weight room.

Other Assessments

A number of other assessments are available to incorporate within your classes. Some will require different means for grading, if that is their purpose. These include portfolios, tactical or game-play assessment, student performances, anecdotal record sheets, and norm-referenced and criterion-referenced assessments.

Portfolios

Portfolios are also an effective tool in assessing student performance and demonstrating that students have accomplished specific objectives in an authentic manner. A portfolio is a collection of multiple assessments made throughout a certain segment of the class. It can include measures of all three learning domains and serves as an excellent tool to assess a student holistically. One of the main advantages of using portfolios is that it allows students who may not excel physically to demonstrate learning and competence in physical education. Melograno (2006) provides good information for teachers interested in developing assessments using portfolios. Examples of items to include in a student portfolio include but should not be limited to the following:

- Tests, assignments, and projects completed in class and as homework
- Fitness score results
- Journal entries
- Performance results on skill tests
- Self-assessments and reflections
- Student goals

If the portfolio is being completed for grade purposes, a rubric should be created to determine how to assign the grade based on student completion. This rubric will help guide students as they put together their portfolios. Several means for evaluating a portfolio are available in Lund and Kirk (2020).

Tactical or Game-Play Assessment

One of the most authentic forms of assessment in physical education occurs in the form of games performance assessment (Mitchell, Oslin, & Griffin, 2007). This type of assessment is authentic in nature because it focuses on the two main aspects of game play: physical performance and decision making. These two components define the nature of game play and provide a teacher and student with accurate information about the student's ability to participate in an authentic setting. Tactical assessments focus on a student's knowledge of what to do during participation and tell a teacher if a student can leave his or her class with the ability to engage in the activity outside the world of physical education. Just about every sporting adventure that students tackle includes a tactical component. Everything from water polo to cricket has tactical problems to solve. In many cases, this type of assessment can provide information critical to the success of a student. For instance, knowing what club to use while golfing is just as important as knowing how to swing the club. Figure 8.23 is an observation sheet that can be used to evaluate a student's ability to solve tactical problems during a game of badminton.

Student Performances

Student performances require students to combine skills and knowledge into a final performance, such as a dance or gymnastics routine, a fitness exercise, a jump-rope routine, a swimming sequence, or an offensive basketball play. Rubrics should be provided to students so that they understand the expectations for the sequences. The performance can be done in class, or it can be recorded for the teacher to watch outside physical education class. The teacher must be cognizant of class time (will individual performances use up a lot of physical education time?) and physical activity outcomes (will most students be sitting if individual performances take place during physical education class?) when determining when and how to evaluate performances.

Anecdotal Record Sheets

A record sheet that contains student names and has room for comments about student performance can be used to assess student progress. Anecdotal records of student progress can be reinforcing to the student and teacher because remembering how much progress has been made over time is often difficult. With anecdotal records, teachers can inform students of their initial skill levels compared with their present performances. When making anecdotal records, record the performance as soon and as accurately as possible. If background information is needed to put the performance in proper context, it should be included.

A digital voice recorder is useful for recording anecdotal information. Comments can be recorded during

WEIGHT ROOM—AEROBIC ACTIVITIES

Name _____ Date _____

List warm-up activities here:

_____ _____ _____ Your initials _____ Teacher initials _____

Treadmill

Before starting:

- Make sure that the safety pin is secured.
- Place your feet on either side of the moving belt and start the machine before stepping on.
- Start the machine at the lowest speed.

Circle which activity you will do on the treadmill for five minutes:

Walking	Jogging	Running

Hold handles or swing arms.   Bend elbows and pump arms.   Pump arms; you should be airborne during this activity.

Rate how you felt during this activity on the following scale:

Easy   Medium   Hard

Select an activity of a different intensity and do it for five minutes:

Walking	Jogging	Running

Hold handles or swing arms.   Bend elbows and pump arms.   Pump arms; you should be airborne during this activity.

Rate how you felt during this activity on the following scale:

Easy   Medium   Hard

FIGURE 8.22   Sample module from a self-paced notebook.

AUTHENTIC ASSESSMENT

Name (doer) _____ Name (observer) _____

Date _____ Activity observed __Badminton Doubles__ _____

Phase of skill	Description of important elements	Errors observed	Possible causes	Corrective feedback
Court positioning	• Remains in critical portions of the court for participation • Recognizes when to assume offensive and defensive positions • Attempts to move opponents from good court positioning			
Court movement	• Quickly moves to position for shot returns, coverage of court, and so on • Following court event, moves back to neutral position • Begins to anticipate where opponents will hit the shuttle and moves in anticipation			
Strategy	• Recognizes strengths and weaknesses of opponents and attempts to exploit each • Attempts to use front-and-back or side-to-side strategy when appropriate • Uses a variety of shots when appropriate			
Skills	• Serves • Clears • Drives • Lobs • Smashes			
Partner recognition	• Attempts to support partner through communication, movement, and encouragement • Displays positive sporting behaviors			

FIGURE 8.23 Sample observation sheet to assess tactical skill in badminton.

observation and transcribed later. This process helps teachers learn the names and behavior patterns of students and leads to better understanding of student performance. Observations should be recorded at the start of the unit and compared with observations made later as instruction proceeds.

Criteria and Uses for Student Evaluation

The evaluation process is crucial in providing feedback to students, teachers, and parents. Teachers are provided with information to make judgments about student performance based on certain criteria. These criteria usually fall under two separate categories: norm-referenced and criterion-referenced evaluations.

Norm-Referenced Evaluations

Performing a norm-referenced evaluation of student performance requires a teacher to use assessment information to rank a student in comparison with other student performances on a similar event. Standardized tests, such as the President's Challenge on Physical Fitness (President's Council on Physical Fitness and Sports, 2004), are reported in this fashion. This information allows a student to know where her or his performance stands in comparison with peers. On a smaller level, teachers may implement this type of evaluation within their own classes. Grading on a curve is an example of a norm-referenced evaluation that teachers might implement. This type of evaluation has several benefits:

- Allows for performance evaluation in relation to peers.
- Is easily administered and collected because most of the measures are outcomes such as number of times and timed events.
- Usually focuses on performance outcomes rather than processes, so it can be used to rank students among themselves and to evaluate overall program effectiveness.

The method also has several disadvantages:

- Students often think they are being unfairly compared with others and that components like improvement and effort are not considered.
- Usually, little information about why a performance was good or bad is communicated with this type of evaluation.
- This method will always rank one student first and one last in performance. In other words, at least one student will fail the task no matter how well he or she does because in relation to peers, he or she performed the worst.

Criterion-Referenced Evaluations

Criterion-referenced evaluation involves comparing a student's performance against a preexisting set of criteria or guidelines. Standardized tests such as the FitnessGram (Cooper Institute, 2017) are reported in this fashion. Much of what is done in a typical physical education class falls under this type of evaluation. When students perform in class to preestablished requirements, criterion-referenced evaluations are performed. In this type of evaluation, the teacher must make appropriate choices in determining the criteria for evaluation. Doing this is not always easy because some students will easily surpass the criteria whereas others will fail the same criteria. Most of the controversy about grading in physical education can be attributed to choosing appropriate criteria for evaluation. Using this type of evaluation, every student in your class can receive an A for his or her performance; likewise, all of them can fail. Therefore, teachers need to choose correct criteria. Criterion-referenced evaluations offer several benefits:

- Evaluation is custom fit for the specific groups or students with whom a teacher is working.

- The information provided is informative in relation to what a student can and cannot do instead of how she or he compares with others.
- These evaluations can explain why students are performing at a certain level.
- Every student can potentially be successful in mastering content.

Criterion-referenced evaluations have two drawbacks:

- The criteria chosen to evaluate performance may not represent appropriate standards.
- Levels of acceptance or quality may be set too high or low for most students. When all students in a class receive an A on a test, the evaluation is probably not sensitive enough to discriminate differences in performance.

Teachers are urged to weigh all the advantages and disadvantages of both types of evaluations to determine which type is the most appropriate for their specific situation. This decision can be crucial in evaluating student and program performance.

Uses for Student Evaluation

Many components are evaluated in physical education. A major part of evaluation is examining the skill learning and development that occurs through the instructional process along with the physical activity levels of students. Even though skill development is a primary focus of physical education, it is not enough; students need to learn about strategy, skill performance techniques, and sport etiquette and develop positive attitudes toward physical activity. Written exams and alternative assessments can evaluate whether students have the requisite knowledge for successful participation. Finally, the area of attitudes and values is important to the program. Students will choose not to participate if their attitudes and values have not developed concurrently with skills and knowledge.

Evaluation can serve several purposes, described in the following sections.

Grading

Performance on valid and reliable instruments offers objective data for grading. Communicating with students and parents is more effective when an objective and systematic tool has been used for evaluation (e.g., rubrics, FitnessGram). Parents and students can see

8

how they compare with others or established criteria and receive a realistic view of their performance. Grades based on objective data carry more credibility and respect both inside and outside the profession.

Motivation

Nothing motivates students more than improvement based on individual effort. Personal improvement documented through evaluation can be clear evidence that effort has been rewarded. Knowing the extent of improvement (or lack of) is difficult if both process and product assessment are not a part of the program. Another factor that motivates students is the setting of achievable goals. If students are unaware of their performance levels and abilities, they are not likely to know what is reasonable and reachable.

Diagnosis

Process assessment often reveals problems or deficiencies. When teaching an entire class, a teacher cannot always sense the ability and progress of each student. Often, more energy is placed on monitoring student behavior than student performance. Assessment performed throughout a unit will focus energy on progress of individual students and reveal those students whose skills are deficient or performed incorrectly.

Placement and Equalization

At times, grouping students homogeneously—that is, placing students with equal ability in groups—is effective. On the other hand, a peer-tutoring method can be used if assessment reveals some skilled performers and others having problems. Student evaluation will help teachers place students with mentor coaches and balance small groups' ability levels when doing so enhances learning.

Program Evaluation

Evaluation of students can reveal the effectiveness of the program, the relevancy of objectives, and the effectiveness of the teacher. If all students pass the evaluation, the goals of the program may be too low. If many fail, the quality of instruction may be inadequate or the standard of performance may be out of reach. Over time, evaluation of students can give direction to the program as objectives and instructional strategies are modified to increase student success. Additionally, the teacher can reflect on her or his teaching style and delivery to improve on previous practices.

Program Support

Results of regular evaluation can be used to validate and support the program. Data gained through evaluation are objective and can reveal what students are expected to learn and how effectively they are learning. Accountability is a buzzword among educators as schools try to document what students are learning to gain public support. When administrators need to make cutbacks in programs, they usually ask faculty members to justify continuation of their programs. Data gained through consistent assessment and evaluation of students are strong and effective means to defend the program.

To Grade or Not To Grade?

Another issue related to grading is whether physical education should be graded. Some believe that the most important purpose of a physical education program is to offer students the opportunity to recreate and exercise. Others think that education should be a primary focus and that a grade is needed to reflect how much students have learned. Arguments are offered on each side of the issue—to grade or not to grade—to help teachers understand and defend the approach they choose. For an in-depth review of grading, the text by Lacy and Williams (2018) is recommended.

Arguments Against Using a Grading System

- Grades are difficult to interpret. A grade means one thing to one teacher and another to a different teacher. When moving to a different school, the meaning of the grade does not transfer, and teachers at the new school may view the grade differently.

- Physical education does not emphasize content and product. Rather, it judges success by improvement of skills. Grades in academic areas reflect achievement and accomplishment because most of what is learned in those content areas is taught and practiced at school, but because grades in physical education reflect improvement and effort, they may be interpreted incorrectly.

- Often, time is limited in physical education, and classes meet only a few days a week. Testing for the purpose of assigning a grade is time consuming and takes away from learning opportunities. Physical educators try to squeeze as much learning as possible into a minimal amount of time, and grading dramatically reduces their instructional time. If teachers expect students to become competent in a specific skill area, more time than is offered in physical education is likely needed to develop those skills.

- Physical education is diverse and broad by definition. Instruction covers all three learning domains—that is, skill development, attitude formation, and content knowledge. Trying to grade all three of these areas is difficult and demands a great deal of time. In addition, which of these three domains is most important, and can any of them be overlooked?

- Grading is done only in areas where standardized instruments have been developed. Fitness testing is the major area in physical education in which a variety of standardized tests have been developed. Because of the dearth of standardized tests in other areas, excessive attention is given to fitness testing.

- Physical education emphasizes physical fitness and skill performance. Genetics strongly controls performance in those areas, making it difficult for all students to achieve—even when they give it their best effort. In addition, when grades are given for physical fitness performance, some students become discouraged because they train and still do not reach standards of high performance (see chapter 15).

Arguments for Using a Grading System

- Giving grades makes physical education like other academic areas in the school curriculum. Physical education gains credibility and respect from parents, teachers, and administrators.

- Grades communicate the performance of students to parents. Parents have a right to know how their children perform in physical education. Teachers in other areas use grades, and parents can easily understand and interpret them; therefore, they should be used in physical education.

- When grades are not given, academic respect is lost. Physical education already suffers from the misguided perception that physical educators do not teach anything; they just "roll out the ball." Lack of a grading system may cause others to believe that little teaching or learning is occurring.

- A grading system gives accountability. When grades are given, administrators and parents often

assume that teaching and student accomplishment have occurred.

- A grading system rewards skilled students. Students are rewarded in academic areas for their intelligence and performance and should be similarly rewarded for accomplishment in physical education settings.

- When teachers use grading systems that apply appropriate criteria for assessment, students can achieve greater success than they can in many other academic areas where success and failure are determined only through performance outcomes.

Grading Considerations

Many approaches are used for grading students. Grading methods vary depending on the philosophies of teachers and districtwide school regulations. This section examines various viewpoints, offers insight into each, and challenges readers to defend the grading procedure they choose.

Educational Objectives Versus Administrative Tasks

Educators generally agree that physical education should help students achieve in four areas: skill development, physical fitness, personal values, and cognitive development. Some grading systems assign weight to each of these areas when compiling a grade. Regardless of the amount of emphasis given to each area, the final grade depends on accomplishment of educational objectives. This approach contrasts with grading on completion of administrative tasks whereby students earn part or all of their grade by showering, attending, participating, being prompt, and wearing the proper uniform. This latter approach grades students on tasks that have little to do with accomplishment of physical education objectives. Furthermore, these tasks are usually documented at the beginning of the period and do little to hold students accountable for their in-class performance.

Consider the conflicts arising when students are graded on achievement of educational objectives versus accomplishment of administrative tasks. Assume that a student in a math class regularly forgets to bring a pencil and is tardy but earns an A grade on all math exams. Does this student earn a final grade of A, or is the student penalized for doing poorly on administrative tasks (tardiness and so on) and given a C grade? Reverse the situation and assume that the student has an outstanding attitude, is never tardy, and always brings the proper supplies to class. At the end of the semester, the student has earned a C grade on exams yet performed all administrative tasks at a high level. Does this student receive a final grade of A? If grades in other curricular areas of the school are earned through accomplishment of educational objectives, it is probably wise to follow suit in the physical education area.

Administrative tasks are usually enforced through school or districtwide regulations. For example, most districts have procedures for dealing with excessive absences or tardiness. Usually, teachers need not further penalize students through a grade reduction. Sometimes students are graded on participation, which is like receiving a grade just because the student is physically present in class. On the other hand, students should be able to choose not to participate in class only when they are excused by the administration or by the school nurse (for sickness or injury). Participation alone should not be used as a factor in assigning grades. Rather, all students should be expected to participate unless excused by administrative edict.

If a student does not attend class, asking the student to repeat the class is defensible. This is usually done by assigning a failing grade. Because instructors do this in other academic areas, excessive absences are usually an acceptable criterion for failing the student. The major theme to remember is that grading systems in physical education should be in line with the grading systems in other subject-matter areas. If physical educators choose to grade otherwise, the grade may be meaningless to other teachers, parents, and students. Differences in grading approaches have caused some school districts to not calculate physical education grades in the overall grade point average or include them in graduation requirements. When grades earned in physical education become unimportant to school requirements, it makes it easy to say that physical education should no longer be required of all students. The bottom line is to grade in a manner that is compatible with other subject matter areas.

Process Versus Product

Another area of concern in evaluation is whether the process or the product of education is more important. Those who emphasize the process of education stress the importance of students leaving school with warm and positive feelings toward physical activity. Those educators state their beliefs in the following manner: "I am not concerned about how many skills my students learn; I just want them to walk out of my class with positive feelings about physical activity." The assumption is that students who feel positive about physical activity will be willing to be active throughout their lifetimes. These teachers assign grades based on the process of trying rather than the product of performance. Students who receive higher grades may not be the most skilled but have shown improvement and effort throughout the semester.

Teachers who reside in the product camp focus primarily on student accomplishment and see effort as something that is laudable but not part of the grading process. Their philosophy might be stated as follows: "I don't really care whether students like me or physical education. What is ultimately important is their performance. After all, the students who are best in math earn the highest grades, so why should it be any different in physical education?" Teachers who focus on product give the highest grade to the best performer, regardless of other factors. Less skilled students, no matter how hard they try, will not receive an above-average grade.

This problem is difficult to resolve in physical education and is always hotly debated. One point of view is that students should learn how society works from the grading system. People are not rewarded in life based on how hard they try, but on their performance. For example, if real estate agents try hard but never sell a house, they will not make any money. The payoff is for selling houses, not for trying hard to sell houses. An opposing viewpoint is that many people in society are rewarded for effort, and doing your best should be rewarded.

The need to develop competency in various physical skills offers support for the product point of view. The opposing view is that to develop competency, the process of obtaining the skill needs to be accomplished. Interests are established based on competency in various areas. A relatively low percentage of adults select new hobbies in areas in which they feel incompetent. To ensure lifetime activity, school physical education programs need to graduate students whose skill competencies allow them to feel comfortable in public view. A grading system that focuses on skill development and performance will encourage the quest toward competency. This grading system may focus on process to obtain the skill or the final product.

A solution to consider is to grade on performance while teaching in a manner that focuses on the process of learning. Much can be said for teaching in a manner that helps students develop a positive attitude toward activity. Attitude development depends largely on how teachers present the material rather than on actual performance. Students, with the help of the instructional process, need to understand that they perform differently from each other as they do in math or science and receive a respectively higher or lower grade. This approach would make physical education like other academic areas in that those who perform best would receive the highest grade.

Relative Improvement

Some physical educators believe that effort, or just doing the best you can, should be the most important factor in assigning grades. To reward effort, these teachers base student grades on the amount that a student improves. This method involves pretesting and posttesting to determine the amount of progress made throughout the grading period. This approach contrasts with basing the grade on absolute performance; because of lack of improvement, the best performer in the class may not receive the highest grade.

Grading on improvement is time consuming and requires that the same test be given at the beginning and end of the semester or unit. The test may or may not be a valid reflection of what has been learned in the class and may not be sensitive enough to reflect improvement made by both poor and outstanding performers. Testing at the beginning of a unit can be discouraging and demoralizing if a student performs poorly in front of peers. It can also be hazardous in some activities, such as gymnastics or archery, which require intensive instruction to prevent accidents or injuries.

Another factor to consider is the issue of performing for a grade. Students learn quickly that if they perform too well on the pretest, they will be penalized on the posttest. Therefore, they perform at a low level so that they can demonstrate a higher degree of improvement on the posttest. A related problem is that improvement is sometimes easier at beginning levels of a skill than it is at high levels of performance. Most teachers are aware of the rapid improvement that beginners make before reaching a learning plateau. A skilled performer may be at a level at which improvement is difficult to achieve. Lack of improvement in this situation would result in a skilled performer receiving a lower grade than a beginner. Perhaps the notion of performing equally as well or better the second time around could be considered.

Grading on Potential

Some teachers choose to grade based on student potential. These teachers may lower a student's grade because the student did not reach his or her potential. On the other hand, a grade may be raised because the teacher thought that the student did not have much ability but did reach his or her potential. In other words, the teacher decides what a student's potential performance level should be and then assigns a grade based on whether he or she reached that level. The grade that a student receives depends on the teacher's subjective perception of that student's genetic limitations. How can any teacher really know the absolute potential of any student? This approach results in students being assigned a grade based on an unknown factor: potential.

This approach depends on the teacher's feelings about the student in question. It is based on intangibles and may result in a grade being assigned because the student is "just like her brothers or sisters." Grades are difficult to defend when they are based on the teacher's subjective beliefs rather than on criteria that can be measured and evaluated. How would a parent react to a teacher's statement that "Your child received a failing grade because he or she just didn't live up to his or her potential"? To be defensible, grading systems need to be based on tangible data gleaned from observable behavior and performance.

Pass–Fail Versus Letter Grades

Another approach to grading involves assigning a pass–fail grade instead of a letter grade. Pass–fail has become more common today because of the push to avoid having physical education grades count in the academic grade point average. This approach prevents students from receiving a low grade in physical education while earning high grades in subject matter areas.

When using a pass–fail grading system, outstanding performers are not rewarded. A student who earns a grade of C or D receives the same final grade as the top performer in the class. This approach reinforces the idea of making a minimal effort to accomplish goals because differing levels of performance are not rewarded. The pass–fail system also does little to show students that they have improved. For example, if a student is performing at the C level and earns a B by the end of the next quarter, the pass grade reflects no change in performance. Grading systems are most effective when they reward improved standards of performance.

Some teachers endorse pass–fail grading because it eases the burden of evaluation. They no longer have to worry about bookkeeping chores because the grade is only grossly indicative of student progress. Recording anything more than the minimum performance required for passing the class becomes unnecessary. Some teachers, therefore, support this grading system because of ease of implementation. That position is inappropriate.

Again, when the grading system in physical education differs from those in other subject matter areas, defending the program in the school setting becomes difficult. If physical education does not require grading integrity, the subject probably should not be counted in the grade point average. The problem lies in the outcome. If the physical education department chooses to operate autonomously from the rest of the school system, it becomes vulnerable to nonsupport and abandonment. Physical education should be considered an integral part of the school system and should be graded in a manner consistent with other subject matter areas.

Program Accountability

One important yet frequently overlooked goal of conducting assessments is to provide accountability for the physical education program. Too often, teachers conduct assessments for the sake of conducting assessments and as a tool to grade students. But a major contribution that assessment can make is providing valuable feedback to teachers on their instructional practices as well as presenting justification for the physical education program in the school. One of the most humbling experiences for teachers can be watching themselves teach. Data from these observations can be used to document teacher progress in several specific areas, such as student activity time, teacher feedback, teacher movement, and student skill practice.

With regard to program accountability, student assessment data should be used to provide information related to student physical activity in physical education, the skill that students are learning, the knowledge that students are gaining related to physical activity and health-related fitness, and the social-emotional benefits of physical education. Assessment allows this information to be provided to parents, administrators, the school board, and community members. As physical educators, we do not take the opportunity often enough to demonstrate to others the positive things we are doing in the gymnasium and other areas in which we teach. In an era of budget cuts, having data to support our programs and the goals and objectives we are trying to accomplish is imperative. Demonstrating that students benefit not only during physical education class but also later in life bodes well for physical education programs everywhere.

SHAPE America offers a checklist for evaluating the entire physical education program across the essential components of physical education, including policy and environment, curriculum, appropriate instruction, and student assessments (SHAPE America, 2015). See the Websites section at the end of this chapter for the reference. Requiring no special training, the checklist asks 19 questions, and it is simple for administrators, teachers, and parents to use. These questions are designed to evaluate your program's strengths and weaknesses. It encourages a plan for improvement where needed.

LEARNING AIDS

STUDY STIMULATORS AND REVIEW QUESTIONS

1. Differentiate between assessment, evaluation, and grading.
2. Briefly describe the basic procedure of doing the FitnessGram PACER test.
3. What are the advantages of doing the PACER test over the 1-mile (1.6 km) run?
4. Explain what criterion-referenced health standards indicate for students.
5. Why is authentic assessment preferred in a physical education environment? Describe two types of authentic assessment you might incorporate into a secondary physical education class.
6. Explain why physical educators should follow the lead of classroom teachers and grade students on performance in class.
7. What is the process versus product dilemma faced by teachers in terms of their grading procedures?
8. Describe the grading procedures you would implement in your secondary physical education class. Defend your system.
9. Why are there so many different points of view regarding grading in physical education?

WEBSITES

Dynamic PE ASAP

DynamicPEASAP.com

FitnessGram/ActivityGram

www.fitnessgram.net

Physical Education Teaching and Curriculum Information

www.pecentral.com

www.pheamerica.org

Presidential Youth Fitness Program

https://pyfp.org

SHAPE America: Physical Education Program Checklist

www.shapeamerica.org/standards/guidelines/upload/Physical-Education-Program-Checklist.pdf

8

REFERENCES AND SUGGESTED READINGS

Abendroth-Smith, J., Kras, J., & Strand, B. (1996). Get aboard the B-BOAT (Biomechanically based observation and analysis for teachers). *Journal of Physical Education, Recreation and Dance, 67*(8), 20–23.

American Association for Health, Physical Education, and Recreation. (1976). *Youth fitness test manual.* Reston, VA: AAHPERD.

Beighle, A., Pangrazi, R. P., & Vincent, S. D. (2001). Pedometers, physical activity, and accountability. *Journal of Physical Education, Recreation & Dance, 72*(9), 16-19.

Blair, S.N., Kohl, H.W., Paffenbarger, R.S., Clark, D.G., Cooper, K.H., & Gibbons, L.W. (1989). Physical fitness and all-cause mortality: A prospective study of healthy men and women. *Journal of the American Medical Association, 17,* 2395–2401.

Block, M.E., Lieberman, L.J., & Connor-Kuntz, F. (1998). Authentic assessment in adapted physical education. *Journal of Physical Education, Recreation and Dance, 69*(3), 48–55.

Chepko, S., & Arnold, R.K. (Eds.). (2000). *Guidelines for physical education programs: Grades K–12 standards, objectives, and assessments.* San Francisco, CA: Benjamin Cummings.

Cooper Institute, Meredith, M., & Welk, G. (Eds.). (2017). *FitnessGram/ActivityGram test administration manual: The journey to MyHealthyZone* (5th ed.). Champaign, IL: Human Kinetics.

Corbin, C., & LeMasurier, G. (2018). *Fitness for life.* Champaign, IL: Human Kinetics.

Corbin, C., & Pangrazi, R. (2008). Appropriate and inappropriate uses of FitnessGram/ActivityGram. In G.J. Welk & M.D. Meredith (Eds.), *FitnessGram/ActivityGram Reference Guide.* Dallas, TX: Cooper Institute.

Corbin, C.B., Welk, G.J., Corbin, W.R., & Welk, K.A. (2008). *Concepts of physical fitness and wellness: A comprehensive lifestyle approach* (14th ed.). Boston, MA: McGraw-Hill.

Cutforth, N., & Parker, M. (1996). Promoting affective development in physical education. *Journal of Physical Education, Recreation and Dance, 67*(7), 19–23.

Fay, T., & Doolittle, S. (2002). Agents for change: From standards to assessment to accountability in physical education. *Journal of Physical Education, Recreation and Dance, 73*(3), 29–33.

Grehaigne, J., & Godbout, P. (1998). Formative assessment in team sports in a tactical approach context. *Journal of Physical Education, Recreation and Dance, 69*(1), 46–51.

Hastie, P.A., Sanders, S.W., & Rowland, R.S. (1998). Where good intentions meet harsh realities: Teaching large classes in physical education. *Journal of Teaching in Physical Education, 18,* 277–289.

Jensen, C.R., & Hirst, C.C. (1980). *Measurement in physical education and athletics.* New York, NY: Macmillan.

Khalil, S., Mohktar, M., & Ibrahim, F. (2014). The theory and fundamentals of bioimpedance analysis in clinical status monitoring and diagnosis of diseases. *Sensors, 14*(6), 10895–10928.

Kleinman, I. (1997). Grading: A powerful teaching tool. *Journal of Physical Education, Recreation and Dance, 68*(5), 29–32.

Lacy, A.C., & Williams, S.M. (2018). *Measurement and evaluation in physical education and exercise science.* New York, NY: Routledge.

Lund, J.L. (2000). *Creating rubrics for physical education.* Reston, VA: NASPE.

Lund, J. & Kirk, M. (2020). *Performance-based assessment for middle and high school physical education* (3rd ed.). Champaign,

IL: Human Kinetics.

Matanin, M., & Tannehill, D. (1994). Assessment and grading in physical education. *Journal of Teaching in Physical Education, 13,* 395–405.

Melograno, V.J. (2006). *Professional and student portfolios for physical education* (2nd ed.). Champaign, IL: Human Kinetics.

Mitchell, S., Oslin, J., & Griffin, L. (2007). *Teaching sport concepts and skills: A tactical games approach* (2nd ed.). Champaign, IL: Human Kinetics.

National Association for Sport and Physical Education. (2004). *Moving into the future: National standards for physical education* (2nd ed.). Reston, VA: Author.

Pangrazi, R.P. & Beighle, A. (2013). *Dynamic physical education for elementary school children* (17th ed.). San Francisco, CA: Benjamin Cummings.

President's Council on Physical Fitness and Sports. (2004). *The president's challenge handbook.* Washington, DC: Author.

Safrit, M.J. (1990). *Introduction to measurement in physical education and exercise science* (2nd ed.). St. Louis, MO: Times Mirror/Mosby.

SHAPE America—Society of Health and Physical Educators. (2013). *National standards for K-12 physical education.* Reston, VA: Author.

SHAPE America—Society of Health and Physical Educators. (2015). *Physical education program checklist* [Guidance document]. Reston, VA: Author.

SHAPE America—Society of Health and Physical Educators. (2019). *PE Metrics: Assessing student performance using national standards & grade level outcomes for K–12 physical education.* Champaign, IL: Human Kinetics.

U.S. Department of Health and Human Services. (2000). *Healthy people 2010: Understanding and improving health.* Washington, DC: U.S. Government Printing Office.

Welk, G.J. (2002). *Physical activity assessments in health-related research.* Champaign, IL: Human Kinetics.

Welk, G.J. & Blair, S.N. (2008). Health benefits of physical activity and fitness in children. In G.J. Welk & M.D. Meredith (Eds.), *FitnessGram/ActivityGram reference guide.* Dallas, TX: Cooper Institute.

Wood, T. (1996). Evaluation: The road less traveled. In S. Silverman & C.D. Ennis (Eds.), *Student learning in physical education* (pp. 171–198). Champaign, IL: Human Kinetics.

Wood, T. (2003). Assessment in physical education: The future is now! In S. Silverman & C.D. Ennis (Eds.), *Student learning in physical education* (pp. 187–203). Champaign, IL: Human Kinetics.

Zhu, W. (1997). Alternative assessment: What, why, how. *Journal of Physical Education, Recreation and Dance, 68*(7), 17–18.

Including Students With Disabilities

9

This chapter focuses on the most common types of disabilities and on ways to modify activities and determine categories of placement for students with disabilities. Every state is required by federal law to develop a plan for identifying, locating, and evaluating all students with disabilities. Due process for students and parents is an important requisite when conducting formal assessment procedures. Assessment plays a vital part in determining proper placement of the student with a disability into physical education. Moving a student to a less restrictive learning environment should be based on achievement of specified competencies necessary in the new environment. Inclusion involves the practice of placing students with disabilities into classes with able peers. An individualized learning environment increases opportunities for successful inclusion. The student with the disability should be held to high expectations and not be permitted to use a disability as a crutch or as an excuse for substandard work.

Learning Objectives

▶ Define adapted physical education and adapted sport.
▶ Understand the implications of Public Law (PL) 94–142 and the Individuals with Disabilities Education Act (IDEA) for physical education.
▶ Develop a plan for identifying, locating, and evaluating all students with disabilities.
▶ Identify essential elements of an individualized educational program and list the stages of development.
▶ List guidelines for successful inclusion experiences.
▶ Describe ways to modify learning experiences in physical education to accommodate students with disabilities.

Defining Adapted Physical Education and Sport

Adapted physical education is best defined as an individualized program designed to meet the unique needs of an individual student, more specifically students with disabilities. This program may include fitness, fundamental motor skills, skills in aquatics, dance, individual and team games, and sports. Quality physical education promotes inclusion of all students. Regardless of the ability level of youth, quality physical education should make adaptations for all students to have success, especially those with a disability. Physical educators often have a range of ability levels in their classes requiring individual instruction, but adapted physical education is typically geared toward meeting long-term (more than 30 days) unique needs as determined by the Individuals

Basketball is a very popular adapted sport.

with Disabilities Education Act (IDEA). Often, these classes include a child diagnosed with mental impairment, speech or language impairment, deafness or other hearing impairment, blindness or other visual impairment, deaf-blindness (the condition of little or no useful sight *and* little or no useful hearing), serious emotional disturbance, orthopedic impairment, autism, traumatic brain injury, a learning disability, multiple disabilities, or other health impairments that require special education (Office of Special Education and Rehabilitation Services, 2007). Adapted physical education may also include children with developmental delays as well as any physical or mental impairment that limits one or more major life activities (Winnick & Porretta, 2017).

Adapted sport refers specifically to sport modified to meet the unique needs of individuals with disabilities. An important responsibility of the physical education teacher is to be aware of adapted sport opportunities for their students, which may include activities through various organizations, including the United States Olympic Committee, Disabled Sports USA, Special Olympics, USA Deaf Sports Federation, U.S. Association of Blind Athletes, National Disability Sport Alliance, and Wheelchair Sports USA (Winnick & Porretta, 2017).

Laws Related to Adapted Physical Education

The **Education for All Handicapped Children Act** (PL 94-142) was passed by Congress in 1975. This legislation introduced new requirements, vocabulary, and concepts into physical education programs across the United States. These concepts include individualized educational programs (IEPs), mainstreaming, least restrictive environments, zero reject, and progressive inclusion. The purpose of the law is clear and concise:

> It is the purpose of this act to assure that all handicapped children have available to them a free appropriate public education which emphasizes special education and related services designed to meet their unique needs, to assure that the rights of handicapped children and their parents or guardians are protected, to assist states and localities to provide for the education of all handicapped children, and to assess and assure the effectiveness of efforts to educate handicapped children. (PL 94-142)

In short, the law requires that all youth with disabilities, ages 3 to 21, receive a free and appropriate education in the least restrictive environment. The law includes youth in public and private care facilities and schools. Youth with disabilities who can learn in regular classes with the use of supplementary aids and services must be educated along with students without disabilities. Physical education is the only specific area mentioned in PL 94-142. The law indicates that the term *special education* "means specially designed instruction, instruction in physical education, home instruction, and instruction in hospitals and institutions." A 1997 amendment, PL 105–17 (also known as IDEA), continues with the objective of providing individuals with a disability the least restrictive environment in the school setting. The Individuals with Disabilities Education Act states, "Physical education services, specially designed if necessary, must be made available to every child with a disability receiving a free appropriate public education." Rehabilitation and social work services are included as related services.

To comply with PL 94-142, secondary schools must locate, identify, and evaluate all students who might have a disability. A screening process must be followed by a formal assessment procedure. An assessment must be made and an IEP developed for each student before placement into a special program can be made. The law states who will be responsible for developing the IEP and what the contents of the IEP will include.

The passage of PL 94-142 shows that a strong commitment has been made to equality and education for all Americans. Before 1970, students with disabilities had limited access to schools and did not have an equal opportunity to participate in school programs. The government also ensured that funding would be made available for quality instruction. The federal mandate reveals the concern of the public for comprehensive education programs for all students regardless of disability.

Least Restrictive Environment

PL 105–17 uses the term **least restrictive environment** to help determine the best placement arrangement of students with disabilities. This concept refers to the idea that not all individuals can do all the same activities in the same environment. However, the concept of zero reject entitles everyone of school age to some aspect of the school program. No one can be totally rejected because of a disability. The focus should be on placing students into settings that offer the best opportunity for educational advancement. Placing a young person in an environment where success is impossible is inappropriate, as is placing a person in a situation where the success of others will be disrupted. But putting a student in a setting that is more restrictive than necessary is debilitating. Special educators speak about inclusion options that offer a variety of opportunities, from participation in regular physical education classes to physical education in a full-time special school. Figure 9.1 shows a series of options that might be available for physical education.

The least restrictive environment varies depending on the unit of instruction and the teaching style. For example, for a student in a wheelchair, a soccer or football unit might be restrictive, whereas in a basketball or disc unit, the environment would not be as restrictive. For a student with emotional disabilities, the direct style of instruction might be the least restrictive environment, whereas a problem-solving method with group cooperation may be too difficult and would be more restrictive. Consistent and regular judgments need to be made considering curriculum content and teaching styles because they can change the type of environment that the student enters. Placing students into a situation and then forgetting about them is shortsighted. Evaluation and modification of environments need to be ongoing. The concept of progressive inclusion focuses on the idea that as students make progress, they should have the opportunity to progress to less restrictive environments and experience more of the mainstream of schools and programs.

9

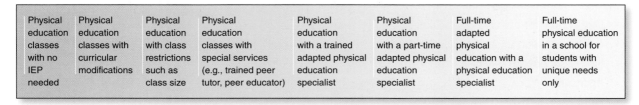

| Physical education classes with no IEP needed | Physical education classes with curricular modifications | Physical education with class restrictions such as class size | Physical education classes with special services (e.g., trained peer tutor, peer educator) | Physical education with a trained adapted physical education specialist | Physical education with a part-time adapted physical education specialist | Full-time adapted physical education with a physical education specialist | Full-time physical education in a school for students with unique needs only |

FIGURE 9.1 Physical education placement options: least to most restrictive environments.

Inclusion

Inclusion refers to the integration of students with disabilities into a regular class to receive physical education. These students often need specialized instruction or adaptations to be successful. Much support has been garnered for inclusive physical education. Experts suggest that it can be more motivating, provides opportunities for social development and age-appropriate play skills, promotes the development of friendships among students with and without disabilities, and provides skilled role models. Arguments against inclusion suggest that it does not allow students with disabilities to get enough attention, teachers are not prepared for successful inclusion, and regular education students will be held back in their development (Winnick & Porretta, 2017). Although including all children in a regular physical education class is typically considered the best approach, a student may be placed in a totally inclusive environment or a totally segregated environment based on the unique needs of the student or the uniqueness of the activity. Lieberman and Houston-Wilson (2018), in their text *Strategies for Inclusion*, provide an example of a continuum of placement options that could be made available to students with disabilities in physical education class (see figure 9.2).

Segregation can be maintained only when it is in the best interests of the student. The purpose of segregated programs is to establish a level of skill and social proficiency that will eventually enable the student to be transferred to a less restricted learning environment. The goal of the process is to place students in the least restrictive environment, where they can benefit most. Students with disabilities, working on their own, have often been denied opportunities to interact with peers and to become a part of the social and academic classroom network.

A. Inclusion Options

- Full inclusion with no adaptations or support (no IEP needed)
- Full inclusion with curriculum adaptations and modifications
- Full inclusion with trained peer tutors
- Full inclusion with paraeducators
- Full inclusion with specialists
- Modified physical education (small class) with able-bodied peers

B. Part-Time Self-Contained and Part-Time Integrated Placement Options

- Split placement without additional support
- Split placement with additional support

C. Community-Based Placement Options

- Part-time community-based and part-time school-based placement
- Full time community-based placement

D. Full-Time Self-Contained Placement Options Within a Regular School District

- Self-contained placement with no additional support
- Reverse integration (typically developing peers attend class with peer with a disability)
- Paraeducator one-to-one support

E. Other Placement Options

- Day school for specific disabilities
- Residential school for specific disabilities
- Home schooling
- Institution
- Hospital

FIGURE 9.2 Continuum of placement options for students with disabilities in physical education.

Reprinted by permission from L. Lieberman and C. Houston-Wilson, *Strategies for Inclusion: Physical Education for Everyone,* 3rd ed. (Champaign, IL: Human Kinetics, 2018), 8.

Students with disabilities often need support personnel during inclusion. Even though the physical education teacher is responsible for all students during class time, students with disabilities may require access to special education teachers, school psychologists, speech therapists, and paraeducators. Support personnel often view physical education as a break from their students, but they are a source of information and support for the physical education teacher in charge and should be there upon request. The physical education teacher must communicate regularly with those personnel to involve them in the students' learning as much as possible. Oftentimes, these people do not have the expertise to know what to do with the students during instruction or practice time. See the later section on Recruiting and Training Paraeducators and Aides.

Screening and Assessment

Every state is required to develop a plan for identifying, locating, and evaluating all students with disabilities. Generally, screening involves all students districtwide and is usually conducted at the start of the school year. Screening tests in physical education include commonly used test batteries such as the FitnessGram (Cooper Institute, 2013), although specialized tests for adapted physical education also exist. A few examples include the Brockport Physical Fitness Test (Winnick & Short, 2014); APEAS II (American Association for Physical Activity and Recreation [AAPAR], 2007); Competency Testing for Adapted Physical Education (CTAPE; Pastorek, 2008); and the Tests of Gross Motor Development-3 (TGMD-3; Ulrich, 2019). Those tests are used to make initial identification of students who need special services.

Assessment is conducted after screening evaluations have been made and appropriate students are referred to special education directors. Assessment is performed by a team of experts, which often includes the physical education specialist. Effective assessment, when used appropriately, can identify the unique physical needs of students with disabilities, assist in the development of physical education goals and objectives, and serve to monitor student progress in the program. The team's focus should be on the needs of the student.

Due Process Guidelines

Due process for students and parents is important during formal assessment procedures. Due process ensures that parents and students are informed of their rights and have the opportunity to challenge educational decisions they believe are unfair or incorrect. To ensure that due process is offered to parents and students, the following guidelines must be followed:

1. Written permission. A written notice must be sent to parents stating that their child has been referred for assessment (a referral may be made by either the parent or school personnel). The notice explains that the district requests permission to conduct an evaluation to determine if special education services are required for the child. Also included in the permission letter must be reasons for testing and the tests to be used. Before assessment can begin, the letter must be signed by the parents and returned to the district.

2. Interpretation of the assessment. Results of the assessment must be interpreted in a meeting that includes the parents. Persons knowledgeable of test procedures need to be present to answer questions that parents ask. At the meeting, parents are told whether their child has any disabilities and what services will be provided.

3. External evaluation. If parents are not satisfied with the results of the assessment, an evaluation outside of school can be requested. The district must provide a list of agencies that can perform such assessments. If the results differ from the school district evaluation, the district must pay for the external evaluation. If the results are similar, parents must pay for the external testing.

4. Negotiation and hearings. If parents and the school district disagree on the results of the assessment, the district is required to negotiate the differences. When negotiations fail, an impartial hearing officer listens to both parties and renders an official decision. This review is usually the final one, but both parties do have the right to appeal to the state department of education, which renders a binding and final decision. Civil action through the legal system can be pursued should the district or parents still disagree. Few cases, however, ever reach this level of long-term disagreement, and educators should not hesitate to serve the needs of students with disabilities based on this concern.

5. Confidentiality. As is the case with other student records, only parents of the child or authorized school personnel can review the student's evaluation. Review by other parties can be done only after the student's parents have given written permission.

Procedures for Ensuring Assessment Standards

PL 94-142 ensures that assessment will be held to certain standards to provide fair and objective results. The following areas are specifically delineated in the law.

Selection of Test Instruments

The test instruments used must provide a valid examination of what they purport to measure. When selecting instruments, all parties must understand how the tests were developed and how they will measure the area of disability. More than one test procedure must be used to determine the student's status or developmental need. Both formal and informal assessment techniques should be used to ensure that the results measure the student's impairment rather than simply reflect the student's shortcomings.

Unfortunately, students must be labeled as disabled to reap the benefits of an adapted education program. The stigmatizing effect of labels and the fallibility of various means of testing students are dilemmas that must be faced. Although current pedagogical practices discourage labeling, in this case, it is necessary because school districts must certify the disability to receive funding.

Administration Procedures

Many disabilities interfere with standard test procedures. For example, many students have communication problems and must be tested in a manner that ensures testing of motor ability rather than communication skills. Many students have visual and hearing disabilities that prevent using tests that rely on these faculties.

A possibility of misdiagnosing and incorrectly classifying students as mentally impaired might be more likely among students from families living in poverty and students of minority ethnic groups. These children may instead be essentially environmentally challenged and in need of expanded experiences. It is subtle discrimination, but it must be replaced with understanding that students differ because of culture, poverty, migrant lifestyle, and language. Many of the tests are based on Caucasian, middle-class students and standards. Students from disadvantaged socioeconomic groups should be assessed with care and sensitivity to determine the validity of the testing procedure.

Team Evaluation

Several experts are used for assessment to help ensure that all facets of the student will be reviewed and evaluated. Evaluation professionals who are well trained and qualified administer the various tests. The school district is responsible for ensuring that this occurs. The team must work with the best interest of the student in mind. The team needs to be aware of several typical barriers to effective team evaluation. These barriers include not communicating effectively, not understanding the individualized education program, not understanding the disability, and not valuing someone else's input. Teamwork is extremely important.

Role of the Physical Education Specialist

The physical education specialist is the point person for assessing and developing an **individualized educational program (IEP)**. An example of an IEP is presented in figure 9.3. The physical educator is responsible for reviewing the health folders of all students to see if any of them have previously been recommended for differing support in the past. Students with differing needs are first observed in the regular physical education setting. Similarly, the physical education teacher should visit with those students to see how they perceive the situation and how they would like to proceed. Usually, an adapted physical educator who specializes in working with students with different needs is called in to do the assessment. Not all districts, however, have an adapted specialist; thus, the physical education teacher is expected to offer feedback about how the student participates in regular physical education classes. The physical education teacher teams with the special education teacher to develop the IEP. The physical education specialist then becomes responsible for implementing the IEP strategies. Figure 9.4 highlights the steps of the IEP process.

Standards for placing students into special programs are necessary for parents to believe that well-defined criteria have been used. Several states have adopted criteria for determining eligibility of students for adapted physical education classes. State guidelines differ but should be followed closely if they exist. Often, standards are based on the administration of standardized tests for which norms or percentiles have been developed. This procedure helps ensure that objective guidelines are used and avoids subjective judgment that may be open to disagreement and controversy.

If a student is determined not to be eligible for special education services, referring the student to programs for secondary students with special needs may be beneficial. These programs deal with areas that are not delineated by PL 94-142, such as obesity, physical fitness, and motor deficiencies. Unfortunately, few secondary schools offer such programs, so eligible students must survive in the regular programs. Physical educators need to show con-

INDIVIDUALIZED EDUCATIONAL PROGRAM

❏ Initial placement   ❏ Reevaluation   ❏ Change of placement   ❏ Review

A. Student Information

Student name _____ Student no. _____ Home school _____
            Last   *first*   *middle*

Date of birth _____ Chronological age _____ (M ____ or F ____) Present placement or grade _____

Parent or guardian name(s) _____ Receiving school _____

Home address _____ Program recommended _____
          Street   *city*   *state*   *zip*

Home phone _____ Work phone _____ Starting date_____

Emergency phone _____ Three-year reevaluation due date _____/_____/_____

Primary language (home) _____ (child) _____ Interpreter needed: Yes ____ No ____

B. Screening Results

Vision screening results: Pass _____ Fail _____   Hearing screening results: Pass _____ Fail _____

Date _____ Comments _____   Date _____ Comments _____

_____   _____

C. Required Observation(s) (All Categories Other Than Regular Teacher)

By _____ _____ By _____ _____ By _____ _____
  Name(s)   *Date(s)*   *Name(s)*   *Date(s)*   *Name(s)*   *Date(s)*

D. Summary of Present Levels of Performance

Educational:

_____

_____

_____

_____

_____

Behavioral:

_____

_____

_____

_____

_____

E. Additional Justification

See comments _____ See addendum _____
                    Initial   *Initial*

FIGURE 9.3   Example of an individualized educational program (IEP).   *(continued)*

F. Placement Recommendation Indicating Least Restrictive Environment

Related services needed: Yes _____   No _____   (*List below.)

Placement recommendation	Person responsible	Amount of time (range)	Entry date on or about	Review reports on or about	Projected ending date	IEP review date
Primary:						
*Related services:						

Transportation needed: Yes _____   No _____   (If yes, submit MPS special education transportation request form.)

Describe extent to which student will participate in regular program.

_____

Page 1 of _____

Report of Multidisciplinary Conference

Date held _____

Student name _____   Student no. _____

G. Program Planning

Long-term goals:

_____

_____

_____

_____

_____

_____

_____

_____

Short-term goals:

_____

_____

_____

_____

_____

_____

_____

_____

H. Evaluation

Evaluation criteria are described in the Individual Implementation Plan (IIP), which is available in the classroom file.

FIGURE 9.3   *(continued)*

I. Placement Committee

The following have been consulted or have participated in the placement and IEP decisions:

Names of members	Position	Present (initial)	Oral report	Written report	Signatures
	Parent or guardian				
	Parent or guardian				
	School administrator				
	Special ed administrator				
	School psychologist				
	Nurse				
	Teacher(s) receiving				
	Teacher(s) referring				
	Interpreter				

Dissenting opinion: Yes _____   No _____   If yes, see comments _____   See addendum _____

Initial   _Initial_

J. Parent (or Guardian) Statement

We agree to the placement recommended in this IEP: Yes _____   No _____

We give our permission to have our child counseled by the professional staff, if necessary: Yes _____ No _____

We understand that placement will be on a continuing trial basis and we will be contacted if any placement changes are contemplated. We are aware that such placement does not guarantee success, but to help our child, we accept the responsibility to cooperate in every way with the school program. We acknowledge that we have been notified of and have received a copy of our due process rights pertaining to special education placement and have a basic understanding of these rights. We acknowledge that we have received a copy of the completed IEP form.

_____

Parent or guardian signature_____

Date_____

Comments:

_____

_____

_____

Page 2 of _____

FIGURE 9.3   _(continued)_

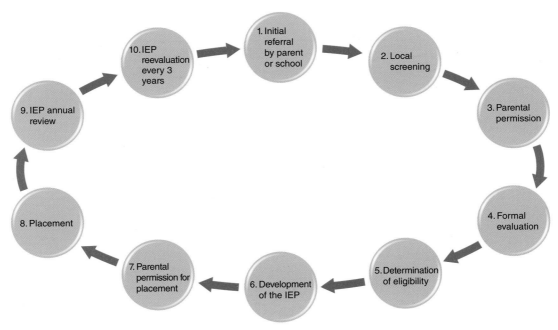

FIGURE 9.4 The steps to the IEP process.

cern for helping students with these problems because obesity and physical fitness are areas with long-term health consequences and are especially important to students and their parents.

Development of the IEP

PL 94-142 requires that an IEP be developed for each student receiving special education and related services. The IEP must be developed by a committee as stipulated by the law. Typically included on the committee are the following members: a local education association representative qualified to provide and supervise the administration of special education, the student's parents, the teachers who have direct responsibility for implementing the IEP, and when appropriate, the student. Other people, such as an independent evaluator, may be included at the discretion of the parents or school district. This program identifies the student's unique qualities and determines educationally relevant strengths and weaknesses. A plan is then devised based on the diagnosis. The IEP must contain the following material:

- Status of the student's level of academic and functional performance
- A statement of measurable short-term and long-term academic and functional goals

- A statement of special education and related services to be provided to the student
- A statement as to what extent the student will be able to participate in regular educational programs
- A statement of alternative assessment accommodations
- The dates for initiation of services and anticipated duration of the services
- A statement of needed transitional services (by law when a child turns 16) to help with the transition from youth to adulthood
- Appropriate objective criteria for determining annually whether the short-term objectives are reached

Developing and sequencing objectives for the student is the first step in writing the IEP. Short- and long-range goals are delineated, and data collection procedures and testing schedules are established to monitor the student's progress. Materials and strategies to be used in implementing the IEP are established followed by a determination of the methods of evaluation to be used to monitor the student's progress and the effectiveness of the program. Movement to a less restrictive environment is based on achievement of specified competencies that are necessary in the new environment.

The IEP must contain a section determining whether specially designed physical education is needed. If not, the student is held to the same expectations as his or her peer group. A student who needs special physical education might have an IEP with specified goals and objectives and still be mainstreamed in regular physical education with goals that do not resemble those of classmates.

Continued and periodic follow-up of the student is necessary. Effective communication between special and regular teachers is essential because the student's progress needs careful monitoring. At the completion of the designated period or school year, a written progress report is filed along with recommendations for action during the coming year or period. A summer program is often an excellent prescription to ensure that school year improvement is maintained. Comprehensive records are maintained so that information about the student's problem and the effects of long-term treatment are always available.

Assistive Technology

As part of the IEP process, IDEA stipulated that assistive technology (AT) must be offered for children with disabilities if it is needed to receive "free and appropriate public education." AT is defined as any piece of equipment, device, or system that helps bypass, work around, or compensate for an individual's specific learning deficits. Such items may be balls and bases that make noise for students with visual impairments, bowling ramps that can accommodate wheelchairs, and bright-colored or lighter balls for students who have difficulty with perceptual development. The school district is responsible for accepting and applying the technology at no cost to parents. The IEP team is responsible for determining whether an assessment for AT is required. Either school district employees or an outside agency may conduct the assessment. Just about any learning problem can be reviewed to see if AT can compensate for the learning difficulty.

Using AT must be a thoughtful and well-planned process, and all involved parties must be on board and supportive. Certainly, it makes much sense to consider the student's strengths and special needs as well as her or his motivation to use the AT. If a student sees little value in using the technology, she or he is not likely to follow through with it. The student is the end user and must find the AT valuable—not embarrassing or worthy of ridicule from peers. Even though it seems obvious that the AT must meet the developmental characteristics of the student, parents or teachers may be overzealous in prescribing inappropriate technology. A trial period with the student and AT is appropriate to see if it is suitable. Parents also can be critical of the success of the prescribed AT. If they do not see a need or are embarrassed that their child needs such help, odds are high they will undermine the student at home. This caution points out the need for the student and parents to be involved in the process of diagnosis and prescription. The following steps help ensure the successful implementation of AT.

1. Identify the needs of the student. Does the student need help with listening, reading, organization, memory, math, and so on? Being as specific as possible in identifying the special needs of the student will make prescription more accurate and effective.

2. Review the AT that is available to meet those needs. SchwabLearning.org has an excellent list of tools and a booklet that explains this approach in detail. It contains a checklist of steps that make the job easier.

3. Use a trial period to see how (or if) the youth and parents adapt to the AT. Did the AT improve the performance of the youth? If not, the technology may have been inappropriate or used incorrectly (if at all) by the student.

4. Review the AT instruments to see if they are user friendly, reliable, and somewhat maintenance free. Another important consideration is technical support when help is required. The quality of support varies widely. Many companies supply AT, and if one product is not satisfactory, certainly other options should be considered.

A Systematic Approach to Successful Inclusion

Inclusion is a legal and moral issue. Educators have the responsibility to see that all students can experience activity and related social experiences. All parents desire the maximum of experiences for their children, and the goal of teachers should be to meet this need. The issue is not whether to include, but how to include effectively. The physical educator must teach a number of students, some with disabilities and diverse impairments. Learning strategies that the instructor is familiar with and has been using successfully may not be appropriate for students with disabilities. The teacher must accept the student as a full-fledged participant and assume the responsibilities that go along with special education. Few disagree that mainstreaming increases the difficulty of offering instruction for all students, but teachers who support it show their concern for the human spirit regardless of condition.

Step 1: Determine How to Teach

The success or failure of the inclusion process depends largely on the interaction between the teacher and the student with a disability. There is no foolproof, teacher-proof system. Purposes and derived goals are perhaps more important to students with disabilities than to peers without disabilities. Proper levels of fitness and skill are vital for healthful living. Such levels enable them to compete with peers. Teachers must accept responsibility for meeting the needs of students, including those with disabilities. Teachers need to be able to judge when referral for special assistance or additional services is in order. Physical education teachers must be able to do the following: (1) analyze and diagnose motor behavior of the students with disabilities, (2) provide appropriate experiences for remediation of motor conditions needing attention, and (3) register data as needed on the student's personal record. Record keeping is important. A short period, perhaps five minutes between classes, could be set aside to accomplish the task promptly. When time between classes is short, the teacher may want to use a tablet computer or smart phone for recording evaluative comments during class time.

To work successfully with students with disabilities, teachers must understand specific impairments and the way that they affect learning. Also, teachers must know how to assess motor and fitness needs and how to structure remediation to meet those needs. They should have alternative strategies in reserve in case the original method fails. Referral to the special education teacher then becomes a last resort. When giving explanations and directions, as a teacher you should use terms that all students, including those with disabilities, can understand. Be sure everyone understands what is to be accomplished before the learning experiences begin, especially when working with the hearing impaired. Concentrate on finding activities in which students can excel. Avoid placing students with disabilities in situations where they could easily fail. Give them opportunities that make the best use of their talents. Stress the special objectives of those with disabilities. Obvious increments of improvement toward terminal objectives are excellent motivators for both students and teachers. Let students know that you as a teacher are vitally interested in their progress.

Using multiple senses or learning styles is an effective way of incorporating universal design for learning.

Universal Design for Learning

Universal design for learning (UDL) is a strategy with the intent of eliminating barriers for individuals, no matter what their special need (Lieberman, 2017). It became accepted as a necessary approach to teaching following the Individuals with Disabilities Act, which addressed the major barriers to educational opportunities for youth. A real-world example is curb cuts on the sidewalk that allow those with assistive devices to travel easier. In the physical education setting, it relates to accommodations that can and should be made for students to experience success in physical activity settings. Such accommodations include modifying equipment, rules, instructions, and the environment when needed. One of the best, most effective ways of incorporating UDL into teaching is by using multiple senses or learning styles. For instance, if a skill can be taught with verbal instructions, visual demonstrations, and kinesthetic learning, it is more likely that a student will learn it.

Step 2: Modify the Curriculum

This step involves reviewing the existing physical education curriculum and determining how it will affect students who have differing needs. An important point to consider is whether certain activities completely exclude certain students. Many students with disabilities have severe developmental lags that become insurmountable if the curriculum is not modified. On the other hand, if the student is going to be included, he or she must be able to accomplish a portion of the program. It also may be that certain activities are limiting, and inclusion is not in the best interest of the student with special needs. A compromise must be reached whereby the physical education teacher makes changes in the curriculum, and included students realize that they may not be able to participate in some activities. The teacher should always try to individualize activities as much as possible so that students with disabilities are smoothly integrated.

Step 3: Modify Instruction and Activities for Student Success

Special education students need additional consideration when participating in group activities, particularly when the activity is competitive. Much depends on the physical condition of the student and the type of disability. Students like to win in competitive situations, and resentment can be created if a team loss is attributed to the presence of a student with a disability. Equalization helps reduce this source of friction. Rules can be mod-ified for everyone so that the student with a disability has a chance to contribute to group success. On the other hand, students need to recognize that everyone, including those with unique needs, has a right to play.

Be aware of situations that might devalue the student socially. Avoid using the degrading method of having captains choose from a group of waiting students. Elimination games should be changed so that points are scored rather than players eliminated (this consideration is important for *all* young people). Determine the most desirable involvement for students with disabilities by analyzing participants' roles in game and sport activities. Assign a role or position that will make the experience as natural or normal as possible.

Students with disabilities must build confidence in their skills before they want to participate with others. Individual activities give them a greater amount of practice time without the pressure of failing in front of peers. The aim of these techniques is to provide more practice opportunities for all students and to avoid highlighting any student's weaknesses in front of peers. Avoid the tendency to underestimate students' abilities.

Many instructional modifications can be made that will not be obvious to other students but will improve the opportunity for student success. For example, factors such as teaching styles, verbal instructions, demonstrations, and the elimination of distractions might easily be manipulated in a manner that improves the lesson for all.

Reflection Check

Making modifications to the lesson has an effect on many people, including students with differing needs, other students in the class, and the teacher. Modifying activities is relatively easy, but making modifications that add to the total environment rather than create unsafe conditions or reduce the educational value of the experience can be quite difficult. When thinking about ways to accommodate all students, take some time to reflect on the total experience. The following questions should be considered as you formulate modifications:

- Do the changes allow students with differing needs to participate successfully yet still be challenged?
- Does the modification make the setting unsafe for students with differing needs as well as for students without disabilities?
- Does the change negatively affect the quality of the educational experience? Is learning seriously hampered because of the changes made?
- Does the change cause an undue burden on the

teacher? This consideration is important because many teachers come to resent students with differing needs because they think that the burden is too great. Certainly, change needs to be made, but it must be reasonable for all parties.

Activities need to be modified because all students have differing needs. In fact, a teacher who seldom or never modifies activities is probably not meeting the needs of many students. Effective teachers always examine an activity and know that they are responsible for making the environment better for all students. Doing the most good for the most students is a good guideline to follow. Table 9.1 illustrates the characteristics and physical education considerations for 10 common disabilities or unique needs that physical education teachers may be presented with. The following are ways to modify curriculum activities to maximize success.

Equipment Modifications

- Lower or enlarge the size of the goal or target. In basketball, the goal can be lowered; in soccer, the goal may be enlarged.

TABLE 9.1 Considerations for Students With Unique Needs

Special need	Characteristics	PE considerations
Autism spectrum (pervasive developmental disorders)	• Impaired social interaction and communication • Delays or dysfunction in language use (autism only) • Stereotypic and repetitive behavior patterns • Difficulty processing sensory information • Short attention span	• Understand the specific disorder within the autism spectrum. • Provide a structured routine. • Use picture and communication boards. • Use parallel talk (e.g., As Tyler throws the ball, the teacher says, "Tyler is throwing the yarn ball."). • Inform the students of transitions ahead of time. • Use demonstration and physical assistance when appropriate. • Isolate one task at a time. • Be cautious of group activities. • Minimize or eliminate wait time. • Develop appropriate behavior reinforcement and use consistently. • Use short instructional bouts. • Speak softly and avoid loud noises. • Use activity stations with pictorial instructions.
Behavioral or emotional disabilities	• Odd or improbable ideas expressed • Temper tantrums or other disruptive behaviors to garner attention • Attention issues such as short attention span, blurting out responses, and inattentiveness • Inappropriate behavior or feeling given a specific context • General feeling of unhappiness • Ongoing, extreme behavior • Inability to relax, restless	• Provide structure and establish routines. • Create a positive, student-friendly physical education environment. • Identify triggers for each student. • Provide contexts for learning social skills. • Create leadership opportunities for students when feasible. • Provide lots of praise and positive reinforcement to the students. • Catch the student doing something positive. • Work with the student on conflict resolution. • Use behavior contracts when appropriate. • Avoid showing negative emotion when dealing with inappropriate behavior. • Allow students to make choices among given activities. • Encourage appropriate verbal expression when frustrated.

Special need	Characteristics	PE considerations
Brain injury (cerebral palsy, traumatic brain injury, and stroke)	• Increased muscle tone or spasticity, possibly leading to permanent contractions and bone deformity • Slow, writhing movements such as facial grimacing and difficulty controlling the head • Classified from I to VIII, with class I being the most involved and class VIII the least • Lack of coordination • Difficulty coordinating movement patterns • Various sensory impairments such as vision • Spasticity • Headaches • Cognitive deficiencies • Seizures • Communication issues • Motor impairment	• Focus on strengthening extensor muscles for spasticity. • Modify activities involving speed or quick movements. • Consider teaching students who fall regularly a safe way to fall. • Assist students with planning movements and allow time to plan. • Minimize loud noises and speak quietly. • Allow rest time because students may fatigue easily. • Incorporate strategies for relaxation into lessons. • Use peer teaching when appropriate. • Allow students to stabilize using an apparatus when performing motor skills. • Use soft equipment to minimize injury. • Provide accommodation for activities involving balance. • Teach body awareness (e.g., "Which foot are you using?"). • Use simple directions. • Minimize distractions by creating routines. • Do not assume that the student has an intellectual delay.
Deaf, hard of hearing, and deaf-blind	• Degree of hearing loss classified by hearing threshold in decibels • Profound hearing loss (deaf) • Hearing loss that makes understanding speech difficult (hard of hearing) • Motor skills of deaf children equal to those of their peers given equal opportunity • Distorted visual and auditory input	• Use visual cues. • Speak normally and avoid yelling. • Use paper and pencil to assist with conversation if needed. • Avoid interruptions to the conversation. • Maintain eye contact. • Use hand-over-hand demonstration for students who are deaf-blind. • Allow students who are deaf-blind to touch equipment. • Learn basic sign language applicable to physical education. • Use a peer tutor to promote social inclusion of students in the class who are deaf. • If applicable, work with an interpreter to enhance the student's experience. • Minimize background noise. • Ensure that the student can see you and your facial expressions. • Include students in class discussion.
Health-impaired conditions (asthma, diabetes mellitus, epilepsy, heart condition, and so on)	• Low blood sugar possibly an issue during activity • Relatively frequent occurrence of seizures (epilepsy) • Breathing issues triggered by external allergens or internal factors	• Refer to the student's health management plan or IEP. • Monitor nutrition intake before PE and physical activity level during PE. • Be aware that for some students physical activity positively affects seizures whereas for others it can trigger seizures in high humidity. • Know symptoms of asthma and treatment of each student. • Consult parents, physicians, and school medical staff to determine appropriate PE activities.

9

(continued)

TABLE 9.1 *(continued)*

Special need	Characteristics	PE considerations
Intellectual disabilities	• Classified from mild mental retardation to profound mental retardation • Wide variety of skills, abilities, and potential • Varied learning rates, which may be slower than peers • Inappropriate social and emotional responses at times • Greater motor delays	• Use peer tutoring. • Move from familiar activities to unfamiliar activities. • Progress slowly with instruction and motor skills. • Allow the student time to process instructions before beginning an activity. • Allow slow transitions between activities. • Develop routines and structure and use consistently. • Teach developmentally appropriate activities rather than age-appropriate activities. • Limit words and use just cues when feasible.
Les autres (amputations, dwarfism, arthritis, muscular dystrophy, and multiple sclerosis)	• Congenital or acquired loss of limb or portion of a limb • Being shorter than 98% of other children that age • Inflammation of joints	• Maintain a positive environment for all students. • Avoid jarring activities. • Ensure successful experiences in all activities. • Integrate strength and endurance activities (including aquatic activities) frequently to combat muscle atrophy. • Use regular stretching and activities that foster flexibility. • Be cautious of twisting activities. • Use balance and agility activities to assist with gait issues.
Specific learning disabilities (learning disabilities, attention deficit/ hyperactive disorder, and developmental coordination disorder)	• Problems processing, storing, and producing information, which results in issues understanding written or spoken words • Learning difficulties in a specific area such as reading or math • Usually not easy to identify by outward physical signs	• Ensure a safe physical and psychological environment. • Choose instructional practices that support behavior management. • Provide class structure so that the child knows what to expect. • Avoid complex instructions and use only one skill cue at a time. • Use supportive positive feedback. • Provide adequate processing time after instruction. • Be aware of potential behavioral issues that may be a product of learning challenges. • Use peer tutoring when appropriate. • Allow students to learn through movement as much as possible. • Include relaxation activities such as yoga and stretching. • Use thoughtful, smooth, and efficient transitions to minimize down time.
Spinal cord disabilities (quadriplegia, paraplegia, polio, spina bifida, and scoliosis)	• Classification of spinal cord injuries by location of the injury on the spinal column • Quadriplegia (or tetraplegia)—a spinal injury that affects all four limbs • Paraplegia—a spinal cord injury that affects the lower limbs • A form of paralysis caused by a viral infection that affects the spinal cord • Loss of motor function	• Emphasize developing appropriate motor skills. • Use stretching to assist with spasticity or increase in muscle tone. • Consider the social needs of students. • Maintain an inclusive PE environment as much as possible because these students have similar interests as peers. • Avoid tumbling rolls and contact if the child has a shunt.

Special need	Characteristics	PE considerations
Visual impairments	• Impairment to vision that affects the educational experience • Ranges from visual impairment to total blindness • Fearfulness and apprehension • Fewer social networks • Delays in motor skills • Holding the head in special positions to improve vision • Posture problems	• Incorporate socialization during PE. • Use peer tutoring. • Ask the student what will work or what he or she needs to succeed. • Maximize the use of the tactile sense, such as touching the foot when teaching how to kick. • Allow the child to touch equipment. • Describe the setting and allow the child to walk through the area and around the boundaries. • Allow the student to take your arm when guiding her. • Use brightly colored equipment and beeper balls. • Keep the teaching area free of clutter. • Ensure that appropriate support services are present. • Support the student in becoming independent in a safe manner.

9

Reprinted by permission from R.P. Pangrazi and A Beighle, *Dynamic Physical Education for Elementary School Children,* 19th ed. (Champaign, IL: Human Kinetics, 2020), 199-201.

- Reduce the weight or modify the size of the projectile. A lighter object will move more slowly and inflict less damage on impact. A larger object will move more slowly, making it easier for students to track visually and catch.

- Modify striking implements by shortening them and reducing their weight. Rackets are much easier to control when shortened.

- If possible, slow the ball by letting out some air. This will reduce the speed of the rebound and make the ball easier to control in a restricted area. It will also keep the ball from rolling away from students.

- Use a stationary object when teaching striking or hitting. The use of a tennis ball fastened to a string or sitting on a tee can offer the student a better opportunity for success.

- When teaching catching, use a soft, lightweight, and slow-moving object. Beach balls and balloons are excellent for beginning catching skills because they allow the student to track movement visually. In addition, foam rubber balls eliminate the fear of being hurt by a thrown or struck projectile.

- Increase the width of rails, lines, and beams when practicing balance. Carrying a long pole will help minimize rapid shifts of balance and is a useful lead-up activity.

- For students with visual impairments, use sound devices in equipment (e.g., beeper balls, balls with a jingle bell inside). Use larger, brightly colored equipment.

Rule Modifications

- Modify the tempo of the game. For example, games might be performed using a brisk walk rather than running. Another way to modify tempo is to stop the game regularly for short instructional bouts. These stoppages allow students to rest if they are fatigued and to refocus on a specific cue or skill.

- Reduce the distance that an object must be thrown or served. Options are to reduce the dimensions of the playing area or add more players to the game. In serving, others can help make the serve playable. For example, teammates can hit the ball over the net as long as it does not touch the floor.

- In games played to a certain number of points, reduce the number required for a win.

- Play the games in a different position. Some games may be played in a sitting or lying position, which is easier and less demanding than standing or running.

- Offer points for hitting an area near the goal or target instead of the actual target. For example, in Five Pass, allow a point to be scored if the final point hits the backboard of the basket instead of requiring it to be through the hoop itself. Because scoring is self-motivating, modification should occur until success is ensured.

- Shorten fitness activities or provide additional breaks.

Instructional Modifications

- When teaching throwing or target skills, allow students the opportunity to throw at maximum velocity without concern for accuracy. Use small balls that students can grasp easily. Fleece balls and beanbags are easy to hold and release.

- Challenge all students to be active at their own pace for a certain time, as opposed to a certain number of trials or laps.

- Increase the amount of encouragement and positive support.

- When possible, separate fitness and sport skill activities. Sport skills will inherently include some fitness, but some students will not try if they must do something cardiorespiratory in nature.

- For balancing, increase the width of the base of support. Students should be taught to keep the feet spread at least shoulder-width apart.

- Lower the center of gravity. This position offers more stability and greater balance to the participant. Place emphasis on bending the knees and leaning slightly forward.

- Increase the surface area of the body parts in contact with the floor or beam. For example, walking flat-footed is easier than walking on tiptoes.

- Provide physical assistance. A barre, cane, or chair can be used to keep the student from falling. The teacher can also allow the student to hold his or her hand.

- For students with visual impairments, use simple language and detailed explanations. Demonstrate within the child's field of vision.

- For students with hearing impairments, provide written lessons and explanations of tasks. Position yourself where students can see you. Use additional demonstrations. Learn as much sign language as possible. Figure 9.5 shows some signs commonly used in physical education.

- Instructional cues are important. These can be provided verbally, by physical or visual demonstration, and through physical assistance or tactile modeling. Help the student learn the appropriate grip by placing your hand on top of hers or his and physically placing it on the racket or piece of equipment correctly.

- Class organization and instruction matters. Determine if whole-group instruction is best for the student with special needs. Or perhaps small groups, stations, partners, or individual work would be more appropriate.

- Teaching style will influence how students with special needs will learn. Direct style is the most common and simple form of teaching style used, but a more student-centered approach (e.g., task style, guided discovery, or problem solving) may be more effective with different types of lessons or skills. These styles are discussed in more detail in chapter 6.

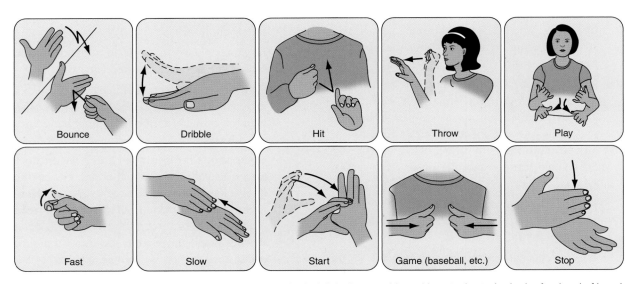

FIGURE 9.5 Learning basic physical education signs can be helpful when working with a student who is deaf or hard of hearing.

Environmental Modifications

- Offer protection when appropriate. Some students are more susceptible to injury because of certain conditions. Use various types of protectors, such as glasses, chest protectors, or face masks.
- Make projectiles easily retrievable. If a great deal of time is spent on recovering the projectile, students will receive few practice trials and feel frustrated. Place them near a backstop or use a goal that rebounds the projectile to the shooter.
- Make sure that surfaces offer good friction. Slick floors and shoes may cause students to fall. Carpets and tumbling mats will increase traction.

Step 4: Determine What Support and Aid Is Necessary

When a student is deemed ready for placement, consultation between the physical education teacher and the special education supervisor is of prime importance. In a setting where emotions and feelings can run high, communication and planning should occur on a regular basis. The reception and acceptance of students with disabilities cannot be left to chance. A scheduled plan must be instituted before the student is mainstreamed. Special and physical education professionals must discuss the needs of the student and the needs of the physical education teacher to develop realistic expectations. The special education teacher may have to participate in a physical education class to ensure a smooth transition. The emphasis should be on what students can do rather than on what they cannot do.

Full information about the needs of the student should be provided to the physical education teacher before the student participates. Physical education teachers must feel able to tell support personnel what kind of help they need. Negative feelings toward students with differing needs can occur if the physical educator thinks that students are dropped into class without being asked what kind of help they need. This procedure should also be implemented when the student moves from one mainstreaming situation to another. Students with and without disabilities need opportunities to make appropriate progress. The educational needs of students with disabilities must be met without jeopardizing the progress of other students. This statement does not rule out activity modifications so that those with disabilities can be included.

Step 5: Teacher Tolerance to All Students

The teacher is advised to help all students understand the issues related to having special needs. A goal should be to have students understand, accept, and live comfortably with persons with disabilities. They should recognize that students with disabilities are functional and worthwhile people who have innate abilities and can make significant contributions to society. The concept of understanding and appreciating individual differences merits positive development and should concentrate on three aspects:

- Recognizing the similarities among all people: their hopes, rights, aspirations, and goals.
- Understanding human differences and focusing on the concept that all people are disabled. For some, disabilities are of such nature and severity that they interfere with normal living.
- Explore ways to deal with those who differ without helping them excessively and stress the acceptance of all students as worthwhile people. Although seeking to understand the needs of an individual with disabilities is important, equally important is avoiding a patronizing attitude and affirming the individual's abilities and self-efficacy.

Training Toward Acceptance

Several activities can be conducted to help students better understand the feelings, differences, and similarities of students with disabilities. Teach students that everybody has a few areas where they feel a deficit or lack confidence in their ability to perform. Talking about similarities rather than differences is a good starting point. Often, some type of disability will cause students to focus on the deficit, which dehumanizes that person. Several strategies can be used to teach better acceptance and understanding of others. The following are some suggestions that can be modified to help students increase their sensitivity to others.

- Ask students to brainstorm as many words or images that come to them when they think of or hear the words *disability, impairment, handicap,* and so on. Write the words on the board and continue to discuss the words mentioned throughout the week. As discussion and feelings about such words continue to surface, create a new list of words and images that occur.
- Discuss successful people who had some type of disability, such as Helen Keller, Ray Charles,

9

Winston Churchill, and Franklin D. Roosevelt. Describe how they succeeded despite having serious disabilities. Try to focus on how they used their existing strengths to succeed. Ask students about friends and family members who have disabilities. Discuss behaviors that teachers and students can use to make students with disabilities feel part of the class setting. Approach those peers and give them a high five or word of encouragement. Identify activities in which they may excel or feel competent. Ask students how they could modify success for all students. Often, students have a good idea of how an activity could be changed or modified to ensure success for all students regardless of disability.

- Discuss how to behave toward students with disabilities. For example, if you are chatting with someone in a wheelchair, seat yourself first and then begin the discussion. If you see a blind person, identify yourself and ask if you can be of assistance. Use a normal tone of voice to avoid startling or treating them in a manner different from that you use with others.

- Check out the school for modifications that have been made to make the school accessible for all. For example, is a sink at the right height available for students in wheelchairs? Does the school have automatic doors? Are the curbs ramped in places? Borrow some wheelchairs and have students try to get around the school without leaving the chair.

- Discuss why a society passes laws to aid those with disabilities. Ask them the purpose of the laws and the way that such laws reflect on our society. Identify the handicapped parking laws and ask students how they feel when someone with or without a visible disability parks in these spots. What do their parents think about this law? Do they sometimes park in a handicapped spot?

Step 6: Integrate Students With Differing Needs Into the Class

After all students, teachers, and aides have undergone preliminary preparation, consideration can be given to integrating the student with a disability into the learning environment. When correctly implemented, mainstreaming allows the student to make educational progress, achieve in those areas outlined in the IEP, learn to accept limitations, observe and model appropriate behavior, and become socially accepted by others. Some guidelines for successful integration of students with disabilities into physical education follow.

- Expect students with disabilities to meet target goals specified in the IEP in addition to participating in the regular program of activities. Meeting this goal can involve resources beyond the physical education class, including special work and homework.

- Build ego strength; stress abilities. Eliminate established practices that unwittingly contribute to embarrassment and failure.

- Foster peer acceptance, which begins when the teacher accepts the student as a functioning, participating member of the class.

- Concentrate on the student's physical education needs and not on the disability. Give strong attention to fundamental skills and physical fitness qualities.

- Provide continual monitoring and periodically assess the student's target goals. Anecdotal and periodic record keeping are implicit in this guideline.

- Be constantly aware of students' feelings and anxieties concerning their progress and integration. Provide positive feedback as a basic practice.

Fitness and Posture for Students With Disabilities

The normalization process has directed attention to posture as a factor in peer acceptance. Because many secondary students with disabilities have low physical fitness levels, posture problems occur in this group. One aim of mainstreaming is to make special needs students less visible in terms of negative stigmas, hence the need to help them achieve fit and confident posture. Values received from an attractive appearance include better acceptance by peers and more employment opportunities later.

Physical fitness is also important for these students. Adequate physical fitness helps the student move through the school day, which may be complicated by a sensory deficit, a mobility problem, or a mental deficiency.

Special care must be given to students who have been excluded from physical education programs. Students who use wheelchairs need special attention to their cardiorespiratory development through activities that stimulate deep breathing. Arm development is important so that they can move in and out of the wheelchair easily.

An idiosyncratic gait or an appearance that gives the impression of abnormality is often a problem for people with disabilities. Early identification of a problem and inclusion of a posture correction program are important. The physical educator is often best qualified to initiate and supervise this program. Informal screening includes several tasks: walking, sitting, and stair climbing. Obesity may need to be considered in amelioration. After identification is made, a more detailed analysis of the subject's posture can follow. The degree of postural abnormality governs whether referral is indicated. Recording a video of movement and posture can provide baseline data from which to monitor corrections. Achieving acceptable posture is both a short-term (progress) and long-term (achievement) goal to be included in the student's IEP. Referral for severe conditions or for postural conditions that are difficult to correct usually involves the support services of a physician or an orthopedic specialist.

The psychosocial aspects of posture should be considered, and attention should be focused on the establishment of a good self-concept and effective social relations. Behavior management can focus on motivation toward better postural habits when standing, walking, sitting, lifting, and general movement. Proper posture should become a habit.

Parental Support

Having parents on the IEP committee spurs their involvement and establishes a line of communication between home and school. Home training or homework may be recommended for many students. If home training is indicated, parents must be committed in terms of time and effort. Their work need not be burdensome but must be done regularly in accordance with the sequenced learning patterns. In addition, the school must supply printed and sequenced learning activities for a systematic approach to homework. Materials should be understandable, and goals should be clear. Parents should see obvious progress in their children as assignments unfold.

Older students with disabilities may accept some responsibility for home training, relegating the parent to the role of an interested, encouraging spectator. Even if homework is not feasible, parental interest and support are positive factors. The parents can help their child realize what skills have been learned and what progress has been made.

Recruiting and Training Paraeducators and Aides

The use of paraeducators and aides can be an effective way of increasing the amount of instruction and practice for students who have special needs. Lieberman (2007) identifies ways to work with paraeducators and aides in the physical education arena. Volunteers are easy to find among various community organizations, such as parent–teacher associations, foster grandparents, and local colleges. High school students who volunteer have been effective with middle school students.

An initial meeting with volunteer aides should explain the type of students with whom they will work and clarify their responsibilities. Aides must learn how to be most effective in assisting the instructor. Training could include learning how to work effectively with individuals, recording data, and developing special materials and instructional supplies. In addition, the potential aides should receive experience in working with young people to see if they are capable and enjoy such work. Physical education specialists must also learn how to work with aides. In some cases, physical educators find the task of organizing and supervising aides to be burdensome if they have not learned specifically what and how to delegate.

Aides can assume many roles that increase the effectiveness of the instructional situation. For example, the aide may gather and locate equipment and supplies before the lesson. They may officiate games and ensure that they run smoothly. Seasoned aides enjoy and can offer one-on-one or small-group instruction to students. Aides should not reduce the need for involvement of the physical education instructor because they only implement instruction strategies that the professional educator has organized and developed. In addition, the physical educator must monitor the quality of the presentations made by the aide.

9

LEARNING AIDS

STUDY STIMULATORS AND REVIEW QUESTIONS

1. Explain the term *least restrictive environment*.
2. Cite the steps associated with development of an individualized educational program (IEP). Indicate the phases of development most important to ensure success.
3. Explain the moral dimension of the inclusion process.
4. Discuss four strategies that will contribute to successful integration of students with disabilities.
5. What is the central purpose of modifying practice or game conditions for students with disabilities?
6. Provide an example modification that can be made with equipment, rules, instruction, and environment.
7. Discuss the recommended teaching strategies for instructing students with mental impairments.
8. Students with visual impairments cannot benefit from demonstrations or other visual cues. Explain what alternative strategies can be used for these students.
9. Why is it especially important to have consistency and routine in the learning environment when students with emotional disabilities are mainstreamed?
10. How can a physical education teacher increase parental involvement when instructing a student with a disability?

WEBSITES

Palaestra

www.palaestra.com

CTCNet

www.ctcnet.org

Children and Adults with Attention-Deficit/Hyperactivity Disorder

www.chadd.org

Autism Society

www.autism-society.org

Blind

www.acb.org
www.nfb.org

Brain Injury Association of America

www.biausa.org

United Cerebral Palsy

www.ucp.org

Children's Disabilities Information

www.childrensdisabilities.info

Deafness and Other Communication Disorders

www.nidcd.nih.gov
www.nad.org

Diabetes

www.diabetes.org

www.diabetes.niddk.nih.gov

National Down Syndrome Society

www.ndss.org

Epilepsy Foundation

www.epilepsyfoundation.org

Learning Disabilities

www.ncld.org

www.ldaamerica.org

www.thearc.org

Muscular Dystrophy Association

www.mdausa.org

Cortland: Physical Education Department

www.cortland.edu/apens

Spina Bifida Association

www.spinabifidaassociation.org

REFERENCES AND SUGGESTED READINGS

AAPAR. (2007). *APEAS II: Adapted Physical Education Assessment Scale, revised.* Reston, VA: Author.

Cooper Institute, Meredith, M., & Welk, G. (Eds.). (2013). *FitnessGram/ActivityGram test administration manual* (updated 4th ed.). Champaign, IL: Human Kinetics.

Lieberman, L.J. (2007). *Paraeducators in physical education.* Champaign, IL: Human Kinetics.

Lieberman, L.J. (2017). The need for universal design for learning. *Journal of Physical Education, Recreation and Dance, 88.*

Lieberman, L.J., & Houston-Wilson, C. (2018). *Strategies for inclusion: A handbook for physical educators.* Champaign, IL: Human Kinetics.

Office of Special Education and Rehabilitation Services. (2007). 34 CFR 300.

Pastorek, P.G. (2008). *Competency testing for adapted physical education.* Baton Rouge, LA: Louisiana Department of Education.

Ulrich, D.A. (2019). *The test of gross motor development* (3rd ed.). Austin, Texas: Pro-Ed.

Winnick, J.P. & Porretta, D. (2017). *Adapted physical education and sport* (6th ed.). Champaign, IL: Human Kinetics.

Winnick, J.P., & Short, F.X. (2014). *The Brockport Physical Fitness Test manual* (2nd ed.). Champaign, IL: Human Kinetics.

9

Safety and Liability

This chapter focuses on the concepts of safety and liability. The practice of safety involves preventing accidents, whereas liability implies a responsibility to perform a duty to a particular group, in this case students in an education setting. Using a safety and liability checklist is a preventive approach to avoiding the possibility of a lawsuit. Negligence involves four major areas: (1) duty to the individual, (2) breach of duty or failure to carry out the required duty, (3) injury to the student, and (4) proximate cause (whether the accident was caused by the teacher not carrying out the duty). Among the many types of negligence are malfeasance, misfeasance, nonfeasance, contributory negligence, and comparative or shared negligence. The major areas of neglect that often lead to lawsuits are supervision of students, instruction of students, equipment and facilities, and athletic participation. Policies and guidelines in these areas need to be written and posted. Teachers need to know the health status of students and adjust their instruction accordingly.

A written plan for emergency care should be approved by the school district and followed to the letter by teachers. The administration of first aid should be undertaken by the physical education instructor only for saving a life; the school nurse can handle other nonemergencies. Accident reports should be filled out immediately while the results of the accident are fresh. A safety and liability checklist can be used to monitor the physical education environment.

Learning Objectives

▶ Develop a working definition of safety that represents the risks inherent in physical education.

▶ Dictate the need for effective record keeping of accidents and purchase of liability insurance.

▶ Write a comprehensive safety checklist for a physical education or athletic program.

▶ Explain why careful planning is a prelude to adequate instruction.

▶ List several guidelines that a teacher should incorporate when planning meaningful and safe instruction.

▶ Write a plan for emergency care when an accident occurs in a physical education class.

▶ Clearly delineate the different types of negligence and give an example of how each situation might occur in the physical education setting.

▶ Identify the different types of defense arguments that are made to prove that the instructor was not negligent. Explain why each defense leaves the teacher at the mercy of the court.

▶ Describe the features of physically active participation that make it a high-risk activity.

▶ Define a set of guidelines that will help minimize the chance of a lawsuit.

School district personnel, including teaching and non-teaching members, are obligated to exercise due care for the safety of students. This duty is manifested as the ability to anticipate reasonably foreseeable dangers and the responsibility to take necessary precautions to prevent problems from occurring. Failure to do so may cause the district and teachers to be the targets of lawsuits.

Compared with other subject matter areas, physical education is particularly vulnerable to accidents and resultant injuries. Each year, more than 200,000 playground injuries are seen by emergency departments in the United States (CDC, 2019). This chapter takes a three-pronged approach designed to minimize the effect of accidents and injury. The first topic covered is safety and the way in which guidelines can be used to create a safe environment for students. Safety requires foresight and procedures that will ensure that the activity area and related equipment are ready for safe use. In addition, rules and checklists are used to assess the area on a regular basis. Proper supervision of students is the second area that needs to be implemented properly. Supervision includes responsibilities for administrators and staff members to ensure that teachers and students have a safe environment and proper equipment. Likewise, supervision includes responsibilities for teachers that must be planned and integrated into all lessons. The final portion of the chapter is about negligence and liability. Most legal situations can be avoided if proper safety and supervision are practiced.

Safety

The major thrust of safety is to prevent situations that cause accidents. Many injuries that occur in sports and physical education could be prevented through proper safety procedures (CDC, 2019). Still, some accidents occur despite precautions, and proper emergency procedures should be established to cope with any situation.

A comprehensive report of injuries was conducted by the U.S. Consumer Product Safety Commission (2010). This report analyzed data gathered through a network of computers in 119 hospital emergency rooms. The sports and activities that produced the most injuries were, in order, football, touch football, baseball, basketball, gymnastics, and skiing. The facility that produced the most disabling injuries was the swimming pool.

Learning to recognize potential high-risk situations is an important factor in preventing accidents. Teachers must possess a clear understanding of the hazards and potential dangers of an activity before they can establish controls. Instructors must not assume that participants are aware of the dangers and risks involved in various activities. Students must be told of all dangers and risks before participation.

Guidelines for Safety

1. In-service sessions in safety should be administered by experienced and knowledgeable teachers.

Learning to recognize potential high-risk situations is an important factor in preventing accidents.

Department heads may be responsible for the training or outside experts can be employed to undertake the responsibility. Giving in-district credit to participating teachers offers strong indication that the district is concerned about using proper safety techniques.

2. Medical records should be reviewed at the start of the school year. Students who have special needs should be identified and noted before the first instructional day. Check the IEPs of students (see chapter 9) because they often contain comprehensive information. If necessary, the teacher or school nurse can call the doctor of a student with disabilities or activity restrictions to inquire about the situation and discuss special needs. Physical education teachers should check with the school nurse about students who have special problems (e.g., epilepsy) or temporary health issues (e.g., medication).

3. Throughout the school year, safety orientations should be conducted with students. Discussions should include potentially dangerous situations, class conduct, and rules for proper use of equipment and apparatus. Teachers should urge students to report any conditions that might cause an accident.

4. Safety rules for specific units of instruction should be discussed at the onset of each unit. Rules should be posted and brought to the attention of students regularly. Posters and bulletin boards can promote safety in an enjoyable and stimulating manner.

5. If paraprofessionals, volunteers, or students are to serve as instructional aides, they should be trained. Caution must be used when using aides because teachers are held responsible if an aide performs a duty incorrectly.

6. Instructional practices need to be monitored for possible hazards. For example, the teacher should match students by size, maturity, and ability in competitive situations. Proper instruction necessary for safe participation should occur before activity. Instructors should be certified physical educators to ensure they are adequately trained to give instruction in various activities. The instructional area should be properly prepared for safe participation; if the area is lacking necessary apparatus and safety devices, instruction should be modified to meet safety standards.

7. An inventory of equipment and apparatus should include a safety checklist. Whenever necessary, equipment in need of repair should be sent to proper agents. If the cost of repair is greater than 40% of the replacement cost, discarding the equipment or apparatus is usually a more economical choice. Report equipment in need of repair to the chain of command for approval.

8. When an injury occurs, it should be recorded and a report should be placed in the student's file. The injury report should also be filed by type of injury such as ankle sprain or broken arm. The report should list the activity and the conditions to facilitate analysis at regular intervals. The analysis may show that injuries are occurring regularly during a specific activity or on a certain piece of equipment. This process gives direction for creating a safer environment or defending the safety record of a sport, activity, or piece of equipment.

9. Teachers need to maintain up-to-date first-aid training and cardiopulmonary resuscitation (CPR) certification. Automated external defibrillator (AED) training should be included as part of CPR certification. Administrators should ensure that teachers meet these standards and should provide training sessions when necessary.

10

TEACHING TIP

A note of caution here is warranted about confidentiality of school records. The Family Education Rights and Privacy Act (FERPA) of 1974 is a federal law that protects the privacy of student educational records. Although medical records are not considered educational records, a wise approach is to check with your school administrator regarding the confidentiality of school medical records.

Emergency Care Plan

Before any emergency arises, teachers should prepare themselves by learning about special health and physical conditions of students. Most schools have a method for identifying students with special health problems. If a student has an issue that may require treatment, a consent-to-treat form should be on file in case the parent or guardian is unavailable. Necessary first-aid materials and supplies should be available in a kit and be readily accessible. Establishing procedures for emergency care and notification of parents in case of injury is of utmost importance in providing a high standard of care for students. To plan properly for emergency care, all physical education teachers should have first-aid training. First aid is immediate and temporary care given at an emergency before a physician is available. Its purpose is to save life, prevent aggravation of injuries, and alleviate severe suffering. You must administer first aid if life-threatening bleeding is occurring or if the victim is unconscious or has stopped breathing. When already injured persons may be further injured if they are not moved, then moving them is permissible. As a rule, an injured person should not be moved unless absolutely necessary. If back or neck injury is indicated, the head must be immobilized and should not be moved without the use of a spine board. The purpose of first aid is to save life. The emergency care plan consists of the following steps:

1. Administration of first aid to the injured student is the number-one priority. Treat only life-threatening injuries and contact emergency personnel and the school nurse for other issues. Contact the building administrator or school safety officer and school nurse immediately. Most schools have an emergency action or care plan and a chain of command to follow. Be sure to know these policies before the school year starts. Emergency care procedures should indicate whether the student can be moved and in what fashion. The person applying first aid must avoid aggravating the injury.

2. Parents should be notified as soon as possible when emergency care is required. Each student's file should list home and emergency telephone numbers where parents can be reached. If possible, the school should have an arrangement with local emergency facilities so that a paramedic unit can be called immediately to the scene of a serious accident.

3. In most cases, the student should be released to a parent or a designated representative. Policies for transportation of injured students should be established and documented.

4. A student accident report should be completed promptly while the details of the accident are clear. Figure 10.1 is an example of an accident form that covers the necessary details. The teacher and principal should both retain copies, and additional copies should be sent to the administrative office.

Safety Committee

Safety should be publicized regularly throughout the school, and a mechanism should exist that allows students, parents, and teachers to voice concerns about unsafe conditions. A safety committee can meet at regular intervals to establish safety policies, rule on requests for allowing high-risk activities, and analyze accidents resulting in serious injuries that have occurred in the school district. This committee develops safety rules that apply districtwide to all teachers. It may determine that certain activities involve too high a risk for the return in student benefit. Establishing acceptable criteria for sport equipment and apparatus is often a function of the safety committee.

The safety committee should include one or more high-level administrators, physical education teachers, health officers (nurses), parents, and students. School administrators are often included when lawsuits are filed against teachers because they are held responsible for program content and curriculum. Their representation on the safety committee is therefore important. Students on the committee may be aware of possible hazards, and parents may voice concerns overlooked by teachers.

Supervision

All activities in a school setting must be supervised, including breaks between classes, lunch periods, and field trips. The responsibilities of the school are critical if supervision is to function properly.

Administrators

Two levels of supervision are required: general and specific. General supervision (e.g., study hall, lunchroom, and so on) refers to broad coverage, when students are not under direct control of a teacher or a designated person. Administrators must plan supervision, designating the areas to be covered and including where and how the supervisor should rotate through those areas. This plan should cover rules of conduct governing student behavior. Rules should be posted prominently on bulletin boards, especially in classrooms. In addition to developing the plan, administrators must select qualified personnel, provide necessary training, and monitor the plan properly.

The general supervisor must be concerned primarily with student behavior, focusing on the student's right to a safe and unthreatening experience. Supervisors must observe the area, looking for breaches of discipline, par-

STUDENT ACCIDENT REPORT

_____ **School**

In all cases, this form should be filed through the school nurse and signed by the principal of the school. The original will be forwarded to the superintendent's office, where it will be initialed and sent to the head nurse. The second copy will be retained by the principal or the school nurse. The third copy should be given to the physical education teacher if the accident is related.

Name of injured _____ Address _____

Phone _____ Grade _____ Home room _____ Age _____

Parents of injured _____

Place of accident _____

Date of accident _____ Hour _____ a.m./p.m. Date reported _____

By whom_____

Parent contact attempted at _____ a.m./p.m. Parent contacted at _____ a.m./p.m.

Describe accident, giving specific location and condition of premises _____

_____

Nature of injury _____
(Describe in detail)

Care given or action taken by nurse or others _____

_____

Reason injured person was on premises_____
(Activity at time—i.e., lunch, physical education, etc.)

Staff member responsible for student supervision at time of accident _____

_____

Is student covered by school-sponsored accident insurance? _____ Yes _____ No

Medical care recommended _____ Yes _____ No

Place taken after accident _____
(Specify home, physician, or hospital, giving name and address)

By whom _____ **At what time** _____ a.m./p.m.

Follow-up by nurse to be sent to central health office

Remedial measures taken _____
(Attach individual remarks if necessary)

School _____ Principal _____

Date _____ Nurse _____

On the back of this sheet, list all persons familiar with the circumstances of the accident, giving name, address, telephone number, age, and location with respect to the accident.

FIGURE 10.1 Sample form for a student accident report.

Reprinted by permission from R.P. Pangrazi and A Beighle, _Dynamic Physical Education for Elementary School Children,_ 19th ed. (Champaign, IL: Human Kinetics, 2020), 233.

ticularly when an individual or group picks on or bullies another student. If the supervisor must leave the area, a qualified substitute must be found to prevent the area from going unsupervised.

Faculty and Staff

General supervision is necessary when students congregate but are not involved in instruction. The supervisor should know the school's plan for supervision and emergency care procedures to follow in case of an accident. Supervision is a positive act that requires the supervisor to be actively involved and moving throughout the area. The number of supervisors is usually determined by the type of activity, the size of the area, and the number and age of the students. At least two supervisors should be on duty (refer to your individual school polices) to ensure that supervision will be uninterrupted if an emergency or situation requires close attention by one of the supervisors. If you think that a situation cannot be safely supervised, you should document it and share it with an administrator. Because physical education teachers are expected to promote physical activity opportunities beyond the school day for students, they should account for adequate supervision during physical activities in the gym (or other school areas) before school, during lunch drop-ins, and after school hours.

TEACHING TIP

One of the more difficult supervision issues occurs when students arrive in the locker room to dress for class. Some students dress quickly and arrive in the gym ready to be active, whereas other students take as much time as possible getting dressed. If you are the only teacher available, you may need to have a supervision plan that is approved by the principal. Because you cannot be in two places at once, the administration must be made aware of this problem and a written supervision plan must be on record.

Specific supervision requires that the instructor be with a certain group of students (i.e., a class). An example is spotting students who are in a weight-training class. If certain pieces of equipment require special care and proper use, post rules and regulations on or near the equipment. Make students aware of the rules and offer appropriate instruction and guidance in applying the

rules. When rules are modified, they should be rewritten in proper form. There is no substitute for documentation when the need to defend policies and approaches arises.

When teaching, arrange and teach the class so that all students are always in view. This guideline implies supervising from the perimeter of the area. Teachers in the center of the area with many students behind them will be unable to supervise a class safely and effectively (see figure 10.2). Equipment and apparatus should not go unsupervised at any time when left accessible to students in the area. An example would be equipment left on the playing field between classes. If other students in the area have easy access to the equipment, they may use it in an unsafe manner, and the teacher can be found liable if an injury occurs.

Teachers should not agree to supervise activities for which they are unqualified to anticipate possible hazards. If this situation arises, a written memo should be sent to administration stating such lack of insight and qualification. Teachers should maintain a copy for their files. The following guidelines will help ensure that supervision is adequate:

1. Be in the immediate vicinity (within sight and hearing) of students.

2. If required to leave, make sure you have an adequate replacement in place before departing. Adequate replacements do not include paraprofessionals, student teachers, custodial help, or untrained teachers (unless approved by the school district).

3. Plan and incorporate your supervision procedures into daily lessons.

4. Remind yourself about what you should look and listen for, where to stand for the most effective view, and what to do if a problem arises.

Instruction

Instructional responsibility rests primarily with the teacher, but administrators have certain defined functions as well because they are responsible for ensuring proper instruction.

Administrators

The administration should review and approve the curriculum on a yearly basis to ensure that it is current and updated. Activities included in the curriculum should be based on contributions they make to the growth and development of young people. Saying that an activity was included "for the fun of it" or "because students liked it" makes little sense in a court of law. Instead,

FIGURE 10.2 Teacher supervising from a place where all students are visible.

activities should be placed in the curriculum because they contribute to program outcomes. Administrators are obligated to support the program with adequate finances to ensure a safe environment. The principal and higher administrators should be requested to visit the program periodically. Familiarity with program content and operation reduces the possibility that practices are occurring without adequate administrative supervision.

Physical Education Teachers

With regard to instruction, the teacher has a duty to protect students from unreasonable physical or mental harm. Ask yourself if students are physically and emotionally safe while in your care. In addition, you must avoid committing any acts or omissions that might cause harm. You are educated, experienced, skilled, and certified in physical education and are expected to foresee situations that could be harmful.

A major area of concern involving instruction is whether the student received adequate instruction before or during activity participation. Adequate instruction means (1) teaching students how to perform activities correctly and use equipment and apparatus properly and (2) teaching students necessary safety procedures. Instructions must be correct and understandable and include proper technique. Otherwise, the instructor can be held liable. The risk involved in an activity must be communicated to the learner.

The age and maturity level of students play an important role in the selection of activities. Younger students require more care, instructions that are easy to comprehend, and clear restrictions in the name of safety. Some students lack appropriate fear of certain activities, and the teacher must be aware of this when discussing safety factors. A daredevil may have little concern about performing a high-risk activity, even if an instructor is nearby. The instructor is responsible for knowing each student's tendencies and providing adequate instruction and supervision.

Careful planning is a necessity. Written curriculum guides and lesson plans offer a well-prepared approach that can withstand scrutiny and examination by other teachers and administrators. Written lesson plans should include proper sequence and progression of skill instruction. Teachers are on defensible grounds if they can show that the progression of activities was based on presentations designed by experts and was followed carefully during the teaching act. District and state guidelines that dictate instructional sequences and restricted activities should be checked closely.

Students must not be forced to participate. If a student is required to perform an activity unwillingly, the teacher may be open to a lawsuit. In a lawsuit dealing with stunts and tumbling, the court held the teacher liable when a student claimed that she was forced to try a stunt called roll over two before adequate instruction was offered. Gymnastics and tumbling are examples of activities that might be open to lawsuits because of lack of adequate instruction. Posting the proper sequence of skills and lead-up activities may be useful to ensure that they have been presented properly. Tread the line carefully between helpfully encouraging and forcing students to try new activities. When introducing new or challenging activities, using challenge by choice may be an appropriate strategy.

For teachers who use running and exercises as punishment, the consequences of such a practice should be examined carefully before implementation. By itself, using some type of physical activity (push-ups or running) is an unacceptable practice because it signals to students that activity is a negative consequence. A teacher's practice of having students perform laps when they misbehave might go unchallenged for years. But if a student is injured while performing physical activity as a punishment, teachers are usually found liable and held responsible for the injury.

Planning a Safe Lesson

Consider the following points as you plan your lesson. If you have any doubt in your mind about whether an activity is unsafe, avoiding it is probably best.

- Make sure that your students are engaged in meaningful and appropriately challenging activities. Sequence all activities so that you present them at the proper developmental level of your students. Many problems occur when snap judgments are made under the daily pressure and strain of teaching.

- Scrutinize high-risk activities to ensure that all safety procedures have been implemented. If in doubt, discuss the activities with other experienced teachers and administrators.

- Ensure that activities taught are adapted to the developmental levels of all students. Students vary widely in maturity and physical development, so activities must be modified or adjusted to ensure that all students can participate safely. For example, overweight students may not be not be able to play positions that demand high amounts of aerobic activity.

- If students' grades are based on the number of activities they attempt, some students may feel forced to try all activities. Make it clear to students that the choice to try an activity they fear belongs to them. If they are afraid of getting hurt, they should be able to choose not to perform an activity.

- Include in written lesson plans necessary safety equipment. The lesson plan should detail and diagram how equipment should be arranged, where mats will be placed, and where the instructor will carry out supervision.

- If a student claims injury or brings a note from parents requesting that the student not participate in physical activity, always honor the communication. Excuses are almost always given to the teacher at the start of the period, which is your busiest time because of other duties (e.g., management and taking attendance). Making a thoughtful judgment at this time is difficult. The school nurse is better qualified to make judgments about health issues and is not under pressure to start a class. If possible, try to work out an arrangement with the school nurse or secretary to review and approve the excuses. If the excuses continue over a long period, the teacher or nurse should have a conference with the parents to rectify the situation.

- Make sure that activities included in the instructional process are in line with your equipment and facilities. An example is the amount of space available. A soccer lead-up activity brought indoors because of inclement weather may no longer be a safe and appropriate activity unless you change the rules and types of balls used.

- The teacher must ensure that students are matched based on size and ability. Just because competitors are the same sex and choose to participate does not absolve the instructor of liability if an injury occurs. The question that courts examine is whether an effort was made to match students according to height, weight, and ability.

- If spotting is required for safe completion of activities, always do it yourself. Students spotting students is not recommended because they are not professionally trained. If an accident occurs while they are spotting, you will be held responsible.

- If students are working independently at stations, distribute carefully constructed and written task cards to help eliminate unsafe practices.

- Participants in extracurricular activities should be required to sign a responsibility waiver form. For example, if you are taking a class off campus to the bowling alley or golf course, a waiver form should be sent home explaining the risks involved in voluntary participation. Although signed waiver slips do not waive the rights of participants (teachers can be found liable if injuries occur), the waiver does clearly communicate the risks involved and may offer a strong assumption of risk defense.

- Have a written emergency care plan posted in the gymnasium. This plan should be approved by health care professionals and should be followed to the letter when an injury occurs.

Equipment and Facilities

School responsibility for equipment and facilities is required for both noninstructional and class use.

Administrators

The principal and the custodian (if approved by the principal) should oversee the fields and playground equipment used for outside activities. Students should be instructed to report broken and unsafe equipment, as well as hazards (e.g., glass, cans, rocks), to the principal's office. If equipment is faulty, it should be removed from the area. The physical education specialist should regularly conduct a thorough inspection of equipment and facilities. Results of the inspection should be filed with the school district safety committee. Administrators should develop a written checklist of equipment and apparatus for the purpose of recording scheduled safety inspections. The date of inspection should be noted to show that inspection occurs at regular intervals. If a potentially dangerous situation exists, rules or warnings should be posted so that students and teachers are made aware of the risk before participation is allowed.

Proper installation of equipment is critical. Climbing equipment and other apparatus that needs to be anchored should be installed by a reputable firm that is licensed, bonded, and guarantees its work. When examining apparatus, inspection of the installation is important. Maintenance of facilities is also important. Grass should be kept short, and the grounds should be inspected for debris. Holes should be filled, and loose gravel should be removed. A finish that prevents excessive slipping should be used on indoor floors. Locker rooms should have a roughened floor finish applied to prevent falls when the floors are wet.

Equipment and facilities used in the physical education program must ensure safe participation. The choice of apparatus and equipment should be based on the growth and developmental levels of the students. For example, allowing middle school students to use climbing equipment designed for high school students may result in a fall that causes injury. Hazards found on playing fields need to be repaired or eliminated. The legal concept of an attractive nuisance implies that some piece of equipment or apparatus, usually left unsupervised, was so attractive to young people that they could not be expected to avoid it. When an injury occurs, even though students may have been using the apparatus incorrectly, teachers and school administrators are often held liable.

Physical Education Teachers

Indoor facilities are of primary concern to physical education instructors. Although the administration is charged with overall responsibility for facilities and equipment, including periodic inspections, the instructor should make a regular safety inspection of the instructional area. If corrective action is needed, the principal or other designated administrator should be notified in writing. Verbal notification is not enough because it offers little legal protection to the instructor.

Proper installation of equipment is critical.

Proper use of equipment and apparatus is important. Regardless of the state of equipment repair, if it is misused, an injury may occur. If equipment has the potential for misuse, students must receive instruction about acceptable ways to participate. Safety instruction should be included in your lesson plan to ensure that all points are covered. Equipment should be purchased based on quality and safety as well as potential use. Many lawsuits occur because of poorly constructed equipment and apparatus. The liability for such equipment may rest with the manufacturer, but this case must be proved, which means that the teacher must state, in writing, the exact specifications of the desired equipment. The process of bidding for lower-priced items may result in the purchase of less-safe equipment. If teachers have specified proper equipment in writing, however, the possibility of being held liable for injury is reduced.

Torts

All students have the right to freedom from injury caused by others or by participation in a program. Courts have ruled that teachers owe their students a duty of care to protect them from harm. Teachers must offer a standard of care that any reasonable and prudent professional with similar training would apply under the given circumstances. A teacher is required to exercise the teaching skill, discretion, and knowledge that members of the profession in good standing normally possess in similar situations. Lawsuits usually occur when citizens believe that this standard of care was not exercised.

In education, a tort is concerned with the teacher–student relationship and is a legal wrong that results in direct or indirect injury to another person or to property. The following legal definition is from *Black's Law Dictionary* (Garner, 2009):

> [A tort is] a private or civil wrong or injury, other than breach of contract, for which the court will provide a remedy in the form of an action for damages. Three elements of every tort action are: existence of legal duty from defendant to plaintiff, breach of duty, and damage as proximate result.

As the result of a tort, the court can give a monetary reward for damages that occurred. The court can also give a monetary reward for punitive damages if a breach of duty can be established. Usually, the court rewards the offended person for damages that occurred because of the negligence of the instructor or other responsible person. Punitive damages are much less common.

Liability

Liability is the responsibility to perform a duty for a particular group. It is an obligation to perform in a way required by law and enforced by court action. Teachers are bound by contract to carry out their duties in a reasonable and prudent manner. Liability is always a legal matter. It must be proved in a court of law that negligence occurred before a person can be held liable. Negligence involves four major areas: (1) duty to the individual, (2) breach of duty or failure to carry out the required duty, (3) injury to the student, and (4) proximate cause (whether the accident was caused by the teacher not carrying out the duty). There are many types of negligence: malfeasance, misfeasance, nonfeasance, contributory negligence, and comparative or shared negligence.

Determination of Negligence

Four major points must be established to determine if a teacher was negligent.

1. Duty. The first point considered is that of duty owed to the participants. Did the school or teacher owe students a duty of care that implies conforming to certain standards of conduct? When examining duty or breach of duty, the court looks at reasonable care that a member of the profession in good standing would provide. In other words, to determine a reasonable standard, the court uses the conduct of other teachers as a standard for comparison.

2. Breach of duty. The teacher must commit a breach of duty by failing to conform to the required duty. After it is established that a duty was required, it must be proved that the teacher did not perform that duty. Two situations are possible: (a) the teacher did something that was not supposed to be done (e.g., left the class alone while leaving campus to buy lunch), or (b) the teacher did not do something that should have been done (e.g., failed to teach an activity using proper progressions).

3. Proximate cause. The failure of the teacher to conform to the required standard must be the proximate cause of the resulting injury. It must be proved that the injury was caused by the teacher's breach of duty. Proving that a breach of duty occurred is not enough. It must simultaneously be shown that the injury was a direct result of the teacher's failure to provide a reasonable standard of care. The plaintiff's expert will try to convince

the court that the requisite standard was not met. In contrast, the defendant will try to show that the teacher met the proper standard of care.

4. Damages. Actual harm must occur if liability is to be established. If no injury or harm occurred, there is no liability. It must be proved that the injured party is entitled to compensatory damages for financial loss or physical discomfort. Actual damages can be physical, emotional, or financial, but the court will award only financial remuneration.

Foreseeability

A key to the issue of negligence is foreseeability. Foreseeability is a requirement under tort law that the consequences of a party's action or inaction could reasonably result in the injury. Courts expect that a trained professional can foresee potentially harmful situations. Was it possible for the teacher to predict and anticipate the danger of the harmful act or situation and to take appropriate measures to prevent it from occurring? If the injured party can prove that the teacher should have foreseen the danger involved in an activity or situation (even in part), the teacher will be found negligent for failing to act in a reasonable and prudent manner. This statement points out the necessity of examining all activities, equipment, and facilities for possible hazards and sources of accident.

Malfeasance

Malfeasance occurs when the teacher does something improper by committing an act that is unlawful and wrongful, with no legal basis (often referred to as an act of commission). Malfeasance is illustrated by the following incident. In a rock-climbing unit, a student is fearful and does not want to participate. The teacher is taken aback and tells the student loudly in front of other students to try it. Although the teacher meant to encourage the student, she or he may have been embarrassed in front of peers. The student tries it, slips, and injures a wrist in a short fall. The student did not want to participate but was forced to do so, which could make the teacher liable for any physical or emotional harm caused.

Misfeasance

Misfeasance occurs when the teacher follows the proper procedures but does not perform according to the required standard of conduct. Misfeasance is based on performance of the proper action but not up to the required standard. It is usually the subpar performance of an act that might have been otherwise lawfully done.

An example of misfeasance could be the teacher offering to spot a student during a tumbling routine and then not spotting properly. If the student is injured following a faulty spot, the teacher can be held liable.

Nonfeasance

Nonfeasance is based on lack of action in carrying out a duty. It is usually an act of omission: The teacher knew the proper procedures but failed to follow them. Teachers can be found negligent if they act or fail to act. Understanding and carrying out proper procedures and duties in a manner befitting members of the profession is essential. In contrast to the misfeasance example, nonfeasance occurs when a teacher knows that spotting certain gymnastic routines is necessary but fails to do so. Courts expect teachers to behave with more skill and insight than parents. Teachers are expected to behave

A professional can foresee potentially harmful situations and should seek to prevent them.

with greater competency because they have been educated to give students a higher standard of professional care than parents.

Contributory Negligence

The situation is different when the injured student is partially or wholly at fault. Students are expected to exercise sensible care and to follow directions or regulations designed to protect them from injury. When the injured party exhibited improper behavior that caused the accident, courts usually rule it to be contributory negligence because the injured party contributed to the resulting harm. This responsibility is directly related to the maturity, ability, and experience of the student. For example, most states have laws specifying that a child under seven years of age is incapable of contributory negligence.

Comparative or Shared Negligence

Under the doctrine of comparative negligence, the injured party can recover damages only if he or she is found to be less negligent than the defendant (the teacher). Where statutes apply, the amount of recovery is generally reduced in proportion to the injured party's participation in the circumstances leading to the injury.

Common Defenses Against Negligence

Negligence must be proved in a court of law. Many times, teachers are negligent in carrying out their duties, yet the injured party does not take the case to court. If a teacher is sued, some of the following defenses are used to show that the teacher's action was not the primary cause of the accident.

Act of God

The act of God defense places the cause of injury on forces beyond the control of the teacher or school. The defense is made that predicting an unsafe condition was impossible and that the injury occurred through an act of God. Typical acts would be a gust of wind that blew over a volleyball standard or a cloudburst of rain that made a surface slick. The act of God defense can be used only in cases in which the injury still would have occurred even though reasonable and prudent action had been taken.

Proximate Cause

The defense of proximate cause attempts to prove that the negligence of the teacher did not cause the accident. A close relationship must be found between the breach of duty by the teacher and the injury that occurred.

This defense is common in cases dealing with proper supervision. A student is participating in a competitive activity supervised by the teacher. As the student drives to the basket, she or he is undercut by another student and hits her or his head in a fall to the floor. Unfortunately, the teacher was observing an adjacent activity and did not see the accident. The defense lawyer will try to show that the accident would have occurred regardless of whether the teacher was there.

Assumption of Risk

Clearly, physical education is a high-risk activity when compared with most other curriculum areas. Assumption of risk implies that the participant assumes the risk of an activity when choosing to be part of that activity. Physical education teachers seldom use the assumption of risk defense because students are rarely allowed to choose to participate or not participate. An instructor for an elective program that allows students to choose desired units of instruction might find this a better defense than an instructor who teaches a totally required program. Athletic and sport club participation occurs by choice, and players must assume greater risk in activities such as football and gymnastics.

Contributory Negligence

Contributory negligence is often used by the defense to convince the court that the injured party acted in a manner that was abnormal. In other words, the injured person did not act in a manner that was typical of students of similar age and maturity. The defense attempts to demonstrate that the activity or equipment in question was used for years with no record of accident. A case is made based on the manner of presentation—how students were taught to act in a safe manner—and that the injured student acted outside the parameters of safe conduct. A key point in this defense is whether the activity was suitable for the age and maturity level of the participants.

Personal Protection: Minimizing the Effects of a Lawsuit

Despite proper care, injuries do occur, and lawsuits may be initiated. Two courses of action are necessary to counteract the effects of a suit.

Liability Insurance

Teachers may be protected by school district liability insurance. Usually, however, teachers must purchase their own policies. Most policies provide legal services to contest a suit and will pay indemnity up to the limits of the policy (liability coverage of $500,000 is most common). Most policies give the insurance company the right to settle out of court. Unfortunately, when this occurs, some may infer that the teacher was guilty even though the circumstances indicate otherwise. Insurance companies usually settle out of court to avoid the excessive legal fees required to try to win the case in court.

Record Keeping

The second course of action is to keep complete records of accidents. Many lawsuits occur months or even years after the accident, when memory of the situation is fuzzy. Accident reports should be filled out immediately after an injury. The teacher should take care to provide no evidence, oral or written, that others could use in a court of law. The teacher should not attempt to make a diagnosis or to specify the supposed cause of the accident in the report.

If newspaper reporters probe for details, the teacher should avoid describing the accident beyond the basic facts. When discussing the accident with administrators, the teacher should describe only the facts recorded on the accident report. School records can be subpoenaed in court proceedings. The point here is not to dissemble but to be cautious and avoid self-incrimination.

Safety and Liability Checklists

The following checklists can be used to monitor the physical education environment. Any situations that deviate from safe and legally sound practices should be rectified immediately.

Supervision and Instruction Checklist

1. Are teachers adequately trained in all the activities they are teaching?

2. Do all teachers have evidence of a necessary level of first-aid training?

3. When supervising, do personnel have access to a written plan of areas to be observed and responsibilities to be carried out?

4. Have students been warned of potential dangers and risks and advised of rules and the reasons for the rules?

5. Are safety rules posted near areas of increased risk?

6. Are lesson plans written? Do they include provi-sions for proper instruction, sequence of activities, and safety? Are all activities taught listed in the district curriculum guide?

7. When a new activity is introduced, are safety precautions and instructions for correct skill performance always communicated to the class?

8. Are the activities taught in the program based on sound curriculum principles? Could the activities and units of instruction be defended based on their educational contributions?

9. Do the methods of instruction recognize individual differences among students, and are the necessary steps taken to meet the needs of all students, regardless of sex, ability, or disability?

10. Are substitute teachers given clear and comprehensive lesson plans so that they can maintain the scope and sequence of instruction?

11. Is the student evaluation plan based on actual performance and objective data rather than on favoritism or arbitrary and capricious standards?

12. Is appropriate dress required for students? This requirement does not imply uniforms—only dress (including shoes) that ensures the safety of the student.

13. When necessary for safety, are students grouped according to ability level, size, or age?

14. Is the class left unsupervised for teacher visits to the office, lounge, or bathroom? Is one teacher ever asked to supervise two or more classes at the same time?

15. If students are used as teacher aides or to spot others, are they given proper instruction and training?

Equipment and Facilities Checklist

1. Is all equipment inspected regularly, and are the inspection results recorded on a form and sent to the proper administrators?

2. Is a log maintained that records the regular occurrence of an inspection, the equipment in need of repair, and the date when repairs were made?

3. Are attractive nuisances eliminated from the gymnasium and playing field?

4. Are specific safety rules posted on facilities and near equipment?

5. Are the following inspected periodically?

10

- Playing field for presence of glass, rocks, and metal objects?
- Fasteners that support equipment, such as climbing ropes, horizontal bars, and baskets?
- Goals for games—such as football, soccer, and field hockey—to be sure they are fastened securely?
- Padded areas, such as goal supports?

6. Are mats placed under apparatus from which a fall is possible?
7. Are playing fields arranged so that participants will not run into each other or be hit by a ball from another game?
8. Are landing pits filled and maintained properly?

Emergency Care Checklist

1. Is a written procedure for emergency care in place?
2. Is a person properly trained in first aid available immediately following an accident?
3. Are emergency telephone numbers readily accessible?
4. Are telephone numbers of parents available?
5. Is an up-to-date first-aid kit available? Is ice immediately available?

6. Are health folders maintained that list restrictions, allergies, and health problems of students?
7. Are health folders reviewed by instructors on a regular basis?
8. Are students participating in extracurricular activities required to have insurance? Is the policy number recorded?
9. Is a plan for treating injuries that involves the local paramedics in place?
10. Are accident reports filed promptly and analyzed regularly?

Student Transportation Checklist

1. Have parents been informed that their students will be transported off campus?
2. Are detailed travel plans approved by the site administrator and kept on file?
3. Are school vehicles used whenever possible?
4. Are drivers properly licensed, and are vehicles insured?
5. If teachers or parents use their vehicles to transport students, are the students, driver, and car owner covered by an insurance rider purchased by the school district?

LEARNING AIDS

STUDY STIMULATORS AND REVIEW QUESTIONS

1. Explain what standard of duty a teacher has from a legal standpoint.
2. Explain what is meant by contributory negligence and provide an example of such.
3. Discuss the responsibilities of the school district administration in the areas of supervision and instruction.
4. Discuss the importance of having a well laid-out lesson plan from a legal defense perspective.
5. Define attractive nuisance and explain how it might pose a risk for teachers.
6. Cite the four elements that must be present to confirm negligence.
7. Explain why having a high-ranking district administrator on the safety committee is important.
8. Describe the basic emergency care process that should be followed when a student suffers a serious injury.
9. Differentiate between malfeasance, misfeasance, and nonfeasance. Cite examples of each as they might occur in the physical education setting.
10. Why is a decision to settle out of court often a mixed blessing for the teacher?

WEBSITES

Legal Issues and Physical Education

http://quizlet.com/5434685/liability-concerns-in-physical-education-flash-cards/

www.heylroyster.com/_data/files/Seminar_2010/2010_CP_C_MSH.pdf

School Safety and Security

www.schoolsecurity.org

https://study.com/academy/lesson/liability-legal-considerations-for-physical-education.html

REFERENCES AND SUGGESTED READINGS

Appenzeller, H. (Ed.) (2012). *Risk management in sport: Issues and strategies* (3rd ed.). Durham, NC: Carolina Academic Press.

Appenzeller, H. (2003). *Managing sports and risk management strategies* (2nd ed.). Durham, NC: Carolina Academic Press.

Carpenter, L.J. (2008). *Legal concepts in sport: A primer* (3rd ed.). Champaign, IL: Sagamore.

Centers for Disease Control and Prevention. (2019). Protect the ones you love: Child injuries are preventable. Retrieved from www.cdc.gov/safechild/sports_injuries/index.html.

Centers for Disease Control and Prevention. (2017). Safe youth, safe schools. Retrieved from www.cdc.gov/features/safe-schools/index.html.

Clement, A. (2004). *Law in sport and physical activity* (3rd ed.). Dania, FL: Sport and Law Press.

Doscher, N., & Walke, N. (1952). The status of liability for school physical education accidents and its relationship to the health program. *Research Quarterly. American Association for Health, Physical Education and Recreation, 23*(3), 280-294.

Dougherty, N.J. (Ed.). (2009). *Principles of safety in physical education and sport* (4th ed.). Reston, VA: American Alliance for Health, Physical Education, Recreation and Dance (AAHPERD).

Dougherty, N.J., Goldberger, A.S., & Carpenter, A.S. (2007). *Sport, physical activity, and the law* (3rd ed.). Champaign, IL: Sagamore.

Garner, B.A. (Ed.). (2009). *Black's law dictionary* (9th ed.). St. Paul, MN: West.

Hart, J.E., & Ritson, R.J. (2002). *Liability and safety in physical education and sport: A practitioner's guide to the legal aspects of teaching and coaching in elementary and secondary schools* (2nd ed.). Reston, VA: AAHPERD.

U.S. Consumer Product Safety Commission. (2010). *Public playground safety handbook*. Publication #325. Washington, DC: U.S. Government Printing Office.

10

Supporting and Advocating for Physical Education

11

This chapter defines advocacy and describes why it is imperative for physical education teachers today. Putting effort into advocating to the right people (stakeholders) and in the right way is important; therefore, strategies for promoting the physical education program are provided. Obtaining resources and materials in support of physical education often requires funding, and fiscal support for the program can be earned in a variety of ways. Professional development, communication with stakeholders, updated equipment, and adequate facilities all lend themselves to the promotion of a quality physical education program.

Learning Objectives

▶ Define advocacy and identify effective methods to advocate for physical education.

▶ Identify three important stakeholders in which advocacy is crucial.

▶ Describe three basic budgeting strategies for a quality physical education program.

▶ List means for fund-raising to support physical education.

▶ Describe ways in which teachers can find physical-education-related professional development opportunities.

▶ Identify why it is essential to maintain an inventory of equipment and facilities to help a physical education program be more effective.

Advocacy and Effective Methods for Physical Education

Advocacy is an aspect of physical education that many teachers feel inept at doing and often are unprepared to carry out. Defined as "the act or process of supporting a cause or proposal" (Merriam-Webster, 2019), the purpose of advocacy is to promote something in an attempt to gain social or political stature, monetary or public support, or backing of policy or program. In this case, we strive to garner support for physical education programs and teachers with the hope of gaining social approval, fiscal support, and buy-in to our mission of instilling the love of lifelong physical activity into all students who complete our programs. In an era of budget cuts and time constraints for physical education because of testing pressures, advocating for physical education is a necessity if we want what is best for students from a holistic standpoint.

Currently, youth are not accumulating recommended levels of physical activity, which is contributing to overweight and obesity levels. Physical education is the only content area in the education system that directly addresses cognitive, affective, and psychomotor learning domains. A plethora of research provides evidence of the multiple benefits of physical activity for youth, including physical, cognitive, and affective (U.S. Department of Health and Human Services, 2018).

In this section, information on previous research related to advocacy is presented, along with suggested strategies for advocating for quality physical education programs to a variety of stakeholders, including school administrators, classroom teachers and colleagues, school board members, the superintendent, and community members. Additionally, means for advocating, such as networking, media, social media, and leveraging state and federal policies, are provided.

Research on Advocacy in Physical Education

One of the standards for national board certification for physical education teachers is that "accomplished physical education teachers will advance their work through advocacy by actively promoting outcomes that benefit students" (National Board for Professional Teaching Standards, 2014, p. 62). SHAPE America offers a plethora of resources that can be found on their website to help teachers advocate for their programs. For instance, SHAPE provides detailed information on current legislation supportive of physical education programs.

Despite the wealth of readily available information to assist with promoting programs, little research exists to identify the best ways to advocate.

One recent campaign, *Let's Move!* focused on healthier lifestyles, with physical activity as one of the major outcomes. *Let's Move!* Active Schools resulted from this in 2013 to ensure that all K through 12 students received 60 minutes per day of physical activity. Physical education is obviously an important component of this movement, because youth who participate in physical education are two to three times more likely to engage in physical activity outside school and are more likely to be active during adulthood (Physical Activity Council, 2019). Campaigns such as this are positive for physical education, in theory, but no research has been provided to show that the advocacy for physical activity in these instances was truly persuasive.

Effective promotion of the physical education program should involve social marketing, which entails product, price, place, and promotion (Tannehill, van der Mars, & MacPhail, 2015). As described elsewhere (Erwin & Centeio, 2020), product is the physical education program itself, or the physical activity that comes from it. Price involves the cost and barriers to engaging in physical education. Place includes the location in which physical education programming occurs. Promotion is the act of informing all the stakeholders what is available to them. All these components must be targeted to sell the physical education program and garner support.

Stakeholders

Who are the stakeholders whom teachers should target for advocacy? The following is a fairly exhaustive list of potential stakeholders for a physical education program.

- Classroom teachers or elective area teachers
- Community members or businesses
- Parent–teacher associations or parent–teacher organizations (parents)
- Legislators
- School (building) administrators
- School board members
- Students
- Superintendent

Determining whom to target depends on what the goal of advocacy is for the program. Different people or entities have bearing on different outcomes. If the goal is to gain social or political stature, classroom teachers or elective area teachers, administrators, school board

Supporting and Advocating for Physical Education

members, the superintendent, and even legislators may be the most important people to target for support. If monetary or public support is the goal, community members or businesses, administrators, and parent–teacher associations may be the best targets for advocacy efforts. If backing of policy or the physical education program tops the list, students, classroom teachers or elective area teachers, parent–teacher associations, and local- or state-level administrators may be the focus. Many of these goals overlap; thus, advocating to all stakeholders is important. Knowing how and when to approach each entity may be key.

Means of Advocacy

Advocacy for physical education programs can be accomplished in multiple ways, including networking and talking or presenting to stakeholders, sharing information through media and social media, influencing state and federal policies, demonstrating the positive aspects or outcomes of your program, featuring student work and successes, and providing data to demonstrate what has been accomplished and what could be accomplished with the resources being requested. Figure 11.1 represents the various levels of advocacy within the nested ecology of advocacy framework. They include the epicenter, micro level, meso level, exo level, and macro level (Erwin & Centeio, 2020). The target audience for each layer is different, depending on the goal.

Epicenter

The epicenter involves children's psychological factors, which influence their attitudes and behaviors towards physical education. Promoting activities during physical education that are enjoyable for all students, provide autonomy, instill connectedness, and are culturally relevant are effective means for advocating the physical education program to youth. Always strive to be on the cutting edge by designing units and lessons that the students can relate to. Drawing on their interests might make movement less daunting for some. For example, if students like a certain YouTuber or video game, try to incorporate that into some aspect of the lesson.

Micro Level

The micro level includes social factors, such as parents and peers, as well as community engagement, which involves people from the local area who might work in business or trade. When advocating at this level, demonstrating the benefit and value of the physical education program from the perspective of those people is important. Why would parents care that physical education at their child's school was of high quality? An answer might be that high-quality physical education provides a break from academic rigor and enhances student health, which helps with academic performance. That benefit might be a selling point for them. For local business people or taxpayers, advocacy might be better framed in terms of showing student outcomes and that what students learn

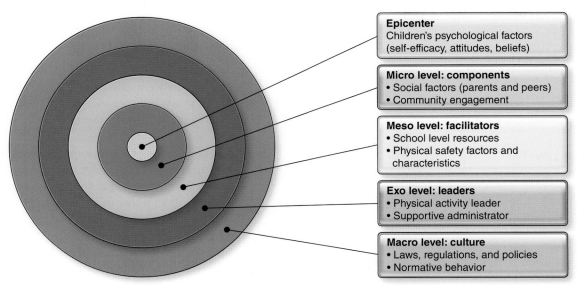

FIGURE 11.1 Nested ecology of advocacy.

Reprinted by permission from H.E. Erwin and E.E. Centeio, "Advocating for CSPSPs279," in *Comprehensive School Physical Activity Programs,* edited by R.L. Carson and C.A. Webster (Champaign, IL: Human Kinetics, 2020), 283.

in physical education helps them become better citizens. Focusing on cooperation and conflict resolution may be aspects that those people see as beneficial to the school and community, which may lead to their support of the program in some way, shape, or form.

Meso Level

The meso level is composed of school-level resources and physical safety factors and characteristics. At this level, advocating for safe facilities is necessary. Disseminating what is expected for students at the secondary level, such as up-to-date equipment that will not chip or give students splinters, may be key to persuading an outside entity to provide some financial support. This level may involve reaching out to the city or county board to discuss the importance of installing appropriate lighting for students as they walk or bike to school or improving the play area behind the school grounds to eliminate potholes. The community may be responsible for upkeep of these types of facilities, but if the need is not brought to their attention, the board will vote to approve upgrades to things that are.

Exo Level

At the exo level, supportive administration is key, along with others in the school building who are physical activity leaders. This effort requires sharing with your administration all the positive outcomes of physical education. You, as the physical education teacher, may need to create your own type of elevator, or stairwell, speech to be ready to promote your program should you happen to have a 30-second time slot with the principal. You may need to request a meeting with your department and the principal to share success stories from your students. Perhaps you can ask your students to create a short video of themselves during physical education that highlights something unique they have the opportunity to do. You can show this product to the administration, revealing that you need more support to continue offering these opportunities to students.

Macro Level

The macro level, the outer shell of the advocacy figure, involves laws, regulations, and policies. At this level, you should use legislation to your advantage, if it exists. If a local or state law requires a specific amount of physical activity per day for your students, ensure that your administration is following it. If proposals are on the table for ROTC or marching band to count in place of physical education credit, you must provide information to demonstrate that your program is more than a drill

sergeant leading troops or a director organizing marching band members. Policy can change, but the process is slow. You must be proactive in knowing what things are being proposed and potentially proposing new school policy yourself. At the same time, you must be reactive in defending your program if proposals come along that may negatively affect physical education.

Multiple position statements exist to support physical education, so either sharing them or pulling data from them to present to stakeholders would provide information on quality programming. Websites for locating this information can be found at the end of the chapter.

Along these lines, developing promotional materials is important to sharing the message of the importance of physical education. Again, these can be borrowed from state or national organizations who regularly lobby for physical education and the health of youth, or you can create your own. Defining who the audience is will help you settle on the type of promotional materials to create. For instance, if students are the target group, social media may be the most effective method (specifically through the apps they use, such as Instagram and Snapchat). If parents are the target group, email, fliers, or social media (specifically Facebook) may be the wisest choice. For administrators and teachers, videos of student engagement during physical education or copies of students' assignments or journals may be most persuasive for garnering support. Community members, school board members, and the superintendent may be most swayed by seeing evidence of the positive outcomes of the program on students' academics or mental health.

Networking and Advocacy

Four key aspects of networking and advocacy are the following:

1. *Educate yourself.* As a physical education teacher, you are likely educated on the topic of teaching physical education concepts to youth. When seeking support from others, however, you must educate yourself about them, their backgrounds, and their passions. The last thing you want to do is secure a spot on the PTA meeting agenda and plan a presentation that focuses on overweight people only to realize that the PTA president and vice-president are severely overweight themselves. That presentation might be a turnoff for them to support the physical education program if they believe that reducing obesity is all you stand for. In this situation, you would be wise to find out who the PTA officers' children are and what types

of activities they enjoy. If one of them is engaged in the local skateboarding association, you could mention skateboarding as a lifelong activity that could be taught during physical education if the resources were provided. You do not need to lose focus on what is best for physical education at the expense of begging for funding, but you can certainly tap into things that resonate with people in decision-making positions.

2. *Volunteer.* As a follow-up to the first point in this section about educating yourself, you will benefit by being involved in the activities and organizations that may have an effect on your program's success. Volunteering to help with the PTA before asking them for resources never hurts. Help out with the drama club at school when asked, because those involved will be more likely to support you when it comes time to ask for their help. Do things to make your school and administration look good in the public eye. They will remember those little things and be more apt to add some money to your budget or give you leeway on things.

3. *Walk the talk.* If you want students to be active and healthy, then you should model those habits for them. Drink water at school. Demonstrate activities and try to participate in one activity per class period so that students know you are willing to do the things you want them to do. Engage in community physical activities. Students are always amazed, even at the secondary level, to see you run at a local 5K or push your child on the swing at a local park. You are obviously allowed to splurge and eat or drink things that are not healthy at times, but everything in moderation is always a good motto to live by and model for students.

4. *Focus your message.* This point goes back to knowing your outcomes. These goals typically include gaining social or political stature, garnering monetary or public support, and backing policy or the physical education program. If advocating for more funds, the message should relate to the effect that funding can have on the program. If vying for social status within the educational environment, the message should focus on the importance of physical education in a student's academic life. Soliciting sponsorship for anything and everything is not the most effective use of time or energy. Narrowing down the purpose will better serve the efforts put forth.

Media and Social Media

Media and social media are quick and efficient ways to promote your physical education program. Media include television and radio, newspapers, magazines and other written materials, and the Internet to transmit

11

If you want students to be active and healthy, then you should model those habits for them.

information to the public. Advertising through television, radio, newspapers, and magazines may cost money, so do the research before determining the avenues for advocacy efforts. Do these venues reach the intended audience? How quickly do you need or want the information to be shared?

Social media specifically include websites and applications that facilitate the creation and sharing of information and ideas through virtual communities and networks to gain input, interaction, sharing of content and collaboration. Prominent examples of social media include school websites, Facebook, Twitter, Wikipedia, Google+, Instagram, Snapchat, and Pinterest. Using these platforms to share ideas and garner support is becoming more prominent. Additionally, they are often free ways to spread the word and to spread it quickly.

But when considering the Internet and websites as ways to advocate for physical education, Kahan and colleagues have recently noted that physical education and physical activity are often not advertised on school websites (Kahan & McKenzie, in press; Kahan, McKenzie, & Khatri, 2019). Thus, physical education teachers may be missing out on opportunities to engage potential support entities (e.g., parents, school board, administration, PTA, and students) through this medium.

Advocacy typically occurs though pictures and videos in media outlets. Pictures can include fliers or advertisements for events, data to support your cause, photographs of students being active during physical education, samples of student work, and student quotations, among others. Videos may be student driven and student created, or they could be clips of students engaging in the physical education program. The intent is to draw the user into your physical education class or program and tie the visual they are seeing to an emotion. Ideally, the emotion will support your physical education program in some way, shape, or form.

State and Federal Policies

State and federal policies exist for education, and some specifically for physical education. The Every Student Succeeds Act (ESSA, 2015) allows federal education programs to promote physical education and physical activity in a variety of ways, such as by providing training on physical activity breaks, integrating physical-education-related measures on state reports cards, and requiring that physical education or physical activity programs be included as indicators of school quality and accountability. Using the standards that this act supports can lead to promoting physical education as a means for more student, teacher, and school accountability.

The National Association of State Boards of Education has a state policy database showing the landscape of state policies related to school health (http://statepolicies.nasbe.org/health). Drastic differences are seen among states, depending on the physical education or physical activity searched. For example, only a single state has policy related to comprehensive school physical activity programs (see chapter 12), 6 have policy related to time for high school physical education, and 16 have policy related to time for middle school physical education.

SHAPE America has information regarding advocacy resources for physical education and physical activity and ways to contact constituents within the state to support funding for physical education and professional development. To locate your state toolkit, visit this site: www.shapeamerica.org/advocacy/advocacyresources_state.aspx. Take advantage of the legislation that supports physical education and use it to your advantage to negotiate for better resources for your program, if possible.

Budget Strategies for Physical Education

Budgeting for physical education is important because quality programs require quality teachers, facilities, and equipment. Typically, the number of full-time employees dedicated to physical education is determined by the administration (and is often influenced by student enrollment). The facilities are also determined by the school board and administration, but you can and should keep them apprised of the condition of the facilities and make the case for new or different facilities as the needs arise. Equipment is one aspect of the budget that is more in the hands of the teachers and, ultimately, the principal.

When planning the budget, program goals, and long-term strategic plan, outcomes or objectives should be prioritized. Budgets can range from $200 per year for one school to purchase equipment and supplies to over $1 million for an entire school district. An excellent resource for understanding the complete budget process is *Organization and Administration of Physical Education* (Greenberg & LoBianco, 2020). The budget involves personnel salaries and benefits, professional and technical services, property services, equipment and supplies, property, other objects, and other financing issues. The focus for most physical education teachers will be equipment and supplies, which are described next.

Equipment and Supplies

Equipment refers to long-standing items such as utility gym standards (for volleyball nets, badminton nets, and so on), equipment carts, and sound systems. Supplies are items with a limited lifespan, such as foam balls, hoops, and badminton rackets. Supplies are typically purchased once per year, whereas equipment may be purchased on rotating years depending on what needs to be replaced. Teachers should understand the budget for equipment and supplies each year and have a plan for spending the money if and when it is provided.

One advocacy point for physical education is to have enough equipment and supplies for students to have optimum practice time. Teachers and administrators would not likely require a student to complete math work without a textbook; therefore, why should they expect students to participate in activity without any equipment? Although some materials can be shared, having enough equipment for each student is ideal and can lead to a better physical education experience.

Purchasing Policies

Equipment and supplies should be purchased based on need, quality, price, and material. Safety of students is the number one concern. Pooling funds from an entire school district is the best use of money, but this procedure may be beyond your control. Request specific items and do not accept anything less than what you pay for.

A good practice is to have one person at the school responsible for keeping records of equipment and supplies and ultimately purchasing or requesting the purchases for the physical education program. A wise practice is to label all materials and to test equipment and supplies for safety purposes every nine weeks or before and after they are used for each unit.

At the beginning and end of each school year, an inventory of all equipment and supplies should be completed to keep up with the condition of the equipment and develop a system for replacing materials should they become lost, stolen, or unusable. Most quality equipment should be expected to last 7 to 10 years (Pangrazi & Beighle, 2019), but some equipment companies guarantee lifetime replacement. In these situations, paying more for the equipment upfront knowing that it is guaranteed to last is often better long term.

Maintaining an updated inventory will help identify which equipment and supplies are needed to maintain a quality physical education program. Figure 11.2 itemizes basic equipment and supplies, listed by priority based on cost, need, and versatility. The first supplies listed are basic coated foam balls that can be used to teach the most skills, so they have the highest priority. The quantity of equipment listed will facilitate an average class size of 30. Of course, each physical education program and class will have different priorities for equipment, so this example is not the gold standard for all secondary physical education programs. It is simply a starting point, meant to be modified for individual programs.

Fund-Raising

Fund-raising is one way to secure additional funding for your physical education program. You can do this on your own or with school groups (i.e., the physical education program) and school organizations (i.e., PTA, booster clubs) if more manpower is needed. If you choose to host your own fund-raiser, you will ultimately secure 100% of the profits (minus what you spend to host it). If you partner with a company that specializes in hosting fund-raisers, less manpower is required, but you will likely secure a smaller percentage of the profit (typically around 50%). Consider carefully the amount of time and effort you have to organize and run a fund-raising effort.

According to Greenberg and LoBianco (2020), you should gather a team of people or groups to secure volunteers and supporters. Select a company with which to partner, ensuring that the company is not in conflict with the goals of your program (e.g., selling candy or cookie dough). Additionally, ensure that you are following any fund-raising procedures that may exist within your school or district.

Multiple strategies will help make the entire fund-raising process smooth:

1. *Form a committee and divide the workload.* Appoint a cochair or chairpersons to assist with various aspects of the fund-raiser so that the work will not be on one person's shoulders.

2. *Motivate your volunteers.* Provide incentives and a way of tracking profit to keep students and volunteers engaged and encouraged throughout the process.

3. *Establish a financial goal.* Know much it will cost to run the fund-raiser (to know how much profit is earned), how large the target audience is (to advertise appropriately), and how much time to allot for sales (to earn the most profit for the time engaged).

4. *Choose a quality product to sell.* A good idea is to poll your potential audience to see what items or

11

Priority	Materials and supplies	Quantity
1	8 in. (20 cm) coated foam balls	36
2	Game cones (18 in. [45 cm])	20
3	Dome cones	36
4	Scarves	72
5	Beanbags	48
6	FitStep Stream pedometers (pack of 30)	2
7	Poly spots (set of 12)	4
8	Jump ropes (speed ropes)	
	8 ft (2.5 m) length	36
	16 ft (5 m) length (long rope jumping)	12
9	Hoops (36 in. [90 cm] diameter)	36
10	Pinnies (four colors, 12 each)	48
11	Discs (9–10 in. [23–25 cm] diameter)	36
12	Ball bags (nylon see-through mesh)	12
13	Basketballs	18
14	Soccer balls	18
15	Volleyballs (lightweight trainers)	18
16	Footballs	18
17	Hockey sticks	36
18	Hockey pucks	36
19	Tennis rackets	36
20	Tennis balls	144
21	Indoor tennis balls	72
22	Badminton rackets	36
23	Badminton shuttlecocks	72
24	Softballs	72
25	Softball bats	12
26	Softball gloves (four to six left-handed)	36
27	Cageball	1
28	Baton	5
29	Medicine balls	18
30	Resistance bands	36
31	Stability balls	36
32	Small hurdles	36
33	Agility ladder	1

FIGURE 11.2 Basic equipment and supplies needed for quality physical education. (continued)

Priority	Materials and supplies	Quantity
1	Sound system	1
2	Electric ball pump	1
3	Parachute and storage bag (28 ft [9 m] diameter)	1
4	Heavy-duty equipment ball carts	4
5	Jumping boxes (8 in. [20 cm] height)	6
6	Jumping boxes (16 in. [40 cm] height)	6
7	Utility gym standards (for volleyball nets and so on)	4
8	Gymnastics mats	12
9	Volleyball net	2
10	Badminton net	6
11	Foldable indoor tennis nets	6
12	Field marker (for chalking lines)	1

FIGURE 11.2 *(continued)*

services they would be most interested in before making a decision on the fund-raiser. Ensure that the product is of high quality.

5. *Set specific beginning and ending dates (Greenberg & LoBianco, 2020).* Having the first and last day set will help guide the pacing of the entire process. Target timelines will help monitor the process and keep students and volunteers motivated as well.

An abundance of fund-raising ideas exists, depending on whether they are self-hosted or hosted by an outside company. A simple list of ideas follows. Other resources are available to provide fund-raising ideas and how-to tutorials. See the Websites section at the end of the chapter.

Fund-Raising Ideas

- Charge a small fee for physical education each semester
- Daddy–daughter dance or mother–son dance
- T-shirt sale
- Outdoor movie night with concessions
- Walk- or jog-a-thon, bike-a-thon, read-a-thon
- Pajama day
- No dress code day
- Talent show
- Dunk tank
- Silent auction or raffle
- Happygrams
- Penny wars
- Restaurant proceeds night
- School supplies
- School spirit apparel
- Grocery store scrip program
- Rent a special parking spot
- Discount cards
- Restaurant gift cards
- Tote bags
- Wrapping paper
- Boosterthon
- Pampered chef
- Thirty-one
- Pedometers
- "Y-ties"
- Green fund-raisers

Crowdfunding is becoming more prevalent as a means to raise money for a cause. It is "the ability to raise small amounts of money for a designated goal from a large number of people, usually through the Internet" (Greenberg & LoBianco, 2020, p. 347). GoFundMe, Kickstarter, GoGetFunding, Indiegogo, RocketHub, and many other crowdfunding sites exist. Physical education teachers have attempted to crowdfund for equipment (i.e., rock-climbing wall), field trips, and even for professional development (i.e., attend a national conference).

Professional Development

Professional development is specialized training to help teachers build on their knowledge, skills, competence, and effectiveness in teaching practices (Great Schools Partnership, 2014). It comes in many forms such as conferences and workshops, trainings, seminars, activity sessions, observing other teachers, professional learning communities, webinars, and mentoring by experienced teachers, among others. Effective professional development includes collaborative efforts that are based on the school and situated so that they can be transferred to the learners' environments (Patton & Parker, 2014). They are also active and involve reflection.

As with most products, professional development typically comes with a price. Some free professional development opportunities are out there, and some of them are of high quality. But some sessions touted as free professional development often lack the rigor of a quality physical education program. Sadly, some professional development products sold at a significant fee are not of the quality they should be. Do your research when it comes to any professional development opportunity, because meeting the quota of hours per year may be a waste of your time and energy.

A good practice is to engage regularly in professional development. But just like practicing a sport skill, the practice must be correct practice if performance is to improve. Student teaching will likely be your last continuous "professional development" before you get a teaching job. After that point, the opportunities are not as prevalent. Therefore, you should discuss professional development requirements (and wishes) with your administrators, preferably when you are initially hired, to learn whether there are hourly requirements each year and whether the administrators will allow you to attend during school time (i.e., pay for a substitute) and pay for the activity. Because of the severe budget cuts in education over the past several years, professional development is an area that has often been reduced or even eliminated. Teachers therefore must pay out of their own pockets or seek out free (oftentimes low-quality) professional development opportunities.

Research shows that professional development helps in-service teachers refine their pedagogical practices for student learning (Darling-Hammond, Hyler, & Gardner, 2017). In fact, teachers leading or mentoring other teachers informally has been found to be especially helpful for continuing professional development (Armour & Yelling, 2007). A variety of frameworks exist regarding quality professional development. Among those, the main points are encouraging teachers to interpret educational issues for themselves, pushing teachers to have ownership of their programs, establishing some type of sustainability, and providing professional development in the school setting (Deglau & O'Sullivan, 2006). Professional development is strongly linked to teacher performance and student outcomes (Yoon, Duncan, Lee, Scarloss, & Shapley, 2007). Therefore, professional development should be valued and practiced continually.

LEARNING AIDS

STUDY STIMULATORS AND REVIEW QUESTIONS

1. What is advocacy, and what are some effective means for advocating for your physical education program?
2. List three important stakeholders for advocacy in your program.
3. What are three basic budgeting strategies for a quality physical education program?
4. Discuss the importance of an equipment and supplies inventory.
5. Describe some steps or strategies to fund-raise for physical education.
6. What is professional development?
7. List at least three different forms of professional development for teachers.

WEBSITES

Budgeting

www.theguardian.com/teacher-network/2016/jun/19/beginners-guide-planning-managing-school-budgets

Fund-Raiser Ideas

www.actionforhealthykids.org/activity/healthy-fundraising
https://cspinet.org/sites/default/files/attachment/schoolfundraising.pdf
www.peacefulplaygrounds.com/download/pdf/dpho-fundraiser-guide.pdf

www.pecentral.org/professional/fundraisers.html

www.pewtrusts.org/en/research-and-analysis/articles/2016/05/24/active-school-fundraisers-support-student-health-school-budgets

Professional Development

www.gophersport.com/blog

www.iphys-ed.com/learn

www.pecentral.org/professional/onsiteworkshops.html

https://peuniverse.com

SHAPE America: Position Statements

www.shapeamerica.org/advocacy/positionstatements/pe/#positionStatements

REFERENCES AND SUGGESTED READINGS

Armour, K.M., & Yelling, M. (2007). Effective professional development for physical education teachers: The role of informal, collaborative learning. *Journal of Teaching in Physical Education, 26*(2), 177–200.

Darling-Hammond, L., Hyler, M.E., & Gardner, M. (2017). *Effective teacher professional development.* Washington, DC: Learning Policy Institute.

Deglau, D., & O'Sullivan, M. (2006). The effects of a long-term professional development program on the beliefs and practices of experienced teachers. *Journal of Teaching in Physical Education, 25,* 379–96.

Erwin, H., & Centeio, E. (2020). Advocating for CSPAPs. In R.L. Carson & C.A. Webster (Eds.) *Comprehensive school physical activity programs: Putting research into evidence-based practice.* Champaign, IL: Human Kinetics.

ESSA. (2015). Every Student Succeeds Act of 2015, Pub. L. No. 114-95 § 114 Stat. 1177 (2015-2016).

Great Schools Partnership. (2014). The glossary of education reform. Retrieved from www.edglossary.org/professional-development/.

Greenberg, J.D., & LoBianco, J.L. (2020). *Organization and administration of physical education: Theory and practice.* Champaign, IL: Human Kinetics.

Kahan, D., & McKenzie, T.L. (in press). School websites: A physical education and physical activity content analysis. *Journal of School Health.*

Kahan, D., McKenzie, T.L., & Khatri, A. (2019). U.S. charter schools neglect promoting physical activity: Content analysis of nationally representative elementary charter school websites. *Preventive Medicine Reports, 14,* 100815. doi.org/10.1016/j.pmedr.2019.01.019

National Board for Professional Teaching Standards. (2014). *Physical education standards for teachers of students ages 3-18+* (2nd ed.). Arlington, VA: Author.

Pangrazi, R. P., & Beighle, A. (2019). *Dynamic physical education for elementary school children* (19th ed.). Champaign, IL: Human Kinetics.

Patton, K., & Parker, M. (2014). Moving from "things to do on Monday" to student learning: Physical education professional development facilitators' views of success. *Journal of Physical Education & Sport Pedagogy, 19*(1), 60–75.

Physical Activity Council. (2019). *The Physical Activity Council's annual study tracking sports, fitness, and recreation participation in the U.S.* Jupiter, FL: Sports Marketing Surveys USA.

Tannehill, D., van der Mars, H., & MacPhail, A. (2015). Comprehensive school physical activity programs. In D. Tannehill, H. van der Mars, & A. MacPhail (Eds.), *Building effective physical education programs.* Burlington, MA: Jones & Bartlett Learning.

U.S. Department of Health and Human Services. (2018). *Physical activity guidelines for Americans* (2nd ed.). Washington, DC: USDHHS.

Yoon, K.S., Duncan, T., Lee, S.W., Scarloss, B., & Shapley, K.L. (2007). *Reviewing the evidence on how teacher professional development affects student achievement.* (Issues & Answers Report, REL 2007–No. 033). Washington, DC: U.S. Department of Education, Institute of Education Sciences, National Center for Education Evaluation and Regional Assistance, Regional Educational Laboratory Southwest. http://ies.ed.gov/ncee/edlabs

11

Comprehensive School Physical Activity Programs

12

The purpose of this chapter to introduce comprehensive school physical activity programs (CSPAP). The chapter provides an explanation of the model and what is recommended. It also provides seven steps to developing the model in schools as well as numerous example ideas of what could be implemented.

Learning Objectives

- ▶ Discuss the five components of a CSPAP.
- ▶ Identify the two goals of a CSPAP.
- ▶ Identify recommendations for each CSPAP component.
- ▶ Discuss strategies for effective implementation.
- ▶ Identify committee members who will be instrumental for CSPAP.
- ▶ Discuss how to assess current program and the planning, implementation. and assessment of a new CSPAP.
- ▶ Develop a mission, vision, goals, and objectives for a CSPAP.
- ▶ Identify examples of activities for each component of a CSPAP.

A comprehensive school physical activity program (CSPAP) is a multicomponent school physical activity model designed to ensure that youth have access to 60 minutes of physical activity opportunities each day. Figure 12.1 visually illustrates a CSPAP.

FIGURE 12.1 Comprehensive school physical activity program.
Copyright, SHAPE America–Society of Health and Physical Educators, www.shapeamerica.org.

The CDC (2013) highlights two goals for a CSPAP:

1. To provide a variety of school-based physical activities to enable all students to participate in 60 minutes of moderate to vigorous physical activity each day

2. To provide coordination among the CSPAP components to maximize understanding, application, and practice of knowledge and skills learned in physical education so that all students will be fully physically educated and well-equipped for a lifetime of physical activity

The key to multicomponent programming is that it combines numerous physical activity opportunities across settings within the school. Components may include (but are not limited to) before- and after-school physical activity (including active transport), school-day physical activity (including classroom and recess), physical education, family and community engagement, and other programming and opportunities for staff in the school. For our purposes, a multicomponent program must have at least two physical activity opportunities and be school based. Table 12.1 shows recommendations that may be included for each of the components of a CSPAP.

Strategies for Development, Implementation, and Evaluation of a CSPAP

The development of a CSPAP should be a coordinated effort, be well planned and implemented, and be evaluated. Strong administrative support is essential. The following seven steps can be followed to develop, design, implement, and assess your CSPAP. The CDC (2013) identified seven steps that they recommend you follow for CSPAP development.

Step 1: Establish a Team and a Leader

The best way to develop and implement a CSPAP is through the use of a strong team or committee committed to promoting physical activity in youth. Ideally, the physical education teacher or teachers will lead the CSPAP effort and identify a team that will assist in the process. The leader (e.g., physical activity leader) should organize meetings, work with community partners, manage any resources available, and work to sustain the program. Carson, Castelli, Beighle, and Erwin (2014) have highlighted that a quality leader is needed to influence school-based physical activity programming. More specifically, Beighle et al. (2009) identified the physical education teacher as the person who should be this leader in schools. These leaders must have organization and administration skills, public health knowledge, advocacy tools, and physical activity backgrounds. Carson (2012) suggested that the physical activity leader needs training and also highlighted that this person should ideally be the physical education teacher. Heidorn and Centeio (2012) identified the role of the physical activity leader to train school personnel to develop and integrate physical activity into academic curricula, provide encouragement, and create opportunities for school personnel to participate in activities themselves. In their research, Jones and colleagues (2014) found that in addition to the physical education teacher, classroom teachers and school staff provide leadership in multicomponent physical activity efforts, suggesting that a group effort is needed to be successful. Goh, Hannon, Webster, and Brusseau (2019) found that the physical education teacher has insufficient time to provide the necessary leadership by her- or himself to implement CSPAP successfully, supporting the notion that a team effort is essential. If resources are available, a stand-alone physical activity leader might have the time and availability to help produce greater improvements in physical activity

TABLE 12.1 Multicomponent Program Recommendations for Secondary Schools

Component	Example recommendation
Quality physical education	• Provides 225 minutes per week of PE for secondary schools • Results in at least 50% of student time during PE in activity • Is enjoyable and teaches students movement, self-management and behavioral skills • Can increase student physical activity, fitness, knowledge, and skills • Includes opportunities to learn, is meaningful, is developmentally appropriate, and assesses student and program effectiveness
Physical activity during school	• Provides students with opportunities to be active throughout the school day • Requires schools to make space, facilities, and equipment available • Is organized and supervised • May include physical activity during advisory and homeroom periods, elective courses, and school transition time • Integrates physical activity into academic coursework or provides activity breaks
Before- and after-school physical activity	• Offers a variety of intramural activities before and after school that are both competitive and noncompetitive to practice what is learned in PE, meet the daily physical activity recommendations, help prepare for learning, and is safe and enjoyable • Promotes active transportation to school (i.e., walking or riding bikes to school) • Can include clubs, intramurals, informal recreation, active homework, and interscholastic sport • May be coordinated with community-based organizations
School staff involvement	• Provides appropriate and ongoing professional learning in physical activity instruction for staff members • Provides wellness programs for staff members that encourage them to model physical activity • Encourages staff members to be active with students in PE and school sport
Family and community involvement	• Involves family members and guardians as volunteers in PE and school sport • Involves family members and guardians in evening and weekend special events • Establishes joint-use and shared-use agreements with community organizations to encourage use of school facilities before and after school

Adapted from Hills, Dengel, and Lubans (2015).

by working directly with physical education teachers, physical activity supervisors, classroom teachers, and before- or after-school program leaders (Brusseau & Burns, 2019). It has also been noted previously that teachers need ongoing professional development, and this practice has been linked to CSPAP effectiveness (Carson et al., 2014). It has also been highlighted that quality leadership and a point person are important for the success of multicomponent programming. When designing a multicomponent physical activity program, a committee that is invested in the health of youth must be established (CDC, 2013). The committee should be made up of members who are also involved in school health or wellness committees. Members might include health and physical education teachers, classroom teachers, school staff, administrators, parents, students, and community members. Table 12.2 highlights some of the roles and responsibilities of committee members. Ideally, if it is not the physical education teacher, a physical activity leader who will be responsible for coordinating school physical activity efforts will be identified from this group.

Step 2: Assess Existing Physical Activity Opportunities

After you have a CSPAP committee, the next step is to examine current practices and policies in your school.

TABLE 12.2 Potential CSPAP Committee Members and Their Roles

Committee member	Role
School administrators	• Gain teacher and staff support and commitment • Allocate resources for program implementation, evaluation, and sustainability • Serve as a model for school teachers and staff
School teachers and staff	• Plan, teach, and infuse more physical activity in lessons and activities • Promote the importance of physical activity throughout the school day • Include more physical activity opportunities before, during, and after school
Students	• Identify activities that are enjoyable • Promote physical activity in school
Parents and parent organizations	• Serve as a role model for their children and encourage them to be active • Help to raise funds and find resources to help with implementation • Encourage administrators and teachers to support and implement physical activity • Volunteer time to assist with and promote physical activity
School health or wellness committee	• Serve on committee • Promote importance of physical activity to decision makers, leaders, and other members of school community • Develop, implement, and enforce school health and physical activity policy and programs
District administrators (e.g., superintendent, physical education coordinator)	• Offer professional development and trainings • Promote and coordinate CSPAP across the district • Provide resources
School board	• Advocate for CSPAP • Provide resources
Community leaders	• Support and promote CSPAP in the community • Volunteer to assist in programming (especially before and after school) • Provide resources
University partners	• Provide trainings • Provide undergraduate and graduate student assistance • Assist with program development and evaluation
Local business	• Donate equipment • Assist with fund-raising
Local media	• Spread the word about CSPAP • Highlight CSPAP successes

Adapted from Centers for Disease Control and Prevention (2013).

A number of assessments may be helpful: School Health Index (www.cdc.gov/healthyschools/shi/index.htm), Physical Education Curriculum Analysis Tool (www.cdc.gov/healthyschools/pecat/index.htm), School Physical Activity Assessment (https://activelivingresearch.org/school-physical-activity-policy-assessment-s-papa-0), and the Health Schools Program Inventory (www.healthiergeneration.org/take-action/schools/the-6-step-process). These tools can be used to assess a variety of indicators across the CSPAP components, and the CSPAP committee should identify the best tool for your school. The results can then be used to develop program objectives and goals and determine which components should be included. After the committee has completed the chosen assessments, a number of questions should be asked and answered (CDC, 2013):

- What strategies, policies, and practices are already in place in your school? Can these be used to develop a CSPAP?
- What strategies, policies, and practices are already being developed to promote physical activity in the school? What needs to be done to ensure that these come to fruition?
- What strategies, polices, and practices are still needed? Which are the top priorities for the committee?

Step 3: Develop a Mission, Vision, Goals, and Objectives for Your CSPAP

The committee can brainstorm a vision (big-picture purpose and framework), mission (general statement of how your will achieve your vision), goals (general statements that need to be accomplished to implement your CSPAP), and objectives (statements of specific milestones that need to be completed to meet your goals). This task requires the committee to identify the ideal CSPAP for your school while considering what you would want students, parents, teachers, and staff to be doing during the program. Goals need to include two parts: who will be affected and what will change. No minimum or maximum number of goals must be established (some programs may have one, whereas others have several). Objectives should be specific, measurable, achievable, realistic, and time-phased. The following is an example of a vision, mission, goal, and objective:

Vision: Get active to learn.

Mission: To provide 60 minutes of daily physical activity opportunity for all children.

Goal: Increase the number of students who are active 60 minutes per day.

- **Objective:** By the end of the year, 50% of students will participate in the morning physical activity program that is at least 10 minutes long.

Step 4: Identify the Changes You Want to See After Program Implementation

A program committee should identify the outcomes that are expected to change because of the program. These outcomes might include changes in knowledge, attitudes, skills, and behaviors. Outcomes are often differentiated as being short, intermediate, or long term. Outcomes require formal data collection to check on program progress. They need to be monitored over time to ensure that steps are being taken to achieve these outcomes. Each outcome needs one or more indicators that will be used to monitor progress. A sample short-term and long-term outcome with indicators might be the following:

Short-term outcome: increase physical activity opportunities at school

Indicator: *number of classrooms providing physical activity breaks*

Long-term outcome: implementation of a policy requiring 225 minutes of physical education per week

Indicator: *number of minutes of physical education each week*

Step 5: Plan CSPAP Activities

The committee must identify the activities that will be implemented by considering the goals and objectives established in step 3. This process requires consideration of time and feasibility of the planned activities as well as a discussion with stakeholders. The physical activity leader needs to identify the equipment and personnel that are currently available as well as what else will be needed for implementation. This task includes an examination of space, staffing, cost, and current offerings. The committee needs to identify which physical activities will be offered (e.g., intramurals, before-school drop-in program, and so on). A useful approach is to survey students to determine their interests and to discuss opportunities with local community organizations (e.g., the local YMCA). Identifying all possible time slots that can be used for physical activity is also essential (for secondary schools, these may include before school, lunch time, study halls, and so on). Classroom teachers should look at times and ways they can build physical activity opportunities into their classrooms. The committee must also work with school staff to determine which space and facilities are available to use during the identified time slots.

12

Although the physical education teacher will most likely serve as the overall leader of the program, others who might lead specific smaller aspects of the implementation should be identified. Is a grade or subject area teacher willing to spearhead the classroom physical activity efforts? Is a paraeducator willing to supervise lunchtime intramurals? Additionally, a budget needs to be created that considers staffing, equipment, facilities, and so on. The budget must be realistic and flexible to meet the program needs. Community and business leaders on your committee can be instrumental in helping to raise funds and in supporting the CSPAP. The budget process should include both immediate needs as well as long terms ways to ensure program sustainability. The planning process also needs to build in communication and marketing strategies to educate students, parents, administrators, teachers, and community members. This effort might include announcements, newsletters, videos, and so on. Getting all these stakeholders engaged and on board is essential to ensuring that the CSPAP hits the ground running. Marketing strategy needs to consider the product, price, place, and promotion. Table 12.3 highlights possible activities that could be planned and implemented for each component of the CSPAP.

Step 6: Implementation

This step requires a process for implementing what was planned in step 5. This plan outlines exactly what will be done, by whom, when, and how. This plan must align with the goals and objectives and requires a list of the tasks, resources, and responsibilities that are required for implementation.

Change is hard and takes time, so the committee should start small and ensure that the implementation is realistic and has a high likelihood of being successful. To do this, a smart approach may be to start with a pilot (a small-scale test) by introducing new components in a few classes or with a smaller group of students before school-wide implementation. A phased approach may also make sense in which a new component is rolled out to a single grade level and additional grade levels are added every two weeks thereafter. After your committee knows that each aspect of the plan can be implemented and that they have been successful (by pilot or phased), a full implementation is in store. Implementation needs to be developmentally appropriate for each student and may require modifications for youth with disabilities.

CSPAP implementation requires ongoing support and communication with stakeholders to keep everyone in the loop on program progress.

Step 7: Evaluation

The systematic collection of information about the activities, characteristics, and outcomes of the program is essential to make judgments about the program, make improvements, and inform decision makers. This information is ultimately used to document the strengths and weaknesses of the CSPAP and plan for changes and improvements to the program.

The two primary types of program evaluation are process and outcome. Process evaluation is the information gathered that allows the program committee and personnel to know if the program is being implemented well. It answers the who, what, when, where, and how much about the program. For example, data might be collected on the types of activities and the program content. This type of evaluation must align with the programs objectives and can be used to improve the CSPAP further. Outcome evaluation is used to assess what happens because of implementing the CSPAP. This data can be used for future planning and assessing the overall effect of the program on the participants. This type of assessment is used when the program is fully implemented and well established.

Evaluation data needs to be high quality, which requires valid and reliable measures. Common approaches might include questionnaires, interviews, document review, and observations of behavior. Questionnaires can be used to ask students, parents, teachers, and school personnel about the program and their experience. Interviews can be used to obtain additional quantitative and qualitative details about the program from stakeholders. Document reviews can include activity logs, meeting minutes, and reports on participation. Observation of behavior, events, and so on can be done directly (e.g., by observing what is happening during classroom activity breaks) or indirectly (e.g., by monitoring youth physical activity with pedometers).

Successful program evaluation requires significant planning and preparation. The CDC (2013) identified six steps that should be followed: Engage the stakeholder, describe the program, focus on evaluation design, gather credible evidence, justify conclusions, and use and share the findings.

TABLE 12.3 Examples of Possible CSPAP Component Activities

CSPAP component	Sample activities
Physical education	• Standards and activity-based physical education • Increase physical education class time and opportunities • Fund-raise for new equipment • Developmentally and culturally appropriate curriculum
Physical activity during school	• School-wide activities through classroom media • Drop-in physical activity in the gym or outside during lunch • Establish physical activity clubs • Allow walking during study halls (or lunch) • Add physical activity to academic lessons • Add intramural program to lunch hour
Before and after school	• Establish an official active commuting program • Before- or after-school intramural program • Interscholastic sports • Sport and physical activity clubs
Staff involvement	• Employee wellness program • Engage in clubs, intramurals, and other physical activity opportunities • Infuse and participate in classroom physical activity • Mode physical activity for students
Family and community engagement	• Create walking trails • Add recreation programs to meet demands of students • Community wellness and physical activity events • Physical activity homework for families • Health and physical activity information for families • School and community partnerships

Based on SHAPE America, *CSPAP Comprehensive School Physical Activity Program* (Reston, VA: SHAPE America, 2013).

LEARNING AIDS

STUDY STIMULATORS AND REVIEW QUESTIONS

1. Define CSPAP and discuss the two CSPAP goals.
2. What should be included in each component in secondary schools?
3. Discuss strategies for preparation, implementation, and assessment of CSPAP.
4. Who should be involved in the CSPAP committee?
5. What is the role of the physical activity leader?

WEBSITES

Comprehensive School Physical Activity Programs

https://shapeamerica.org/cspap/what.aspx
https://cdc.gov/healthyschools/professional_development/e-learning/CSPAP/index.html
https://actionforhealthykids.org/activity/comprehensive-school-physical-activity-programs

12

REFERENCES AND SUGGESTED READINGS

American Alliance for Health, Physical Education, Recreation and Dance. (2013). *Comprehensive school physical activity programs: Helping all students achieve 60 minutes of physical activity each day.* Reston, VA: SHAPE America.

Beighle, A., Erwin, H., Castelli, D., & Ernst, M. (2009) Preparing physical educators for the role of physical activity director. *Journal of Physical Education, Recreation & Dance, 80,* 24–29.

Brusseau, T.A., & Burns, R. (2018). The physical activity leader and comprehensive school physical activity program effectiveness. *Biomedical Human Kinetics, 10*(1), 127–133. https://doi.org/10.1515/bhk-2018-0019

Carson, R. (2012). Certification and duties of a director of physical activity. *Journal of Physical Education, Recreation & Dance, 83*(6), 16-29.

Carson, R.L., Castelli, D.M., Beighle, A., & Erwin, H. (2014). School-based physical activity promotion: A conceptual framework for research and practice. *Childhood Obes*ity, *10,* 100–116.

Carson, R.L., Castelli, D.M., Pulling Kuhn, A.C, Moore, J.B., Beets, M.W., Beighle, A., . . . & Glowacki, E.M. (2014). Impact of trained champions of comprehensive school and sedentary behaviors. *Preventive Medicine, 69,* S12–S19.

Castelli, D.M., Carson, R.L., & Kulinna, P.H. (2017). PETE programs creating teacher leaders to integrate comprehensive school physical activity programs. *Journal of Physical Education, Recreation and Dance, 88,* 8–10.

Centeio, E.E., McCaughtry, N., Gutuskey, L., Garn, A.C., Somers, C., Shen, B., . . . & Kulik, N.L. (2014). Chapter 8: Physical activity change through comprehensive school physical activity programs in urban elementary schools. *Journal of Teaching in Physical Education, 33*(4), 573–591.

Centers for Disease Control and Prevention. (2013). *Comprehensive school physical activity programs: A guide for schools.* Atlanta, GA: U.S. Department of Health and Human Services.

Erwin, H., Beighle, A., Carson, R.L., & Castelli, D.M. (2013). Comprehensive school-based physical activity promotion: A review. *Quest, 65*(4), 412–428.

Goh, T.L., Webster, C., Brusseau, T., & Hannon, J. (2019). Infusing physical activity leadership training in PETE programs through university–school partnerships: Principals' and graduate students' experiences. *Physical Educator, 76*(1), 238-257.

Heidorn, B., & Centeio, E. (2012). The director of physical activity and staff involvement. *Journal of Physical Education, Recreation & Dance, 83*(7), 13-26.

Hills, A.P., Dengel, D.R., & Lubans, D.R. (2015). Supporting public health priorities: recommendations for physical education and physical activity promotion in schools. *Progress in Cardiovascular Diseases, 57*(4), 368-374.

Jones, E.M., Taliaferro, A.R., Elliott, E.M., Bulger, S.M., Kristjansson, A.L., Neal, W., & Allar, I. (2014). Feasibility study of comprehensive school physical activity programs in Appalachian communities: the McDowell CHOICES project. *Journal of Teaching in Physical Education, 33*(4), 467-491.

Metzler, M., Barrett-Williams, S., Hunt, K., Marquis, J., & Trent, M. (2015). *Final report: Establishing a comprehensive school physical activity program.* Atlanta, GA: Centers for Disease Control and Prevention and Georgia State University Seed Award Program for Social and Behavioral Science Research.

Intramurals, Physical Activity Programs, and Athletics

This chapter summarizes the role of intramurals, physical activity programs, and athletics in the total school program. These opportunities should be available to all students and be conducted in a manner that contributes to educational objectives. The intramural program is a voluntary activity that enables students to develop interest and competence in a wide range of physical activities. Intramurals have the potential to offer something of interest to all students in the school. Physical activity programs are filled with students who have a common interest in a particular sport or physical activity. These programs are usually organized and funded by students and provide them with an opportunity to be active at school outside the regular class time (i.e., before school, during the lunch hour, or after school). The school athletic program should contribute to educational goals. The way that an athletic program is conducted determines whether it is a positive or negative experience for students.

Learning Objectives

▶ Explain the relationship and the differences between intramurals, physical activity programs, and athletics.
▶ Set up a student interest survey that could be used to determine the activities to be offered in these programs.
▶ Discuss the issues regarding programs such as leadership, motivation, facilities, officials, competition, and tournament construction.
▶ Defend the values of a properly organized and conducted athletic program.
▶ Explain many possible detrimental effects of an athletic program.
▶ Identify procedures for developing a high-quality athletic program.
▶ Defend the implementation of intramural, physical activity, and athletic programs in an educational setting.

School-sponsored cocurricular programs that focus on sports, games, and physical activities are especially important to many students because they provide motivation beyond the academic classroom setting. Valuable lessons are learned that enhance and shape physical skills, knowledge, social skills, and attitudes. Physical educators should be involved in the overall planning and delivery of these programs to ensure that the educational value of these programs is enhanced and that all participants are treated with respect. Many school districts that have cut back offerings in these areas are reconsidering their previous position and planning to reinstitute traditional after-school programs. These programs serve a valuable function for students. They provide adolescents with positive alternatives to youth crimes, gangs, violence, dropout problems, discipline problems, and drug experimentation, and they provide further opportunities for engagement in physical activity for health-related benefits. The activities are important for students who are exploring and searching for programs in which they can be involved, and they serve as additional physical activity opportunities for students who may be cut from athletic teams in the exclusionary athletic environment.

Intramurals and physical activity programs are rarely priority items in middle and high schools. In school districts, the athletic program is the number one after-school activity and receives most of the facilities, money, and qualified personnel. Additionally, in districts that have strong athletics at the high school level, many middle school athletic programs are inadequate or nonexistent. Quality programs should be offered in all three areas: athletics, intramurals, and physical activity programs. The combination of all of these can serve the needs of many students while offering physical activity and recreation in a school-sanctioned setting.

Studies have revealed that a high percentage of students who participate in athletics in elementary school dropout or are eliminated during the secondary school years. This finding would not be alarming (considering that athletic programs are for the elite) if other avenues were available to students who want to enjoy sports and physical activities, like the club sport environment practiced in Europe and Australia. Some of the best and most economical approaches include intramural programs and physical activity programs. But if the school district does not hire or train qualified personnel to administer them, these programs soon become second rate and fail to attract participants. A key word is *hire*, which implies that someone is being paid to run the programs, indicating their importance. The ensuing discussion offers direction for developing quality programs in all these areas, which are based on student interest and conducted through student input and energy.

Intramurals

An intramural program is an organized activity for students that is an extension of the physical education program. Three characteristics of an intramural program include (1) student attendance and participation are voluntary; (2) all students are given an equal opportunity to participate, regardless of their physical ability; and (3) students are able to take part in planning, organizing, and administering the program (National Association for Sport and Physical Education, 2002b). The intramural program can be a site, as recommended by the National Intramural-Recreational Sports Association (2004), for engagement in physical activity for health-related benefits, skill development, social interaction, recreational participation, and application of knowledge gained in the physical education program. Supervisory personnel, equipment, and facilities for the intramural program should be funded by the school district. In some cases, fees might be required if the activity involves private facilities such as climbing walls, bowling alleys, skating rinks, or horseback riding stables.

TEACHING TIP

Private funding is often available for certain programs from organizations such as the United States Tennis Association and the Professional Golf Association. These and other organizations are often available to stage after-school activities, which may include intramurals at the secondary level.

Intramurals may be the program that offers culminating outdoor activity events such as hiking and skiing. These activities often cannot occur during physical education because of time restrictions. In addition, teachers conducting a program may use one program to spark interest in the other. The intramural program is a social meeting ground for students. Students participate in activities they may enjoy and use throughout their lives.

Who participates in an intramural program? Ideally, every student in the school takes part. The program should offer something of interest to all students and provide appropriate competitive experiences for students of all sizes, shapes, and skill levels. All students need to have many opportunities to find success and enjoyment in the program, regardless of their physical stature or ability level. When starting an intramural program, however, the administrator may begin small by offering the opportunity to one grade level per day of the week, for instance.

Why have an intramural program? An intramural program offers students an opportunity to develop interest and competence in a wide range of recreational activities. The program also gives students an opportunity to develop and maintain a reasonable level of fitness. Evidence has shown that if people do not develop competence and confidence during their school years in their ability to participate in recreational activities, they seldom participate in later life. In the intramural program, students learn to compete against and cooperate with each other in an environment that has little at stake in terms of winning and losing. Additionally, the embarrassment of performing in front of peers is rarely an issue. The program can be a setting for developing lifelong friendships.

The intramural program can also be a place to learn leadership and followership skills. Students learn to compromise and assert themselves. Through these programs, students, parents, and teachers can become closer friends. Finally, the program offers students a place to spend some of their out-of-school time in a supervised setting, rather than walking the streets with nothing to do. Few programs for youth offer so many benefits at such low cost to society.

Recreation Versus Competition

A successful intramural program should attract all types of students. The question often arises about whether competition or recreation should be featured. If the focus is on competition, then tournaments that identify champions and reinforce winners are featured. Competition emphasizes practicing as much as possible, playing only the best participants, and avoiding mistakes as much as possible. This focus is not far from athletic programs, which are exclusionary in nature.

If recreation is featured, emphasis is placed on participation and playing all teams an equal number of times. Tournament and league standings are not highlighted or posted, and students play each game as an entity in itself. Rewarding recreation emphasizes attendance and participation, and all students are expected to play the same amount. Awards and trophies are not offered, but certificates of participation are sometimes given.

Which direction should the intramural program take? As usual, no easy answer exists, but several points need to be considered. Students who have been cut from

an athletic program may still want to compete. Other students may not have participated on an athletic team after the elementary school years and simply want a positive experience. Most secondary students prefer an intramural program that is a mixture of both recreation and competition. Students want the opportunity to match skills and wits with an opponent in a competitive setting. They also want to have an opportunity to relax, play, and communicate with peers. The best programs probably offer students a balance of competition and recreation.

TEACHING TIP

One way to accomplish a balance of competition and recreation is to require all team members to have equal playing time, while still recognizing winners. This approach requires, in team sports, cooperation among teams to determine which balance of players are on the court or field at the same time, when to substitute players, and how to strive for a common goal while remaining inclusive.

Types of Activities

The types and varieties of activities offered to students are the heart of the intramural program. Activities that meet the desires of all students should be offered. In some cases, the intramural program is an outgrowth of the athletic program rather than the physical education program and has been directed by athletic coaches. The result is probably a program conducted in a manner like the athletic program and intended to recruit for future athletic teams. In most cases, this type of program is inappropriate. The scope of intramural activities should be unlimited and dictated by students. If students are expected to participate in the program during their free time, it must cater to their desires and wants. The intramural program should not be regarded as minor league for athletes who might make the varsity team later.

Use a student survey to determine student interests and to establish the magnitude of those interests. Surveys can be conducted by homeroom teachers and returned when they are completed. A compilation of results is posted so that students can clearly see that the activities offered are a result of their expressed interests. The survey is a strong tool when bargaining with the administration for program facilities and equipment. When principals

Dynamic Physical Education for Secondary School Students

understand that many students desire certain activities, the physical educator has some leverage to gain program support. Figure 13.1 is a sample of the type of survey that could be administered. The survey will also indicate to students the number and variety of activities that can be offered. After a survey has been administered and

compiled, information about desired activities, times to offer the program, and qualified supervisors are identified. A program that matches student interests is easier to develop if a diagnostic instrument like the one in figure 13.1 is administered.

HIGH SCHOOL INTRAMURAL

Name _____ Date _____

1. Would you participate in the intramural program if activities were offered that interest you?

   Yes _____   No _____   If no, why not?

2. What do you like most about the present intramural program?

3. What do you like least about the present intramural program?

4. If you choose not to participate, would you be willing to help in the program in other roles? Check those ways in which you could offer your aid.

   Officiating _____   Publicity _____   Secretarial _____   Scorekeeping _____   Other (identify) _____

5. A program can emphasize competition, recreation, or a combination of both. Which would you desire?

   Competition _____   Recreation _____   Both _____

6. What days and what time of the day would be best for your participation?

Day	Time
Monday	_____ _____
Tuesday	_____ _____
Wednesday	_____ _____
Thursday	_____ _____
Friday	_____ _____
Saturday	_____ _____

7. Should awards be given to winning participants?

   Yes _____   No _____   Please justify your answer.

8. Please list any other points that would make the program better suit your needs.

9. The following is a list of activities that might be offered. Please circle five activities that you would most like to be offered in the intramural program. If an activity that you want is not offered, please write it in the blank at the end of the form.

Archery	Billiards	Cross country	Flickerball
Badminton	Bowling	Darts	Floor hockey
Bait and fly casting	Box hockey	Decathlon	Disc golf
Basketball	Cards	Deck tennis	Golf
One on one	Checkers	Fencing	Driving
Two on two	Chess	Field hockey	Putting
Other	Cooperative games	Figure skating	Gymnastics
Free-throw shooting	Croquet	Flag football	Handball

FIGURE 13.1 Sample high school intramural survey.

(continued)

306

Horseshoes	Riflery	Steeplechase	Water polo
Ice hockey	Roller hockey	Swimming	Weightlifting
Judo	Roller skating	Table tennis	Wrestling
Kite flying	Shuffleboard	Tennis	
Lacrosse	Skiing	Tetherball	
Lawn bowling	Soccer	Track and field	
Marbles	Softball	Tumbling	
New games	Fast pitch	Volleyball	
Orienteering	Slow pitch	Two player	
Paddle tennis	One pitch	Volley tennis	
Relays	Speed-a-way	Water basketball	

Others _____

10. Do you know any experts who could teach and help organize any of the activities designated above? If so, please describe how they can be contacted.

FIGURE 13.1 *(continued)*

Leadership

Leadership of an intramural program is a joint obligation. School districts should fund personnel to supervise the program and minimize liability problems. Whoever is in charge should recognize that other teachers and staff in the building who want to help may need guidance on the issues related to administering an effective intramural program. Additionally, some staff may have specific hobbies that they would be willing to direct as part of the program. Students also have a responsibility to organize committees and to implement a successful program. They should develop the policies, rules, and procedures that guide the program.

An effective way to ensure student input and energy for implementing the intramural program is to develop an intramural council. The council consists of 6 to 10 students, balanced by gender and grade level. This group makes the final decisions about the wide-ranging aspects of the program. Committees of productive students who report to the council are developed and maintained. Some of the following committees might be organized to serve the intramural council.

- Activity development. The activity development committee is responsible for selecting intramural activities, largely based on the student interest surveys, as well as securing facilities, equipment, and personnel necessary for implementation.

- Rules and regulations. The rules and regulations committee develops guidelines for administering the program. This committee is also the enforcement body when rule infractions occur.

- Scheduling and statistics. The scheduling and statistics committee schedules games and contests, maintains school intramural records and league standings, and oversees other related matters.

- Referees. The officiating committee recruits referees, trains them, and interprets and makes rulings dealing with protests.

- Public relations. The public relations committee develops materials for promoting the program, seeks funding from private organizations, and sponsors car washes, raffles, and other fund-raising activities.

- Safety. The safety committee develops an approved list of procedures for first aid and emergency situations, and provides a trained student capable of administering first aid who can be present at activities.

- Participation. One of the primary roles for leadership in any intramural program is developing the standards for participation. Although the rules committee will be charged with enforcing the rules of the program, the leader of the program determines minimum qualifications for

13

participation. Some schools use criteria such as grade point averages or student status in regard to school discipline or attendance as criteria for participation. The program should reflect the values of the school but should not make participation criteria so difficult that a majority of students are excluded. Keep in mind that using grades as a criterion for participation may exclude some of the students who need physical activity the most. An effective intramural leader will find the right balance between punitive restrictions and unlimited participation.

The formation of the student intramural council should not supersede the need for qualified adult personnel, and the school district should be willing to hire adequate help. Without district funding, administrative commitment to the program is usually limited, which ultimately leads to program failure.

Motivating Students to Participate

Many methods are available for promoting intramural programs and encouraging participation. Regardless of the method used, students must see the benefits of participating if the program is to work. The program must exude a spirit and be an "in" thing to do. Some of the following suggestions have been used with success in varying situations and can be modified to meet the needs of a particular school.

- Intramural bulletin board. Bulletin boards, located throughout the school, display schedules, standings, and future activities. Photos of participants can be posted and labeled.
- Patches or other tokens. Winners or all participants (depending on the competitive versus recreational nature of the program) are awarded arm patches with a school designation, the year, and activity. Several schools have school money (e.g., Bronco Bucks) that can be given to students to buy school supplies from the school store. Some successful programs have awarded patches or other tokens for participating in a certain number of activities regardless of whether the participant won or lost.
- T-shirts. T-shirts can be given to winners or participants. The school can hold a T-shirt day when teachers and participants wear their shirts to school.
- Point-total chart. Points are given for winning first, second, third, or fourth place in an activity,

or points can be awarded to the class with the highest participation rate. The points may be awarded to homeroom teams or on an individual basis. The point-total chart keeps a running tally throughout the year. These students or classes can be recognized at a school assembly.

- Trophies. Trophies are awarded to homerooms based on point totals at the end of the school year. An excellent idea is to award an outstanding participant trophy to those who earned the most participant points.
- Newspaper reports or morning announcements. Newspaper articles written by students can be placed in the school or local newspaper. Articles motivate best when they explicitly name students. Specific student information can be presented over the school system in the morning announcements.
- Field trips. Field trips are awarded to all participants at the end of the activity. For instance, at the end of the basketball tournament, all participants might attend a college or professional game together.
- Extramural competition. A play-day activity can be organized between one or more schools that have similar activities. The participants meet at one school on a Saturday and compete against each other. These students are nonathletes; the play day provides an opportunity for them to compete in a setting similar to athletic competition.
- Committee acknowledgment. Volunteers who serve on the various committees for the program are rewarded with the recognition they deserve. Student participants will be more likely to serve on committees if they feel appreciated for doing so.

Two schools of thought are involved in promoting intramural programs. One awards notoriety and trophies to winners, whereas the other offers awards and equal publicity to all participants. A case can be made for both approaches. A consideration is that winners already receive reinforcement, but those of lesser accomplishment may need additional positive strokes to ensure equal publicity for all students in the program.

Facilities and Equipment

Without proper facilities and equipment, an intramural program has little chance for success. A major problem is the conflict between athletics and intramurals. Much time and money has been poured into athletic programs, and athletics often take priority in terms of facility use. At best, the programs should compromise on the use of facilities at opportune times, such as during the final game of the intramural tournament. One point to make is that intramurals have the propensity to affect many more students than athletics do, so they should be provided with ample time to use facilities and equipment.

Another way to work through the facility problem is to schedule program activities out of season. For example, scheduling intramural basketball programs in the fall or spring would alleviate the conflict. Alternatively, intramural activities can be scheduled during low-demand times such as before school, during the noon hour, and later in the evening. Community facilities, such as churches, the YMCA or YWCA, and city park and recreation areas, can be used at times to increase the number of participants who can be accommodated, particularly if those facilities are located near the school. Scheduling becomes paramount in ensuring that facilities will be available. The scheduling committee should work with the athletic director and staging director to avoid conflicts.

The school district should provide equipment for intramurals. Some successful programs have been funded by student activities, such as car washes or raffles, but in general, when the district chooses not to give fund-

ing, the program is held in low esteem. If the program involves private facilities, such as bowling alleys, golf courses, and skating rinks, club members usually receive reduced rates. Having an equipment committee to determine how and when money will be spent is effective. The committee is responsible for maintaining and repairing equipment. The school provides a storage area for intramural equipment used solely by intramurals. A conflict usually occurs when physical education program equipment is used for the intramural program. When equipment is lost or damaged, hard feelings or loss of program support may result.

Officials

Critical to the success of any athletic endeavor is the quality of the officiating. The intramural program should be officiated by students. Chapter 2 discussed incorporating student roles of officiating in the sport education model. Thinking that teachers will be willing to work all games is unrealistic. A sound approach is to develop an officiating committee that is responsible for acquiring and training officials. Many students who do not play competitively are willing to officiate and enjoy being an integral part of an event. An alternative is to have students call their own games or events.

Students should be recruited as soon as possible so that they can acquire experience and work confidently

13

Extramural competitions can increase the appeal of an intramural program.

with experienced officials. They should be trained in rules and game mechanics before a tournament and be allowed to practice with as little pressure as possible. The word of the officials is absolute. Disagreements are filed and resolved through proper protest channels.

Scheduling officials and ensuring that they make their assignments is crucial. An organized plan needs to be implemented. A master chart should be posted where student officials can initial to verify that they have accepted the assignment for the game.

Officials can be given points for the number of games they work; they can also be awarded patches, T-shirts, and trophies for their accomplishments in a fashion similar to participants. Without some recognition, students will have little motivation for carrying out the thankless obligations of officiating.

Equating Competition

All participants need to know they have an opportunity to succeed in the intramural setting. Students fail to participate if they foresee a constant diet of losing or other negative experiences. Grouping by ability has both advantages and disadvantages. Having skilled and unskilled players together can be awkward when the activity demands a great deal of progression and skill performance. In those cases, having similarly skilled students play together and compete against teams of similar ability is probably better. But placing less skilled athletes with skilled athletes may improve the performance level of the unskilled students and enhance their confidence. This method also provides opportunities for skilled students to aid the less skilled.

When grouping for teams, try the following methods. Allow students to choose competition levels. Provide the opportunity for both recreation and competitive games so that students can choose the intensity at which they would like to participate. By allowing students to choose their level of competition, they will be more likely to choose one that is comfortable to them. In addition, students will experience less embarrassment when they are not placed in a game in which the other participants do not match their ability level.

Homerooms can compete against homerooms. This method of grouping is the most heterogeneous. Students of varying skill levels will then play on the same team. Grouping by homeroom may be effective if homeroom assignments are random. Another method is to use divisions of competition. Depending on the activity, students are grouped by ability, size, or age. Homerooms could sponsor two or more teams of different ability that

play in different leagues. The advantage of homeroom sponsorship lies in the camaraderie developed among students and the possibility of enhancing the classroom relationships. Probably the best solution is to equalize the competition regardless of homeroom assignments or other segregating factors. Choosing teams that are somewhat equal can be done in the following ways:

- Leaders are elected by the students. The leaders then choose teams in a private session held away from the rest of the participants. To further strengthen the idea of fair play, leaders might even choose teams without knowing which team they will be on. In so doing, leaders will ensure that each team is equally strong.
- Students are arranged by height or weight. The names of students within a certain range are put in one box, and those of a different range of heights or weights are placed in another box. Teams are then selected by drawing the names of an equal number of students of similar size for each team.

Whatever method is used to form teams, be sensitive to maintaining a balance of competition and preventing embarrassing situations. Teams should never be selected in such a fashion that the poorest player is chosen last. The intramural experience should be a positive experience that all students anticipate it with enthusiasm. If the program is to succeed, participants are needed and all should be treated as important and meaningful people.

Tournaments

A variety of tournaments can be organized to carry out the intramural program. The type will depend on the number of entries; the number of sessions or days the tournament will continue; the facilities and equipment available; and the number of officials, scorers, and other helpers on hand. The following types of tournaments are often used with success.

Round-Robin Tournament

The round-robin tournament is a good choice when adequate time is available for play. In this type of tournament, every team or individual plays every other team or individual once. Final standings are based on win–loss percentages. To determine the amount of time the tournament will take, the following formula can be used:

$$TI (TI - 1)/2$$

where TI = number of teams or individuals.

For example, if there are five teams in a softball unit, 5 (5 – 1)/2 = 10 games are to be scheduled.

To arrange a tournament for an odd number of teams, each team should be assigned a number. (Number the teams down the right column and up the left column.) All numbers rotate, and the last number each time draws a bye. The team not playing at the time can serve as officials or referees, scorekeepers, and managers. An example using seven teams follows:

Round 1	Round 5
7	3 (assign duties to these teams)
6—1	2—4
5—2	1—5
4—3	7—6

Round 2	Round 6
6	2 (assign duties to these teams)
5—7	1—3
4—1	7—4
3—2	6—5

Round 3	Round 7
5	1 (assign duties to these teams)
4—6	7—2
3—7	6—3
2—1	5—4

Round 4
4 (assign duties to these teams)
3—5
2—6
1—7

To arrange a tournament for an even number of teams, the plan is similar except that the position of team 1 remains stationary and the other teams revolve around it until the combinations are completed. No byes occur in this plan. An example of an eight-team tournament follows.

Round 1	Round 5
1—2	1—5
8—3	4—6
7—4	3—7
6—5	2—8

Round 2	Round 6
1—8	1—4
7—2	3—5
6—3	2—6
5—4	8—7

Round 3	Round 7
1—7	1—3
6—8	2—4
5—2	8—5
4—3	7—6

Round 4
1—6
5—7
4—8
3—2

Ladder Tournament

A ladder format is used for an ongoing tournament administered by a teacher or informally by students. Teams are ranked, and competition occurs by challenging a higher ranked opponent. Supervision is minimal. Various arrangements are possible, but participants usually challenge only those opponents who are two steps above their current ranking. If the challenger wins, that person or team changes places with the loser. The teacher can establish an initial ranking, or positions can be drawn from a hat.

Pyramid Tournament

A pyramid tournament is like a ladder tournament, but more challenge and variety are possible because a wider choice of opponents is available (see figure 13.2). In the pyramid tournament, any player can challenge any opponent one level above his or her present ranking. In another variation, a player must challenge someone at his or her level and beat that person before he or she can challenge a person at a higher level.

Elimination Tournament

The disadvantage of the elimination tournament is that poorer teams are eliminated first and do not get to play as many games as more proficient teams. The skilled thus get better, and less skilled students sit out without an opportunity to improve. The advantage of the elimination tournament is that it can be completed in less time than, for example, a round-robin tournament. Double-elimination tournaments are somewhat better than single-elimination events because a team must lose twice before being relegated to the sidelines. Students come to intramurals to play rather than sit on the side and watch others play. Figure 13.3 is an example of a simple single-elimination tournament with six teams. An alternative to a true elimination tournament is to place the teams who have lost in a round-robin tournament.

13

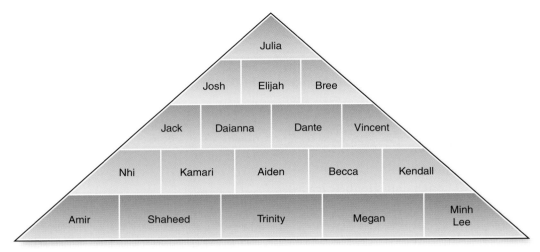

FIGURE 13.2 Pyramid tournament chart.

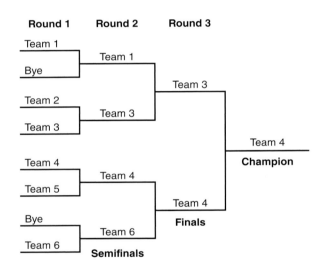

FIGURE 13.3 Sample single-elimination tournament chart.

Physical Activity Programs

Physical activity programs are filled with students bonded by their common interest in some sport or activity. The concept originated in Europe and has become more common in the United States, largely because of the inability of school districts to fund a wide variety of activities. The programs are for students, run by students, and often funded by the students. They offer young people the chance to organize and participate in a club that meets the specific needs of a group and the opportunity to socialize with friends.

Developing a Physical Activity Program Network

Physical activity program are often administered by guidelines set by the intramural director in a school district. The clubs can be an outgrowth of either the intramural or athletic program. The types of physical activity programs to be offered are usually dictated by students, although a teacher or staff member in the building who has a particular interest or hobby may want to host a program. The following steps are typical of a system for developing a physical activity program network in the school setting.

1. *Determine the interests of students.* A survey instrument (see figure 13.1) is used to determine student interests in and concerns for physical activity programs. Developing one or two clubs first is a good way to demonstrate the effectiveness of this approach to the district administrators.

2. *Meet with interested students.* Before meeting with students, find a faculty member or some other person to serve as the program's advisor. Oftentimes, the advisor has a keen interest in the area and at least some expertise. For example, appointing someone as an advisor to the backpacking program is foolish if he or she has never backpacked. The first meeting should include a discussion of the dues necessary for conducting activities. If the cost is prohibitive, many students may choose not to participate. Students should also discuss the joys and dangers of participating in the activity. Discuss school guidelines for programs so that students understand the parameters involved.

3. *Develop a constitution.* After the initial meeting, interested students meet again to develop a constitution. This document delineates membership requirements, the function and selection of officers, and meeting dates. An outline form can be used to aid in the development of similar program constitutions.

4. *Establish rules and regulations.* Programs need to determine the scope of their organization and the requirements of members to retain active membership. If competition is involved, travel funding and housing requirements are explicitly outlined. The need for adult chaperones and drivers and the need for a waiver of responsibility signed by parents are vital parts of the rules. The basic premise of rules is to eliminate misunderstandings and to encourage a safe, liability-free club setting.

5. *Seek funding, facilities, and equipment.* With the help of the advisor, students should determine what facilities and equipment are available and when they can be scheduled. Seeking outside funding from private organizations and service clubs is important. In some cases, school time may be given for clubs to conduct meeting and planning sessions. Appropriate facilities such as bowling alleys or swimming pools need to be contacted to see if one or two hours per week can be reserved for activities.

6. *Organize participation and competition.* After facilities, equipment, and participants have been determined, a participation event will need to be organized. The event, whether intramural or extramural, should be carefully planned to provide the participants a rich and rewarding experience.

7. *Conduct a periodic evaluation.* Programs should be evaluated on a regular basis to see whether interest is waning, whether the needs of students are being met, and whether the manner of conduct needs to be modified. When programs are developed based on the interests of students, that interest can sometimes decrease to such an extent that the program should be discontinued. New student interests may develop and result in new programs. A periodic evaluation can result in a new club advisor, better ways to facilitate program goals, or an attempt to stimulate renewed interest in the program.

Implementing an Out-of-School Physical Activity Program

The following areas should be considered when developing a physical activity program that occurs beyond the school day. School district personnel need to be aware of these points if a successful program is to be implemented.

Liability

Students who participate in the program should have liability insurance. Depending on the activity, regular school insurance may cover the student during participation. But if the activity is exceptionally risky (e.g., skiing or rugby), supplementary insurance is usually needed. Parents must certify that the student is covered by their insurance policy if students choose not to purchase insurance offered by the district's carrier.

A signed parental responsibility waiver form is necessary for participation in activities. Although the form does not waive the student's right to sue and seek redress, a signed form communicates to the school district that the parents approve and are aware of their student's participation in the program.

Instructors and advisors to the program must be competent to administer the activity. If the school district advisor lacks proper training, experts outside the school should be secured. These experts may be parents or interested community volunteers. In most cases, the responsibility for supplying a safe environment falls on the school district.

Procedures for handling injuries are important and may involve having a physician on call. Written procedures should be available and understood by all program members in case an accident occurs. For example, what steps will be taken if someone is injured on a backpacking trip? Accidents do happen, and fewer problems occur if proper emergency procedures are in place for such an occurrence.

Budget

Ideally, the school district funds physical activity programs. In some cases, student fees are assessed at the start of the school year and distributed on an equal basis to all clubs. This money provides a financial foundation, but almost all programs require additional funding. The most common methods used are car washes, rummage sales, sales of old and outdated equipment, and donations. When travel and lodging are necessary, students are usually expected to absorb the cost. School districts often provide a bus if the activity is scheduled when buses are available. Travel by private car is the least acceptable

13

method of transport because of the possibility of an accident and subsequent liability problems.

Many programs have an equipment bank where equipment is stored for use year after year. An adequate source of equipment is developed over a period of years. Used equipment from local colleges and high school athletic programs can sometimes be secured to augment the equipment bank.

Coaching

Qualified coaches and other school-affiliated advisors are usually involved in administration of the athletic and intramural programs. Therefore, program advisors and coaches may have to be selected from the community. The school district should undertake some type of screening to see that the advisors are properly qualified. The programs must be conducted at a time when those people are available; many potential advisors are working during the school day. If the activity is recreational in nature, interested parents may carry out the supervisory responsibilities. All adults involved should be approved by the school district and required to sign a form agreeing to abide by district policies.

Facilities

Facilities usually must be scheduled at low-use times. Physical activity programs are often last in line for facilities, after the athletic and intramural programs. Facilities need to be found in the community if the clubs involve sports offered interscholastically. For example, city parks have softball fields that can be used. Some school districts choose not to approve programs dealing with sports offered at the intramural and interscholastic level. The philosophy behind this ruling is that activities should offer opportunities not available through other avenues. If that is the case, then most programs will be conducted in facilities such as bowling alleys, swimming pools, ski areas, skating rinks, riflery and archery ranges, and racquetball clubs.

Achievement Clubs

Many of the activities suggested in the intramurals section for motivating students can be used with program activities. In addition, some programs can be formed for which students are eligible only after they have met predetermined standards of achievement. Examples might be a jogging group, bike-riding program, distance swimming program, and weightlifting group. In each case, students join the program and are a part of the group only after they have met the minimum standards.

Interscholastic Athletics

The interscholastic athletic program usually stands at the top of the pyramid in terms of attention, time, and money focused on the program. Sports in the school setting should contribute to the educational purposes of the institution. Arguments abound about whether the athletic program is a negative or positive influence on students. Athletics are not inherently good or bad; the way in which the athletic program is conducted makes it a positive or negative experience for participants. Students can certainly have a positive experience through a competitive sports program (Siedentop & van der Mars, 2012).

Values of an Athletic Program

A strong athletic program can develop a sense of belonging among the participants. Students like to see what they can accomplish by themselves and with the help of peers. Team sports teach them that they can reach goals only if teammates are willing to cooperate. It quickly becomes apparent that cooperation precedes competition. Conducting a competitive game is impossible when teammates do not cooperate and follow the established rules.

Athletics teach students that the journey is more important than the destination, that the process is more important than the product. The work done to reach a goal is the essence of an athletic experience, and students learn that after the victory or defeat, continued hard work is still necessary. This lesson may carry over to adult life and help the participant continue to succeed.

Athletics give students something to talk about and something to do. Many of the problems of youth arise because of boredom and having little to do when the school day is over. Athletics give status to participants and make them feel important. The program allows students to share their positive accomplishments with others and appreciate the accomplishments of friends.

The athletic program serves as a laboratory for gifted students. It offers students a chance to perfect their skills to a high level with the aid of a knowledgeable coach. Students who are athletically gifted are appreciated and rewarded for their accomplishments. The athletic program brings a community of people together for a common cause. Parents and business people develop pride in their communities and find a common ground for communication. The athletic team can be a unifying factor that brings together people of all backgrounds.

Participation in athletics can teach students how to

maintain a high level of physical fitness and to care for their bodies. They learn about the need for self-discipline when attempting to reach a goal. The importance of making sacrifices, following training rules, and practicing regularly become an attitudinal set of the participants. Students must practice sportsmanship and self-control if they are to find success. Rules and regulations become an integral part of sport participation and illustrate to students the importance of following predetermined rules. Students learn they are penalized when they break rules, and those unwilling to cooperate are seldom welcome to participate. Finally, the athletic program shows students how highly regarded and important excellence is to people. Athletics should try to embody excellence and the Olympic ideal. Students set goals and make sacrifices to achieve excellence without any guarantee of success. Participating is athletics should be a privilege to students, not a right. Therefore, students must maintain certain standards, determined by administrators, coaches, and staff at the school, if they want to be a member of the team. These standards may include grades and behavior in and out of school.

Detrimental Aspects of an Athletic Program

The athletic program mobilizes large amounts of time, energy, and money to aid a relatively small number of participants. The exclusionary nature of athletics leads to neglect of less skilled performers. In contrast, an athlete who receives special attention can develop the attitude that athletes are better than others and are eligible for personal favors and special attention. Student-athletes may develop a value set that is detrimental when their playing days are over.

Participation in athletic programs often interrupts the educational environment. Athletes leave school to go on trips or receive released time to practice during a final-period physical education class. The athlete may begin to believe that being a successful athlete is more important than being a good citizen in the community and a competent student. Another possible effect of the athletic program is a loss of personal identity. Athletes are told when to eat, when to practice, when they can have free time, and when to study. They may soon begin to wonder

A school's athletic program can bring communities together.

if they can make any important decisions for themselves and whether they have the right to live their own lives.

The pressures of coaching are apparent to all who have filled a head coaching position in a major sport. This pressure is often unjust and can lead to unacceptable coaching behavior. Athletic coaching is a good example of holding an individual accountable for the result (winning) regardless of how that individual reaches the goal. When this situation occurs, students may suffer from the coach's lack of concern about personal problems and injuries. Until the process and product of coaching receive equal emphasis, the athletic setting will be less than a positive and developmental experience (Steinberg, Singer, & Murphy, 1999).

At times, parents and community members can become so deeply involved in the athletic program that they apply pressure on students to win at all costs. Student-athletes begin to feel that if they do not win, they will not be accepted as an integral part of the community. The athletic program then becomes an incessant effort on the part of students to achieve the adults' goals. In these situations, adults forget that the athletic program was developed to contribute to the students' personal growth. When the program becomes an adult program with adult goals, students cannot separate what is important from what is not. Other concerns for athletes are injury and burnout. All participants assume the risk of injury through involvement. If the desire to win exceeds the desire to provide a safe environment, then some students may be ordered to play with an injury or may receive injuries caused by lack of proper care and treatment. Concern for the health of participants is the paramount program goal. Overemphasizing the importance of sports participation also leads to burnout, which defeats the overarching purpose of physical education and other programs related to physical activity engagement.

Developing a Quality Athletic Program

Depending on how it is organized and presented, an athletic program can be a positive or negative experience for students. The following guidelines, if heeded, help ensure meaningful experiences for participants. All districts must interpret the guidelines based on their specific situations, but a program is not likely to be worthwhile if districts deviate from the guidelines to a large degree.

1. *The athletic program should be voluntary.* All students who choose to participate should have an opportunity to compete. All athletes should have the opportunity to play if they have practiced and disciplined themselves. Cutting players from a squad is an accepted practice, but players should be able to compete in another arena, which may be a junior varsity, C squad, or strong intramural or physical activity club program. If athletics is regarded as an educational experience, all students have the right to receive that experience.

2. *The program should be based on the maturation level of participants.* This point is particularly important at the middle school level because these students exhibit a wide range of development. Grouping by age, ability, or size may be necessary if the program is to be meaningful.

3. *The athletic program should be an out-of-school program.* The practice of giving a period of school time for practice is discriminatory and runs counter to the established rule that an academic education is the school's priority. Along the same lines, excusing athletes from physical education is difficult to justify. If the program is educational, then all students, regardless of background, should benefit from it.

4. *The athletic program should offer a broad spectrum of activities for participants.* The fewer activities offered, the fewer the participants. The program should also be balanced in offering activities to all groups—skilled and unskilled, boys and girls, able-bodied students and those with disabilities.

5. *Organization of the athletic program should meet the needs of students.* The concerns of the spectators should be met only after the program has been developed. Many sports are dropped because they do not draw large numbers of spectators or make money. If this trend continues, football and basketball might represent the total athletic program.

6. *All participants should be certified as medically healthy by a physician.* The program should be evaluated regularly in terms of safety practices to ensure that proper procedures are conducted.

7. *Procedures to be followed after an accident must be written, posted, and sent to parents.* Most districts ask that parents sign a waiver of responsibility form before a student can participate. This is an opportune time to explain the safety and first-aid procedures being followed. Insurance for all participants is necessary. Many states (e.g., New York) have specific guidelines and requirements such as having an automated external defibrillator (AED) on site for all athletic contests.

8. *The program should emphasize enjoyment and participation.* As idealistic as this may sound to many coaches, skill development and a positive experience are benefits that students can take with them after graduation. People might well question what has been gained if students win most of their games but lose the desire to participate in sports after they leave school.

9. *Physical conditioning should be an important phase of the program.* Preconditioning is essential to the safety and welfare of players and should precede intense, early-season practice sessions.

10. *Facilities should be shared by all facets of the athletic, intramural, and physical activity club programs.* Athletics are understandably expected to take priority, but someone needs to direct the situation so that all programs are given acceptable use of the facilities and equipment.

11. *Awards, trophies, and other incentives used to identify outstanding achievement should be minimized.* Excellence can be rewarded, but with proper discretion. If an excessive number of awards are given, they become meaningless.

12. *The athletic program should be constantly evaluated.* In some cases, the program is seldom scrutinized until an infraction occurs. Periodic evaluations by the athletic director, principal, and coaching staff can aid in preventing problems. Evaluation can serve to improve offerings for both boys and girls, upgrade scheduling efficiency, and show the need for in-service training.

Athletic Council

To help ensure that a quality athletic program is maintained, many school districts organize an athletic council. The council is a districtwide body composed of the superintendent (or a representative), principals, the athletic director for the district, coaches from each school, and student representatives from each school. All schools, sports, and genders should be equally represented.

The athletic council plans and evaluates the total district program and deals with issues such as finances, facilities, and personnel. The council promotes the athletic program and serves as a screening body when outside parties become involved. This body is responsible for evaluating coaches and hearing grievances. Sometimes, for example, parents have a concern but are hesitant to approach the coach involved. The council

hears such cases confidentially without revealing the plaintiff's identity. The council can enhance the image of the coaching community. It can be a place where coaches work together to achieve the highest ideals and reach common goals. In summary, the council should be an asset for coaches, administrators, and athletes.

Securing Qualified Coaches

Qualified coaches are the cornerstone of a sound athletic program. Most coaches are highly motivated and dedicated. In most cases, they are motivated by their enjoyment of sport rather than the financial remuneration, because coaching is not a highly paid profession. An athletic director recently calculated that assistant coaches were receiving about 50 cents per hour. Most coaches enter the profession because they were successful athletes and found positive experiences in the athletic program, but being an outstanding athlete seldom guarantees success in coaching. Coaches need to have a wide range of abilities. The following attributes are characteristics of successful coaches:

- *Display strong character.* The coach should be a model for athletes to emulate. How the coach relates to others, how she or he maintains personal fitness, and whether she or he displays honesty, integrity, and other personal qualities often teach students more about athletics than the actual participation experience (Alberts, 2003). Many administrators find cause for concern when coaches swear, drink, or smoke excessively, and most students cannot deal with the double standard of a coach who advocates team fitness but does not practice fitness, who tells them to be respectful but yells when a mistake is made, and who preaches honesty but shows them how to foul without being caught. Many athletes remember their coach much longer than they remember the actual playing experience. The coach should be remembered for positive experiences.

- *Have knowledge of growth and development patterns.* The coach must have a strong background in motor development and motor learning. Understanding the physical limits of athletes is as important as understanding their capabilities under pressure. The coach should also have some knowledge of psychology and the emotional development of secondary-level students. Knowing when to reinforce, when to scold, and when to praise are key components of a successful coaching career.

13

- *Have knowledge of the activity.* Coaches should know the fundamentals of the sport they are coaching and the best ways to present and teach the basic skills. A good coach understands strategy and knows when to use various types of game plans. The coach must be an excellent teacher, and in many cases, the best coaches are regarded as the best teachers. Concurrent with knowledge of the sport is the ability to plan carefully. Both teaching and coaching demand a high degree of planning to succeed. Like effective physical educators, effective coaches always attempt to account for every minute of practice time to minimize idle or wasted time.

Coaching Certification

The need for certification in the coaching profession is substantial. Many still believe that anyone can coach—regardless of background or training. Unfortunately, almost anyone can find the opportunity to coach because of the lack of certification requirements and standards. Each state sets the specific requirements for coaches within the schools in that state. Some states have an age requirement only, whereas others require a teaching certificate or a specific coaching education program, such as the American Sport Education Program, which is available through Human Kinetics (Martens, 2012).

Training of Coaches

Training in many areas is necessary for coaches to be productive and motivating. A National Association for Sport and Physical Education (NASPE) task force of the American Alliance for Health, Physical Education, Recreation and Dance (AAHPERD) developed a resource text on coaching standards called *Quality Coaches, Quality Sports: National Standards for Sport Coaches* (2006). The task force identified 40 standards in the following

eight domains:

Philosophy and ethics

Safety and injury prevention

Growth and development

Physical conditioning

Organization and administration

Sport skills, tactics, and strategies

Teaching and communication

Evaluation

Coaching is a weighty responsibility, and regardless of certification, coaches should seek the best possible training.

Teaching–Coaching Role Conflict

A personal conflict often occurs when teachers choose to coach. Particularly in physical education, a teacher required to coach long hours has a difficult task. Many physical education instructors are hired not for their expertise in teaching but for their ability to coach more than one sport. This policy can result in teaching takes second place to coaching, and most of the teacher's planning and energy is dedicated to the coaching assignment.

Teachers who also coach often end up working 10- to 12-hour days. The pay is low, but the rewards can be great. Coaching ability is scrutinized regularly in terms of the won–loss record, and teachers may become caught up in the pressure of trying to be winning coaches for fear of losing their positions. In this situation, only a strong and gifted person can place equal emphasis on teaching and coaching. Physical educators should not lose sight of the fact that about 90% of their salary comes from teaching and the remaining 10% from coaching. Many more students are affected by the outstanding teacher than by the effective coach. The ability to perform well in both roles is a difficult challenge, particularly when most contingencies apply to the coaching role (Darst & Pangrazi, 1996).

LEARNING AIDS

STUDY STIMULATORS AND REVIEW QUESTIONS

1. Outline the components of a total physical education program and explain which types of students each serves.
2. Discuss the importance of advocating for intramural, physical activity club, and out-of-class physical activity programs for students during or beyond the school day.
3. Explain why an intramural program that offers both recreational and competitive opportunities has greater appeal to the student population.
4. Discuss the importance of having students dictate the direction and focus of the intramural program.
5. Defend an intramural program about to be eliminated because of a district budget crisis.
6. Construct a round-robin tournament with 10 teams.
7. What are the differences between an intramural program, a physical activity club, and an out-of-class physical activity program?
8. Explain why a school is less likely to have a basketball club than a bowling club.
9. Discuss the possible values and detrimental effects of an interscholastic athletic program.
10. Why do secondary teachers often experience the teaching–coaching role conflict?

WEBSITES

American Sport Education Program

www.asep.com

Character Counts!

www.charactercounts.org

National Alliance for Youth Sports!

www.nays.org

National Association of Sports Officials

www.naso.org

National Federation of State High School Associations

www.nfhs.org

Positive Coaching Alliance

www.positivecoach.org

McREL International

www.mcrel.org

13

REFERENCES AND SUGGESTED READINGS

Alberts, C. (2003). *Coaching issues & dilemmas: Character building through sport participation.* Reston, VA: NASPE.

Beighle, A., Erwin, H., Castelli, D., & Ernst, M. (2009). Preparing physical educators for the role of physical activity director. *Journal of Physical Education, Recreation and Dance, 80*(4), 24–28.

Brewer, J.D., Luebbers, P.E., & Shane, S.D. (2009). Increasing student physical activity during the school day: Opportunities for the physical educator. *Strategies, 22*(3), 20–23.

Bucher, C., & Krotee, M. (2002). *Management of physical education and sport.* Boston, MA: McGraw-Hill.

Carr, G. (2004). *Sport mechanics for coaches* (2nd ed.). Champaign, IL: Human Kinetics.

Cassidy, T., Jones, R., & Potrac, P. (2004). *Understanding sports coaching.* New York, NY: Routledge.

Castelli, D.M., & Beighle, A. (2007). The physical education teacher as school activity director. *Journal of Physical Education, Recreation and Dance, 78*(5), 25–28.

Darst, P., & Pangrazi, R. (1996). The teaching/coaching challenge. *Teaching Secondary Physical Education, 2*(6), 4–5.

Faber, L., Hodges-Kulinna, P., & Darst, P.W., (2007). Strategies for physical activity promotion beyond the physical education classroom. *Journal of Physical Education, Recreation and Dance, 78*(9), 27–30.

Flegel, M. (2004). *Sport first aid* (3rd ed.). Champaign, IL: Human Kinetics.

Martens, R. (2012). *Successful coaching* (4th ed.). Champaign, IL: Human Kinetics.

McMullen, J. (2010) Experiences of PETE majors participating in an out-of-class-time physical activity promotion and facilitation-based internship course. Unpublished doctoral dissertation, Arizona State University.

National Association for Sport and Physical Education. (2006). *Quality coaches, quality sports: National standards for sport coaches* (2nd ed.). Reston, VA: AAHPERD.

National Association for Sport and Physical Education. (2002a). *Co-curricular physical activity and sport programs for middle school students.* Reston, VA: AAHPERD.

National Association for Sport and Physical Education. (2002b). *Guidelines for after school physical activity and intramural programs.* Reston, VA: AAHPERD.

National Intramural-Recreational Sports Association. (2004). Mission and bylaws. Retrieved from www.nirsa.org.

Sharkey, B., & Gaskill, S. (2006). *Sport physiology for coaches.* Champaign, IL: Human Kinetics.

Siedentop, D., & van der Mars, H. (2012). *Introduction to physical education, fitness, and sport* (8th ed.). Boston, MA: McGraw-Hill.

Steinberg, G.M., Singer, R.N., & Murphy, M. (1999). Lack of control in coaching: Potential complications and strategies to help coaches. *Journal of Physical Education, Recreation and Dance, 70*(8), 39–42.

Introductory Activities

This chapter provides rationale for using daily introductory activities for secondary school physical education and presents a variety of activity ideas that can be used to start each lesson. Introductory activities are vigorous in nature, consist primarily of gross locomotor movements, are not rigidly structured, and allow considerable freedom of movement. They are meant to engage students in physical activity quickly and serve as a psychological and physiological warm-up for the ensuing portion of the lesson. They are characterized by minimal instruction time and maximum movement time. Introductory activities should be selected with the interests, developmental levels, and physical abilities of the students in mind. Introductory activities can be novel and challenging. They can also allow students to be creative. In a 30-minute lesson, the introductory activity period generally lasts 2 or 3 minutes (or 6%–10% of the lesson as suggested by Pangrazi & Beighle, 2020) and emphasizes enthusiasm and motivation. A longer lesson might have a 5- to 10-minute introductory activity. Students should develop introductory activities that will be useful to them as a warm-up for activities they intend to pursue for a lifetime. As long as the activities are vigorous and emphasize large-muscle movement, they can be used in this part of the lesson.

Learning Objectives

▶ Discuss the objectives of introductory activities for secondary school physical education.
▶ Select appropriate introductory activities for students taking a specific unit of activity.
▶ Characterize the various features of the introductory phase of the lesson.
▶ Develop a new or modified introductory activity.

The beginning of the lesson is important in establishing the tone for the class period, which helps promote a successful experience for students and the teacher. Even though the introductory activity takes a small amount of time in the lesson, it supports a positive well-managed start. All students come to PE after a break. They have been talking with friends and want to continue chatting. Successful teachers get the class on board with them immediately by establishing move and freeze signals quickly; otherwise, chances are that the lesson and student behavior will go downhill from that point.

All lessons should start by having students enter the space with nothing more than a command to "jog around the area." When a signal is given, the class freezes in the ready position and stops talking. A good rule is to jog and freeze a class three times to reinforce attentive behavior. If the entire class is on task, then an enjoyable introductory activity is played as a reward to the class for being attentive and ready to learn. If the class is not attentive, then the best approach may be to skip the introductory activity and work on class management skills (see chapter 7). Allied to this approach is the fact that starting an inattentive class with an exciting introductory activity is unwise because doing so will only make the problem worse. By ensuring that the class is well managed and on task, you express your personal expectation that before students can enjoy class activities, all must be attentive and ready to participate properly.

Most students desire immediate activity when they arrive for class, and introductory activities meet this need. Introductory activities may be vigorous and incorporate large-muscle activity in their execution. An objective of introductory activities is to use movements basic to sport and leisure pursuits. When appropriate, explain how the activities apply to their personal activity interests. Introductory activities serve as a psychological and physiological warm-up for the rest of the lesson. Introductory activities should be selected with the interests and developmental levels of the students in mind. Middle school students, because of their rapid growth spurts, need activities that emphasize body control, coordination, and agility. High school students like to know how introductory activities are related to activities in which they have developed competency and interest.

To teach leadership skills, teachers can ask students to direct others with introductory activities they have learned previously. Alternatively, students can self-organize with supervision from the PE teacher. They need opportunities to lead and become independent thinkers. Inform the class of the goal and the desired outcome. Students can develop introductory activities suited to their needs. As long as the activities help students approach or reach their target heart rate and emphasize large-muscle movement, they can be used in this part of the lesson. Introductory activity may also place demands on the cardiorespiratory system, so they can be used as the fitness portion of the lesson in future classes. A large variety of introductory activities should be taught and presented to show students that many acceptable methods can be used to prepare for ensuing physical activity.

The introductory activities in this chapter are roughly grouped into the following categories:

- Agility activities—The activities in this group are designed to improve the aerobic power and agility of students. They are demanding and should be done in short bouts so that excessive fatigue does not become an issue. Emphasis is on quick feet and fast response to commands.

- Locomotor challenges—This set of activities gives students a variety of challenges while they perform sport movements that include but are not limited to sliding, leaping, jumping and hopping, and the grapevine step. Students should be encouraged to perform the sport movements in an athletic position.

- Individual activities—These activities have students performing individual challenges while they compete against other students. Students are encouraged to see how many times they can perform an activity.

- Partner and small-group activities—These cooperative activities require working with a partner or small group. These activities include a variety of tag games that can be played in small groups or as a single class. Some of the activities may excite a class, so you should use them only if you are able to get the attention of the class quickly when the activity is over.

Agility Activities

Seat Roll

Students begin on all fours with their heads up, looking at the instructor. When the teacher gives a left- or right-hand signal, students respond quickly by rolling in that direction on their seat. Seat rolls can be alternated with running in place or with rope jumping to increase the aerobic challenge.

Arkansas Flip

Students begin in the same position as the seat roll. They flip over to the left or right, without touching their seats to the floor, so that they are in a crab position (half flip). The flip should be a quick, continuous movement. Students can wait for the next signal in the crab position or, if the teacher designates, can continue over to an all-fours position with the head up (full flip).

Quarter Eagle

Students are in a ready position with the head up, arms flexed in front of the body, knees slightly bent, and feet straight ahead and shoulder-width apart. The instructor gives a hand signal left or right. The class responds by making a quarter jump turn in that direction and returning to the starting position as quickly as possible.

A variation involves having participants move on a verbal signal such as "Go." The students then make a quarter turn to the left or right and wait for the next signal. They continue to make quarter turns on each signal.

Wave Activity

In the wave activity, students are in ready position. They shuffle (without a crossover step) left, right, backward, or forward on signal. A useful variation is to place an obstacle (boundary cone) for students to shuffle over.

Variations

1. Same as the original except that students use a crossover step.
2. Same as the original except that students are on all fours.
3. Students are between two cones or bags and are running rapidly in place. On a hand signal to the left or right, the performer steps over the obstacle in the corresponding direction and moves the feet in place while waiting for the next signal.
4. Same as the previous variation except that students move left or right with both feet together (ski hop). Emphasis is on watching the signal and moving quickly.

Log Roll (Three-Person Roll)

Students are in groups of three to start the log roll. The instructor gives a signal left or right. The middle person does a roll (with the body extended) in that direction (see figure 14.1a), while the person on that side jumps up and over the top of the middle person (see figure 14.1b) and rolls toward the third person (see figure 14.1c), who jumps over the rolling person and rolls the other direction (see figure 14.1d). The activity continues with each

person rolling several times. The objective is to roll with the body straight, get up quickly, and not touch anybody while jumping over them.

FIGURE 14.1 Log roll.

Square Activity

The class forms several 10-yard (m) squares with boundary cones. Students stand in the middle of each side of the square and face the center. On signal, they shuffle around the square to the left or right, depending on the signal of the teacher. A student can be in the center of the square to give a direction signal.

Lateral Shuffle

Place two cones about 5 yards (m) apart. A student stands in the middle and shuffles quickly back and forth between the cones, touching the cone each time. Students try to make as many touches as possible in 15 seconds. Set up enough pairs of cones so that all students can participate simultaneously.

Rooster Hop Activity

Students hop 10 yards (m) on one leg in the following sequence: (1) left hand touching the right toe, which is on the ground; (2) right hand touching the left toe on the ground; (3) right hand touching the right toe on the ground; and (4) left hand touching the left toe on the ground (see figure 14.2). Students can be challenged to develop different combinations and tasks.

FIGURE 14.2   Rooster hop activity.

Weave Activity

The weave activity is like the wave activity except that students shuffle in and out of a series of obstacles such as cones, blocking dummies, or boards. They use a shuffling step rather than a crossover step.

Running Weave Activity

Students run through the maze of obstacles with a regular running stride. A stopwatch can be used to challenge students to improve their times, and the maze can be arranged in many ways. Let students set up the maze and time each other. Use the carioca (or grapevine) step as a variation.

Burpee-Flip Activity

The burpee-flip can be done in small groups or in unison with the entire class. The teacher calls out the number, and students yell the number while performing the movement. The sequence is as follows:

1. Standing position
2. Bend the knees, hands on the floor or ground
3. Legs kick back into an all-fours position, head up
4. Half flip right to a crab position
5. Half flip right to an all-fours position

This activity can also be done with a left flip or with two flips, one left and one right, and so forth. Let students try this activity with a small group. Challenge them to stay together and to continue enlarging the group. Participants must call the numbers for their group.

Another variation is to put in a push-up before the flip. Step 4 would be the down motion, and step 5 would be the up motion. Use caution to ensure that students are far enough apart in case one student flips the wrong way.

All-Fours Circle

Students lie on their bellies with heads close together and legs extended outward like the spokes of a wheel (see figure 14.3). One person starts by placing the hands in the center and moving around the circle over the other students without touching anyone. The last person who is passed is the next participant. The activity can be done with 4 to 12 people.

FIGURE 14.3   All-fours circle.

Coffee Grinder Square

With the coffee grinder square (see figure 14.4), students start at one corner of the square, run to the next corner, and perform a coffee grinder on the right arm (arm extended on the ground, supporting the body weight, while the feet walk 360 degrees around the arm). At the next corner, they put their left arms down and do another coffee grinder. This action continues through the four corners. The square should be marked with something flat, such as beanbags or spots. Students should move in the same direction around the square.

FIGURE 14.4 Coffee grinder square.

Flash Activity

To begin the flash activity, students stand in a ready position facing the teacher (see figure 14.5). The teacher says, "Feet," and students stutter the feet. The teacher then flashes the following hand signals:

1. Hands up: Students jump up and return to stuttering feet.

2. Hands down: Students touch the floor and return to stuttering feet.

3. Hands right: Students shuffle right with hands in defensive position.

4. Hands left: Students shuffle left with hands in defensive position.

5. Hands make a circle: Students do a forward roll and get up stuttering.

FIGURE 14.5 Flash activity.

Locomotor Challenges

The following activities can be done with locomotor movements such as sliding, carioca steps, power skipping, running, and jumping. The locomotor movement is then combined with a challenging activity used in sport such as a pivot, stop, or change of direction.

Move and Change Direction

Starting in scattered formation, students run in any direction and change direction on signal. The change in direction can be specified or student selected. If specified, the commands might be "Reverse, right angle, 45 degrees," or "Left turn." The change in direction should be made quickly in pivotlike fashion. This can also be done with levels or speeds.

Move and Change the Type of Locomotion

Students move using a specified locomotor movement. On signal, they change to another type of movement. Challenges can be given to do the movements forward, backward, sideways, or diagonally.

Move and Quickly Stop

Students move throughout the area and quickly stop under control. Emphasis should be placed on stopping in athletic position using proper technique. Students should lower the center of gravity, widen the base of support, and place one foot in front of the other to absorb the force.

Move and Perform Athletic Movement

Students move and stop on signal. They then perform an athletic skill move, such as a basketball jump shot, leaping football pass catch, volleyball spike, or soccer kick. Students should emphasize correct form and timing. A variation of the activity is for students to move with a partner and throw a pass on signal, punt a ball, or shoot a basket. The partner catches the ball or rebounds the shot.

Move, Stop, and Pivot

Students move under control throughout the area. On signal, they stop, pivot, and resume moving. Emphasis should be placed on making a sharp pivot and a rapid acceleration. The skill is like running a pass pattern in football.

14

Move and Perform a Fitness Task

The class moves throughout the area. When a signal is given, students perform a predesignated fitness task. Examples of tasks are push-ups, sit-ups, squat thrusts, and crab kicks. Variations of these tasks, such as push-ups with shoulder taps, push-ups with a hand wave, push-ups while high fiving with a partner, can also be included. The fitness tasks can be written on a card and flashed to the class to signal the next challenge.

Move and Perform a Stretch

The class is challenged to run throughout the area. On signal, students stop and perform a designated stretching activity for 10 to 30 seconds. (See chapter 15 for a comprehensive list of stretching exercises.) A list of stretches that covers all body parts can be posted so that students perform a different stretch after each signal. A motivational supplement to this introductory activity is interval music that plays for a certain time (e.g., 30 seconds) and goes silent for a certain time (e.g., 15 seconds). Students run while the music is on and perform the stretch led by the teacher during the silent time.

Individual Activities

Dribblerama

Students are divided into two groups, one on each half of the playing area. All students have a basketball or soccer ball. Everyone dribbles a ball on his or her own side. While dribbling, students try to knock the ball out of other students' control while maintaining control of their own basketball or soccer ball. If a student's ball is knocked away, that student retrieves it, moves to the other side, and continues playing there.

Number Challenges

Students are challenged to move and perform to a set of three to four numbers. For example, the given set of numbers might be 25, 10, and 30. The first number would signify some type of sport movement, the second number a set of stretching exercises, and the last an activity with equipment. Implemented, this challenge might be 25 running steps, 10 repetitions of a stretching activity, and 30 rope-jumping turns.

Four Corners

A square or rectangle is marked using four boundary cones. Students spread out around the perimeter of the square or rectangle. On signal, they move in the same direction around the perimeter. As they pass a corner,

they change the movement they are doing. On the short sides, some of the challenges would be to perform lunges, move in crab position, or creep forward using the measuring-worm technique (i.e., standing with legs straight, students reach down to touch toes and move out with their hands in small increments until their hands are about 5 feet (1.5 m) away from their feet; then they move their feet in small increments into their hands until their feet meet their hands). The movements can be noted by a sign at each cone.

Gauntlet Run

Students line up at one end of a football field or an area of similar size. Challenges are placed every 10 yards. Examples of challenges might be to jump over hurdles, crawl through hoops, run through tires, perform a long jump to a certain distance, hop backwards, high-jump over a bar, do a forward roll, or perform a sport movement. Students can begin with different challenges so that the activity does not become a race. Emphasis should be placed on warming up and achieving quality movement.

Rubber Band

Students begin from a central point with the instructor. On signal, the students move away from the instructor using a designated movement such as a jump, run, power skip, slide, carioca movement, or walk. On the second signal, students sprint back to the instructor's position where they form a tight circle around the teacher. The cycle is repeated with different movements. As a variation, students can perform one or two stretching activities when they return to the teacher.

Rope-Jumping Circuit

Each student has a jump rope. On the first signal, they begin jumping rope. On the second signal, they drop the rope and perform a stretching activity. A third signal can be used to designate performing a light, easy run. Emphasis should be placed on warming up students for fitness activity rather than offering an intense workout.

Ball Activities

Each student has a ball and dribbles it throughout the area while moving. On signal, students stop and move the ball behind the back, around each leg, and overhead. Emphasis is on learning to handle the ball as well as on moving. A variation is to drop one ball on signal and play catch with a partner until the signal to resume dribbling is given.

Beanbag Touch and Go

Spread different colored beanbags throughout the area. On signal, students run to a beanbag, touch it, and resume running. To increase the challenge, the color of the beanbag can be specified, and the touch must be made with a designated body part. An example might be, "Touch six yellow beanbags with your left hand." Students can also move to a beanbag, perform a 90-degree pivot (or 180 degrees), and resume running. This activity can also be conducted with cones or poly spots.

Vanishing Beanbags

Spread beanbags throughout the area, one per student. Students move around the area until a signal is given. On the signal, they find a beanbag and kneel on it or straddle it. The instructor then signals for the class to move again, and one or more beanbags are removed during this interval. Now when students are signaled to find a beanbag, some will be left without one. The challenge is to avoid being left out more than five times. Locomotor movements and different body parts can be specified to add challenge and variety. This activity can also be done with cones or poly spots.

Hoops and Plyometrics

Each student has a hoop and rolls it alongside or carries it while jogging. On the signal, the hoops are dropped, and students are challenged to move in and out of as many hoops as possible during the time given. The number and color of hoops to move in and out of can be specified, as can the type of activity to perform. Students can be asked to do plyometric-type movements with two feet, one foot, or alternating feet. When the teacher gives the next signal, students pick up their hoops and resume jogging with them or rolling them.

Musical Hoops

This activity is like musical chairs. Hoops are spread over the floor space, and each student puts one or both feet in a hoop (depending on how many hoops are available). Play music with random pauses. The teacher collects some of the hoops during the music so that some students will be left without one when the music stops. Students are challenged to avoid being left out two times in a row. The sport movement can be changed each round.

Sport Movements

Two parallel lines marked with boundary cones are placed 10 to 20 yards (m) apart. Half of the class lines up on one line and the other half on the opposite line. On signal, students perform a locomotor movement from one line to the other. Students must be careful as they cross over in the middle of the cones. Examples of movements include sliding, doing carioca, walking, doing crossover steps, or performing power skips.

Rhythm Nation

Using station signs, cards, or verbal instructions, the students are given three or four dance steps (e.g., grapevine, step touch, cha-cha). Their task is to perform the steps, in any order, for eight counts each. Play upbeat music for the students to practice. The steps can be changed up after the students have an opportunity to practice. This introductory activity can also be done in small groups.

Seek and Find

A set of cards with names of objects in the physical education space are scattered face down near the center of the playing area. These cards may include terms such as *bleachers*, *end line*, *free-throw line*, *door*, *light switch*, among others. On "Go," students flip over a card, run to touch that object, and return to the center to grab another card. Their challenge is to flip over as many cards as possible during the allotted time.

Partner and Small-Group Activities

Birdie in the Cage

In groups of five to seven, students position themselves in circle formation with two in the middle. Those around the circle try to make good passes while keeping the ball away from the "birdies" in the middle. Students switch places if their ball is touched or blocked.

Hoarders

Group students evenly at five or six hoops and place a variety of items such as soft balls, yarn balls, rubber chickens, scarves, or beanbags in the center of the playing area. The purpose is to obtain as many items as possible in the hoop when time is called. Students may carry one item at a time. Items must be carried (not thrown or passed). Students may not defend their hoop. One way to incorporate health content is to signal red items as muscle, yellow as fat. Groups should try to gain muscle and get rid of fat. This activity can also be done using different colors as food groups.

14

Hook 'Em

Start with students in partners sitting toe to toe, holding wrists. They should lean back and work together to try to stand up. Next, they try sitting back to back and hooking elbows, trying to stand. Partners then join another set of partners to form a group of four. They try forward group stands and then hooking elbows. Continue doubling the number of students in each group as they find success.

Marking

Marking is an excellent activity for learning to elude an opponent and learning to stay near someone defensively. Partners are selected, and one elects to stay near the other. On the first signal, the challenge is to stay as close as possible to the partner attempting to get away. When a second signal is given, both partners must immediately freeze. If the chaser can reach out and "mark" the partner, the chaser scores a point. Roles are reversed each time a signal is given. Locomotor movements can be changed for each round, for example, walking, fast walking, jogging, sliding, and doing carioca.

Marking With Addition or Multiplication

With a partner, students perform a rock–paper–scissors sequence and then display a number from one to five with one hand. Students quickly add or multiply the numbers. Whoever calls out the correct sum or product of the two numbers first runs and tries to get away from her or his partner. Students can line up with their partners in a scattered formation or in a line at midcourt facing their partners. The teacher can control all the starts and stops or allow students to start and stop on their own.

Pac-Man

Students must walk on any line on the gym floor. About five students are given a Pac-Man designation (carrying a ball or rubber chicken, and so on). The Pac-Men are the taggers. Students move along the lines and try to avoid being tagged. Pac-Men try to tag the others and give them the piece of equipment after tagging them. Locomotor movements can be changed for each round. The teacher should specify whether students may jump lines or pass others.

Pentabridge Hustle

To start the pentabridge hustle, students form groups of five. They spread out as far as possible in the playing area and form individual bridges that another person can move under (see figure 14.6). On signal, the first person in the group of five moves under the other four bridging students, runs ahead 6 to10 steps, and forms

a bridge. The next person in sequence moves under the four bridges. This sequence becomes a continuous movement activity. Activity success depends on making sure that students form bridges that are quite a distance apart so that enough running occurs to ensure warm-up. This activity can also be modified by forming bridges and having the moving students step over the bridges.

FIGURE 14.6 Pentabridge hustle.

Over, Under, and Around

To begin this activity, students find a partner. One person gets in position on all fours or in bridge position, and the other stands alongside, ready to begin the movement challenge (see figure 14.7). The challenge is given to move over, go under, and run around the partner a certain number of times. For example, one partner moves over the other 5 times, goes under 8 times, and runs around 10 times. When the task is completed, partners change positions and repeat the challenge. To increase motivation, the challenge can be made to move over, under, and around different students. For a more difficult challenge, the students move on all fours slowly throughout the area.

FIGURE 14.7 Over, under, and around.

Variation: Have three students work together. Two students hold hands, and the third student goes over the hands, around the group, and then under the hands for 15 seconds; then everyone changes places. This variation is excellent for a situation where students cannot get on all fours because of the grass, heat, or teaching area.

New Leader

Students work in small groups. The task is to move continuously in a productive fashion that will warm up the group. One person begins as the leader. When a signal is given, a new leader steps up and leads the next activity.

One Behind

Students are in groups of three. One person is the leader, and he or she begins an exercise. The leader moves on to a second exercise, and the next person begins the first activity. Each person in the group is one behind the person in front of them in terms of the activity.

Tag Games

A variety of tag games can be used to motivate students to move. These activities are excellent for teaching students to elude and chase each other while staying under control. Some simple tag game rules include using the back of hand to touch another person and tagging only the areas of arms, legs, and torso. Examples of tag games include the following:

1. Balance tag. To be safe, students balance in a stipulated position (e.g., one hand and one foot on the floor or one foot on the floor).

2. Push-up tag. Students assume the push-up or another designated position to avoid being tagged.

3. Blob tag. Two people begin by being "it." When they tag someone, they hold hands or lock elbows. As more people are tagged, the chain or blob of people becomes long, and only those at the end of the chain are eligible to tag.

4. Addition tag. This is like blob tag, but students try to move across the gym floor (or a rectangle area) with their partners and avoid the taggers in the middle of the floor. If tagged, the partners trade places or stay in the middle to make it more difficult for others to cross the floor. The locomotor movement is changed to add variety and more of a challenge.

5. Frozen tag. When tagged, the person must freeze in a designated position (e.g., stork stand or straddle stretch position). To be able to resume play, a classmate must high five the frozen person.

6. Spider tag. Students stand back to back with a partner with the elbows hooked. A pair of people are "it" and chase the other pairs. If a pair is tagged (or becomes unhooked), they are "it."

7. Triangle-plus-one tag. Three students hold hands to form a triangle. One person in the triangle is the leader. The fourth person outside the triangle tries to tag the leader. The triangle moves around to avoid getting the leader tagged. Leader and tagger are changed often.

8. Triangle-and-two tag. Students are in groups of five. Three students hold hands and form a triangle. One other student is the chaser, and the other student is a fugitive trying to keep from being tagged. The triangle tries to help the fugitive stay untagged by moving around and blocking the chaser. Rules include no jumping over the triangle or pushing the triangle out of the way. The triangle must stay together. The chaser must go around the triangle to tag. Students switch roles after a tag or a certain amount of time.

9. Fugitive tag. One person is the fugitive and is given a head start. The partner is a police officer trying to tag the fugitive. Flag belts can be used by the fugitive. Various movements can be used.

10. Fastest tag. All students are "it" at the same time. Use only short bouts of activity to be safe. Start a new bout often in this warm-up period. Start students with a walk, then slide, then skip, and then carioca steps. When students are tagged, they can kneel and then tag others from that position. Focus students on safety and have students watch where they are moving and stay under control at all times.

11. Clothespin tag. Students place two or three clothespins on the back of their shirts. The game starts in a scatter formation with specific boundaries, usually marked by boundary cones. When the game is started, students try to grab other students' clothespins and try to avoid getting their clothespins taken. As students acquire other clothespins, they place them on the front of their shirts. The game should be stopped and started often, and the means of locomotion (walk, jog, slide, carioca steps) should be changed.

12. Heads and tails tag. The teacher flips a large coin or floor spot with the picture of a head and a tail of a donkey taped on opposite sides of the spot. Half the students are heads (they put a hand on their head), and half are tails (they put a hand on their tail). Whichever side comes up is the winner and chaser of the opposite group. Modify the type of movement to add a variation.

14

13. Help me tag. Start with four or five taggers in a large area. Three or four students hold a rubber chicken as a safe area. Three students can be touching a chicken at one time. The chicken must be passed on before 30 seconds or the holder becomes a tagger. Students can yell, "Help me," for a chicken when they are about to be tagged.

14. Hospital tag. Four or five taggers have some type of softball or equipment for tagging (no throwing or hard hitting). If a student is tagged, he or she must hold the injury with the other hand. If tagged twice, the student must hold each wound with a hand. On the third tag, student must go to one knee and wait for a rehab high five from a classmate. Change the taggers often.

15. True or false partner tag. Students face a partner down the middle line in the gym. A safe zone is about 10 yards (m) behind each line. The teacher calls out a true or false question, and the line that has the correct answer (either the true line or the false line) chases the other group and tags them before they reach the safe zone. If a student gets tagged outside the safe zone, he or she changes sides.

16. Four corners tag. Student are in groups of six or more in single file line facing in toward the middle of a square. Each group is on the corner of the square made by poly spots or some type of court or field markers. In the middle of the square are a tagger and a loose person. When the teacher says, "Go," the loose person tries to get to a safe position at the end of one of the four lines, hooks on, and yells, "Go." The front person is now the loose person trying to get to a safe position. Multiple games should be going at the same time. Change the tagger often if he or she is having a hard time tagging someone.

Jumping Jack Countdown

Students are in groups. Choose two leaders to stand in front of the group. The teacher chooses a number of jumping jacks. If the number is 10, the leaders say, "Ready, go," and the whole group does 10 jumping jacks together. If a student does an incorrect number, she or he jogs around the group until the activity ends. After performing the 10 jumping jacks, the group does one fewer each time. The leaders can help the group or try to mess them up depending on how many times the class has done the intro.

Cross the Line

Students are divided into two even groups, standing on opposing sidelines. One team huddles and puts a paper clip in one of the teammate's hands. The remaining students on that team balls up their fists to keep the location of the paper clip hidden. On "Go," the offense moves across the space. The defense moves forward, and each student may tag only one person. After a student tags another, both stand still. If the person with the paperclip makes it across the opposite sideline without being tagged, that team earns a point.

Triplet Stoop

Students walk around the gym floor on the out-of-bounds line for the basketball court. One student is inside the line, one is on the line, and the third is outside the line. When the music starts, all students walk together with their line of three. The teacher blows one whistle, the inside person changes directions, the middle person stays still, and the outside person continues walking. When the music stops, the students run back to their middle person and stoop down. The fastest group to stoop is the winner.

Follow the Leader

Students are grouped by pairs. On signal, the leader performs all types of movements to elude his or her partner. Zigzags, rolls, 360-degree turns, and jumps are encouraged. Partners switch after 30 seconds. The same activity can be done with one leader and two or more followers.

Hoops on the Ground

Students run around the area where hoops are spread. When the teacher calls a number, students must get that number of students inside one hoop in five seconds or less.

Mirror Activity in Place

Each student faces a partner (see figure 14.8). One person is the leader and makes a quick movement with the hands, head, legs, or body. The partner tries to be a mirror and perform the exact same movement. The leader must pause briefly between movements. Leader and partner exchange places after 30 seconds.

FIGURE 14.8 Mirror activity in place.

Formation Rhythmic Running

The class begins in a circular formation. Students move to a drumbeat or other steady beat. They attempt to run rhythmically to the beat, lifting the knees and maintaining a formation or line with even spacing between students. Challenges can be added, such as clapping hands on the first beat, stamping the feet on the third beat, and thrusting a hand into the air on the fourth beat of a four-count rhythm.

As students become experienced at maintaining the formation and rhythm of the activity, they can be led into different formations such as a rectangle, square, triangle, or line. Students can also wind up and unwind the line and can learn to cross in front of each other to break a line.

Loose Caboose

All students are hooked together in groups of two or three by having the rear person put their hands on the shoulders of the person in front of him or her. The teacher picks several students to move without a partner. These students are called the loose cabooses. The loose cabooses try to hook on with another set of students by grabbing the waist of the rear student. When this happens, the front student is now loose and attempts to hook on with another pair of students. The teacher can vary the means of locomotion for the students.

Flag Grab

All students have a flag belt and are scattered around the gym. On the start signal, students try to grab the flags of others while trying to avoid getting their flag taken. Students drop the flags they took immediately, and the other students put the flags back on and continue in the game. Teachers vary the movements to include walk, jog, slide, and carioca steps.

Running High Fives

Use a music interval of 15 seconds on and 15 seconds off. When the music is playing, students walk the first interval, then jog, slide, skip, do carioca, or stretch. When the music goes off, students give high fives to other students. After a couple of intervals, students can give low fives, then alternate between high and low fives, then medium fives, then alternate between right hand and left hand, and so on as the teacher varies the activity.

Standing High Fives

Students get a partner about the same height and stand facing one another. Students start with a jump and right-hand high five, then use the left hand, and then use both hands. Next, students add a quarter turn and the various high fives. Next, students add a half turn and then the high fives. Then they add a three-quarter turn and, finally, a full turn. Students should try turning to the right and left and using both hands with each turn. Encourage body control and teamwork.

Surf's Up!

Students stand back to back with a partner along the center line. Each jumps and counts to three, then turns and shows surfer (hands out like riding a wave), shark (hands above head like a fin), or wave (hands above head rounded to front). Shark eats surfer, surfer rides the wave, and wave overtakes the shark. Whoever wins runs back to their sideline while the partner chases. If the winner makes it across line without being tagged, he or she earns a point. If the chaser tags the partner before crossing line, he or she earns a point. See figure 14.9 for an example of a surfer, a shark, and a wave.

FIGURE 14.9 Surf's Up!

Quick Hands With Beanbags

Students sit facing a partner with legs crossed or extended. One beanbag is placed on the floor equally between the two partners. The teacher calls out, "Right" or "Left," and the students try to grab the beanbag with the hand that was called by the teacher. The same activity can be performed from a push-up position or a sit-up position. Partners face each other and quickly try to grab the beanbag with the right or left hand, as called by the teacher.

Builders and Destroyers

Place about 30 cones on the gym floor in a scatter formation with half the cones tipped over. Half of the students are the builders trying to set up all the cones, and the other half of the students are the destroyers tipping over the cones. After 15 to 20 seconds, stop the activity

14

and see how many cones are in each position. Challenge the groups to improve that number during the next attempt.

Hoops Circle Pass

Divide the class into three or four groups that form circles while holding hands. A hoop is started between two connected hands. The hoop is passed around the circle without letting go of hands. Students need to work together to help others through the hoop in the most efficient manner. After a couple of practice runs, a race can be held to see which group performs the passing techniques the fastest.

Quick Lineup

The class is divided into four equal groups. Each group decides on a team name and lines up single file, facing one assigned side of the teacher (front, back, right side, or left side). All students close their eyes, and the teacher moves to a new position and rotates her or his body position. On the teacher's signal, students run to the new position, line up in the same order, facing the same side of the teacher, and yell out their team name as they finish. The first team finished gets a point.

Moving Throw and Catch

Students move and play catch with a partner under control from about 5 yards (m) apart. Any type of ball, beanbag, throton, rubber chicken, or other item can be used for this activity. Students need to remain safe and under control with their movements and equipment. Teachers can stop the action often and do a large group stretch or exercise to maintain control. The locomotor movements can be changed to add variety for this activity. Challenge students to add different pivots, such as front, back, 90 degrees, 180 degrees, or 360 degrees during this activity.

LEARNING AIDS

STUDY STIMULATORS AND REVIEW QUESTIONS

1. Explain the primary purposes of introductory activities.
2. Describe the characteristics of an effective introductory activity.
3. Cite four reasons for using introductory activities in secondary school lessons.
4. Why should the interests, physical abilities, and developmental levels of students be considered in the selection of introductory activities?
5. Discuss the transition from introductory activities to physical fitness activities. Why is this transition important in secondary classes?
6. Why should the introductory activity be short in length (two to three minutes) with an atmosphere of enthusiasm, motivation, and fun?
7. What can a teacher do to make an introductory activity novel and challenging for students?

WEBSITES

Human Kinetics
www.humankinetics.com

SHAPE America
www.shapeamerica.org

Physical Education Teaching and Curriculum Information
www.pecentral.org
www.pheamerica.org

Physical Fitness

This chapter explains the importance of including physical fitness activities in the lesson plan and identifies novel strategies and techniques that can be used to implement fitness into the lesson structure. A variety of exercises and techniques that can be used to develop physical fitness are discussed. Fitness is defined into two categories: health related and skill related. Health-related fitness is selected for the vast majority of people. A selected few who want to improve their athletic performance or personal accomplishments will choose skill-related fitness as their outcome of choice.

Fitness performance is strongly controlled by genetic factors, including how students respond to training. The relationship between activity and fitness performance is quite weak and leads to misconceptions about the importance of training and passing fitness tests. Newer fitness tests evaluate the amount of fitness necessary for good health using criterion standards. Secondary school students need the opportunity to experience and select fitness routines that are useful and motivating to them personally. Physical fitness activities should be offered as a positive contribution to total wellness. These activities should not be used as punishment. Using a variety of fitness routines helps motivate students toward a lifetime of fitness activities. The school physical education program should help students make the transition into community-based physical activity programs, particularly health and fitness clubs. Instruction and participation relative to physical fitness should be done in a positive atmosphere.

Learning Objectives

▶ Differentiate between skill-related and health-related physical fitness.

▶ Identify the various components of physical fitness and the way in which they can be measured and evaluated.

▶ Describe the effect that physical fitness can have on the overall wellness of a person.

▶ Explain the relationship between fitness and activity and the effect that this relationship has on performance on fitness tests.

▶ Cite strategies and techniques to motivate students to develop and maintain physical fitness.

▶ Demonstrate the instructional procedures associated with exercise routines included in this chapter.

▶ Develop new and different physical fitness routines that will accomplish fitness objectives and motivate students to continue to be active for a lifetime.

Most students want to be fit and active. Physical education programs should make time for fitness development to teach students that fitness is important for a healthy lifestyle, but physical fitness activities should be offered as a positive contribution to total wellness. They should be something that benefits those who participate and not be used as punishment for misbehavior.

Fitness of America's Youth

A popular point of view among physical education teachers is that youth today are less fit than they were in the past. This opinion is often used as justification for more physical education time in the schools. But no longitudinal studies have been done to support this claim. Historical evidence indicates that youth may have had slight increases in muscular strength and endurance. For example, when data were compared across four national youth fitness surveys (1957 to 1985) conducted by the American Alliance for Health, Physical Education, Recreation and Dance (AAHPERD) and the President's Council on Physical Fitness and Sports, the only items used in all four surveys were pull-ups and the flexed-arm hang. Young people, both boys and girls, showed an increase in upper-body strength when these two items were compared over four decades (Corbin & Pangrazi, 1992). Unfortunately, comparing other fitness results across generations is difficult, because the testing procedures have constantly changed or evolved.

The area where youths have shown a serious and documented decline is body composition. Obesity has more than doubled in children and tripled in adolescents in the past 30 years (Skinner, Ravanbakht, Skelton, Perrin, & Armstrong, 2018). Currently, 40% of youths age 12 through 19 years old are overweight or obese (Skinner et al., 2018). This large increase in overweight youths takes its toll on fitness scores. Common sense dictates that if someone can do 50 push-ups at normal weight, putting 20 pounds (9 kg) of sand on his or her back will decrease the number of push-ups he or she is able to perform. Body fat is dead weight and does not contribute to muscular or cardiorespiratory performance. Thus, as being overweight increases at a rapid rate among youths, all strength and aerobic performance scores decrease. Recent FitnessGram results support this by indicating that 54% of middle school youth and 66% of high school youth fail to meet the desired levels of cardiorespiratory fitness set by experts (Welk, Meredith, Ihmels, & Seeger, 2010).

Genetic Endowment and Fitness Performance

Physical fitness tests often lead students down a path of failure regardless of how much they train to improve. Heredity has a direct effect on all aspects of health-related fitness (Corbin, Welk, Corbin, & Welk, 2008). Various other factors, such as environment, nutrition, and maturation, affect fitness performance as reflected in physical fitness test scores. Research clearly shows that heredity and maturation strongly influence fitness scores (Corbin, 2012; Pangrazi & Corbin, 2008). In fact, these factors may have more to do with youth fitness scores than activity level. Lifestyle and environmental factors can also make a difference. For example, nutrition is a lifestyle factor that can influence test scores, and environmental conditions (heat, humidity, and pollution) strongly modify test performances. Fitness performance is only partially determined by activity and training.

Some youths have a definite advantage on tests because of the types of muscle fibers they inherit. Others inherit a predisposition to perform well on tests. In other words, even in an untrained state, some students score better because of heredity. On the other hand, some students who train will not score as well as others who are untrained because of their genetic predispositions. Beyond heredity lies another genetic factor that predisposes some young people to higher performance. Research has shown that trainability is inherited (Bouchard, 2012), which means that some people receive more benefit from training (regular physical activity) than others. As an example, assume that two students perform the same amount of activity throughout a semester. Student A shows dramatic improvement immediately, whereas student B does not. Student A simply responds more favorably to training than student B does. Student A inherited a system that is responsive to exercise. Student A not only gets fit and scores well on the test but also gets feedback that says, "The activity works—it makes me fit." The less responsive student scores poorly, receives no feedback, and concludes, "Activity doesn't improve my fitness, so why try?" The unfortunate thing is that student B will improve in fitness but to a lesser degree than student A and will take longer to show improvement. Student B will probably never achieve the fitness level attained by student A. Trainability and genetic endowment differences limit performance, so having different expectations for students is important.

Does this mean that little is gained by helping students become more active? Certainly not. Although heredity plays an important role in fitness, all young people benefit from regular physical activity. Some students will not show much improvement in their physical performance, but physical activity will offer them health benefits. Regardless of desired outcomes, less gifted students will always need more encouragement and positive feedback because their improvement will be in smaller increments and of lesser magnitude.

Relationship Between Fitness Results and Activity

Teachers and parents want to believe that fitness in young people is primarily a reflection of how active they are. A common belief is that adolescents score poorly on fitness tests because they are not active enough and spend too much time in sedentary activity like playing video games, watching TV, and being on their phones. The mistaken belief that being physically active builds fitness may lead teachers to the conclusion that students who score high on fitness tests are active, and those who do not score well are inactive. Physical activity is an important variable in fitness development, but other factors can be of equal or greater importance. If teachers make the mistake of assuming that a student who achieves low scores on a fitness test is inactive, misunderstandings and misinterpretations can result.

For example, consider the problems that occur when teachers mistakenly assume that fitness and activity are highly related. If students are encouraged to do regular exercise and training to improve their fitness scores, many will take the challenge seriously. When fitness tests are given, students will expect to do well on the tests if they have been training regularly, and, of course, teachers will also expect them to do well. If, however, they receive scores that are lower than expected, they will be disappointed. They will be especially discouraged if the teacher concludes that their low fitness status reflects their lack of training and not being active. A conclusion such as, "You are not as fit as you should be compared with other students; therefore, you have not been active," is often not true. This type of dialogue from teachers will cause the student to lose self-esteem, and the student and teacher will lose respect for one another.

The other side of this issue can just as easily be untrue, that is, assuming that students who perform well on fitness tests are training the hardest and being the most active. Young people who are genetically gifted may be inactive yet still perform well on fitness tests. Students are always aware of peers who do not train, are not active, and maintain poor health habits yet still perform well on fitness tests. If teachers do not teach students why these cases occur, students soon question the integrity

All young people benefit from regular physical activity.

of the teacher. Students need to learn that some people are gifted in fitness performance. Such students can more easily show fitness improvement over those who lack the genetic predisposition for fitness performance.

Health-Related and Skill-Related Physical Fitness

A general definition regarding the precise nature of physical fitness has never been universally accepted. But two types of physical fitness are often recognized: **health-related physical fitness** and **skill-related physical fitness**. The differentiation between physical fitness related to functional health and physical performance related to athletic ability makes it easier to develop proper fitness objectives and goals for students. Health-related fitness is characterized by moderate and regular physical activity as described in chapter 16. The lifestyle activities in described in chapter 19 are often used by adults as a medium to maintain health-related fitness. These activities are designed for the masses who are generally unwilling to exercise at high intensities. Health-related activities can be integrated into regular everyday lifestyles.

In contrast, skill-related physical fitness includes not only the health-related components but also components that are in part controlled by genetic factors. Skill-related fitness is the right choice for people who want to perform at a high level (usually in an athletic setting) but is less useful for the masses because it requires training and exercising at high intensities. In addition, many people cannot reach high levels of skill-related fitness because of their genetic limitations. The following discussion describes and contrasts the differences between health-related and skill-related fitness.

Health-Related Physical Fitness

Teaching health-related fitness should be a focus in physical education. The benefit of health-related fitness is that all students can improve their health status through daily physical activity. Health-related fitness is an important marker shown to predict cardiovascular disease, morbidity, and mortality (Morrow, Tucker, Jackson, Martin, Greenleaf, & Petrie, 2013). Health-related fitness is one of the few areas where all students can succeed regardless of ability level and genetic limitations. Students can be assured, "If you are willing to be active, you will enhance your health status." In contrast, skill-related fitness is oriented toward sport performance and

is influenced by genetic traits and abilities. A primary reason for teaching health-related fitness is that it gives students activity habits they can use throughout their lifespans.

Health-related physical fitness includes those aspects of physiological function that offer protection from diseases related to a sedentary lifestyle. It can be improved or maintained through regular physical activity. Specific components include cardiorespiratory fitness, body composition (ratio of leanness to fatness), muscular strength and endurance, and flexibility. When measuring health-related fitness, criterion standards are used to indicate levels of good health. The FitnessGram (Going, Lohman, & Eisenmann, 2014) uses criterion-referenced health standards that represent good health instead of traditional percentile rankings often found in skill-related fitness tests. These standards represent a level of fitness that offers some degree of protection against diseases resulting from sedentary living.

The FitnessGram, in conjunction with the Presidential Youth Fitness Program, focuses on the process and promotion of health-related fitness (Presidential Youth Fitness Program, 2017). The true emphasis is on personal goals and achievement of age- and gender-appropriate standards, as opposed to comparisons to peers. The actual tool uses an approach that classifies fitness performance into three categories: healthy fitness zone (HFZ), needs improvement—some risk, and needs improvement—high risk. All students are encouraged to score in the HFZ, but scoring outside the HFZ offers little health advantage. The goal is for all students to achieve and move their personal performance into the HFZ.

Health-Related Fitness Components

Health-related physical fitness includes aspects of physiological function that offer protection from diseases caused by a sedentary lifestyle. Health-related fitness is often called functional fitness because it helps ensure that a person will be able to function effectively in everyday tasks. Such fitness can be improved or maintained through daily moderate physical activity. Specific components include cardiorespiratory endurance, body composition (ratio of leanness to fatness), muscular strength and endurance, flexibility, and more recently, power. The first five are the components measured in the FitnessGram test (Going, Lohman, & Eisenmann, 2014). The following are the major components of health-related fitness.

Cardiorespiratory Endurance

Aerobic fitness is important for a healthy lifestyle and may be the most important element of fitness. **Cardiorespiratory endurance** is the ability of the heart, the blood vessels, and the respiratory system to deliver oxygen efficiently over an extended period. At least 60 minutes of moderate to vigorous aerobic activity should be accumulated daily (United State Department of Health and Human Services, 2012) to ensure good health. Activities that stimulate development in this area are walking, jogging, biking, rope jumping, aerobic dance, swimming, and active sports such as basketball and soccer.

The exercise prescription model is best for people interested in cardiorespiratory or aerobic fitness improvement. To improve health-related cardiorespiratory fitness, the FITT (frequency, intensity, time, and type) formula is used to identify the necessary exercise prescription. Working out for the sake of fitness improvement should be done at least three days per week (frequency), at a heart rate of 70 to 85% of predicted maximum heart rate (intensity), and for at least 20 minutes (time) (American College of Sports Medicine [ACSM], 2013). Maximum heart rate is calculated roughly as 208 minus 0.7 × age. Thus, the maximum heart rate for a 15-year-old student would be 208 − 0.7 × 15 = 198. For this student, 70 to 85% of 198 would mean keeping the heart rate between 139 and 168 beats per minute while participating in aerobic activities. Calculating target heart rate zones may be useful in determining which level of activity is necessary for youth to improve cardiorespiratory fitness. For example, to maintain low fitness levels, youths may need to participate regularly in activity at 55 to 65% of their max heart rate. For good fitness, youths may need to participate regularly in activity at 75 to 90% of max heart rate. More specific calculations can be found in *Physical Best: Physical Education for Lifelong Fitness and Health* (SHAPE America/Conkle, 2020).

Heart rate monitors, although not necessary, provide an exciting tool for teaching about cardiorespiratory fitness. These instruments provide accurate information and eliminate the need for the manual calculation of heart rates (SHAPE America/Conkle, 2020). Heart rate monitors are typically worn across the chest (the newest versions calculate heart rate at the wrist) and transmit to a wrist receiver that provides instant feedback on heart rate. This device provides continuous personal feedback and can serve as a self- or teacher-directed assessment. Students will immediately know if the activity they are participating in is causing their heart rate to rise and if it is within their target heart rate zone. Heart rate monitors do take some training and getting used to. Teachers will need to spend time allowing students to get comfortable wearing the instruments and teaching their proper use. Swaim and Edwards (2002, 2003) provide a middle and high school fitness program specifically designed around the heart rate monitor. Heart rate monitors can be used with any fitness or physical activity to monitor its effect on the heart.

Body Composition

Body composition is an integral part of health-related fitness. Body composition is the proportion of body fat to lean body mass. After the thickness of selected skinfolds has been measured, the percentage of body fat can be extrapolated from tables. The conversion of skinfold thickness to percent body fat can be a less accurate measure, but it is easier to communicate to parents than skinfold thickness. Considering that the wellness status of people depends on body composition, students must learn about concepts and consequences in this area.

A much less intrusive way to determine body composition is by using the body mass index (BMI). BMI is a number calculated by using a person's weight and height. BMI is being used in many states to evaluate body fatness among students. The method is generally reliable and has the advantage of providing feedback without touching the body. In some instances, however, a highly conditioned athlete may have a high BMI but a low body fat percentage. Teachers must understand and be able to explain this result to students and parents. Research shows that BMI correlates to direct measures of body fat such as underwater weight. The Centers for Disease Control and Prevention (CDC) and the American Academy of Pediatrics recommend that BMI be used to screen for overweight youths. For teenagers, a sex- and age-specific table of percentiles is used to determine BMI. Research (Burns, Hannon, Brusseau, Shultz, & Eisenman, 2013) has highlighted bioelectrical impedance and waist-to-height ratio as valid alternative measures for examining body composition in youths that are easy and affordable options in the physical education setting.

Flexibility

Flexibility is the range of movement through which a joint or sequence of joints can move. Inactive people lose flexibility, but frequent movement helps retain the range of movement. Stretching activities increase the length of muscles, tendons, and ligaments. The ligaments and

15

tendons retain their elasticity through constant use. People who are flexible may be less subject to injury in sport, usually possess sound posture, and have less lower-back pain.

Muscular Strength and Endurance

Muscular strength is the ability of muscles to exert force; it is an important fitness component that facilitates learning motor skills. Most activities in physical education do not build strength in the areas where it is most needed: the arm–shoulder girdle and the abdominal region. **Muscular endurance** is the ability to exert force over an extended period. Endurance postpones the onset of fatigue so that activity can be performed for lengthy periods. Most sport activities require that muscular skills, such as throwing, kicking, and striking, be performed many times without fatigue.

Power

Power is the ability to transfer energy explosively into force. Power has been identified as a combined compo-

nent of fitness (health-related and skill-related) because of its association with strength and speed (Corbin, Janz, & Baptista, 2014). The Institute of Medicine (2012) linked power to health, specifically suggesting that power is associated with wellness, quality of life, reduced risk of chronic disease and early death, and better bone health.

Skill-Related Fitness Components

Skill-related fitness includes those physical qualities that enable a person to perform in sport activities. Skill-related fitness is closely related to athletic ability. The traits of speed, agility, coordination, and so on form the basis of the ability to excel in sports. Because skill-related fitness is strongly influenced by a person's natural or inherited traits, most students will find it difficult to achieve. In contrast to health-related tests, skill-related fitness tests often use norm-referenced standards that rank students compared with their peers. For some students, the goal becomes trying to do better than other students rather than learning to do the best they can regardless of peer scores.

Stretching activities can help students improve flexibility.

Skill-related fitness components are useful for performing motor tasks related to sports and athletics. The ability to perform well depends largely on the genetic endowment of the person. Although all students can perform adequately in health-related fitness activities, it is difficult, if not impossible, for many young people to excel in this area of fitness. Asking students to try harder only adds to their frustration if they lack native ability because they see their more skilled friends perform well without effort. When skill-related fitness is taught, it should be accompanied by an explanation of why some students can perform well with a minimum of effort, whereas others, no matter how hard they try, never excel. Many examples can be used to illustrate genetic differences, such as speed, jumping ability, strength, and physical size in people. The bottom line for teachers is to understand that some students will want to work hard to improve their fitness performance, whereas a majority will probably be satisfied to play, be active, and enjoy their bodies in a less demanding manner. For these students, health-related fitness will be an important outcome.

Skill-related physical fitness includes the health-related items listed previously plus the following:

Agility

Agility is the ability of the body to change position rapidly and accurately while moving. Wrestling, dance, and football are examples of sports and activities that require agility.

Balance

Balance refers to the body's ability to maintain a state of equilibrium while remaining stationary or moving. Maintaining balance is essential to all sports but is especially important in the performance of gymnastic activities.

Coordination

Coordination is the ability of the body to perform more than one motor task smoothly and successfully at the same time. Needed for football, baseball, tennis, soccer, and other sports that require eye–hand and eye–foot skills, coordination can be developed by repeatedly practicing the skill to be learned.

Power

As identified earlier, power is the ability to transfer energy explosively into force. To develop power, a person must practice activities required to improve strength but at a faster rate involving sudden bursts of energy. Skills requiring power include high jumping, long jumping, performing the shot put, throwing, and kicking.

Reaction Time

Reaction time is the response time needed to move after recognizing the need to act. Reaction time is important for fast starts in swimming or track, for reacting to a thrown or batted ball in baseball, or when dodging an opponent in many team sports.

Speed

Speed is the ability of the body to perform movement in a short time. Usually associated with running forward, speed is essential for the successful performance of most sports and general locomotor movement skills.

Creating a Positive Fitness Experience

How the fitness program is taught increases the possibility of students being turned on to activity. Fitness activity in and of itself is neither good nor bad. Instead, how fitness activities are taught influences how students feel about making fitness a part of their lifestyles. Physical educators should keep in mind that most youths (unless the class is designed for athletes) are more interested in good health than high levels of skill-related fitness. Consider the following strategies to make activity a positive learning experience.

Individualize Fitness Workloads

Students expected to participate in fitness activities who find themselves unable to perform exercises are not likely to develop a positive attitude toward physical activity. Allow students to determine personal workloads and capabilities through goal setting and program planning. Students can individualize their goals and plan according to what they want to accomplish. One student may want to make the soccer team, and another would prefer to hike a nearby gorge. Some may simply be focused on looking better. Use time (instead of repetitions and distance) as the workload variable and ask students to do the best they can within the time limit. People dislike and fear experiences of failure they perceive to be forced on them from an external source. Voluntary long-term exercise is more probable when people are internally driven to do their best. Fitness experiences that give control to students offer better opportunity for development of positive attitudes toward activity.

15

TEACHING TIP

Individualized fitness workloads are especially important for youth who may be overweight, have a disability, or typically do not enjoy physical education class. When possible, provide all students with multiple options when introducing fitness activities so that the students can work at a level comfortable to them.

Present a Variety of Physical Fitness Routines and Exercises

Teaching a variety of fitness opportunities decreases the monotony of doing the same routines week after week and increases the likelihood that students will experience fitness activities that are enjoyable. Most students are willing to accept activities they dislike if they know there will be a chance to experience routines they enjoy in the near future. A yearlong routine of doing calisthenics and running a mile forces students, regardless of ability and interest, to participate in the same routine whether they like it or not. When young people know that a new and exciting routine is on the horizon, their tolerance for routines or activities they dislike will increase. Avoiding potential boredom by systematically changing fitness activities is an effective method of helping students perceive fitness in a positive way.

Provide Meaningful Feedback

Teacher feedback contributes to the way that students view fitness activities. Immediate, accurate, and specific feedback regarding performance encourages continued participation. Provided in a positive manner, this feedback can stimulate youths to extend their participation habits outside the confines of the gymnasium. Reinforce everybody, not just those who perform at high levels. All students need feedback and reinforcement.

Teach Physical Skills and Fitness

Physical education programs teach skill development and fitness. Some states mandate fitness testing, which may make teachers worry that their students will not pass. This concern can lead to the skill development portion of physical education being sacrificed to increase the emphasis on teaching fitness. Fitness testing should be used for educational purposes and to help students set goals and measure progress. Skills are the tools that

most adults use to attain fitness. Most people maintain fitness through various skill-based activities such as tennis, badminton, swimming, golf, basketball, aerobics, cycling, and the like. People have a much greater propensity to participate as adults if they feel competent in an activity. Skills and physical activity go hand in hand for an active lifestyle.

Be a Positive Role Model

Appearance, attitude, and actions speak loudly about teachers and their values regarding fitness. Teachers who display physical vitality, take pride in being active, participate in fitness activities with students, and are physically fit positively influence young people to maintain an active lifestyle. Teachers cannot be expected to complete a fitness routine each period, five days a week, but they must exercise with a class periodically to assure students they are willing to do what they ask them to do.

Foster the Attitudes of Students

Attitudes dictate whether youths choose to participate in activity. Teachers and parents sometimes take the approach of forcing fitness on students to "make them all fit." Resentment may be the result. Training does not equate to lifetime fitness. When students are trained without concern for their feelings, the result may be fit students who dislike physical activity. When a negative attitude develops, changing it is difficult. This caution does not mean that young people should avoid fitness activity; it means that fitness participation must be a positive and success-based experience. Avoid funneling all students into one type of fitness activity. For example, running may be an inappropriate activity for overweight youth, and lean, uncoordinated students may not enjoy contact activities. The fitness experience must be a challenge rather than a threat. A challenge is an experience that participants believe they can accomplish. In contrast, a threat appears to be an impossible undertaking—one that is not worth trying. As a final note, remember that whether activity is a challenge or a threat depends on the perceptions of the learner, not the instructor. Listen to students express their concerns. Do not tell them, "Do it for your own good."

Start Easy and Progress Slowly

Fitness development is a journey, not a destination. No teacher wants students to become fit in school only to become inactive as adults. A rule of thumb is to allow students to start at a level they can accomplish. This idea

COMBINING FITNESS WITH SPORT SKILLS

A great way to introduce fitness activities into physical education is by combining fitness with sport skills. For example, when teaching basketball, a physical education teacher might use the task style by alternating basketball and fitness stations. This approach allows students to move on from fitness and into basketball activity every 30 seconds to 2 minutes depending on the length of the station. Brusseau, Darst, and Johnson (2009) provide two examples that illustrate this concept. Figure 15.1 shows an example of how stations could be set up to incorporate basketball skill practice with fitness practice. The stations are as follows:

Skill Activities

Shooting: Students shoot on goal.

Dribbling: Students dribble around obstacles (cones).

Passing: Students make consecutive passes with partner or against a wall or board.

One-versus-one: Students work on dribbling and shooting with a defender.

Free choice: Students choose a skill to practice.

Fitness Activities

Toe touches: Students alternate touches on top of a ball.

Ball jumps: Students jump over a ball or line on field.

Ball crunches: Students perform sit-up variation with a ball between the knees.

Fitness choice: Students choose their own fitness activity.

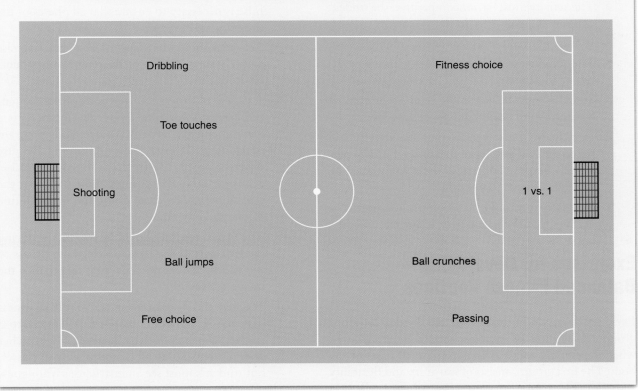

FIGURE 15.1 Setup for basketball skill and fitness stations.

Reprinted by permission from T.A. Brusseau, P.W. Darst, and T.G. Johnson, "Combining Fitness and Skill Tasks," *Journal of Physical Education, Recreation, and Dance* 80 (2009): 50-52.

15

means offering the option of self-directed workloads within a specified time frame. Do not force students into heavy workloads too soon. Starting a fitness program at a level that is too easy is impossible. Start with success and gradually increase the workload to avoid the discouragement of failure and excessive muscle soreness. When students successfully accomplish activities, they learn a system of self-talk that expresses exercise behavior in a positive light. They avoid the common practice of self-criticism that can occur when they fail to live up to their own or others' standards.

Encourage Activities That Are Positively Addicting

Teachers want students to exercise throughout adulthood. Certain activities may be more likely to stimulate exercise outside school. Glasser (1985), in his book *Positive Addiction*, suggests that if the following activity conditions are met, exercise will become positively addicting and a necessary part of a person's life. These steps imply that many individual activities, including walking, jogging, hiking, biking, and the like, are activities that students might regularly use for fitness during adulthood.

- The activity must be noncompetitive; the student chooses and wants to do it.
- It must not require a great deal of mental effort.
- The activity can be done alone—without a partner or teammates.
- Students must believe in the value of the exercise for improving health and general welfare.
- Participants must believe that the activity will become easier and more meaningful if they persist. To become addicting, the activity must be done for at least six months.
- The activity should be accomplished in such a manner that the participant is not self-critical.

Exercises for Developing Balanced Fitness Routines

Exercises discussed in this section are divided into four groups. All groups of exercises should be represented when developing routines that exercise all parts of the body. The first group consists of warm-up and flexibility activities. These groups of exercises primarily develop

muscular strength and endurance in the upper body, midsection, and lower body. When exercise routines are planned, they should contain a balance of activities from all groups. The following instructional procedures (and exercises to avoid) should be considered carefully when developing exercise routines.

Instructional Procedures

Fitness instruction is exclusively dedicated to the presentation of a variety of fitness activities. The following suggestions can aid in the successful implementation of the fitness module.

1. Fitness instruction should be preceded by a two- to three-minute warm-up period. The introductory activity is useful for this purpose because it allows young people the opportunity to loosen up and prepare for strenuous activity.

2. The fitness portion of the daily lesson, including the warm-up, should not extend beyond 15 to 20 minutes. Some argue that more time is needed to develop adequate fitness. But a limited amount of time is available for fitness and skill instruction. Because skill instruction is part of a balanced physical education program, compromise is necessary to ensure that all phases of the program are covered.

3. Activities should be vigorous in nature, exercise all body parts, and cover the major components of fitness.

4. A variety of fitness routines comprising sequential exercises for total body development is a recommended alternative to a yearlong program of regimented calisthenics and running. Because different people like different forms of exercise, a diverse array of routines should replace the traditional approach of doing the same routine day in and day out.

5. The fitness routine should be conducted during the first part of the lesson. Relegating fitness to the end of the lesson does little to enhance the image of exercise.

6. Teachers should assume an active role in fitness instruction. Students respond positively to a teacher who is a positive role model. The teacher does not have to do all exercises with all classes, but students must see an instructor's willingness to exercise.

7. When determining workloads for exercise, the available alternatives are time, speed, or repetitions. Basing workloads on time rather than on a specified number of repetitions is the best approach because students can adjust their workloads within personal limits. Having students perform as many repetitions as they are capable of in a given amount of time will result in successful and positive feelings about activity.

8. Using music to time fitness activity segments allows teachers the freedom to move throughout the area and offer individualized instruction. Participation and instruction should be enthusiastic and focus on positive outcomes. If the instructor does not enjoy physical fitness participation, such an attitude will be apparent to students.

9. Fitness activities should never be assigned as punishment. Such a practice teaches students that push-ups and running are things they must do when they misbehave. The opportunity to exercise should be a privilege as well as an enjoyable experience. Think of the money that adults spend to join a health club. Take a positive approach and offer students a chance to jog with a friend when they do something well. This activity allows them the opportunity not only to visit with the friend but also to exercise on a positive note. Be an effective salesperson; sell the joy of activity and benefits of physical fitness to students.

10. When introducing a new exercise, the teacher should demonstrate it, break it down into components, and explain its value. Students should practice it at a slower-than-normal pace and then increase speed. Proper form should be emphasized.

11. Proper form is important when performing exercises. For instance, in exercises that require the arms to be held in front of the body or overhead, the abdominal wall needs to be contracted to maintain proper positioning of the pelvis. The feet should be pointed reasonably straight ahead, the chest should be up, and the head and shoulders should be in good postural alignment.

12. Vary the aerobic activity used in classes. Too often, such activity consists of everybody running a lap. This practice is boring and does little to meet the personal needs of all students. Exercise alternatives to running might be interval training, rope jumping, obstacle courses, astronaut drills, brisk walking, rhythmic aerobic exercise, and parachute movements.

Flexibility Exercises

The multiple types of flexibility exercises, or stretches, include static, dynamic, and ballistic (Burkhart & Dlugolecki, 2020). **Ballistic stretches** involve quick bouncing movements to produce the stretch. Although considered necessary for sport movements, ballistic stretches are *not* recommended to be used in general physical education classes. **Static stretches**, which are low and sustained stretches in which the individual reaches the point of mild discomfort, can gradually improve flexibility. This type of stretching is considered generally safe and should be used for flexibility training and as a cool-down. Static stretches are not recommended for warm-ups. **Dynamic stretches** involve moving parts of the body, gradually increasing range of motion or speed of movement or both. Dynamic stretching is considered an active warm-up that helps prepare the body for more strenuous activity. The flexibility exercises in this section increase the range of motion at various joints.

Lower-Leg Stretches

Lower-Leg Stretch

Stand facing a wall with the feet about shoulder-width apart. Place the palms of the hands on the wall at eye level. Walk away from the wall, keeping the body straight, until the stretch is felt in the lower portion of the calf. The feet should remain flat on the floor during the stretch.

Achilles Tendon Stretch

Stand facing a wall with the forearms on it. Place the forehead on the back of the hands. Back 2 to 3 feet (60 to 90 cm) away from the wall, bend, and move one leg closer to the wall. Flex the bent leg with the foot on the floor until the stretch is felt in the Achilles tendon area. The feet should remain flat on the floor as the leg closest to the wall is flexed. Repeat, flexing the other leg.

Balance Beam Stretch

Place one foot in front of the other, about 3 feet (90 cm) apart. The feet should be in line as though you are walking a balance beam. Bend the forward leg at the knee, lean forward, and keep the rear foot flat on the floor. Repeat with the opposite leg forward. The calf of the rear leg should be stretched.

15

Upper-Leg Stretches

Bear Hug

Stand with one leg forward and the other to the rear. Bend the forward knee as much as possible while keeping the rear foot flat on the floor. Repeat the exercise with the other foot forward. Variation: Different muscles can be stretched by turning the hips slightly in either direction. To increase the stretching motion, look over the shoulder and toward the rear foot.

Leg Pickup

Sit on the floor with the legs spread. Reach forward and grab the outside of the ankle with one hand and the outside of the knee with the other. Pick up the leg and pull the ankle toward the chin. The back of the upper leg should be stretched. Repeat the stretch, lifting the other leg.

Side Leg Stretch

Lie on the floor on the left side. Reach down with the right hand and grab the ankle. Pull the ankle and upper leg toward the rear of the body. Pull the ankle as near to the buttocks as possible and hold, stretching the front of the thigh. Repeat with the other side of the body.

New Hurdler's Stretch

Sit on the floor with one leg forward and the other leg bent at the knee with the foot tucked into the crotch. Lean gradually forward, bending at the hips and tucking the head. Allow the forward leg to flex at the knee, which stretches the back of the thigh. Next, lean backward, away from the forward leg, to stretch the top of the thigh. Repeat, reversing leg positions.

Groin Stretch

Sit on the floor with the legs spread as far apart and kept as straight as possible. Slowly lean forward from the hips and reach with the hands. Do not bend at the neck and shoulders because doing so puts pressure on the lower back. Stretch and hold in three positions: left, right, and directly ahead.

Lower-Back Stretches

Back Bender

Stand with the feet about shoulder-width apart. Bend the knees slightly and gradually bend the lower back, starting at the hips. Relax the arms and neck and let the upper body hang. If more stretch is desired, gradually straighten the legs.

Ankle Hold

From a standing position with the knees bent, reach down and hold both ankles with the hands. Gradually straighten the legs, applying the stretch to the lower back.

Sitting Toe Touch

Sit on the floor with the legs straight and together. Reach forward and grab the lower legs. Gradually walk the hands down the legs toward the ankles; continue to walk the hands down and touch the toes. Bend from the hips, not the upper back.

Feet-Together Stretch

Sit with the knees bent and the soles of the feet touching. Reach forward with the hands and grasp the ankles. Gently bend forward from the hips, applying stretch to the inside of the legs and lower back. To increase the stretching effect, place the elbows on or near the knees and press them toward the floor.

Cross-Legged Stretch

Sit on the floor with the legs crossed and tucked toward the buttocks. Lean forward with the elbows in front of the knees. To stretch the sides of the lower back, lean forward to the left and then the right.

Body Twist

Figure 15.2 shows the body twist. Sit on the floor with the right leg straight. Lift the left leg over the right leg and place it on the floor outside the right knee. Move the right elbow outside the upper left thigh and use it to maintain pressure on the leg. Lean back and support the upper body with the left hand. Rotate the upper body toward the left hand and arm. Reverse the position and stretch the other side of the body.

FIGURE 15.2 Body twist.

Table Stretch

Stand facing a table, chair, or similar platform. Place one leg on the table while maintaining the weight on the other leg. Lean forward from the hips to apply stretch to the hamstrings and lower back. Repeat with the other leg on the table. Variation: Stand with the side of the body facing the table. Place one leg on the table and bend toward the table to stretch the inside of the leg. Repeat with the other side of the body facing the table.

Back Stretches

Back Roller Stretch

Curl up by holding the lower legs with the arms. Tuck the head gently on the knees. Tip backward and then roll back and forth gently. The rolling action should be slow and should stretch the length of the back. Variation: Perform the same stretch but cross the legs and tuck them close to the buttocks.

Straight-Leg Roller

In a sitting position, roll backward and allow the legs to move overhead. Support the hips with the hands to control the stretch. The legs can be straightened and moved to different positions to vary the intensity and location of the stretch.

Squat Stretch

Begin in a standing position with the legs shoulder-width apart and the feet pointed outward. Gradually move to a squatting position, keeping the feet flat on the floor if possible. If balance is a problem, the stretch can be done while leaning against a wall.

Side-of-the-Body Stretches

Wall Stretch

Stand with one side toward the wall. Lean toward the wall and support the body with the hand. Walk away until the feet are 2 to 3 feet (60 to 90 cm) from the wall. While supporting the weight in the leaning position, bend the body toward the wall, stretching the side. Reverse and stretch the other side.

Elbow Grab Stretch

In a standing position with the feet spread, raise the hands above the head. Grab the elbows with the hands. Lean to the side and pull the elbow in that direction. Reverse and pull to the opposite side.

Standing Hip Bend

Stand with one hand on the hip and the other arm overhead. Bend to the side with the hand resting on the hip. The arm overhead should point and move in the direction of the stretch with a slight bend at the elbow. Reverse and stretch the opposite side.

Sitting Side Stretch

Sit on the floor with the legs spread as far apart as possible. Lift the arms overhead and reach toward one foot. Reverse and stretch in the opposite direction. Try to maintain an erect upper body.

Arm and Shoulder Girdle Stretches

Arm and Shoulder Stretch

Standing, extend the arms and place the palms of the hands together. Move the arms upward and overhead. Lift the arms as high as possible over the head.

Elbow Puller

Bend the right arm and place it behind the head. Reach to the right elbow with the left hand. Pull the elbow to the left to stretch the triceps and the top of the shoulders. Reverse the positions of the arms and repeat.

Elbow Pusher

Place the right arm over the left shoulder. Push the right elbow toward the body with the left hand and hold. Repeat in the opposite direction.

Wishbone Stretch

Move the arms behind the back and clasp hands. Keep the arms straight and raise the hands toward the ceiling to stretch the shoulder girdle. Variation: Stand near a wall (back toward the wall) and place the hands on it. Gently bend at the knees and lower the body while keeping the hands at the same level.

Exercises for Upper-Body Development

Push-Ups

The basic push-up is done from the front-leaning rest position. Only the hands and toes are on the floor, and the body is kept as straight as possible. The exercise is a two-count movement as the body is lowered by bending only at the elbows and then returned to the starting position.

As the body is lowered, only the chest touches the floor before the return to the starting position. The push-up should be done with controlled movement. The

15

arms can be adjusted together or apart, depending on the muscles desired to be exercised. As the arms are moved closer together, greater demands are placed on the triceps. Spreading the arms beyond shoulder width increases the workload on the muscles across the chest (pectorals). Variation: If performing a full push-up is difficult, the half (knee) push-up is excellent. Movement is the same as the push-up, but the body is supported by the hands and knees.

Inclined Wall Push-Ups

This exercise can be done with either the feet or the hands on the wall. The hands version is easier and should precede the push-up with feet on the wall. In the hands version, the hands are placed on the wall, and the feet walk as far from the wall as possible. The farther the performer's feet move from the wall, the more inclined and difficult the push-up is.

When the student can do the inclined push-up with the hands on the wall, the feet-on-the-wall version can be attempted. This exercise is like doing a push-up in the handstand position and demands a great deal of strength. As the hands are walked closer to the wall, the incline becomes less, and greater demand is placed on the shoulder girdle muscles.

Reclining Partner Pull-Ups

Students find a partner of similar strength. One partner assumes a supine position on the floor, and the other stands in a straddle position at chest level. Partners use a wristlock grip with both hands. The standing partner stands erect, while the partner in the supine position attempts to do a reclining pull-up (see figure 15.3). The upward pull is done completely by the person in supine position bending at the elbows. The standing person's task is to remain rigid and erect.

The person in the supine position should start this exercise with the feet against a wall. This position will prevent the person from sliding and keep the focus of the activity on upper-body development.

FIGURE 15.3 Reclining partner pull-ups.

Rocking Chair

The exerciser moves to a prone position on the floor. With the arms out to the sides of the body, the back is arched to raise the upper body off the floor. While the upper body is elevated, different activities and arm positions can be attempted. For example, arm circling, waving, clapping hands, or placing the hands behind the head can add challenge to this upper-back and shoulder development activity. Variation: The lower body can be elevated instead of the upper body. Various movements can then be done with the legs. In either exercise, a partner may be required to hold the half of the body not being moved.

Crab Walk

This activity can be modified in several ways to develop trunk and upper-body strength. The crab position is an inverted walk on all fours. The belly faces the ceiling, and the weight is supported on the hands and feet. Crab walking can be done in all directions and should be performed with the trunk as straight as possible. Variations: The crab kick can be executed from this position by alternating forward kicks of the left and right leg. The double crab kick is done by kicking both feet forward and then backward simultaneously.

Exercises for the Midsection

Reverse Curl

Lie on the back with the hands on the floor to the sides of the body. Curl the knees to the chest. The upper body remains on the floor. Try to lift the buttocks and lower the back off the floor. To increase the challenge, do not return the feet to the floor after each repetition, lowering them to within 1 to 2 inches (2.5 to 5 cm) off the floor. This activity requires greater abdominal strength because there is no resting period (feet on floor).

Pelvis Tilter

Lie on the back with feet flat on the floor, knees bent, arms out in wing position, and palms up. Flatten the lower back, bringing it closer to the floor by tensing the lower abdominals and lifting up on the pelvis. Hold for 8 to 12 counts. Tense slowly and release slowly.

Knee Touch Curl-Up

Lie on the back with feet flat and knees bent, and with hands flat on top of thighs. Leading with the chin, slide the hands forward until the fingers touch the kneecaps and gradually curl the head and shoulders until the shoulder blades are lifted off the floor. Hold for eight counts and return to the original position. To avoid stress on the lower back, do not curl up to the sitting position.

Curl-up

Lie on the back with feet flat, knees bent, and arms on the floor at the side of the body with palms down. Lift the head and shoulders to a 45-degree angle and then back in a two-count pattern. The hands should slide forward on the floor 3 to 4 inches (7.5 to 10.0 cm). The curl-up can also be done as an eight-count exercise, moving up on one count, holding for six counts, and moving down on the last count.

Curl-up With Twist

Lie on the back with feet flat and knees bent. Arms are folded and placed across the chest with hands on shoulders. Do a partial curl-up and twist the chest to the left. Repeat, turning the chest to the right.

Leg Extension

Sit on the floor with legs extended and hands on hips. With a quick, vigorous action, raise the knees and bring both heels as close to the seat as possible (see figure 15.4). The movement is a drag with the toes touching lightly. Return to the original position.

FIGURE 15.4   Leg extension.

Abdominal Cruncher

Lie in supine position with feet flat, knees bent, and palms of hands cupped over the ears (not behind the head). An alternate position is to fold the arms across the chest and place the hands on the shoulders. Tuck the chin and curl upward until the shoulder blades leave the floor. Return to the floor with a slow uncurling.

Plank Variations

Create a bridge with the body in which only the toes and forearms (forearms are directly under the chest) are touching the ground. Keep the back as flat as possible, while making sure that the hips do not raise or sag. Be-

ginners can start by holding this position for 10 seconds; more advanced performers can hold it as long as possible. The side plank requires the bridge to be on one forearm and the outside of one foot, the body still needs to be straight, and both sides should be done.

Exercises for the Lower Body

Squat Jumps

Begin in a squatting position with one foot slightly ahead of the other. Take part of the weight with the hands in front of the body. Jump as high as possible and return to the squatting position. Taking some of the body weight with the hands prevents stressing the knee joints.

Treadmill

Begin on all fours with one foot forward and one behind. Rapidly alternate foot positions while taking the weight of the body on the arms. The movement of the feet can be varied by moving both feet forward and back simultaneously or by moving the feet apart and together.

Jumping Jacks

Begin in standing position with the arms at the sides and feet together. Simultaneously lift the arms overhead and spread the legs on the first count. On the second count, return arms and legs to the starting position. Variations: Feet and arm movements can be varied. The arms can be moved in front of the body, behind the body, and in different patterns. The legs can be split forward and backward, crossed in front of each other, and swung to the front of the body.

Running in Place

Running in place is most beneficial when the upper leg is lifted parallel to the floor. The thighs can touch the hands held slightly above the parallel line to encourage the high lift.

Side-Leg Flex

Lie on the side on the floor. Rest the head in the right hand and place the left hand along the side of the body. On the first count, lift the left leg and arm and point them toward the ceiling. Return to the starting position on the second count. Rotate to the other side of the body after performing the desired number of repetitions. Variation: The double side-leg flex is an exercise that demands more effort. Both legs are lifted simultaneously as far off the floor as possible.

15

Front-Leg Kick

From a standing position, alternately kick each leg forward and as high as possible. This exercise should be done rhythmically so that all movement occurs on the toes. When the leg is kicked upward, the arm on the same side should be moved forward to touch the toe of the lifted leg.

Avoiding Harmful Practices and Exercises

The following points contraindicate certain exercise practices and should be considered when offering fitness instruction. For in-depth coverage of contraindicated exercises, consult *Concepts of Fitness and Wellness* by Corbin and colleagues (2013).

1. The following techniques should be avoided when performing abdominal exercises that lift the head and trunk off the floor:

   - *Avoid placing the hands behind the head or high on the neck.* This positioning may cause hyperflexion and injury to the discs when the elbows swing forward to help pull the body up.

   - *Keep the knees bent.* Straight legs cause the hip flexor muscles to be used earlier and more forcefully, making it difficult to maintain a proper pelvic tilt.

   - *Do not hold the feet on the floor.* Having another student secure the feet places more force on the lumbar vertebrae and may lead to lumbar hyperextension.

   - *Do not lift the buttocks and lumbar region off the floor.* This also causes the hip flexor muscles to contract vigorously.

2. Numerous types of stretching activities have been used to develop flexibility. Ballistic stretching (strong bouncing movements) formerly was the most common stretching method used, but it has been discouraged for many years because it was thought to increase delayed-onset muscle soreness. Dynamic stretching includes moving parts of the body and gradually increasing the range of motion. The term *dynamic stretching* is often used interchangeably with *ballistic stretching*, but dynamic stretching avoids bouncy movements.

3. If forward flexion is done from a sitting position to touch the toes, the bend should be from the hips, not from the waist, and should be done with one leg flexed. To conform with this concern, the new FitnessGram sit-and-reach test item is performed with one leg flexed to reduce stress on the lower back.

4. Straight-leg raises from a supine position should be avoided because they may strain the lower back. The problem can be somewhat alleviated by placing the hands under the small of the back, but avoiding such exercises is probably best.

5. Deep knee bends (full squats) and the duck walk should be avoided. They may cause damage to the knee joints and have little developmental value. Much more beneficial is flexing the knee joint to 90 degrees and returning to a standing position.

6. When doing stretching exercises from a standing position, the knees should not be hyperextended. The knee joint should be relaxed rather than locked. Having students do their stretching with bent knees is often effective in reminding them not to hyperextend the joint. In all stretching activities, participants should be allowed to judge their range of motion. Expecting all students to be able to touch their toes is unrealistic. To alleviate concern about touching the toes from this position, students can do so from a sitting position with one leg flexed.

7. Activities that place stress on the neck should be avoided. Examples of activities in which caution should be used are the inverted bicycle, wrestler's bridge, and abdominal exercises with the hands behind the head.

8. The so-called hurdler's stretch should be avoided. This activity is done in the sitting position with one leg forward and the other leg bent and to the rear. Using this stretch places undue pressure on the knee joint of the bent leg. Substitute a stretch using a similar position with one leg straight forward and the other leg bent with the foot placed in the crotch area.

9. Stretches that demand excessive back arching should be avoided. For example, while lying in the prone position, the student reaches back and grabs the ankles. By pulling and arching, the exerciser can hyperextend the lower back. This action places stress on the discs and stretches the abdominal muscles (not needed by most people).

Activities and Routines for Developing Fitness

The following are methods of organizing exercises and aerobic activities to develop total body fitness. All the routines should enhance muscular strength and endurance, as well as cardiorespiratory endurance.

Teacher and Student Leader Exercise Routines

During the first part of the school year, teachers should lead and teach all exercises to ensure that students learn them correctly. In addition, teachers should stay involved in fitness activities throughout the year to demonstrate their willingness to do the activities they are asking students to perform. In some cases, teachers ask students to exercise and maintain fitness while they choose not to do either. Pushing others to be fit is difficult if the teacher does not make a similar personal commitment.

When students have learned a wide repertoire of exercises, they can begin to lead the exercise routines. Leading means not only starting and stopping the exercises but also designing well-balanced routines that offer total body development. Students can be guided in performing the desired number of repetitions and counting exercises correctly as they are performed. In any case, students should not be forced to lead the exercises; leading should be a personal choice.

More than one student leader can be used at a time. For example, if four leaders are selected, each can be thinking of the exercises to choose when it is his or her turn. Leaders can be placed on four sides of the class, and the class can rotate one-quarter turn to face a new leader after each exercise. If a leader cannot think of an appropriate exercise, the class can be asked to volunteer one. In any case, emphasis should be placed on learning to weave together a set of exercises that offers total body development. Continuous movement activity should also be added to the exercise routines to ensure cardiorespiratory endurance development.

Group Leader Exercises

Group leader exercises offer students the opportunity to develop fitness routines without teacher intervention. Group leaders take their group to a designated area and lead them through a fitness routine. Giving a blank exercise card to each leader a few days before the student will lead is helpful. The leader can develop a routine and write down the exercises and repetitions or duration of each.

Students who have learned a wide repertoire of exercises can help lead exercises.

Leaders can also assign members of the group to lead or to offer certain activities. A number of exercises can be specified to develop a particular area of the body. For example, ask leaders to develop a routine that has two exercises for the arm–shoulder girdle area, two for the abdominal region, one for the legs, three for flexibility, and two minutes of continuous movement. The responsibility for planning a fitness routine that is balanced and developmental should shift gradually from the teacher to the students.

Exercises to Music

Without question, music increases the motivational level of students during exercise. Although many commercial exercise-to-music playlists are available, they all suffer from two major problems: They seldom meet the specific workload requirements of different groups of students, and they cannot provide the necessary systematic overload. Teachers therefore need to develop their own homemade exercise-to-music playlists that they can tailor to meet the needs of a specific class or grade.

Homemade playlists are one option. Music that is currently popular can be combined with exercises that students have already learned. Avoid music that might affront some members of the community. Instrumental versions of songs may be best to avoid playing lyrics. Either the teacher or a group of students can make the playlist. When students create the playlist, they have control over the selection, sequence, and number of exercises and repetitions. The routines can be adapted to needs and characteristics of the group. Procedures for starting and stopping exercises can be incorporated easily in the playlist.

Continuous Movement Activities

In order to maintain higher intensity for a fitness activity, continuous movement activities are often incorporated. These can include jogging, rope jumping, and four corners activity, among others.

Jogging

Jogging is running at a slow pace. It is faster than walking but slower than sprinting. Jogging is an excellent conditioner for the cardiorespiratory system, and virtually all students can do it. It does not require specialized equipment or specialized skill.

Any one of three approaches can be used to develop a jogging program. The first is the jog–walk approach, which emphasizes the amount of time that students are involved in continuous movement. Students determine how far they can jog before they need to slow down and walk. Students continue walking until they are again ready to jog. The goal is to decrease the length and time of the walking episodes and to increase the time spent jogging.

A second approach to increasing endurance through jogging is to set up definite and measured intervals. An example would be setting up cones to mark jogging intervals of 110 yards (100 m) and walking intervals of 55 yards (50 m). As the fitness level increases, the length of the jogging interval is increased and the walking interval is decreased.

Finally, the workload can be increased by increasing either the duration or the pace of the jogging. The goal is either to maintain a constant pace over a longer distance or to run the same distance at an increased pace. Increasing the speed is usually the less desirable alternative because the intensity of the exercise may discourage students.

Jogging is performed in an erect body position with a minimal amount of leaning. Excessive leaning is less efficient and demands a greater amount of energy. The elbows should be bent, and the arms should be carried in a relaxed manner. Most joggers strike the ground with a flat foot, allowing the force of impact to be absorbed over a larger surface area, which seems to be more desirable. Some joggers land on the heel and then rotate to the toe. In either case, trying to change a jogger's foot action is often ineffective.

Jogging should be a noncompetitive activity. Students should be encouraged to look for self-improvement instead of comparing their performance with others. An enjoyable technique is to ask students to jog with a partner who has similar ability. They should be encouraged to talk and visit while they jog. Suggest that if they find it difficult to talk while jogging, they are probably running too fast.

Endurance and continuous activity should be rewarded. Teachers sometimes ask students to run a certain distance, and then they reward those who complete the distance first. This practice is discouraging to most of the joggers. Students should be permitted to run in any direction they desire until a certain amount of time has elapsed. This approach prevents the situation in which a few gifted runners finish first and must sit and wait for the rest of the class to complete a given distance.

A general rule of thumb for beginning a jogging program is to ask students to walk and jog continuously for 5 minutes. Increase the amount of time 1 minute per week up to 15 minutes. Students can increase the total amount of time, while they also try to reduce the amount of walking. Ideas for an instructional unit on jogging can be found in chapter 19.

Rope Jumping

Rope jumping is a demanding activity that requires little equipment. For some participants, it can be a valuable approach to cardiorespiratory fitness. The energy demands of rope jumping are similar to those of jogging. Rope jumping can be performed for a specified amount of time or for a specified number of jumps.

A variety of activities can be done with a jump rope to help avoid the monotony and excessive fatigue of continuous jumping. The rope can be turned at fast or slow speeds while various foot steps are performed. If rope jumping is used for the fitness portion of the lesson, it should be alternated with stretching activities to give students an opportunity to recover from aerobic demands. See chapter 19 for ideas on developing a unit of instruction on rope jumping.

Four Corners

A large rectangle is formed using four cones as markers. Students move continually around the perimeter of the rectangle. At each corner, a different movement is performed. Examples of activity alternatives that can be performed on the long sides of the rectangle are jogging, power skipping, sliding, jumping, and hopping. On the short sides of the rectangle, movements requiring slower, more concentrated attention (for example, lunges and inchworms) can be performed. An interesting variation is to set up tumbling activities or tires and challenge students to go over, around, and through them. The need for continuous movement should be emphasized, and the rectangle should be large enough to provide a challenging workload for the cardiorespiratory system.

Interval Training

Interval training involves carefully controlling the work and rest intervals of the participant. Intervals of work (exercise) and rest can be measured in distance, repetitions, or time. Interval training is done by monitoring the heart rate. The student first needs to get the heart rate up to 120 to 140 beats per minute with a warm-up routine. Strenuous activity is then performed to push the heart rate into the 170 to 180 beats-per-minute range. At this point, the student begins the rest interval (usually walking) until the heart rate returns to 120 to 140 beats per minute. Theoretically, the amount of time it takes for the heart rate to return to 120 to 140 beats per minute should not exceed 90 seconds. The major advantage of interval training is that endurance can be increased markedly in a short time.

Interval training can be used with various locomotor movements. For example, the following work and rest activities can be alternated. Intervals can be measured in either distance or time.

Work activities	Rest activities
Brisk walking	Slow walking
Jogging	Walking
Sprinting	Jogging
Rope jumping	Walking
Jumping in place	Walking

Circuit Training

Exercise stations are organized into a circuit for the sake of fitness development. Each of the stations contributes, in part, to the total fitness of the participant. The components of fitness—flexibility, muscular strength and endurance, and cardiorespiratory endurance—are represented in the circuit.

Development of a Circuit

1. If the circuit is to be used as a group activity, all class members must be capable of performing each of the exercises.

2. Organize the stations so that different muscle groups or fitness components are exercised; in other words, consecutive stations should not place demands on the same area of the body.

3. Students should know how to perform all the activities correctly. Proper form is important. Instruction can be done verbally, or descriptive posters can be placed at each station.

4. Distribute students evenly among the stations at the beginning of the exercise bout. A rotation plan ensures that students move to the correct station.

5. Measure dosage in time or repetitions. Students can move on their own to the next station if they have completed the required number of repetitions. If a time criterion is used, the class moves as a whole when students have exercised for the specified period.

6. To increase the demands on the cardiorespiratory system, one or two of the stations can include rope jumping or running in place. An alternative is to have students run around the perimeter of the entire circuit a certain number of times before they move to the next station.

15

7. The circuit should contain at least 10 stations. The result of participation in the circuit is a total body workout.

Timing and Dosage

Workload at each station should be based on time, and students should be asked to do their best within that time. Signals to start exercising, stop exercising, and rotate to the next stations are given to allow accurate timing of intervals. A reasonable expectation for beginning circuit training is 40 seconds per station. The amount of rest between stations can be monitored to increase or decrease the workload. An effective way of timing the circuit is to use a playlist of popular music that students enjoy and that includes signals to stop and start activities at proper intervals. Following are two interval workouts that incorporate hoops and core exercises.

Hoop Cardio Circuit

1. Jumping jacks
2. Waist spin (hoop)
3. High knees
4. Squat and spin (hoop)
5. Ski jumps
6. Lunge spin (hoop)
7. Burpees
8. Arm spin (hoop)
9. Plank jacks
10. Arm and waist spin (hoop)

Cardio Core Circuit

1. Mountain climbers
2. Low jacks (jacks while squatting)
3. High plank hold (hold a push-up position)
4. Star jumps
5. Low plank toe touches (elbow plank, touch floor with left toe, swing leg out and touch ground to left of body with left toe, swing leg back in, repeat on right side)
6. Jumping jacks
7. Crunches
8. Jumping rope
9. 6-inch (15 cm) leg hold (lie on back with hands under bottom, raise both feet 6 inches [15 cm] off ground and hold)
10. High knees

Reprinted by permission from Angela Stark.

Figure 15.5 is an example of a circuit that might be developed for middle school students.

Nine-station course

1 Rope jumping	2 Push-ups	3 Agility run	4 Arm circles
8 Windmill	2 Treadmill	3 Crab walk	4 Rowing

9
Hula-hooping (or any relaxing "fun" activity)

FIGURE 15.5 Circuit-training stations.

Astronaut Drills

Astronaut drills are continuous movement activities that combine exercises with walking and jogging. Students move randomly throughout the area or follow each other in a circle formation. The drills begin with brisk walking. On signal, the teacher or selected students lead the class in exercises or stunt activities. If a movement is not developed immediately, the class runs or walks in place. Combinations of the following activities can be arranged to develop a demanding routine:

1. Perform various locomotor movements such as hopping, running, jumping, leaping, skipping, and running on the toes.
2. Perform exercises such as arm circles, body twists, and trunk and upper-body stretches while moving around the area.
3. Perform stationary exercises such as push-ups, sit-ups, and jumping jacks to stress development of the upper body and abdominal wall.

Students move throughout the area and perform as many exercises as possible. They can also develop individual routines that control the amounts of time allotted for movement activity and stationary activity. The following is an example of an astronaut drill that might be implemented. The duration of the movements is timed, and students are encouraged to do the best they can within the specified time.

1. Walk throughout the area.
2. Run and hurdle.
3. Stop and perform push-ups.

4. Walk and do arm circles.

5. Do a crab walk.

6. Stop, find a friend, and perform partner strength exercises.

7. Hop for a period of time on each foot.

8. Walk on all fours (bear crawl).

9. Run, with the knees lifted as high as possible.

10. Stop and perform a treadmill.

11. Repeat the previous steps.

Continuity Exercises

Continuity exercises can be done in squad formation or scatter formation. Because each student has a jump rope, students must have plenty of room to avoid hitting each other. Performers alternate between rope jumping and exercises. Rope jumping is done for timed episodes with music to help maintain the rhythm. At the signal to stop rope jumping, students quickly drop the rope and move into position for the exercise. Selected exercises should be performed in a down position with a leader who says, "Ready," and the students respond, "One-two," while performing the exercise. For each repetition, students wait until the command "Ready" is given. Students are allowed to monitor their own speed and intensity. The following is an example of a routine:

- *1st signal.* Begin rope jumping.
- *2nd signal.* Stop jumping, drop ropes, and move to the push-up position. On each command of "Ready," do one push-up.
- *3rd signal.* Resume rope jumping.
- *4th signal.* Drop ropes and move into supine position on the floor with the arms overhead, prepared to do the rowing exercise. On the command "Ready," perform the exercise.
- *5th signal.* Resume rope jumping.
- *6th signal.* Drop the ropes and move into crab position. Prepare to do the double crab kick. On the signal "Ready," extend both feet forward and back.
- *7th signal.* Resume rope jumping.
- *8th signal.* Move into position for the side-leg flex exercise. On the command "Ready," lift the upper leg and return it to the starting position.
- *9th signal.* Resume rope jumping.
- *10th signal.* Move into position for the reclining partner pull-up. On signal, pull the body up

on count 1, and return to the floor on count 2. Switch positions with your partner after performing the proper number of repetitions.

The number of repetitions and the duration of the rope-jumping episodes should be determined by the fitness levels of the students. More exercises can be added to the routine. Instructors can use an audio device to signal the start and finish of the rope-jumping episodes. Continuity exercises are an example of interval training. The rope jumping stresses the cardiorespiratory system, and the exercises develop strength and allow the performer to recover.

Partner Resistance Exercises

Partner resistance exercises are enjoyable for students because they offer variable workloads and a chance to work with a partner. Partners must be matched in size and strength so that they can challenge each other. The exercises should be performed throughout the full range of motion at each joint and take 8 to 12 seconds each to complete. The partner providing the resistance gives the "Begin" command and counts the duration of the exercise. Each student does three sets of each exercise as the partners alternate the exercise and resistance roles.

The following are examples of exercises that can be performed. Challenge students to invent their own partner resistance exercises and to develop a set of exercises that strengthens all body parts.

Arm Curl-Ups

The exerciser keeps the upper arms against the sides of the body, bends the elbows, and turns the palms up. The partner puts fists in the exerciser's palms. The exerciser then attempts to curl the forearms upward to the shoulders. To develop the opposite set of muscles, the exerciser pushes down in the opposite direction, starting with the palms at shoulder level.

Forearm Flex

The exerciser places the hands, palms down, on the partner's shoulders. The exerciser attempts to push the partner into the floor. The partner may slowly lower the body to allow the exerciser to move through the full range of motion. The exerciser can try the exercise with the palms up.

Fist Pull-Apart

The exerciser places the fists together in front of the body at shoulder level. The exerciser attempts to pull the

15

hands apart, while the partner forces them together with pressure on the elbows. The exerciser reverses this exercise and begins with the fists apart. The partner tries to push them together by grasping the wrists.

Pec-Deck

The exerciser holds the arms up at a 90-degree angle at shoulder height. The exerciser then pushes the arms together in front of the body, similar to the motion on a pec-deck machine. The exercise may be reversed by having resistance provided on the inside or outside of the arms, depending on which direction the exerciser is moving.

Butterfly

The exerciser holds the arms straight, forming a right angle with the side of the body (see figure 15.6). The partner attempts to hold the arms down, while the exerciser lifts with straight arms to the sides. The exerciser can try the activity by starting with the arms above the head and then moving them down to the sides against partner's effort to hold them up.

FIGURE 15.6   Butterfly.

Camelback

The exerciser is on all fours with the head up. The partner sits or pushes on the exerciser's back, while the exerciser tries to hump the back like a camel.

Back Builder

The exerciser spreads the legs and bends forward at the waist with the head up. The partner faces the exerciser and clasps the hands together behind the exerciser's neck. The exerciser then attempts to stand upright, while the partner pulls downward.

Scissors

The exerciser lies on one side, while the partner straddles him or her and holds the upper leg down. The exerciser attempts to raise the top leg. The exercise is reversed and performed with the other leg.

Bear Trap

The exerciser performs as in the scissors but spreads the legs first and attempts to move them together, while the partner holds them apart.

Knee Bender

The exerciser lies in prone position with legs straight and arms ahead on the floor. The partner places the hands on the back of exerciser's ankle. The exerciser attempts to flex the knee, while the partner applies pressure. Reverse legs. The exerciser can try this exercise in the opposite direction with the knee joint at a 90-degree angle.

Resistance Push-Up

The exerciser is in push-up position with arms bent so that the body is halfway up from the floor. The partner straddles or stands alongside the exerciser's head and puts pressure on the top of the shoulders by pushing down. The partner must judge the amount of pressure to apply to prevent the exerciser from collapsing.

Aerobic movements such as walking, jogging, sliding, skipping, and so on can be alternated with the partner resistance exercises to create a balanced fitness routine. A recommended format is to devote 45 seconds to partner resistance and 20 to 30 seconds to aerobic movements. Creative signs can help structure this routine.

Challenge Courses

Challenge courses, or parcourses, are popular throughout the country. Various stations are developed, and the participants move from station to station as they cover the course. The type of movement done between stations can also place demands on the participants' body systems. Courses can be run for time, or repetitions can be increased to ensure balanced fitness development. Courses should be developed to exercise all parts of the body. A variety of activities, such as stretching, vaulting, agility runs, climbing, hanging and chinning, and crawling, can be included to place demands on all aspects of fitness. Figure 15.7 represents an indoor challenge course that might be constructed for students.

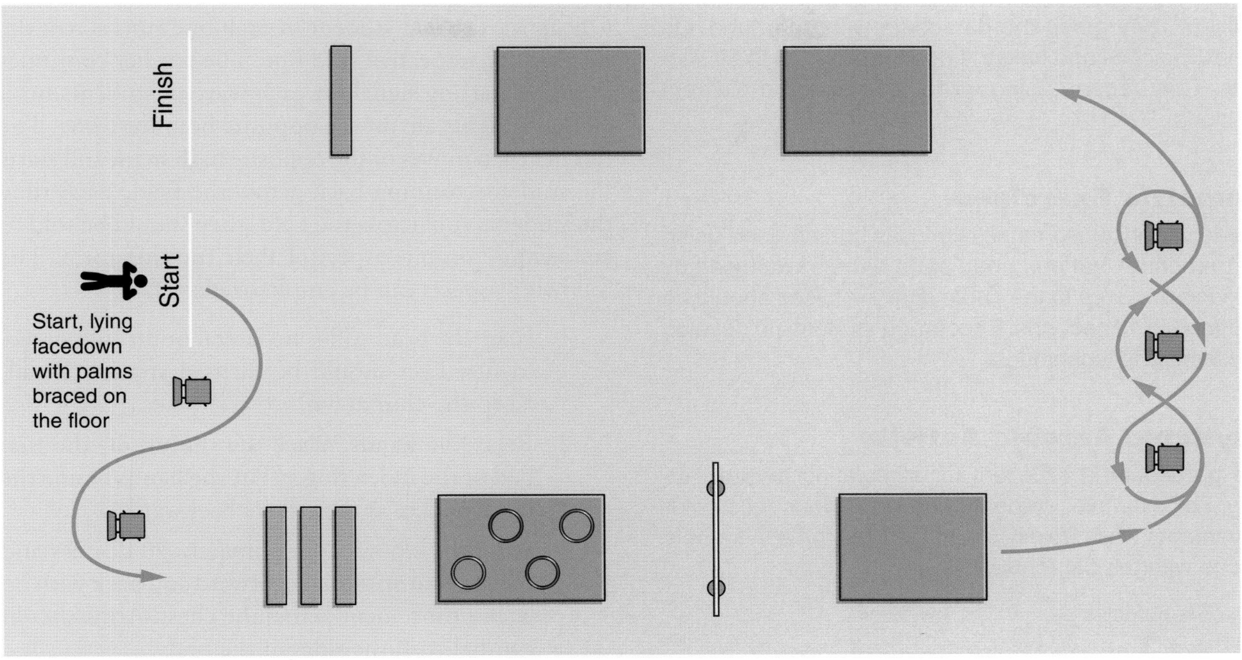

10. Cross the finish line.

9. Vault 36 in. box or horse.

8. Do a forward roll the length of the mat.

7. Climb to the top of a rope or hang for 20 sec.

6. Do an agility run (figure eight) around 3 chairs.

Finish

Start

Start, lying facedown with palms braced on the floor

1. Run around 2 chairs.

2. Hurdle over 3 benches.

3. Crawl through 4 tires.

4. High jump over a 30 in. high bar.

5. Do a crab walk the length of the mat, feet first.

FIGURE 15.7   Challenge course.

Parachute Exercises

The parachute can be used to develop fitness activities that are exciting and challenging. Through these activities, students work together to enhance their fitness. They should be encouraged to develop personalized group activities. The following are examples of exercises that use the parachute.

Toe Toucher

Students sit with the feet extended under the parachute and hold it taut with a two-hand grip, drawing it to the chin. They bend forward and touch the grip to the toes. They then return the parachute to the stretched position.

Curl-Up

Students extend the body under the parachute in curl-up position so that it comes up to the chin when held taut. They do curl-ups, returning each time to the stretched position. Encourage students to work together and snap the parachute tight each time they recline.

Dorsal Lift

In prone position, students lie with the head toward the chute. They grasp the chute with the arms extended overhead. On signal, they raise the chute off the floor while simultaneously raising the head and chest. Encourage students to lift the chute high enough so they can see a friend across the way.

Sitting Leg Lift

In a sitting position with the legs under the chute, students lift the legs on signal while holding the chute taut and lift the chute off the floor. They hold the position for 6 to 10 seconds and try to keep the legs straight. As a variation, they can start in a supine position with the legs under the parachute and do a V-seat.

Sitting Pulls

Students sit with their backs to the parachute. They grasp it and raise it overhead. On signal, they try to pull the parachute down to the knees. Other variations are done facing the parachute and raising it above the head, lowering it to eye level, and lowering it to waist level. Emphasis should be placed on using the arms and shoulder girdle to apply force rather than leaning.

15

All-Fours Pulls

Students get on the floor in a crab-, bear-, or seal-walk position. They grasp the parachute with one hand. On signal, they pull and hold the contraction for 6 to 10 seconds. They repeat, using the other hand and different positions.

Isometric Exercises

A wide variety of isometric exercises can be done using the parachute. Various body parts can be exercised by applying pressure to the chute. The exercises should be held for 6 to 10 seconds. Encourage students to develop new isometric techniques.

Rhythmic Aerobic Activity

The parachute is excellent for stimulating aerobic activity. For example, students can do various locomotor movements while holding on to the parachute. A sample routine with the parachute follows:

1. Skip clockwise.
2. Skip counterclockwise.
3. Jump to the center of the parachute.
4. Hop backward and tighten the chute.
5. Slowly lift the parachute overhead.
6. Slowly lower the parachute to the toes.
7. Quickly lift the parachute overhead.
8. Quickly lower the parachute to the toes.
9. Repeat steps 5 through 8.
10. Run clockwise with the parachute held overhead.
11. Run backward with the parachute held at waist level.
12. Make a dome.
13. Repeat steps 10 through 12.
14. Finish with a parachute lift and release.

Running Activities and Drills

A number of running drills and activities can be used to improve running techniques, agility, and fitness, depending on how they are administered. Aerobic ability varies widely in classes, and many students may not be able to do much running because of being overweight and having other disabilities. Offer other options or allow them to perform the drill while walking.

Form Running

This drill works well on a football field using the yard lines as markers. A group of students lines up on the boundary line at the goal line, 10-yard line, 20-yard line,

30-yard line, and so forth. The teacher stands on the hash mark closest to the students, on about the 25-yard line. On signal, the first student in each line runs across the field on the respective yard line. The teacher continues to give a starting signal for each wave of students until all the students are on the opposite boundary line. The teacher then moves to the opposite hash mark and starts the students running back across the field. Each time the students run across the field, they should be told to concentrate on one aspect of their running form. The following aspects can be emphasized:

1. Keep the head still—no lateral or turning movements. Eyes should be focused straight ahead. Keep the chin down.
2. Relax the hands. Place the thumb on the first pad of the index finger. Put the hands beside the front pocket as they move backward.
3. Bend the elbows approximately 90 degrees and move the arms straight forward and back with no lateral movement across the chest. Arms should gently brush the sides of the body.
4. Align the feet straight ahead. The knees drive straight ahead rather than upward. High knee action can be used as another variation, although it is not necessary for good running form. The heel of the foot should come close to the buttocks.
5. Align the foot, knee, and hip. The body tilts forward about 5 degrees from the feet, not from the hips.
6. The length of the stride is usually shorter for longer runs (i.e., a longer stride for sprinting and a shorter stride for distance running).

Give students only one aspect of running form to concentrate on during each trip across the field so that they can emphasize and overlearn each point. Beginning slowly and increasing the speed gradually works best. Start the drill at half speed, proceed to three-quarter speed, and finally increase to full speed.

This same drill format can be used with other running activities.

1. Backward running. Students stay on the line. They roll the shoulders forward and keep them forward while running. They should emphasize the forward and backward movement of the arm by pulling that arm through with each step.
2. Crossover-step backward. The teacher stands on the boundary line, and the first wave of students moves 5 yards (m) out on their respective yard lines facing the teacher. The teacher gives a left-

or right-hand signal. The students start backward with a crossover step. When the teacher changes the direction signal, students rotate their hips and do a crossover step on the opposite side. Students must keep their eyes on the teacher and concentrate on rotating their hips and staying on the line.

3. Crossover-step forward. As students run forward, they concentrate on stepping across the line with each step. They should start slowly and increase the speed gradually.

4. Carioca step. Students stand sideways on the line with their arms held out, parallel to the ground. On signal, the students move sideways down the line by using a crossover step in front and a return step, a crossover step in back, and finally another step. They repeat the process for the length of the field. Students should make sure that they lead with both the right and left shoulder.

5. Shuffle sideways. Students stand sideways on the line in a ready position (feet shoulder-width apart, knees bent, head up, arms flexed in front of the body). On signal, students shuffle down the line without a crossover step. Students should also lead with both the left and right sides. A variation is to have students spread out down the line and face the teacher, who is standing in front of the entire group. The teacher gives a left- or right-hand signal to start the group moving.

Form-running drills can be done without lines if necessary. Use boundary cones to mark the beginning and end of each running section. Another variation is to place cones at one-third and two-thirds of the distance and ask students to vary their speed in each third. For example, students could jog the first third, sprint the second, and ease to three-quarter speed during the last third. Or they can change the type of running during each third. The following combinations might be used:

1. Jog, shuffle right, and shuffle left
2. Carioca step, shuffle, and sprint
3. Backward run, crossover left, and crossover right
4. Form run, crossover front, and form run
5. Carioca step left, carioca step right, and sprint

Walk–Jog–Sprint

In this continuous movement activity, the teacher controls the speed of movement with a whistle signal. Three whistles mean sprint, two mean jog, and one means walk. The students start by walking around a given area (track, field, or boundary cone). The teacher alternates the periods of jogging, sprinting, and walking for a number of minutes or for a given distance. The goal is to build up the time or distance progressively.

Pace Work

Students need to practice running at an even pace for a given distance, such as an 8- or 10-minute mile (5 or 6 min per km). Pacing can be practiced by running shorter segments of the distance at the correct speed. Using a marked track is easiest, but a workable track can be developed through placement of boundary cones. Using a rectangle is helpful for ease of measurement. Place a cone at every corner and in the middle of each side. Put an equal number of students at each cone. Students are challenged to run distances in a given time. For example, the first challenge may be to run the distance marked as close to 30 seconds as possible. Having a timer visible is best, but the teacher can also yell out times in increments of 5 seconds to help. Next, the class may be challenged to run the same distance in 25 seconds. Finally, they may be challenged to run that distance in 35 seconds. As students begin to understand how to pace themselves around the marked area, they can then be encouraged to run two laps, then three laps, then four laps using a certain pace (or a self-selected pace).

Random Running

Random running is a simple and effective way to improve cardiorespiratory fitness. The emphasis is on long, slow distance (LSD) running. Students are allowed to run randomly throughout the area at a pace that is comfortable for them. They are encouraged to find a partner and to talk while jogging.

Students who need to walk can do so without experiencing the stigma of finishing last during a run. The distance each student runs is not charted. Effort is acknowledged, rather than speed or distance-running ability. Emphasis is placed on being active, involved, and moving during the entire episode rather than on seeing how far the student can run or jog.

Students can begin with a 10-minute random running episode three times per week. The duration of the run can be increased 1 minute per week until students achieve a 20-minute episode. This approach allows most students to increase their workload in a gradual and palatable manner.

Fartlek

Fartlek is a form of training developed in Sweden in the 1930s and 1940s. (The term *fartlek* means "speed play.")

15

The training is aerobic in nature and entails hard but untimed long-distance efforts over topographic challenges. The hilly terrain is run at varied tempos. Fartlek is usually done on soft surfaces. A typical workout for an athlete in training might be as follows:

1. Five to 10 minutes of easy jogging
2. Steady, intense speed for 1 to 2 kilometers
3. Five minutes of rapid walking
4. Easy running broken by 50 to 60 meters of accelerated runs that cause moderate fatigue
5. Easy running with two to five intermittent swift strides every 100 meters until moderate fatigue results
6. Full uphill effort for 150 to 200 meters
7. One minute of fast-paced running on level ground
8. Easy running for 5 to 10 meters

This workout illustrates the variation involved in fartlek. Students can perform a workout that lasts 10 to 20 minutes and encompasses the many tempos and geographic features described. The run challenges can be written on cards, and students select runs of varying difficulty (easy, moderate, difficult, and strenuous).

Monopoly Fitness

Place students in groups of two to three at 12 to 14 fitness stations around the perimeter of the area. Station ideas could include stretch-band exercises, stretches, jump-rope activities, strength-development exercises, and jump-band activities. Students perform curls with exercise tubes as shown in figure 15.8. Have a student roll the dice. All students add the numbers when the dice stop rolling and jog forward the corresponding number of stations. They then perform the exercise listed at that station. Students may repeat some stations. Use music intervals to signal when to exercise and when to roll the dice.

FIGURE 15.8 Curls with exercise tubes on a fitness circuit.

Jump-Bands Circuit

Arrange this fitness routine as a circuit of stations around the area. Place students in groups of four with two jumpers and two band holders. Exercisers use the basic four-count step of "in, in, out, out." Students are encouraged to make a quick choice while working at each station and to choose an activity that will challenge their own levels of fitness. Other stations that can be integrated into this circuit include abdominal strength choices, upper-body strength choices, and flexibility choices. An interval of 30 seconds of music and 10 seconds of silence can be used to signal station changes.

Cardio-Choice Fitness

Create a circuit with several stations around the perimeter of the area. Use four cardio-choice signs, one placed in each corner of the room. Students are encouraged to make a quick choice while working at each station and to choose an activity that will challenge their personal levels of fitness. Other stations in the circuit include abdominal strength choices, upper-body strength choices, and flexibility choices. An interval of 30 seconds of music and 10 seconds of pause can be used to signal rotation to the next station and free the teacher to observe. Cardio-choice signs include the following: Cardio-choice A (two of each)—power walk and talk with a friend, jump rope, slide halfway, pivot, and do carioca steps; and cardio-choice B (two of each)—jog around the perimeter of the area, jump rope, and do step-ups.

Fitness Scavenger Hunt

Students can work together in teams or small groups. The teams stay together and hunt for the exercise area of the gym or field space. The teams are given a laminated sheet or card that lists the area to find and the activities to perform at the designated area. The sheets could have 8 to 12 activities, depending on how long the fitness segment of the lesson is going to last. Each group can be assigned a different starting point to ensure that students are spread across all areas and that a backup of students does not occur at one of the fitness areas. Examples of entries on the exercise sheet or card could be the following:

- Run to each corner of the gym and perform 25 curl-ups. All team members should work together.
- Run to the open set of bleachers and perform 25 step-ups on the first row. The count should be "up, up, down, down," with the steps.

- Do carioca steps to each of the other groups and tell them they are doing a good job.
- Jog to the tumbling mats and perform two sitting stretches; hold each for eight counts.
- Run and find the short jump ropes. Complete 25 jumps at a fast-time pace.
- Jog and touch five walls, two different red lines, and three different black lines. Stay together with your group.
- Jog to the "Jumping jacks" sign and perform 25 jumping jacks with at least four different variations in arm or foot patterns.

Students can complete all seven activities and then return to their squads and wait for the next activity.

Rabbit in the Hat Fitness

In this variation of the fitness scavenger hunt, various fitness activities are written on index cards and then placed in a "hat" (shoe box). The shoe box can then be placed at the center of the gym or at another convenient place for students to pick up and return the cards. Students can work alone or with a partner. Partners take turns selecting the fitness card from the box. The activities can be like the scavenger hunt activities or could include ballhandling skills with a specific area designated for the use of equipment. Examples could include the following:

- Dribble the basketball down and back up the length of the gym.
- Do a crab walk across the width of the gym.
- Jog and shake hands with eight different people. Tell them to have a good day.
- Perform two layup shots at three different baskets.
- Slide to the drinking fountain and get a drink.
- Do carioca steps around the basketball court two times.
- Perform a mirror drill with a partner for 30 seconds.
- Jog over and tell your teacher that physical education is a fun activity.
- Perform three partner resistance exercises with a different partner.

Music can be programmed on a playlist for 30-second intervals to structure the transitions for students. A 10-second interval without music could be used for getting a new card. Students could then perform as many repetitions as possible while the music is playing. This method allows more individualization for students with varying fitness and skill abilities. Students should be challenged to do as many activities as possible and try to improve as the units continue.

Partner Racetrack Fitness

Students begin work with a partner at one of five or six stations in the gym or on a field outside. The stations are arranged in a circle or rectangle around the area. Each station has a sign with five or six exercises or stretches to perform. On the start signal, one partner begins the first exercise or stretch on the card, while the other partner jogs around the perimeter of the stations. After the jogging partner returns, the partners switch roles and move down the list of activities on the cards. The teacher can also change the locomotor movement for the students going around the cones. For example, in addition to jogging, students could do carioca steps, slide, run backward, skip, or hurdle around the stations. The signs at the stations could include stretches, jumping jacks, crab kicks, treadmills, sit-ups, push-ups, body twists, and other variations. Continuous music could be used to motivate students. Stability balls and medicine balls can be added to the racetrack stations.

Uno Fitness

This activity was provided by Jo Geddes, Lexington, Kentucky. Organize students into groups of four with an Uno exercise card sheet and a stack of Uno cards. One student draws a card from the group, and students complete the activity based on the number or symbol and color:

- Red: sit-ups
- Blue: push-ups
- Yellow: burpees
- Green: lunges
- Skip card: one-lap jog around the gym
- Reverse card: one-lap jog backward around the gym
- Wild Draw 4 card: four repetitions of every exercise
- Wild card: 20-second rest

Reprinted by permission from Jo Geddes.

The Twelve Ways of Fitness

This add-on fitness game uses 12 student leaders. It follows the same format as the song "The Twelve Days of Christmas." Students could be in groups of 12, or a large group could be used with the student leaders. Each student adds on the next number of exercises. Here is an example:

1. Push-up (1st student leader)
2. Sit-ups (2nd leader adds on)
3. Coffee grinders (3rd leader adds on)
4. Crab kicks (4th leader adds on)
5. Golden rests (5th leader adds on)
6. Leaping leaps (6th leader adds on)
7. Jumping jacks (7th leader adds on)
8. Forward lunges (8th leader adds on)
9. Carioca steps (9th leader adds on)
10. Skipping skips (10th leader adds on)
11. Rooster hops (11th leader adds on)
12. Running steps (last student leader adds on)

Long Jump-Rope Fitness Routine

Students are in groups of three with a long jump rope. Two students turn the rope, and the third student is the jumper. When the music comes on, the jumper makes three jumps and begins running a figure eight around the turners. Jumpers make three jumps each time they enter the center of the figure eight. The focus is on entering the jumping area with the turning rope, making the three jumps, and then continuing around the figure eight. When the music stops, a new jumper starts and the former jumper becomes a turner. The music should be programmed for 30 to 45 seconds of music and 10 to 15 seconds of no music for change time.

Jump and Jog Fitness

Set up five or six cones in a circle around the gym with two or three jump ropes at each cone. Students need to get a partner and start at one of the cones. One partner jumps rope at the cone, while the other partner jogs around the circle. Partners switch roles with the completion of each lap. Teachers can vary the student movement around the cones with the following: walk, jog, slide, do carioca steps, power skip, and perform butt kickers (heels hit the butt).

As students improve their rope-jumping skills, the teacher can vary the foot patterns with the following:

two-foot basic step, jog step, side swings (left and right), jumping-jack step, ski jump step, scissors step, crossovers, and double jumps. Teachers can also stop the action and lead the class in a strength or flexibility exercise and then return the students to the jump and jog activities.

Cone Interval

This activity was provided by Jo Geddes, Lexington, Kentucky. Place six to eight cones on the sideline with a variety of strength station signs. Place students in partners. One partner completes the strength station, while the other one performs a locomotor skill from sideline to sideline. After 60-second intervals, students switch. After each of the pair completes that station, they rotate down the sideline to the next station. They repeat taking turns at the new station. Figure 15.9 shows sample station signs.

Reprinted by permission from Angela Stark.

Circuit Training Fitness With a Jog

Create stations for jumping rope, crab kicks, stretching, and doing sit-ups, treadmills, arm circles, agility runs, and push-ups. Students exercise for 30 seconds at each station for the first week and have 5 to 10 seconds to move up to the next station. During the next week, the station intervals can be longer, and a jog around the circuit stations can be added before moving up. The jog can be varied with a slide, power skip, carioca steps, and backward run. Variations for each station can be added or substituted. Station cards can have two or three variations of the exercise.

Partner Resistance and Aerobic Movement Fitness

Students alternate between a partner resistance activity and an aerobic activity. The intervals should be 45 to 60 seconds for the partner resistance activities and 30 seconds for the aerobic movement intervals. Students can work with a partner at a station that has a card listing the various resistance activities and aerobic activities. The resistance activities can be grouped into upper-body and lower-body activities. Each resistance activity should take 8 to 10 seconds through the full range of motion. Partners should provide enough resistance to allow the exerciser to complete the repetition in 8 to 10 seconds. After one repetition, the partners change roles. The aerobic activities can be done in place (jumping-jack variations) or moving around the stations (jog, skip, or

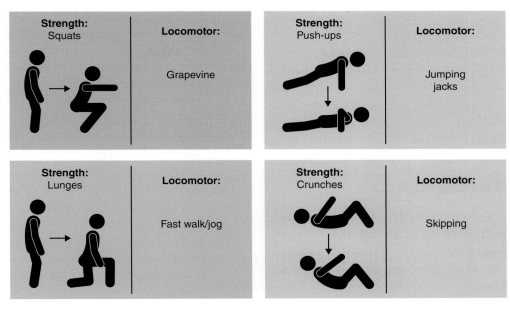

FIGURE 15.9 Sample station signs for cone interval.

slide). Several variations will be demonstrated. See the section Partner Resistance Exercises earlier in the chapter for complete descriptions of the activities.

Health Club Workouts

This group of activities is generally taught in health clubs. An important outcome for quality physical education programs is to graduate students who feel comfortable joining a health club. Students must leave high school having the perceived competence to participate with older adults. Many people will not join community clubs and organizations because they believe they are incompetent and will embarrass themselves. Clubs offer many popular activities, including spinning, aerobic dance, kickboxing, and Pilates. The intent of the following activities is to stimulate teachers to teach and stay current with activities taught in nearby health clubs. These activities change regularly, and course instruction in physical education will have to stay current to be relevant to juniors and seniors taking physical education classes.

Aerobics Workouts

At present, many types of aerobic activities are taught in health clubs. Aerobic dance is the basis for many variations of rhythmic exercise now implemented.

These routines develop a high level of cardiorespiratory fitness as well as strength and flexibility. Popular music is used to increase enjoyment of the activity. Rhythmic aerobic exercise consists of a mixture of fundamental movements—dance steps, swinging movements, and stretching exercises. Routines are developed to music that has a definite and obvious beat. Other variations of aerobic dance are step aerobics and low-impact aerobics. These activities are popular because they eliminate some of the stress on the legs and joints. The height of the steps can help determine the desired workload.

The activities and routines should ease the burden of learning. If the movement patterns are too difficult, students become self-conscious and discouraged. Use the following points as guidelines when teaching new aerobic exercise routines.

- Alternate the intensity of the activities to allow allows interval training to be built into the routines. Stretching movements can be alternated with demanding locomotor movements.

- Routines motivate more students when they appear not to be dance activities. The challenge is to develop demanding routines that increase the endurance of all participants. All students should feel comfortable performing the routines.

- Follow-the-leader activities work well with students after they have developed a repertoire of

15

movements. Each student can be responsible for leading one activity.

- Energetic and positive teachers strongly influence the success of the presentations. Students need to see teachers enjoying fitness activities.

- The following steps and movements can be used to develop a variety of routines. Most are performed to four counts, although this can be varied depending on the skill of the students.

Running and Walking Steps

1. Directional runs can be done forward, backward, diagonally, sideways, or turning.

2. Rhythmic runs integrate a specific movement (knee lift, clap, jump, and jump–turn) on the fourth beat.

3. Runs with stunts are performed while lifting the knees, kicking up the heels, or slapping the thighs or heels. Runs can also be done with the legs extended, such as the goose step.

4. Runs with the arms in various positions can include the arms on the head, straight up or down, or on the hips.

Movements on the Floor

1. Sit-ups or curl-ups can be used in many ways. For example, use four counts: (1) up to the knees, (2) touch the floor, (3) back to the knees, and (4) return to the floor. A V-seat can be held for two counts and rested for two counts.

2. Side-leg raises can be done with a straight leg on the side, or the lower leg can be extended while positioned on your back with bent knees.

3. Alternate leg raises are performed in supine position with one leg raised to meet the opposite hand. Repeat using the opposite leg or both legs.

4. Push-ups can be done in two- or four-count movements. A four count would be as follows: (1) halfway down, (2) touch chest to floor, (3) halfway up, and (4) arms fully extended.

5. Crab kicks and treadmills can be performed to four-count movements.

Standing Movements

1. Lunge variations. To perform a lunge, step forward onto the right foot while bending at the

knees and extending the arms into the air (counts one and two). Return to the starting position by bringing the right foot back and pulling arms into a jogging position (counts three and four). Vary the exercise by changing the direction of the move or the depth and speed of the lunge.

2. Side bends. Begin with the feet apart. Reach overhead while bending to the side. This movement is usually done to four beats: (1) reach, (2) bend, (3) return, and (4) arm down.

3. Reaches. Alternate reaching upward with the right and left arms. Reaches can be done sideways also and are usually two-count movements.

4. Arm and shoulder circles. Make arm circles with one or both arms. Vary the size and speed of the circles. Shoulder shrugs can be done in similar fashion.

Jumping-Jacks Variations

1. Arms alternately extended. Jump with the arms alternately extended upward and pulled into the chest.

2. Side jumping jacks. Use regular arm action while keeping the feet together for jumping forward, backward, and sideways.

3. Variations with feet. Try forward stride alternating, forward and side stride alternating, kicks or knee lifts, crossing the feet, and a heel–toe step.

Bounce Steps

1. Bounce and clap. The step is like the slow-time jump-rope step. Clap on every other bounce.

2. Bounce, turn, and clap. Make a quarter- or half-turn with each jump.

3. Three bounces and clap. Bounce three times and then clap and bounce on the fourth beat. Turns can be performed using the four counts.

4. Bounce and rock side to side. Transfer weight from side to side and forward and backward. Add clapping or arm swinging.

5. Bounce with body twist. Hold the arms at shoulder level and twist the lower body back and forth on each bounce.

6. Bounce with floor patterns. Bounce and make different floor patterns such as a box, diagonal, or triangle.

7. Bounce with kick variations. Perform kick vari-

ations such as knee lift, kick, knee lift, and kick; double kicks, knee lift, and slap knees; kick and clap under the knees. Combine the kicks with two- or four-count turns.

Activities With Manipulative Equipment

1. Jump ropes. Using the jump rope, perform basic steps such as forward, backward, slow time, and fast time. Jump on one foot, cross arms, and jump while jogging. Swing the rope from side to side with the handles in one hand and jump over it.
2. Beanbags. Toss and catch beanbags while performing various locomotor movements. For more challenge, use different tosses.
3. Hoops. Rhythmically swing the hoop around different body parts. Perform different locomotor movements around and over hoops.
4. Balls. Bounce, toss, and dribble balls; add locomotor movements while performing tasks.

Sample Routine

1. March, moving arms in large circles.
2. Hold a side lunge position and circle the right arm. Do reverse circling with the left arm.
3. Bounce forward twice, slapping thighs; then bounce backward twice, thrusting arms in the air.
4. Bounce and clap. Perform a quarter turn on every second bounce. Perform movement clockwise and counterclockwise.
5. Do a grapevine step with a clap on the fourth beat. Repeat it to the left.
6. Perform a jumping-jack variation, extending arms up and out.
7. Bounce and twist.
8. Do a two-count version of side jumping jacks.
9. Bounce, bounce, bounce, and clap to a four-count movement.
10. Do rhythmic running with a clap on the fourth beat. While running, move into a circle formation.
11. Bounce and twist.
12. Perform side leg raises with each leg.
13. Do rhythmic running with a clap on every fourth beat.

Strength Training

Most teachers accomplish strength development through strength training. Physical education teachers should instruct students in the use of weights and weight machines for proper development with an emphasis on safety. Using strength training as an instructional unit is often difficult because of lack of equipment and facilities.

Strength-training routines should develop all major body parts. A comprehensive program prevents the excessive development of specific body parts, which can lead to postural or joint problems. Exercises should be performed through the full range of motion. If training is done for a specific sport, analyze the sport and develop exercises that replicate the range of motion it uses.

Strength exercises should be performed at a speed similar to the movements performed in various physical activities. If a student is involved in an activity requiring speed, then the exercises should be performed at a similar speed. Similarly, if a student is training for activities that demand high levels of endurance, the exercises should be designed to increase this attribute. When the sport or activity demands strength, the training program can be geared to develop muscular strength. In each case, students should understand program differences and be able to develop a personal program. For an in-depth discussion of strength training, see chapter 19.

Safety

Students must know and practice necessary safety precautions. The following points should be clear and reinforced regularly. Post safety rules as a further reminder and to avoid possible lawsuits.

- Perform warm-up exercises before intense lifting. These exercises may be a set of calisthenics or a set of strength exercises at a lower level.
- Use correct form to prevent injury as well as to develop strength. When a heavy weight is lifted from the floor, the lift should be done with bent knees, straight back, and head up.
- Spot weightlifters. Spotters are necessary when near-maximum weight is lifted. Exercises such as the bench press, squats, and declined presses should always have two students present to spot.
- Check equipment regularly. Weights should be checked by the instructor before each period and by students each time they use them. Collars should be tightly fastened, cables checked, and bolts on machines periodically tightened.
- Wear wide leather practice belts when heavy

15

lifting is performed. A belt prevents injury to the lower back and abdominal wall.

- Explain all exercises in class before implementation. Discuss proper form, points of safety, and necessary spotting before students participate.

Repetitions and Sets

Many theories address the number of repetitions and sets that need to be performed to achieve optimum results. Repetitions are the number of times a participant performs an exercise to make a set. Each set, in turn, consists of a specified number of repetitions of the same exercise. Determining the proper number of repetitions or sets is difficult. Dozens of experts have researched this area without agreement. For physical education classes, a middle-of-the-road approach is probably best. Three sets of 10 repetitions should be performed for each exercise.

Strength or Endurance?

Muscular strength and endurance are developed using different methods. If maximum strength is desired, the exercise program should emphasize heavy weight and fewer repetitions. If endurance is the desired outcome, the program should emphasize a high number of repetitions with less weight. Some strength and endurance will be developed regardless of the type of program, but major gains will depend on the selected emphasis.

Frequency and Rest Intervals

Frequency is the number of workouts per week. The most common pattern is lifting every other day, leaving three days to recover and dissipate waste products. Some participants alternate by exercising the upper body and the lower body on different days. This pattern results in a six-day program while retaining the day of rest between workouts.

The rest interval between repetitions and sets can be timed carefully to increase the intensity of the workout. By organizing the exercises in a circuit stressing different muscle groups, the amount of time needed for a total workout can be reduced. In other words, less recovery time is needed between sets if the next exercise places demands on a different group of muscles.

Body Bar Exercises

Body Bars are fitness equipment that can be used to supplement the strength-training component of the health club physical education program. Developed in 1987, Body Bars are fitness bars that are available in regular length, which is 4 feet (1.2 m) long (3, 6, 9, 12, 15, 18, and 24 pounds [1.4, 2.7, 4.1, 5.4, 6.8, 8.2, and 10.9 kg]), mini-length, which is 2 feet (60 cm) long (4 and 6 pounds [1.8 and 2.7 kg]), and the heavy model, which is 5 feet (1.5 m) long (30 and 36 pounds [13.6 and 16.3 kg]). Flex bars are also available in 3- and 4-foot (90 and 120 cm) lengths with varying resistance to match students' abilities. Most high school girls should consider the regular length at 18 pounds (8.2 kg). Boys should consider the 18- or 24-pound (8.2 or 10.9 kg) versions or the heavier models, but the approach is still individual. Having a variety of lengths and weights is useful.

Body Bars can be combined with stability balls or medicine balls in a variety of lessons and circuit-training situations. We suggest the following lifts with Body Bars, which are explained in chapter 19 in the section Strength Training.

Lower Body

- Squat—quadriceps
- Squats with military press—quadriceps and deltoids
- Squats with toe raises—quadriceps and gastrocnemius muscles
- Lunges—gluteus maximus
- Straight leg dead lift—hamstrings
- Wide leg squats and plies—adductors
- Toe raises—gastrocnemius muscles

Upper Body

Figure 15.10 depicts a student performing pull-ups using a Body Bar with the help of two other students.

- Bench press—pectorals
- Bent-over rows—latissimus dorsi
- Military press—deltoids
- Forward raises—deltoids
- Standing rowing—deltoids
- Arm curls—biceps
- Arm curl sevens—biceps (seven counts halfway up and continue seven counts for the second half of the repetition, followed by seven counts for the full range of motion during the next repetition)
- Triceps extensions—triceps

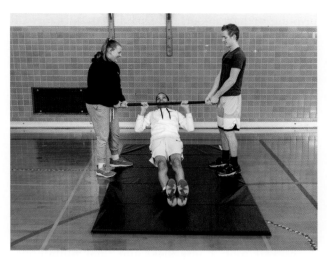

FIGURE 15.10   Pull-ups using a Body Bar and two partners.

Core

- Sit-ups with bar at chest. In figure 15.11, a student performs sit-ups using a Body Bar with a partner. The standing partner can perform an arm curl with each repetition.
- Bar on shelf sit-ups. Sit-up with bar at the chest and then a military press at the top of the sit-up.

FIGURE 15.11   Partner sit-ups with a Body Bar.

Unit Planning

Chapter 19 contains several ideas and activities for a unit on strength training that can be modified or augmented to meet the needs of the instructor, the students, and the physical education program.

Weightlifting and Powerlifting

Experts (e.g., Kozub & Brusseau, 2012) have suggested that introducing the lifetime strength events such as weightlifting and powerlifting in high school physical education programs offers a variety of students another strength-based lifetime activity. Both weightlifting and powerlifting have novice competitions and are two of the fastest growing masters levels sports. These sports are much different from lifting weights for health or improved sports performance. These athletes spend many hours perfecting their technique and training for the specific lifts used in these sports. Powerlifting includes the squat, bench press, and deadlift in which the top lift in each category is combined for an overall total weight lifted. Weightlifting has a similar scoring system with two lifts—the snatch and clean and jerk. When taught in physical education class, these sports are often best presented as a 10-week elective that focuses on developing proper technique, skills, and safe spotting practices to encourage students to view lifting as a lifetime activity. Students should never lift maximally in a physical education setting, and the proper equipment and setting are required when introducing these lifts. Kozub and Brusseau (2012) provide a sample 10-week block plan as well as a breakdown of the lifts and spotting needed in a physical education setting.

Cardio Kickboxing

Cardio kickboxing is a popular physical activity that is offered in many health clubs and fitness centers to attract new participants and motivate continuing members. Cardio kickboxing—also sometimes known as aerobic kickboxing, Tae Bo, or cardio karate—is a rhythmic repetition of boxing jabs and punches, karate kicks and blows, and the movements or elements of aerobic dance. This activity can be used to attract and challenge all levels of students in the schools. Cardio kickboxing can be incorporated into the program as a standalone unit or as part of a variety of fitness routines in each day's lesson. Instructional videos are available that offer easy-to-understand instruction in developing lessons and kickboxing routines. Start with a direct instruction style with students in a scatter formation by leading students through basic techniques on the boxer's stance and shuffle. Then progress into various punches and kicks. After students have learned and are comfortable with the basic skills, a variety of routines can be introduced to incorporate all the skills.

Boxer's Stance

The boxer's stance is the ready position for most kicks and punching activities. Hands are held about chin high, and the dominant hand is slightly behind the opposite hand in most cases. Carry the weight on the balls of the feet, with the feet pointed straight ahead and the dom-

15

inant foot to the rear of the front foot. Most punches require a weight transfer and a pivot off the rear foot.

Boxer's Center Jog Stance

This stance involves bouncing on both feet. The hands are up to the chin, and the feet are even, parallel, and shoulder-width apart. This stance is used to lead into the boxer's stance described previously. It is also an effective position to practice bobbing and weaving to each side by dropping the head and upper body.

Punches and Blocks: Jab, Cross, Uppercut, Hook, Blocks, and Flutter Jabs

The jab is with the lead arm, and it snaps forward and back. The cross is made with the rear arm and involves a shoulder turn and a pivot on the rear foot. The uppercut involves dropping the knee and starting a circular windmill motion with the arm. This motion is followed by rotating the hips and extending the knee upward as the punch comes up and forward. The hook can be performed with either arm and involves a slight drop of the arm and a rounded hooking motion to hit the side of the target. Blocks involve moving either arm upward in an L shape to block a punch. Flutter jabs can be done from the center jog stance and involve a burst of continuous jabs.

Kicks: Front, Side, and Roundhouse

The front kick involves a step with the opposite foot followed by bringing the knee up with a flexed ankle and extending the kick forward. The right side kick involves stepping sideways with the right foot and then crossing over with the left foot, bringing the right knee up and extending the kick to the side (see figure 15.12). The roundhouse kick involves stepping forward with the opposite foot, raising the kicking leg to a flexed position,

pivoting on the rear foot, and exploding the kick forward with the toes pointed.

An effective lesson sequence involves the following:

1. Boxer's jog with bobbing and weaving, jabs, and blocks
2. Left jabs and right jabs
3. Left hooks and right hooks
4. Left uppercuts and right uppercuts
5. Left jab combos (jab, jab, cross) and right jab combos
6. Left forward kicks and right forward kicks
7. Left side kicks and right side kicks
8. Left roundhouse kicks and right roundhouse kicks
9. Left combo kicks and right combo kicks

After these skills have been introduced in a scatter formation and students are comfortable performing them, all these combinations can be put into fun and challenging routines with music. One option is to have students moving in waves across the length of the floor in continuous movement. When all students get to the opposite end of the floor, give them a new variation routine to follow for going back across the floor. Remind students to focus on their skills and to do their best. The next instructional variation is to have partners or small groups work with the sparring mitts to practice striking the mitts (see figure 15.13). Remind students that this class is *not* a self-defense class and that the focus is on the physical workout. The kicks and punches may be the same as those used in a self-defense class, but students are not taught the overall philosophy of self-defense and need to be careful with these ideas.

FIGURE 15.12 Side kicks in cardio kickboxing.

FIGURE 15.13 Sparring with partners wearing sparring mitts.

Stability Balls

Exercise, or stability, balls have been gaining popularity with schools and health clubs and offer an activity that can be done at home, at work, or in a club. The physical education program is an excellent place to get started and learn the basics of the balls. Activities on the balls can be modified many ways by varying the position of the ball to ensure that all students are being challenged and can find success quickly. The ball provides an unstable base for exercising and adds challenge for the core muscles of the abdomen, back, sides, and buttocks. Many stretching and flexibility activities can be done on the balls. Work on the balls helps to remind students about good posture and proper alignment of the body. Work on the balls can tie to other activity programs such as strength training with hand weights or stretch bands, yoga activities, and Pilates. Students can even do a line dance such as the "Macarena" using the arms and upper body. They can use the balls to personalize their workouts and improve their performance in other sports or activities. Balls are available in varying sizes and quality, so researching prices and sizes is important.

Basic Skills for the Stability or Exercise Ball

Students need to be taught safety for getting on and off the ball and staying on it. They must always use two hands and both feet in a stable position and move slowly and carefully. Many activities are performed with the ball against the wall or with a partner for stability. Getting used to the motion of the ball takes time and practice.

Basic Sit, Lie on All Fours

Some basic positions serve as starting points for many of the exercises. In the sitting position, the feet should be shoulder-width apart with the thighs parallel to the ground and a 90-degree angle formed with the lower legs. Good posture should always be practiced (head up, shoulders back, belly in and relaxed). Have students move into the lying position on all fours and move around slightly side to side, forward and back, and in a circular motion to get comfortable on the balls.

Hand Walk With the Ball (Push-Up Variations)

From the all-fours position, move forward by walking the hands forward until the hips and thighs are on the ball. Try to work under control and balance. Continue to move forward until the knees are on the ball and then forward until the shins and ankles are on the ball. If you can, try some slight push-ups in any of these positions.

Sit-Ups on the Ball

Move to a lying position on the ball. Roll forward and lower the buttocks toward the floor while keeping the upper body more vertical. Try crunches from this position. Continue to roll back farther up on the ball to increase the difficulty of the curl-ups. Hold the hands near the ears and add a slight twist to each side as you come up.

Squats With the Ball

Move the feet to a shoulder-width position with the ball pressed against a wall. Position the ball in the lower-back area. Slowly roll down on the ball into a squat position with the thighs parallel to the floor. Add small dumbbells to increase the challenge.

Superhero Challenge

A more challenging skill involving multiple muscle groups begins in the all-fours position. Then lift the left arm and the right leg in superhero style. Work on balance and then try the opposite side. Next, try both hands held in the air with one leg and then switch legs. Eventually, try both arms and legs in the air like the real superhero.

Additional Stability Ball Exercises

See the section Strength Training in chapter 19 for ideas.

Lower Body

- Wall squats—quadriceps
- Lunges with Russian twist—gluteus maximus
- Woodchoppers with toe raise—quadriceps and gastrocnemius muscles (place the ball up, over, and behind the head and then down to the toes)
- Glute lift (two legs or one leg)—gluteus maximus
- Hamstring press—hamstrings
- Hamstring lift—hamstrings
- Adductor presses—adductors
- Bent-over glute raises—gluteus maximus

Upper Body

- Bench press with Body Bar—pectorals (see figure 15.14)
- Flies with dumbbells—pectorals
- Push-ups with legs on ball—pectorals
- One handed bent-over rows with dumbbell—latissimus dorsi
- Military press with Body Bar or dumbbells—deltoids
- Lateral raises with dumbbells—deltoids

15

- Forward raises with Body Bar or dumbbells while performing wall squats—deltoids
- Arm curls sitting or preacher curls—biceps
- Triceps extensions sitting or lying with Body Bar or dumbbells—triceps
- Kickbacks with dumbbells—triceps
- Dips—triceps

FIGURE 15.14 Bench press with Body Bar.

Core

- Crunches
- Hand-to-opposite-knee crunches
- Plank
- Plank knees to chest
- Plank to V
- Russian twists (in partial sit-up position, twist left and right, and touch the ball to the floor)
- Ball-on-shelf sit-ups
- Hand-to-feet switch
- Suitcase with ball and barbells (sit on ball and then tilt left and right as if holding a suitcase)
- Side twists with wall
- Rollouts
- Sit, lie, sit

Stability Ball Fitness Routine

Students work with a partner and a stability ball. Partner A performs any type of locomotor movement once or twice around the perimeter (basketball floor, gymnasium, rectangle of cones, and so on), while partner B performs an exercise on the stability ball.

- Partner A performs sit-ups, balancing on the stability ball, while partner B jogs around the perimeter twice. Upon his or her return, partners switch roles and repeat the exercise.
- Partner A performs push-ups on the stability ball, while partner B performs a basketball slide around the perimeter once. When partner B returns, partner A slides while partner B performs push-ups.
- Partner A performs a supine reverse trunk curl, while partner B performs carioca steps around the perimeter once. The reverse trunk curl is done by lying flat on the floor with both feet on top of the ball; partner A grips the ball with heels and hamstrings and pulls the ball into the body. Partner A repeats the action until partner B returns. Partners then switch activities.
- Partner A uses the stability ball to perform wall squats against a wall, while Partner B performs a two-step around the perimeter once. The partners switch roles.
- Partner A performs a hamstring curl, while partner B jogs backward around the perimeter. The hamstring curl is performed by lying face down on the floor and the stability ball, resting on top of the hamstrings. Partner A uses his or her heels to squeeze the ball against the gluteus maximus for five to seven seconds. He or she squeezes and releases the ball until partner B returns. The partners switch roles.
- Partner A performs a side-lying abduction, while partner B jogs around the perimeter twice. Abduction is performed by starting in a side-lying position with the bottom leg bent. The top leg is extended out to the side with the foot resting on the floor. Both hands are supported on the front of the ball. Partner A slowly abducts the top leg until it is parallel to the floor, pauses at the top, and then lowers the leg. Partner A repeats this activity until partner B completes one lap. Partner A then switches sides, while partner B jogs the second lap. After that, partners switch roles.

- Partner A performs a side-lying adduction, while partner B skips around the perimeter twice. Adduction starts in a side-lying position on the floor with an elevated leg. The ball is centered under the ankle. The lower leg is flexed to 90 degrees and rests on the floor under the top leg. The head rests on one arm, and the other arm is on the floor in front of the body. Partner A adducts the lower leg until it lifts off the floor 3 to 4 inches (7.5 to 10.0 cm), pauses at the top, and then lowers the leg. Partner A repeats this activity until partner B finishes his or her first lap; partner A then switch legs as partner B does the second lap. After that, partners switch roles.

- Partner A performs a supine leg curl, while partner B performs carioca steps around the perimeter once. This exercise begins in a supine position with the heels on top of the ball. The hands rest on the floor, and the lower back and buttocks are slightly off the floor. Partner A curls the ball in toward the buttocks and rolls it back to the starting position. Partner A repeats the exercise until partner B returns. Partners then switch roles.

- Partner A performs a Russian twist, while partner B performs power skips around the perimeter once. The twist begins with the performer sitting on the floor and the ball on one side of the body. Partner A begins by touching the ball to the floor on each side of his or her body continuously and as fast as possible, but not sacrificing good technique for speed. (An advanced version requires the performer to keep his or her feet 3 inches [7.5 cm] off the ground throughout the routine). Partner A performs this until partner B returns, when the partners switch roles.

Reprinted by permission from Ron Schoenwetter.

Medicine Balls

The medicine ball has gained popularity and can add a nice challenge for students in a fitness workout. Medicine balls can be used in a variety of ways to focus on all parts of the body. After students become comfortable with them, they can be used in a circuit with combinations of other pieces of equipment such as jump bands, jump ropes, and stability balls. Students should start with a partner who has about the same height or strength. Most girls should start with a 2-kilogram (4.4 lb) ball, and boys should start with a 3-kilogram (6.6 lb) ball. Organize students in two lines facing each other and use the length of the gym to avoid injuries with overthrows, missed catches, and runaway balls. Use a ball that bounces and has a good grip.

Students work in pairs with partners of their choice. Each pair is equipped with a 2-kilogram (4.4 lb) medicine ball.

Warm-Ups

Around the World

One partner has a medicine ball, and a partner faces him or her. Partners begin by holding the ball or the hands above the head. Partner A rotates in a clockwise direction, taking the ball all the way to the floor and then back above the head. Partner B does the same without the ball. They do this five times and then switch directions for five rotations. Partners then exchange the ball and repeat the activity.

Good Mornings

Partners again face each other about 10 feet (3 m) apart with one ball. Keeping the back straight and the ball or hands above the head, both partners bend at the waist and back up to a straight position. Keeping the head up and back straight is important.

Wood Choppers

The student holds the ball between the legs, takes it up above the head, and returns it down between the legs (simulating chopping wood).

Lower-Body and Upper-Body Exercises

Overhead Lunges or Power Squats

Partners are side by side with one holding the medicine ball above the head. Partners perform 10 walking lunges. They then exchange the ball, change direction, and continue the activity. They perform three times each. Keeping the knee parallel to the toe when lunging is important.

Toss Series A

Chest toss, overhead toss, underhand toss, combinations

- Chest toss. Partners face each other approximately 5 to 10 feet (1.5 to 3.0 m) apart. Partners perform a chest pass with the ball back and forth for about 20 seconds. They must keep the hands out to give the partner a target and to catch the ball safely.

- Overhead toss. Partners stand approximately 5 to 10 feet (1.5 to 3.0 m) apart. They perform the over-

15

head pass back and forth for approximately 20 seconds, tossing the ball above the partner's head.

- Underhand toss. Partners stand approximately 5 to 10 feet (1.5 to 3.0 m) apart. Using both hands, partners toss the medicine ball back and forth with an underhand motion for about 20 seconds.

- Combinations. After completing the previous three exercises, partner put them together into a combination routine. They complete 10 repetitions of each, one after the other for 60 seconds.

Toss Series B

Left lateral toss, right lateral toss, chest squat toss, combinations

- Left lateral toss. Partners face each other approximately 5 to 10 feet (1.5 to 3.0 m) apart. The partner with the ball twists to his or her left and tosses the medicine ball to the partner. After catching the ball, the second partner twists to the left and tosses the ball back to the first partner. Both partners must bend down as they twist. They perform the exercise for 10 repetitions each.

- Right lateral toss. Partners face each other approximately 5 to 10 feet (1.5 to 3.0 m) apart. The partner with the ball twists to his or her right and tosses the medicine ball to the partner. After catching the ball, the second partner twists to the right and tosses the ball back to the first partner. Both partners must bend down as they twist. They perform the exercise for 10 repetitions each.

- Chest squat toss. Partners face each other approximately 5 to 10 feet (1.5 to 3.0 m) apart. Both partners simultaneously perform a squat. As the partner with the medicine ball comes up out of the squat, he or she gives a chest pass to the partner. Both partners perform squats again. As the partner with the ball comes out of the squat, he or she gives a chest pass back to the partner. They perform the exercise for 10 repetitions each.

- Combinations. After partners complete the previous three exercises, they put them together into a combination routine. Partners complete 10 repetitions of each, one after the other for 60 seconds.

Cardiorespiratory Exercises

1, 2, 3, Switch Chest Passes

Partners face each other approximately 5 to 10 feet (1.5 to 3.0 m) apart. They perform three chest passes (total) and then run to switch places with each other. They continue the exercise for 10 repetitions.

Chest Pass Switch

Partners face each other approximately 5 to 10 feet (1.5 to 3.0 m) apart. Partner A gives a chest pass to partner B; partners then switch places. The exercise continues for 20 repetitions.

Roll Pass

Sets of partners form two single-file lines approximately 10 feet (3 m) apart. The first two partners begin with partner A rolling the medicine ball diagonally down the court or field. Both partners run in a straight line down the court. Partner B must pick up the ball and make a diagonal pass back to partner A. At this point, the next group of two begin. They continue until they have reached the end of the exercise area. After they finish, partners move to the outside of the area and hustle back to the original lines. They perform the exercise five times each.

Chest Pass

Partners begin in the formation they used for the roll pass. The partners slide down the court while performing chest passes back and forth. The passer must lead the partner to the spot where he or she will be at the completion of the pass. After reaching the end of the designated area, partners move to the outside of the area and return to the line. They perform the exercise five times each.

1, 2, 3, Switch

This exercise is the same as the chest pass (previous activity) except that partners must switch places after every third chest pass as they slide down the court. After reaching the end of the designated area, partners move to the outside of the area and return to the line. They perform the exercise five times each.

Abdominal Exercises

Russian Twists

Partners sit in pairs, facing the same direction about 5 feet (1.5 m) apart and keeping their feet slightly off the ground. The partner on the right side starts with the ball. He or she taps the ball on the ground to the right side, left side, and then right side. After the third tap, he or she passes the ball to the partner on the left. He or she catches the ball, repeats the same exercise (left, right, left), and then passes the ball back to the first partner. They perform the sequence approximately five times each. Figure 15.15 shows the Russian twist with a partner toss.

FIGURE 15.15   Russian twists.

Straddle Chest Passes

Partners face each other in a sit-up position. The partner with the medicine ball performs a sit-up and makes a chest pass to his or her partner, who is in the upright sit-up position. The partner catches the ball and performs a sit-up. They repeat the sequence approximately 10 times each.

Chest Pass Sit-Ups

This exercise is performed the same way as straddle chest passes with one difference. Both partners perform a sit-up simultaneously as they pass and catch the medicine ball. They repeat the sequence approximately 10 to 15 times.

Standing Twists

Partners stand back to back. The partner with the ball turns to his or her left and hands the medicine ball off to the partner, who is turning to his or her right. Partners work quickly but must maintain a quality position throughout. This pattern continues about 10 to 15 times. Partners then change the direction of the handoff for another set of 10 to 15.

Upper-Body Exercises

Plank Hold

Partner A assumes the plank position on the floor. Partner B places the medicine ball on his or her partner's back. Partner A must keep the ball steady for approximately 30 seconds. Partners then switch roles and repeat.

Trunk or Plank Rolls

Partners face each other in a push-up position about 3 feet (1 m) apart. One partner rolls the ball diagonally across to his or her partner. The second partner receives the pass with one hand, rolls the ball to the other hand, and then passes diagonally back to the first partner. The activity continues for 10 transfer passes. Directions of the ball can be changed to use both hands many times.

Cool-Down

Cool-Down or Stretch

Partners sit facing each other on the floor with feet spread in a straddle position. The student with the medicine ball begins to roll the ball slowly with the fingers toward the partner, stretching the hamstrings and lower back. At the peak of the stretch, he or she slowly releases the ball to the partner, who receives the ball and repeats the stretch. They perform the sequence five times each.

Reprinted by permission from Maria Corte.

Pilates

The Pilates training program originated with Joseph Pilates in Germany nearly a hundred years ago. The program has evolved over that time into a popular worldwide exercise program that has attracted millions of people of varying ages and physical abilities. It focuses on good posture, proper breathing, and fundamental exercises that stretch and strengthen the muscles. Pilates is a set of exercises done in a dynamic and rhythmic sequence to produce a low-intensity, calorie-burning workout that sculpts the muscles. In addition, Pilates works the core muscle groups (abdominal, lower back, hips, and buttocks) to produce a streamlined, longer, leaner body look. Advocates argue that Pilates makes them look and feel great. Pilates can be added to a physical education program in many ways. Many books and videos describe different combinations of Pilates that can be used to get students started on a program.

The following is an example of a beginner sequence of exercises.

Stretch With Knee Away

On your back, pull your knees up to your chest, flatten your lower back, and hold this pose. Then slowly lower your knees to one side and then the other.

Spinal Rotation

Sitting in a slight straddle position with the legs extended and the arms out to the side, slowly rotate the upper body to the left and right.

15

The Hundred

On your back with the legs at a 90-degree angle, lift the shoulders and arms up slightly and exhale five times, pressing the hands down, and then exhale five times pressing the hands upward. Increase the number of repetitions until you can do this sequence 10 times for 100 breaths.

Abdominal Strengthener

Lie on your back with hands behind the head and knees flexed; exhale and curl up slowly using just the abdominal muscles. Repeat five to six times.

Lower Abdominal Strengthener

Use the same position as before with a mat under the hips. Start the knees at 90 degrees with the ankles crossed and slowly curl the hips up toward your chest.

Rolling Ball

Sit curled up by hugging the ankles and curling the spine. Slowly roll backward while maintaining the position. Repeat five to six times.

Single-Leg Stretch

Lie on your back with one leg extended about 12 inches (30 cm) off the floor. Flex the other leg and bring the knee to the chest. Hold the flexed leg and raise the shoulders slowly. Hold the position while rotating the position of the legs.

Double Straight Leg

Lie on your back with your hands behind your head and your legs pointed toward the ceiling while held tight together. Lift the chin and shoulders slightly off the mat and lower the legs about 1 foot (30 cm). Keep the lower back tight to the floor. Repeat five to six times.

Forward Spine Stretch and Roll-Ups

Start in a sitting position with the legs and arms extended forward. Stretch forward and exhale. Repeat five to six times and then add the roll-up by slowly going backward to the mat with the arms extended.

Bridge

Lie on your back with the arms extended, the palms down, and the knees bent. Lift the upper body upward using only the abdominal muscles. Hold for eight counts and repeat several times.

Back Strengthener

Start in an all-fours position. Lift and extend the opposite arm and leg, hold the position for several seconds, and then switch arms and legs. Repeat several times.

Side Plank With an Oblique Twist

In figure 15.16, students demonstrate the (a) starting position of Pilates exercise side plank with twist and (b) the twist down to the floor.

FIGURE 15.16   Side plank with an oblique twist.

Total Rest Pose

Start in an all-fours position. Push the hips to your heels and your abdomen to your thighs. Slowly extend the arms forward with your palms flat on the floor and hold for a longer count.

Yoga

Yoga is one of the most popular fitness practices today. Considering the fast pace and multiple activities of our lives, yoga can provide a mental and physical focus that helps people deal with their lives. It can be implemented into the physical education program as a brief 10- to 15-minute fitness routine as a part of a four-part lesson, as a two-week unit that meets daily, or as part of a semester unit that combines many health-club activities such as Pilates, kickboxing, and stability and medicine ball routines. Yoga has grown in popularity because of the variety of holistic mind–body benefits it can provide for students of any ability, from excellent athletes to students of average skills and anyone in between. Yoga has many different forms and variations. Many of these forms focus on multiple topics including breathing, diet, personal behavior, meditation, relaxation, stress management, and health promotion. Yoga can be a wonderful addition to your program.

Power Yoga

Power yoga is an active form of yoga that links a flowing sequence of poses together in continuous succession. The sequence of poses or postures are designed to warm up the body, increase circulation, improve muscular strength and endurance, increase flexibility and range of motion, and relieve mental and physical stress.

Strength Yoga

Strength yoga incorporates more challenging arm balancing poses into the power yoga sequence to help develop muscular strength in the upper body and improve posture. This workout is effective in improving physical performance and confidence, releasing tension, and promoting peace of mind.

Basic Beginning Poses

The following are recommended poses for beginning classes. Students need to learn these yoga terms and poses. Beginners will need some time to get comfortable with them and feel as if they are having success. Detailed information on all these poses is available from many sources including the Internet. Most state and district SHAPE America associations will provide yoga information and certifications.

- Basic sitting
- Breathing arms
- Child's pose
- Downward-facing dog
- Mountain pose
- Stork to knee
- Stork to thigh
- Side bending

- Star (see figure 15.17)
- Forward lunge
- Plank
- Seal
- Triangle (see figure 15.18)
- Forward lunge with yoga arms
- Proud warrior
- Downward-facing dog with leg lift
- Side one arm
- Side one arm with leg lift
- Sun salutation (see figure 15.19)
- Triceps plank
- L sit
- Rocking horse
- Relaxation supine with breathing
- Yoga sitting
- Side leans

FIGURE 15.17   Star pose.

FIGURE 15.18   Triangle pose.

15

FIGURE 15.19   Sun salutation pose.

CrossFit

An increasingly popular physical education activity, CrossFit is designed as an all-encompassing fitness activity. For example, CrossFit includes activities that will help develop both health- and skill-related fitness including cardiorespiratory endurance, stamina, strength, power, speed, flexibility, agility, accuracy, balance, and coordination. Youth CrossFit programming typically uses randomized functional fitness exercises that students perform at as high an intensity as possible for the individual student. Adjustments should be made to meet the varying ability of students in the class. CrossFit in physical education should use a time component that has youths moving quickly from one exercise to the next to create a high-intensity workout. Staple activities such as box jumps, jump roping, and sprints help develop the cardiorespiratory endurance needed to be successful

across all sports and physical activities taught in physical education class. An example of a basic CrossFit workout that could be implemented with novice secondary students follows:

Warm-Up (Three Times)
- 5 burpees
- 5 squats
- Bear crawl
- 10 mountain climbers
- Bar hangs

Basic Dot Drill (10 Times)
- 3 broad jumps
- 5 jumping jacks

Workout of the Day (Three Rounds)
- 400-meter run
- 21 kettlebell swings (12 or 8 kg)
- 12 push-ups

High Intensity Interval Training (HIIT) is similar to CrossFit in that it combines short bursts of intense exercise with periods of rest or lower-intensity activities (Logan, Harris, Duncan, & Schofield, 2014). A typical workout follows a 4:4 ratio of four-minute intervals with a three-minute recovery period in between. The key is to increase the heart rate to 80% of its capacity during the high-intensity intervals. A shorter interval routine is 10:1, which includes 10 one-minute bouts of intense exercise with one minute of recovery in between.

LEARNING AIDS

STUDY STIMULATORS AND REVIEW QUESTIONS

1. What are the main differences between the criterion-referenced and norm-referenced fitness tests?
2. Identify the different types of standards often used with health-related and skill-related fitness tests.
3. Explain the influence of heredity on students' ability to perform well on physical fitness tests.
4. What are the consequences of the belief that physical activity and fitness performance are highly related?
5. Discuss the basis for the recommendation that every U.S. adult should accumulate 60 minutes or more of moderate to vigorous physical activity on most, preferably all, days of the week.
6. Discuss four strategies that teachers should employ to create a more positive fitness experiences for students.
7. What guidelines are offered for flexibility and stretching exercises?
8. Describe some activities that could be incorporated into a physical education class for fitness using stability balls.

9. Why might it be important to incorporate health club workouts with the fitness portion of physical education? How does this potentially influence the students and lifelong physical activity engagement?

10. What legacy should a quality physical education program offer its graduates?

WEBSITES

Fitness for Youth

www.americanheart.org/presenter
www.cdc.gov/nccdphp/dash/presphysactrpt
www.fitnessgram.net
www.fitnessforlife.org
www.presidentschallenge.org

REFERENCES AND SUGGESTED READINGS

American College of Sports Medicine. (2013). *Guidelines for exercise testing and prescription* (9th ed.). Baltimore, MD: Williams and Wilkins.

Bouchard, C. (2012). Genomic predictors of trainability. *Experimental Physiology, 97*(3), 347–352.

Brusseau, T.A., Darst, P.W., & Johnson, T.G. (2009). Incorporating fitness and skill tasks together. *Journal of Physical Education, Recreation and Dance, 80,* 50–52.

Burkhart, E.A., & Dlugolecki, P.C. (2020). Flexibility. In S. Ayers & M.J. Sariscsany (Eds.)., *Physical best for lifelong fitness* (3rd ed.). Reston, VA: SHAPE America.

Burns, R., Hannon, J.C., Brusseau, T.A., Shultz, B., & Eisenman, P. (2013). Indices of abdominal adiposity and cardio-respiratory fitness test performance in middle-school students. *Journal of Obesity.* doi:10.1155/2013/912460

Corbin, C.B. (2012). C.H. McCloy lecture: Fifty years of advancements in fitness and activity research. *Research Quarterly for Exercise and Sport, 83*(1), 1–11.

Corbin, C.B., Janz, K.F., & Baptista, F. (2014). Good health: The power of power. *Journal of Physical Education, Recreation and Dance, 88*(9), 28–35.

Corbin, C.B., & Pangrazi, R.P. (1992). Are American children and youth fit? *Research Quarterly for Exercise and Sport, 63*(2), 96–106.

Corbin, C.B., & Pangrazi, R.P. (2004). *Physical activity for children: A statement of guidelines for children ages 5–12* (2nd ed.). Reston, VA: National Association for Sport and Physical Education.

Corbin, C.B., Welk, G.J., Corbin, W.R., & Welk, K.A. (2013). *Concepts of fitness and wellness: A comprehensive lifestyle approach* (10th ed.). Boston, MA: McGraw-Hill.

Glasser, W. (1985). *Positive addiction.* New York, NY: Harper and Row.

Going, S. B., Lohman, T. G., & Eisenmann, J. C. (2014). *FITNESSGRAM/ACTIVITYGRAM reference guide* (updated 4th ed.). Dallas, TX: Cooper Institute.

Institute of Medicine. (2012). *Fitness measures and health outcomes in youth.* Washington, DC: National Academies.

Kozub, F.M., & Brusseau, T.A. (2012). Powerlifting: A suitable high school curricular elective and after school intramural program. *Journal of Physical Education, Recreation and Dance, 83,* 34–41.

Logan, G. R., Harris, N., Duncan, S., & Schofield, G. (2014). A review of adolescent high-intensity interval training. *Sports Medicine, 44*(8), 1071-1085.

Morrow Jr., J.R., Tucker, J.S., Jackson, A.W., Martin, S.B., Greenleaf, C.A., & Petrie, T.A. (2013). Meeting physical activity guidelines and health-related fitness in youth. *American Journal of Preventive Medicine, 44*(5), 439–444.

Pangrazi, R.P., & Corbin, C.B. (2008). Factors that influence physical fitness in children and adolescents. In G.J. Welk & M.D. Meredith (Eds.), *FitnessGram/ActivityGram reference guide* (pp. 52–60). Dallas, TX: Cooper Institute.

Presidential Youth Fitness Program. (2017). *Presidential Youth Fitness Program physical educator resource guide* (Internet resource). Washington, DC: National Fitness Foundation.

SHAPE America/Conkle. (2020). *Physical best: Physical education for lifelong fitness and health* (4th ed.). T. Conkle (Ed.). Reston, VA: SHAPE America.

Skinner, A.C., Ravanbakht, S.N., Skelton, J.A., Perrin, E.M., & Armstrong, S.C. (2018). Prevalence of obesity and severe obesity in US children, 1999–2016. *Pediatrics, 141*(3), e20173459.

Swaim, D., & Edwards, S. (2003*). High school healthy hearts in the zone: A heart rate monitoring program for lifelong fitness.* Champaign, IL: Human Kinetics.

15

Swaim, D., & Edwards, S. (2002). *Middle school healthy hearts in the zone: A heart rate monitoring program for lifelong fitness.* Champaign, IL: Human Kinetics.

Welk, G.J., Meredith, M.D., Ihmels, M., & Seeger, C. (2010). Distribution of health-related physical fitness in Texas youth: A demographic and geographic analysis. *Research Quarterly for Exercise and Sport, 81*(supp 3), S6–S15.

U.S. Department of Health and Human Services. (2012). Physical activity guidelines for Americans midcourse report subcommittee of the President's Council on Fitness, Sports, & Nutrition. *Physical activity guidelines for Americans midcourse report: Strategies to increase physical activity among youth.* Washington, DC: U.S. Department of Health and Human Services.

Healthy Lifestyles

This chapter focuses on teaching basic concepts of health and related components that can be enhanced within the physical education setting. The chapter offers the methodology for holding discussions to develop an understanding and insight into behavior necessary to maintain optimum health. A state of general health and personal functioning helps determine the quality of life. Discussion sessions must include the opportunity for students to have the psychological freedom to explore alternative lifestyles. A difficult skill for students to learn is independent decision making based on careful consideration of alternatives and consequences rather than peer pressure. Teachers can help students understand the requisites of quality health by offering a discussion session that is structured so that students can feel comfortable. Focus setting, clarifying, acknowledging, and staying silent are behaviors that teachers need to learn to use when conducting discussion sessions.

To ensure total body development, exercises must follow principles of exercise. Stress affects performance and is not unique to any age group. Being overweight is associated with various degenerative diseases and can be curtailed through a reduction of caloric consumption and increased activity. Substance abuse among students is common and serves to stimulate the onset of emotional problems and degenerative diseases.

Learning Objectives

► Conduct a discussion session with students that successfully allows clarification and understanding of healthy lifestyle concepts.
► Describe how concepts for healthy living can be achieved through a properly structured instructional program of physical education.
► Understand the basic function of the skeletal, muscular, and cardiorespiratory systems.
► Explain how health instruction can be integrated into the physical education setting at the middle and high school level.
► Delineate the type of teacher behavior that enhances the development of self-concept among students.
► Identify risk factors associated with degenerative diseases.
► Discuss factors that are roadblocks to healthy lifestyles.
► Explain how stress reduction can be accomplished.
► Describe how students can learn to evaluate their levels of physical fitness.
► List a plan for improving self-control by altering behavior.

The need for teaching students how to maintain personal health for a lifetime becomes apparent when the skyrocketing costs of minimal health care are examined. Health insurance policies cost 5 to 10% of a person's gross income. A short stay in the hospital may incur a bill for thousands of dollars, but despite costs, most Americans continue to put little or no effort into maintaining a healthy lifestyle. Good health allows a person to participate fully in life. Having the energy and enthusiasm to undertake activities after a full day of work is characteristic of people who are well. A healthy person is not only free of sickness or other malady but also is happy, vibrant, and able to solve personal problems.

Teaching students how to achieve a lasting state of healthiness lends credibility to the physical education profession. For many years, physical educators were seen solely as teachers of physical skills who had little concern for the knowledge and comprehension involved in physical performance. Teachers often pushed students without considering their abilities and personal issues (i.e., "Learn the skill or else!"). Today, most experts agree; physical education must reach beyond fitness and skill development and teach students how to maintain a healthy lifestyle throughout life, not only physically but also mentally and emotionally. No trophies or other extrinsic rewards are received for achieving it. Health is a personal matter. When a person achieves it, she or he is directly rewarded with a full lifestyle. Physical education programs must graduate students who know the what, why, and how of maintaining a healthy mind and body. Maintaining personal health must be considered a primary objective of secondary school physical education.

Why teach health concepts in the physical education setting? Although teachers are often resistant to teaching material other than skills and fitness, the knowledge related to health maintenance remains with people for a lifetime. This long-lasting gift is one of the few that teachers can offer students. Achieving an optimal level of health is unique and personal. Skills and fitness levels that are useful to one person may be less important to another. Teachers must teach students how to search for a healthy lifestyle that is unique to them and how to maintain it once found.

At present, the credibility of the physical education profession is strained. Instructors often teach students skills and activities they will never use again. For example, students may spend 6 weeks each year from middle school through the sophomore year of high school involved in flag football—thus 24 weeks of flag football. The possibility is strong that few students will play football after graduation from high school. Few people play flag football after age 25, yet nearly a year of physical education was spent playing and learning a sport seldom used for maintaining a healthy lifestyle in adulthood. The point here is not to belittle football or to ask for its elimination; it is to suggest that physical education is often dominated by activities that students will not use after they leave school.

TEACHING TIP

What are the skills and activities that students will use when they become mature adults and then aging adults? Because few adults play team sports as they age, offering a curriculum dominated by team sports is a mistake. Gough (2018) offers statistics that give some insight into the type of activities that adults use to stay healthy. The most common outdoor physical activities are running and jogging, fishing, biking, hiking, and camping, in that order. Over 45 million people participate in running and jogging, fishing, and biking annually. More than 40 million hike or camp each year. These skills are all individual activities that do not require a lot of money and facilities for daily participation. Will your program graduate students who know how to maintain a healthy lifestyle using these activities?

Teaching students how to maintain a state of personal health makes activity purposeful. Students begin to understand why certain activities and games are selected in place of others. Selection of activities for a lifetime of physical involvement occurs when students are exposed to a wide range of instructional units. A systematic approach to a broad curriculum ensures that students know that they can follow many pathways to personal fitness and health.

Integrating Health Concepts

This chapter is designed for physical education teachers who are asked to integrate health education into the physical education program. Most often, this assignment is required of teachers at the middle school level, so most of the following concepts and learning activities are geared to that level. The topics covered in this chapter are divided into three areas.

- How does the body work?—This topic includes basics of the skeletal, muscular, and cardiovascular systems. Emphasis is on the concepts that all students should know, followed by learning activities that can be assigned or discussed in class to further understanding. Much of the information is related to the body in an exercise and activity setting and the way that it responds to exercise and physical activity. Basic principles of training and fitness also are covered in this section.

- Barriers to healthy living—This section deals with behaviors that are harmful to the body if not managed or avoided by students. The emphasis is on developing a basic understanding of stress, mental health, nutrition and weight management, substance abuse, personal safety, and first aid. The instructional focus is not to preach and mandate what students should do but to help students understand how to make thoughtful decisions that contribute to their overall health.

- Teaching health maintenance—Understanding how the body works and how poor health habits can damage it is important, but knowledge is not enough. Students need to learn and practice behaviors related to health-related fitness, stress management, and self-control. This section teaches students how to evaluate their health status and modify their behavior when necessary. Steps for modifying personal behavior help students monitor, prioritize, and set personal goals.

Each of the areas includes concepts that students need to understand. These concepts provide direction for both the teacher and students. The concepts should give students a general idea of what is important and which areas they must understand to achieve proper functioning. The concepts, when taken as a whole, offer a framework to help initiate discussions that examine the pros and cons of personal decisions related to health maintenance. This approach contrasts with giving students a set of objectives that must be learned, leaving little room for student input and inquiry.

The suggested learning activities offer laboratory experiences that add substance to basic instructional concepts. The laboratory experiences are simple, yet they clearly illustrate how the body functions in different settings. Many of these experiences can be done in 5 or 10 minutes by a whole class. They are excellent rainy day activities or homework assignments. Ask students to develop a notebook of activities and lab experiences

that they can use as a reference. An excellent resource for laboratory activities and instructional lesson plans is *Fitness for Life: Teacher Web Resources* (Corbin & LeMasurier, 2014). Sample lessons are available online at www.fitnessforlife.org. *Lesson Planning for Skills-Based Health Education: Meeting Secondary-Level National Standards* (Benes & Alperin, 2019) is designed to help teachers implement a skills-based approach to health education in secondary schools, whether building a new curriculum or seeking to supplement an existing one. Skills-based learning activities, lessons, units, and assessments can be used as is or modified for particular class needs. All activities are organized to map to the skills addressed in the National Health Education Standards and are aligned with the standards' development model.

How Does the Body Work?

A basic understanding of how the body functions helps students maintain a healthy body. The three major systems discussed here are the skeletal, muscular, and cardiorespiratory systems. A brief discussion of each is provided, and learning activities are offered to enhance student understanding.

Skeletal System

The skeletal system is the framework of the body. The bones act as a system of levers and are linked together at various points called joints. The joints are held together by ligaments, which are tough and unable to stretch. In a joint injury, when the bones are moved beyond normal limits, it is the ligaments that are most often injured.

Joints that are freely movable are called synovial joints. Synovial fluid is secreted to lubricate the joint and reduce friction. A thin layer of cartilage also reduces friction at the ends of the bones. A disk, or meniscus, forms a pad between many of the weight-bearing joints and absorbs shock. When the cartilage is damaged, the joint becomes less able to move easily, and arthritis often occurs.

The skeletal system is not a static system; it changes and adapts in response to the demands placed on it. The bones act as a mineral reserve for the body, but they can become deformed because of dietary deficiency. Muscular activity increases the stress placed on bones, and the bones respond to this added stress by increasing in diameter and by becoming denser and more resistant to breakage. The bones also can change shape because of regular stress. Athletes whose skeletal systems are conditioned may gain a mechanical advantage in performing certain skills.

16

The bones are connected to make three types of levers, with the joint acting as the fulcrum. The muscles apply force to the joints, and the body weight or an external object provides the resistance. The levers are classified as first-, second-, or third-class levers (Behnke, 2012). Although rare in the human body, a first-class lever has the axis (fulcrum) located between the weight (resistance) and the force. One example is the joint between the head and the first vertebra (see figure 16.1*a*). The weight is the head, the axis is the joint, and the muscular action come from the posterior muscles attaching to the skull. In second-class levers, the weight (resistance) is located between the axis (fulcrum) and the force. A common example of a second-class lever occurs when someone stands on tiptoes (see figure 16.1*b*). The axis is formed by the metatarsophalangeal joints, the resistance is the weight of the body, and the force is applied to the calcaneus bone (heel) by the gastrocnemius and soleus muscles through the Achilles tendon. The most common levers in the human body are third-class levers in which force is applied between the resistance (weight) and the axis (fulcrum). One example can be seen in the elbow joint (see figure 16.1*c*). The joint is the axis (fulcrum). The resistance (weight) is the forearm, wrist, and hand. The force is the biceps muscle when the elbow is flexed.

Basic Concepts

1. The skeletal system consists of 206 bones and determines the external appearance of the body. This network of bones is somewhat malleable and can be reshaped, made denser, and strengthened.

2. Joints are located where two or more bones are fastened together by ligaments to allow movement that is restricted by the range of motion. The range of motion at various joints can be increased by regularly performing flexibility exercises. The most flexible people have the greatest range of motion at a combination of joints.

3. Ligaments and muscles hold the bones together. The stronger the muscles become, the stronger the ligaments and tendons become in response. The result is a stronger joint that is more resistant to injury.

4. Efficient posture occurs when the bones are properly aligned. Alignment depends on the muscular system to hold the bones in correct position. Poor posture occurs when the muscles are weak and increased stress is placed on the joints.

5. The bones meet at joints to establish levers. Movement occurs when muscles apply force (by contraction only) to the bones.

6. The attachment of the muscle to the bone determines the mechanical advantage that can be gained at the joint. Generally, muscles that attach farther from the joint generate more force. But there is a trade-off. When the attachment is farther from the joint, the amount of speed generated is less, and vice versa.

7. The human body has three types of lever arrangements. These are classified by the placement of the fulcrum, force, and resistance. The majority of levers in the body are third-class levers in which the point of force (produced by the muscles) lies between the fulcrum (joint) and the point of resistance (the weight of the object to be moved).

Suggested Learning Activities

1. Identify and locate the bones of major significance in movement. (Approximately 167 bones are capable of moving.) Some that can be assigned are as follows:
   - Arm–shoulder girdle—radius, ulna, humerus, scapula, clavicle
   - Back–pelvis—spinal column, pelvis, coccyx
   - Thigh–leg—femur, tibia, fibula, patella
   - Chest—sternum, ribs

2. Identify the type of movement possible at selected joints. Use various terms to identify the movements (e.g., extension, flexion, adduction, abduction, pronation, supination, and plantar flexion).

3. Diagram and list the types of levers found in the body. Illustrate the force, fulcrum, and resistance points. Identify muscle attachments and their effect on generating force or speed in movement.

4. Obtain animal bones and analyze the various parts of the bone. Identify the bone marrow, growth plates, epiphyses, ligaments, tendons, muscle origins and attachments, and cartilage.

5. Study outdated X-ray films of children to see the various rates of ossification. Note differences in bone shape and structure between individuals.

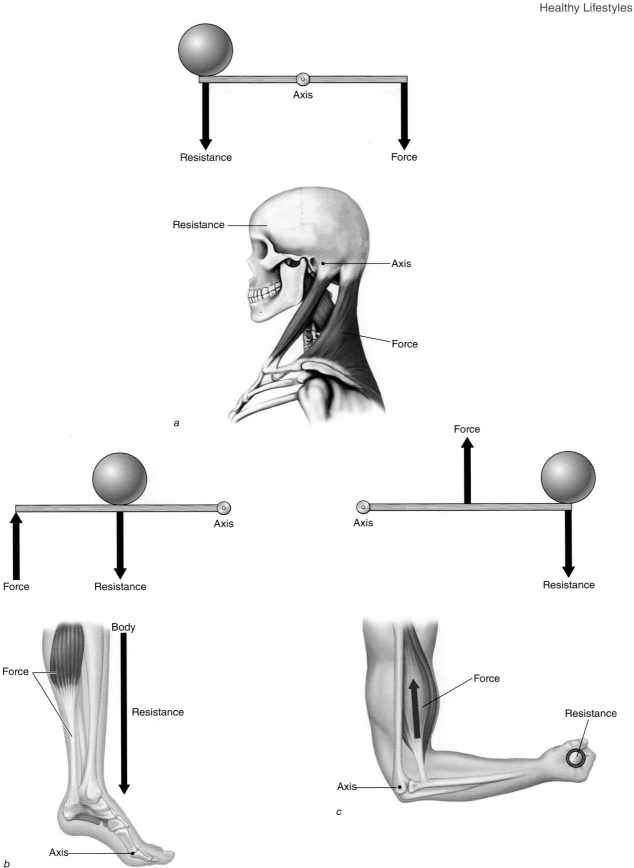

FIGURE 16.1 Levers of three types are found in human joints: (*a*) first class, (*b*) second class, and (*c*) third class.

16

Muscular System

The muscular system (see figure 16.2) is complex. Muscles apply force to the bones to create movement and always create movement through contraction. When one set of muscles contracts, the other set relaxes. Muscles are always paired. The muscle (or group of muscles) that relaxes while another set contracts is called the antagonistic muscle. The muscles located on the anterior side of the body are flexors and reduce the angle of a joint while the body is standing. Muscles on the posterior side of the body produce extension and a return from flexion.

Humans have two types of muscle fibers, commonly referred to as slow-twitch and fast-twitch fibers. Slow-twitch fibers respond efficiently to aerobic activity, whereas fast-twitch fibers are suited to anaerobic activity. This difference explains, in part, why people perform physical activities at varying levels. People are born with a set ratio of fast- and slow-twitch fibers. Those with a higher ratio of slow-twitch fibers are better able to perform in endurance activities; those with a greater percentage of fast-twitch fibers might excel in activities of high intensity and short duration.

Strength gains occur when muscles are overloaded. Therefore, more weight must be lifted on a regular basis if gains are to occur. Exercises should overload as many muscle groups as possible to ensure total body development. Both the flexors and extensors should receive equal amounts of overload exercise to main-

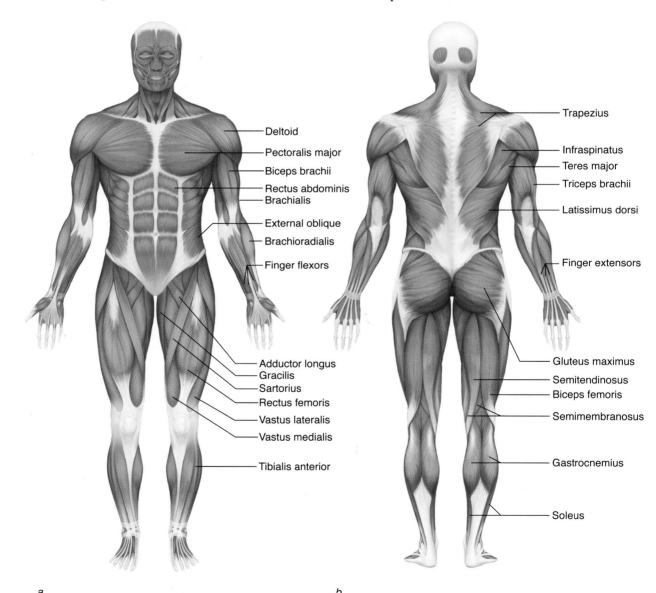

Deltoid
Pectoralis major
Biceps brachii
Rectus abdominis
Brachialis
External oblique
Brachioradialis
Finger flexors
Adductor longus
Gracilis
Sartorius
Rectus femoris
Vastus lateralis
Vastus medialis
Tibialis anterior

Trapezius
Infraspinatus
Teres major
Triceps brachii
Latissimus dorsi
Finger extensors
Gluteus maximus
Semitendinosus
Biceps femoris
Semimembranosus
Gastrocnemius
Soleus

a   b

FIGURE 16.2   The (a) front view and (b) rear view of the muscular system.

tain a proper balance between the two muscle groups. Muscular strength appears to be an important factor in performing motor skills.

Muscular exercises should be performed throughout the full range of motion to maintain maximum flexibility. Strenuous exercise such as weightlifting should be done every other day so that the muscles have an opportunity to heal and regenerate. Maintaining muscular strength throughout life is important. If exercises are not done to maintain strength, muscle atrophy occurs. The average American gains 1 pound (.45 kg) of weight per year after age 25. This annual increment results in 30 pounds (14 kg) of excess weight by age 55. During the same period, bone and muscle mass decreases by approximately .5 pound (.2 kg) per year, which results in a total gain of 45 pounds (20 kg) of body fat (Kenney et al., 2015).

Basic Concepts

1. Muscles contract and apply force by pulling only. They never push. When movement in the opposite direction is desired, the antagonistic muscles must contract.

2. A reduction in joint angle is called flexion; an increase in the joint angle is extension. Generally, the flexor muscles are on the anterior side of the body, and the extensors are on the posterior side.

3. Exercises should focus on developing the flexors and extensors equally if proper posture and joint integrity are to be maintained.

4. Muscles can be attached directly to the bone. A tendon, such as the Achilles, can also be the source of attachment. The origin of the muscle is the fixed portion of the muscle; the insertion is the moving part of the muscle.

5. Progression involving gradual overloading of muscles is necessary to increase muscular strength and endurance. Regular strength-development exercises result in an increase in the width (girth) of a muscle. Females rarely attain similar results from strenuous exercise because the hormone testosterone, present in greater quantities in males, is responsible for the increase in muscle size.

6. Different types of training are necessary to develop muscular strength and muscular endurance. Heavier amounts of weight and fewer repetitions cause a greater increase in strength, whereas lighter weight and more repetitions enhance muscular endurance.

7. Different types of muscular contractions include isometric (without movement), isotonic (with movement), and eccentric (movement that lengthens the muscle from a contracted state). The contraction most commonly used for developing strength and endurance is isotonic.

8. Stretching can increase flexibility. Flexibility (the range of motion at a joint) increases because of a lengthening of connective tissue that surrounds the muscle fibers.

9. Muscle soreness occurs when the workload is applied too intensely. The soreness probably results from muscle tissue damage. Static stretching may alleviate the pain and help prepare the body for continued activity.

10. The principle of specificity is important in developing muscular strength. Only those muscles that are exercised will develop. No carryover results from exercising other muscle groups (i.e., strengthening the arms will not cause an increase in leg strength).

Suggested Learning Activities

1. Identify major muscle groups and their functions at the joints. Discuss the origins and insertions of the muscles.

2. Study muscles from animals under a microscope. Show stained biopsies of human muscle fiber that reveal fast- and slow-twitch muscle fibers.

3. Perform some skill-related activities that might reveal which individuals appear to be endowed with more fast-twitch than slow-twitch fibers. Examples might be the standing long jump, vertical jump, and an endurance activity such as the mile run.

4. Develop a personal strength profile for students. Measure the strength of various muscle groups using a dynamometer and set goals for well-rounded strength development.

5. Perform an action research project. As an example, pretest students for strength and divide them into equal groups. Have one group train for 12 weeks using muscular endurance techniques while the other trains for 12 weeks using muscular strength techniques. Retest them and compare the results of the two groups after training.

6. Identify various sports and games, and determine what type of training will achieve maximum results.

7. Discuss certain exercises that should be avoided, such as straight-leg sit-ups and deep knee bends.

16

8. Have students identify why backache occurs in more than 70% of Americans. Prescribe a program of exercise that could remedy most of these back problems.

Cardiorespiratory System

The cardiorespiratory system consists of the heart (see figure 16.3), lungs, arteries, capillaries, and veins. The heart is a muscle that pumps blood throughout the circulatory system—arteries, capillaries, and veins. The coronary arteries bring the heart a rich supply of blood. Heart disease occurs when fatty deposits block or seriously impede the flow of blood to the heart.

The heart has two chambers and is, in effect, divided in half with each side providing different functions. The left side of the heart pumps blood carrying nutrients and oxygen to the body through the arteries to the capillaries, where the nutrients and oxygen are exchanged for waste products and carbon dioxide. The waste-carrying blood is returned through the veins to the right side of the heart, from which the blood is routed through the lungs to discharge the carbon dioxide and pick up oxygen. This oxygen-renewed blood returns to the left side of the heart to complete the circuit.

Each time the heart beats, it pumps blood through both chambers. The beat is called the pulse; its impact travels through the body. Pulse is measured in number of beats per minute. A pulse rate of 75 means that the heart is beating 75 times each minute. The cardiac output is determined by the pulse rate and the stroke volume, which is the amount of blood discharged by each beat.

The pulse is measured by placing the two middle fingers of the right hand on the thumb side of the subject's wrist while the subject is seated. Taking the pulse at the wrist is usually preferable to using the carotid artery because pressure on the carotid can decrease blood flow to the brain and cause lightheadedness or fainting.

The respiratory system includes the entryways (nose and mouth), the trachea (or windpipe), the primary bronchi, and the lungs. Figure 16.4 shows the components of the respiratory system.

Breathing consists of inhaling and exhaling air. Air contains 21% oxygen, which is necessary for life. Inspiration is assisted by muscular contraction, and expiration is accomplished by a relaxing of the muscles. Inspiration occurs when the intercostal muscles and the diaphragm contract. This increases the size of the chest cavity, and expansion of the lungs causes air to flow in as a result of reduced air pressure. When the muscles are relaxed, the size of the chest cavity is reduced, the pressure is increased, and air flows from the lungs.

The primary function of the lungs is to provide oxygen to the cells on demand. The amount of oxygen needed varies depending on activity level. When a person exercises strenuously, the rate of respiration increases to bring more oxygen to tissues. If the amount of oxygen carried to the cells is adequate to maintain the level of activity, the activity is termed *aerobic*, or *endurance exercise*. Examples are walking, jogging, and bicycling for distance. If, because of high-intensity activity, the body is not capable of bringing enough oxygen to the cells, the body will continue to operate for a short time without oxygen. The result is an oxygen debt, which must be repaid later. In this case, the activity is termed *anaerobic exercise*.

The respiratory rate returns to normal after exercise. The recovery rate will be faster if the oxygen

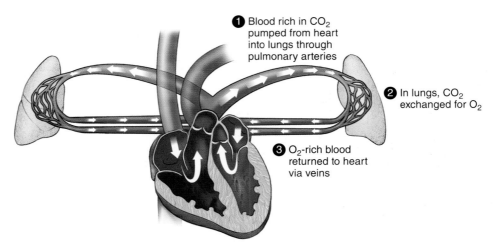

❶ Blood rich in CO_2 pumped from heart into lungs through pulmonary arteries

❷ In lungs, CO_2 exchanged for O_2

❸ O_2-rich blood returned to heart via veins

FIGURE 16.3 Structure of the heart.

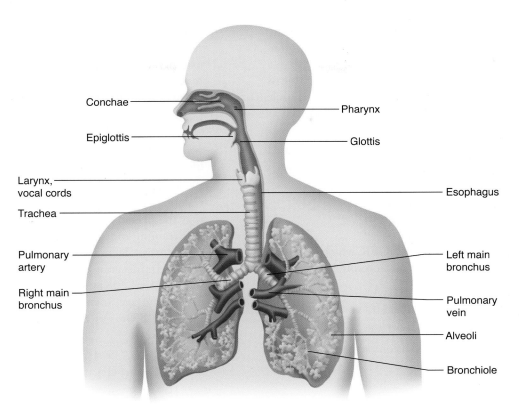

FIGURE 16.4 The respiratory system.

debt incurred during exercise was small. A person has recovered from the exertion of exercise when blood pressure, heart rate, and ventilation rate have returned to pre-exercise levels.

Basic Concepts

1. The heart is a muscular organ that must be exercised like other muscles to maintain maximum efficiency. Effective heart exercise is activity that is usually of low to moderate intensity and long duration, which is aerobic in nature.

2. Pulse rate varies among people. In most people it will slow down at rest because of training. Resting pulse rate is sometimes used as an indicator of the state of training. Not all people respond to training (show many of the effects mentioned in this section) because much of it is genetically controlled. In addition, the amount of improvement from the same amount of physical activity will vary a great deal among people.

3. Cardiorespiratory training appears to decrease the susceptibility of people to heart disease. The earlier in life that a person begins an active lifestyle, the better the chance of retarding the onset of cardiovascular disease.

4. Moderate to vigorous physical activity (MVPA), such as jogging, brisk walking, bicycling, changes the chemistry of the blood and lowers cholesterol levels. There are two types of lipoproteins—high-density lipoproteins (HDLs) and low-density lipoproteins (LDLs)—and exercise appears to increase the ratio of HDLs to LDLs. The ratio is important because HDLs seem to prevent harmful plaque from building up in the arteries.

5. Hypokinetic (inactivity) diseases are somewhat influenced by gender, heredity, race, and age. Many of these diseases can be prevented, however, by controlling factors such as smoking, being overweight, inactivity, improper diet, and high blood pressure.

6. The heart grows stronger and larger when the body is involved in MVPA of 30 minutes or more. A larger and stronger heart results in a greater stroke volume per beat.

16

7. If weight control is a concern, maintaining muscle mass is important. Severe dieting often results not only in a loss of fat cells but also in a loss of muscle tissue. Because muscle tissue burns twice as many calories as fat tissue does, muscle mass is important for weight control as well as for cosmetic and performance reasons.

8. The vital capacity of the lungs can be increased through regular MVPA, which makes the oxygen exchange system more efficient.

Suggested Learning Activities

1. Discuss the acronym DANGER, which is defined as follows, in regard to cardiorespiratory disease:
   - Do not smoke.
   - Avoid foods high in fat and cholesterol.
   - Now control high blood pressure and diabetes.
   - Get medical examinations at least every other year.
   - Exercise moderately each day.
   - Reduce weight if carrying excess fat.

2. Compare resting pulse rates among students. Look for differences between sexes, ages, and states of training. Try taking the resting pulse rate in different positions.

3. Examine the effect that exercise has on heart rate. Record the resting heart rate. Have each person run in place for one minute. Take the pulse rate immediately and record it. Continue taking the pulse rate at two-minute intervals three to five times to demonstrate recovery rate. Discuss individual differences in maximum heart rate and recovery heart rate.

4. Teach students how to take blood pressure. Exercise for one minute as described previously and monitor the effect that exercise has on blood pressure.

5. Demonstrate the effects on the cardiorespiratory system of carrying excess weight. Identify two students who weigh the same, are of the same sex, are in similar training states, and do not carry excess weight. Monitor their resting heart rate before starting. Ask one person to perform the upcoming task while carrying two 10-pound (4.5 kg) weights. Set two markers 20 yards (m) apart and have both students run back and forth between the cones 10 times. Immediately after

they finish, monitor their heart rates and recovery rates as described previously. Discuss the fact that excessive body fat is merely dead weight that must be moved and note how the excess weight decreases physical performance.

6. Compare heart rates after two- or three-minute bouts of different types of exercise. Experiment with walking, jogging, sprinting, rope jumping, bicycling, and performing calisthenics. Discuss the differences.

7. Calculate the heart rate training zone to ensure that the person is not under- or overexercising. The training zone heart rate can be calculated in several ways. Here is an example of one:

   Determine your estimated maximum heart rate by taking 208 beats per minute (bpm) minus $0.7 \times$ your age; then multiply the difference by 70% and 85%. An example for a student who is 15 follows:

   $$208 - 0.7 \times 15 = 198 \text{ bpm}$$
   $$198 \times 70 = 139 \text{ bpm}$$
   $$198 \times 85 = 168 \text{ bpm}$$

8. Identify resting respiratory rates. Have students try different types of exercise and compare the effects that each has on the respiratory rate.

Barriers to Healthy Living

Healthy living involves two major parts: participating in healthy behaviors and avoiding behaviors that are contrary to good health. Teaching behaviors to avoid should not be done by preaching and telling students what they should or should not do. Instead, emphasis should be placed on showing students the pros and cons of various practices and the consequences of making certain decisions. Every student should graduate from your program knowing that health maintenance is their sole responsibility. The ultimate responsibility rests with the student, not the teacher.

This section covers stress, nutrition and weight control, substance abuse, and personal safety. All are areas where behaviors detrimental to health can be modified or avoided to enhance quality of life. Students can make decisions in these areas, which affect how they live and, sometimes, whether they will live.

Stress

Stress is the body's reaction to certain situations in life. Everyone experiences some stress. Stress, by itself, is probably not harmful, but handling stress is critical in determining the effect it will have on a person's life. Stress affects many students. Often, students are seen as carefree and without worries, but quite the opposite is usually the case. Students live under the stress of others' expectations, peer pressure, sexual mores, and the necessity of becoming an independent being. If teachers appreciate that students are subject to stress, they can begin to deal with them in ways that alleviate possible stressors and allow stress release. In this way, teachers can have an influence on students' self-concept and worldviews.

Psychologically, stress may take the form of excitement, fear, or anger. Physical changes also accompany psychological stress; for example, heart rate increases, blood pressure rises, ventilation rate increases, perspiration increases, body temperature may rise, and the pupils may dilate. This response to stress once aided human beings in survival and is labeled the fight-or-flight syndrome. When a situation arises that may cause harm, the body's endocrine system prepares it to fight or to flee the situation. People often speak of the "adrenaline flowing" when they are scared or worried about upcoming situations.

Unfortunately, our society and schools offer few opportunities to relieve tension through activity, and few people find the motivation to do so. The resulting tension and stress that build up cause people to expend a great deal of energy in unproductive ways. People often feel fatigued when they are unable to release stress. Many nervous habits, such as constant movement while sitting, playing with an item in the hands, and various facial twitches, are the body's attempts to relieve tension.

The ultimate question when dealing with stress might be "What does it matter if I'm under stress? All people are." It matters because excessive stress has many detrimental effects on the body. It increases the risk of heart disease and can lead to insomnia and hypertension. Indigestion is common in stressed people, as is constipation. Many backaches and general body aches originate through stress. Doctors are diagnosing more and more psychosomatic diseases, those with no physical prognoses that appear to be caused by stress. Another serious problem associated with unrelieved stress is the tendency of people to try to cope by using substances such as alcohol, tobacco, and drug abuse.

People who feel stressed demonstrate behavior characterized by some of the following patterns:

- Moving everywhere rapidly, even when doing so is unnecessary.

- Feeling bored and impatient (for example, with classes) and with how others are doing things.

- Trying to coprocess (do two or more things simultaneously, referred to as polyphasic thought or action).

- Always feeling busy and feeling uneasy when taking time to do nothing or do something relaxing.

- Needing to do everything faster and more efficiently than everyone else.

- Exhibiting many strong gestures, such as clenching the fists, banging a hand on the table, or dramatically waving the arms.

TEACHING TIP

Most people learn who they are by reflecting and talking with friends who care about them. Most people find it difficult to sense that they are stressed. If you ask them what is stressing them, most will answer, "Nothing." A class activity that can help them understand stress is to create a "signs of stress" instrument. Create a group discussion about identifying signs of stress and then post the results as a list that students can refer to and share with others.

Learning to cope with stressful situations is important. The first step involves developing an awareness of what types of situations cause stress. Sharing situations with others often releases the tension and allows students to feel they are normal and are maturing properly. In the physical education setting, place emphasis on the role that activity can play in stress reduction. Involvement in enjoyable and success-oriented physical activities decreases tension. This involvement has a side effect because the required concentration will provide a diversion from worries and stressors. Note, however, that if the activity is not enjoyable and the student fails to find success, stress may actually increase.

Some experts believe that exercise applies stress to the body in a systematic fashion and thus prepares the individual to deal with other stressful situations. Physical education can provide a variety of physical activities to help students relieve tension. Another beneficial strategy is to teach various relaxation techniques that help relieve general body stress. These are discussed in a later section in this chapter.

16

Basic Concepts

1. Stress affects all people to varying degrees. Some stress is necessary to stimulate performance and increase motivation.

2. The amount of stress that a person can cope with depends on how it is perceived. Positive self-concepts help people accept threatening situations in a less stressful manner.

3. When people have difficulty dealing with stress through productive methods, such as exercise, relaxation activities, and talks with friends, they often attempt to relieve stress through unhealthy and potentially dangerous means such as alcohol, tobacco, and drug usage.

4. Stress causes changes in perceptible bodily functions. An awareness of these changes is necessary if students are to recognize when they are under stress and need to cope with its effects.

5. Stress appears to increase susceptibility to many diseases and causes psychosomatic illnesses.

6. Exercise is an excellent way to relieve stress and tension when the activity is perceived as enjoyable and success oriented.

7. Stress is a risk factor that influences the onset of heart disease.

8. Among the various ways of relieving stress are exercise, expressing feelings to friends, developing problem-solving skills, and performing accepted relaxation techniques.

Suggested Learning Activities

1. Hold an isometric contraction at the elbow joint. With the other hand, feel the contraction in the biceps and triceps. Repeat the activity with other muscle groups. Discuss how stress causes generalized body tension that can result in tensed muscles and an increase in general body fatigue. Learning to recognize muscle tension is a desired outcome of this discussion.

2. Discuss the concept of choking under pressure. How does this phenomenon relate to athletic performance? What happens when stress is greater than the person's ability to cope with it? Discuss how some level of stress increases performance, whereas too much stress decreases it. Why do professional athletes hire personal consultants to help them improve performance?

3. Discuss the importance of perception in stressful situations. How is stress perceived? Should students admit when they are worried or scared? Is the best approach to be tough and not tell anyone how you feel? Is it better to keep emotions inside or to share feelings with others?

4. Discuss the importance of finding activities in which students believe they are successful. How are positive self-concepts developed? Why are some people able to cope with failure and losing better than others?

5. Discuss situations in physical activity settings that give rise to increased stress, such as failing in front of others, not being selected for a team, being ridiculed for a poor performance, or losing a game that was personally important. How could these situations be handled differently?

6. Identify physical activities that seem to relieve tension and stress. Discuss the relationship between involvement in activity and the reduction of stress.

7. Identify and discuss unproductive attempts to relieve stress such as drinking, smoking, and drug abuse. Why are these methods chosen rather than exercise, discussions, or relaxation activities?

8. Discuss the many effects of stress on health. Give students a stress inventory to see how much stress they are under, and discuss ways of reducing this pressure.

9. Teach relaxation techniques such as deep breathing, progressive muscle relaxation, and personal meditation. Emphasize the importance of taking time for these activities daily. Just as brushing the teeth is necessary for healthy dentition, relaxation is necessary for a healthy body and mind.

Nutrition and Weight Management

Proper nutrition is an important component of physical fitness and performance. For many students, a major area of concern deals with the balance between caloric intake and expenditure to maintain proper weight. Students should understand the theory and principles for maintaining an optimum level of body weight. Discuss the effect of empty calories through excessive ingestion of junk foods. Explain the importance of a balanced diet to help the body grow and develop. Point out that the role of exercise in weight control and muscle development is as important as a balanced diet.

Students need to understand the elements of a balanced diet. A balanced diet draws from each of the basic food groups; emphasis should be given to proportionality, moderation, and variety. MyPlate from the U.S. Department of Agriculture (2013a) replaces the MyPyramid that previously offered dietary guidelines for Americans of all ages (see figure 16.5). MyPlate is designed to remind people to eat healthfully and is not intended to change consumer behavior alone. The icon illustrates the five food groups that should be part of a meal. Allied to the icon is the ChooseMyPlate website (www.choosemyplate.gov). A great deal of information is available for the public and professionals. The focus of the messages is to balance calories; increase the consumption of fruits, vegetables, and whole grains; switch to fat-free or low-fat milk; and decrease consumption of foods that are high in sodium and sugar.

Depending on the criteria used, anywhere from 30 to 50% of students are overweight, meaning that their body weight is over the accepted limits for their age, sex, and body build. The ChooseMyPlate website can deliver all the relevant information to students in an easy to understand manner. It provides an efficient and easy way for students to develop awareness of the caloric content of foods as well as the nutritional value. They can count calories and practice consistency in the number of calories they ingest. Coupled with this awareness should be some comprehension of the number of calories expended through various types of physical activity (see figure 16.6). When caloric intake exceeds

caloric expenditure, becoming overweight is the result. A well-documented and common cause of becoming overweight is inactivity. Some experts believe overweight students do not eat more than normal-weight students; rather, they exercise less. Regardless of the cause, a balance of caloric intake and expenditure is the key to weight management.

Being overweight is a roadblock to optimal health. Life insurance companies view overweight people as risks because of their shorter life expectancy. Excessive body fat makes the heart work harder, increases the chance of having high blood pressure, and lowers the possibility

Activity	Calories per hour
Moderate activity	**200–350**
Bicycling (5.5 mph [9 km/h])	210
Walking (2.5 mph [4 km/h])	210
Gardening	220
Canoeing (2.5 mph [4 km/h])	230
Golf	250
Lawn mowing (power mower)	250
Lawn mowing (hand mower)	270
Bowling	270
Fencing	300
Rowing (2.5 mph [4 km/h])	300
Swimming (.25 mph [.4 km/h])	300
Walking (3.75 mph [6 km/h])	300
Badminton	350
Horseback riding (trotting)	350
Square dancing	350
Volleyball	350
Roller skating	350
Vigorous activity	**Over 350**
Table tennis	360
Ice skating (10 mph [16 km/h])	400
Tennis	420
Waterskiing	480
Hill climbing (100 ft/h [30 m/h])	490
Skiing (10 mph [16 km/h])	600
Squash and handball	600
Cycling (13 mph [21 km/h])	660
Scull rowing (race)	840
Running (10 mph [16 km/h])	900

16

FIGURE 16.5 MyPlate icon.
USDA's Center for Nutrition Policy and Promotion.

FIGURE 16.6 Caloric expenditure.
Adapted from the President's Council on Physical Fitness and Sports (Washington, D.C.).

of recovery from a heart attack. Even more detrimental to students is the psychological effect that being overweight has on self-concept development. Students of normal weight find it much easier to perform physical tasks because strength in relationship to body weight is a critical performance factor. Overweight students are often punished more severely than normal-weight students for the same type of deviance and may receive lower grades for a similar quality of work.

TEACHING TIP

Most people overestimate how active they are and underestimate how much they eat. In addition, many people believe that if they exercise, they can eat whatever they like, regardless of the number of calories. Not true. For example, jogging 1 mile (1.6 km) burns about 100 calories. Suppose you jog 4 miles (6.4 km) and burn around 400 calories. Then you decide to go to a well-known fast-food provider and have a cheeseburger, small side of fries, and a small coke. You clean your plate and consume 1,160 calories. Your fast-food meal resulted in your consuming three times as many calories as you burned during your jog. Initiate a class discussion about the number of calories that snacks and treats can add to daily food intake. Then show how many miles (kilometers) they would have to walk or jog to burn off those excess calories. Discuss how easy it is to eat more calories than you can burn through exercise.

Basic Concepts

1. Log onto the ChooseMyPlate website at www.choosemyplate.gov and become familiar with creating a balanced and healthy diet. Identify foods to eat more often and foods to eat less often. Discuss portion size and making half of your plate fruits and vegetables.

2. Caloric expenditure (body functions plus exercise) and intake (eating) must be balanced to maintain a healthy weight. A weight-reducing program should include a reduction in caloric intake and an increase in daily exercise.

3. Activities vary in the energy they require. Individual needs must be considered in the selection of activities to promote weight control and maintain physical fitness.

4. Junk foods add little if any nutritional value to the diet and are usually high in calories. Foods and beverages such as sugar, margarine and butter, oils, and alcohol are high in calories but make little or no contribution in terms of nutrition.

5. Excessive weight makes performing physical tasks difficult. This impediment results in less success and in less motivation to be active, thus increasing the tendency toward being overweight.

6. Being overweight increases the risk of heart disease and related diseases such as diabetes.

7. Many overweight students do not consume more calories than normal-weight students do; they are simply less active.

8. Vitamins are not nutrients but are catalysts that facilitate metabolic processes. Certain vitamin deficiencies can produce various diseases.

9. Various foods are excellent sources of specific nutrients. Students should be able to identify which foods to ingest to provide a balance of the needed nutrients, vitamins, and minerals.

Suggested Learning Activities

1. Post a list of activities and their energy demands on the bulletin board. Discuss the need for selecting activities that will burn enough calories to balance caloric intake.

2. Maintain a food diary. Record all food eaten daily and the number of calories in each. Compare the number of calories ingested with the number of calories expended.

3. Maintain a nutritious-food diary. Keep a log of foods eaten daily and categorize each into major food groups. Determine the percentage of carbohydrate, protein, and fat in relation to all the food ingested during each day.

4. Develop a desirable and practical balanced diet that can be followed for one week. Arrange with parents to facilitate the diet within their budget restrictions.

5. Calculate the recommended daily allowance (RDA) for various nutrients. Compare a daily intake with the recommendations for various minerals and vitamins.

6. Bring various foods to class that have labels offering nutrition information. Determine which foods are good buys for desired nutrients.

7. Develop an activity diary. For one week, record all activity over and above maintenance activities. Calculate the number of calories burned per day.

8. Discuss and analyze how people respond to physically fit and athletic people. Contrast the ways in which overweight people are discriminated against in various situations.

Substance Abuse

Substance abuse is defined as the harmful use of alcohol, tobacco, or drugs. If students are expected to make wise and meaningful decisions, they must understand how various substances affect their physical and psychological being. Facts, both pro and con, should be presented in a nonjudgmental environment, without moralizing and preaching. Students will have difficulty making good personal decisions if most of the information they receive is from peers or moralizing adults.

Alcohol, tobacco, and drugs are usually detrimental to total health. The use and misuse of these substances should be discussed objectively with students because much of the information they receive is from biased sources, such as parents, peers, and various media formats. The physical education teacher can promote discussions and fact-seeking sessions that relate to a healthy lifestyle. Many times, the physical educator is the only person who focuses on health promotion. But if the instructor believes that an issue has only one acceptable point of view, avoiding a discussion might be best. Telling students only the reasons for behaving the way you want them to behave often results in a strong reaction in the opposite direction.

Alcohol has both short-term and long-term effects. Short-term effects vary as a result of the depressant effect that alcohol has on the central nervous system. Some people become relaxed, others become aggressive or angry, and some become active to differing degrees. Ultimately, a lack of coordination and confusion occur if a great deal of alcohol is ingested. The long-term effects of alcohol abuse may be liver damage, heart disease, and malnutrition. The greatest concern surrounding long-term drinking is the possibility of alcoholism. Most agree that alcoholism has the following components: loss of control of alcohol intake, presence of functional or structural damage (physical and psychological), and dependence on alcohol to maintain an acceptable level of functioning.

Students usually drink for any of the following reasons: curiosity, the desire to celebrate with parents, peer pressure, the desire to be like adults and appear more mature, rebelliousness, the desire to emulate role models, or addiction (i.e., they are alcoholics). Some students are ambivalent about alcohol; they know its detrimental effects, yet they see many of their friends and peers using it. The problem is a difficult one and an understanding of both moderate use and abstinence is needed. An understanding of how to cope with peer pressure to drink alcohol is also needed and is discussed in the next section on basic concepts.

Tobacco use is common among middle and high school students. Smoking significantly increases the possibility of heart attacks, strokes, and cancer. Chronic bronchitis and emphysema are prevalent diseases among smokers. A recent study revealed that the average lifespan of long-term smokers is seven years shorter than that of nonsmokers. Students need to understand the effect of smoking on a healthy body. Along with gaining this knowledge, they should examine why people choose to smoke. Overall, the percentage of people smoking has declined. Among those who choose to smoke, the fastest growing group is young girls and women. Students will always make the final decision for their individual behaviors, but before they do so, they need to thoroughly understand the ramifications of smoking.

TEACHING TIP

Most young people are unable to imagine their mortality and think that they will live forever regardless of their behavior or will be able to avoid the long-term consequences of abusing alcohol, tobacco, and drugs. For that reason, scare tactics usually do not work. A better approach is to use straight talk to teach them the facts and consequences of unhealthy behavior.

The use of performance-enhancing drugs in athletics should be discussed. If you are uncomfortable dealing with these topics, agencies outside the school are available to discuss substance abuse in an objective manner with students. Vet and clear the agency with your campus administrator to ensure they are valid, reputable, and reliable. The intent is to enhance students' awareness so that they learn about alternatives to and consequences of doping and illicit or performance-enhancing drug use. Substance abuse is contrary to the whole concept of personal health. Physical educators need to accept the challenge of increasing student understanding and knowledge regarding drug use. The National Institute of Health (NIH) has developed an excellent website filled with information for teachers and students. Funded by the National Institute of Drug Abuse, the website is located at www.drugabuse.gov.

Basic Concepts

1. The earlier a person begins to smoke, the greater the risk is to functional health.

2. People smoke for psychological reasons.

3. Young people may choose substance abuse because of curiosity, status, or peer pressure.

4. Choosing a lifestyle independently of peers requires courage.

5. Students can make wise and purposeful decisions about substance abuse only when they understand all the alternatives and consequences.

6. Substance abuse is often an attempt to cope with stress. Exercise and relaxation are much more productive, healthy methods of coping.

7. The use of alcohol, tobacco, and drugs always carries the risk of addiction. When people are addicted, they are no longer in charge of their lifestyles. All people, to some degree, are subject to addiction; no one is immune.

8. Spending time and effort developing personal competencies is more productive than abusing substances. Personal competency in many areas reduces the need to be like everyone else and contributes to a positive self-concept.

9. The use of harmful substances frequently reduces the pleasure that people can receive from experiencing the world. Physical performance often declines because of substance abuse.

10. People can drink and smoke and still excel at athletics, but their maximum performance level may be lower and the ultimate effect will be harmful. Students see many professional athletes who smoke and drink. They know that this behavior occurs, but they should understand that the choice is undesirable from a health standpoint.

Suggested Learning Activities

1. Identify and discuss the reasons why people choose or choose not to become involved in substance abuse.

2. Discuss the importance of making personal decisions based on what is best for the person. Why do people follow others and allow them to influence decisions, even when those decisions are not in a person's best interest?

3. Develop a bulletin board that illustrates the many ways that the tobacco, alcohol, and drug industries use to try to get young people to buy their products. Reserve a spot for advertisements (if any can be found) that admonish and encourage students to abstain or moderate the use of various substances.

4. Students often see professional and college athletes smoking and drinking on television while hearing that those habits impair performance. Discuss why these athletes can perform at a high level even though they may drink or smoke.

5. Students often choose to be part of a peer group at any cost. Discuss how our society often respects and honors individuals who have the courage to go their own way. Examples might be Helen Keller, Martin Luther King, Jr., and others.

6. Identify and discuss the ways in which people choose to relieve and dissipate stress. Discuss productive releases of tension such as recreation, hobbies, and sports.

7. Bring in speakers who are knowledgeable about the effects and uses of alcohol, tobacco, and drugs. If necessary, bring in a pair of speakers who might debate both sides of an issue.

8. Develop visual aids that identify the various effects that alcohol, tobacco, and drugs have on the body.

9. Log on to the Internet and find resources that are available for helping people with substance abuse issues.

Safety and First Aid

Safety and first aid are often part of the physical education program because more accidents occur in physical education than in any other area of the school curriculum. Safety is an attitude and concern for the welfare and health of self and others. An accident is an unplanned event or act that may result in injury or death. Often, accidents occur when they could have been prevented. The following are the most common causes of accidents: lack of knowledge and understanding of risks; lack of skill and competence to perform tasks safely, such as riding a bike or driving a car; false sense of security that leads people to think that accidents happen only to others; fatigue or illness that affects physical and mental performance; drugs and alcohol; and strong emotional states (e.g., anger, fear, or worry) that cause people to do things they might not otherwise do.

Traffic accidents result in many deaths that could be prevented. Wearing seat belts reduces the risk of dying by 50%. Drinking alcohol while driving increases the risk of an accident 20-fold compared with not drinking. Driver education and awareness of the possibility of serious injury should be a part of the health program.

Bicycles are involved in numerous accidents. Automobile drivers have difficulty seeing bicycles, and the resulting accidents are often serious. The physical education setting is often the only place where bicycle safety training occurs. Classes in bicycling for safety and fitness are usually well received by middle and high school students.

Swimming-related accidents are the second-leading cause of accidental death among young adults. More than 50% of all drownings occur when people unexpectedly find themselves in water. Another major cause of death from drowning is alcohol ingestion. Swimming and drinking do not mix well. Physical education programs should teach all students to swim and learn water-safety rules during their school careers.

Physical education and sports are sources of injury in the school setting. Proper safety procedures and first-aid techniques should be taught. Students should know how to stop bleeding, treat shock, administer cardiopulmonary resuscitation (CPR), and use an automated external defibrillator (AED). Many physical education programs now include a required unit of instruction dealing with these topics. Bystanders could save an estimated 100,000 to 200,000 lives if they knew CPR. The American Red Cross estimates that with training and access to AEDs, 50,000 lives could be saved.

Basic Concepts

1. Accidents are unplanned events or acts that may result in injury or death. Most accidents could be prevented if people were adequately prepared and understood the necessary competencies and risks involved.

2. Wearing seat belts and not drinking alcohol while driving will dramatically decrease the risk of death by automobile accident.

3. Car drivers do not often see bicycles. Bicycling safety classes can help lower the number of bicycle accidents.

4. Swimming-related accidents are the second-leading cause of accidental death among young people. Instructional swimming programs and avoiding alcohol will dramatically decrease the risk of death by drowning.

5. Thousands of lives could be saved if all people knew how to perform CPR and use an AED.

6. All students should know how to stop bleeding and administer CPR.

7. Basic first-aid procedures to prevent further injury to victims are competencies that all students should possess.

Suggested Learning Activities

1. Discuss the causes of different types of accidents and the ways that many accidents could be avoided.

2. Identify the types of accidents that happen to different age groups and the reasons for these differences.

3. Identify the role of alcohol and drugs in causing accidents. Why are these substances used in recreational settings?

4. Develop a bulletin board that illustrates how to care for shock victims. Practice the steps in a mock procedure.

5. Have an "accident day" to stage various types of accidents that demand treatments such as stopping bleeding, using an AED, and performing CPR. Identify where the AEDs are located in a school setting.

6. Outline the steps to follow in case of a home fire. Discuss how many fires could be prevented.

7. Conduct a bicycle safety fair. Have students design bulletin boards and displays that explain and emphasize bicycle safety.

Teaching Health Maintenance

The health of students can be seriously impaired when safety issues are dealt with incorrectly. But consuming proper nutrition, avoiding substance abuse, and practicing proper safety when bicycling or driving a car can protect the health of participants. The purpose of this section is to help students learn maintenance behaviors. Health maintenance focuses on a three-pronged

16

approach: (1) health-related fitness, (2) stress reduction, and (3) self-evaluation. Discussions here are not covered in depth because other textbooks deal specifically with these areas. For example, for a source that helps students develop lifetime fitness, see the Corbin and LeMasurier (2014) text listed in the References and Suggested Readings section at the end of this chapter.

Health-Related Fitness

Health-related fitness is directly related to the wellness of people and generally consists of cardiorespiratory fitness, strength, muscular endurance, flexibility, and body fatness. Cardiorespiratory fitness is the most important phase of fitness for wellness. Cardiorespiratory fitness is a complex concept, but simply put, it involves efficient functioning of the heart, blood, and blood vessels to supply oxygen to the body during aerobic activity. Strength refers to the ability of a muscle or muscle group to exert force. Without strength, a low standard of performance can be expected because muscles will fatigue before a person can perform well. Muscular endurance refers to the ability of a muscle or muscle group to exert effort over time. Endurance uses strength and postpones fatigue so that the effort can be expended for long periods. Cardiorespiratory fitness also plays a key role in how long people can perform an activity. Flexibility is a person's range of movement at the joints. It allows freedom of movement and ready adjustment of the body for various movements. Body fatness refers to the percentage of body weight that is fat. People who are physically fit generally have a lower percentage of body fat than those who are unfit. For males in high school, 11 to 15% body fat is a reasonable range, and 20 to 25% is acceptable for females (Corbin & LeMasurier, 2014).

Teachers should help students to develop a health-related fitness plan they can use to monitor themselves throughout life. The basic steps for such a plan are as follows:

1. Identify present areas of fitness and weakness through pretesting with the FitnessGram test (Meredith & Welk, 2010). This test shows students the criterion level they need to achieve for good health.
2. Identify the activities that the students are currently performing by having them fill out a survey that lists a wide variety of activities. Post a chart that shows the components of health-related fitness enhanced by each activity. A good source for surveys and lists of activity benefits is *Fitness for Life* by Corbin and LeMasurier (2014).

3. Select some activities that build health-related fitness components that each student needs, as identified in step 1. Each student will begin to have a personalized plan that is meaningful to him or her.
4. Plan a weeklong activity program that contains activities that are enjoyable and help alleviate weaknesses in various component areas. Evaluate the weeklong program and develop a month-long program to provide longer-range goals. In the program, delineate the frequency of exercise, the intensity, and the amount of time to be spent exercising.

Stress Reduction

Many methods are recommended for learning to cope with stress. Only a few of the most popular in the school setting are covered here. The following textbooks are resources to help in this area: *Stress Management: A Wellness Approach* (Tummers, 2013), *Comprehensive Stress Management* (Greenberg, 2013), and *Fitness for Life* (Corbin & LeMasurier, 2014). In addition, there are a variety of apps that target stress management and mindfulness practices, especially for youth. Because technology changes constantly, we cannot recommend specific ones, but they can be searched easily on the Internet or in app stores on phones.

In an earlier section, exercise was discussed as an excellent method of controlling stress. It appears to allow negative feelings to dissipate and positive feelings to replace them. Many people believe that the relaxed feeling that occurs after an exercise bout is the best part of activity.

Many deep-breathing exercises are available. The relaxation response advocated by Benson & Klipper (2000) is supposed to replicate the effects of transcendental meditation. People sit comfortably and quietly and breathe deeply through the nose. The person says the word "one" on each exhale. Twenty-minute bouts, once or twice a day, are recommended.

Another popular method is progressive muscle relaxation. With this technique, a muscle or muscle group is first tensed and then relaxed slowly and smoothly. All the major parts of the body are in turn relaxed as the person works down from the head to the toes. Mindfulness is a current popular approach to enriching life and relaxing. The basic approach is to accept life as it comes and avoid passing judgment on what occurs. Focus on one topic at a time and forget multitasking. Mindfulness is practiced by focusing on the immediate surroundings and staying in the present versus thinking about the past. A book by Wheeler (2007) is a straightforward and easy to use book for students and teacher.

Regardless of the activity choice selected for relaxation, students should be taught the importance of taking time to relax. An important learning situation is to take four or five minutes at the end of a class to sit down and relax. By setting aside this time, the instructor communicates to students that relaxation is indeed important.

The concept of mindfulness, a practice of fully engaging in the present moment as opposed to dwelling in the past or being concerned with what the future may hold (Lu, 2012), has caught on in schools as a way to help students and staff focus on the present and manage self-regulation (Mulhearn, Kulinna, & Lorenz, 2017). Mindful practices include intentionally prompting and teaching students to focus on their actions in a movement, try to complete each action in its own unique moment, and incorporate conscious breathing with all physical activities (Lu, 2012).

Avoiding multitasking is another way to promote mindful practice during physical education. In a world of competing interests, listening to music may motivate some students to be active during physical education, but it can serve as a distraction for others if the purpose is to be present in the moment. Mindfulness is all about individuality, so allowing students to determine what works best for them may be a key ingredient to turning them on to physical activity for a lifetime. Accepting self and others, appreciating the surroundings, and focusing on the process of the skill or activity are all points to highlight when encouraging students to be mindful (Lu, 2012). Including these strategies within a physical education setting may improve student interest, skill performance, behavior, and kinesthetic awareness (Mulhearn et al., 2017).

Self-Evaluation and Behavior Self-Control

Knowing that a goal of physical education is to help students for a lifetime, it is imperative that they leave a high school program with the skills to self-evaluate and moderate their own behaviors related to health. Next, we provide some means for teaching these practices to students.

Self-Evaluation

An important step in maintaining good health is being able to self-evaluate on a regular basis. People ultimately answer to themselves, so students need not share the results of their evaluations. Many inventories, such as drinking and smoking scales, are available from various governmental agencies. Students can begin to see the extent of a problem and whether they are improving. Students should be taught to evaluate their own health-related physical fitness. Each of the health-related fitness items can be evaluated easily using the Fitness-Gram (Meredith & Welk, 2010). If students are not given time in the physical education program to evaluate their own fitness, they will probably not take the time for evaluation after they leave school. An effective technique is to give each student a self-testing card that has room for recording four to five testing episodes. Students can regularly test themselves and record their performances. If desired, instructors can file the cards and return them when it is time for another testing period. This system allows students to monitor their personal health-related fitness in a number of areas.

Modifying Personal Behavior

Students can be taught how to monitor their personal health behavior. Behavior modification is a systematic approach to solving problems. It involves keeping records of behavior to understand the positive and negative variables that influence behavior. The following steps help students learn to manipulate their behavior.

1. *Maintain behavior records.* Students monitor their activity patterns and record the performances on personal charts. Many websites and technologies allow activity monitoring. Examples include inexpensive Fitbits; apps such as NFL Play 60, MyNetDiary, and MyFitnessPal; and websites such as TeenBEAT out of California. These platforms allow students to observe their patterns of exercise, the duration of the exercise, and the intensity of effort. Such observation becomes self-reinforcing when, for example, students see clearly that they are exercising only two days per week and showing little gain, or when they observe rapid improvement after exercising five days per week for several weeks. Another advantage of recording behavior is that the routine act of recording reminds the performer that the behavior must be done. This routine reinforcement causes the behavior performance to improve.

2. *Develop a priority schedule.* If students want to exercise regularly, they must schedule the activity and make it a high-priority item. In other

16

words, they must exercise before doing other less important tasks. Scheduling the activity for a certain number of days at a specified time is most effective.

3. *Analyze restrictive factors.* Even after they have analyzed behavior and set priorities, students may find that they are not following desired behavior patterns. The reasons for lack of adherence must be analyzed and other changes implemented to increase the probability of carrying out the behavior. For example, the time of day for exercise may have to be changed. Exercising for two shorter periods per day instead of one longer period might be a solution. Exercising with a friend or changing the mode of exercise is another possible solution.

4. *Establish rewards.* To continue the activity over a long period, establishing personal contingencies that are available after performing the desired behavior can be helpful. For example, students might relax and watch television immediately after exercise or take a long, hot shower. Regardless of the reward, it must be meaningful and worthwhile to the individual. Verbalizing internally after each exercise routine is also effective as a contingency. A person might say to her- or himself, "I feel better and look stronger after every bout of exercise." In any case, if students can identify something positive that occurs because of or after the exercise bout, they will tend to continue on the path of wellness.

LEARNING AIDS

STUDY STIMULATORS AND REVIEW QUESTIONS

1. Define health education and discuss how it can be integrated into secondary physical education.
2. Describe several ideas for teaching health concepts in physical education.
3. What can teachers do to develop awareness and decision-making skills for students? Specifically, discuss the importance of coping and decision-making skills.
4. Identify several teaching behaviors critical to leading effective class discussions.
5. What areas of understanding do students need to master before they can develop a value for personal health? Include several knowledge concepts and learning experiences for each area.
6. Discuss the importance of proper nutrition for youth.
7. Describe various types of substance abuse as they apply to secondary school students.
8. What concepts of safety and first aid are important for healthy living?

WEBSITES

Healthy Lifestyles

www.actionforhealthykids.org
www.aap.org
http://cdc.gov/physicalactivity/everyone/guidelines/index.html
www.medlineplus.gov

ChooseMyPlate

www.choosemyplate.gov

Stress Management

http://mindfulnessinschools.weebly.com/mindful-physical-activities.html
www.mindtools.com/smpage.html
www.stress.org
www.the-guided-meditation-site.com

Substance Abuse

www.drugabuse.gov

www.alcoholism.about.com

www.samhsa.gov

REFERENCES AND SUGGESTED READINGS

Behnke, R.S. (2012). *Kinetic anatomy* (3rd ed.). Champaign, IL: Human Kinetics.

Benson, H., with Klipper, M.Z. (2000). *The relaxation response* (updated and expanded edition). New York, NY: Harper-Collins.

Blonna, R. (2012). *Coping with stress in a changing world* (5th ed.). Boston, MA: McGraw-Hill.

Corbin, C., & LeMasurier, G. (2014). *Fitness for life* (6th ed.). Champaign, IL: Human Kinetics.

Corbin, C.B., Welk, G., Corbin, W.G., & Welk, K.M. (2007). *Concepts of physical fitness and wellness: A comprehensive lifestyle approach* (7th ed.). Boston, MA: McGraw-Hill.

Fahey, T.D., Insel, P.M., & Roth, W.T. (2013). *Fit and well: Core concepts and labs in physical fitness and wellness* (10th ed.). Boston, MA: McGraw-Hill.

Gough, C. (2018). Physical activity – statistics & facts. Retrieved from https://www.statista.com/topics/1749/physical-activity/#dossierSummary__chapter4.

Greenberg, J.S. (2013). *Comprehensive stress management* (13th ed.). Boston, MA: McGraw-Hill.

Hoeger, W.W.K., & Hoeger, S.A. (2013). *Fitness and wellness* (10th ed.). Belmont, CA: Wadsworth.

Jackson, A.W., Morrow, J.R., Jr., Hill, D.W., & Dishman, R.K. (2004). *Physical activity for health and fitness* (updated edition). Champaign, IL: Human Kinetics.

Kenney, W. L., Wilmore, J. H., & Costill, D. L. (2015). *Physiology of sport and exercise*. (6th ed.). Champaign, IL: Human Kinetics.

Lu, C. (2012). Integrating mindfulness into school physical activity programming. *Teaching & Learning, 7*(1), 37–46.

Meredith, M.D., & Welk, G.J. (2010). *FitnessGram and ActivityGram test administration manual* (4th ed.). Dallas, TX: Cooper Institute.

Mulhearn, S.C., Kulinna, P.H., & Lorenz, K.A. (2017). Harvesting harmony: Mindfulness in physical education. *Journal of Physical Education, Recreation and Dance, 88*(6), 44–50.

Tummers, N.E. (2013). *Stress management: A wellness approach.* Champaign, IL: Human Kinetics.

U.S. Department of Agriculture. (2013a). ChooseMyPlate. Retrieved from www.choosemyplate.gov.

Wheeler, C.M. (2007). *10 simple solutions to stress.* Oakland, CA: New Harbinger.

16

Nontraditional Activities

This chapter offers a variety of activities and games that are not often included in physical education classes. Activities such as juggling, handling beanbags, stunts, and cooperative challenges are novel to physical education classes. Presentation of these activities is best done in a low-key manner with emphasis on enjoyment and working with peers toward common goals.

Learning Objectives

▶ Identify a number of activities that are nontraditional in most physical education programs.
▶ Teach basic techniques of juggling.
▶ Understand how activities in this chapter can be used to motivate less skilled students.
▶ Teach a variety of novel games and activities in a relaxed, recreational setting.
▶ Challenge students to create cooperative activities that augment those found in this chapter.

The activities in this chapter offer students and teachers a change of pace from longer units of instruction. Most students find the activities personally challenging because they require some new and different skill sets. The activities can be used on rainy day schedules, shortened-period days, or as a short one- or two-week unit. The activities incorporate equipment not often used in typical secondary physical education programs, and they do not require a large instructional space. Some students who do not enjoy group or team activities will be motivated by the opportunity to learn individual skills. For example, the introductory progression of juggling skills can be taught in the first lesson. After they learn the rudimentary skills, some students may choose to progress to more challenging tasks, whereas others remain at a lower level.

Besides using them to manage space or weather issues, nontraditional activities can serve as a change of pace to break up a longer unit of instruction. Encourage students to help each other master the new tasks, emphasizing and reinforcing cooperation. These activities create a different environment that may be more meaningful for some students.

Individual, Partner, and Small-Group Units of Instruction

Activities in this area include the use of beanbags, hoops, jump bands, juggling, stunts and combatives, and wands. Place instructional focus primarily on individual skill development and allow students to progress at an optimum rate of development. Students can develop new and different challenges that the rest of the class can try.

Beanbags

A good size for beanbags is about 6 by 6 inches (15 by 15 cm) because they can be balanced on various body parts and used for personal challenges. Beanbags can be used for juggling activities as well as for many of the challenge activities listed here. Students should try to master the stunts with both the right and left hands.

The following challenges can be taken in any order.

1. Toss the beanbag overhead and catch it on the back of the hand. Try catching on different body parts, such as the shoulder, knee, and foot.

2. Toss the beanbag, make a half-turn, and catch it. Try making a different number of turns (full, double, and so forth).

3. Toss the beanbag, clap the hands, and catch it. Try clapping the hands a specified number of times. Clap the hands around different parts of the body.

4. Toss the beanbag and touch various body parts or objects. For example, toss it and touch the toes, shoulders, and hips before catching it. Specify objects to touch, such as the wall, floor, or a line.

5. Toss the beanbag, move to various body positions, and catch it. Suggested positions are sitting, kneeling, adopting a supine or prone position, and moving to the side.

6. Reverse task 5 by tossing the beanbag from some of the suggested positions and then resuming the standing position.

7. Toss the beanbag and perform various stunts before catching it, such as heel clicks, heel slaps, a jump with a full turn, and a push-up.

8. Toss the beanbag from behind the back and catch it. Toss it overhead and catch it behind the back.

9. Toss the beanbag, move, and catch it. Cover as much ground as possible between the toss and catch. Move forward, backward, and sideways, using steps such as the carioca, shuffle, and slide.

10. Toss the beanbag with various body parts (feet, knees, shoulders) and catch it with the hands or other body parts. Try to develop as much height on the toss as possible.

11. Perform some of the stunts with a beanbag in each hand. Catch the bags simultaneously.

12. Play a balance tag game. Specify a body part on which the bag must be balanced while moving. Designate who is "it." If the beanbag falls off or is touched with the hands, the player must freeze and is subject to being tagged.

13. Try partner activities. Play catch with a partner using two or three beanbags. Toss and catch the beanbags using various body parts.

Hoops

A hoop with a diameter of 42 inches (1.07 m) is usually the best size for middle and high school students. This hoop is large enough for them to move their bodies through and over. Encourage students to master the activities with both sides of their bodies. Emphasize creating new routines with the hoops. The following are suggested ideas:

1. Spin the hoop like a top and see how long the hoop will continue to spin. While the hoop is spinning, see how many times it can be jumped.

2. Twirl a hoop using various body parts (waist, knees, ankles, neck, wrist). Twirl a hoop from the neck to the knees and back up to the neck. Twirl it on a wrist and then change it to the other wrist. Pass the hoop to a partner while twirling it.

3. Try many of the hooping challenges while using two or more hoops. Twirl a hoop on two or more body parts.

4. Play catch with a partner while twirling a hoop. Catch more than one object and twirl more than one hoop.

5. Jump or hop through a hoop held by a partner. Vary the challenge by altering the angle and height of the hoop. Try jumping through two or more parallel hoops without touching them.

6. Roll the hoop like a spare tire. Change direction on signal. Roll two or more hoops at the same time.

7. Use the hoop in place of a jump rope. Jump the hoop forward, backward, and sideways. Perform various foot stunts like toe touching, a rocker step, and heel-and-toe movement while jumping.

8. Roll the hoop forward with a reverse spin. The spin should cause it to return to the thrower. As the hoop returns, try some of the following challenges: Jump the hoop, move through it, kick it up with the toe and catch it, and pick it up with the arm and begin twirling it on the arm.

9. Play catch with the hoop with a partner. Use two or more hoops and throw them alternately as well as simultaneously.

10. Employ the hoop relay. Break into equal-size groups. Join hands and place a hoop on a pair of joined hands. The object is to pass the hoop around the circle without releasing the hand grip. The first group to get the hoop around the circle is declared the winner.

Jump Bands

Jump bands can be used to create several challenging movement tasks. Groups of different sizes can use jump bands, although three students is the most used choice. Two students attach the jump bands around the lower legs or ankle area with Velcro and jump rhythmically to music, while one or more students jump in and out of the bands with specific foot patterns (see figure 17.1). Students with the bands on their legs can adjust them up or down, depending on the skill and fitness of the jumpers. Beginners should start with the bands as low as possible on their legs. The bands can be raised to increase the intensity of the workout because the jumpers have to elevate higher to get over the bands. Change jumpers and holders often to equalize jumping demands and development of skills. The jump bands demand teamwork from all involved. Many creative opportunities are also possible with different steps and partner activities.

FIGURE 17.1 Movement task with jump bands.

Jump bands can be used with rhythmic activities such as tinikling or lummi sticks. A wide variety of rhythmic foot pattern skills can be developed with a group of three students working together. Larger group activities can be challenging as well. Another variation with jump bands is to use them as part of a fitness circuit (see the section Jump-Bands Circuit in chapter 15). In a fitness circuit, students rotate from a jump-band station for cardiorespiratory work to a flexibility station, to a strength station, and then back to another cardiorespiratory station with the jump bands, and so on. Stations can incorporate medicine balls and stability balls to add variety to the circuit.

Beginning Jump-Band Steps

Music should incorporate a 4/4 rhythm with popular, upbeat songs. The following steps are suggested:

1. Students with the jump bands on should follow an "out, out, in, in" pattern. They should practice together without the music and then with the music.

2. The jumper starts with the right side facing the bands. When the bands go apart, the jumper moves the right foot in and then hops on the

17

right foot. The jumper then crosses the left foot over to the out position and then hops on the left foot. The jumper then crosses the right foot over to the in position and hops on the right foot. The sequence should be "in, in, out, out." After becoming comfortable with one side facing the bands, the jumper should start with the opposite side facing the bands.

3. The next sequence should be in on the right, change to the left, out on the right, pause, and start over from the opposite side. The jumper then switches to the left foot, starting the sequence "in, change, out, pause."

4. The next sequence is with two feet together, starting with the right or left side. The sequence is "in, pause, out, pause." The jumper switches sides after becoming comfortable.

5. The next variation is to add a spin (90 degrees, 180 degrees, and so on) to each step while moving in and out of the bands. The jumper starts with a small spin and then increases the spin after becoming comfortable.

Advanced Jump-Band Ideas

Rotating in a Circle

Students with the bands slowly rotate in a circle while the jumper is working on his or her steps. After a while, the students switch the rotation to the opposite direction.

Tic-Tac-Toe

Two groups join together and form a tic-tac-toe formation with the jump bands. The jumpers start in one corner and follow single file in a clockwise direction through the four jumping areas, continuing forward to the next set of bands. Then they all change directions and go counterclockwise. Another variation is for the jump-band group to start rotating slowly in a circle as described previously.

Snake the Line

A large group activity can set up with two long vertical lines of jump bands covering the length of the gym. The people in the middle of the lines have two sets of jump bands on their legs (one in front and one in back). These people should practice as a large group to coordinate their "out, out, in, in" sequence. The jumpers can begin weaving through the jump bands in a snakelike fashion. If you have enough jump bands for two lines, the stu- dents can go down one line and come back crossing the other line for continuous activity.

Juggling

Juggling offers a challenge to secondary school students. Using lightweight juggling scarves is an excellent way to teach introductory skills. The lightweight, sheer scarves move slowly and allow students to master the proper arm and hand movements. Plastic grocery bags are an inexpensive alternative to the scarves if the budget is limited. After students learn the movement pattern, beanbags, juggle bags (small, round beanbags), and fleece balls can be used before proceeding to rings and clubs.

Juggling with scarves teaches students the correct patterns of object movement, but it does not transfer automatically to juggling with faster-moving objects such as fleece balls, tennis balls, rings, and hoops. Therefore, two distinct sections for juggling are offered: a section on learning to juggle with scarves and a section explaining juggling with balls. Juggling with scarves will bring success to a majority of the class, and youngsters who have mastered the scarves can move to balls and other objects.

Juggling With Scarves

Scarves are held by the fingertips near the center. To throw the scarf, it should be lifted and pulled into the air above eye level. Scarves are caught by clawing, a downward motion of the hand, and grabbing the scarf from above as it is falling. Scarf juggling is used to teach proper habits (e.g., tossing the scarves straight up in line with the body rather than forward or backward). Many instructors remind students to imagine they are in a phone booth to emphasize tossing and catching without moving.

Cascading

Cascading is the easiest pattern for juggling three objects. The following sequence can be used to learn this basic technique.

1. One scarf. Hold the scarf in the center. Quickly move the arm across the chest and toss the scarf with the palm out. Reach out with the other hand and catch the scarf in a straight, downward motion (clawing). Toss the scarf with this hand using the motion and claw it with the opposite hand. Repeat the tossing and clawing sequence. The scarf should move in a figure-eight pattern as shown in figure 17.2.

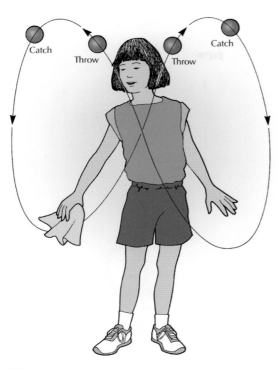

FIGURE 17.2   Cascading with one scarf.

2.   Two scarves. Hold a scarf with the fingertips in each hand. Toss the first one across the body as described in step 1. When it reaches its peak, look at it, and toss the second scarf across the body in the opposite direction. The first scarf thrown is caught (clawed) by the hand throwing the second scarf and vice versa (see figure 17.3). Verbal cues such as "toss," "claw," "toss," "claw" are helpful.

FIGURE 17.3   Cascading with two scarves.

3.   Three scarves. Hold a scarf in each hand by the fingertips. Hold the third scarf with the ring and little finger against the palm of the hand. Throw the first scarf from the hand holding two scarves. Toss this scarf from the fingertips across the chest as learned earlier. When scarf 1 reaches its peak, throw scarf 2 from the other hand across the body. As this hand starts to come down, it catches scarf 1. When scarf 2 reaches its peak, throw scarf 3 in the same path as scarf 1. To complete the cycle, as the hand comes down from throwing scarf 3, it catches scarf 2. The cycle is started over by throwing scarf 1 with the opposite hand. Figure 17.4 illustrates the figure-eight motion used in cascading with three scarves. Tosses are always alternated between left and right hands with a smooth, even rhythm.

FIGURE 17.4   Cascading with three scarves.

Reverse Cascading

Reverse cascading involves tossing the scarves from waist level to the outside of the body and allowing the scarves to drop down the midline of the body (see figure 17.5).

1.   One scarf. Begin by holding the scarf as described in the previous cascading section. The throw goes away from the midline of the body over the top, so the scarf is released and falls down the center of the body. Catch it with the opposite hand and toss it in a similar fashion on the opposite side of the body.

17

2. Two scarves. Begin with a scarf in each hand. Toss the first as described in step 1. When it begins its descent, toss the second scarf. Catch the first scarf, then the second, and repeat the pattern in a toss, "toss, catch, catch manner."

3. Three scarves. Think of a large funnel fixed at eye level directly in front of the juggler. The goal is to drop all scarves through this funnel so that they drop straight down the center of the body. Begin with three scarves as described earlier for three-scarf cascading. Toss the first scarf from the hand holding two scarves.

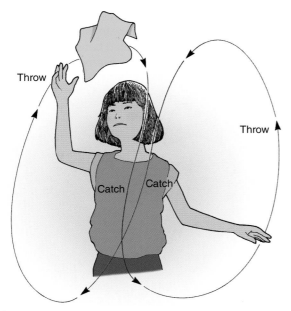

FIGURE 17.5 Reverse cascading.

Column Juggling

Column juggling is so named because the scarves move straight up and down as though they were inside a large pipe or column and do not cross the body. To perform three-scarf column juggling, begin with two scarves in one hand and one in the other hand. Start with a scarf from the hand that has two scarves and toss it straight up the midline of the body overhead. When this scarf reaches its peak, toss the other two scarves upward along the sides of the body (see figure 17.6). Catch the first scarf with either hand and toss it upward again. Catch the other two scarves and toss them upward, continuing the pattern.

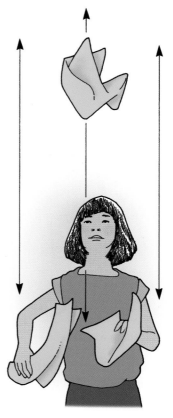

FIGURE 17.6 Column juggling.

Showering

Showering is more difficult than cascading because of the rapid movement of the hands. Less time is available for catching and tossing. The scarves move in a circle following each other. It should be practiced in both directions for maximum challenge. Figure 17.7 illustrates the cycle.

Start with two scarves in the right hand and one in the other. Begin by throwing the first two scarves from the right hand. Toss the scarves in a large circle away from the midline of the body and overhead as high as possible. After releasing the second scarf, toss the third scarf across from the left hand and throw it in the same path with the right hand. All scarves are caught with the left hand and passed to the right hand.

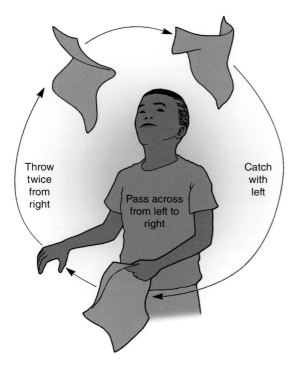

FIGURE 17.7 Showering with three scarves.

Juggling Challenges

- While cascading, toss a scarf under one leg.
- While cascading, toss a scarf from behind the back.
- Instead of catching one of the scarves, blow it upward with a strong breath of air.
- Begin cascading by tossing the first scarf into the air with a foot. Lay the scarf across the foot and kick it into the air.
- Try juggling three scarves with one hand. Do not worry about establishing a pattern, just catch the lowest scarf each time. Try both regular and reverse cascading as well as column juggling.
- While doing column juggling, toss up one scarf, hold the other two, and make a full turn. Resume juggling.
- Try juggling more than three scarves (up to six) while facing a partner.
- Juggle three scarves while standing side by side with a partner and with inside arms around each other. This variation is easy to do, because it is regular three-scarf cascading.

Juggling With Balls

Juggling with balls requires accurate, consistent tossing, which should be the first emphasis. The tosses should be thrown to the same height on both sides of the body, about 2 to 2-1/2 feet (60 to 75 cm) upward and across the body because the ball is tossed from one hand to the other. Students should practice tossing the ball parallel to the body; the most common problem in juggling is that the juggler tosses the balls forward and then has to move forward to catch them.

The fingers, not the palms, should be used in tossing and catching. Stress relaxed wrist action. Encourage students to look upward to watch the balls at the peak of their flight, rather than watch the hands. They should focus on where the ball peaks, not the hands. Two balls must be carried in the starting hand, and the art of releasing only one must be mastered. Progression should be working successively with one ball, then two balls, and finally three balls.

Recommended Progression for Cascading

1. Using one ball and only one hand, toss the ball upward 2 to 2-1/2 feet (60 to 75 cm) and catch it with the same hand. Begin with the dominant hand and later practice with the other. Toss quickly, with wrist action. Then handle the ball alternately with right and left hands, tossing from one hand to the other.

2. Now, with one ball in each hand, alternate tossing a ball upward and catching it in the same hand so that one ball is always in the air. Begin again with a ball in each hand. Toss across the body to the other hand. To keep the balls from colliding, toss under the incoming ball. After acquiring some expertise, alternate the two kinds of tosses by doing a set number (four to six) of each before shifting to the other.

3. Hold two balls in the starting hand and one in the other. Toss one of the balls in the starting hand, toss the ball from the other hand, and then toss the third ball. Keep the balls moving in a figure-eight pattern (see figure 17.8).

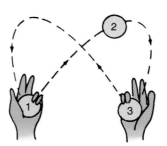

FIGURE 17.8 Cascading with three balls.

Recommended Progression for Showering

1. The showering motion is usually counterclockwise. Hold one ball in each hand. Begin by tossing with the right hand on an inward path and then immediately toss the other ball from the left hand directly across the body to the right hand. Continue this action until it is smooth.

2. Now, hold two balls in the right hand and one in the left. Toss the first ball from the right hand on an inward path and immediately toss the second on the same path. At about the same time, toss the ball from the left hand directly across the body to the right hand (see figure 17.9).

3. A few students may be able to change from cascading to showering and vice versa. This skill presents considerable challenge.

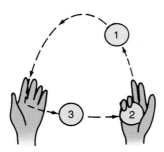

FIGURE 17.9   Showering with three balls.

Stunts, Pyramids, and Combatives

This unit emphasizes personal challenge and brief competitive episodes. Students enjoy the chance to pit their strength and coordination skills against others. Combatives should be conducted between opponents of approximately the same skill level and size. Change partners often so that animosity is less likely to develop. The contests start and stop by mutual agreement, and either party can terminate the contest immediately. Avoid running tournaments to determine a class champion in combative activities. Instead, emphasize enjoying the activity, learning personal strengths and weaknesses, and being able to challenge a number of opponents.

Stunts, on the other hand, require that students work cooperatively to accomplish them successfully and are an excellent way to help students learn more about their peers. Teachers must emphasize safety when teaching these activities and include this information within the lesson plan for documentation. As you teach activities, you will need to determine if you want to teach activities that require spotting. If you do, spot only one student at a time. Be aware that some students will not want an adult's hands on them. Asking students to spot one another is not appropriate because of the liability that may ensue. Also, offer activities as choices so that students are never forced into something that they do not feel comfortable doing. Use mats when possible. Partner activities work best when partners are approximately the same size.

Individual Stunts

Leg Dip

Extend both hands and one leg forward while balancing on the other leg. Lower the body until the seat touches the heel and then return to the standing position. Do this without the aid of the arms and without losing balance.

Behind-the-Back Touch

Start in a standing position with the arms extended behind the back and hands clasped. Squat slowly and touch the floor with an extended finger and then return to the standing position.

Knee Jump

Kneel on the floor with the seat on the heels and the toes pointing backward. In one continuous motion, swing the arms forward and jump to the feet. If successful, try to perform a half-turn during the jump.

Wall Climb

Take a push-up position with the feet against the wall. Walk up the wall with the feet to a handstand position and then return to the push-up position.

Popover

While in push-up position, propel the body upward and do a half-turn to the inverted push-up position. Pop over to the regular push-up position.

Double Heel Click

Jump upward and click the heels twice. If successful, try to perform a triple heel click before landing.

Push-Up Inversion

Begin in a push-up position. Push strongly off the floor and bring the legs through the arms in one smooth motion, assuming the inverted push-up position. Return to the original position with a strong movement backward.

Jump Through

Hold the left toe with the right hand. Jump the right foot through without losing the grip on the toe. Try the stunt with the other foot.

Sitting Liftoff

Sit on the floor with the legs extended forward. Place the hands on the floor somewhere between the hips and knees, depending on the balance point. Lift the entire body off the floor in a balanced position. The stunt can be learned in stages—first with the heels remaining on the floor and then with the heels held off the floor by a friend.

Jumping Toe Touch

Begin in a standing position with the hands held in front of the body shoulder-width apart and palms down. When ready, jump up and bring the feet quickly forward so that the toe tips touch the hands in front of the body. The attempt should be to bring the hands to the feet, lifting the feet as high as possible.

Leg Circling

In a squatting position with both hands on the floor, place the left knee between the arms and extend the right leg to the side. Swing the right leg forward and under the lifted right arm, under the left leg and arm, and back to the starting position. Perform several circles in succession. Try circling with the other leg.

Partner and Group Stunts

Leapfrog

One student forms the base by standing stiff legged, bending over, and placing the hands on the knees. The other student runs and leaps over the base by performing a light push-off on the back of the base. A number of students can form bases to create a series of leaps for the moving student.

Caterpillar

One student is on hands and knees, acting as the support. Another student, facing the same direction, places the hands about 2 feet (60 cm) in front of the support's hands. The second student then places her or his legs on top of the support and locks them together at the ankles. Five to six students can continue this process and then begin walking when everyone is in place.

Knee Stand

The base student is in a crab position. The other student stands on the knees of the base. A spotter may be nec-

essary to help the second student come to a balanced position.

Cooperative Scooter

Two students face each other and sit with toes under the seat of the other. They join arms by holding each other's arms at the wrist or above. Students scoot forward or backward by cooperatively lifting the feet when the other lifts the seat. Progress is made by alternately flexing and extending the knees and hips.

Spider Walk

The base student is in a sitting position with his or her back against a wall. The next student backs up and sits lightly on the knees of the base. More students can be added in similar fashion. The hands should be placed around the waist of the person in front. Walking is done by moving the feet on the same side together.

Triple High Jump

Students form groups of three and join hands. One of the students is designated as the performer and jumps over the joined arms of the other two. The performer is assisted in the jump by an upward lift from the others. The hands to be jumped over should be clasped lightly and released if the jumper does not gain enough height.

Octopus

Eight to twelve students work together to develop this activity. Half of the students form a circle with hands joined, while each student in the other half finds a pair of joined hands to lean backward on, placing the weight on the heels. Each of the leaners then joins hands behind the backs of the others, thus creating two separate groups with joined hands. The octopus begins moving slowly around the circle, taking small sidesteps. The stunt is brought to a climax by moving as fast as possible.

Double-Bear Walk

The base student is on hands and knees. The top student assumes the same position with the hands on the shoulders and the knees over the hips of the base. They move slowly throughout the area without losing balance.

Double-Crab Walk

The bottom student moves into a crab position. The top performer straddles the base and assumes the crab position with the hands on the shoulders and the feet on the knees of the base. They move slowly throughout the area.

17

Back Balance

Students work with a partner. One partner lies in the supine position and becomes the base. The base bends the knees, and the balancer places the small of the back on the soles of the base's feet. The balancer then lies back and balances in a layout position (see figure 17.10).

FIGURE 17.10 Back balance.

Sitting Balance

The base assumes a supine position on the floor and then raises the legs and positions the feet so that the soles are parallel to the floor (looks like an L from the side). The balancer straddles the base so that the partners are looking at each other. The balancer sits on the soles of the base's feet, and the base holds the ankles of the balancer. The balancer should extend her or his legs as much as possible.

Abdominal Balance

The base assumes a supine position on the floor and then raises the legs and positions the feet so that the soles are parallel to the floor (looks like an L from the side). The balancer faces the base and places the abdomen on the soles of the base's feet. The base grasps the hands of the balancer and extends the legs to move the performer into a balanced position. The balancer should attempt to arch the back, raise the head, and extend the arms to the sides.

Seat Press

The base lies on the floor with the knees bent and the feet flat on the floor. The balancer straddles the base, facing the feet of the base. The two join hands, and the top partner sits on the joined hands supported by the base. The balancer's legs are placed on the knees of the base.

Minipyramids

Students can work in groups of three to five to develop various types of pyramids. Some examples are shown in figure 17.11. Encourage the class to develop different types of pyramids and allow time for them to share their creations with the rest of the class. Examples are the hip–shoulder stand, double-crab stand (see figure 17.11a), double-bear stand (see figure 17.11b), and shoulder stand (see figure 17.11c). Caution students to select a partner of similar size and to stand on the proper points of support.

FIGURE 17.11 Minipyramids.

Combatives

The following list should give insight into the many types of combatives, but it is certainly not exhaustive.

Standing Hand Wrestle

Contestants place the toes of their right feet together and grasp right hands in a handshake grip. The left foot is moved to the rear for support. The goal is to force the opponent to move either foot.

Finger Wrestle

Opponents stand on the right foot and hold the left foot with the left hand. They hook the index fingers of their right hands and attempt to push each other off balance.

Flag Grab

Contestants have a flag tucked in the belt and attempt to keep others from pulling it out. At the same time, they try to collect as many flags as possible from opponents.

Palm Wrestle

Contestants face each other, standing 12 inches (30 cm) apart. The palms of the opponents are placed together and must remain there for the duration of the contest. The goal is to push the opponent off balance.

Toe Dance

Contestants begin by placing their hands on the opponents' shoulders. The goal is to step on top of the toes of the opponents. A variation can be to see how many toe touches can be accumulated in a specified time.

Seat Pull-Up

Opponents sit on the floor, facing each other, with the knees bent and the soles of the contestants' shoes together. Players bend forward, grasp hands firmly, and attempt to pull the opponent's seat off the floor. Unless a contestant is sitting upright in position when the opponent is lifted from the floor, the contest is a draw.

Back-to-Back Takedown

Contestants sit back to back and lock elbows. They spread the feet widely to form a broad base of support. Both players attempt to pull the other to the left and touch the opponent's shoulder (or elbow) to the floor. As a variation, they can attempt the contest by pulling in the opposite direction.

Tug-of-War

Partners pull each other using a tug-of-war rope. Tug-of-war ropes are easily made from 10 feet (3 m) of 3/16- or 1/4-inch (5 or 6 mm) nylon rope and two sections of 5/8-inch (16 mm) garden hose that is 2 feet (60 cm) long. The rope is threaded through the garden hose, which serves as a handle, and tied with a bowline knot to form a loop at each end of the rope. Change partners often so that students have a chance to compete with many others and are not subjected to losing constantly or to seldom being challenged. Limit the pulling bouts to 5 to 10 seconds. Pulling immediately stops if one of the partners loses balance or falls.

Partners can have contests using some of the following suggested positions and activities.

Different Positions

Facing, back-to-back, side-to-side, one-handed, two-handed, and crab positions are a few suggested variations, with the rope hooked over the foot, in a push-up position, and on all fours.

Balance Pulls

Students begin in a stationary position. The goal is to cause the opponent to move the feet or lose balance.

Pick-Up Contest

Bowling pins are placed behind the contestants. The goal is to pull and move backward in order to pick up the clubs.

Multiple Rope Pulls

Ropes can be twisted together so that four to six students can become involved in the contest.

Pick Up and Pull

The ropes are laid on the floor between two contestants. On signal, the two opponents run to the rope, pick it up, and begin the tug-of-war.

Team Tug-of-War

Small groups and classes can have contests with the large commercially available tug-of-war ropes. Most are 50 feet (15 m) in length and at least 1 inch (2.5 cm) in diameter. Avoid using ropes that have large loops on each end because students cannot easily release or step outside the loop when the other team gains momentum.

17

A suggested manner for conducting team tugs-of-war is to tie a marker in the middle of the rope. Two parallel lines are drawn 10 to 20 feet (3 to 6 m) apart. The pull starts with the marker in the middle of the two lines. The goal is to pull the marker over the other team's line. Variations for pulls are to try pulling with the rope overhead, having opponents pull with their backs to each other, pulling with one hand on the ground or in the air, or pulling from a seated position.

Wands

Wands provide challenge through balance and flexibility activities that students can perform individually. Wands are usually made from 5/8-inch or 3/4-inch (16 or 19 mm) dowels and should be 42 inches (1.07 m) long. They can be painted, and rubber tips can be placed on the ends to soften the noise they make when they fall on the floor. When using wands, ensure that you have instructed students regarding safety.

Wand Whirl

Stand a wand in front of the body and balance it with one finger. Release the wand, perform a full turn, and catch the wand. Try the activity in both directions. Try catching it with one finger on top of the wand.

Thread the Needle

Hold the wand in both hands near the ankles. Without letting go of the wand, step over the wand and through the space between the arms. Return to the starting position. Try passing the wand under the feet side to side, one foot at a time, holding the wand in front of and behind the body.

Thread the Needle (Jumping)

Perform the same stunt as the previous activity except jump over the wand and pass it under the feet simultaneously.

Wand Kickover

Balance the wand in front of the body with one hand. Release the wand, kick a leg over, and catch the wand. Try kicking in both directions using both legs. Try catching the wand with one finger.

Walk Under

Grasp the wand with the right hand. Twist under the right arm without letting go of the wand, without taking it off the floor, and without touching the knee to the floor. Try using the left arm.

Broomstick Balance

Balance the wand vertically in one hand. Begin by walking while balancing and then attempt to balance the wand in a stationary position. Try walking in different directions, using both hands, and balancing the wand on different body parts.

Wand Walk-Down

Start in a straddle stance with legs straight. Hold a wand near one end with the other end of the wand above the head and pointed toward the ceiling. Bend backward, place the wand on the floor behind, and walk the hands down the wand. Return to a standing position. If the wands do not have rubber tips, a spotter may have to stabilize the wand end on the floor.

Partner Exchange

Partners face each other, each balancing a wand in front of her- or himself. On signal, each runs to the other's wand and catches it before it hits the floor. Challenge can be added by increasing the distance, using two wands, and performing stunts such as a full turn or heel click before catching the wand.

Reaction Time

One partner holds the wand horizontally. The other places one hand directly above the wand, palm down. The first partner drops the wand, and the second partner tries to catch it before it hits the floor. This can also be tried with the wand held vertically. The other person forms a V with the thumb and fingers and is challenged to catch the wand. Marks can be placed on the wand, and students are challenged to catch the wand on certain marks.

Wand Wrestle

A student holds a wand in the vertical position with a partner. The goal is to move the wand to the horizontal plane. One person is designated to move the wand horizontally, while the other resists the attempt. Roles are reversed after each bout.

Wand Release

Partners sit facing each other with the legs straight and the soles of the feet together. Together, they hold a wand horizontally at chest level. A win occurs when one person causes the other to release the grip on the wand. Neither player is allowed to leave or modify the starting position.

Isometric Exercises

Perform isometric exercises. Examples are attempting to twist the wand, to stretch the wand, to compress the wand, or to pull it against various body parts. Many stretching activities can also be done using wands.

Novel Team Games and Activities

The following activities are enjoyable because they demand few specialized skills yet require teamwork. The games help develop camaraderie among students, and teams can be reorganized periodically to equalize the competition. Rules listed are only starting points; students and teachers can modify any and all of the rules as they desire.

Cageball Games

Cageballs come in many sizes (see figure 17.12). The most common size is 2 feet (60 cm) in diameter, which is an easy size to store and inflate. The next size is 4 feet (1.2 m) in diameter, which makes the games more interesting at the high school level. Drawbacks to the larger size are storage, expense, and inflation time. The largest cageballs, often termed *earth balls,* are 5 or 6 feet (1.5 or 1.8 m) in diameter. These can be kicked, batted, and tossed. Students should not be allowed to mount the ball and roll it, because injuries in those circumstances are common.

FIGURE 17.12 When planning for cageball activities, set aside time for storing and inflating cageballs.

Crab Cageball

Divide students into four teams. Use cones to delineate the corners of a square. One team forms one side of the square, and a different team makes up each side. All players sit with hands behind them for support. Each team is numbered from right to left beginning with the number 1. The cageball is placed in the middle of the square. The instructor or another student calls out a number, and one member from each team (with the number called) performs a crab walk to the center and attempts to kick the cageball over the other teams. A team has a point scored against it when (1) the ball is kicked over or through the team, (2) a team member touches the ball with the arms or hands, or (3) a player stands to block or stop the ball. The team with the fewest points is declared the winner.

Long Team Cageball

Divide players into two teams. The teams move into sitting positions in two lines facing each other 10 to 15 feet (3 to 5 m) apart. The teacher rolls or throws a cageball between the two lines. The object is for one team to kick the ball over the other team. A point is scored against a team when the ball goes over or through a line. The team with the fewer points wins. Again, a point is awarded if a player stands or touches the ball with the hands. More than one cageball can be used simultaneously.

Cageball Football

The game is played on a large playing field. Divide the class into two teams. The object of the game is to carry the cageball across the goal line. The only way the ball can be advanced, however, is when it is in the air. Whenever the ball is on the ground, it can be moved only backward or sideways. This game is best played with a 4-foot (1.2 m) or larger cageball.

Cageball Target Throw

The cageball is used as a target in this game. Divide the class into two teams and place them on opposite sides of the gym. A center line divides the area in half, and teams can move only in their half. Use cones to mark the goal line near the ends of the playing area. Center the cageball between the teams. Each team is given a number of playground balls or volleyballs for throwing at the cageball. The object is to move the cageball across the opponent's goal line by hitting it with the volleyballs. Players cannot touch the cageball. If a player touches it, regardless of intent, the point goes to the other team.

17

Scooter Cageball Soccer

Each has a scooter. The ball may be advanced by using the feet only. The object is to score a goal in a fashion similar to soccer. Penalty shots are awarded for rough play, touching the ball with the hands, and leaving the scooter.

Scoop Activities and Games

Scoops can be used for throwing and catching activities as well as games like modified lacrosse or Ultimate (see sections in chapters 18 and 19, respectively). A variety of challenging throwing and catching skills can be performed with either hand. Examples include overhand throws, sidearm throws, and underhand throws. Catching skills involve a different positioning of the scoop for throws above and below the waist, as well as forehand and backhand position of the scoop. Additional skills include scooping the ball off the ground and cradling the ball while running (see the section Lacrosse in chapter 18). Balls of different sizes can be used depending on the skills of the students. Students should start with a softball-sized whiffle ball and progress to balls that are smaller, harder, or bounce more. The scoops are an excellent lead-up game for lacrosse because the skills are similar. The rules for Ultimate (chapter 19) can be used for a game with the scoops.

Flickerball Games

Flickerball is a game similar to team handball and Ultimate in which a team tries to advance a ball or object down the field or court and score a goal by throwing the object through or into a goal. On an outdoor field, the goals can be 4-foot-by-8-foot (1.2 by 2.4 m) pieces of plywood permanently placed on poles so that they are about 8 feet high. A 2- or 3-foot (60 to 90 cm) square is cut out of the center of the goal. A ball that goes through the hole earns more points than a ball that hits the plywood. Local rules and variations can be applied. Usually a 3-point type of basketball crease is set up to keep the players farther from the goal. The size of the crease can vary according to the situation. A "rules of three" approach can be applied to force students to pass within three seconds, to make at least three passes before shooting, and, for defenders, to keep at least 3 feet (1 m) from the player with the ball. The player with the ball can take up to three steps and then must pass or shoot. Turnovers or free passes occur when any of the rules of three are violated. Players advance the ball up the field by passing to teammates. If the game is played indoors, a target such as a mat on the wall or a standing goal can be substituted for the goals. Various types of footballs, foam balls, rugby balls, and discs can be used for the games to add variety to the unit.

Potato Ball Games

Potato ball is usually played with a regular or modified football. Other types of balls can be used, including playground balls, Nerf balls, or foam playground balls. The game is similar to Ultimate except that players can run or throw the ball. The game involves continuous movement until a touchdown is scored by running or throwing to a teammate across the goal line. The game is usually played on a football field or across a football field. Students advance the ball toward the goal line by running or passing to teammates in any direction—forward, sideways, or backward. A turnover occurs when a student is tagged while holding the ball, when an incomplete pass occurs, or when an interception occurs. Play starts immediately when the opposing team picks up the ball. The game works best by advancing the ball up the field with short, controlled passes.

Eclipse Ball Games

Eclipse ball is a racket game that combines elements from badminton, racquetball, tennis, and volleyball. It is played on a standard volleyball court with a special eclipse ball. A modified tennis racket or any other similar racket is used to serve the ball and hit forehands and backhands. Four to six players can be on a team, depending on the size of the court. The game is designed to foster long rallies with second chances because the ball is allowed to bounce and to be played off of the back walls with special rules for keeping the rally alive. A "play it" situation is possible when one team is at fault and the opposing team desires to gamble for more points. For example, if a player hits the ball out of bounds and an opposing team player thinks that he or she can keep a rally alive, the player yells, "Play it," and continues to play for the point, which is now worth 2 points instead of the normal 1 point. Each additional "Play it" call adds 2 points more to the rally so that a rally may be worth many points. Local rules for each school or facility can be developed.

Spikeball

Spikeball is a netball game that combines elements from volleyball and four square. It is played two versus two around a small round net approximately 36 inches (90 cm) in diameter, placed 9 inches (23 cm) above the ground. The ball is 12 inches (30 cm) in circumference. The first player serves the ball with the hand down toward the net so that it bounces off the net at the opponents. After the ball is hit, there are no boundaries.

From there on out, each team has up to three possible hits to control the ball and bounce it back off the net to the other team. When a team cannot return the ball onto the net within their three touches or the ball bounces more than once on the net, the rally is over. Games are typically played to 11, 15, or 21. Rules for your class can be modified as you see fit.

Recreational Activities

Many other recreational activities can be used as mini-units or as a change of pace. Rules and regulations usually accompany the purchase of equipment and are specific to the situation. The authors have had success with the following activities:

- Ladder ball
- Kan jam
- Tetherball
- Shuffleboard
- Deck tennis
- Tennis volleyball
- Table tennis
- Pillow polo
- Sacket
- Horseshoes
- Lawn bowling
- Global ball
- Pickleball

Relays

When not overused, relays are enjoyable activities for students. To keep the atmosphere vibrant and the students motivated, the teams should be changed often to equalize the ability of various groups. If the same team wins every bout, the outcome is predetermined and the rest of the class will not be motivated. Another motivator is frequent changing of the relay. The relay can be run once to show students how it is to be conducted and then one to three times for competition. All relay teams should have the same number of persons. Change the order of the squads so that different students get a chance to run the starting and finishing legs. Define the signals to start the relay and tell students what position they must assume when finished (sitting, kneeling, or some alternative position).

Potato Relays

Potato relays have been played for years. A small box to hold the objects (potatoes) is placed in front of each group. Four circles (hoops can be used) are placed 10 to 15 feet (3 to 5 m) apart in front of each group. The goal is for the first runner to pick up an object from the box and carry it to one of the hoops, come back, pick up another object, and place it in another hoop. The runner does this until all the hoops are filled. The next person picks up the objects one at a time from the hoops and places them back in the box. The pattern is repeated until all members of the group have had a turn.

Bowling Pin Relay

Four bowling pins per squad are spaced evenly in front of each squad in a fashion similar to the potato relay. The first person in line lays down all the pins, and the next person stands them up. Players can use only one hand.

Over-and-Under Ball Relay

Each team is spread out in open squad formation so that players are 10 to 15 feet (3 to 5 m) apart. The first person in line passes the ball backward overhead to the nearest teammate. That person throws it backward between the legs to another teammate, and the pattern repeats. When the ball gets to the end of the squad, that person runs to the front of the squad and passes the ball backward. The process is repeated until all players have had a turn at the end and front of the squad.

Stepping-Stone Relay

Two small carpet squares are used per squad. The first person in line is the mover and helps the next person in line move down and back. The only way to advance in this relay is by standing on a carpet square and moving to another. Moving or standing on the floor is illegal. The mover picks up the rear carpet square and moves it in front of the advancing player so that the next step can be taken. All players must play both roles before the relay is completed.

Pass-and-Squat Relay

Players are spread out 10 to 15 feet (3 to 5 m) apart. The first person in line turns around, faces the rest of the squad, and throws a volleyball or soccer ball to the first person in line, who returns the throw and squats. The leader now throws the ball to the next person until all members have received a throw and have squatted. When the ball is thrown to the last player, that person dribbles the ball to the front of the squad and repeats the pattern.

Fetch Relay

Squads line up and place one member at the other end of the playing area, 10 to 20 yards (m) away. This person runs back to the squad and fetches the next person. The person who has just been fetched in turn runs back and fetches the next person. The pattern continues until all members have been fetched to the opposite end of the playing area.

Snowball Relay

This relay is similar to the fetch relay, except that after one person has been fetched, both players run back and pick up another player. The pattern continues until most squad members are running back and forth, picking up the remaining members. This relay can be exhausting for the first few people in line and should not be run too often.

Sport Skill Relays

Many sport skills can be used for relays. For example, students can dribble the basketball down the court, make a basket, and return. The problem with relays of this type is that success is predicated on the skill of the participants. If some students are less skilled in basketball, the relay can be a source of embarrassment, causing those students to be blamed for losing the relay. An instructor who uses sport skill relays is wise to include a variety of skills and to develop many different types of relays.

Spread-Eagle Relay

Break the class into groups of 8 to 10 students. They lie on the floor and form a circle with their heads toward the center. They join hands and spread their legs. Participants in each group are numbered, beginning with one through the number of group members. When a number is called, that person stands up, runs around the circle, and then resumes the prone position on the floor. The runner must place both feet between each pair of legs. The first person to return to the starting position earns a point for that group. The group with the most points wins.

Cooperative Activities

Cooperative activities require students to work together. They can be used early in the year as mixers to help students get to know one another. The emphasis is on enjoyment and accomplishment.

Commonalities

Put enough hoops out for half the students in the class. The class walks or moves around the gym until the music stops or the teacher blows a whistle. Two students put one foot in the same hoop. The two must talk to each other and come up with two traits they have in common that are not visible to anyone. The students then repeat this activity and find a new partner or group of three and complete the same task. The groups can get bigger and bigger as the teacher chooses. This activity is an excellent way for class members to get to know each other and for the teacher to learn about the students in the class.

Picnic Name Game

Have your class stand in a circle. The first person starts by saying his or her first name and showing a movement that he or she is bringing to the picnic; the move must start with the same letter as the person's first name (e.g., Paul is bringing a push-up or Jessica is bringing a jumping jack.). The next person repeats the name and the movement of all the previous people and then adds his or her name and the move that he or she is bringing to the picnic. This procedure continues until the last person has spoken everyone's name and done each movement.

Group Name Juggling

Ask the class to stand in a circle. The first person calls out the name of one person in the circle and then passes a soft ball (or any piece of appropriate equipment) underhand to that person. This process continues until all members of the circle have been called and received a pass. After the group gets the hang of the game, more pieces of equipment can be added and the speed of the game can be increased. To add fun, use a rubber chicken, pig, or fish or all three at the same time. If your class size is large, start with two or three circles. Periodically rotate several people to new circles to increase the learning of classmates' names.

Mass Stand Up

Start with two people sitting back to back. They lock elbows and try to stand up. Increase the number to three people, then four, and so forth. See how many people can stand up simultaneously. Try the same thing in a sitting position; students face a partner with hands locked, feet flat, and toes touching. Add people to this position.

Circle Sit

Have students stand and form a circle holding hands. They close the circle so that shoulders are touching. Then they move the right side of the body toward the center of the circle and move inward, eliminating gaps. Now they sit on the knees of the person behind them. When everyone has assumed the sitting position, they try walking in this position. Next, they can put the left side toward the center and sit on a new partner's knees.

Word or Team Sounds

Students all close their eyes. Someone is designated to move throughout the group and assign a word or sound such as "Grr," "Wow," Colts, Rockets, or other football, basketball, or baseball team names to the players. The number of words assigned determines the number of groups formed. This is a useful way to organize groups. When the command is given, the only noises that can be made are those that resemble the word. Students must keep their eyes closed and move throughout the area in search of another person who has been assigned the same word. For example, people assigned to be Buckeyes or Sun Devils search for their counterparts by saying "Buckeyes" or "Sun Devils" and listening for others saying the same words.

Entanglement

Divide the class into two or more groups. Each group makes a tight circle with arms pointing toward the middle. In each group, students hold someone's hand until everybody is holding hands. Each person must hold a hand of two different people and not hold the hands of the people on either side. On signal, the two groups race to see which group can untangle first without disjoining hands. The group may end up in either one large circle or two smaller, connecting circles. People can be facing different directions when finished.

Bulldozer

Students lie in prone position side by side and as close as possible on the floor. The end person rolls on top of the next person and down the line of people. When that person gets to the end of the line, the next person starts the roll. Two teams can be formed and a relay race conducted.

Addition Tag

Two students are selected to be "it." They must hold hands and can tag only with their outside hands. When they tag someone, that person must hook on. As the process continues, the tagging line becomes longer and longer. Regardless of the length of the line, only the hand on each end of the line is eligible to tag.

Team Paper, Scissors, and Rock

Two teams huddle up on half of the gym or field space. Team members decide as a group which of the three choices (paper, scissors, or rock) they will reveal as a team when the game begins. The team members come out to the midcourt line and face each other with one foot on the line. The teacher counts, "One, two, three, show." The teams reveal their group decision on the word "show" with the appropriate hand signal. Members of the winning team chase members of the losing team and try to tag them before they reach a safe zone, which is about 10 to 20 yards (m) from the starting line (paper covers rock, rock breaks scissors, and scissors cut paper). A person who is tagged must switch teams. After each round, team members huddle again and decide their next choice.

Chicken Baseball

Two teams of about nine people compete. The game starts with each team in a single-file line. The first person in line on team 1 has a rubber chicken. The first person in line on team 2 is ready to run around the line. At the start of the game, the rubber chicken is passed back over the head of the first person, between the legs of the next person, over the head of the third person, and so on until the last person gets the chicken. She or he then throws it as far as possible and yells, "Chicken." Meanwhile, the first person on team 2 is running around his or her team and getting points for each lap completed while team 1 is passing the chicken. When "chicken" is yelled, all members of team 2 run to the chicken and begin passing it back in the previously described manner while team 1 is accumulating points by having its last person run laps around the group. The teams have to work together to line up quickly and take turns running the laps around the group.

17

LEARNING AIDS

WEBSITES

Adventure Activities

www.adventurehardware.com
www.pa.org

Eclipse Ball

www.eclipseball.com

Flickerball

https://en.wikipedia.org/wiki/Flickerball

Pickleball

www.pickleball.com

Speed Stacks

www.speedstacks.com

REFERENCES AND SUGGESTED READINGS

Barney, D., & Mauch, L. (2003). Jump bands: Success and fun with rhythms. *Teaching Elementary Physical Education*, *14*(6), 14–16.

Orlick, T. (2006). *Cooperative sports and games book* (2nd ed). Champaign, IL: Human Kinetics.

Pangrazi, R.P., & Beighle, A. (2020). *Dynamic physical education for elementary school children* (19th ed.). Champaign, IL: Human Kinetics.

Panicucci, J., Constable, N.S., Hunt, L., Kohut, L., & Rheingold, A. (2003). *Adventure curriculum for physical education: High school*. Hamilton, MA: Project Adventure.

Rohnke, K. (2012). *Funn 'n games*. Dubuque, IA: Kendall/Hunt.

Rohnke, K. (2013). *A small book about large group games*. Dubuque, IA: Kendall/Hunt.

Sports

Chapter 18 presents a series of beginning-level units for a wide variety of team and individual sports. These units are designed to serve as a framework for developing units that meet the needs of your individual students. These units are not all inclusive, but they provide lead-up activities and skills needed to be proficient in the individual games. Each unit includes a sequence for teaching game skills, ideas for effectively teaching these skills, options for lesson skill or game organization, lead-up activities and games, and potential student learning objectives. The activities include both traditional and modified team and individual sports. Additional references are provided to assist in further development of units.

Learning Objectives

► Identify lead-up games and learning activities necessary to teach a beginning unit in a variety of team and individual sports.
► Identify the proper sequence of skills for a variety of sports.
► Describe various ideas to teach a variety of team and individual sports.
► List a series of suggested performance objectives for both team and individual sports.
► Identify references and suggested readings that can be used to develop units in a variety of sports.

Archery

Archery has long been recognized as an appealing activity for students of both sexes, of all ages, and for those with disabilities. The two most popular forms are target archery and field archery. Target archery, the most popular archery activity taught in secondary school programs, involves shooting a specific number of arrows from a given distance at a target with 5 or 10 concentric circles. Scoring is completed by adding up the points for each arrow striking the target. Field archery involves 28 stationary targets of assorted sizes and shapes placed at varying distances. Field shooting requires a larger area and considerable safety procedures. It is especially appealing to those who hunt and bowfish. Many families participate together, because all family members can enjoy archery activities. Archery can be inactive, so incorporating active introductory and fitness activities into each lesson during this unit is appropriate.

Sequence of Skills

The following is a breakdown of the skills necessary to successfully participate in archery.

Bracing the Bow

Several methods are used for stringing, or bracing, the bow. One method involves using a bow stringer device made of a 5-foot (1.5 m) rope with a leather cup on each end. The cups are put on both ends of the bow with the string hanging down toward the ground in front of the body. After placing one string loop in position, place one foot on the center of the bow stringer and pull the bow straight up with one hand. Use the free hand to slide the free string loop into place. To unstring the bow, reverse the process.

Another stringing technique is called the step-through method. Start by placing the bottom string loop in position. Then put the bottom curve of the bow across the top of the right ankle, and step between the string and the bow with the left foot. Use the left hand to bend the bow against the left thigh until the string loop can be moved into place with the right hand. Be sure to keep the face away from the bow tip.

Establishing a Stance

The feet should straddle the shooting line and be shoulder-width apart (the stance can be square or slightly open). The toes should be in a direct line with the target. The knees should be relaxed, and a comfortable standing posture should be maintained.

Nocking the Arrow

The bow should be held horizontally in the left hand, and the nock (or butt end) of the arrow should be placed on the nocking point (a small knot in the string that ensures that the arrow will be parallel to the sight) of the string. The odd-colored feather should face away from the bow. Use the index finger of the left hand to steady the arrow on the arrow rest.

Extending and Drawing

The string is on the first joint of three fingers of the right hand. The index finger is above the arrow, and the next two fingers are below the arrow. Rotate the bow to a vertical position with the left arm parallel to the ground. Extend the left arm and draw the string toward the body with the right hand. Keep the right elbow parallel to the ground. Be sure to keep the fingers of the bow hand loose and relaxed.

Anchoring and Holding

The string should touch the nose, lips, and chin, while the index finger touches under the center of the chin. The anchor point should be the same for every shot.

Aiming

Target archery has two basic methods of aiming—point of aim and bowsights. The beginner should probably use the point-of-aim technique, which involves finding a spot somewhere on a vertical line drawn above, through, and below the middle of the target. This point of aim will vary according to the distance from the target. To locate the point, align the eye and the arrow with an object on the vertical line through the center of the target. Shoot several rounds and then adjust the point of aim up or down accordingly. A mechanical bowsight can be mounted on the bow and used by aligning the center of the target through the aperture (a scope or opening to view down range). The aperture is then adjusted up or down, or left or right, depending on the pattern of the arrows for that shooting distance. The aperture position is then noted for each distance and is used in the future.

Releasing and Experiencing Afterhold

As the arrow is released, the back muscles remain tight while the string fingers relax. The relaxed drawing hand moves backward slightly along the neck. The bow arm and head remain steady until the arrow hits the target (afterhold).

Retrieving Arrows

Arrows in a target should be removed by placing the arrow between the index and middle finger of the left hand. The palm of the hand should be away from the target facing the archer. The right hand should be placed on the arrow close to the target. The arrow is removed by gently twisting and pulling at the same angle at which the arrow entered. If the fletching (feathers or plastic material used to stabilize the flight of the arrow) is inside the target, the arrow should be pulled through the target. Arrows should be carried with the points together and the feathers spread out to prevent damage.

Ideas for Effective Instruction

This section highlights numerous ideas to allow for more effective instruction.

Equipment

The composition of bows is primarily wood, fiberglass, or a laminated combination of the two. Both straight and recurved bows are available. The recurved bow has curved ends to provide additional leverage, which increases the velocity of the arrow. Bows also have different weights and lengths. Archers should select a bow based on their strength and skill. Starting with a lighter bow and progressing to a heavier one as skill and strength develop is best. In class situations, teachers should try to have a variety of bows available for different ability levels.

Arrow shafts are made of wood, fiberglass, or aluminum. The beginning archer needs to use arrows of the proper length. A good method for determining proper length is to have someone hold a measuring stick against the sternum, perpendicular to the body, while the person extends the arms with the palms on either side of the measuring stick. The point at which the fingertips touch the measuring stick is the correct arrow length. For beginners, long arrows are better. Many types of points and feathers are available.

To protect fingers and promote smooth release, many types of finger tabs and shooting gloves are available. An arm guard should be used to prevent the bowstring from slapping the bow arm and to keep long clothing sleeves snug to the body. Movable and stationary quivers are used to transport arrows and sometimes to support the bow while retrieving arrows.

General Rules

1. Archers must straddle a shooting line. Arrows should always be pointed downrange.

2. An end of six arrows is usually shot at one time. A round consists of a number of ends shot at several distances.

3. Values for rings in a target are as follows:

5-Ring Scoring
Gold = 9
Red = 7
Blue = 5
Black = 3
White = 1

10-Ring Scoring
Gold = 10, 9
Red = 8, 7
Blue = 6, 5
Black = 4, 3
White = 2, 1

4. An arrow that bisects two colors scores the higher of the two values.

5. An arrow that bounces off a target or passes through a target is given 7 points if a witness is present.

6. The petticoat, or outside area of the target, counts as a miss.

Organization and Skill Work

Beginning students can experience success quickly if the instructor moves the target close to them (10 yards [m] or less). Students can then move away from the target as their skill levels increase. A safe environment is important. Make sure that students follow strict rules for shooting procedures (i.e., always point the bow down range, shoot only when commanded, retrieve arrows only when cleared to do so, and so on). Partner work is useful for checking form, reminding about safety procedures, and giving feedback. A form for a rating scale or checklist for shooting can be useful and motivating to some students. Several checklists are available from the sources listed at the end of the unit.

Time should be spent with partners and observers to make sure they are actively involved in the learning process and concentrating on the specific shooting skills. Make sure that all students are mentally involved, even when they are not shooting. Depending on the number of sets of bows and arrows you have and the number of students in the class, other activities may need to

18

be available for some students to engage in while the remaining students are focusing on archery skills. This approach will help increase both practice opportunities and physical activity.

Lead-Up Games and Learning Activities

This section highlights numerous lead-up games and learning activities to help develop the skills to participate in archery.

Relays

Each team (2-5 students) has one target, and each person has one arrow. On the teacher's signal, the first person in line shoots and then goes to the end of the line. All team members shoot one arrow, and the team score is then tallied. The team with the highest score is the winner.

Turkey Shoot

Each team (2-3 students) draws a turkey about the size of a target on a piece of paper. The turkey is placed on the target. Each team tries to hit the turkey as many times as possible.

Tic-Tac-Toe or Bingo

Balloons or a target with squares are placed on the regular target—three rows of three for tic-tac-toe and five rows of five for bingo. The object is to hit three or five in a row vertically, horizontally, or diagonally. The game can be for individuals or teams.

Target Work-Up

Start with four or five students on a target. Students shoot an end of four arrows and tally the score. The highest scorer moves up one target, and the lowest scorer moves down a target. This activity can be for individuals or partners.

Tape Shooting

Place two pieces of masking tape across the target, one vertically and one horizontally. The object is to hit either piece of tape. This activity can also be an individual or team event.

Suggested Performance Objectives

The following are possible objectives that might be used in an archery unit.

Core Objectives

Objectives 1, 2, and 3 should be completed before the student is allowed to shoot on the range.

1. On a written test covering safety rules, archery terminology, and scoring, the student scores at least 70% (two attempts allowed).
2. The student demonstrates how to brace and unbrace the bow. Grading is on a pass–fail basis.
3. The student demonstrates the nine steps of the shooting technique (i.e., stand, nock, extend, draw, anchor, hold, aim, release, and afterhold). Grading is on a pass–fail basis.
4. At a distance of 10 yards (m), the student hits the target at least five of six times and scores a minimum of 28 points.
5. At a distance of 15 yards (m), the student hits the target four of six times and scores a minimum of 24 points.
6. At a distance of 20 yards (m), the student hits the target four of six times and scores a minimum of 24 points.
7. The student participates in a minimum of two out of three novelty archery events.

Optional Activities (Extra Credit)

1. On a written test covering safety rules, archery terminology, and scoring, the student scores 100%.
2. At a distance of 10 yards (m), the student hits the target six of six times and scores at least 40 points.
3. At a distance of 15 yards (m), the student hits the target five of six times and scores at least 40 points.
4. At a distance of 20 yards (m), the student hits the target five of six times and scores at least 38 points.
5. The student writes a two-page report on the history of archery, complete with bibliography.
6. The student participates in all three days of novelty archery events.
7. The student designs and puts up a bulletin board about archery.

Badminton

Badminton is popular in schools, from middle and high school through college. Competition at the college level is popular nationally and internationally. The activity is considered a lifetime sport, and everyone can enjoy it in a recreational setting. The game is played with a shuttlecock and racket on a court with a net set at a height of 5 feet (1.5 m). The court is marked for both doubles and singles competition. A toss of a coin or a spin of the racket determines service or court choice. The game begins with a serve from the right-hand service court to an opponent standing in the opposite right-hand service court.

Sequence of Skills

The following is a breakdown of the skills necessary to successfully participate in badminton.

Grips

Forehand

With the racket lying across the palm and fingers of the racket hand, the index finger should be separated from the rest of the fingers. Wrap the thumb around the other side of the handle. The grip resembles a handshake and is called the pistol grip. This grip is used for serving and forehand shots.

Backhand

Move the thumb to a straightened position and to the right of the handle. Rotate the rest of the hand one-fourth of a turn to the right (if right-handed). Regardless of the grip used, the player should contact the shuttlecock as early and as high as possible. This method gives the player a better angle for return and for more controlled shots and forces an opponent to move quickly.

Serves

Ready Position and Preparatory Action

Stand with the nonracket foot forward and the weight mainly on the racket foot. The feet should be approximately 12 to 15 inches (30 to 40 cm) apart. The nonracket shoulder is toward the receiver, and the racket is held waist high and behind the body. Keep the wrist cocked.

The shuttlecock must be contacted below the waist at the instant of the serve. Either a forehand or backhand shot may be used, but the forehand is most common. Until the serve is delivered, the server and receiver must be in their legal service courts. Part of both players' feet must remain in contact with the ground.

Singles Service

Review the ready position. Extend the nonracket arm and drop the shuttlecock before starting to move the racket forward. As weight shifts to the front foot, rotate the shoulders and hips. As contact is made below the waist, the wrist and forearm rotate. The racket arm

should follow through high and be extended over the left shoulder at completion of service. Most serves will be long and high. A short serve, however, can be effective if the opponent is playing too deep.

Doubles Service

The stance is similar to that used for the singles serve. Contact the shuttlecock closer to waist height and slightly more toward the server's racket-hand side. Guide the shuttlecock instead of hitting it. The wrist does not uncock. Just before contacting the shuttlecock, shift the weight from the racket foot to the nonracket foot. Little follow-through or rotation occurs. The shuttlecock should peak in height just before the net and be descending as it clears the net.

Forehand Shots

Clear

Get in ready position with the feet and shoulders parallel to the net. Hold the racket slightly to the backhand side and bend the knees slightly. Contact the shuttlecock as high as possible and in front of the body. The racket face should be tilted upward, and the shuttlecock should clear the opponent's racket and land close to the back line.

Drop

When contact with the shuttlecock is made, the racket face should be flat and pointing ahead or slightly downward. Guide the shuttlecock gently over the net. Remember to follow through. The shuttlecock should drop just over the net into the opponent's forecourt.

Smash

Extend the arm when hitting the shuttlecock in front of the body. Perform rotation of the wrist and forearm quickly. The downward angle of the racket face is more important than racket speed. The shot should be attempted only from the front three-fourths of the court.

Backhand Shots

Ready Position

From the forehand position, turn so that the racket shoulder faces the net. The weight should be on the nonracket foot, the racket shoulder should be up, and the forearm should be slightly down and across the chest. While shifting the weight to the racket foot, the body rotates toward the net. As the wrist leads, the racket extends upward. The racket arm and elbow should be fully extended at contact. The thumb should not point upward.

18

Clear

Hitting hard and upward, contact the shuttlecock as high as possible and hit it over the opponent's racket. Make contact in front of the body with the racket face flat to the target.

Drop

While guiding the shuttlecock over the net, the racket should be flat and pointed ahead or slightly downward. The shuttlecock should land close to the net.

Underhand Shots

Ready Position

Place the racket foot forward and the racket face parallel to the ground. Cock the wrist and make contact as close to net height as possible.

Forehand Net Clear

The forehand net clear is a high, deep shot similar to the singles deep serve. Turn the shoulder slightly toward the net and cock the wrist. An inward rotation of the wrist and a lifting of the forearm occur just before contact. Proceed to follow through with the elbow slightly bent.

Backhand Net Clear

The racket foot is forward, and the racket shoulder is turned to the net. Contact the shuttlecock as close to net height as possible. While moving toward the net, cock the wrist. Use an outward rotation for the backhand. The shot is high and deep into the opponent's court.

Forehand Net Drop

Review the forehand net clear. The net drop is guided over the net with a lifting motion. The shuttlecock should drop quickly.

Backhand Net Drop

This motion is the same as the forehand net drop except that the backhand grip is used. The shuttlecock should be contacted close to net height.

Ready Position for Receiving

The feet should be parallel and positioned slightly wider than shoulder-width apart. Bend the knees slightly with the weight forward. Hold the racket with the head up and to the backhand side of the body.

Doubles Strategy

Up and Back

One player plays close shots, while the partner plays deep shots.

Side by Side

Each partner plays half of the court and is responsible for both close and deep shots in his or her half of the court.

Combination

Both side-by-side and up-and-back formations are used. Regardless of the strategy, partners should always call for the shot (e.g., "Mine!") to avoid accidental injuries.

Ideas for Effective Instruction

This section highlights numerous ideas to allow for more effective instruction.

Rackets and Shuttlecocks

The racket frame can be made of metal or wood. It is usually 26 inches (66 cm) long and weighs between 3.75 and 5.5 ounces (100 and 150 g). Nylon is commonly the choice of material for stringing the racket. The metal frame rackets are desirable because they do not warp or require a press for storage.

The shuttlecock weighs between 73 and 85 grains, and it has 14 to 16 feathers. If authentic feathers are used, the shuttlecocks should be stored in a damp place. If nylon feathers are used, the shuttlecocks will be more durable and reasonably priced, which are desirable qualities in the school setting.

Net

The top of the net is 5 feet (1.5 m) from the floor at its midpoint and 5 feet, 1 inch (1.55 m) from the floor at the posts. The net is 30 inches (76 cm) in height and 20 feet (6 m) long.

Court

Figure 18.1 shows the court dimensions for badminton.

Games and Match

Eleven points make a game in women's singles. All doubles and men's singles games are 15 points. A match consists of two games out of three. As soon as a side wins two games, the match is over. The winner of the previous game serves the next game. Players change courts after the first and second games. In the third game, players change after 8 points in a 15-point game and after 6 points in an 11-point game.

Scoring

Only the serving side scores and continues to do so until an error is committed.

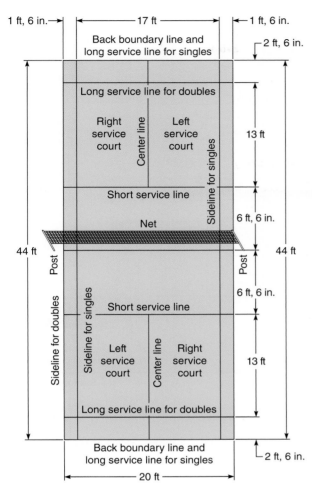

FIGURE 18.1 Court dimensions for badminton.

Setting

If the score becomes tied, the game may be extended by the player or side first reaching the tied score. In a 15-point game, the set may occur at 13–13 (setting to 5 points) or 14–14 (setting to 3 points). In an 11-point game, the score may be set at 10–10 (setting to 2 points) or 9–9 (setting to 3 points). A set game continues, but the score called is now 0–0, or "love all." The first player or side to reach the set score wins. If a side chooses not to set, the regular game is completed.

Singles Play

The first serve is taken from the right service court and received crosscourt (diagonally) in the opponent's right service court. All serves on 0 or an even score are served and received in the right-hand court. All serves on an odd score are served and received in the left service court.

Doubles Play

In the first inning, the first service is one hand (one player serves) only. In all other innings, the serving team gets to use two hands (both players have the opportunity to serve before the other team gets to serve). At the beginning of each inning, the player in the right court serves first. Partners rotate only after winning a point.

Even and odd scores are served from the same court as in singles play. If a player serves out of turn or from the incorrect service court and wins the rally, a let will be called. The let must be claimed by the receiving team before the next serve.

If a player standing in the incorrect court takes the serve and wins the rally, it will be a let, provided that the let is claimed before the next serve. If either of these cases occurs and the side at fault loses the rally, the mistake stands, and the players' positions are not corrected for the rest of the game.

Faults

A fault committed by the serving side (in-side) results in a side out, whereas a fault committed by the receiving side (out-side) results in a point for the server. A fault occurs in any of the following situations:

1. During the serve, the server contacts the shuttlecock above the waist or holds the racket head above the hand.

2. During the serve, the shuttlecock does not fall within the boundaries of the diagonal service court.

3. During the serve, some part of both feet of the server and receiver do not remain in contact with the court, inside the boundary lines, until the shuttlecock leaves the racket of the server. Feet on the boundary lines are considered out of bounds.

Organization and Skill Work

An effective way to add variety and skill work to classes is to create a series of stations. The stations can be arranged to use the space available in the gymnasium and can focus on badminton skills, conditioning activities, or a combination of both (see figure 18.2).

Partner activities are helpful with accompanying rating scales or checklists like the one following.

Partner Activities: Low Doubles Serve

You will need one badminton racket and five shuttlecocks per couple. One person is the server, and the

18

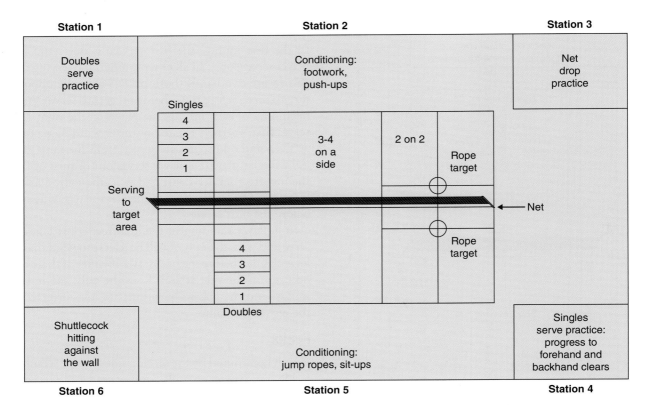

FIGURE 18.2 Badminton skill station setup.

other is the helper with a trained eye. The server follows these steps, and the helper checks off the skills as they are completed.

1. Standing behind the 6-foot, 6-inch (2 m) line from the wall, drop the bird and hit it underhand against the wall. Repeat this at least five times. The trained eye must be looking for and giving feedback on the following criteria:

   a. Keep both feet on the ground until after the shuttlecock is contacted.

   b. Hold the shuttlecock at chest height.

   c. Contact the shuttlecock below waist level.

   d. Keep the racket head below the wrist at the point of contact.

   e. Keep the wrist firm and cocked throughout the stroke.

   f. Guide the shuttlecock instead of hitting it.

2. From the same position behind the line, direct three of five serves above the 5-foot, 1-inch (1.55 m) line on the wall and below the 18-inch (45 cm) line above it. Switch positions, and if you

were serving, become the helper. Help your partner and remember that you are the trained eye who sees what your partner is doing. Your partner repeats the first two steps.

3. Move to the court and take about five practice serves. Keep the serve under the 18-inch (45 cm) line. Now do five serves and have your partner record your score. This score is to help you determine your accuracy. Switch positions again and repeat step 3.

4. Now try step 3 using your backhand.

Tournament play works well for badminton. Ladder, pyramid, or round-robin tournaments can add a competitive flavor to the class. The use of marking tape on the floor and walls, jump ropes on the court, fleece balls, and task cards can give the teacher more stations for a circuit. This setup enables students to progress at a personalized skill level. Minigames or lead-up games played on the courts allow skill work, competition, and enjoyment. Regulation games and tournament play can gradually replace the lead-up games. Students should also be trained as scorekeepers and line or service judges.

Lead-Up Games and Learning Activities

This section highlights numerous lead-up games and learning activities to help develop the skills to participate in badminton.

Doubles Drop

After students learn the short serve and underhand drop, they can play a doubles drop game between the net and the short service line. Points are scored for dropping a shot between the net and short service line.

Overhead Clear

After students learn the long serve and the overhead clear, they can attempt an overhead clear rally. They try to keep the shuttlecock in play at least 5 times in a row, then 10 times in a row, 15 times, and so forth.

Designated Shots

After students learn the underhand clear, they can work on a designated shots rally. They start with a short serve, return with an underhand drop, return with an underhand clear, and return with an overhead clear. They keep performing overhead and underhand clears.

Server Versus Receiver

After students learn the flick serve and push return, they can play a server versus receiver game. The receiver tries to return as many of the server's 20 serves as possible—10 from the right and 10 from the left. The server gets a point each time the receiver misses the return. The receiver gets a point if the server misses the serve. They then reverse the server and receiver roles.

Clear Smash

After students learn the smash, they can play a long serve and overhead clear game. They start with a long serve, return with an overhead clear, and keep hitting clears until someone makes a short clear shot, which the opponent then smashes. The server is awarded a point if the smash is not returned or loses a point if the smash is returned. They repeat the rally and try to make points by well-placed smashes.

Drive Rally

After students learn the drive shot, organize a drive rally with four players. Players drive crosscourt and down the alley. If the drive shot is too high, they smash it.

Advanced Combination Drill

Players start the rally with a long serve and return with an overhead drop, return with an underhand drop, return with an underhand clear to the opponent's backhand side, return with a backhand overhead clear, and return with an overhead clear unless the return shot is short. If the shot is short, they use a smash.

Volleyball Badminton

Four players are on each team. Assigned positions rotate as in volleyball.

Three per Team

Alternate servers, and the up player plays the net shots.

Name the Shot

After five days of the badminton unit, challenge students to name their shots (see figure 18.3).

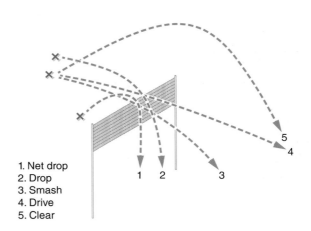

1. Net drop
2. Drop
3. Smash
4. Drive
5. Clear

FIGURE 18.3　Name the shot.

Suggested Performance Objectives

The following are possible objectives that might be used in a badminton unit.

Core Objectives

All directions given are for right-handed players.

Short or Low Serves

1. Standing 6 feet, 6 inches (2 m) from the wall, serve the shuttlecock 10 times in a row between the 5-foot (1.5 m) and 6-foot (1.8 m) marks on the wall.

18

2. Standing behind the short service line on the right side of the court, serve the shuttlecock crosscourt over the net 10 times and place 7 out of 10 in the court.

3. Repeat step 2 from the left side of the service court.

4. Standing behind the short service line, next to the center line in the right court, serve the shuttlecock crosscourt over the net, between the net and a rope 1 foot (30 cm) above it. Repeat this five times in a row from the right and then five times from the left.

5. Standing behind the short service line, next to the center line in the right-hand court, serve 10 short serves in a row to the receiver's backhand side on the court.

6. Repeat step 5, standing in the left-hand court.

Long Serves

7. Standing to the right of and next to the center line, 12 feet (3.5 m) from the net, serve 10 long serves in a row to the opposite court.

8. Repeat step 7 from the left service court.

9. Repeat step 8, but the serves must land in the backhand area marked on the court. Serve five long serves in a row to this area.

Underhand Clears: Forehand and Backhand

10. Standing between the net and the short service line, drop the shuttlecock and hit 10 underhand clears in a row on the forehand side, to the back 4 feet (1.2 m) of the court marked for doubles.

11. Repeat step 10 on the backhand side.

12. Standing 6 feet (1.8 m) behind the short service line, hit five underhand clears in a row on the forehand side to the back 4 feet (1.2 m) of the doubles court.

13. Repeat step 12 on the backhand side.

Drops

14. Standing just behind the short service line on the right court, hit a tossed shuttlecock from your partner in an underhand drop on the forehand side. Return 10 drops in a row from the forehand side.

15. Repeat step 14 on the backhand side.

16. Repeat steps 14 and 15 from the left court.

17. Standing anywhere just behind the short service line, hit a shuttlecock barely tossed over the net by your partner, alternating between your forehand and backhand on the toss. Hit 10 underhand drops in a row back between the net and a rope stretched 1 foot (30 cm) above the net.

Overhead Clears: Forehand

18. Standing within 12 feet (3.5 m) of the net, your partner hits underhand clears. Return 10 shuttlecocks in a row with an overhead forehand clear into the doubles court, at least 10 feet (3 m) from the net.

19. Repeat step 18, returning 10 in a row to the back 4 feet (1.2 m) of the doubles court.

20. Repeat step 18, returning 10 in a row, alternating from right court to left court at least 10 feet (3 m) from the net.

Attendance and Participation

21. Arrive on time for class, dressed, and ready to participate (one-third of a point per day, up to six points maximum).

22. Participate in 15 games: 13 doubles and two singles.

Optional Objectives

1. Standing next to the center line on the right court and just behind the short service line, serve the shuttle five times in a row to the back 3 feet (90 cm) of the doubles service court. Repeat on the left.

2. Standing in the right receiving court for doubles, return five short serves in a row either to the server's backhand side or down the side alley next to the server. Repeat on the left.

3. Standing 6 feet (1.8 m) from the short service line next to the center line on the right court, return five long serves in a row to the backhand side of the server with an overhead clear.

4. Repeat step 3, standing in the left court.

5. A server sets up short, high shots 6 to 8 inches (15 to 20 cm) from the net. Standing 6 feet (1.8 m) from the short service line, smash five in a row within 15 feet (5 m) of the net.

6. Repeat step 5, smashing five in a row down the left side of the court.

7. Repeat step 5, smashing five in a row down the right side of the court.

8. Standing within 10 feet (3 m) of the short service line, return 10 of your opponent's smashes back over the net as smashes.

9. Standing within the last 5 feet (1.5 m) of the back court, hit an overhead drop off your opponent's clears to you. Hit five shuttlecock drops to the right court side between the net and the short service line.

10. Repeat step 9 on the left court between the net and the short service line.

11. Stand on the center line, 6 feet (1.8 m) from the short service line. Your partner sets up low, flat serves down the forehand alley. Hit five forehand drives in a row down that alley.

12. Repeat step 11, hitting five backhand drives down the backhand-side alley.

13. Standing within 12 feet (3.5 m) of the net, from a high clear setup by a partner, backhand five overhead clears in a row to the back 6 feet (1.8 m) of the doubles court.

14. Standing 15 feet (5 m) or farther from the net, backhand five overhead clears in a row to the back 4 feet (1.2 m) of the doubles court.

Skill Tests

Badminton courts can be marked in many ways to provide students with a challenge in perfecting their skills (see figure 18.4). Using white shoe polish or floor tape, number portions of the target area in an ascending manner, from the easiest to the most difficult shots. Courts can be marked for deep serves, low serves, clears, drops, and drives. The teacher determines the number of attempts that each student is allowed.

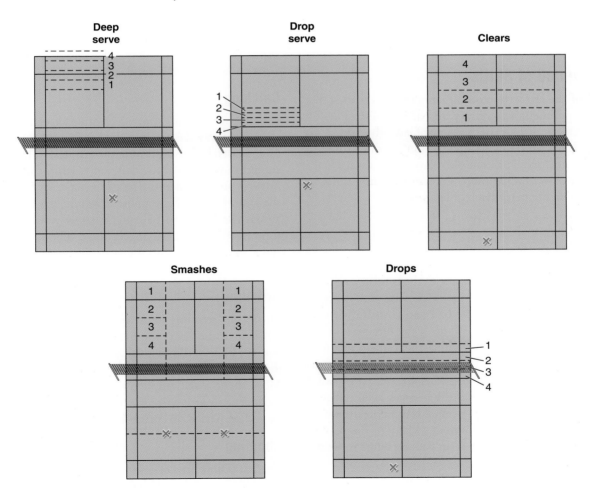

FIGURE 18.4 Badminton skills test.

Basketball

Basketball is a popular game played by many participants on school yards. It was invented in 1891 at Springfield College by Dr. Naismith, who used peach baskets and a soccer ball. The game offers reinforcement to participants when they make a basket and is one of the few team sports requiring skills that people can practice individually. The game demands great cardiorespiratory endurance and development of fine motor skills.

Basketball instruction should focus on developing skills and competence so that students leave school with the ability to participate in recreational games later in life. At the middle school level, emphasis should be on lead-up games that allow all students to find success and enjoyment. As students develop the skills necessary to play the game well, instruction during the high school years can concentrate on strategy and teamwork. Highly skilled and interested students should be offered additional opportunities to play through intramural programs, recreational leagues, or interscholastic competition.

Sequence of Skills

One of the attractive components of basketball is that little equipment is necessary for participation. The following skills are basic to the game of basketball. Students never learn these skills to perfection, so offer time for regular practice. For example, players can always make a better pass, develop more efficient dribbling skills, or shoot a higher percentage of baskets.

Passing

Regardless of the pass used, certain points should be emphasized. The ball should be handled with the fingertips. As the ball makes contact with the hands, the elbows should bend and the hands should move toward the body so that they "give" with the ball and absorb the force. The passer should step forward in the direction of the receiver. The ball is released with a quick straightening of the elbows and a snap of the wrists. The arms and fingers are fully extended, and the palms are turned outward for the follow-through after the ball has been released. A passer should anticipate where his or her teammate is going to be when the ball arrives. Many of the passing drills should therefore focus on passing while moving.

Chest Pass

The chest pass is used frequently in basketball for passes up to 20 feet (6 m). The ball is held at chest level with the fingers spread on both sides of the ball. One foot is ahead of the other in a stride position. The elbows remain close to the body, and the ball is propelled by extending the arms, snapping the wrists, and stepping toward the target.

Bounce Pass

The bounce pass is used to transfer the ball to a closely guarded teammate. It is directed to a spot on the floor closer to the receiver than to the passer. The ball should rebound to waist level of the receiver. Passing form is similar to that used for the chest pass.

Flip Pass

The flip pass is used for a close-range exchange. The ball is flipped somewhat upward to a teammate. It is used often as a pass to a player cutting to the basket for a layup shot.

Two-Handed Overhead Pass

This pass is used against a shorter opponent, usually in the back court. The passer is in a short stride position holding the ball overhead. The momentum of the pass comes from a forceful wrist and finger snap. The upper arms remain relatively in place.

Catching

For effective catching, the receiver must keep the eyes on the ball, follow the ball into the hands, and concentrate on the catch before beginning the next task. The receiver should move toward the ball and reach for it with the fingers spread. When the pass is at waist level or above, the thumbs should be pointed in and the fingers up. When the ball is to be caught below waist level, the thumbs are out and the fingers down. The hands should "give" and move toward the body to absorb the force of the throw and thus make the ball more catchable.

Dribbling

Dribbling requires bent knees and crouching. The forearm of the dribbling hand is parallel to the floor, and the ball should be pushed toward the floor, rather than slapped. The ball is controlled with the fingertips. Most of the force supplied to the ball should be from the wrist, so arm movement is minimized. Emphasis should be placed on controlling the ball.

Shooting

Certain points are common to all shooting. The body should be squared up with the basket whenever possible. The ball is held with the fingers spread, and the elbow of the shooting hand should always be directly behind the ball. The eyes are fixed on the rim, and the ball is shot with a slight backspin on it. The arm is extended on follow-through with the wrist flexed.

Layup Shots

For a right-handed layup, the player approaches the basket from the right side at an angle of about 45 degrees. The ball is released with the right hand, and the weight is on the left foot. As the body is elevated off the floor by the left foot, the ball is released 12 to 18 inches (30 to 45 cm) above the basket on the backboard. For a left-handed shot, the sequence is the opposite. The shooter should always reach toward the spot on the backboard with the shooting hand. Students should practice shooting with either hand.

One-Hand Push Shots (Free-Throw Shot)

The push shot is used primarily for shooting free throws. Few people shoot a one-hand shot from a set position. The ball is held at shoulder level in the nonshooting hand. The shooting hand is behind the ball, the fingertips are touching the ball, and the wrist is cocked. The legs are shoulder-width apart, and the knees are slightly bent. To shoot, the player straightens the legs and pushes forward with the forearm and wrist. The wrist should be bent over on follow-through, and the arm should be straight.

Jump Shots

The jump shot is the most popular shot in basketball because it is difficult to block. The hands are in the same position as described for the one-hand push shot. After the shooter jumps, the ball is placed just above and in front of the head. The elbow must be kept under the ball so that the shooting hand moves in a straight line toward the basket. The wrist snaps on release. The shot should be performed using a jump in an upward plane. Leaning forward, sideways, or backward will make the shot much less consistent. The jump shot is sometimes difficult for middle school students. They often learn the wrong motor pattern of throwing the ball instead of shooting it. If this is the case, use a smaller ball, a lower basket, or both to develop the correct pattern.

Rebounding

Rebounding is the ability to gain possession of the ball after a shot is missed. To rebound successfully, boxing out or blocking out is required. A player does this by taking a position between the basket and opponent. The player spreads the feet wide, spreads the body wide by holding the elbows away from the body, and bends the legs to create a solid base position. A good rebounder

maintains contact with the opponent and aggressively slides or moves to stay between her or him and the basket. After establishing the box-out position, the player needs to anticipate where the ball will bounce off the rim or backboard and jump high and grab the ball with two hands.

Ideas for Effective Instruction

Drills used in basketball should simulate game conditions as closely as possible. Rarely in basketball do players stand still. Passing drills, therefore, should include player movement, shooting drills should require movement and pressure, and dribbling drills under control should include looking away from the ball.

Baskets can be lowered to 8.5 to 9.0 feet (2.60 to 2.75 m) to increase the level of success. This basket height will also help develop better shooting patterns in the weaker, smaller players. Note that almost all students will select the lower basket when they have a choice of a basket at regulation height and another, lowered basket. Most people are motivated by being able to make the shot and thus shoot a higher percentage.

The program should concentrate on skill development and include many drills. Basketball offers endless drill possibilities, and using many drills gives variety and breadth to the instructional program. The drills should offer each student as much practice as possible in a stipulated amount of time. Lining up a squad of eight players to take turns makes little sense. Use as many balls as possible. In some cases, students may be willing to bring one from home for class use. Having more baskets and balls means that more students will have an opportunity to practice and learn skills.

Many basketball drills can be used to enhance passing, dribbling, and shooting, but the lead-up games in the following section encourage skill practice while introducing competition and game play. When possible, therefore, isolate skills and practice them in lead-up games to maintain a high level of student motivation.

Lead-Up Games and Learning Activities

This section highlights numerous lead-up games and learning activities to help develop the skills to participate in basketball.

Keep-Away

The essence of the game is to make as many consecutive passes as possible without losing control to the opposite team. Teams may consist of 5 to 10 players. Use colored vests so that players can identify their teammates. The

18

game is started with a jump ball, and the goal is to maintain control. Each defensive player must stay with a designated opponent, rather than be part of a swarming zone defense. As soon as possession is lost, the team taking possession starts counting passes. The team that makes the most consecutive passes within a designated time is the winner.

Five Passes

This game is like keep-away, but the object is to make five consecutive passes. As soon this goal has been reached, the ball is turned over to the other team. Students are not allowed to travel with the ball. Two or three dribbles may be allowed between passes. Players may hold the ball for only three seconds.

Dribble Tag

The playing area is divided into two equal parts. All players begin dribbling in one-half of the area. The object of this game is to maintain a continuous dribble while avoiding being tagged by another player. If tagged or if control of the ball is lost, the player must move to the other half of the playing area and practice dribbling without the pressure of competition.

Dribble Keep-Away

The area is divided into two equal parts. All players start in one-half of the area and begin dribbling. The goal is to maintain control of the dribble while trying to disrupt the dribble of an opponent. If control of the ball is lost, the player moves to the other side of the area and practices.

Around the World

Shooting spots are marked on the floor with tape. Players are in groups of three. A player begins at the first spot and continues until he or she misses a shot. The player can then wait for another turn or take a second "risk" shot. If the player makes the risk shot, he or she continues "around the world." If the player misses the shot, he or she must start over on the next turn. The winner is the player who goes around the world first. A variation is to count the number of shots that players take to move around the world. The person who makes the circuit with the fewest shots is the winner.

Twenty-One

Players are in groups of three or four. Each player receives a long shot (distance must be designated) and a follow-up shot. The long shot, if made, counts 2 points, and the follow-up shot counts 1 point. The follow-up shot must be taken from the spot where the ball was recovered. The first player to score 21 points is the winner. A variation is to play team 21, in which the first team of players to score 21 is declared the winner.

Horse

Players work in groups of two to four and shoot in a predetermined order. The first player shoots from any place on the court. If the player makes the shot, the next player must make the same type of shot from the same position. If the next player misses the shot, that player receives an H, and the following player can shoot any shot desired. No penalty is assigned for a missed shot unless the previous player has made a shot. A player is disqualified if the letters spelling HORSE are accumulated. The winner is the last remaining player.

Sideline Basketball

The class is divided into two teams, each lined up along one side of the court, facing the other. The game is played by three or four active players from each team. The remainder of the players stand on the sideline and can catch and pass the ball to the active players, but they may not shoot or enter the playing floor. They must keep one foot completely out of bounds at all times.

Active players play regular basketball with one variation; they may pass and receive the ball from sideline players. The game starts with the active players occupying their own half of the court. The ball is taken out of bounds under its own basket by the team that was scored on. Play continues until one team scores or until a designated time (2 or 3 minutes) has elapsed. The active players then move to the left side of their line, and three new active players come out from the right. All other players move down three places in the line.

No official out of bounds on the sides is called. The players on that side of the floor simply recover the ball and put it into play without delay with a pass to an active player. Out of bounds on the ends is the same as in regular basketball. If one of the sideline players enters the court and touches the ball, it is a violation, and the ball is awarded out of bounds on the other side to a sideline player. Free throws are awarded when a player is fouled. Sideline players may pass to each other and should be well spaced along the side.

Half-Court Basketball

Teams of two to four work best for this variation. The game is like regulation basketball with the following exceptions. When a defensive player recovers the ball, either from a rebound or an interception, the ball must be taken back to midcourt before offensive play can begin. After a basket is made, the ball must also be taken to midcourt. For out-of-bounds and ballhandling violations, the ball is awarded to the opponents' out of bounds at a spot near the place where the violation occurred. The ball, in this case, does not have to be taken to midcourt. If a foul occurs, the ball is given to the offended team, or regulation foul shooting can be done.

Three on Three

For many lead-up games, the number of players on a team varies. The advantage of playing half-court basketball with only two or three players on a team is that each player gets to handle the ball more. Regulation rules are followed.

The game three on three can be played with four or five teams. An offensive team of three stands forward of the midcourt line, while another team is on defense. The other teams wait behind midcourt for their turns. A scrimmage is over when one team scores. The defensive team then goes on offense, and a new team comes in to play defense. The old offensive team goes to the rear of the line of waiting players. The game can be varied so that the winning team stays on after a basket is scored. Caution must be used with the winner-stay-on approach because the better players may get much more practice than the less skilled performers. Make the teams as equal as possible so that all have a chance to win.

Suggested Performance Objectives

The following are examples of performance objectives that might be used in a beginning basketball class. The standards may have to be adjusted depending on the skill level and age of the students.

Core Objectives

Dribbling Tasks

1. In a stationary position, execute a right-hand dribble 10 consecutive times.
2. Perform task 1 except use the left hand.
3. At reduced speed, dribble the ball with the right hand from the baseline to the midcourt line without losing control.
4. At reduced speed, dribble the ball with the left hand from the midcourt line to the baseline without losing the dribble.

Passing Tasks

5. Standing 10 feet (3 m) from the target on the wall, throw 10 consecutive two-hand chest passes.
6. Standing 10 feet (3 m) from a partner, execute 8 of 10 consecutive two-hand passes.
7. Standing 10 feet (3 m) from the target, throw 10 consecutive two-hand bounce passes.
8. Standing 10 feet (3 m) from a partner, execute 8 of 10 consecutive bounce passes.
9. Standing 10 feet (3 m) from the target, throw 10 consecutive two-hand overhead passes.
10. Standing 10 feet (3 m) from a partner, execute 8 of 10 consecutive two-hand overhead passes.

Shooting Tasks

11. Starting from the right side about 20 feet (6 m) from the basket, dribble the ball toward the basket and make four of six lay-ups using the backboard.
12. Perform task 11 but start from the left side.
13. Standing 6 feet (1.8 m) from the basket (right side), make four of six bank shots.
14. Perform task 13 but use the left side.
15. Standing at the free-throw line, make 5 of 10 consecutive set shots.
16. Standing 10 (3 m) feet from the basket, make 5 of 10 jump shots.

Rebounding Tasks

17. Standing with the feet shoulder-width apart and with both hands at shoulder level, jump up and touch the target on the wall three consecutive times using both hands.
18. Standing 2 to 3 feet (60 to 90 cm) from the basket, toss the ball off the right side of the backboard and rebound it with both hands five consecutive times.
19. Perform task 18 but use the left side.
20. Standing 2 to 3 feet (60 to 90 cm) from the basket, toss the ball off the right side of the backboard, rebound it using both hands, pivot right, and make an overhead pass or chest pass to a partner. Repeat five consecutive times.
21. Perform task 20 but use the left side and pivot left.

18

431

Optional Objectives

1. Officiate at least one regulation game during class time, using correct calls and signals.
2. Write a one-page report on the game of basketball.
3. Make a list of 15 basketball terms and define them.
4. Write a one-page report on a basketball article or book.
5. Perform a figure-eight ballhandling technique by weaving the ball around one leg and then around the other leg, forming a figure eight, successfully for 10 seconds.
6. Make 8 of 10 bank shots from anywhere outside the foul lane.
7. Make 9 of 10 free throws.

Field Hockey

Field hockey is a popular team sport that has been played predominantly by females in the United States. Many clubs across the country are affiliated with the United States Field Hockey Association and offer playing experiences for participants ages 6 to 60. In other countries, the game is also played by males and is a popular Olympic sport. Many high schools and colleges offer field hockey competition for girls and women.

The regulation game is played with 11 players on each team. The object of the game is to move a ball with a stick into the opponent's goal, which is 12 feet (3.7 m) wide and 7 feet (2.1 m) high. The game is started with a pass back to teammates in the center of the field. Besides the goalkeeper, a team usually has three forwards, three links, three backs, and one sweeper. The field is 60 by 100 yards (55 by 92 m) with a 16-yard (14.6 m) striking circle (see figure 18.5).

Hockey equipment includes the ball, sticks, shin guards, mouth guards, and the goalkeeper's helmet with mask, chest protector, gloves, full-length leg pads, and kickers for the shoes. The ball is composed of cork and twine and is covered in leather. Sticks vary in length from 30 to 37 inches (76 to 94 cm). Middle school students use sticks 30 to 34 inches (76 to 86 cm) long, and high school students use sticks 35 to 37 inches (89 to 94 cm) long. All regulation sticks have a flat surface on one side and a rounded surface on the other. Only the flat side can be used for legal hits.

The game can be modified in several ways for secondary physical education units. The number of players and

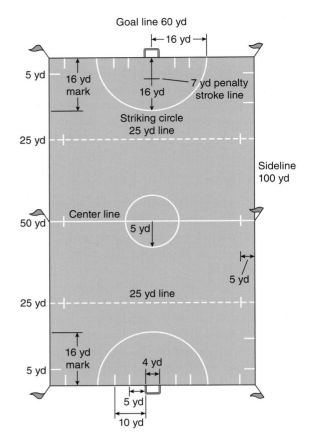

FIGURE 18.5 Field markings and dimensions for field hockey.

the field size can be reduced. Goals can be improvised by using boundary cones, high-jump standards, or even soccer goals. A whiffle ball or a rubber or plastic ball can be used, and plastic sticks that are flat on both sides are available. A flat plastic puck is recommended for play on the gymnasium floor. Goalies can wear a face mask, chest protector, and shin guards from softball or lacrosse equipment. If the goalie equipment is not available, then the game should be played without a goalie. Both boys and girls can enjoy the game in a coeducational unit. Field hockey can be played indoors, outdoors, or on a concrete surface. Physical educators often use floor hockey while inside the gymnasium. Floor hockey has many of the same tactics and skills as field hockey, and most of the skills in this section can be adapted for floor hockey.

Sequence of Skills

The following is a breakdown of the skills necessary to successfully participate in field hockey.

Gripping

Grip in is the basic grip. The left hand is placed on the top of the stick as though shaking hands. The right hand is placed 6 to 8 inches (15 to 20 cm) below the left hand. The palms of the hands face each other in most situations. The right hand can slide up the stick for a drive shot and for a reverse stick. The lower position is used for dribbling and for most passes.

Dribbling

Dribbling is propelling the ball downfield in a controlled manner. It can be done straight down the field or zig-zagging to the left and right. In straight dribbling, the arms are kept in front of the body. The flat side of the stick faces forward. Short, controlled taps on the ball are used. The ball should remain in front of the body. The zigzag dribble moves the ball left and right by using a forehand tap to the left and a reverse stick tap to the right. In the reverse stick, the stick is turned over so that the toe of the stick is pointing down. This type of dribble requires a lot of practice and stick control. The taps to the left and right should be short and controlled. Dribbling can also include dragging the ball with the flat side of the stick. The stick stays in contact with the ball as it is being dragged downfield.

Passing and Shooting

The drive shot is the most forceful pass for longer distances and goal shots. The hands are together, and the stick comes back and forward in a manner like a short-ened golf swing. The stick cannot be lifted higher than the shoulder in either the backswing or follow-through. Drive shots can be straight, to the left, or to the right.

The push pass is used for shorter, more accurate passes. The pass is usually executed quickly off the dribble. No backswing occurs. The right hand is lower on the stick, and the ball is pushed or swept along the ground.

The scoop is a pass or shot lofted into the air using a shoveling motion for a shot or to get over an opponent's stick. The top of the stick must be tilted backward so that the blade is behind and under the ball to give it loft as the force is applied. The flick pass or shot is the most popular aerial shot. It gets off the ground about knee high and is an extension of the push pass (pushing slightly below the center of the ball to ensure that it rises off the ground). The flick is a popular shot on goal.

A slap hit is a modified drive shot or pass that uses a short backswing and does not require a change in the position of the hands. The pass can be used with the hands apart in the normal hand position for ballhandling.

Fielding

Fielding refers to stopping and controlling a moving ball and must be practiced with balls coming from the right, left, and center. The face of the stick and the body position need to be adjusted according to the direction in which the ball is traveling. The front fielding position is similar to the straight dribbling position and is used for balls rolling straight toward a person. Balls coming from the left require a regular forehand position with the blade facing to the left. For balls coming from the right, the stick must intercept the ball before it reaches the body. The blade must be turned so that it is facing to the right. Fielding requires the ability to absorb the ball's momentum by "giving" with the stick, depending on the speed of the ball.

Tackling and Dodging

Tackling is attempting to take the ball away from an opponent. Tackles can be made straight on or from the left or the right side of an opponent. Timing is important because the ball must be picked off while it is away from the opponent's stick. The stick is carried low, and the tackler must concentrate on the ball and on the opponent's stick. The speed of the opponent and the ball must be considered. The tackle should not be a reckless striking of the stick.

Dodging is a skill for evading a tackler and maintaining control of the ball. A dodge can be executed to the left or right side of the tackler, and a scoop shot can be used to go over an opponent's stick. If a dodge is made to the left, the dodger should move the ball 90 degrees to the left just before the tackle. A dodger moving around to the left is on the stick side, which is the right, of the opponent. This maneuver is a stick-side dodge. A dodge to the right involves moving the ball to the right of the opponent, but the dodger's body must move around the other side of the tackler, that is, the ball goes to the right but the person goes to the left (nonstick-side dodge). A reverse stick technique can also be used for a nonstick-side dodge. The player uses the reverse stick to pull the ball across the body to the nonstick side of the defender and then steps forward with the left foot and pushes the ball past the defender.

Bully or Face-Off

The bully is used only when simultaneous fouls occur. Two players face each other in the middle of the field with their respective sticks facing the direction of the goal where they can score. The bully starts with the two players striking the ground on their own side of the ball

18

and then touching sticks above the ball. They repeat this action three times and then attempt to control the ball or to pass it to a teammate.

Goalkeeping

The goalkeeper can kick the ball or block the ball with the body, hands, or stick. Most balls are blocked with the legs or feet, hence the padding on those areas. Most clears away from the goal are with a kick. The goalie cannot hold the ball or throw the ball away from the goal.

Ideas for Effective Instruction

Drills can be set up for partner work at several stations. Dribbling, passing, fielding, shooting, tackling, dodging, and goalkeeping can be specific stations with varying tasks to be practiced. Use the performance objectives detailed here for the tasks at each station. Set up boundary cones, stopwatches, targets, baskets, and other instructional devices for challenging skill work. Arrange classes so that students spend several minutes working at each station. The station work can then be followed by several small group drills, such as three on three, keep-away, or three-person weave. A modified or regulation game could follow the group work. This variety of learning activities helps keep students active and motivated.

Remind students continually about the importance of safe stick handling. High sticking (taking the stick above the waist) is extremely dangerous, and rules must be enforced tightly. Body checking, tripping, and hooking (using the blade of the stick to impede the movement of an opponent) with the stick should also be forbidden. A free hit or penalty corner can be used as a penalty for these violations, depending on where the penalty occurs. The teacher must be clear about the rules, regulations, and penalties that are enforced in the game.

Lead-Up Games and Learning Activities

This section highlights numerous lead-up games and learning activities to help develop the skills to participate in field hockey.

Sit-Up Sticks

This activity is a fun warm-up and fitness idea in which partners face each other in a typical sit-up position. On the start signal, partners perform a sit-up and pass one hockey stick back and forth at the top of each sit-up. A challenge would be to see how many passes partners can make in 30 seconds.

Three-Person Weave

The ball is started by the center person and passed to the person on either the left or the right. The person making the pass always runs behind the person who receives the pass. The person receiving the pass then dribbles to the center to become the middle person. This procedure continues downfield.

Partner Passing

Partners stand apart and try to hit and complete as many passes as possible in 30 seconds. Each hit is counted. For variations, students can try the same activity with three people in a triangle, four in a square, or five in a circle.

Circle Keep-Away

Students form a circle with one person in the middle. The people in the circle try to keep the ball away from the center person. This game can also be played with only three people. The person in the middle is rotated after one minute.

Circle Dribble

A student dribbles the ball around the circle as fast as possible, concluding the dribble at the next person in the circle. All members of the circle go around quickly. Circles compete against each other or against the clock. A variation is to dribble in and out of the players standing in the circle.

Star Drill

Five classmates make a star formation. Number 1 passes to 2, 2 to 3, and so forth. After passing the ball, the passer runs and takes the receiver's spot. The passer always follows the pass, and more than one person can be in line. The game can also be played against another team or against the clock.

Defensive Squares Drill

Set up several squares with boundary cones. The size of the squares can vary depending on the ability of the students. Smaller squares make the drill more demanding for the offensive player. A defensive player is in the square, and an offensive player tries to dribble through the square. The defensive player tries to keep the offensive player from dribbling through the square.

Dribble and Hit for Distance

Half of the class or group line up 5 yards (m) behind a drive line. A partner is downfield about 50 yards (m). On signal, the hitters dribble the 5 yards (m) and hit a drive shot as far as possible. The partner stands over the ball, and a winner is determined. Partners change places after several hits.

No-Goalie Field Hockey

The game is played without a goalie. Person-to-person defense can be used. The goal size can be modified if necessary.

End Zone Hockey

The entire end line of the field is the goal area. Each team designates a certain number of goalies and field players. The goalies must spread out over the entire goal line to cover it properly. Goalies and field players change places after a specified number of minutes.

Sideline Hockey

Part of each team lines up on one sideline, and the rest of each team is on the field. The sideline players keep the ball from going out of bounds, and they can also pass to the field players. A regulation goal and goalie are used in the game. The sideline and field players switch after three minutes of play. This game can be varied by putting members of each team on both sidelines, thus adding another challenge to the game.

Square Hockey

The game is played on a large square. Each team defends two sides of the square. Some team members are on the square sides as goalies, and others are on the field trying to hit the ball past either of the two end lines. At the start of the game, the teacher can have all students stand on the square and count off. Several numbers can then be called, and those students become the field players.

Half-Circle Hockey

This game is like square hockey, but each team forms one-half of a circle. The half circles connect, and the object is to push the ball through the opponent's half circle. If the ball comes to rest inside the circle, it belongs to the team nearer the ball. That team can take a shot from the point where the ball stopped.

Modified Field Hockey

1. A pass back is used to start the game and after each goal.
2. A legal hit is used when the ball goes out of bounds.
3. A short corner (or penalty corner) shot is awarded to the offense when the ball goes past the end line within the striking circle, last touching off a defender. The short corner is taken 10 yards (m) from the goal on the end line, and the defensive team is allowed to have only five players, including the goalie, to defend. The offensive team is allowed to include all players if they choose; the remaining defensive players are required to be beyond half field.
4. A long corner shot is awarded to the offense when the ball goes past the end line outside the striking circle, last touching off a defender. The long corner involves all players and is taken from the sideline approximately 5 yards (m) from the corner.
5. A defensive hit is awarded to the defensive team when the ball goes over the end line off an offensive player.
6. The striking circle is the 16-yard (m) half circle around the goal. A free shot is awarded for a foul occurring anywhere outside the striking circle. All players must be 5 yards (m) away when the shot is hit.
7. A penalty corner is awarded for a defensive foul inside the striking circle.
8. Offside occurs when an offensive player gains an advantage within the 25-yard (m) line. A defensive hit is awarded at the top of the circle.
9. High sticking occurs when a player raises the stick above the shoulder. The penalty is a free hit or a penalty corner if it occurs in the striking circle.
10. Advancing occurs when a player uses any part of the body to advance the ball. The penalty is a free hit or a penalty corner.
11. Hooking, tripping, or dangerous stick use involves using the stick to slow down or trip an opponent. The penalty is a free hit or penalty corner.
12. Body checking is vigorous use of the body for blocking and other maneuvers. The penalty is a free hit or penalty corner.

Suggested Performance Objectives

These performance objectives can be used to structure the learning activities for station work. They can also be tied to a motivational scheme for earning grades or winning an entry into a playing situation. Teachers might develop a contract from these objectives, which can be modified according to the ability levels of the students in a specific situation. If the objectives are too

18

hard or too easy, they should be rewritten to provide a fair challenge and a successful experience for students.

1. Dribble the ball for 30 yards (m) three consecutive times, always using proper technique (straight dribble).

2. Dribble the ball through an obstacle course and back in 30 seconds or less (straight dribble).

3. Dribble the ball toward a target and execute a nonstick dodge in three of five attempts without losing control.

4. Dribble the ball toward a target and execute a stick-side dodge around the target in three of five attempts without losing control.

5. With a partner, push pass the ball back and forth (jogging speed) for 30 yards two consecutive times.

6. Use a push pass to direct the ball to a target three of five times from a distance of 10 yards (m).

7. Shoot three of five drive shots into the goal from 10 yards (m) with no goalie.

8. Scoop the ball over an obstacle into a basket three consecutive times from within a stick-length distance.

9. Dribble the ball from the center of the field toward the goal and hit three drive shots three consecutive times without a goalie.

10. Execute proper fielding of the ball from the front, right, and left sides passed by a partner from 10 to 15 yards (m) with no goalie away (five times from each side).

11. Dribble the ball for 30 yards (m) with no goalie three consecutive times using proper technique at all times (zigzag dribble).

12. Dribble the ball through an obstacle course and back in 30 seconds or less (zigzag dribble).

13. Dribble the ball toward a goal and score two of five drive shots past a goalie from 10 yards (m) with no goalie.

14. Execute a three-person weave passing drill from 15 to 30 yards (m) with no goalie two consecutive times.

15. Hit two of five penalty shots past a goalie.

16. Execute a proper tackle from the left, right, and center.

17. Scoop and run with the ball for 25 yards (m) with no goalie.

18. Dribble 5 yards (m) with no goalie and then execute a scoop shot. Repeat five consecutive times.

19. Flick three of five balls into the left and right corners of the goal.

Flag Football

Football is the United States' favorite spectator sport. Students hold professional football players in high esteem. The shape of the football makes throwing and catching more difficult and challenging than similar maneuvers in other sports. Flag and touch football are variations of the game of football, modified so that the game can be played without the padding and equipment necessary for tackle football. Flag football is usually the more enjoyable sport because it eliminates the arguments about whether someone was touched. Flag football is often taught with modified footballs (i.e., junior balls or Nerf balls) because many students have difficulty gripping a regulation ball.

Sequence of Skills

The following is a breakdown of the skills necessary to successfully participate in flag football.

Passing

Passing is used to advance the ball downfield to a teammate. The passer looks at the receiver and points the shoulder opposite the throwing arm toward the receiver. The ball is brought up to the throwing shoulder with both hands. The fingers of the throwing hand are placed across the laces of the ball. The weight is transferred to the rear leg in preparation for the throw. On throwing, the weight is transferred forward, and a step is taken with the front foot in the direction of the receiver. The throwing arm is extended, and the wrist is flicked upon release of the ball. The longer the throw is, the higher the angle of release is.

Lateral Passing

Lateral passing is pitching the ball underhand to a teammate. The ball must be tossed sideways or backward to be a legal lateral that can then be passed again. No attempt is made to make the ball spiral as it does in a pass.

Catching

Because the football is a large and heavy object and can be thrown with great velocity, the catcher must "give" and bring the ball in toward the body. In a stationary position, the catcher faces the thrower and plants the feet about shoulder-width apart. To catch a ball on the run, the catcher observes the ball by looking over the shoulder. The fingers should be spread and the arms extended to meet the ball. This positioning allows the receiver to "give" with the ball and bring it in toward the body to absorb the force of the throw. Students should develop the habit of tucking the ball in close to the body after each catch.

Carrying the Ball

The ball is carried with the arm on the outside, and the end of the ball is tucked into the notch formed by the elbow and arm. The fingers cradle the forward part of the ball.

Centering

The center moves into position with the feet well spread and the toes pointed straight ahead. The knees are bent in preparation for forward movement. The dominant hand reaches forward slightly and is placed across the laces of the ball, which is resting on the ground before her or him. The other hand is on the side near the back and guides the ball. The head is between the legs, and the center's eyes are on the quarterback. The arms are extended, and the ball is propelled by pulling both arms backward and upward. The ball should spiral on its way to the quarterback.

When centering in T formation, only one hand is used. The quarterback places the throwing hand in the crotch of the center and the other hand below with the hands touching at the base of the palms. The ball is given a one-quarter turn as it is centered and placed sideways in the quarterback's hands.

Developing a Stance

Ends and backs use the two-point stance so that they can see downfield. The feet are spread shoulder-width apart, and the knees are bent slightly. The hands can be placed just above the knees. In the past, the three- and four-point stances were used, but many youth football organizations have rules against them to prevent head injuries.

Blocking

The purpose of blocking is to prevent the defensive player from getting the flag of the ball carrier. Blocking is accomplished by keeping the body between the defensive player and the ball carrier. Knocking the defensive player down is not necessary to accomplish a successful block.

- **Shoulder blocking:** The shoulder block starts from a three- or four-point stance. The blocker moves forward and makes shoulder contact at the chest level of the opponent. The head should be placed between the opponent and the ball carrier to move the defensive player away from the ball carrier. The elbows are out and the hands are held near the chest.

- **Pass blocking:** The pass block is used when the quarterback is dropping back to throw a pass. The block can begin from any of the described stances. The blocker moves slightly backward with the rear foot as the opponent charges. The blocker should attempt to stay between the quarterback and the rusher.

Exchanging the Ball

The handoff is made with the inside hand (nearest the receiver). The ball is held with both hands until the ball carrier is about 6 feet (1.8 m) away. It is then shifted to the hand nearer the receiver, with the elbow bent partially away from the body. The receiver comes toward the quarterback with the near arm bent and carried in front of the chest, with the palm down. The other arm is carried about waist high, with the palm up. As the ball is exchanged, the receiver clamps down on the ball to secure it.

Punting

The punter starts in standing position with both arms fully extended to receive the ball. The kicking foot is placed slightly forward. After receiving the ball, the kicker takes two steps forward, beginning with the dominant foot. The ball is slightly turned in and held at waist height. The kicking leg is swung forward, and at impact, the knee is straightened to provide maximum force. The toes are pointed, and the long axis of the ball makes contact on the top of the instep. The ball should be dropped rather than tossed into the air. A good drop is required for effective punting to occur.

Ideas for Effective Instruction

Because many drills are available for flag football, this section describes the rules and equipment necessary for them. Most of the prerequisites for developing a sound flag football program are listed and discussed.

Uniforms

Rubber-soled shoes should be worn. Metal cleats or spikes are not allowed, nor is any hard surface padding or helmets.

Flags

Flags are available in two colors for team play. All flags should be similar in terms of being able to be pulled loose from players. The flag belts have two flags attached, one at each hip. The pulling of either flag downs the ball carrier.

18

Downed Ball

To down a ball carrier, either flag must be withdrawn from the waist by a tackler. The tackler must stop at the point of tackle and hold up the hand with the withdrawn flag. Ball carriers cannot deliberately touch their own flags or defend them in any manner. These acts result in a penalty of 15-yard loss from the point of the foul and loss of a down.

Dead Ball

The ball is ruled dead on a fumble when it hits the ground or on a wild center when it hits the ground. When a fumble rolls out of bounds, the ball is returned to the team that last had full possession of it.

Loss of Flags

If the flag is inadvertently lost, that player is ineligible to handle the ball. The ball then becomes dead if the player is behind the line of scrimmage or the pass is called incomplete. A player cannot deliberately withdraw an opponent's flag unless that opponent is in possession of the ball. Such conduct is penalized as unsportsmanlike for a penalty of 15 yards.

Charging and Tackling

The ball carrier may not run through a defensive player but must attempt to evade the tackler. The tackler must not hold, push, or run through the ball carrier; he or she must play the flag rather than the person. The officials make these judgment calls and may award a penalty of 15 yards and loss of a down offensively and 15 yards defensively.

Tackling

Tackling is not permitted. The ball is declared dead when a defensive player pulls one of the runner's flags. Action against the runner, other than pulling the flag, is unnecessary roughness and carries a penalty of 15 yards from the point of the foul and loss of a down offensively and 15 yards from the point of the foul defensively.

Hacking

The ball carrier cannot hack, push, or straight-arm another player. These actions result in a penalty of 15 yards from the point of the foul and loss of a down.

Blocking

Line blocking is the same as in regulation football. In open-field (out-of-the-line) line blocking, no part of the blocker's body, except the feet, shall be in contact with the ground during the block. Blocking is a type of body checking. The blocker is in an upright position and cannot use the hands or extended arms. Any rough tactics, such as attempting to run over or batter down an opponent, is penalized as unnecessary roughness. Unnecessary roughness may be declared if the blocker uses knees or elbows in blocking, carrying a penalty of 15 yards and loss of a down offensively and 15 yards and a first down defensively.

Passing

A forward pass may be thrown from any point behind the line of scrimmage. The passer is declared down if a flag is withdrawn by a defensive player or if a flag falls out on its own before the passer's arm is engaged in the throwing motion. The officials make this decision.

Downs

A team has four downs to advance the ball from wherever the team takes over to score. If the team fails to score in four downs, its opponents gain possession of the ball at the spot where the ball is declared dead on the fourth down. To obtain a first down, the offensive team must complete three forward passes out of four downs. A forward pass is a pass thrown from behind the line of scrimmage past the line of scrimmage.

Miscellaneous Penalties

The following penalties should be explained and discussed with students.

Illegal use of flags (i.e., covering them)	5 yards
Offensive use of hands	15 yards
Defensive illegal use of hands	15 yards
Offsides	5 yards
Pushing ball carrier out of bounds	15 yards
Ball carrier pushing the interference	15 yards
Ineligible person downfield	5 yards
Illegal procedure	5 yards

Lead-Up Games and Learning Activities

The following lead-up games can be enjoyable ways to broaden the variety of activities in a football unit. They also prevent one student from dominating a skilled position while others simply go through the motions of blocking.

Five Passes

The game can be played on a football field, but the size of the field is not critical; any large area is satisfactory. Players scatter on the field. The object of the game is for one team (identified by pinnies, which are side markers worn by participants) to make five consecutive passes to five different players without losing control of the ball. This sequence scores a point. The defense may play the ball only and may not make personal contact. If a player takes more than three steps when in possession of the ball, the ball is given to the other team.

No penalty is assessed when the ball hits the ground. It remains in play, but this event interrupts the five-pass sequence, which starts over. Students should call aloud the number of consecutive passes.

Kick Over

The game is played on a football field with a 10-yard end zone. Teams are scattered at opposite ends of the field. The object is to punt the ball over the other team's goal line. If the ball is caught in the end zone, no score results. A ball kicked into the end zone and not caught scores a goal. If the ball is kicked beyond the end zone on the fly, a score is made regardless of whether the ball is caught.

Play is started by one team with a punt from a point 20 to 30 feet (6 to 9 m) in front of its own goal line. On a punt, if the ball is not caught, the team must kick from the point of recovery. If the ball is caught, the team also kicks from the point of recovery. When the ball is caught, three long strides are allowed to advance the ball for a kick. Number the students so that they all kick in rotation and receive equal practice.

Fourth Down

Six to eight players are on a team and play in an area roughly half the size of a football field. Every play is a fourth down, which means that the play must score or the team loses the ball. No kicking is permitted, and players may pass at any time from any spot in any direction. A series of passes can occur on any play, either from behind or beyond the line of scrimmage.

The teams start in the middle of the field with possession determined by a coin toss. The ball is put into play by centering. The quarterback receiving the ball runs or passes to any teammate. The receiver has the same options. No blocking is permitted. After each touchdown, the ball is brought to the center of the field, and the nonscoring team resumes play. The ball is downed when the ball carrier's flag is pulled. If a player makes an incomplete pass beyond the line of scrimmage, the ball is brought to the spot from which it was thrown.

Positions are rotated so that everyone has a chance to be the quarterback. The rotation occurs after every down. The quarterback rotates to center, which ensures that everyone plays all positions.

Captain Football

The game is played on half of a football field. Five yards beyond each goal is a 2-by-2-yard square, which is the box. The teams must be identified with pinnies. The object of the game is to complete a pass to the captain in the box.

To begin, the players line up at opposite ends of the field. One team kicks off from its 10-yard line to the other team. The game then becomes keep-away. One team is trying to secure possession of the ball, and the other team is trying to retain possession until a successful pass can be made to the captain in the box. To score a touchdown, the captain must catch the ball on the fly and keep both feet in the box.

A player may run sideways or backward when in possession of the ball. Players may not run forward, but they are allowed momentum (two steps) if receiving or intercepting a ball. Taking more than two steps is penalized by loss of possession.

The captain is allowed three attempts to catch a pass or one successful goal before a new player is rotated into the box. A ball hitting the ground inbounds remains in play. Players may not bat or kick a free ball. The penalty is the awarding of the ball to the other team out of bounds.

Aerial Ball

Aerial ball is like flag football with the following differences. The ball may be passed at any time. It can be thrown at any time beyond the line of scrimmage—immediately after an interception, during a kickoff, or during a received kick. Players have four downs to score a touchdown. If the ball is thrown from behind the line of scrimmage and an incomplete pass results, the ball is returned to the previous spot on the line of scrimmage. If the pass originates otherwise and is incomplete, the ball is placed at the point from which the pass was thrown.

Because the ball can be passed at any time, no downfield blocking is permitted. A player may screen the ball carrier but cannot make a block. Screening is defined as running between the ball carrier and the defense.

Suggested Performance Objectives

The following are possible objectives that might be used in a flag football unit.

Core Objectives

1. Throw 10 overhand passes to the chest area of a partner who is standing 10 yards (m) away.

18

Practice correct holding, point of release, and follow-through techniques of passing.

2. Throw three or four consecutive passes beyond a target positioned 20 yards (m) away.

3. Facing the opposite direction from a partner 5 yards (m) away, execute a proper center stance with feet well spread, toes pointed straight ahead, knees bent, and two hands on the ball. Snap the ball back through the legs 10 consecutive times.

4. With a partner centering the ball, punt the ball one time from a distance of 10 yards (m) using proper technique to another set of partners 15 yards (m) away.

5. Perform task 4 except at a distance of 10 to 20 yards (m).

6. Punt the ball three consecutive times within the boundary lines of the field and beyond a distance of 20 yards (m).

7. With a partner, run a quick pass pattern (5- to 7-yard pattern) and catch the ball two of three times.

8. With a partner, run a 10- to 15-yard (m) down-and-in pass pattern and catch the ball two of three times.

9. With a partner, run a 10- to 15-yard (m) down-and-out pass pattern and catch the ball two of three times.

10. With a partner, run a 5- to 7-yard (m) hook pattern and catch the ball two of three times.

Optional Objectives

1. With a partner centering the ball, punt the football three consecutive times from a distance of 10 yards, using proper technique to another set of partners 15 yards (m) away.

2. Perform task 1 but at a distance of 20 yards. (m)

3. As a center, snap the ball four of six times through a tire positioned 5 yards (m) away.

4. Throw three of four consecutive passes beyond a target positioned 20 yards (m) away.

5. Throw four of six passes through a tire from a distance of 10 yards (m).

Lacrosse

Lacrosse is played in the United States, Australia, and England, and it is the national sport of Canada. In the United States, lacrosse is most popular in the Middle Atlantic states. Native Americans originated the game as early as the 16th century. They played each game with more than 100 players and often with as many as 1,000 players.

Lacrosse is a wide-open game that offers aerobic activity for players. The game can be easily modified to suit all skill and age levels. Examples of modified games are soft lacrosse, which is played in a gym or on a field with a lacrosse stick, ball, and goals; plastic lacrosse, which is played with modified plastic sticks and does not require as much skill as regulation lacrosse; box lacrosse, which is played in an arena or lacrosse box and requires the highest skill; and field lacrosse, which is played on a soccer-size field with a playing area behind each goal.

Sequence of Skills

The following is a breakdown of the skills necessary to successfully participate in lacrosse.

Gripping the Stick

Position the dominant hand at least halfway down the handle of the stick with the palm up. The other hand grips the stick at the end with the palm down. The stick should be held close to the body with relaxed hands and wrists.

Throwing

Bring the head of the stick backward while keeping the eyes focused on the target. Step with the opposite foot in the direction of the throw. Keep the elbows high and throw overhand to improve accuracy. The hands should be kept shoulder-width apart (do not push the ball). Break the wrists on follow-through; the head of the stick points to the target at the end of the throw.

Catching

Reach to meet the ball and "give" with the arms when the ball makes contact with the stick. Move the feet and align the body with the path of the oncoming ball. When catching, allow the dominant hand to slide on the handle for better stick control. The following techniques are used for catching balls at various levels:

1. Above the shoulders. Extend the crosse in the path of the ball. When the ball is caught, rotate the dominant hand sharply inward to protect it from a defender.

2. Between the shoulders and knees. Extend the face of the stick directly toward the ball. When the ball is caught, move the head of the crosse upward.

3. Below the knees. Rotate the handle outward and upward following the reception.

4. Head high. Put the face of the crosse directly in the path of the ball and drop the head and shoulders to the left. Rotate the crosse inward with the dominant hand upon reception.

5. Ball on the weak-hand side of the body. Bring the dominant hand across the body to put the crosse in the path of the ball. Cross the leg on the dominant side in front of the other leg while turning the body. After the catch, move the head of the crosse upward.

Scooping

When fielding ground balls, bend the knees and the back. Keep the butt end of the stick away from the midline of the body. Scoop up the ball with a slight shovel motion. As soon as the ball enters the stick, the player needs to break to the right or left to elude the defender.

Dodging

An offensive player who has the ball uses four basic dodges in an attempt to evade the defender:

1. Face dodge. The player with the ball fakes throwing the ball. When the crosse is about even with the head, it is twisted to the nondominant side. The offensive player then drops the shoulders and head slightly to the nondominant side, brings the leg on the dominant side across the other leg, and runs around the defender.

2. Change-of-pace dodge. The offensive player runs quickly in one direction, stops suddenly, and reverses directions. This pattern of movement continues until the opportunity arises to move past the defender.

3. Toss dodge. When the offensive player meets the defender, the ball is tossed on the ground or in the air past the defender. The player then moves past the defender and recovers the ball.

4. Force dodge. The offensive player approaches the defender with the back side of the body, causing the defender to retreat. The offensive player fakes to the left and right until an opportunity occurs to run past the defender.

Goaltending

The main duties of the goalie are to stop the ball, direct the defense, and start the offense by passing the ball out to the side or down the field. The goalie should have the feet shoulder-width apart and the knees bent. She or he should decrease the shooting angle for the offensive player by moving in an arc about 3 feet (1 m) from the goal mouth with short shuffle steps. When the ball is behind the goal, the goalie should operate in the same arc, favoring the ball side. If regulation equipment is lacking, the goalie can wear a softball catcher's mask and chest protector during shooting drills and games.

Ideas for Effective Instruction

This section highlights numerous ideas to allow for more effective instruction.

Equipment

The lacrosse ball is solid rubber and white or orange in color. It is slightly smaller than a baseball but just as hard. A modified ball, such as a tennis ball, may be appropriate when introducing lacrosse to beginners because the regulation ball can be dangerous for inexperienced players. When dropped from a height of 6 feet (1.8 m) above a solid wooden floor, it must bounce 43 to 51 inches (1.09 to 1.30 m). The lacrosse stick may be 40 to 72 inches (1.02 to 1.83 m) long except for the goalie's stick, which may be any length. For physical education, plastic sticks and balls are recommended. The net of the stick is between 6.5 and 10 inches (16 and 25 cm) wide. The net is made of gut, rawhide, or nylon. Players wear gloves and a helmet with a face mask in regulation lacrosse.

Game Play

Lacrosse is often played in football stadiums. In physical education classes, it can be played on any field, gym, or court with portable goals. The regulation field is 110 yards (101 m) long with the goals 80 yards (73 m) apart, leaving 15 yards (m) behind each goal. The field is 60 yards (55 m) wide, but current rules allow for the width to be reduced to 53-1/3 yards (49 m), which is the width of a football field (see figure 18.6). A rectangular box 35 by 40 yards (m) surrounds each goal and is called the goal area. The goal consists of two vertical posts joined by a top crossbar. The posts are 6 feet (1.8 m) apart, and the top crossbar is 6 feet (1.8 m) from the ground.

A team consists of 10 players, including a goalie, three midfielders, three attackers, and three defenders. The goalie guards the goal and receives support from the defenders. The defenders must remain in their half of the field. The midfielders serve as rovers and roam the entire field, operating as both offensive and defensive

18

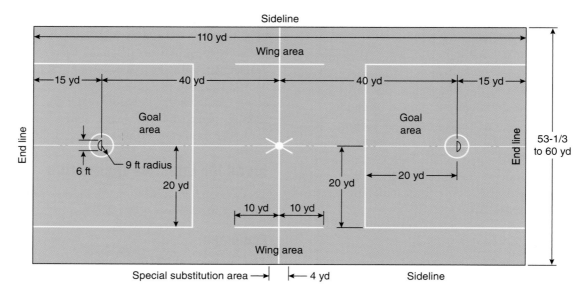

FIGURE 18.6 Markings and dimensions of a lacrosse field.

players. One of the midfielders handles each face-off and is called the center. The attackers remain in the offensive half of the field and attempt shots on goal. The attackers, defenders, and goalies often play the entire game, but the midfielders are often substituted.

Basic Rules

Face-Off

Play begins with a face-off (a draw) at the start of each quarter and after a goal is scored. The ball is placed between the back side of the opponents' sticks. All players must be in their assigned positions for the face-off. On signal, players in the wing areas are released, but all other players are confined until a player gains possession of the ball, the ball goes out of bounds, or the ball crosses either of the goal-line areas.

Off-Side Rule

Each team must have three players located on its attack half and four players on its defensive half of the field. This rule prevents piling up around the goal.

Out of Bounds

When a player throws or carries the ball out of bounds, the opposing team gets possession. But when a loose ball goes out of bounds as a result of a shot taken at the goal, it is awarded to the team whose player is closest to it at the exact time it rolls out of bounds.

Checking

Body checking to dislodge the ball is allowed in regu-lation play. Football blocks can be legally made on the player with the ball or on those going for a loose ball 5 yards (m) away. Checking an opponent with the body or stick is a common practice.

Illegal Procedure

An illegal procedure occurs when (1) an offensive player steps in the opponent's crease when the ball is in the attacking half of the field, or (2) a defending player with the ball runs through the crease.

Penalty Box

There are two types of fouls: personal and technical. Personal fouls are more serious than technical fouls and result in suspension for one to three minutes based on the severity and intention of the foul. Personal fouls are assigned for illegal personal contact, tripping, and unsportsmanlike conduct. Technical fouls usually result in a 30-second suspension from the game if the player does not have the ball. If the offending team has the ball, it loses possession of the ball.

Technical fouls are assigned for the following infrac-tions:

- Interfering with an opponent without the ball
- Holding any part of the opponent's body
- Pushing, particularly from the rear
- Acting illegally with the stick or playing the game without the stick
- Withholding the ball from play by lying on it or trapping it longer than necessary to gain control

Modified Rules

The regulation rules for lacrosse can be modified for use in a physical education setting where equipment and facilities are limited. The following are various modifications:

1. The number of players can be reduced to fewer than 10 so that players have more opportunity to handle the ball. Try assigning players to zones so that all students have the opportunity to play the ball. This modification helps prevent the dominant players from hogging the ball.

2. No stick or body contact is allowed. Encourage students to play the ball rather than the opponent. If a violation occurs, a penalty shot is awarded at the spot of the infraction.

3. Players must always keep both hands on their sticks. A penalty shot is awarded at the spot of an infraction.

4. If a ball goes out of bounds, the team that did not touch it last may run it in (grab the ball and run onto the field) or pass it in.

5. To steal the ball from an opponent, only stick-on-stick tactics may be used (no body contact).

6. To encourage teamwork and passing skills, two passes must be made before each shot on goal.

7. Play should be continuous without any stalling tactics. If problems develop in this area, add a time limit for holding the ball. For example, if the ball is held more than five seconds, it is turned over to the other team at the point of infraction.

8. The ball is a free ball when it is on the ground or in the air. Stick contact is allowed at those times without body contact.

Organization and Skill Work

A number of drills and lead-up games can be used to teach the fundamentals of lacrosse. See the units on basketball, soccer, and field hockey for additional activities that can be modified for lacrosse.

Drills

Throwing and Catching

1. Practice throwing the ball against a wall.
2. With a partner, begin throwing and catching in close proximity. Gradually move apart to throw longer passes.

3. Play keep-away in groups of three.

4. Use the jack-in-the-box drill. The jack is located midway between the two other players, each with a ball. The jack receives a pass from one of the end players, who is about 10 yards (m) away. The jack passes the ball back to that player, rotates 180 degrees, and receives a pass from the other end player. Change jack players frequently.

5. Use buddy passing for learning to pass on the move. Buddies jog around the area and pass back and forth to each other. Increase the challenge by giving each a ball.

6. Use the three-person rush and three-person weave, like the common basketball drills.

Scooping

Organize the class into groups of three. Two students are positioned on one side with the third student across from them, 30 feet (10 m) away. The ball is placed in the middle. One of the two students positioned on the same side runs to the ball, scoops it up, and carries it a few steps before dropping it. Continuing forward, the student runs behind the player on the opposite side. This player runs forward, scoops up the ball, carries it a few steps, drops it, and moves forward behind the remaining student. The pattern continues.

Shooting

A line of four to five students face the goal. A feeder behind the goal passes the ball to a shooter who cuts toward the goal or moves to a different position. After the shot on goal, the shooter becomes the feeder. Rotate goalies frequently.

Dodging

Practice all types of dodges with a partner, using one ball per two students.

Defending

Three players form a circle with a 20-yard (m) radius. Two offensive players try to keep the ball away from the defensive player while remaining in the circle.

Lead-Up Games

Three-Seconds, No Steps

Players cannot take any steps with the ball. In addition, if they hold the ball longer than three seconds, it is turned over to the other team.

Half-Court Lacrosse

The offensive team gets five attempts to score. Each

18

shot on goal counts as an offensive attempt. Offense and defense switch roles after the five attempts.

Five Touch

At least five members of a team must touch the ball before a goal can be scored.

Rugby

Rugby is a game that requires many of the skills used in football. The oval ball may be kicked, carried, or passed from hand to hand. Teams score by grounding the ball beyond the opponents' goal line or by kicking it between the opponents' goal posts. Rugby football started at Rugby School in England in 1823 and has been played in the United States since the late 19th century. It has evolved in its most common form to be played by two teams of 15 players each.

The object of the game is to advance the ball into the opponents' end zone, called the try zone. The ball must be touched to the ground by a player in the try zone to be awarded a try. As in American football, the ball is advanced by running the ball up the field. The opponents must stop the advance by tackling the player with the ball. Passing the ball backward is allowed in rugby; conversely, passing the ball forward or dropping the ball forward results in a turnover. Rugby is a fast-moving game because when a player is tackled to the ground, he or she has approximately one second to release the ball to begin play again. Several modifications, including touch instead of tackle, should be made to the official rugby rules for it to be considered an appropriate and safe activity for a physical education class.

Sequence of Skills

The following is a breakdown of the skills necessary to successfully participate in rugby.

Passing

Using both hands, hold the ball in front of body. Move hands laterally across body toward the target and step with foot closer to the target.

Receiving a Pass

Hold the hands outstretched and watch the ball. Give with the ball and bring it toward the body.

Running With the Ball

Keep eyes up to see teammates and opponents. Tuck the ball close to body and hold it in front with two hands.

Stay near teammates so that you can pass the ball quickly. Try to create space between you and the opponents while keeping teammates nearby.

Ideas for Effective Instruction

This section delineates the rules and equipment necessary to perform the many drills available for rugby. Most of the prerequisites for developing a sound rugby unit are listed and discussed.

Starting the Game

Teams set up on the center of the field. The defense must be 10 steps away from the ball. Play begins by rock–paper–scissors to determine possession, and an offensive player then taps the ball with his or her foot.

Rules

1. The ball may only be passed backward.

2. The ball carrier is the only person who may be touched or tagged.

3. Defenders should play person-to-person coverage, each guarding the person across from her or him.

4. If the ball is dropped or goes out of bounds, a scrum is formed. Offensive and defensive lines of four players each are formed. These players interlock arms and face each other. The referee rolls the ball between the lines. Each line attempts to roll the ball to a teammate behind them with their feet. After it is rolled back, the ball may be picked up and run with or passed.

5. Officially, the number of passes or touches that may be made before possession changes is unlimited. For physical education, teachers are encouraged to limit the number of passes or touches before possession changes (e.g., five). A defensive player's tags of the ball carrier is considered a touch. At this point, the defensive player should freeze, raise her or his hand and yell, "Touch!" At the spot of the touch, the offense places the ball on the ground for a roll ball.

6. For a roll ball, the offensive player who was touched or tagged places the ball on the ground and rolls it behind with her or his foot. The defense must remain 10 steps back and cannot move until the ball is lifted off the ground for a run or pass.

7. A try, worth 5 points, is scored if the offense taps

the ball on the ground in the opponents' try zone. The point value for the try can be changed at the discretion of the teacher.

8. A dropped goal, worth 3 points, is scored during open play. The ball must hit the ground immediately before it is kicked and pass through uprights and above the crossbar of the goal posts for it to count. Again, the point value for a dropped goal can be changed at the teacher's discretion.

Lead-Up Games and Learning Activities

The following lead-up games can be enjoyable ways to broaden the variety of activities in a rugby unit. They prevent one student from dominating a skilled position while others simply go through the motions of blocking.

Five Passes

The game can be played on a field; any large area is satisfactory. Players scatter on the field. The object of the game is for one team (identified by pinnies, which are side-markers worn by participants) to make five consecutive passes backward to five different players without losing control of the ball. This sequence scores a point. The defense may play the ball only and may not make personal contact. If a player takes more than three steps when in possession of the ball, the ball is given to the other team.

No penalty is assessed when the ball hits the ground. It remains in play, but this interrupts the five-pass sequence, which starts over. Students should call aloud the number of consecutive passes.

Kick Over

The game is played on a field with a 10-yard (m) try zone. Teams are scattered at opposite ends of the field. The object is to punt the ball over the other team's goal line. If the ball is caught in the try zone, no score results. A ball kicked into the try zone and not caught scores a goal. If the ball is kicked beyond the try zone on the fly, a score is made regardless of whether the ball is caught.

Play is started by one team with a punt from a point 20 to 30 feet (6 to 9 m) in front of its own goal line. On a punt, if the ball is not caught, the team must kick from the point of recovery. If the ball is caught, the team also kicks from the point of recovery. When the ball is caught, three long strides are allowed to advance the ball for a kick. Number the students so that they all kick in rotation and receive equal practice.

Final Play

Six to eight players on each team play in an area roughly half the size of a football field. Every play is the last play, which means that the play must score or the team loses the ball. No kicking is permitted, and players may pass at any time from any spot in any direction. There can be a series of passes or runs on any play.

The teams start in the middle of the field with possession determined by rock–paper–scissors. The ball is put into play by tapping. The player receiving the ball runs or passes to any teammate. No blocking is permitted. After each try, the ball is brought to the center of the field, and the opposing team resumes play. The ball is downed when the player is touched or the ball is dropped. Positions should be rotated each play.

Try Zone Force

The game is played on half of a football field. Ten feet (3 m) beyond each goal are three to five hoops. The teams must be identified with pinnies. The object of the game is to complete a try in one of the hoops.

To begin, the players line up at opposite ends of the field. One team begins by tapping at midfield. The game then becomes keep-away; one team tries to secure possession of the ball, and the other team tries to retain possession until they can make a successful pass or run to tap the ball to the ground in one of the hoops to score a point.

A player may run or pass backward when in possession of the ball. Loss of possession occurs when a player is touched or the ball is dropped.

Suggested Performance Objectives

The following are possible objectives that might be used in a rugby unit.

Core Objectives

1. Throw 10 backward passes to the chest area of a partner who is standing 10 yards (m) away. Practice correct holding, point of release, and follow-through techniques of passing.

2. Throw three or four consecutive passes beyond a target positioned 5 to 10 yards (m) away.

3. With a partner, punt the ball one time from a distance of 10 yards (m) using proper technique, to another set of partners 15 yards (m) away.

4. Perform task 3 except at a distance of 10 to 20 yards (m).

18

5. Punt the ball three consecutive times within the boundary lines of the field and beyond a distance of 20 yards (m).

6. With a partner, run and catch the ball two of three times.

Optional Objectives

1. With a partner, punt the ball three consecutive times from a distance of 10 yards (m), using proper technique, to another set of partners 15 yards (m) away.

2. Perform task 1 but at a distance of 20 yards (m).

3. Throw three of four consecutive passes beyond a target positioned 5 yards (m) away.

4. Throw four of six passes through a tire from a distance of 10 yards (m).

Soccer

Soccer, the most popular game in the world, is now rapidly gaining popularity among youth in the United States. Many sport clubs and programs run by organizations such as the YMCA, YWCA, Boys Clubs, and municipal recreation departments sponsor soccer teams, and many school districts include soccer in their intramural and athletic programs. Soccer is known throughout the rest of the world as football and is said to have originated in England around the 10th century, although the Romans played a similar game. Soccer was brought to the United States about 1870, and women played the game in an organized fashion in 1919. From a physical education standpoint, one of the advantages of soccer is that it is one of the few sports that depends primarily on eye–foot coordination for success. Almost all kickers in American football are soccer-style kickers. The long hours of kicking practice have contributed to their success.

The object of the game is to move the ball down the field by foot, body, or head contact to score goals and to prevent the opposing team from scoring. Soccer demands teamwork and the coordination of individual skills into group goals. Position play becomes important as students become more skilled. The game is excellent for cardiorespiratory development because it demands a great deal of running and body control.

Sequence of Skills

The skills of soccer are difficult to master, so instructors should teach the skills through short practice sessions. Many drills and lead-up games can be used to make the practice sessions interesting and novel.

Dribbling

The purpose of dribbling in soccer is like its purpose in basketball—to maintain control of the ball and advance it before passing it off to a teammate or shooting on goal. Players advance the ball by pushing it with the inside or outside of the front of the foot. The player should keep the ball close during the dribble, rather than kicking it and then running after it. Practice should involve learning to run in different patterns such as weaving, dodging, and twisting or turning with the ball.

Kicking

The purpose of the kick is to pass the ball to a teammate or to take a shot on goal. When passing, the performer plants the nonkicking foot alongside the ball with the foot pointing in the desired direction of the kick. The ball is contacted with the inside portion of the instep of the foot. The body weight shifts forward after the kick. The pass can also be made with the outside of the foot, although this kick will not move the ball as great a distance or with as much velocity. This kick is useful for passing without breaking stride or for passing to the side.

In kicking for a shot on goal, the procedure is similar to that used for the inside-of-the-foot kick. The nonkicking foot is planted alongside the ball with the toes pointing in the direction of the goal. The ball is contacted on the instep, followed by a snap of the lower leg and follow-through.

Trapping

The purpose of trapping is to deflect a moving ball and bring it under control so that it may be advanced or passed. Any part of the body may contact the ball except the hands or arms. Effective trapping results in the ball dropping in front of the body in position to be advanced. The sole-of-the-foot trap is most commonly used and is often called wedging. The ball is contacted between the foot and the ground just as the ball hits the ground. The ball is swept away under control immediately after the trap. The shin trap is done by moving to meet the ball just as it hits the ground in front of the lower legs. The ball is trapped between the inside of the lower leg and the ground. The chest trap is executed by arching the trunk of the body backward and giving with the ball on contact. The giving occurs with the body collapsing so that the ball does not rebound and instead drops in front of the player.

Heading

Heading can be an effective way of propelling a ball in the air to a teammate or on goal. The player should strike the ball with the head, rather than wait for the ball to hit the head. The player leans backward as the ball approaches. The head is up, and the eyes follow the ball. On contact, the head moves forward and strikes the ball near the hairline on the forehead. The body also swings forward to complete the follow-through.

Tackling

Tackling is used defensively to take the ball away from an offensive player who is dribbling or attempting to pass. The single-leg tackle is used when approaching an opponent directly, from behind, or from the side. Effective tackling depends in large part on anticipating the opponent's next move with the foot. One leg reaches for the ball, while the weight is supported on the other. The knees should be bent to maintain good balance. Focus should be on a clean tackle rather than on body contact. The object is to reach out and bring the ball to the body or to kick the ball away and then continue to pursue it.

Goalkeeping

Goalkeeping involves stopping shots by catching or otherwise stopping the ball. Goalkeepers should become adept at catching low, rolling balls; at diving on rolling balls; at catching airborne balls waist high and below; and at catching airborne balls waist high and above. The diving movements are the reason that the goalkeeper may choose to wear knee, elbow, and hip pads.

Students should get in the habit of catching low, rolling balls in much the same manner as a baseball outfielder: They get down on one knee, with the body behind the ball to act as a backstop, and catch it with both hands, fingers pointing toward the ground. If diving for a ball is necessary, the goalkeeper must throw the body behind it and cradle it with the hands. The body should always be between the goal and the ball.

The goalkeeper may also punch the ball to deflect it if it is not catchable. The ball can be deflected off other body parts if it cannot be punched.

After catching the ball, the goalkeeper throws it to a teammate. The ball can also be kicked, but this technique is less desirable because it is less accurate. Effective throws allow teammates to place the ball in action immediately.

Ideas for Effective Instruction

Soccer is played with two teams of 11 players each. For young players, however, decreasing the size of the teams is more effective. Smaller teams allow each player to handle the ball more often and to be an integral part of the soccer team.

Many of the drills, such as dribbling, kicking, and punting, can be learned individually. Having one ball per player will ensure the maximum amount of practice time. Many types of balls can be used besides a regulation soccer ball. Playground balls (8-1/2 inches [22 cm] in diameter) can be used if they are deflated slightly. Many students will play a more aggressive game of soccer if a foam-rubber training ball is used. They become less fearful of being hit by the ball and are willing to kick it with maximum velocity.

Field sizes can be reduced to increase the activity level of the game. The regulation game is played on a field with dimensions illustrated in figure 18.7. Soccer is meant to be played on grass. If a hard surface is used, deflate the ball so that it is not as lively and will not bounce so readily.

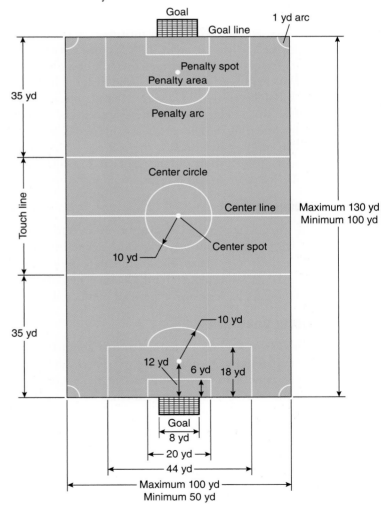

FIGURE 18.7 Regulation soccer field.

The drills used for developing soccer skills should help all participants achieve proper form. For example, if students are asked to pass and trap together, drills should focus on developing both skills. But students are sometimes asked to kick with velocity, so the students trapping are fearful of getting hurt. Those students then develop an improper trapping style.

Lead-Up Games and Learning Activities

The following lead-up games are excellent for getting students involved in soccer activities. The games emphasize participation and action. The lead-up activities are often more fun for most students than an actual soccer game because the activities develop specific skills in which students may lack expertise.

Circle Kickball

Players are in circle formation. They kick the ball with the side of the foot back and forth inside the circle. The object is to kick the ball out of the circle beneath shoulder level. A point is scored against each of the players where the ball left the circle. If the lost ball is clearly the fault of a single player, however, then the point is scored against that player only. Players who kick the ball over the shoulders of the circle players have a point scored against them. Players with the fewest points scored against them are the winners. The game works well with a foam training ball because the ball can be kicked at someone from a short distance and can be played with smaller teams to maximize practice opportunity.

Soccer Croquet

The game is like croquet in that the object is to hit one ball with another. One player kicks a ball and tries to hit another ball lying ahead. Kickers alternate until a hit is made, which scores a point for the kicker. The game continues until a player scores a specified number of points.

Soccer Keep-Away

Players are spaced evenly around a circle about 10 yards (m) in diameter. One player is in the center. The object of the game is to keep the player in the center from touching the ball. Players pass the ball back and forth as in soccer. If the center player touches the ball with a foot, the person who kicked the ball goes in the center. If a player makes an error, he or she changes places with the person in the center.

Diagonal Soccer

Two corners are marked off with cones 5 feet (1.5 m) from the corners on both sides, outlining triangular dead areas. Each team lines up and protects two adjacent sides of the square. The size of the area depends on the size of the class (more students require more playing area) and must be adjusted accordingly. Dead areas on opposite corners mark the opposing team's goal line. To begin competition, three players from each team move into the playing area in their own half of the space. These are the active players. During play, they may roam anywhere in the square. The other players act as line guards.

To score, the active players must kick the ball through the opposing team's line (beneath shoulder height). When a score is made, active players rotate to the sidelines, and new players take their places. Players on the sidelines may block the ball with their bodies but cannot use their hands. The team against which the point was scored starts the ball for the next point. Only active players may score. A point is scored for the opponents whenever any of the following occurs:

- A team allows the ball to go through its line below shoulder height.
- A team touches the ball illegally.
- A team kicks the ball over the other team's line above shoulder height.

Sideline Soccer

The teams line up on the sidelines of a large square with the end lines open. Three active players from each team are called from the end of the team line. These players remain active until a point is scored, and then they rotate to the other end of the line.

The object is to kick the ball over the end line, which has no defenders, between cones that define the scoring area. The active players on each team compete against each other, aided by their teammates on the sidelines.

To start play, a referee drops the ball between two opposing players at the center of the field. To score, the ball must be kicked last by an active player and must go over the end line at or below shoulder height. Regular rules prevail, with the restrictions of no pushing, holding, tripping, or other rough play. For out of bounds, the team on the side of the field where the ball went out of bounds is awarded a free kick near that spot. No score can result from a free kick. Violation of the touch rule also results in a free kick.

Line Soccer

Two goal lines are drawn 180 to 210 feet (55 to 65 m) apart. A restraining line is drawn 15 feet (5 m) in front of and parallel to each goal line. Field width can vary from 90 to 105 feet (25 to 35 m). Each team stands on one goal line, which it defends. The referee stands in the center of the field, holding a ball. At the whistle, three players (or more if the teams are large) run to the center from the right side of each line and become active players. The referee drops the ball to the ground, and the players try to kick it through the other team defending the goal line. The players in the field may advance by kicking only.

A score is made when an active player kicks the ball through the opposing team and over the end line, providing the kick was made from outside the restraining line. Place cones on the field corners to define the goal line. A player rotation system should be set up.

Line players act as goalies and are permitted to catch the ball. After being caught, the ball must be laid down immediately and either rolled or kicked. It cannot be punted or drop-kicked. One point is scored when the ball is kicked through the opponent's goal line below shoulder level. One point is also scored in cases of a personal foul involving pushing, kicking, tripping, or similar acts.

For illegal touching by the active players, a direct free kick is given from a point 12 yards (m) in front of the penalized team's goal line. All active players on the defending team must be standing to one side until the ball is kicked; only goalies may defend. A time limit of two minutes should be set for any group of active players. When no goal is scored during this time, a halt is called at the end of two minutes and players are changed.

An out-of-bounds ball is awarded to the opponents of the team that last touched the ball. Players use the regular soccer throw-in from out of bounds. If the ball goes over the shoulders of the defenders at the end line, any end-line player may retrieve the ball and put it into play with a throw or kick.

Minisoccer

The playing area can be adjusted depending on the size and skill of the players. A reasonable playing area is probably 150 by 225 feet (45 by 70 m). A goal, 24 feet (7 m) wide, is on each end of the field, marked by jumping standards. A 12-foot (3.5 m) semicircle on each end outlines the penalty area. The center of the semicircle is at the center of the goal.

The game follows the general rules of soccer. Each team has a goalkeeper. The corner kick, not played in other lead-up games, needs to be introduced. This kick is used when the ball goes over the end line but not through the goal and was last touched by the defense. The ball is taken to the nearest corner for a direct free kick, and a goal can be scored from the kick. If the attacking team last touched the ball, a goalkeeper kick is awarded. The goalkeeper puts the ball down and

placekicks it forward. Players should rotate positions at regular intervals. The forwards play in the front half of the field and the backs in the back half, but neither position is restricted to those areas entirely. All may cross the center line without penalty.

A foul by the defense within its penalty area (semicircle) results in a penalty kick, taken from a point 12 yards (m) distant, directly in front of the goal. Only the goalkeeper is allowed to defend. The ball is in play, and others wait outside the penalty area. Emphasize position play and encourage the lines of three to spread out and hold their positions.

Suggested Performance Objectives

The following objectives are designed for three skill levels: introductory, intermediate, and advanced. The objectives can be used in intermediate or advanced soccer classes or in a heterogeneously grouped class to challenge students of varying abilities.

Introductory Unit: Core Objectives

Kicking

1. Execute a push pass, low drive, and lofted drive. Satisfy the instructor that you understand these techniques and can execute them with the preferred foot. (All objectives may be performed with the preferred foot.)

Passing

2. Make three of five push passes from 10 yards (m) to your partner.
3. Make three of five low-drive passes from 15 yards (m) to your partner.
4. Make three of five loft-drive passes from 20 yards (m) to your partner.

Dribbling

5. Dribble 20 yards (m) twice with one or both feet. The ball must not stray more than 5 yards (m) from the feet.

Shooting

6. Shoot the ball with the preferred foot from 18 yards (m) into an empty goal 8 of 10 times.

Heading

7. Head the ball back to the tossing partner 8 of 10 times over a distance of 5 yards (m). The partner must be able to catch the ball.

18

Control of the Ball

8. Control three of five passes on the ground using the feet only.
9. Control three of five passes in the air using the head, chest, or thigh.

Game Situation

10. Show an understanding of pass, run, and control in a minisoccer game situation.

Rules of the Game

11. Score 80% on a rules-of-the-game test. One retake is permissible.

Introductory Unit: Optional Objectives

Goalkeeping

1. Save 6 of 10 shots from 18 yards (m). The shots must be on target.
2. Punt the ball 25 yards (m) four of five times.

Juggling

3. Keep the ball in the air with at least 10 consecutive touches. Hands or arms may not be used.

Field Dimensions

4. Diagram a full-size soccer field and give dimensions.

Grading

5. Achieve 13 passing grades for a unit pass. The instructor reserves the right to lower the number of required passing grades for the unit as necessary.

Intermediate Unit: Core Objectives

Kicking

1. Satisfy the instructor that you understand the techniques of the push pass, low drive, and lofted drive and can execute them with both feet.

Passing

2. Complete four of five push passes with the preferred foot from 10 yards (m). The passes must go between two cones placed 5 yards (m) apart. Complete three of five passes with the nonpreferred foot.

3. Complete four of five low-drive passes with the preferred foot from 10 yards (m). The passes must go between two cones placed 8 yards (m) apart. Complete three of five passes with the nonpreferred foot.
4. Complete four of five lofted-drive passes with the preferred foot from 10 yards (m). The passes must go over an obstacle 6 feet (1.8 m) high. Complete three of five passes with the nonpreferred foot.

Dribbling

5. Dribble through six cones over 25 yards (m) four times with no misses. Both feet must be used.
6. Dribble around an advancing goalkeeper and score a goal three of five times.

Shooting

7. Shoot the ball with the preferred foot from 18 yards (m) into an empty goal 9 of 10 times.
8. Shoot the ball with the nonpreferred foot from 18 yards (m) into an empty goal 7 of 10 times.

Heading

9. Head the ball to a serving partner 9 of 10 times over a distance of 10 yards (m). The partner must be able to catch the ball before it touches the ground.

Control of the Ball

10. Control four of five passes on the ground. Use the feet only.
11. Control four of five passes in the air. Use the head, chest, and thighs.

Corner Kick

12. Propel three of five corner kicks inside the penalty area. The ball may not touch the ground between the corner and the penalty area.

Throw-In

13. Throw the ball with two hands to a partner 10 yards (m) away four of five times. The partner must be able to catch the ball.

Juggling

14. Juggle the ball at least 10 consecutive times without allowing it to touch the ground.

Tackling

15. Successfully complete three of five front block tackles on a partner dribbling a ball at a walking pace.

Goalkeeping

16. Kick goal kicks at least 20 yards (m) in the air four of five times.

17. Punt the ball 25 yards (m) four of five times.

18. Save at least 6 of 10 on-target shots from the 18-yard (m) line.

Rules of the Game

19. Score 80% on a rules-of-the-game test. One retest is allowed.

Intermediate Unit: Optional Objectives

Officiating

1. Help officiate at least two games.

2. Know the roles of the referee and linesmen.

3. Know the correct positioning of officials at corner kicks, goal kicks, and penalties.

Volleying

4. Volley four of five goals from outside the goal area with the preferred foot.

Swerving or Bending the Ball

5. Bend the ball into the goal from the goal line three of five times with the preferred foot.

Penalty Kicks

6. Score 7 of 10 penalty kicks against a recognized peer goalkeeper.

Power and Distance Kicking

7. Score two of five goals into an empty goal from the halfway line.

Grading

8. Make 20 passing grades for a unit completion.

Advanced Unit: Basic Objectives

Passing

1. Make four of five push passes with the preferred foot from a distance of 10 yards (m) between two cones, placed 5 yards (m) apart, while running with the ball. Complete three of five passes with the nonpreferred foot.

2. Make four of five low-drive passes with the preferred foot from a distance of 15 yards (m) between two cones, placed 8 yards (m) apart, while running with the ball. Complete three of five passes with the nonpreferred foot.

Dribbling

3. Dribble through nine cones over 40 yards (m) and back to the start in 30 seconds or less. Use both feet and do not omit any cones.

4. Dribble around an advancing goalkeeper and score four of five times. Beat the goalkeeper to the left at least once and to the right at least once.

Shooting

5. Score 10 of 10 shots into an empty goal from outside the 18-yard line (m) with the preferred foot and score 9 of 10 shots with the nonpreferred foot.

6. Score 8 of 10 penalty kicks against a recognized peer goalkeeper.

7. Volley four of five goals from a serving partner, from outside the goal area, with the preferred foot, and three of five with the nonpreferred foot.

8. Serve or bend the ball from the goal line into the goal three of six times with the preferred foot. Place the ball within 1 foot (30 cm) of the line any distance from the post.

Heading

9. Head the ball back to a serving partner 9 of 10 times over a distance of 10 yards (m). The partner must be able to catch the ball.

10. Head the ball back and forth with a partner a minimum of 10 times without allowing the ball to touch the ground.

11. Head 9 of 10 serves from a partner into an empty goal from a distance of 10 yards (m).

Control of the Ball

12. Control 9 of 10 passes on the ground with the preferred foot.

13. Control 8 of 10 passes on the ground with the nonpreferred foot.

14. Control 9 of 10 passes from a partner with the head.

15. Control 9 of 10 serves from a partner with the chest.

16. Control 9 of 10 serves from a partner with the preferred thigh and 8 of 10 with the nonpreferred thigh.

18

Corner Kick

17. Kick 9 of 10 corner kicks into the penalty area with the preferred foot from the preferred side. The ball may not touch the ground between the corner and the penalty area.

18. Kick 8 of 10 corner kicks into the penalty area from the nonpreferred side (same conditions as task 17).

Throw-In

19. Throw the ball with both hands to a partner 15 yards (m) away 9 of 10 times. The throw must be placed so the partner is able to catch the ball with his or feet.

20. Throw the ball to a moving partner at least 10 yards (m) away. The partner must be able to catch the ball with his or her feet.

Juggling

21. Juggle the ball at least 20 times without it touching the ground. The head, foot, and thigh must be used. Start with the ball on the ground and get it into the air using the feet.

22. Juggle the ball with a partner. At least 10 passes must be made. No restrictions are placed on the number of touches by each player.

Tackling

23. Use a block tackle on a partner jogging with the ball 8 of 10 times successfully.

24. Use a slide tackle on a partner jogging with the ball three of five times successfully.

Goalkeeping

25. Kick four of five goal kicks at least 20 yards (m) in the air before the ball hits the ground.

26. Punt the ball at least 30 yards (m) four of five times.

27. Save 7 of 10 shots on target from outside the 18-yard (m) line.

Game Rules and Strategy

28. Demonstrate a thorough understanding of the rules of the game and principles of strategy.

Grading

29. Achieve a score of 80% or higher on a test covering the rules of the game. One retake is allowed.

Advanced Unit: Optional Objectives

Officiating

1. Officiate at least three games.

Grading

2. To complete the unit successfully, earn 26 passing grades.

Softball

Softball raises controversy among physical education teachers. Some instructors believe it is a game in which players catch only varicose veins from standing around. On the other hand, because softball is a less active game, adults often play it for many years. When participants develop skills, the game can be enjoyable. If skill is lacking, emphasis should be placed on development of skills and individual practice.

Softball can be taught effectively by using stations. This method gives students ample practice in many skills and avoids the situation in which students play only one position and specialize in skills. Softball can be played coeducationally, and many of the lead-up games make the activity enjoyable and suited to students' ability levels.

Sequence of Skills

The following is a breakdown of the skills necessary to successfully participate in softball.

Equipment and Facilities

Softball is played on a diamond with the dimensions shown in figure 18.8. Lines can be applied to the field with chalk or can be burned into the grass with a solvent that kills the grass and leaves a brown line.

Softball requires some specialized equipment. When ordering gloves, about 20% should be left-handed, and enough balls should be ordered so that each student has one. This quantity allows many drills to be undertaken without waiting for balls to be returned. Available equipment should include a set of bases for each diamond; bats of varying sizes (aluminum bats are the most durable); fielders' gloves; a catcher's glove, protector, and face mask; and batting tees. For less experienced players, the soft softball is desirable because it helps alleviate the fear of the ball that some players have. When a regulation softball is used, students often learn to dodge the ball rather than catch it. Some teachers have had success with the large 16-inch (40 cm) ball. It moves slower,

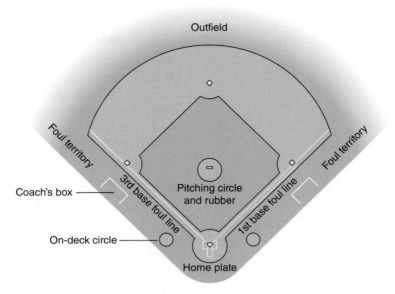

FIGURE 18.8 Softball diamonds.

cannot be hit as far, and allows the game to be played in a smaller area. The drawback is that the large ball is difficult to throw because of its size.

Catching

Catching involves moving the body into the path of the ball. Players hold their hands in two ways to catch fly balls. For a low ball, the fielder keeps the fingers in and the thumbs turned outward. For a ball above waist level, the thumbs are turned inward and the fingers are outward. The arms and hands extend and reach for the ball. As the ball comes into the glove, the arms, hands, and body give to create a soft home for the ball.

When catching grounders, the fielder moves into the path of the ball, then moves toward the ball, and catches it on a good hop. The fielder keeps the eyes on the ball and follows it into the glove. The feet are spread, the seat is kept down, and the hands are carried low and in front. The weight is on the balls of the feet or on the toes, and the knees are bent to lower the body. As the ball is caught, the fielder straightens up, takes a step in the direction of the throw, and makes the throw.

Throwing

The ball is generally held with a three- or four-fingered grip. Smaller students usually have to use the four-fingered grip. The fingers should be spaced evenly, and the ball should be held with the fingertips.

Because throwing is a complex motor pattern, breaking the skill into component parts is difficult. At best, throwing skills can be slowed down about 10% to

teach proper throwing technique. If a mature pattern of throwing has not been developed, students should focus on throwing for velocity rather than accuracy. After proper form has been learned, accuracy becomes the prime objective.

Overhand Throw

The player stands with the side opposite the throwing arm facing the target. The hand with the ball is brought back, over the head, at just above shoulder height. The nonthrowing hand is raised in front of the body. The weight is on the rear foot (away from the target), and the front foot is advanced toward the target. The arm comes forward with the elbow leading, and the ball is thrown with a downward snap of the wrist. The weight of the body shifts simultaneously with the throw to the front foot. The rear foot rotates forward, and the throwing hand ends facing the ground during the follow-through. The eyes should be kept on the target throughout the throw.

Sidearm Throw

The sidearm throw is like the overhand throw, except that the entire motion is kept near a horizontal plane. The sidearm throw, which uses a quick, whiplike motion, is for shorter, quicker throws than the overhand. The sidearm throw should be used only for short infield throws because the sideways motion causes a spin on the ball, which results in a curved path.

Underhand Throw

The underhand throw is used for short distances such as throwing to the pitcher covering first base or to the

453

person covering second base. The player faces the target, and the hand is swung backward with the palm facing forward. The arm is then moved forward in a pendulum swing with the elbow slightly bent. The weight shifts to the front foot during the toss.

Pitching

The pitcher must begin with both feet touching the rubber. The pitcher holds the ball in front of the body while facing home plate. The pitching hand is brought backward in a pendulum swing, and the wrist is cocked at the back of the swing. The pitcher steps forward on the opposite foot and swings the arm forward. The wrist is snapped, and the ball is released from the fingertips as the arm finishes moving in an upward, lifting fashion. The follow-through should be accompanied by a forward step of the foot on the throwing side so that the player is in a fielding position.

Fielding

Infielders should assume the ready position in a semi-crouch; the legs are shoulder-width apart, the knees are bent slightly, and the hands are on or in front of the knees. The weight is distributed evenly on both feet so that the player can move easily to the left or right. To field a grounder, the fielder moves as quickly as possible into the path of the ball, then moves forward, and plays the ball on a good hop. The glove should be kept near the ground and raised only as the ball rises. (A common mistake is not putting the glove down soon enough.) The eyes follow the ball into the glove, and the head is kept down. As the fielder catches the ball, she or he straightens up, takes a step in the direction of the throw, and releases the ball.

To catch a ground ball in the outfield, the player should employ the sure-stop method. This technique involves using the body as a barrier. The fielder drops to one knee to block the ball with the body if the catch is missed. This method should be used when runners are on base.

Batting

The bat is gripped with the dominant hand above and adjacent to the nondominant hand. The feet should be positioned comfortably apart, and the front of the body faces the plate. The knees are slightly bent, and the weight is distributed equally on both feet. The player holds the hands and the bat shoulder high and slightly behind the rear foot. The elbows are away from the body, the wrists are cocked, and the bat is held in an upward position. The ball should be followed with the eyes as long as possible. The stride begins by stepping toward the ball with the front foot. The hips are rotated, followed by the trunk and forward shoulder. The arms are extended, the wrists are snapped, and contact is made with the ball in front of the forward hip. Various grips on the bat can be tried, including the choke and long grip.

Batters should avoid using poor techniques such as lifting the front foot high off the ground, stepping back with the rear foot, dropping the elbows, or crouching or bending forward.

Base Running

After a hit, the batter should run hard with the head up and eyes looking down the base path. The runner moves past the bag, tagging it in the process, and turns out into foul territory, unless it is an extra-base hit. If it is an extra-base hit, the runner swings 5 to 6 feet (1.5 to 1.8 m) to the right of the baseline about two-thirds of the way down the base path and makes the turn toward second.

Runners on base must stay in contact with the base until the pitcher releases the ball. The runner faces the next base, with one foot forward and the other foot touching the base in a push-off position. The knees are flexed, and the upper body leans toward the next base.

Ideas for Effective Instruction

Safety is important, and throwing the bat is a constant issue. The members of the batting team should stand behind the backstop or on the side opposite the batter. Techniques to make the batter think about the bat are requiring the player to carry the bat to first base, to change ends of the bat before dropping it, or to place the bat in a circle before running. Eliminating sliding as an option in physical education is best because it can lead to injury if the proper equipment is not available. The catcher should always wear protective gear. In the early stages of practice, soft softballs can be used.

Many of the lead-up games were developed to increase the number of people who get to bat in each inning. One strategy for effective batting practice is to have a member of the batting team pitch so that the ball is easy to hit. Players should rotate positions often. Another idea is to have players rotate to a new position each inning. This approach has the effect of making the players supportive of each other, considering that the quality of the game depends on all the participating players.

Station teaching is effective for developing softball skills. This method ensures that participants have the opportunity to practice a wide variety of activities. Players who are particularly skilled in an activity can help others. Teachers should position themselves at a different station each day to ensure that they have instructed all students at all stations over a one- to two-week period. The following stations can be used by placing task cards at each station so that students know exactly what is expected of them.

Station 1: Catching Ground Balls

One person rolls, and the other person catches the ball.

1. Roll the ball straight to the person.
2. Roll the ball to the left side. Increase the distance.
3. Roll the ball to the right side. Increase the distance.
4. Roll the ball in an unpredictable direction.
5. Bat the ball in different directions. Start at 5 yards (m) and increase the distance up to 20 yards (m) from the fielder.

Station 2: Batting

1. Work in groups of three with a batting tee. One person fields, one bats, and the other shags the ball. Hit 10 balls.
2. Perform item 1, except pitch the ball to the batter.
3. As the batter, try placing the ball. Call the direction where you are going to hit the ball and then do so.

Station 3: Base Running

1. Run the bases using a circle technique. Have a partner time you.
2. Run the bases using a clover technique. Decide which you prefer and which allows you to run the bases faster.
3. Bunt and run to first. Have your partner time you.
4. Play the game In a Pickle in groups of three. (See game description in the section Lead-Up Games and Learning Activities.)

Station 4: Throwing

1. One person stands at each base, and a catcher is behind home plate. Practice throwing to each of the bases from each position. Rotate positions after each person has made three throws.
2. Throw the ball from the outfield. Throw the ball through a cutoff person. Make five throws and rotate to catcher position.

3. If you are not throwing, back up the other positions and act as a cutoff person.

Station 5: Fly Balls

1. Throw fly balls back and forth.
2. Vary the height and direction of the throw so that teammates must move into the flight of the ball.
3. Make teammates move backward and forward to catch the ball.
4. Bat some flies and play the game Five Hundred (see next section for description).

Lead-Up Games and Learning Activities

This section highlights numerous lead-up games and learning activities to help develop the skills to participate in softball.

Over-the-Line Softball

Over the line is a popular modified lead–up game incorporating softball skills. It is best as a three-versus-three game, but it can be modified to include more players. Offensive players try to hit the ball over a line about 20 yards (m) from home plate and into a zone that is 20 yards (m) wide and as long as possible. Batters do not run the bases. The game can be started from a batting tee, a soft toss, or a pitch from a teammate, depending on the skill level of the students. The ball must land on the fly in the zone area to be a base hit. Three hits equal a run, and a ball hit over the head of all the fielders is a home run. Outs are made by hitting two fouls, one strike, a fly caught by a fielder, or a hit ball landing on any of the lines or being a ground ball. All these rules can be modified for a local situation. A good area to play on is a marked football field because the yard lines can serve as the boundaries. The sideline of the field is the line to hit over, and home plate is backed up 20 yards (m). A fun variation is to divide the hitting zone into three areas with cones and award a single, a double, or a triple a ball that lands in the respective area.

Two-Pitch Softball

Two-pitch softball is played like regulation softball except that a member of the team at bat pitches. Every member of the team must have an opportunity to pitch. The batter receives only two pitched balls to hit, and a ball that is not hit fair is an out. The pitcher does not field the ball, and no balls or strikes are called.

18

In a Pickle

A base runner is "in a pickle" when caught between two bases and in danger of being tagged out. To begin, each of two fielders is on a base and a runner is in the middle. The goal is for the player in the middle to get to a base safely. If successful, that person scores a point. In either case, rotation occurs.

Pepper

This game is one of the older skill games in baseball. A line of four to six players is about 10 yards (m) in front of and facing a batter. A player tosses the ball to the batter, who attempts to hit controlled grounders back to him or her. The next player pitches. The batter stays at bat for a while and then rotates to the field.

Five Hundred

A batter hits balls to a group of fielders. The goal is to score 500 points. When a fielder reaches the total, that person becomes the new batter. Fielders earn 100 points for catching a fly ball, 75 points for catching a ball on one bounce, 50 points for catching a ball after two bounces, and 25 points for any other ball. The points must total exactly 500 or the total just earned is subtracted from the fielder's score. Points are also subtracted if a player makes an error.

Home Run

The critical players are a batter, a catcher, a pitcher, and one fielder. All other players are fielders and take positions throughout the area. The batter hits a pitch and on a fair ball must run to first base and back home before the ball can be returned to the catcher. The batter is out whenever any of the following occur: A fly ball is caught; a strikeout occurs; or, on a fair ball, the ball beats the batter back to home plate. The number of home runs per batter can be limited, and a rotation plan should be developed. The distance to first base can be varied based on the strength and skill of the players.

Work-Up

In this game players rotate positions each time an out is made. The game is played using regulation softball rules. Three batters are up at bat. After each out, the players move up one position, and the player making the last out goes to right field. The pitcher moves up to catcher, the person on first base moves to pitcher, and all others move up one position. If a fly ball is caught, the batter and the person catching the ball exchange places.

Babe Ruth Ball

The outfield is divided into three sections: left, center, and right field. The batter calls the field to which she or he will hit the ball. The pitcher throws pitches that the batter can hit easily. The batter remains in position as long as she or he hits the ball to the designated field. Field choices are rotated. The batter gets only one swing but may let a pitch go by. There is no base running.

Speedy Baseball

Speedy baseball is played like regular softball with the following exceptions:

1. The pitcher is from the team at bat and must not interfere with or touch a batted ball on penalty of the batter being called out.

2. The team coming to bat does not wait for the fielding team to get set. Because it has its own pitcher, the pitcher gets the ball to the batter just as quickly as the batter can grab a bat and get ready. The fielding team members must hustle to get to their places.

3. Only one pitch is allowed per batter. If batters do not hit a fair ball, they are out. The pitch is made from about two-thirds of the normal pitching distance.

4. No stealing is permitted.

5. No bunting is permitted. The batter must take a full swing.

Suggested Performance Objectives

The following are performance objectives that might be used in a softball unit.

Core Objectives

Throwing Tasks

1. Standing 45 feet (14 m) from a partner who is inside a hoop, complete five consecutive underhand pitches to that person without causing him or her to move outside the hoop.

2. Standing 60 feet (18 m) from a partner who is inside a hoop, complete five overhand throws to that person without forcing him or her to move more than 1 foot (30 cm) outside the hoop.

3. Be able to demonstrate the proper stance, windup, and delivery of the windmill pitch to the instructor.

4. From a designated area of the outfield, situated 150 feet (45 m) away for boys or 100 feet away (30 m) for girls, throw the softball through the air directly to a circle 10 feet (3 m) wide chalked in front of home plate. To count, the throw must bounce only once before landing or going through the circle. Student must make three of five throws to qualify for points.

5. Display pitching skills by striking out three or more batters or by allowing no more than five base hits in an actual game.

6. From an outfield or relay position, throw out a base runner at any base in an actual game.

Fielding Tasks

7. Demonstrating correct fielding stance, cleanly field five consecutive ground balls or fly balls hit by a partner.

8. Play a game of Pepper with a group of no more than six players, demonstrating good bat control, eye–hand coordination, and fielding skills.

9. Play a game of Five Hundred with no more than five players and demonstrate skills in catching flies and line drives and in fielding ground balls.

10. In an actual game situation, participate in a successful double play.

11. Perform a diving or over-the-head catch in an actual game situation.

Hitting Tasks

12. Watch a film or read an article on hitting.

13. Using a batting tee, hit five consecutive softballs, on the fly or on the ground, past the 80-foot (25 m) semicircle line marked off in chalk.

14. Execute proper bunting form and ability by dumping three of five attempts into designated bunting areas along the first or third baselines.

15. In an actual game, make two or more base hits.

16. Hit a triple or home run in an actual game.

17. During an actual game, observe an opponent or a teammate's swing. Write down the strong and weak points of that particular swing and bring them to the instructor's attention. The instructor will then match observations with your critique.

Optional Objectives

1. Make a diagram of an official softball diamond on poster board. Illustrate proper field dimensions.

2. On a piece of paper, show how batting average and earned run average are computed.

3. Watch a college or fast-pitch softball game on television or at the actual setting. Record the score, place, teams, and date of the contest. List the strengths and weaknesses of each team, and note how weaknesses could be corrected.

4. Umpire a game for three or more innings.

5. Keep accurate score in an official score book for three or more innings.

Speed-a-Way

The game of speed-a-way was originated in 1950 by Marjorie Larsen, but it spent 10 years in experimental stages before its arrival on the field. It is a dynamic game that combines the challenges of soccer, basketball, speedball, field ball, and field hockey. It was created as a game that could serve as a lead-up for field hockey and bring enjoyment to participants without their having to learn complicated rules and techniques.

Speed-a-way is intended for students from middle school through college. With the emphasis on student success, the game employs a variety of fundamental movements such as running, throwing, catching, and kicking. Participants have many opportunities for vigorous activity, competition, and team cooperation.

The area in which speed-a-way is played is the same as that used for field hockey. The recommended size is 100 by 60 yards (91 by 55 m). This rectangle is divided into four parts with alleys and striking circles. Speed-a-way has an official ball, but a soccer or playground ball can be substituted. The game consists of four quarters of 8 minutes each, with a 2-minute rest period between quarters and a 10-minute rest period between halves. Substitutions can be made when the ball is dead.

Speed-a-way is played with two teams of 11 players. Each player wears a set of flags. Players line up on their half of the field at the beginning of each quarter and after each score. The ball is put into play by a push kick backward from the center of the field. The object of the game is to advance the ball through the opponent's territory by means of kicking, dribbling, heading, or

18

shouldering a ground ball; by throwing an aerial ball; or by running with an aerial ball. A field goal (3 points) is scored by kicking the ball between the opponent's goalposts from within the striking circle. (If football or speedball goalposts are used, a dropkick over the bar scores 4 points.) A touchdown (2 points) is scored by running across the goal line with the ball or by passing it to a teammate who is already over the goal line but not between the goalposts. An aerial ball is one that has been converted from the ground with the feet.

Rules

1. The defense can pull the flags of offensive players only when they are carrying the ball.

2. If flags are pulled before the ball leaves the offensive player's hand, the defensive team gains possession. Everyone moves 5 yards (m) away before play can be continued.

3. To carry the ball in his or her hands, a player must first legally lift the ball up and catch it. This action is usually done with the feet. A player can lift the ball to a teammate, or a player can lift the ball to him-or herself with the feet.

4. If the ball goes out of bounds over the goal line (not between the goalposts) and is last touched by the offense, the goalie gets possession. The goalie may punt, placekick, throw, or run the ball out of the goal area. After the goalie leaves the striking circle, the opposition can pull the goalie's flag. In the striking circle, however, the goalie is safe. Goalies may go anywhere on the field they desire, but they can use their hands only inside the striking circle.

5. If the ball goes out of bounds over the goal line (not between the posts) and is last touched by the defense, the offense receives a corner kick on the side where the ball went out.

6. When a ball goes out of bounds over a sideline, a player from the opposing team uses a two-handed overhead toss to put the ball in play.

7. A player holding the pivot foot in position cannot have her or his flag pulled for three seconds.

8. No contact is allowed during guarding. A player can be guarded by only one player.

Safety Precautions

Because the game of speed-a-way is fast moving, the safety of the game depends on the instruction that players receive and the quality of officiating. A player should be taught that good position is an essential safety factor in speed-a-way. Good body control and skill in the fundamentals of running, starting, and stopping quickly should be encouraged to eliminate body contact. Players should be taught how to control the ball, to evade and dodge an opponent, to throw the ball, and to lift the ball to another teammate. The technique of guarding or tackling an opponent who is in possession of the ball is most important in the prevention of unnecessary body contact. Team play and its value in preventing injury should be emphasized. Players should always be safety conscious and follow the rules.

During the game, referees should be alert to the dangerous elements of the game. All harmful body contact—such as obstructing, pushing, charging, tripping, and dangerous kicking (kicking an opponent or kicking the ball directly into an opponent)—should be called immediately. Speed-a-way can be a low-risk and nonthreatening game when taught and conducted with safety as a priority.

Lead-Up Games and Learning Activities

This section highlights numerous lead-up games and learning activities to help develop the skills to participate in speed-a-way.

Circle Kickball

Ten to twenty players form a circle and use a speed-a-way, soccer, or playground ball. The skills used are kicking and trapping. Players kick the ball back and forth inside the circle. The object of the game is for a player to kick the ball out of the circle below the shoulder level of any other circle player. Each time a player achieves this, he or she collects a point. Any player who kicks the ball over the shoulders of a circle player gives back a point already earned.

Croquet Ball

Students play in pairs or groups of three. Each student has a ball. The object of this game is for one ball to hit another. Each hit scores a point. The first player kicks her or his ball out 10 to 15 yards (m) ahead. The next player kicks her or his ball and tries to hit the ball lying ahead. Alternate kicking continues until a hit is made. The game continues until a player scores a designated number of points. If three play, turns are taken in sequence. If a successful hit is made on one ball, the kicker gets an immediate try at the other.

Touch Ball

Eight to ten students form a circle, and one player is in the center. One ball is used. The students are spaced around a circle about 10 yards (m) in diameter. The ball is thrown or passed back and forth. If the center player touches the ball, the circle player who last touched the ball moves into the center.

Pin Kickball

Two teams of 7 to 10 players face each other 20 yards (m) apart. Six or seven pins and two balls are needed. The object is to knock down the pins. Each pin is worth a point. Kicks should be made from the line behind which the team is standing. Players should concentrate on performing controlled traps and accurate kicks. The number of players per team and the number of pins used can be varied.

Team Handball

Team handball is an exciting and challenging game that combines skills from basketball, soccer, water polo, and hockey. It involves running, dribbling, jumping, passing, catching, throwing, and goaltending. The object of the game is to move a small soccer ball down the field by passing and dribbling and then to throw the ball into a goal area that is 3 meters wide and 2 meters high. The game is relatively simple to learn, and both sexes can enjoy it. Team handball is inexpensive to add to the curriculum and can be played indoors, outdoors, or on a tennis court. Virtually any space can be adapted or mod-ified for team handball. The play is rapid and involves continuous running, so the sport is a good cardiorespiratory activity. Because the game is relatively new to the United States, many students will be inexperienced. A unit on team handball can provide students with a fresh challenge and increased motivation, and teachers should enjoy introducing a new activity.

Basic Rules

In regulation play, each team has six court players and one goalie. The six court players cover the entire court. A player is allowed three steps before and after dribbling the ball. There is no limit on the number of dribbles. Dribbling, however, is discouraged because passing is more effective. A double dribble is a violation. A player can hold the ball for only three seconds before passing, dribbling, or shooting. No player except the goalie can kick the ball in any way.

The court is marked (see figure 18.9) with a 6-meter goal area, a 7-meter penalty line, and a 9-meter free-throw line. The goal is 2 by 3 meters. The goal area inside the 6-meter line is for the goalie only. Other players are not allowed in this area. The 7-meter line is used for a major penalty shot, and the 9-meter line is used for a minor penalty shot. A regulation court is 20 by 40 meters.

One point is awarded for a goal. Violations and penalties are similar to those of basketball. A free throw is taken from the point of the violation, and defense must remain 3 meters away while protecting the goal. A penalty throw is awarded from the 7-meter line for a major violation. A major violation occurs when an

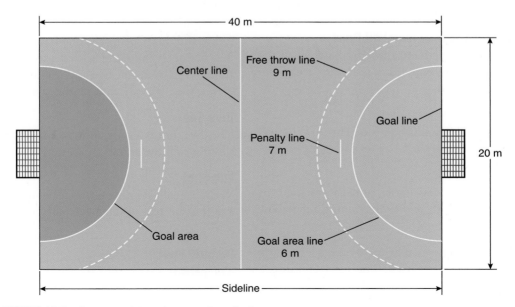

FIGURE 18.9 Court markings for team handball.

offensive player who is inside the 9-meter line in a good shooting position is fouled. During a penalty throw, all players must be behind the 9-meter line.*

The official team handball looks like a small soccer ball. The men's ball is 23 inches (58 cm) in circumference, and the women's ball is 21 inches (53 cm). A smaller minihandball is available for younger students. Most sporting goods dealers sell handballs. Playground balls and small volleyballs can be substituted if necessary. The goals can be improvised by using boundary cones, tape on the wall, rope through a chain-link fence, soccer goals, field hockey goals, or homemade regulation goals. The floor lines can be established by marking the floor with tape or by putting boundary cones along the area where the lines should be. A basketball court can be easily modified for team handball by setting boundary cones along the goal area and by using the free-throw lane for the width of the goal.

*Specific rules of team handball are available from the United States Team Handball Federation, www.usateamhandball.org.

Sequence of Skills

Team handball is a good unit to follow basketball, soccer, or water polo because it uses many of the same skills and techniques.

Passing

Team handball is a passing game, and many different passes can be used for short and medium ranges. The passing fundamentals are like those of basketball.

Chest, Bounce, and Overhead Passes

All are two-handed passes, like those in basketball.

One-Handed Shoulder or Baseball Pass

This pass is like an overhand throw in baseball. If the student cannot grip the ball, it can rest on a flexed hand with the fingers spread.

Sidearm Pass

This pass is like the shoulder pass except that the ball is released to the side of the body to avoid a defender.

Shovel Pass

This one- or two-handed underhand pass is used for releasing the ball quickly and thus avoiding a defender.

Handoff Pass

This pass is like the one used by a quarterback handing off the ball to a running back. The receiver forms a pocket for the ball.

Roller Pass

The ball is simply rolled along the floor to a teammate when all other passing lanes are blocked.

Hook Pass

This pass is like the hook shot in basketball in that the passer hooks the ball over or around a defender. A jump may be added before the pass.

Jump Pass

Usually made with a shoulder pass, the jump pass occurs when the passer jumps over or around a defender and throws the ball.

Behind-the-Back Pass

Like the basketball pass, this pass can be effective because the smaller ball is easier to control than a basketball.

Dribbling

Dribbling in handball is the same as the basketball skill, but the ball is harder to control because it is small and the ball surface is uneven. Players need to get used to taking the legal three steps before and after dribbling, as well as the three-second holding rule. Dribbling should be practiced some but in general should be discouraged in team handball.

Goal Shooting

All the aforementioned passes can also be used for shots on goal. The following shots are the most popular.

Jump Shot

Because the offensive player can jump outside the goal area and land in the goal area after a shot, the jump shot is the most popular shot. Shooters run three steps, jump, and shoot, using the one-handed shoulder throw. The action is the same as that used for a one-handed shoulder pass, except that it is a shot on goal. The shot can be used with or without a defender.

Dive Shot

The dive shot is a good shot on either wing because the shooter can dive or fall away from an opponent.

Lob Shot

When a goalie comes out too far to defend, the shooter can lob the ball up and over the goalie's outstretched arms.

Penalty Shot

The penalty shot is the one-on-one free shot with only the goalie defending. The shooter must keep one foot stationary and cannot touch the seven-meter penalty line until the ball is thrown. The ball must be shot within three seconds. The goalie must be 3 meters or more away from the shooter. The shoulder or sidearm throw is usually most efficient for this shot.

Behind-the-Back

The shooter can fake a shot to the right and then bring the ball behind the back and the defender for a shot. The behind-the-back shot can be executed to either side.

Goal shooting involves the following general principles:

1. Attack the high or low corners on each shot.
2. Shoot primarily between the 6- and 9-meter lines.
3. Find the open offensive player to take the shot.
4. Do not force a shot that is not open.
5. Do not shoot too far down on the wings because the angle is too extreme.
6. Use the floor or ground to bounce shots into the goal.
7. Try jump shots toward the goal, which are usually effective. The ball must be released before the shooter lands in the goal area.
8. Develop a wide variety of goal shots.

Goaltending

The position of goalie, the most important defender on the team, requires quick hands and feet and fast reaction time. All parts of the body can be used to deflect shots. The goalie also starts the offense after saving shots. The goalie needs to learn how to cut down shooting angles by moving out from the goal, depending on where the ball is located on the court. Goalies should practice saving shots in all four corners of the goal. They need to understand all the rules governing the goalkeeper.

Defensive Strategy

The defensive strategy is like that used in basketball in that person-to-person and zone defenses are popular. Beginning players should start with the person-to-person defense and learn how to stay with an offensive player. Zone defenses can be 6-0, 5-1, 4-2, and 3-3; each person plays an area or zone. The back players in the zone are back against the goal line, and the front players are just inside the 9-meter line. The zone rotates with the ball as passes are made around the court.

Offensive Strategy

The offense starts the game with a throw-on (pass to a teammate) from the center line. A throw-on also initiates play after each goal. All six offensive players line up at the center line, and one teammate throws the ball to another. The defense is in position, using either a zone or person-to-person defense. Offensive strategy is like that used in basketball with picks, screens, rolls, and movement to open up shots on goal. With a zone defense, short, quick passes are made in an overloaded portion of the zone.

Ideas for Effective Instruction

Set up learning stations for passing, shooting, goaltending, dribbling, and defensive work. The performance objectives in this section are useful for structuring practice time at each station. Students can play with Nerf or comparable foam-rubber balls, playground balls, and volleyballs to get more practice attempts and to help beginning goalies perfect their skills. Group drills from basketball are applicable to team handball defense, offense, passing, and dribbling. Include various instructional devices for targets in passing, timing for dribbling through cones, or narrowing the goal area for shots to the corners. Penalty shots should be practiced daily. Competitive drills are enjoyable and motivating for most students.

Modified Games

This section highlights numerous modified games to help develop the skills to participate in handball.

No Bounce, No Steps, and No Contact

Students are forced to pass the ball rather than dribble. The walking or traveling rule from basketball is in effect because students are usually comfortable with it. The no-contact rule gives the offense an advantage. The three-second rule should remain in effect to force quick passes and deter holding the ball.

Three Bounces, Three Steps, and No Contact

This game is closer to the regulation game and provides a gradual adjustment to the team handball rules. A variation would have the three-bounce and three-second rules but with no steps allowed. Getting students used to the three-step rule is difficult.

Sideline Team Handball

Sideline handball can be played when space is limited and the class is crowded. Extra team members spread out along each sideline. These sideline players can receive passes from teammates and can help pass the ball down the court. Sideline members can only pass the ball, however, and the three-second rule applies to

18

them. One sideline can be devoted to one team, and the other sideline to the other team. A challenging variation is to have players of both teams on each sideline. This distribution forces the active players to sharpen their passing skills.

Five Passes

This game is similar to keep-away, but the object is to make five consecutive passes. As soon as these have been made, the ball is turned over to the other team. Students are not allowed to travel with the ball. Two or three dribbles may be allowed between passes. Players may hold the ball for only three seconds. This game should be played on a team handball court with the proper handball.

Suggested Performance Objectives

1. Dribble the ball with the right hand (standing position) 10 consecutive times.
2. Perform task 1 but with the left hand.
3. Dribble the ball with the right hand (moving forward) from the center line to the goal line without losing the dribble.
4. Perform task 3 but with the left hand.
5. Pass the ball to a partner standing 10 feet (3 m) away with a two-handed chest pass to the chest area (between chin and waist) 8 of 10 times.
6. Pass the ball to a partner standing 10 feet (3 m) away with a two-handed bounce pass to the waist area 8 of 10 times.
7. Pass the ball to a partner standing 10 feet (3 m) away with a two-handed overhead pass to the chest area 8 of 10 times.
8. Pass the ball to a partner standing 10 feet (3 m) away with a one-handed overhead pass to the chest area 8 of 10 times.
9. While running from the center line, alternately pass a two-handed chest and bounce pass that a partner can catch running at a parallel distance of 12 feet (3.5 m). Three of four passes should hit the partner.
10. While standing 7 meters from the goal, hit three of five goals.
11. Defend three of five attempted shots taken by a partner from a distance of 7 meters.
12. Dribble the ball with the right hand (moving forward) from the center line to the goal area

without losing the dribble. Jump up and make a goal three of five times.
13. From 6 meters away, hit a target five consecutive times with the following passes: roller, hook, jump, shovel, one-handed shoulder, sidearm, and behind the back.
14. From 9 meters away, hit two of five goals.
15. From 9 meters away, defend four of five goal shots.
16. Dribble through a set of six cones in 25 seconds.

Track and Field

Track and field events consist of running, jumping, weight throwing, and vaulting. Running events include sprinting short distances, running middle and longer distances, and hurdling over barriers. Relay races with four team members are run over various distances. The jumping events include the high jump, long jump, and triple jump. The throwing events are the shot put, discus, javelin, and hammer throw. The vaulting event is the pole vault.

In the United States, instruction in track and field activities as part of the physical education program began in the late 1890s. Both men and women have been interested in pursuing these events for various reasons. The tremendous variety of skills necessary for running, jumping, throwing, and vaulting provides an exciting challenge.

Track and field should continue to be an important part of the secondary school physical education program. Students with different body types can find success in some track and field activity. All students should have the opportunity to explore and experience the wide variety of challenges of this unit.

Secondary schools have changed to metric distances for the running events. These distances vary some from state to state and from men's events to women's events. The men's running events usually include the following: 100, 200, 400, 800, 1,600, and 3,200 meters; 400-, and 1,600-meter relays; 110-meter-high hurdles; and 400-meter intermediate hurdles. The field events for men usually include the high jump, long jump, triple jump, pole vault, shot put, discus, javelin, and hammer throw (only in certain states). Women's running events are similar to the men's, but the women run only one hurdle race, which is 100 meters. The 1,600-meter relay race is sometimes replaced with a medley relay consisting of 100, 100, 200, and 400 meters. In the field events, the women do not pole-vault, triple jump, or throw the hammer. Note that women are finally being allowed officially to run longer distances (such as 1,600 and 3,200 meters). The 1984 Olympic Games in Los Angeles marked the first Olympic marathon for women.

Sequence of Skills

Because track and field is a highly specialized area that includes many specific skills and techniques for each of the running, jumping, vaulting, and throwing events, adequately covering all these activities in a limited space is difficult. Several good texts are available with in-depth information about specific events and the skills involved. Much of what should be taught will depend on the abilities of the students, the length of time allotted to the unit, and the equipment available for instruction. Teachers developing units for track and field should refer to the suggested readings.

Ideas for Instruction

Each event in track and field can serve as a learning station for students. After students are introduced to the events, they can rotate from station to station and work on each activity. Keep a clipboard at each station with records of each day's best performances in an activity. The day-to-day records can be used for motivation and as evidence of individual improvement. A class track meet is an enjoyable culminating activity. Teams can be organized to complete in a regulation dual meet.

Volleyball

Because volleyball was adopted as an Olympic sport in 1964, it has gained a great deal of visibility through the media. It continues to grow in popularity in the United States and throughout the world. Beach volleyball, the newest edition of the sport, is also an Olympic sport, and it has added to the popularity of the sport. The sport has adopted a new rally-scoring method in which scoring occurs for either team on every serve. In the United States, volleyball is a vigorous sport that many pursue in school, club, and recreational leagues. Volleyball is challenging, lends itself to coeducational participation, and can be modified in several ways to suit the abilities of many students.

Most states offer competitive volleyball for girls in the secondary schools, and many states are adding volleyball for boys. Secondary physical education programs should offer coeducational volleyball classes to encourage the participation of both boys and girls. Because of the increased recreational volleyball offerings in YMCAs, community centers, and municipal recreational programs, students will be able to participate in and enjoy this activity for many years.

Sequence of Skills

Volleyball is difficult to play without a basic skills foundation. Help students master these skills before beginning regulation games. Devising modified games for beginning students is important because they will not be able to play a regulation game. (A few students would dominate, and the remaining students would quickly become frustrated.) The type of ball, the height of the net, and the rules of the game can all be adjusted to ensure a successful experience for beginning students.

Serving

Underhand Serve

The underhand serve position starts with the left leg forward and both knees bent slightly. The ball is held in the left hand about waist height. The right arm starts with a long backswing and then comes forward, the right hand striking the ball just below the midline. The striking hand can be open or slightly closed, and the heel of the hand should contact the ball. The body weight is transferred from the rear foot to the front foot as the ball is contacted. The arm swing follow-through should be in a straight line.

Overhand Serve

The overhand floater serve has no spin on the ball. The legs are staggered, with the left leg forward. The ball is held about shoulder height with the left hand under the ball and the right hand behind it. The ball is tossed 2 to 3 feet (60 to 90 cm) up above the right shoulder. The right arm is brought back, behind the ear, and then extended fully to hit the ball. The heel of the hand strikes the ball slightly below the midline. Little follow-through is used because the ball should float or wobble like a knuckle ball.

Students who lack the strength or ability to get the ball over the net can begin serving closer to the net, and the net can be lowered. As students develop skill, they should move back gradually to the regulation distance. Targets can be placed on the floor for work on accuracy as skill improves.

18

Passing and Setting

This skill involves moving the ball from one teammate to another. Forearm passes are used primarily for receiving a serve or a spike. Overhand set passes are used primarily for setting the ball into position for a spike. All passes require quick footwork while keeping a low center of gravity, which is necessary for getting under the ball.

Forearm Passes

In the forearm bump pass, the ball is hit off the forearms. The feet are about shoulder-width apart, and one foot is ahead of the other. The knees are bent, and the arms are extended forward. The forearms are rolled outward to provide a flat, parallel surface for the ball. The elbows must be locked together on contact with the ball. The upward movement of the arms and legs depends on the speed of the ball and on the required distance of the pass. Passers must watch the ball carefully. Forearm passes can be made in different directions and with one arm if necessary.

Overhand or Set Passes

In overhand passes, the body is set up under the ball, which is directly above the passer's nose. The hands are cupped to form a triangle-shaped window. The knees are bent, and the legs are about shoulder-width apart and in a stride position. The ball is contacted simultaneously with the fingers and thumbs of both hands. The legs, body, and arms uncoil into the ball in one smooth movement. Sets can be made from a front position facing the target and from a back position with the back to the target.

Spiking

Spiking is an offensive maneuver that involves hitting the ball above the net and downward into the opponent's court. A spiker usually takes three or four steps toward the net. A final step with the right foot followed by a close step with the left foot precedes takeoff. With both feet together, the spiker then jumps vertically straight up. The arms swing forward during the jump. As the arms come forward to about shoulder height, the back begins to arch, and the right arm is cocked behind the head. The left arm starts the forward motion downward, and the right arm uncoils and attacks the ball. The elbow leads the striking arm and shoulder. The striking hand is open and rigid, and the palm of the hand strikes the ball.

Blocking

Blocking is a defensive maneuver used to stop the ball from going over the net. Any of the three players on the front line can block. Blockers can jump and reach over the net, as long as the ball has not been touched by the offensive player. Blockers should leave the floor slightly after the spiker. The takeoff starts with the legs bent at the knees. After the jump, the arms extend fully upward, as high as possible. The fingers are spread as wide as possible. The hands are held rigid and no wider apart than the width of the ball. As the blocker comes down, the arms are drawn back to the body, and the feet and legs absorb the landing.

Ideas for Effective Instruction

Volleyball lends itself to station work on passes, sets, serves, and spikes. The performance objectives listed at the end of this unit can be posted on task cards at the various stations. A class period could include work on the performance objectives, group skill work, and a modified game. The height of the net, the rules of the game, and the type of ball used can be adjusted so that inexperienced students can keep the ball in play. Foam rubber balls and beach balls are excellent for beginners.

Many passing, setting, and serving activities can be done with partners. Having one partner toss the ball and the other partner pass or set is a good introductory drill. A smooth wall is useful for passing and setting practice, and small groups in a circle can also be effective for passing and setting. For serving practice, several players can line up along both baselines of a court and serve several balls at a time. Servers can practice anywhere along the baseline. Beginning servers should always move closer to the net.

Setting and spiking drills can be arranged with a setter in the center forward position and a line of spikers in either the on-hand or off-hand position. The spiker tosses the ball to the setter and awaits a setup for a spike. Several ball chasers on the other side of the net can be useful. Net recovery shots can be practiced on a properly stretched net. One partner tosses the ball into the net, and the other player tries to recover the ball with a forearm pass.

Competitive situations are fun for drill work (e.g., sets in a row, passes with a partner, serves to a target area, or spikes to an area). These competitive challenges can be individual, with partners, or among small groups. The objectives included here offer many challenges that can be modified for students of different ability levels.

Lead-Up and Modified Games

This section highlights numerous lead-up and modified games to help develop the skills to participate in volleyball.

Leader Ball

Organize students into several teams. The leader of each team stands about 5 yards (m) away from teammates. The teammates can be in single file or standing side by side facing the leader. The leader uses a forearm pass or set and hits the ball to the first person in line. That person hits the ball back to the leader and goes quickly to the end of the line. The object is to hit the ball to all teammates quicker than the other teams do.

Zigzag Relay

Half of the players on one team stand side by side about 2 to 3 yards (m) apart and face the other half of their team. The ball is started at one end and passed or set, back and forth, down the line across a distance of 5 yards (m). The object is to control the ball and move it down the line quickly. The winning team is the fastest in getting the ball up and down the line to all team members. More than one ball can be added for variety.

Keep It Afloat

A group must keep the ball up in the air or against a wall for a specified amount of time. The group can be in a circle or arranged single file for the wall drill. Passes, sets, or both can be used.

Beach Ball or Nerf Ball Volleyball

Regulation rules are followed except that the server must move up close to the net. A beach ball or Nerf ball is easier to control than a regular volleyball.

One-Bounce Volleyball

Regular rules are followed except that the ball can bounce one time on each side. The bounce can occur after the serve, pass, or set. A variation of this game is to allow two or three bounces.

Volley Tennis

The game can be played on a tennis court or on a volleyball court. The net is set up on the ground, as in tennis, and the ball is put in play with a serve. It may bounce once or can be passed directly to a teammate. The ball should be hit three times before going over the net. Spiking is common because of the low net.

Sitting or Kneeling Volleyball

Sitting or kneeling volleyball is a good indoor game to play on a mat or in the gym. The net is lowered according to the general size and ability level of the players. An overhead pass starts the game. Court size and number of players can vary.

Serve and Catch

Serve and catch is started with a ball on each side of the net. Several balls are served at the same time, and all balls must be caught on the other side. After the balls are caught, they can be served from the opposing serving area. The object is to catch the ball and quickly serve so that the opponent cannot catch the ball. A scorer from each side is necessary.

Rotation Under the Net

The game, played with two, three, or four people on a team, starts with one team on each side of the net and with two or three other teams waiting in line to enter the game. The teacher begins the game by tossing the ball up on either side of the net. The ball must be hit three times, with the third hit going over the net. No spiking is allowed. The winning team rotates under the net, a new team rotates into its place, and the losing team rotates off the court and becomes the last team in line. The teacher throws the ball up in the air quickly as the teams are rotating. All teams must move quickly to the proper court. The game is fast moving and involves passing, setting, and court coverage. The game is good for high school students who have developed passing and setting skills.

Three-Hit Volleyball

Three-hit volleyball is like regular volleyball, except that the ball must be hit three times on a side with the third hit going over the net.

Minivolleyball

This modified game is for students ages 9 to 12. The net is 6 feet, 10 inches (2.08 m), and the court is 15 by 40 feet (4.6 by 12.2 m). Three students are on a team—two frontline players and one backline player. The game uses regulation volleyball rules.

Blind-Man Volleyball

A cover is put over the net so that players cannot see what is happening on the other side. Regulation volleyball rules are followed. Teams must be ready because they never know when the ball is coming over the net. A scorer is necessary for both sides of the net.

Regulation Volleyball—Serves Modified

Regulation rules are followed, but the server can have two attempts. Alternatively, the service distance can be shortened.

18

Suggested Performance Objectives

Performance objectives have been used successfully with volleyball units at both the middle and high school levels. The following list can help structure a learning environment for volleyball activities. These can be modified according to the abilities of the students and the facilities available.

Core Objectives

Forearm Pass

1. Bump 12 consecutive forearm passes against the wall at a height of at least 10 feet (3 m).
2. Bump 12 consecutive forearm passes into the air at a height of at least 10 feet (3 m).
3. Bump 10 consecutive forearm passes over the net with the instructor or a classmate.

Overhead Set Pass

4. Hit 15 consecutive set passes against the wall at a height of at least 10 feet (3 m).
5. Hit 15 consecutive set passes into the air at a height of at least 10 feet (3 m).
6. Hit 12 consecutive set passes over the net with the instructor or a classmate.

Serves

7. Hit three consecutive underhand serves into the right half of the court.
8. Hit three of four underhand serves into the left half of the court.
9. Hit three consecutive overhand serves inbounds.

Attendance and Participation

10. Be dressed and ready to participate at 8:00 a.m.
11. Participate in 15 games.
12. Score 90% or better on a rules, strategies, and techniques test.

Optional Objectives

1. Standing 2 feet (60 cm) from the backline, bump three of five forearm passes into an 8-foot (2.5 m) circle surrounding the setter's position. The height must be at least 10 feet (3 m). The instructor or a classmate throws the ball.
2. Bump three of five forearm passes over the net at a height of at least 12 feet (3.5 m) that land inbounds and not more than 8 feet (2.5 m) from the backline.
3. Standing in the setter's position (center forward), hit three consecutive overhead sets at least 10 feet (3 m) high that land in a 5-foot (1.5 m) circle where the spiker would be located. The instructor or a classmate throws the ball.
4. Hit three of five overhead passes over the net at least 12 feet (3.5 m) high that land inbounds and not more than 8 feet (2.5 m) from the backline.
5. Standing in the setter's position (center forward), hit three of five back sets at least 10 feet (3 m) high that land in a 5-foot (1.5 m) circle where the spiker would be located. The instructor or a classmate throws the ball.
6. Volley 12 consecutive times over the net with the instructor or a classmate by alternating forearm passes and overhead passes.
7. Alternate forearm passes and overhead passes in the air at a height of 10 feet (3 m) or more 12 consecutive times.
8. Spike three of four sets inbounds from an on-hand position—three-step approach, jump, extend arm, hand contact.
9. Spike three of five sets inbounds from an off-hand position.
10. Recover three consecutive balls from the net. Recoveries must be playable—that is, 8 feet (2.5 m) high in the playing area.
11. Hit three consecutive overhand serves into the right half of the court.
12. Hit three of four overhand serves into the left half of the court.
13. Hit three of five overhand serves under a rope 15 feet (5 m) high that land in the back half of the court.
14. Officiate at least three games using proper calls and signals.
15. Coach a team for the class tournament, including planning strategy, making substitutions, and scheduling.
16. Devise and carry out a research project that deals with volleyball. Check with the instructor for ideas.

LEARNING AIDS

WEBSITES

Archery

www.usarchery.org

Badminton

www.usabadminton.org

www.worldbadminton.net

Basketball

www.yboa.org

Field Hockey

www.teamusa.org/usa-field-hockey

Flag Football

www.usffa.org

Lacrosse

www.lacrosse.org

www.lax.com

Soccer

www.soccer.org

www.ussoccer.com

Softball

www.softball.mb.ca

www.usasoftball.com

Team Handball

www.usateamhandball.org

Track and Field

www.usatf.org

Volleyball

www.avca.org

www.usavolleyball.org

18

REFERENCES AND SUGGESTED READINGS

Casten, C. (2011). *Lesson plans for dynamic physical education for secondary school students* (7th ed.). San Francisco, CA: Pearson Higher Education/Benjamin Cummings.

Archery

Fronske, H. (2008). *Teaching cues for sport skills* (4th ed.). San Francisco, CA: Pearson Higher Education/Benjamin Cummings.

Haywood, K.M. (2002). Archery. In N. Dougherty (Ed.), *Physical activity and sport for the secondary school student* (5th ed.). Reston, VA: NASPE and American Association for Health, Physical Education, Recreation and Dance (AAHPERD).

Haywood, K.M., & Lewis, C.S. (2006). *Archery: Steps to success* (3rd ed.). Champaign, IL: Human Kinetics.

Kentucky Department of Education. (2002). *Archery standards-based unit of study, grades 6–8*. Frankfort, KY: Author.

McCracken, B. (2001). *It's not just gym anymore: Teaching secondary students how to be active for life*. Champaign, IL: Human Kinetics.

McKinney, W.C., & McKinney, M.W. (1996). *Archery* (8th ed.). Dubuque, IA: Brown & Benchmark.

Mood, D.P., Musker, F.F., & Rink, J.E. (2007). *Sports and recreational activities* (14th ed.). Boston, MA: McGraw-Hill.

Schmottlach, N., & McManama, J. (2010). *The physical education handbook* (12th ed.). San Francisco, CA: Pearson Higher Education/Benjamin Cummings.

Badminton

Bloss, M.V. (2001). *Badminton*. Boston, MA: McGraw-Hill.

Fronske, H. (2008). *Teaching cues for sport skills* (4th ed.). San Francisco, CA: Pearson Higher Education/Benjamin Cummings.

Mood, D.P., Musker, F.F., & Rink, J.E. (2007). *Sports and recreational activities* (14th ed.). Boston, MA: McGraw-Hill.

National Association for Girls and Women in Sport. (1982). *Tennis-badminton-squash guide*. Reston, VA: AAHPERD.

Paup, D.C. (2002). Badminton. In N. Dougherty (Ed.), *Physical activity and sport for the secondary school student* (5th ed.). Reston, VA: NASPE and AAHPERD.

Schmottlach, N., & McManama, J. (2010). *The physical education handbook* (12th ed.). San Francisco, CA: Pearson Higher Education/Benjamin Cummings.

Basketball

Bryant, J. (2002). Basketball. In N. Dougherty (Ed.), *Physical activity and sport for the secondary school student* (5th ed.). Reston, VA: NASPE and AAHPERD.

Fronske, H. (2008). *Teaching cues for sport skills* (4th ed.). San Francisco, CA: Pearson Higher Education/Benjamin Cummings.

Mood, D.P., Musker, F.F., & Rink, J.E. (2007). *Sports and recreational activities* (14th ed.). Boston, MA: McGraw-Hill.

Schmottlach, N., & McManama, J. (2010). *The physical education handbook* (12th ed.). San Francisco, CA: Pearson Higher Education/Benjamin Cummings.

Summitt, P.H., & Jennings, D. (1991). *Basketball: Fundamentals and team play*. Dubuque, IA: Brown & Benchmark.

Wissel, H. (2004). *Basketball: Steps to success* (2nd ed.). Champaign, IL: Human Kinetics.

Field Hockey

Fronske, H. (2008). *Teaching cues for sport skills* (4th ed.). San Francisco, CA: Pearson Higher Education/Benjamin Cummings.

Gray, G.R. (2002). Floor hockey. In N. Dougherty (Ed.), *Physical activity and sport for the secondary school student* (5th ed.). Reston, VA: NASPE and AAHPERD.

Mood, D.P., Musker, F.F., & Rink, J.E. (2007). *Sports and recreational activities* (14th ed.). Boston, MA: McGraw-Hill.

Schmottlach, N., & McManama, J. (2010). *The physical education handbook* (12th ed.). San Francisco, CA: Pearson Higher Education/Benjamin Cummings.

Whitney, M.G. (Ed.). *Eagle*. Colorado Springs, CO: United States Field Hockey Association (USFHA).

Flag Football

Domitrovitz, M. (2002). Flag football. In N. Dougherty (Ed.), *Physical activity and sport for the secondary school student* (5th ed.). Reston, VA: NASPE and AAHPERD.

Fronske, H. (2008). *Teaching cues for sport skills* (4th ed.). San Francisco, CA: Pearson Higher Education/Benjamin Cummings.

Mood, D.P., Musker, F.F., & Rink, J.E. (2007). *Sports and recreational activities* (14th ed.). Boston, MA: McGraw-Hill.

Schmottlach, N., & McManama, J. (2010). *The physical education handbook* (12th ed.). San Francisco, CA: Pearson Higher Education/Benjamin Cummings.

Lacrosse

Fronske, H. (2008). *Teaching cues for sport skills* (4th ed.). San Francisco, CA: Pearson Higher Education/Benjamin Cummings.

Hutcherson, K. (2002). Lacrosse. In N. Dougherty (Ed.), *Physical activity and sport for the secondary school student* (5th ed.). Reston, VA: NASPE and AAHPERD.

Mood, D.P., Musker, F.F., & Rink, J.E. (2007). *Sports and recreational activities* (14th ed.). Boston, MA: McGraw-Hill.

Schmottlach, N., & McManama, J. (2010). *The physical education handbook* (12th ed.). San Francisco, CA: Pearson Higher Education/Benjamin Cummings.

Rugby

Mood, D., Musker, F.F., & Rink, J.E. (1999). *Sports and recreational activities* (12th ed.). Boston, MA: McGraw-Hill.

Soccer

Fronske, H. (2008). *Teaching cues for sport skills* (4th ed.). San Francisco, CA: Pearson Higher Education/Benjamin Cummings.

Luxbacher, J. (2005). *Teaching soccer: Steps to success* (3rd ed.). Champaign, IL: Human Kinetics.

Mood, D.P., Musker, F.F., & Rink, J.E. (2007). *Sports and recreational activities* (14th ed.). Boston, MA: McGraw-Hill.

Schmottlach, N., & McManama, J. (2010). *The physical education handbook* (12th ed.). San Francisco, CA: Pearson Higher Education/Benjamin Cummings.

Weinberg, W. (2002). Soccer. In N. Dougherty (Ed.), *Physical activity and sport for the secondary school student* (5th ed.). Reston, VA: NASPE and AAHPERD.

Softball

Fronske, H. (2008). *Teaching cues for sport skills* (4th ed.). San Francisco, CA: Pearson Higher Education/Benjamin Cummings.

Mood, D.P., Musker, F.F., & Rink, J.E. (2007). *Sports and recreational activities* (14th ed.). Boston, MA: McGraw-Hill.

Potter, D.L. (2007). *Softball: Steps to success* (3rd ed.). Champaign, IL: Human Kinetics.

Ransdall, L.B., & Taylor, A. (2002). Softball. In N. Dougherty (Ed.), *Physical activity and sport for the secondary school student* (5th ed.). Reston, VA: NASPE and AAHPERD.

Schmottlach, N., & McManama, J. (2010). *The physical education handbook* (12th ed.). San Francisco, CA: Pearson Higher Education/Benjamin Cummings.

Team Handball

Dwight, M.P., & Cavanaugh, M. (2002). Team handball. In N. Dougherty (Ed.), *Physical activity and sport for the secondary school student* (5th ed.). Reston, VA: NASPE and AAHPERD.

Fronske, H. (2008). *Teaching cues for sport skills* (4th ed.). San Francisco, CA: Pearson Higher Education/Benjamin Cummings.

Mood, D.P., Musker, F.F., & Rink, J.E. (2007). *Sports and recreational activities* (14th ed.). Boston, MA: McGraw-Hill.

Schmottlach, N., & McManama, J. (2010). *The physical education handbook* (12th ed.). San Francisco, CA: Pearson Higher Education/Benjamin Cummings.

Track and Field

Bowerman, W. (1972). *Coaching track and field*. Boston, MA: Houghton Mifflin.

Doherty, J. (1976). *Track and field omnibook* (3rd ed.). Los Altos, CA: Track and Field News Press.

Fronske, H. (2008). *Teaching cues for sport skills* (4th ed.). San Francisco, CA: Pearson Higher Education/Benjamin Cummings.

Knop, N. (2002). Track and field. In N. Dougherty (Ed.), *Physical activity and sport for the secondary school student* (5th ed.). Reston, VA: NASPE and AAHPERD.

National Federation of High School Associations. (2006). *Officiating track and field and cross country*. Champaign, IL: Human Kinetics.

Schmottlach, N., & McManama, J. (2010). *The physical education handbook* (12th ed.). San Francisco, CA: Pearson Higher Education/Benjamin Cummings.

Volleyball

American Sport Education Program. (2007). *Coaching youth volleyball* (4th ed.). Champaign, IL: Human Kinetics.

Fronske, H. (2008). *Teaching cues for sport skills* (4th ed.). San Francisco, CA: Pearson Higher Education/Benjamin Cummings.

Mood, D.P., Musker, F.F., & Rink, J.E. (2007). *Sports and recreational activities* (14th ed.). Boston, MA: McGraw-Hill.

Schmottlach, N., & McManama, J. (2010). *The physical education handbook* (12th ed.). San Francisco, CA: Pearson Higher Education/Benjamin Cummings.

Viera, B.L. (2002). Volleyball. In N. Dougherty (Ed.), *Physical activity and sport for the secondary school student* (5th ed.). Reston, VA: NASPE and AAHPERD.

18

Lifestyle Activities

Lifestyle activities are self-selected physical activities that take place during a person's daily routine. These lifestyle activities can easily be incorporated into students' lives, both now and in the future. Physical educators should try especially hard to offer as many of these activities as possible. The activities will become more important to students as they grow older and as they try to keep activity in their lifestyle. Students should start learning and doing these activities early in their lives and continue participating into the future. These activities expand the scope of physical education programs for teachers and students.

Learning Objectives

▶ Explain the sequence of skills for each activity.
▶ Discuss the ideas for effective instruction and organization and skill work possibilities.
▶ Set up lead-up games and learning activities.
▶ Organize objectives, tests, and rating forms or scales for all lifestyle activities covered in this chapter.

Bowling

The game of bowling today is a form of kingpins, the first bowling game to use finger holes in the ball. The sport has changed from a simple game played outdoors to a complex mechanized game played in large modern facilities. Bowling has become one of our most widely enjoyed recreational activities. Any family member may participate because the game is suitable for all ages and genders. Bowling can be played in any season, and facilities are usually available at most times of the day. Leagues are popular, and many businesses sponsor employee leagues. Schools have intramural leagues, and many bowling establishments organize leagues for children. National organizations usually sanction these leagues.

The play in bowling consists of rolling balls down a wooden alley with the object of knocking over 10 wooden pins positioned at the far end of the alley. The bowler stands any distance behind the foul line and takes three, four, or five steps before releasing the ball down the alley. If the player touches the alley beyond the foul line, a foul is called, and the ball counts as one ball bowled. No score is made on a foul, and the pins knocked down are immediately replaced. In bowling and duckpins, the pins knocked down after the first ball rolled are cleared away before the next ball is rolled. In candlepins, knocked-down pins are not cleared away. Each bowler has 10 frames in which to knock down as many pins as possible. A bowler who knocks down all the pins in 10 frames of bowling attains a perfect score of 300.

Sequence of Skills

The following is a breakdown of the skills necessary to successfully participate in bowling.

Picking Up the Ball

Place the hands on opposite sides of the ball and lift it to a comfortable position in front of the body before placing the fingers and thumb in the holes. Avoid placing the thumb and fingers in the holes to pick up the ball because this method places strain on the bowling hand.

Gripping the Ball

Holding the ball in the left hand (if right-handed), place the two middle fingers in the holes first and then slip the thumb in the thumbhole. Do not squeeze the ball with the fingertips, but maintain contact by slightly pressing the palm side of the fingers and thumb toward the palm area of the ball. The little finger and index finger are relaxed and flat on the ball.

Developing a Stance

The stance is the stationary position that the bowler holds before approaching the foul line. The development of a stance, which varies among bowlers, is essential for consistency in bowling. To locate the starting position, stand with the back to the foul line, walk four-and-a-half steps, stop, turn, and face the pins. The number of steps will vary with the three-, four-, or five-step approach. Standing erect, place the feet parallel to each other or place the left foot slightly in front of the right foot. The feet should be about 1-1/2 inches (4 cm) apart. The weight is on the left foot, and the knees are slightly bent. The head is up, and the shoulders are level.

Hold the ball at waist level and slightly to the right. The arm is straight from the shoulder to the wrist. Push the ball out during the first step and swing it down directly below the shoulder. Keep the wrist straight and stiff during the pendulum swing. The elbow moves back alongside the body and should not be braced on the hip. The nonbowling hand supports the ball. The shoulders, hips, and feet are square with the pins when the stance is established.

After learning the basic stance, the bowler can develop a personal style. Some leading bowlers hold the ball approximately level with the chin and a few inches (5 to 10 cm) from the body. Proficient bowlers usually hold the ball at waist level and a few inches (5 to 10 cm) away from the body. The upper torso leans slightly forward. Taller bowlers sometimes use a half crouch and a shorter backswing.

Aiming

The method of aim should be decided after the footwork, timing, and method of rolling the ball have been established. The bowler should then experiment to find the preferable method of aim. Spot bowling (described as follows) is recommended.

1. Pin bowling. The bowler looks at the pins and draws an imaginary line between the point of delivery and the point on the pins at which to aim the ball. This line will be the route of the ball. The usual point to hit is the 1–3 pocket.

2. Spot bowling. The bowler draws an imaginary line from the point of delivery to some spot down the lane, usually at the division boards where the maple meets pine. Most lanes have triangular markings for spot bowlers.

Approaching and Making the Delivery

One-Step Delivery

The one-step delivery should be learned before the three-, four-, or five-step delivery. The stance for the one-step delivery differs from the general stance discussed previously. The foot opposite the bowling arm is behind. Extend the bowling hand, and after extension, drop the hand slowly to the side and simultaneously lean forward, bending the knees. Keep the arm relaxed and the wrist straight. Swing the arm forward to eye level, back to waist level, and forward again to eye level. Assume the stance for the one-step delivery. The hands are at waist height as if gripping the ball. Push the arms forward, release the left hand, and complete the pendulum swing.

Repeat the push away and the pendulum swing, but as the arm swings forward (at the completion of the swing), slide ahead on the foot opposite the bowling arm. Keep the shoulders straight and the body facing straight ahead. Practice the simultaneous movement of arm and foot. No ball is necessary when first learning the approach and delivery. When the timing is learned, add the ball.

Four-Step Delivery

The four-step delivery is the most popular. The stance is with the opposite foot forward, as presented earlier. Starting with the right foot, take four brisk walking strides forward. Repeat the four-step walk, making the fourth step a slide. At the completion of the slide, the full body weight should be on the sliding foot, knee bent, and shoulders parallel to the foul line. The forward foot should be pointed toward the pins.

To coordinate the delivery, the bowler should assume the stance, start the four-step walk, and push the ball out, down, back, and forward so that the arm movements coordinate with the steps (one, two, three, slide). As the foot slides, the ball comes forward and is released. At the release, the thumb is out, and the fingers and wrist are turning and lifting the ball. The right leg swings forward for balance, and the right arm, which was straight throughout the backswing, bends at the elbow for the follow-through. The body then straightens to get more lift on the ball.

Different types of balls can be bowled, depending on how the ball is released.

1. Straight ball. The wrist and forearm are kept straight throughout the entire delivery. The thumb is on top of the ball, at a 12-o'clock position, and the index finger is at 2 o'clock.

2. Hook ball. The ball is held throughout the approach, delivery, and release, with the thumb at 10 o'clock and the index finger at 12 o'clock. If the ball hooks too much, move the thumb toward the 12-o'clock position.

Ideas for Effective Instruction

This section highlights numerous ideas to allow for more effective instruction.

Gymnasium Bowling Sets

Gymnasium bowling sets are available through many equipment dealers. They usually contain 10 plastic pins, a triangular sheet for pin setup, score sheets, and a hard plastic ball. Sizes of the finger holes vary and so may the weight of the ball. An in-school instructional video is available through the Bowling Foundation, including a teaching curriculum that has many good ideas for using the gymnasium equipment. For contact information, see the Websites section at the end of this chapter.

Score Sheets

Score sheets can be drawn and duplicated. Sheets are included in gym sets, or the instructor can check with a local establishment about purchase or a possible donation.

General Rules and Scoring

1. A game consists of 10 frames. Each bowler is allowed two deliveries in each frame, with the exception of the 10th frame, in which three are allowed if a spare or strike is scored.

2. The score is an accumulated total of pins knocked down plus bonus points for spares and strikes.

3. If all 10 pins are knocked down on the first ball rolled, it is a strike. The scorer counts 10 plus the total of the next two balls rolled.

4. If all pins are knocked down with two balls rolled, it is a spare. The scorer counts 10 plus the number of pins knocked down on the next ball rolled.

5. If no pins are knocked down when a ball is rolled, the bowler is charged with an error. This includes gutter balls.

6. If pins left after the first ball constitute a split, a circle is made on the score sheet around the number of pins knocked down.

7. A foul results if the bowler steps across the foul line.

19

Etiquette

1. Take your turn promptly.
2. The bowler to the right has the right of way. Wait until the bowler on the right is finished before assuming a stance.
3. Continue your approach.
4. Step back off the approach after delivery.
5. Use your ball only and use the same ball throughout the game.
6. Do not talk to a player who is on the approach.
7. Respect all equipment and the bowling establishment.
8. Although competition is encouraged, be gracious in any case.
9. Return all equipment to its proper place.

Organization and Skill Work

Teach skills in sequence. After teaching the basic grip and stance (group situation), use stations for skill practice. Depending on the unit structure, students can work at stations on skills to be checked off, or they may be involved in lead-up games, minitournaments (using gym sets), or practice at a bowling facility. Because bowling skills are perfected through constant practice, the unit should be designed for maximum activity.

If space is available, mock lanes can be made. Using mock lanes can enhance the number of students involved in activity while using a smaller space. Students are able to practice approaching, releasing, and spotting without pins. They can work in pairs, taking turns practicing and rolling back the ball. Team games with the mock lanes and gymnasium bowling sets can be enjoyable. Hand out score sheets and have students record their scores. Scorers sign their names, and score sheets are checked for correct scoring procedure. Games with mock lanes and gymnasium sets can be used as a lead-up to bowling at a nearby facility.

Lead-Up Games and Learning Activities

This section highlights numerous lead-up games and learning activities to help develop the skills to participate in bowling.

Red Pin

Use regulation alleys or lanes set up on the gym floor. One pin is painted red (tape may be substituted). The bowler rolls one ball in each frame. The bowler scores only if the red pin is upset. The pinsetter makes no attempt to place the red pin in a specific location. It will occur in random placement. Because only one ball is rolled, no spares are scored. Strikes are possible and should be scored as in regulation bowling. This activity can be used for team or individual competition.

Scotch Bowling

This activity can be played on regulation lanes or in a gym with marked lanes. Students choose a partner and decide who will roll the first ball. Partners then alternate throughout the game, which is scored like regulation bowling.

Shuffle-Bowl

The game is played on a shuffleboard court, using shuffleboard cues, discs, and bowling pins. The discs are slid at the pins. Play and scoring are carried out as in regulation bowling.

Three Pins

Regulation equipment or the gymnasium with marked lanes can be used for play. The bowler attempts to knock down the 1–2–3 combination by hitting the 1–3 pocket (right side of pins; 1–2, if left-handed, left sides of pins). One ball is allowed for each turn. Players start with 20 points. Three pins down subtracts 3 points, two down subtracts 2 points, and one pin down subtracts 1 point. The first player to reach 0 points is the winner.

Soccer Bowling

Any open area, indoors or outdoors, is suitable for play. Soccer balls and wooden pins are used, and the game is scored like regulation bowling. Balls are kicked instead of rolled.

Basket Bowling

Play in an alley marked on the gym floor. Allow a 15-foot (5 m) approach. Use two indoor softballs and a metal wastebasket propped up on its side with two bricks or similar objects facing the foul line. Five to ten players and one retriever make up a team. Each player attempts to roll two balls into the wastebasket. Rotate and trade places with the retriever. One point is scored for each basket made, and the high scorer wins. If teams play against one another, use a time limit.

Each player is allowed five turns. If the bowler steps over the foul line, 1 point is subtracted. If the ball is bounced on the alley, 1 point is subtracted. An official scorekeeper and judge are necessary.

Suggested Performance Objectives

The following are possible objectives that can drive the lessons in this activity.

Objectives

1. Bowl six games at any lane. Keep score and turn in the score sheet to the instructor. On a separate sheet, state the two basic rules for scoring. List and explain the symbols used in scoring.

2. Research and write a paper on the history of bowling using at least four sources. The paper should be typed and double-spaced and include a bibliography.

3. Learn the correct way to pick up and hold the ball. Be able to demonstrate the hand positions, footwork, and release. In addition, be able to demonstrate the hand position that creates a hook, a straight ball, and a backup ball. Performance is evaluated on the basis of an oral explanation to the instructor.

4. Watch at least one tournament, either live or on television, for an hour, or observe an hour of league bowling. Report in writing about how this type of bowling differs from open bowling.

5. Obtain a rule book from the Women's International Bowling Congress (WIBC) and find out what special prizes are awarded in sanctioned leagues. Illustrate and explain the patches and award procedures.

6. Visit a lane and ask the operator for an inspection of an automatic pinsetter in operation. Find out how to operate the ball clearer, how to turn on the teleprompter, and how to reset the pins. Discover where the trouble bell and the foul-line indicator are located and how the foul line operates. When ready, take a short quiz from the instructor about this information.

7. Make a poster diagramming a lane. Enlarge and make offset drawings of the approach area and the pin-fall area. Write a short paper telling how a bowler might use this information when bowling.

8. Compile a list of 15 bowling terms and a definition of each.

9. Take a written examination on bowling covering etiquette, scoring, handicaps, averages, techniques, terminology, history, and rules.

10. Demonstrate the proper stance, the four-step delivery, and the position of the hands on each step.

11. Write a paper describing the following: moonlight bowling, headpin tournament, and 3–6–9 tournament.

12. Practice spare bowling of a single pin until you make 4 out of 10 shots. (Have the proprietor take all but one pin out of the rack, and shoot at any set that the automatic pinspotter provides.) When ready, test yourself by trying 10 consecutive shots. Record the score as either a miss or a spare. Use any score sheet provided by the alley and turn it in for credit.

Rating Form

A rating form (see figure 19.1) is useful for partner work and when facilities are limited. The form enables students who are not participating actively to be cognitively involved. The instructor should spend some time helping students learn to use the form correctly.

Disc Games

Playing with a disc is an exciting lifetime physical activity that can offer success and challenge at all ability levels. Disc activities can be played on almost any size field or gymnasium area and can be used with individuals, small groups, or teams. The International Frisbee Disc Association, which numbers more than 100,000 members, has statistics showing that more discs are sold yearly in the United States than footballs and basketballs combined. An annual world championship held in the Rose Bowl draws large crowds to watch competitors focus on distance, accuracy, freestyle moves, and other games.

A number of factors make disc sports an attractive new activity for physical education. A disc is generally inexpensive, depending on the type and quality of the disc. Disc activities provides excellent skills practice in throwing, catching, and eye–hand coordination and offers many interesting individual challenges and team activities. The low injury risk and the attraction to students are positive factors. The sport can be effective in a coeducational environment and offers flexibility in terms of participants' ages and abilities and in terms of program space and time. Both team and individual skills can be learned with disc activities and used for a lifetime of enjoyment.

Sequence of Skills

The following is a breakdown of the skills necessary to successfully participate in disc games.

19

BOWLING RATING

	Bowler											
Approach												
Push away on first step												
Push away: out and down—elbow straight												
Backswing: straight—in line with boards												
Backswing: to shoulder level												
Steps: smooth, gliding, even rhythm												
Steps: length and speed increase												
Slide on left foot												
Release												
Shoulders: parallel to foul line												
Shoulders: level												
Upper body: inclined forward												
Left foot: in line with boards												
Weight: balanced on left foot												
Thumb: in 12-o'clock position												
Ball: first strikes alley 1-1/2 ft (45 cm) in front of left foot												
Follow-through: straight and to shoulder height												
Aim												
Approach: straight, in line with boards												
Release: proper dot or dots at foul line												
Route: crosses proper dart												
Location where ball strikes pins? (e.g., 1–3, 1, 3, 1–2)												

Place a (✓) in proper square if the item is performed correctly.

Place a (—) if it is not correct.

FIGURE 19.1 Bowling rating form.

Throws

Backhand Throw

The thumb is on the top of the disc, and the fingers are under the rim. The index finger can also be placed on the outside lip of the disc. Coil the wrist and arm across the chest. Step forward and release the disc (keeping it level) with a snap of the wrist.

Backhand (Across-the-Chest) Curves

Use the same technique as the straight backhand but release the disc at an angle, with the lower side being the desired direction. Throw curves both left and right by tilting the disc.

Underhand or Bowling Throw

Use a backhand grip or put the index finger on the lip of the disc. Step with the opposite foot, bring the disc underhand past the body, and release it level, about waist height, with a wrist snap.

Thumber Throw

Hook the thumb under the disc and put the four fingers on top (palm of hand to underside of the disc). Bring the disc down from the ear in a sidearm motion and release it when the disc is even with the body. Avoid a follow-through with the disc.

Sidearm Throw

Put the index and middle finger under the disc and the thumb on top. The two fingers can be together on the lip, or one can be on the lip and one in the middle of the disc. Release the disc in a motion similar to that used for the thumber.

Overhand Wrist Flip

Grip the disc with the fingers on top and the thumb under the lip. Cock the wrist backward and start the throw behind the back at shoulder level. Flip the wrist forward to a point in line with the body.

Catches

Sandwich Catch

Catch the disc with one hand on top, the other on the bottom, and the disc in the middle. Alternate hands from top to bottom on different occasions.

C-Catch

Make a C with the thumb and fingers. Watch the disc into the C and close the fingers on the disc. Throws below the waist should have the thumb up, and those above the waist should have the thumb down.

Additional Skills

- Skip-throws off the ground. Tip the forward edge down and throw the disc so that it skips off the ground to a partner.
- Tipping. Use the finger, knee, head, toe, heel, or elbow. Watch the disc make contact with the various body parts and tip the disc in the air.
- Catches. Catch the disc with the finger, behind the back and head, between the legs, or with one hand.
- Air brushing. Hold the disc on one finger while striking the disc on its side to give it rotation.

Ideas for Effective Instruction

Instruction can begin by having partners, positioned about 5 yards (m) apart, work on the basic backhand throw and sandwich catch. As students improve, have them move farther apart and use the backhand curves with the C-catch and the one-handed catch. Be sure to keep beginning students spread out and away from buildings, fences, and other obstacles because the disc is difficult to control. Next, introduce the underhand throw, thumber, sidearm, and several fancy catches.

After students have the basic idea, create four stations that focus on accuracy, distance, accuracy and distance combined, and loft time. Many station variations can be designed to challenge students. Check the following section on activities for specific ideas. Disc golf is a particularly good activity for beginners with few developed skills.

Lead-Up Games and Learning Activities

This section highlights numerous lead-up games and learning activities to help develop the skills to participate in disc games.

Throw for Distance

Set up five or six cones at varying distances and let students experiment with different throws for distance.

Throw for Distance and Accuracy

Mark a line with varying distances and have students throw as far as possible on the line. Subtract the distance of the landing point away from the line from the total distance thrown. Students should develop both distance and accuracy.

Throw for Accuracy

Make a large circular target, about 9 or 10 feet (2.7 or 3.0 m) in diameter, on the ground with rope or jump ropes. Set cones at 10-, 15-, 20-, and 25-yard (m) distances. Let students have five attempts at each distance, and record the number of accurate throws. Another variation is to hang a hoop from a tree or goalpost and have students throw through the hoop. Award 1 point for hitting the hoop and 2 points for going through the hoop.

Time Aloft

Record the time from release of the disc until it hits the ground.

Throw and Catch With Self

The object of this activity is to throw the disc as far forward as possible and then run and catch it. A starting line where the disc must be released is designated, and distance is measured from that line. The disc must be caught.

19

Follow the Leader

One player makes a specific throw, and the second player must try to make the same throw. The first player must match the catch of the second player.

Twenty-One

Players stand 10 yards (m) apart and throw the disc back and forth. The throws must be accurate and catchable. One point is awarded for a two-handed catch and 2 points for a one-handed catch. A player must score 21 points and win by 2 points.

Disc Tennis

This game is the same as regular tennis, but the player must catch the disc and throw from that spot. The serve starts to the right of the center mark and must go to the opposite backcourt, not into the service box.

Ultimate

Ultimate is a team game played by seven or more on a side. The object is to move the disc down the field by passing and to score by passing across the goal line to a teammate. The person with the disc can only pivot and pass to a teammate. If the disc is grounded without being caught or intercepted, or if it goes out of bounds, the defending team gains possession. This game can be modified and played with fewer players per team for more throwing and catching opportunities.

Power Disc

Five to seven players on a team stand behind a line 15 yards (m) from the opponents' line. The goal line is 10 yards (m) wide. The object is to throw so hard that the opponents cannot make a one-handed catch. The disc can be tipped by several people as long as a one-handed catch is used. The receiving team gets a point if the throw is too high, too wide, or too low. The height is determined by having team members stretch their arms straight up, usually 7 to 8 feet (2.1 to 2.4 m) high. The first team to score 21 points wins. Use extra caution with beginners and younger students. Move the goals back a bit and match ability levels.

Disc Soccer

The game is played like soccer, but the disc is thrown to teammates and at the goal. If the disc is dropped, the defenders play offense. Rules can be modified to include two goalies and limitations on the number of steps possible.

Disc Softball

The game is similar to regular softball. The pitcher throws the disc to the batter, who must catch the disc and throw it into play past the pitcher. If the batter drops the pitch, it is a strike. No bunting or stealing is allowed. The other rules of softball apply.

Disc Shuffleboard

Two players compete against two players. The game is played on a basketball court, and the goal is to score by throwing the disc into the opponent's key. Throwers stand outside the out-of-bounds line under the basket. The key is divided into two areas: the circular area around the free-throw line is worth 2 points, and the larger lane area is worth 1 point. Different-colored discs are used to make scorekeeping easier.

Disc Golf

Disc golf is a favorite game of many students. Boundary cones with numbers can be used for tees, and holes can be boxes, hoops, trees, tires, garbage cans, or any other available equipment on the school grounds. Put the course together on a map for students and start them at different holes to decrease the time spent waiting to tee off. Regulation golf rules apply. The students can jog between throws for increased activity.

General Guidelines

Disc golf is played like regular golf. One stroke is counted each time the disc is thrown and when a penalty is incurred. The object is to earn the lowest score.

Tee Throws

Tee throws must be completed within or behind the designated tee area.

Lie

The lie is the spot on or directly underneath the spot where the previous throw landed.

Throwing Order

The player whose disc is the farthest from the hole throws first. The player with the least number of throws on the previous hole tees off first.

Fairway Throws

Fairway throws must be made from behind the lie of the previous throw. A running approach to the throw is allowed.

Dog Leg

A dog leg is one or more designated trees or poles in the fairway that must be passed on the outside when approaching the hole. The penalty for missing a dog leg is two strokes.

Putt Throw

A putt throw is any throw within 10 feet (3 m) of the hole. A player may not move past the point of the lie in making the putt throw. Falling or jumping putts are not allowed.

Unplayable Lies

Any disc that comes to rest 6 or more feet (2 m) above the ground is unplayable. The next throw must be played from a new lie directly underneath the unplayable lie (one-stroke penalty).

Out of Bounds

A throw that lands out of bounds must be played from the point where the disc went out (one-stroke penalty).

Course Courtesy

Players should not throw until the players ahead are out of range.

Completion of Hole

A disc that comes to rest in the hole (box or hoop) or strikes the designated hole (tree or pole) constitutes successful completion of that hole.

Around Nine

A target is set up with nine different throwing positions around it, each 2 feet (60 cm) farther away (see figure 19.2). The throwing positions can be clockwise or counterclockwise around the target. They can also be in a straight line from the target. Points are awarded based on the throwing position number (for example, number 7 means 7 points for hitting the target). The game can be played indoors or outdoors.

One Step

This game is a variation of power disc. Opponents stand 20 to 30 yards (m) apart. The object is to throw the disc accurately so that the opponent can catch it while taking only one step. If the throw is off target, the thrower receives 1 point. If the throw is accurate and the receiver drops the disc, the receiver is awarded 1 point. The first player to reach 5 points loses the match.

Novel Discs

Spin Jammer discs have a special cone underneath the disc for spinning it on the index finger. Many different spinning activities can be performed as an individual or with partners and small groups of students. Some examples include spinning the disc and catching it on the index finger with either hand, passing it back and forth on the index finger with a partner, or passing it around a group of three students to see how many passes can be made before the disc stalls out. See figure 19.3 for an example of a programmed practice sheet for Spin Jammer skills. Students will enjoy the change of pace and the ease in which they can learn to do a variety of tricks with the Spin Jammer. The Spin Jammers can also be used for all regular throws, catches, and games in this chapter.

Double-Disc

This unique disc is made up of two discs that fit together and are designed to separate during a proper throw after about 10 yards (m). The challenge for students is to catch both discs without dropping either. Groups of three or

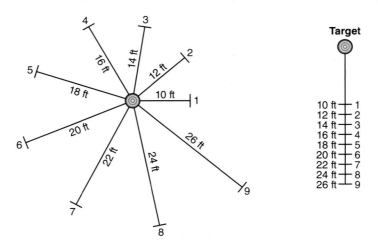

FIGURE 19.2 Around nine.

SPIN JAMMER DISC SKILLS

Name _____ Class period _____ Date_____

Partner _____

Self	Peer	Teacher	Skills

			Spin and catch it 10 times.
			  Right hand
			  Left hand

			Pass the spinning disc to a partner 10 times.
			  Right hand
			  Left hand

			Pop the spinning disc and catch it 10 times.
			  Right hand
			  Left hand
			Pop the spinning disc to a partner 10 times.
			  Right hand
			  Left hand

			Make a backhand throw to a partner 10 times, who uses a sandwich catch. Dominant hand

			Make a bowling throw (underhand) to a partner 10 times.
			  C-catch
			  Dominant hand

			Make 10 backhand curves, left and right.
			Make 10 sidearm throws.
			Perform several types of fancy catches—one handed, left or right; under the leg, left or right; a behind the back, left or right. Perform at least five in a row of each.
			Make 10 thumber throws.

FIGURE 19.3 Example of a programmed practice sheet for a Spin Jammer.

four students can perform this challenging activity by having one student throw the discs while two or three students try to catch one of the discs as they separate. This activity can become part of a disc unit with a variety of discs and different activities.

Suggested Performance Objectives

1. Throw 10 consecutive backhands through a hoop from 10 yards (m).
2. Perform objective 1 using underhand throws.
3. Perform objective 1 using sidearm throws.
4. Perform objective 1 using thumber throws.
5. Perform objective 1 using overhand wrist flips.
6. Throw a disc 30 yards (m) or more using two different throws.
7. Curve the disc around a tree so that it lands in a designated target area on three of five attempts.
8. Perform objective 7 but use the opposite curve.
9. Make 10 consecutive sandwich catches.
10. Make 10 consecutive thumbs-down catches above the waist.
11. Perform objective 10 with thumbs-up catches below the waist.
12. Catch three of five discs behind the head, behind the back, or between the legs.
13. Make five consecutive one-handed catches with both the left and right hands.
14. Throw five consecutive skips into a target area.
15. Score 30 or less on a round of disc golf.

The listed ideas are just a few of the possibilities for challenging students with disc performance objectives. The objectives could be combined with a grading scheme or used with learning stations for skill development. Activities need to be field-tested to establish fair distances and criterion levels for students of various ages and abilities. Figure 19.4 is a three-week disc unit block plan for middle school students.

Rainy Day Activities

1. Review and teach rules and strategies for the various disc games.
2. Set up a short putting (disc golf) course in the gym, hallway, or locker room.
3. Review grips, throws, releases, and so forth.
4. Discuss disc literature and have students read and report on specific information.
5. Discuss the various types and sizes of discs and the purpose of each type.
6. Set up an indoor tossing accuracy test and let students work at improving their accuracy.
7. Develop a crossword puzzle or disc word searches.
8. Assign a group of students to develop a crossword puzzle or a word search.
9. Devise and give a test on terminology.
10. Discuss with students the skills and activities associated with discs and ways that playing with discs can fit into their lifestyles.
11. Have students develop rules and regulations for a new game that will be played when the weather clears.
12. Invite a local disc club or expert to class to give a demonstration and instruction on disc techniques and skills.

Golf

Each weekend millions of golfers everywhere try to obtain a tee-off time to hit and chase a little white ball around an 18-hole golf course. Golf may appear to be a simple sport, but it is a complex activity that requires the participant to use many different shots or strokes (e.g., wood shots, long-iron shots, short-iron shots, pitching, chipping, and putting). Golf is challenging and proves to be fascinating to people of all abilities and ages, from 8 to 80. Golf is truly a lifetime sport that all people can enjoy.

Sequence of Skills

The two primary methods of teaching golf are the swing, or whole, method and the position, or part, method. Both approaches lead to the same result—square ball contact with good acceleration. Both teaching methods can be effective, but the whole method seems easier and faster to learn, which makes it better suited to the limited time available for a physical education unit. The order of skills to be learned in a beginning class follows: grip; stance; alignment; iron shots—half swing, three-quarter swing, and full swing; wood shots—half swing, three-quarter swing, and full swing; putting; chipping; pitching; and the bunker shot.

19

Introduction	Review	Review	Review	Review
What is a disc? Types Activities Backhand throw Sandwich catch Backhand curves C-catch Underhand throw	Backhands—curves Underhands Catches **Teach** Disc golf **Activity** Play six holes of golf	Throws—catches **Teach** Thumber Sidearm Overhand wrist flip **Activities** Four stations: Distance Accuracy Curves Partner work	Throws—catches **Teach** Fancy catches **Activities** Follow the leader Twenty-one One step	Fancy catches **Teach** Throw to self **Activities** Disc softball Disc soccer
Review All throws **Teach** Skipping Tipping Brushing **Activities** Four stations: Distance with accuracy Self-catch Accuracy Partner work	**Review** All catches **Teach** Freestyle **Activity** Ultimate	**Review** Skipping, tipping, brushing, freestyle **Activities** Four Stations Disc tennis Disc golf	**Activity** Nine holes of disc golf	**Activities** Four stations: Around nine Follow the leader Twenty-one One step
Review Skills for station work **Activities** Four Stations Disc softball	**Activities** Ultimate Disc soccer	**Activities** Station work Evaluation Around nine Follow the leader Twenty-one One step	**Activity** Nine holes of disc golf	**Activities** Station work Evaluation Ultimate Disc softball

FIGURE 19.4 Disc block plan.

Grip

Encourage students to use the overlap grip (80% of all golfers use this grip). Place the left hand on the club in the following manner: First, support the club with the right hand and let the left hand hang naturally at the side; then, bring the left hand in until it contacts the grip of the club and wrap it around. (Checkpoint: The V formed by the thumb and index finger should point directly to the center of the body, and two knuckles should be visible on the left hand when looking straight down at the grip.) Place the right hand by letting it also

hang naturally at the side. Bring it in to meet the club and wrap the fingers around the club so that the little finger of the right hand lies over the index finger of the left hand. The thumb of the left hand should fit nicely into the palm of the right hand. (Checkpoint: The V formed by the thumb and index finger of the right hand should point to the center of the body or slightly to the right of center.) A final check on the grip is to extend all fingers and let the club fall to the ground. If the grip is correct, the club will fall straight down between the legs and feet.

Stance

The golf stance should be both comfortable and relaxed. There is a slight bend in the knees and at the waist. The arms and shoulders are relaxed. The feet are shoulder-width apart for the driver and closer together for the shorter clubs. The ball is positioned within a 6-inch (15 cm) span, starting inside the left heel for the driver and moving toward the center of the stance for the wedge.

Lift the club straight out in front of the body at waist level and swing it back and forth, similar to a baseball bat swing. After three or four swings, return to a balanced position in the center. Bend forward from the waist until the club touches the ground. Now relax, and the club will move in slightly closer to the body. The waist bend lowers the club, not the arms. The relationship between arms and body remains the same until relaxation occurs. (Checkpoint: The preceding check can be applied to every club in the bag; it illustrates how far forward or back the ball must be played and the distance that the student should stand from the ball.)

Alignment

A simple procedure for achieving alignment involves the following steps:

1. Stand about 10 feet (3 m) behind the ball and draw an imaginary line from the flag to the ball.
2. Move to the side of the ball and set the clubface square to the target line. Both feet should be together with the ball centered.
3. Grip the club first and then spread the feet apart on a line parallel to the target line. The ball should be in line with the target, and the feet should be on a parallel line just left of the target. The distance between the toes and the ball is approximately 1-1/2 feet (45 cm).

Half Swing

Each student's swing will vary according to the person's stature, degree of relaxation, understanding of the swing, and natural ability. The half swing is started by bringing the club halfway back to a position parallel to the ground and then letting the club swing forward to the same position in front. The swing should be like the swing of a pendulum, and the grass should be brushed in both the backswing and forward swing. When the club is parallel to the ground in the backswing, the toe of the club should point straight up, and the grip end of the club should match the line of the feet. At the end of the

forward swing, the toe should be straight up again, and the far end of the club should match the line of the feet. After students can do a half swing, introduce the ball. Tell them to concentrate on swinging the club correctly and on the proper alignment procedures.

Three-Quarter Swing

The three-quarter swing is simply an extension of the half swing. The hands reach approximately shoulder height on the backswing and on the forward swing. Many students may be at this point already because most usually swing longer than they think do.

Full Swing

A full swing is characterized by a club shaft that is parallel to, or almost parallel to, the ground at the top of the backswing. The full swing is a further extension of the half and three-quarter swings. At the top of the backswing, the clubhead should point to the ground, and the shaft should point toward the target. The club face will thus be square, and the plane will be correct.

The golf swing actually begins at the top of the backswing. The backswing is simply preparation. Students should visualize the full swing as a circle drawn in the air with the clubhead. The circle starts at the top of the backswing and ends at the finish of the forward swing. Students should watch the clubhead draw the actual circle two or three times, always keeping the circle out in front. This routine will help them maintain one plane throughout the swing.

At this point, students should have the feel of the full swing, and they can experiment with different irons. They should try the 5 iron, the 9 iron, and finally the 3 iron. Concentration is still on the swing, because the same swing is used with every club. After students develop patterns of error, such as slicing, they can begin to focus on changing a specific aspect of the total swing.

Woods

The same progression should be used to teach wood shots from the half swing to the full swing. The first wood hit should be the 3 wood from the tee. Next, students can move to the driver, or 1 wood, from the tee, and then experiment with the 3 wood off the ground. Students should move halfway down the club's grip to begin swinging. They tee the ball so that the top edge of the club comes one-quarter to one-half of the way up the ball. The stance will be at its widest (shoulder-width), and the ball will automatically be positioned forward, inside the left heel.

19

Putting

Resembling the pendulum of a clock, the putter is an extension of the arms and shoulders and swings as one unit an equal distance back and forward. The feel is best obtained by having students grip as far down the shaft as they can reach. They square the putter to the target line and stroke straight back and straight through. Have students try the following putting techniques:

1. Use a reverse overlap grip in which the index finger of the left hand lies over the little finger of the right. This positioning allows the whole right hand to be on the club for control.

2. The stance may be wide or narrow, and the ball may be centered in the stance or forward, remaining inside the left heel. If the ball is forward, a slight weight shift to the left must accompany this stance.

3. Place the dominant eye directly over the ball to improve visualization of the target line.

4. Feel the putter accelerating through contact. Doing this may require shortening the backswing slightly.

5. If the ball misses the hole, overshooting the putt is preferable.

6. Keep the putter blade low to the ground to ensure good ball contact.

Learn to judge the break, or the roll of the green, by standing behind the ball and looking at the line between the ball and the hole and also at the slant of the entire green. Visualize throwing a pail of water toward the hole, and picture which way the water would run. For most putts (that is, 4 feet [1.2 m] or less) play the ball to the opposite inside edge of the cup. If the putt is longer, gradually move to the edge of the cup and eventually outside the cup as a point of aim. The point of aim may be a spot on the imaginary line to the hole or a point even with the hole but to one side. In both cases, the break takes the ball into the hole.

Chip, Pitch, and Bunker Shots

A chip shot is used when the ball is slightly off the green and there is room to hit the ball approximately halfway to the hole. The ball must land on the green and roll close to the hole. If there is not enough room to roll the ball to the hole, then a higher trajectory pitch shot is used. The pitch shot should land at the target. The bunker shot is used for coming out of a sand trap.

A chip shot usually requires a 7 iron and a putting-type stroke. A good technique is to have the students stand off the green and toss the ball underhand so that it rolls to within 4 feet (1.2 m) of the hole. Students then place a tee in the green where the ball hit. The tee becomes the target for the chip shot.

The pitch shot should be practiced at different distances with different-sized targets (the greater the distance, the larger the target). Baskets, hoops, and parachutes are possibilities at 10, 30, and 50 yards (m). The 9 iron or wedge is used with a one-quarter, one-half, or three-quarter swing, depending on the distance and the circumstances. Students should learn to make a smooth swing and to let the loft of the club hit the ball. The ball should land at the target and roll slightly forward.

The long-jump landing pit can be used for bunker shot practice. Students should use a wedge or 9 iron and concentrate on the following:

1. Open the club face as you line up the shot.

2. Line up 2 inches (5 cm) behind the ball and focus on that spot, not on the ball.

3. Barely scrape the sand with a one-quarter through full swing, depending on the distance required to land the ball.

4. Always follow through with the club.

Ideas for Effective Instruction

Introduce and stress safety rules on the first day of class. A golf ball or club can cause serious damage, so the instructor must demand strict adherence to safety rules. If the class is large and space is limited, safety officers may be appointed to help manage ball retrieving, changing from station to station, and other responsibilities assigned by the instructor.

The following are safety suggestions that may help in class organization:

1. Allow ample swing space between students for any group formation.

2. Do not carry clubs while retrieving balls.

3. If space is limited, take students to the back of the line for individual correction.

4. Do not retrieve balls until instructed.

5. Group the left-handed players together at the far end of the hitting line, facing the right-handed players.

6. Be certain that equipment is always in top condition and tell students to notify the instructor if equipment needs repair.

7. Caution students never to swing toward one another, even without a ball.

Start students with a high iron (7, 8, or 9) so that they will experience success quicker. Students need to understand that developing a golf swing takes a lot of practice and is not an easy skill to master. Make sure to avoid overloading students with information and provide ample practice time. Depending on the amount of equipment available, you may want to assign partner work and use a swing rating form. This approach motivates students without clubs to be more involved cognitively and improves their observation skills.

Learning stations can be arranged in the gymnasium or in outdoor fields. An example of an indoor facility, including irons, woods, chipping, pitching, and putting, is shown in figure 19.5. An outdoor area could be arranged in a similar manner (e.g., around a football or baseball field).

Lead-Up Games and Learning Activities

This section highlights numerous lead-up games and learning activities to help develop the skills to participate in golf.

Modified Courses

Many teachers set up a short golf course in the field space they have available. Broomsticks, traffic cones,

and hoops can serve as pins, tees, and holes. A power mower can be used to shape the fairways and greens. If digging holes is impossible, students can "hole out" when the ball strikes the target or when they are within a club's length of the target. Whiffle balls, plastic balls, or regular golf balls can be used, depending on what is available. All types of hazards can be set up using tires, hurdles, jump ropes, and cones. Specific course etiquette and rules can be taught with a modified course.

Putting

Miniature putting courses can be set up on smooth grass surfaces, carpeted areas, old carpet pieces, blankets, towels, mats, canvas, and even smooth floors if a whiffle ball is used. Paper cups, pieces of colored paper, shoe boxes, bleach containers, cans, and jars are possibilities for holes.

Partner Golf

Playing on a regular course or on a putting course, partners alternate hitting or putting toward the pin. If the class size is large, use groups of three or four.

Target Golf

Establish several concentric circles and point values around a target. Use rope, jump ropes, or chalk to mark the circles. The distance and size of the circles can vary according to the club used. This activity can be done with individuals or teams.

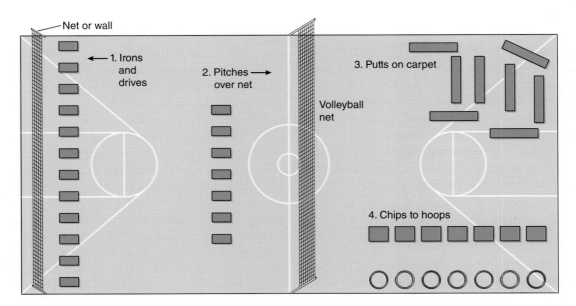

FIGURE 19.5 Setup for golf learning stations.

19

Rainy Day Activities

Rainy days are a good time to have a "spell down" with questions on rules, fundamentals, etiquette, and types of matches. Crossword puzzles and word searches are available in the suggested readings. Short putting courses can be set up in the indoor space available.

Skill Tests

Many of the drills and game situations already mentioned can be used for evaluation. Here are a few other possibilities:

1. Parachute. Count the number of 7-, 8-, or 9-iron shots that land on the parachute in 10 trials.
2. Putting. Play nine holes on a practice green and keep score. Ideally, each student would score two per hole to par the course.
3. Chipping. Count the number of balls that end up inside a circle with a 4-foot (1.2 m) radius.
4. Pitching. Pitch 10 balls at each station (10, 20, and 40 yards [m]) and count the number of balls that land inside the target area.
5. Bunker shot. Arrange a string in a circle with a 10-foot (3 m) radius around one hole and count the number of bunker shots that finish inside the circle after 10 trials.

A rating scale can be used as part of an evaluation scheme or as a part of the learning activities done with partners (see figure 19.6).

In-Line Skating

In-line skating may be best presented as a one-week miniunit. Many schools can rent the skates and safety gear for a reasonable fee for the unit. Fund-raising activities can provide the money for the rental. The following is an example of a daily agenda of lessons that could be presented in class for secondary students.

Day 1: The instructor goes over the class rules for the unit. The basic rules are as follows:

- Always wear the required equipment when skating.
- Never use the wall to stop.
- When falling, always fall forward.
- Never attempt to help keep someone from falling, which could lead to your falling as well.
- Always listen to the whistle commands.

- Enjoy skating and make it a part of your lifetime physical activity plan.

Students are then introduced to the equipment required for the unit. All students must wear wrist guards, elbow pads, and kneepads, and it is recommended that they wear helmets as well. Students are shown where to get their equipment and how to put it on correctly. Students who are proficient with in-line skating can help those who may be inexperienced. After students have equipment on, the instructor leads the class through a daily stretch routine. This sequence should include stretching both arms across the body and performing triceps stretches, wrist rotations, cross-legged oblique stretches, hurdler's stretches, sit-ups, and push-ups. Skills for the first day are getting up on the feet, skating slowly with body weight leaning forward, and performing the brake stop. Students are then shown the proper way to place equipment back in the proper bins as pairs. The use of mats or carpeted areas (if available) may be helpful for true beginners to start.

Day 2: The instructor quickly reviews skills previously taught. Skills for the day are learning to fall properly and performing the T-stop. When falling, students should lean forward and fall on all fours with their chins up. Most of the body weight is taken on the kneepads while the wrist guards guide the student into a sprawl forward. This skill should be practiced frequently under control. Students should never fall backward for obvious reasons. When teaching the T-stop, students drag one skate behind the body, which slows them to a stop. Students are encouraged to try both the T-stop and the brake stop and choose the one they like best.

Day 3: The instructor reviews the previous skills taught. Skills for the day include skating backward and using the crossover step when turning. When skating backward, students work in pairs. One student pushes his or her partner slowly, while the skater uses a figure-eight pattern with her or his skates to gain momentum. Partners switch roles and perform the activity again. When either skater feels confident enough, he or she can work on skating backward. The crossover step is simply stepping the right foot over the left foot while turning left and performing the opposite for turning right. Students are given tag games to play for the game segment of the lesson. Various adaptations of virtually any tag game can be used. Another game to use is called vanishing plates. Paper plates or beanbags for all but one student are placed on the floor or ground. Students skate freely until the instructor signals to grab a plate. The student who does not get a plate is out and must skate around the perimeter until the next game begins. For each round, one plate is

GOLF

1. Grip (4 points, 1 each)

____ Right-hand V is straight up or slightly right

____ Two knuckles of left hand are showing.

____ Grip tension is correct.

____ Hands are completely on grip of club.

2. Stance (4 points, 1/2 each)

____ Feet are a proper width apart.

____ Standing proper distance from ball.

____ Weight is even over feet (ask).

____ Knees are bent properly.

____ Proper bend from waist.

____ Arms are hanging naturally.

____ No unnecessary tension in arms and hands.

____ No unnecessary tension in legs.

3. Alignment (3 points, 1 each)

____ Not left of target.

____ Not right of target.

____ Proper sequence of address. (Draw imaginary line and pick a spot on the line. Set club square, feet together. Place right foot first on parallel line. Take last look at target.)

4. Swing (10 points, 1 each)

____ One-piece takeaway with the club.

____ Head does not move up and down.

____ Head does not move back and forth.

____ Left arm is extended.

____ A complete coil is present.

____ Club toe up to target—backswing—at parallel level.

____ Club toe up to target—forward swing—at parallel level.

____ Club accelerates through ball.

____ Club continues after contact.

____ Facing target at the finish.

Points	Performance
10	Good contact, good trajectory, good direction
9	Good contact, good trajectory, fair direction
8	Good contact, fair trajectory, fair direction
6	Fair contact, fair trajectory, fair direction
4	Two items fair, one item barely acceptable
2	One item fair, two items barely acceptable
0	Miss or near miss

FIGURE 19.6 Golf rating scale.

19

taken away from the field. Games usually last one to two minutes. If time allows, students are given time for free skating during parts of the period.

Day 4: The instructor begins with a review. The skill for the day is going from forward to backward skating without stopping and returning to forward skating again. Skaters use a partial T-stop and turn the other skate to do this. Not all students are able to perform this maneuver, so students should be given a variety of choices. The period concludes with a limbo contest. Students are prohibited from leaning backward. They must crouch and lean forward when going under the limbo bar. Start the bar high and give students plenty

of opportunities for practice and success. Each time the class goes through once, the bar is lowered. Students are not allowed to have anything other than their skates hit the floor as they pass under the bar. Students who touch the floor are eliminated and must skate freely around the area while the contest goes on. The last student who clears the bar is the winner. Limbo music helps make this a fun event. A high-jump bar from track and field works well for a limbo bar. The bar can be raised for students who are uncomfortable when they first try the activity. Students who do not feel comfortable performing the limbo can assist in holding the bar at the start of the activity to become more comfortable.

Day 5: The instructor reviews skills previously taught and may add new skills. An obstacle course is set up around the area, including tunnels made from folding mats, figure eights with large cones, and small jumps with hoops. Beanbags and balls can be available for students to pick up and move to other areas without stopping. Students must be instructed to be aware of those around them. The outside of the course is reserved for less accomplished skaters, and the inside track is for more experienced skaters. This setup will help keep accidents from happening. To wrap up the day, the instructor reviews the week and talks with students about places to skate and skating as a lifetime activity.

Jogging

Joggers and road races are probably the most visible forms of the fitness renaissance. Millions take to the road regularly for fitness and sport reasons. Various types of distances for running events have become popular with men and women of all ages. Marathons, triathlons, and 15K, 10K, 5K, and 2-mile (3.2 km) fun runs are offered virtually every weekend. People in all areas of the country run in all kinds of weather. Secondary students in physical education programs should have positive experiences with running because this potential lifetime activity can contribute to fitness and be a form of play. Jogging is an easy, inexpensive activity that people can do individually or with a group.

Sequence of Skills

Jogging is simply slow running. It differs from walking in that both feet leave the ground during the flight, or airborne, phase. In walking, one foot is always in contact with the ground.

Running Form

Teachers should spend time working on running form, emphasizing one aspect of form with each drill. Students can overlearn the position of the head, hands, arms, knees, feet, and body lean. In distance running, the stride is shorter than it is in sprinting, and the heel of the foot should strike the ground before the ball of the foot. Breathing should be natural, through both the nose and mouth.

Program Design

Students need to understand how to design a jogging program to meet their individual objectives. Programs will differ according to those objectives. Some students want to lose weight, others may want to condition themselves for a particular activity or sport, and still others want to improve their time in 10K races. Program goals may vary, but students should all understand how the principles of frequency, intensity, and duration apply to a running program. Proper warm-up, cool-down, and stretching and strengthening activities must be taught.

Equipment

Runners must obtain adequate running shoes. They should have a well-cushioned, elevated heel and a durable bottom surface. The toes should not rub the front of the shoe, and the tongue and lining should be padded. The sole must be flexible and have two layers for absorbing shock. An arch support should be built into running shoes.

The remaining equipment (shorts, socks, sweat suits, rain suits, jackets, hats, mittens, and so forth) is a matter of personal preference depending on the weather. Comfort is the key, so loose-fitting, nonirritating material is preferred. Extremely cold and warm weather can be dangerous. Students should understand how to prevent problems by dressing properly and avoiding extreme weather.

Ideas for Effective Instruction

Beginners should understand that jogging is an individual activity that can be noncompetitive. Being a competitive runner is a personal choice. Teachers should reinforce this attitude by reducing the emphasis on running races in a jogging unit. The unit emphasis should be on personal improvement and individual goal accomplishment.

Jog–Walk–Jog

Beginners can be given a distance to cover by alternating jogging and walking. They progress by gradually reducing the walking and increasing the jogging. Students can be assigned different distances, depending on their ability. This technique can be used for jogging on a track. For example, students can jog the straightaways and walk the curves for 1 mile (1,600 m).

Timed Runs

Students can be given a set time of a certain number of minutes. They then try to jog continuously for the designated time. (Teachers blow a whistle every minute or half minute.)

Other Running Activities

Refer to chapter 15 for descriptions of activities such as

form running, file running, walk–sprint–jog, pace work, random running, and fartlek. All can be modified for a jogging unit.

Group Runs

Divide students into small groups of similar ability. The group can run together for a certain time or distance. They should be encouraged to use the talk test during the run, referring to the ability to carry on a conversation during a run as an indicator of proper jogging intensity.

Training Heart Rate

After students have learned about training heart rates (see chapter 15), they can check their heart rates at rest before running, after running so many minutes, and again immediately after a run. This practice will help them understand the concepts of training heart rate, recovery heart rate, and jogging at sufficient intensity.

Orienteering Runs

A jogging unit can include several orienteering meets that emphasize running from point to point on the school grounds. Draw a map with 10 checkpoints that students must find. Each checkpoint has a secret clue, such as a letter, word, color, or team name. Students can work alone or with a partner. (See chapter 20 for more orienteering ideas.)

Cross Country Runs

Map out a cross-country course around the school grounds and in neighboring areas, and hold a meet with a chute for finishers and numbers distributed for the finishing positions. Arrange teams and establish categories for beginners, intermediates, and advanced runners. Set time limits and allow students to run time trials to determine their category or team. Students can choose to be on a team or to run for individual improvement.

Exercise Trails

Set up an exercise trail around the school grounds with several stations for stretching and strengthening various muscle groups. Use a boundary cone with a sign to mark each station and give students a rough map showing the location of each station. After completing a station activity, students jog to the next station. The stations can be set up so that students get a total body workout. After a certain period, the trail can be modified.

Runs With Equipment

Some students with special interests may want to run with a piece of equipment (e.g., dribbling a soccer ball or a basketball). Others may want to carry a football or roll a hoop. Let students be creative, as long as they are engaged in a safe activity. Running with equipment adds variety to activities and is a good motivational device. Consider allowing students to run while listening to music by allowing them a day (or every day) to bring a smartphone with earbuds.

Distance Cards and Maps

Many people enjoy keeping a record of the distance covered. Goals can be established for a given period. Students can jog across the state by coloring in a route or moving a pin to a given point as they accumulate distance. Distance cards or charts can be kept individually, or they can be posted in the locker room or on a bulletin board. Individual or group competitions can be set up based on the distance accumulated.

Rainy Day Activities

Many of these activities (rating forms, pace work, timed runs) can be modified for running in the gymnasium. If the gym is not available, teachers can discuss running topics with students, such as training methods, safety, injuries, equipment, health benefits, exercise and calories, marathons, and the female runner. The References and Suggested Readings section is filled with discussion topics.

Racquetball

The game of racquetball is a direct descendant of the game of paddleball, which was first played in the 1920s. In the 1940s a racket with strings was introduced, and it became known as a paddle racket. The sport grew in popularity, and in 1969 the International Racquetball Association was established, and racquetball was born. Within the last 10 years, the game has grown tremendously in popularity. This growth has brought about a comparable increase in the number of facilities, changes in racket style, and a livelier ball. A Nielson Company survey found that racquetball was the fastest-growing participation sport from 1976 to 1979.

Racquetball can be played on a one-, three-, or four-walled court. The most popular is the enclosed four-wall court with a ceiling, but the other types of courts are more common at the middle and high school levels. The game can be played with two people (singles), three people (cutthroat), or four people (doubles). The object is to win each rally by serving or returning the ball so that the opponent is unable to keep the ball in play. A

19

rally is over when a side makes an error or is unable to return the ball to the front wall before it touches the floor twice. Note that a player can score only when serving.

Sequence of Skills

The following is a breakdown of the skills necessary to successfully participate in racquetball.

Grip, Eastern Style

Forehand

Form a V on the top bevel of the handle with the thumb and index finger. Rest the thumb on the knuckle of the middle finger on the left side bevel of the handle. The palm of the hand should be approximately level with the bottom of the racket. The index finger should be in a pistol-grip position.

Backhand

Rotate one-quarter turn to the left (counterclockwise). The V is now on the upper part of the left bevel.

Ready Position

The feet should be shoulder-width apart and the knees slightly flexed. The back is bent slightly forward, and the head is up. The weight is on the balls of the feet. The racket should be in front of the body at about chest height. Stand in the middle of the court, approximately 4 feet (1.2 m) behind the short line.

Forehand

From the ready position, pivot until facing the right sidewall with the left shoulder forward. Bring the wrist back beside the right ear and point the racket toward the ceiling. The weight is on the back foot. Start the forward swing with the racket and shift the weight from the back to the front foot. Rotate the shoulders and hips toward the front wall. Contact with the ball should be in line with the instep of the front foot. Keep the eyes on the ball and follow through across the body.

Backhand

Follow the same technique as the forehand but contact the ball when it is about 6 inches (15 cm) from the lead foot.

Backwall Shot

Proper setup position is the key to any backwall shot. Watch the ball carefully and set up with the weight on the rear foot and the racket by the ear. Step forward and stroke into the ball at the proper position, as stated in the previous discussion.

Serve

Drive

Hit the serve low and hard to the back corner where the back and sidewalls join. This serve usually goes to the receiver's backhand.

Crosscourt Z

Serve so that the ball strikes the front wall 3 to 4 feet (90 to 120 cm) from the sidewall, rebounds to the sidewall, and bounces deep in the opposite corner. The speed and height of the serve can be varied to create different angles for the opponent.

Lob

The lob is a change-of-pace serve that hits high on the front wall and stays close to the sidewall. It should land deep in the backcourt and drop straight down.

Ceiling Shot

The ceiling shot is a defensive shot to move the opponent back and to open up the front center court. The shot can be hit with a forehand, backhand, or overhead stroke, depending on the position of the ball. If the ball is above the head, an overhead shot can be used. Otherwise, a forehand or backhand can be used. The overhead shot is like a tennis serve. The elbow leads the movement, and the arm stretches overhead to contact the ball with an extended arm. The object is to place the shot close to the front wall on the ceiling. It is usually hit to the opponent's backhand side, tightly against the sidewall.

Passing Shot

The passing shot is an offensive shot hit low and hard to either side of the opponent, just out of reach. The object is to keep the ball close to the sidewall and low enough so that the ball does not come off the back wall to any degree. The shot is a wise choice when the opponent is out of center position to either side of the court.

Kill Shot

The kill is an offensive shot hit low on the front wall. It is impossible to return if hit accurately because it is too low. It can be hit straight into the front wall, or it can be hit off the sidewall into the front wall.

Ideas for Effective Instruction

Rackets are made of wood, fiberglass, aluminum, and various other combinations such as graphite and fiberglass. They have different weights, shapes, strings, and grip sizes. Wood rackets are cheaper but heavier; fiberglass rackets are lighter but less durable. Aluminum is lightweight and durable but expensive. Grips are usually leather or rubber. Leather seems to provide a better grip but is not as durable, as rubber. Grip size is the circumference of the handle in inches, such as 4-1/8 and 4-5/8 (10.5 and 11.7 cm).

Racquetballs are quite lively and will break after some usage, so having extras is a good idea. Eye guards are available as a safety measure, and some players may want to wear a glove to provide a better grip.

A good approach is to have two students working in one court, one on each side. If more students must be placed on each court, then designate partners and have one hitting and one chasing balls or throwing setups. Have two hitters and two nonhitters per court. The nonhitter can perform a variety of functions, such as analyzing strokes, checking safety, or using a rating scale. Keep the hitters close to the sidewalls to give everyone enough room.

Skill work can be accomplished easily by practicing performance objectives. The best approach is to start with a bounce-and-hit method and progress to a setup throw off the wall. Either of these methods can be done alone or with a partner. Some students need to practice bouncing the ball and throwing the ball off the wall. Take time to show students how to perform these skills.

Stress the importance of safety on the court because of the confined area and the dangerous implements. Players should be encouraged to wear eye guards and should be reminded never to turn around and expose the face to a person hitting from behind them. All players must tie the wrist strings snugly around the wrist to avoid losing control of the racket and injuring others. Finally, players should be reminded that the rules of racquetball stress safety. Whenever there is any chance of endangering the opponent either by hitting with the racket or by making body contact, they should let the ball go and play the point over.

Lead-Up Games and Learning Activities

This section highlights numerous lead-up games and learning activities to help develop the skills to participate in racquetball.

Ceiling Games

This change-of-pace game requires students to use the ceiling shot. After the serve, a certain number of shots must hit the ceiling before or after hitting the front wall. If the ball does not hit the ceiling, it is a point or side-out. A useful variation is to change the required number of ceiling shots that a person must hit each time. For example, start with one and then increase the required number. Alternatively, require all ceiling shots be hit after the serve.

Five Points and Out

This modified game allows five or fewer serves each time the serve changes hands. After 5 points are scored, opponents change positions (server to receiver). The opponents change positions normally if a side-out is forced before the 5 points are scored. This modification keeps opponents from dominating the scoring through an exceptionally strong serve.

Eight-Ball Rally

After the serve, each person must hit the ball four times before a point can be scored. This modification forces a longer rally and encourages work on different shots.

Backhand Rally

After the serve, a player must hit a certain number of backhand shots before a point is scored or a side-out is forced. Start with one required backhand and then increase the number gradually.

Accuracy Drills

Students can work on their accuracy by hitting to targets marked on the floor and walls. Jump ropes, boundary cones, boxes, and masking tape are useful for constructing targets. Challenge the entire class to make five lob serves, five forehands, five backhands, five Z serves, and five drive serves to the target areas. Kill shots off the back wall and sidewalls can be practiced to marked areas on the front wall. Announce the winner in each category. Vary the size of the targets and the designated skills each day.

Cutthroat and Doubles

Cutthroat is played with three people. The server plays the other two players. Doubles is two players versus two.

Rotation

Rotation involves students playing a five-minute game. After a whistle is blown, students rotate to the court on the left if they are ahead and stay where they are if behind. The object of the game is to move up to the last court. Rotation is also enjoyable when playing doubles. Teammates move ahead a court if they are leading when the whistle blows.

19

Example Objectives

Forehand Drive

1. Standing 3 feet (90 cm) behind the short line and 3 feet (90 cm) from the sidewall, bounce the ball off the sidewall. After the ball bounces on the floor, execute a proper forehand drive, hitting the front wall below the 8-foot (2.4 m) line four consecutive times.

2. Standing 3 feet (90 cm) behind the receiving line and 3 feet (90 cm) from the sidewall, bounce the ball off the sidewall in the same manner task 1 and execute a proper forehand drive, hitting the front wall below the 8-foot (2.4 m) line four consecutive times.

3. Standing 3 feet (90 cm) behind the service line and in the middle of the court, feed the ball to the front wall and then execute a proper forehand drive below the 8-foot (2.4 m) line three of four times.

4. Standing 3 feet (90 cm) behind the short line and in the middle of the court, feed the ball to the front wall and then execute a proper forehand drive below the 8-foot (2.4 m) line three of four times.

Backhand Drive

5. Repeat task 1 using a proper backhand drive.
6. Repeat task 2 using a proper backhand drive.
7. Repeat task 3 using a proper backhand drive.
8. Repeat task 4 using a proper backhand drive.

Back-Wall Shot

9. Standing approximately 10 feet (3 m) from the back wall, bounce the ball off the floor and then off the back wall and execute a forehand back-wall shot, hitting the front wall below the 8-foot (2.4 m) line three of four times.

10. Repeat task 9 using the backhand back-wall shot.

11. Standing approximately in the middle of the court, feed the ball to the front wall so that it bounces off the floor and the back wall and execute a forehand back-wall shot, hitting the front wall below the 8-foot (2.4 m) line three of four times.

12. Repeat task 11 using the backhand drive.

Serves

13. Hit three of five drive serves to the left court that land within 3 feet (90 cm) of the sidewall in the back court and are otherwise legal.

14. Hit three of five crosscourt serves to the left court that land within 3 feet (90 cm) of the sidewall and are otherwise legal.

15. Hit three of five lob serves to the left court that land within 3 feet (90 cm) of the sidewall, do not bounce out from the back more than 3 feet (90 cm), and are otherwise legal.

16. Repeat task 13 to the right court.
17. Repeat task 14 to the right court.
18. Repeat task 15 to the right court.

Ceiling Shot

19. Standing in the backcourt, bounce the ball high enough to execute a proper overhand forehand ceiling shot so that the ball hits the ceiling, front wall, floor, and the back wall low three of four times.

20. Repeat task 19 using the regular forehand stroke.

Pinch Shot

21. Standing at midcourt, bounce the ball and execute a proper forehand pinch shot so that the ball hits the sidewall and front wall, bounces at least two times, and hits the other sidewall three of four times.

22. Repeat task 21 using the backhand stroke.

Intermediate and Advanced Skills

23. Repeat task 1, hitting the front wall below the 3-foot (90 cm) line.

24. Repeat task 2, hitting the front wall below the 3-foot (90 cm) line.

25. Repeat task 3, hitting the front wall below the 3-foot (90 cm) line.

26. Repeat task 4, hitting the front wall below the 3-foot (90 cm) line.

27. Repeat task 1 using a proper backhand drive and hitting the front wall below the 3-foot (90 cm) line.

28. Repeat task 2 using a proper backhand drive and hitting the front wall below the 3-foot (90 cm) line.

29. Repeat task 3 using a proper backhand drive and hitting the front wall below the 3-foot (90 cm) line.

30. Repeat task 4 using a proper backhand drive and hitting the front wall below the 3-foot (90 cm) line.

31. Repeat task 9, hitting the front wall below the 3-foot (90 cm) line.

32. Repeat task 9 using the backhand back-wall shot and hitting the front wall below the 3-foot (90 cm) line.

33. Repeat task 11, hitting the front wall below the 3-foot (90 cm) line.

34. Repeat task 11 using the backhand drive and hitting the front wall below the 3-foot (90 cm) line.

35. Repeat task 19 using the backhand stroke.

36. Repeat task 20 using the backhand stroke.

37. Repeat task 21 with feed off the front wall.

38. Repeat task 22 with feed off the front wall.

39. Repeat task 1, hitting the front wall below the 1-foot (30 cm) line (kill shot) three of four times.

40. Repeat task 3, hitting the front wall below the 1-foot (30 cm) line three of four times.

41. Repeat task 14 using the backhand in the right court three of four times.

42. Repeat task 15 using the backhand in the right court three of four times.

Rainy Day Activities

1. Review rules and strategies for serving, court position, passing shots, singles play, cutthroat, and doubles play.

2. Have students critique several racquetball articles or a chapter from an activity book.

3. Develop a crossword puzzle or word searches about racquetball.

4. Assign a group of students to develop a crossword puzzle or word search.

5. Work on serving against a wall indoors. Speed and distances can be modified according to the available space.

6. Have on hand a variety of rackets, balls, gloves, and eye guards and discuss the advantages of each.

7. Show videos on racquetball.

8. Devise and administer a test on terms and strategy.

9. Discuss caloric expenditure from playing racquetball.

10. Point out the health-related benefits of playing racquetball.

Rhythmic Activity

The urge to express themselves rhythmically has been characteristic of people throughout time. Dances have been done as religious rituals, as national and cultural customs, and as declarations of war. Current dances are borrowed from many cultures and groups, both ancient and modern. Because the United States is a melting pot of cultures, we have a broad and diverse range of folk dances representing many peoples.

Every generation dances. Students must learn the dances of the past as they develop new dances unique to their group. They can learn a variety of social skills through social dancing. Often, if people are not taught dance skills during the school-aged years, they are hesitant to participate in later years. The rhythmic program should thus be viewed as an integral part of the physical education program. If dance skills are not taught as part of the program, they probably will not be taught at all.

Sequence of Skills

The program should consist of four major parts: square dance, folk and round dances, social dance steps, and country swing and western dance. So many skills and dances can be taught that listing all the activities here is impossible. Another concern is that different geographic areas have favorite dances and rhythmic activities peculiar to each. One book cannot offer activities that would be comprehensive enough in the rhythms area to suit all readers. Several resources are available with supplementary and comprehensive coverage, including *Dance Teaching Methods and Curriculum Design, Second Edition* (Kassing, 2020); *Lesson Planning for Middle School Physical Education* (Doan, MacDonald, & Chepko, 2017) and *Lesson Planning for High School Physical Education* (MacDonald, Doan, & Chepko, 2017), which include dance units written by PE teachers for PE teachers; *Beginning Hip-Hop Dance* (Durden, 2018); *Dance Units for Middle School* (Fey, 2011); *Traditional Barn Dances With Calls & Fiddling* (Laufman & Laufman, 2009); and *Dance a While* (Pittman, Waller, & Dark, 2009).

Rope Jumping

People of all ages and ability levels enjoy rope jumping, which can be a demanding activity. The American Heart Association has endorsed rope jumping for years because of its positive effects on cardiorespiratory endurance. It is an inexpensive activity that can be done in a limited

19

space, indoors or outside. Through rope jumping, students develop rhythm, timing, and coordination, as well as fitness. The numerous jumping activities can challenge all ability levels. The rope can be turned many ways at varying speeds, and the jumper can use a variety of foot patterns. Individual, partner, and small-group activities are available.

Rope jumping is a useful carryover activity that can be enjoyed throughout life. Developing creative rope-jumping routines and skills can be a challenge to students. Because of the rhythmic aspect of jumping rope, teachers should add popular music to enhance students' motivational level.

Body Position and Rhythm

Jumping rope requires proper body position and alignment. The head should be up and the eyes looking ahead. Good balance is necessary, with the feet, ankles, and legs close together. The body is erect during the jump. The knees flex and extend slightly with each jump. The elbows are kept close to the body at approximately a 90-degree angle. The basic jump should be straight up and down and about 1 inch (2.5 cm) high. The rope should be turned primarily with the wrists and forearms. Effective jumpers land on the balls of their feet and stay in one spot.

The speed at which the rope turns is referred to as the rhythm. Slow-time (half-time) rhythm involves turning the rope 60 to 90 revolutions per minute. The student jumps, rebounds, and then jumps again as the rope comes through. A rebound is a slight bend at the knee to carry or keep the rhythm. The student does not actually leave the ground during a rebound. Slow time is the easiest rhythm for beginners. Fast-time rhythm involves turning the rope 120 to 180 turns per minute. No rebound occurs because the rope and the feet must move faster. In double-time rhythm, the rope is turned at the same speed as slow time, but instead of using a rebound, the performer executes a different type of step while the rope is coming around. Double-time rhythm is the most difficult to learn, because the feet and the turning of the rope must be coordinated. The feet must move quickly while the rope turns slowly.

Sequence of Skills

Several types of ropes are useful for teaching the skill to secondary students. Sash cord and hard-weave synthetic ropes can be used, but the best jump ropes are made of plastic links with a plastic handle that turns. The rope should be heavy enough to maintain a rhythmic rotation. The length of the rope will vary according to the height of the student. Proper length

can be determined by standing in the middle of the rope and pulling the ends up to the armpits or slightly higher. If the ends of the rope reach beyond that area, students can wrap the extra rope around the hands or use a longer rope if the one tested is too short. Most secondary students need an 8-, 9-, or 10-foot (2.4, 2.7, or 3.0 m) jump rope.

Individual Steps

The following foot patterns can be used with all three rhythm patterns—slow time, fast time, and double time. Students should try the patterns in slow time before moving on to fast and double time.

Two-Foot Basic Step

The student jumps over the rope with the feet together. In slow time, a rebound occurs after each turn of the rope.

Alternate-Foot Step (Jog Step)

The student alternates feet with every jump. The unweighted leg is bent slightly at the knee. A variation can have the student jump a consecutive number of times on one foot before switching feet. For example, a student might jump five times on the right foot and then five on the left foot. With a fast-time rhythm, this step looks like jogging.

Side Swings—Left or Right

The student moves the rope to either side of the body and jumps off both feet in time with the rope. The student does not actually jump over the rope. This technique is good for working on timing and cardiorespiratory fitness because it is demanding.

Swing Step Forward or Sideways

This step is the same as the jog step, except the unweighted leg swings forward or sideways rather than backward. The student can alternate the forward swing with the side swing on each foot.

Rocker Step

The student starts with one leg in front of the other. As the rope comes around, the weight is shifted from the front leg to the back leg and alternates each time the rope goes around. The student rocks back and forth, from front foot to back foot.

Legs Spread Forward and Backward (Scissors)

The student starts with one leg forward and one leg back, like the starting position for the rocker step. As the rope turns, the front leg is shifted back and the back leg is shifted forward. The position of the legs shifts each time the rope is turned.

Legs Crossed Sideways (Jumping Jack)

The student starts with the legs straddled sideways. As the rope is turned, the legs are crossed with the right leg in front. Another straddle position is next, and then the legs are crossed again with the left leg in front. This sequence is repeated. The jump can also be executed with the feet coming together, instead of crossing each time, similar to the foot pattern of a jumping-jack exercise.

Toe Touches Forward or Backward

The student starts with one foot forward. The toe of the forward foot is pointed down and touches the ground. As the rope turns, the feet trade places, and the opposite toe touches the ground. For the backward toe touch, the foot starts in a backward position with the toe touching. The feet then alternate positions with each jump.

Shuffle Step

The student starts with the weight on the left foot and the toe of the right foot touching the heel of the left foot. As the rope turns, the student steps to the right and the feet trade places. The left toe is now touching the right heel. The student repeats the step in the opposite direction.

Ski Jump

The student keeps both feet together and jumps to the left and right sideways over a line. This motion is like that of a skier. The jump can be performed with the rope going forward or backward.

Heel–Toe Jump

The student jumps off the right foot and extends the left leg forward, touching the heel to the ground. On the next jump the left foot is brought back beside the right foot with the toe touching the ground. The student repeats the pattern with the right foot touching the heel and then the toe.

Heel Click

The student starts by completing several sideways swing steps in preparation for this pattern. As the leg swings out to the side, the opposite foot is brought up and the heels are touched together. The heel click can be completed on either side.

Crossing Arms

Crossing the arms can be added to all the basic foot patterns. In crossing the arms, the hands actually trade places. The hands must be brought all the way across the body and kept low. The upper body crouches forward slightly from the waist. Crossing can also be used for backward jumping. Students can learn to cross and uncross after a certain number of jumps.

Double Turns

A double turn occurs when the rope passes under the feet twice during the same jump. The student must jump higher and rotate the rope faster. The jump should be about 6 inches (15 cm) high, and a slight forward crouch is necessary to speed up the turn. Students should try consecutive double turns forward or backward. They can also try various foot patterns with double turns.

Sideways Jumping

The rope is turned sideways with one hand over the head and the other hand extended down between the legs in front of the body. As the rope is turned, the student jumps the rope one leg at a time. The weight is shifted back and forth between the legs as the rope turns around the body. Students can turn the rope either left or right, and either hand can be held overhead. Students should try the technique several ways.

Shifting From Forward to Backward Jumping

Students can change jumping direction is several ways. The first way is to begin jumping forward. As the rope starts downward, the student executes a left- or right-side swing. A half-turn should be made in the same direction as the rope. As the rope is coming out of the side swing, the student must bring it up in a backward motion. This motion can be completed to either side, as long as the turn is toward the rope side.

Another way to execute the shift is to make a half-turn while the rope is above the head with the arms extended upward. The rope will hesitate slightly and then should be brought down in the opposite direction. A final shifting strategy is from a cross-arm position. As the rope is going overhead, the student uncrosses the arms and makes a half-turn. This action starts the rope turning in the opposite direction. The key is to uncross the arms and turn simultaneously.

Partner Activities

19

Using one rope, partners can perform a variety of challenging combinations. The partners can start jumping together, or one person can run into position after the other partner has started jumping. Partner activities can be fun with students the same size. They are more challenging when performed with students of varying sizes.

1. One person turns the rope forward or backward.
   a. The partner faces the turner for a specific number of jumps.
   b. Partners are back to back for a specific number of jumps.

c. The partner turns in place—quarter turn, half-turn, and so on.

d. The partner dribbles a basketball while jumping.

e. Partners match foot patterns (e.g., jog step, swing step).

f. Partners complete double turns.

2. Two students turn the rope forward or backward.

a. Partners stand side by side, facing the same direction.

b. Partners face opposite directions.

c. Partners repeat activities 2a and 2b with elbows locked.

d. Partners repeat 2a, 2b, and 2c while hopping on one foot.

e. Partners are back to back turning one rope with the right or left hand.

f. Partners repeat variation 2e while turning in a circle—both directions.

3. Three students jump together with one turning the rope, one in front, and the third in back. They can do this forward and backward.

4. Two students, each with a rope, face each other. One student turns the rope forward, and the other turns backward, so that the ropes are going in the same direction. Partners jump over both ropes on one jump. Students should then change their rope direction.

5. One student turns the rope. The partner comes in from the side, takes one handle of the rope, and begins turning. The partner must time the entrance so that the rhythm of the rope remains constant. The partner then leaves and enters from the other side. This stunt can be performed with a forward or backward turn.

6. Partners face each other, turning one rope with the right hand. One partner turns to the left and exits from jumping while continuing to turn the rope for the other partner. After several turns, the partner who was out returns to the starting position. A variation can be tried with the partner turning to the right one-quarter turn.

Ideas for Effective Instruction

Rope jumping is a good example of an activity that students can improve on with practice. Remind students

constantly that they will perfect these skills only with regular practice. Such reminders help keep students from becoming discouraged.

Students should first try new jumping techniques without the rope to get the basic idea. They can then try the stunt with a slow-time rhythm and a rebound after each movement. As they improve, they can try fast time and double time. Some students may need to practice turning the rope in one hand to the side of the body to develop the necessary rhythm. Students should practice timing their jumps with the rope turning at the side. An instructor might do some partner jumping with a student who is having trouble with timing. Another effective instructional strategy is to use a movie, videotape, or loop film to give students a visual model of the skill. Because jumping is a high-intensity activity, allow students some opportunities to rest between different jumps. Several strategies are listed in the References and Suggested Readings section at the end of this chapter.

Students need plenty of room for practicing. Care should be taken because the ropes can be dangerous to a person's face and eyes. Horseplay with the jump ropes should not be tolerated. Ropes can be color-coded for various sizes. Students can help distribute and collect the ropes so that they do not become tangled. Student helpers can hold their arms out to the sides, and other students can place the ropes over their arms. Music with different tempos provides a challenge and motivates many students.

Lead-Up Games and Learning Activities

In addition to the foot patterns, rhythms, turning patterns, and partner activities that have been mentioned, other effective learning activities can be done individually, in small groups, or with the entire class.

Follow the Leader

Students can work with a partner, a small group, or the entire class—moving forward, backward, diagonally, or sideways—following a designated leader. Various foot patterns can also be used while moving.

Leader in the Circle

The students follow the leader, who is in the center of a circle. This activity can be done with large or small circles. The leader calls the name of the next leader after a designated time or after a certain number of foot patterns have been executed.

Relays

Many different jump-rope relays can be played with boundary cones and various types of jumps.

1. Jog-step down around the cone and back (forward turns).
2. Perform variation 1 but with backward turns.
3. Jog-step backward using forward turns.
4. Perform variation 3 but with backward turns.
5. Hop to the cone on one foot and hop back on the other.
6. Ski-jump down and forward swing-step back.
7. Jog-step through a series of six cones, do 10 sit-ups, and jog-step back.
8. Use a two-foot basic step going down, do five rocker steps, do five scissor steps, and come back with a two-foot basic step.
9. Partners (side by side with one rope, elbows locked, both facing forward) go down forward and come back backward.
10. Partners (side by side with one rope, one person facing forward, the other facing backward) go down and back with a forward turn.

Routines

Various routines can be developed individually with guidelines for foot patterns, change of direction, crossing over, changing levels, rope speed, and routine length. Small groups can also make up routines, choose music, and perform together. Partner routines can be developed with two people using one rope. An example of the guidelines for a small-group routine follows:

- Two minutes or less—five members per group
- Two changes of direction (e.g., forward, backward, diagonal)
- Two changes of floor pattern (e.g., circle, square, back to back)
- Two changes of levels (e.g., high, low)
- Five changes of foot patterns (e.g., rocker, basic two-step)
- One change of rope direction
- One double turn

Rainy Day Activities

All jump-rope activities are good for rainy days because they can be performed indoors in a limited space. Hallways and gymnasium foyers are possible areas for jump-rope activities. Students can work on individual skills if space is limited. A rotation schedule may have to be arranged so that some students are practicing while partners are observing and using a rating scale or checking off performance objectives. Students can also devote time to learning the appropriate terminology for foot patterns and rhythms.

Strength Training

Various forms of strength training have become extremely popular activities for general conditioning. Adults and students of all ages are lifting weights and working on resistance machines in schools, health clubs, YMCAs, and in their homes. Current research has made women aware of the misconceptions about and benefits of resistance training. Coaches and athletes involved in different sports are using extensive strength-training programs to improve performance. Strength training is now well entrenched in the activity habits of society. A properly developed strength-training program can produce positive changes in body composition and performance. People engaged in strength training look better, feel better, and perform daily activities better. All these results have contributed to the popularity of the sport.

Many types of strength-training equipment are available. Machines such as the Hammer Strength, Smith Machines, Universal Gym, Nautilus equipment, the Orthotron, and the Cybex II are used commonly for training programs. Each machine offers different advantages. Free weights, including different types of dumbbells and barbells, are still popular and are available in most weight rooms. Physical education teachers need to analyze such factors as cost, space, objectives, and usage before purchasing strength-training equipment.

Sequence of Skills

The following is a breakdown of the skills necessary to successfully participate in strength training.

Principles, Terminology, and Safety

Beginning strength trainers need to understand the basic principles of training relative to their specific objectives. Students must understand the definitions of strength, endurance, flexibility, warm-up, cool-down, sets, repetitions, frequency, rest intervals, and the various types of lifts for specific muscle groups. A student's objectives should determine the type and number of lifts. Proper form must be understood to gain maximum benefits and to complete the activities safely. Spotting techniques are a necessity for certain lifts, especially with heavy weights. Safety in the weightlifting area must be stressed

19

constantly. Chapter 15 gives general information on those aspects of strength training. Additional specific information is available in the section References and Suggested Readings at the end of this chapter.

Spotting

Spotters are people who stand by a lifter to provide help when necessary. Spotters are concerned about preventing a weight from falling or slipping if the lifter cannot control the weight. All students should understand the spotting procedures for a specific lift. They can check the equipment for proper alignment, tightened collars, and so forth, and they can be aware of the position of other students in the area. Specific attention should be paid to each lift, especially with heavier weights.

Breathing

Lifters should try to be consistent and natural in their breathing. Most experts agree that breathing should follow a pattern of exhaling during exertion and inhaling as the weight is returned to the starting position. With heavy weights, many lifters take a deep breath before the lift and hold the breath until the final exertion. The final exhalation helps complete the lift. Care is necessary, because holding the breath too long can make a person light-headed and may even cause him or her to faint.

Grips

The three major grips are the overhand, underhand, and alternating. These grips are used with different types of lifts; for example, the overhand grip with the palms down is used for the bench press, the underhand grip with the palms up is used for curls, and the alternating grip with one palm up and the other down is used with the dead lift.

Body Position

With free weights, the lifter must get the feet, arms, and body aligned properly for lifting and removing weights from power racks or squat stands. Carelessness in alignment can result in an unbalanced position that can result in dropping the weights or in poor lifting technique. Each lift requires a different position, depending on whether the bar is lifted from the floor or from a rack. Spotters must understand the type of lift to be executed and their specific responsibilities. For example, with a back squat, the following steps should be followed:

1. Check the collars to see that they are tightened.
2. Grip the bar and space the hands wider than the shoulders.
3. Align the middle of the back under the midpoint of the bar.
4. Use a pad or towel to cushion the bar against the back.
5. Bend the knees and align the body vertically under the bar.
6. Keep the head up and lift the weight straight up.
7. Move out from the rack and assume a comfortable foot position about shoulder-width apart.
8. Perform the lift with a spotter on either side of the bar.

Upper-Body Lifts

Bench Press

Use an overhand grip with the hands slightly wider than the shoulders. Bring the bar down to the chest (see figure 19.7a) and press up over the shoulders (figure 19.7b). Exhale on the press upward.

FIGURE 19.7 Bench press.

Curl

Use an underhand grip with the arms about shoulder-width apart (see figure 19.8a). Curl the bar up the shoulders and extend downward slowly to a straight-arm position (figure 19.8b). Use an underhand grip to perform a reverse curl.

FIGURE 19.9 Bent rowing.

FIGURE 19.8 Curl.

Bent or Upright Row

Both lifts use an overhand grip about shoulder-width apart. The bent position starts with the barbell on the floor and the body bent at the hips (see figure 19.9a). Bend the knees slightly. Pull the bar to the chest and keep the back stable (figure 19.9b). The upright position (see figure 19.10a) starts with the bar across the thighs. Pull the bar up to the chin area (figure 19.10b) and return it slowly.

FIGURE 19.10 Upright row.

19

Military Press

Use an overhand grip slightly wider than the shoulders in a standing or sitting position (see figure 19.11a). Press the bar upward from the chest (figure 19.11b) and return. A variation brings the bar down behind the head and then back up.

FIGURE 19.11 Military press.

Bench Pullover

Lying on a bench, grip the bar overhand and pull it straight up and over the face from the floor (see figure 19.12).

FIGURE 19.12 Bench pullover.

Shoulder Shrugs

With a straight barbell across the thighs or with two dumbbells at the sides of the body (see figure 19.13), raise or shrug the shoulders as high as possible and then return to the starting position.

FIGURE 19.13 Shoulder shrugs.

Triceps Extension

A barbell, two dumbbells, or a machine can be used. With the barbell, start the weight bar overhead with an overhand grip, lower it slowly behind the head, and then extend it back to the starting position. With a machine, bring the bar down in front of the body.

Lateral Raises

Perform lateral raises using an overhand grip with dumbbells. A standing or bent position can be used. Start with the weights at the sides or on the floor and are raise them laterally with straight arms.

Lower-Body Lifts

Front and Back Squat

Use an overhand grip with the bar across the front of the shoulders or across the upper-back muscles. Bend the knees to a position in which the thighs are parallel to the floor.

Dead Lift

Start in a squat position with the weight on the floor, the feet about shoulder-width apart, and an alternating grip. Keep the arms straight and the back flat while lifting the weight and coming to an erect position with the bar across the thighs.

Power Clean

The power clean is a complex lift that starts in the same position as the dead lift but with an overhand grip. The lift includes a start, an acceleration, and a catch phase. The bar is pulled up, past the waist, and ends above the chest. The lifter must control both the weight and the body as the weight moves through the starting position to the catch position.

Leg Curls and Extensions

These lifts call for a machine attached to a bench. The extension starts with the lifter in a sitting position with the feet under a lower, padded section. The arms grip the sides of the bench, and the upper body is leaning slightly back. The legs are extended until they are parallel to the floor. The leg curl uses the upper padded section of the machine. The lifter is on the belly, and the heels are hooked behind the pad. The heels are then pulled up toward the buttocks and lowered.

Heel raises

The student begins on the balls of the feet and the toes over a stable board or step, or standing on a flat surface. The lifter holds a weight in each hand at the sides (see figure 19.14a). The heels are then raised (figure 19.14b) and lowered.

FIGURE 19.14 Heel raises.

Lead-Up Games and Learning Activities

This section highlights numerous lead-up games and learning activities to help develop the skills to participate in strength training.

Circuit Training

An effective strategy for organizing the activities in the weight room is to set up a circuit with several stations. The students can be divided into groups and rotated after a certain number of minutes. Students perform a specific number of sets and repetitions at each station.

Students should keep a daily log of the sets, repetitions, and weights they lifted. These records are important in organizing a progression and should help to motivate the students. Depending on the equipment and facilities available, a good approach is to develop a circuit for both lower-body exercises and upper-body exercises. Students can alternate upper- and lower-body workouts. Aerobic conditioning activities can also be alternated with the resistance training. Many teachers like to add variety to the circuit routines by changing stations regularly.

Partner Resistance Activities

Chapter 15 describes several partner resistance activities that can be used to supplement and add variety to a strength-training unit. These activities can be added to a circuit or be scheduled as an entire day's lesson. They are useful in situations in which equipment is limited. For example, while students are waiting their turns to use a weight machine, they can perform several resistance activities. Various stretch bands are also available for certain situations.

Muscle of the Day

Another good learning activity is to present students with information about one muscle at the end of each lesson. The name of the muscle and its functions are written on a card and placed on the wall of the weight room. A quick review of the muscles previously covered and a presentation of information about a new muscle take place each day. This activity can conclude each day's workout.

Motivational Devices

Resistance training offers tangible evidence of improvement in the various lifts. This improvement can be tied to many different motivational devices: T-shirts, certificates, and membership in a club are popular examples of awards for lifting certain amounts of weight. These items can be quite simple yet are effective and meaningful for

19

CLUB REQUIREMENTS

Requirements—To become a member, you must lift a combined total of 5.2 times your weight. The three required lifts are bench press, dead lift, and squat.

Weight		Required total		Weight		Required total
100–109	=	520		170–179	=	884
110–119	=	572		180–189	=	936
120–129	=	624		190–199	=	988
130–139	=	676		200–209	=	1,040
140–149	=	728		210–219	=	1,092
150–159	=	780		220 and up	=	1,144
160–169	=	832				

Each participant is allowed three tries for each lift. Weight may be added to the previous lift, but it may not be subtracted from the previous lift.

Name _____ Date _____ Class 10 11 12

Body weight _____ Required total lift _____

	First	Second	Third	Best of three lifts
Bench press	____	____	____	____
Dead lift	____	____	____	____
Squat	____	____	____	____
Total				

Coach's signature _____

FIGURE 19.15 Motivational club criteria for weightlifting.

many students. Figure 19.15 is a good example of motivational club criteria that could be used. The club could be available to students in the weight-training classes.

Swimming and Aquatics

An aquatics instructional program in the secondary schools is an excellent addition to a balanced curriculum. Unfortunately, many school districts do not have the facilities necessary to implement swimming and related aquatics programs. A solution that is often feasible is to bus students to swimming pools outside the school. These facilities may be municipal pools, YMCA and YWCA pools, or the pools of various private organizations.

Swimming classes require teacher expertise in the area. Rotating teaching responsibilities is mandatory so that teachers with experience teach the swimming instructional program. Those with less experience can teach aquatic games. The aquatic games component focuses on learning to adjust to the water. All aquatics teachers, regardless of assignment, should have the American Red Cross Water Safety Instruction certification.

The pool should be clean and warm. Nothing turns off students faster than having to swim in a pool that is inadequately heated. A pool with a uniform depth of 3 to 4 feet (90 to 120 cm) of water is often preferable for teaching nonswimmers because students can stand up immediately if they have a problem. This setup offers beginning swimmers a measure of confidence. For intermediate and advanced swimmers, a standard pool, which can be used for diving as well as swimming, is preferable.

Keep lessons short in terms of time spent in the water. Students tire easily when learning new skills, and they can practice some skills out of the water. Because swimming is an important life skill, students should leave the class with a positive feeling about the instruction. Introducing students to any new activity is difficult, and most students need extra encouragement and patience as they begin to overcome their fears of the water.

Sequence of Skills

A difficult aspect of teaching swimming to middle and high school students is the tremendous range of ability and experience that students bring to the class. Some students may not know how to swim, whereas others may have been swimming competitively since they were three years old. This circumstance necessitates homogeneous groupings according to ability. The skills to be taught may therefore range from drown proofing and survival skills to the criteria in American Red Cross Water Safety Instruction certification.

Because aquatics is a highly specialized activity involving specific skills that must be learned, developing meaningful lead-up activities is challenging. We recommend texts listed at the end of this section to teachers interested in creating a meaningful instructional program. They include chapters on developing a successful instructional program, which includes teaching essential aquatic skills, springboard-diving skills, and lifesaving skills. Chapters

are also offered on the evaluation of swimming skills. Of particular help to the less experienced teacher is a series of performance analysis sheets to help in evaluating various strokes and dives. We have included a section on swimming/aquatics safety, a suggested five-day block plan for secondary students (see figure 19.16), a set of detailed lesson plans for those five days (see figure 19.17), and a partner task assessment sheet to assess aquatics skills (see figure 19.18).

Aquatics Safety

To ensure the safety of all people in an aquatics center, facility rules must be clearly defined. Every staff member and student must strictly adhere to facility rules and safety responsibilities, which include identifying potential hazards and enforcing pool rules at all times. Rules should be posted in a highly visible location and clearly state student expectations. Students should be oriented to expectations and held accountable to strict adherence to ensure a safe environment. The rules should state both physical and behavioral expectations in and out of the pool, and they should encompass physical entry and exit of the pool, including diving regulations. In addition to pool rules, an emergency action plan (EAP) must be posted.

An EAP is a well-written document that outlines systematic procedures to follow in an emergency. An emergency is any situation that may be of immediate threat or serious injury to one or more individuals. Emergencies include passive drowning; potential head,

	Monday	Tuesday	Wednesday	Thursday	Friday
Introductory activity	Pool rules and EAP Pool entry and exit	Practice EAP	Marking	Partner resistance kicking	Lazy river
Fitness	Lazy river	Flutter kick	Water aerobics	Treading water	Racetrack fitness in the water
Lesson	Water safety: Treading water Breathing Back floating	Front crawl stroke	Breathing Front crawl stroke	Backstroke skills	Partner task assessment sheet
Activity	Water volleyball	Team relay: kicking with boards	Water basketball	Five passes	Water disc game

EAP = Emergency action plan.

FIGURE 19.16 Aquatics block plan.

AQUATICS LESSON—DAY 1

Performance Objectives (Student Outcomes)

Students will know the pool rules and be able to follow them.

Students will learn and demonstrate how to enter and exit the pool safely.

Students will demonstrate how to properly respond to the emergency action plan (EAP).

Students will learn how to float and tread water to show movement skills and safety activities.

Introductory Activity: Pool Rules, EAP

(The EAP should be reviewed and practiced before the swim unit.)

Before entering the pool, students should be instructed on the pool rules, which should be posted in the aquatics area. The following pool rules include specific behavior in and out of the water.

- Follow all directions.
- No running in the pool area.
- No diving into the pool.
- Do not enter the pool until instructed.
- Enter the pool feet first in a cleared area.
- Stay off the lane line.
- When changing lanes, go under the lane lines, not over them.
- When the emergency sound airs, clear the pool immediately, go directly to the bleachers, and sit quietly.

After reviewing pool rules, students learn how to respond to an EAP and rehearse EAP requirements. Then they practice pool entry and exit procedures.

Fitness: Lazy River

Students walk slowly in the shallow end of the pool, as if they are wading through a river. Students walk in their own personal space. Teacher calls out new directions every 30 to 60 seconds. Examples of student walking directions include normal steps, short steps, long steps, backward steps, side steps, and leg crossovers.

Lesson: Water Safety Skills—Treading Water, Breathing, Front Floating

Treading water: Teach students to tread in chest-high water. The objective is to keep the body upright and use a rhythmic motion. Begin with arm movements; students cup the hands and use a sculling motion. Hands must be in front of the student and submerged. After students have practiced arm movements, teach two methods of leg movements: simulation of bicycle leg pumping and a scissors kick.

Breathing: Teach breathing in waist-high water. Have students take a breath, fully submerge, and exhale, blowing bubbles. Have students reemerge for air and repeat the process.

Front float: Using partner assistance, teach students how to float in waist-high water, keeping their faces in the water and spreading their arms out to the side. Teach students how to recover by having them bring their knees to the chest and their hands to their sides.

Activity: Water Volleyball

Divide students into two equal groups on each side of the net in the shallow end of the pool. Use a beach ball and have students focus on noncompetitive rallying.

Materials needed:

- Pool rules sheets for each student
- Emergency action plan
- Pool volleyball net
- Beach balls

FIGURE 19.17 Aquatic lessons for five days.

(continued)

AQUATICS LESSON—DAY 2

Performance Objectives (Student Outcomes)

Students will perform an emergency action plan (EAP) response (rehearsal).

Student will learn and demonstrate how to enter and exit the pool safely.

Students will demonstrate how to respond properly to the EAP.

Students will learn how to float and tread water to show movement skills and a safety measure.

Students will show proper arm techniques in the crawl stroke (turning head to the side).

Introductory Activity: Practice EAP

Students rehearse the EAP and understand its significance.

Fitness: Flutter Kick

Holding onto the edge of the pool with both hands, students practice a flutter kick. The kicking motion originates from the hips, with a 12- to 15-inch (30 to 40 cm) range in kicking. Students focus on keeping the legs straight and toes pointed. Students then team with partners and take turns practicing a flutter kick using a kickboard.

Lesson: Front Crawl Stroke

Teach proper breathing technique and arm movement in waist-high water in a stationary position before students attempt the front crawl stroke.

Arm stroke: Arms alternate using the following movement skills: entry, down sweep, in sweep, upsweep, recovery. While one arm is in recovery, the other enters the water. Students do this on the side of the pool, first using the wall for support. Then students use kickboards with their hands extended to practice the skill.

Activity: Team Relay: Kicking with Boards

Divide students into teams of four to six. Teams do a relay of one lap of the pool, performing a flutter kick and using a kickboard. Students start in the water (no diving).

Materials needed:

- Kickboards
- Aids: an instructional video to demonstrate proper movement skills (optional)

AQUATICS LESSON—DAY 3

19

Performance Objectives (Student Outcomes)

Students will work cooperatively using the proper kicking technique.

Students will work on their cardiorespiratory fitness doing water aerobics.

Students will learn breathing and how to complete the front crawl.

Introductory Activity: Marking

Have students in waist-high water, grouped with partners of similar ability. On "Go," one partner walks, trying to lose his or her partner. On signal, both stop. The chaser must try to reach out and touch the partner to mark her or him. If the partner can be marked, that player receives a point. If the chaser cannot mark the partner, the walking partner receives a point. Partners then switch, and the chaser becomes the leading walker.

FIGURE 19.17 *(continued)*

Fitness: Water Aerobics

Students warm up with walking activities in the water. They alternate periods of cardiorespiratory work (60 seconds) with resting or muscular strength activities (30 seconds).

Cardiorespiratory movements may include the following: walk forward, walk backward, jog forward, jog backward, march in place, jumping jacks, treading water, scissor kicks, jumping in place, and side-to-side ski jumping. They may also perform the following rest or muscular strength movements: arm curls, calf raises, quadriceps stretches, hamstring stretches, back floating, practice of crawl-style breathing, and triceps stretches.

Lesson: Breathing, Front Crawl Stroke

Breathing: With the face in the water, students exhale by blowing bubbles into the water. They inhale by turning the head sideways, taking a breath, and returning the face to the water. For a breath, the head turns to the side of the recovering arm.

Leg movement: Using the flutter kick, students work on breathing by using kickboards and turning the head to the side. When they need a breath, they take one by turning the head to the side.

Front crawl stroke: Combine all the elements of front crawl and attempt the full stroke.

Activity: Water Basketball

Tie down flotation basketball hoops on each side of the shallow end of the pool. Divide class into two equal teams. Students play noncontact water basketball. A student cannot hold the ball longer than three seconds. A team must make three passes before attempting to shoot a basket.

Materials needed:

- Music interval playlist for water aerobics
- Kickboards and other flotation devices for student assistance
- Two flotation basketball baskets
- One water basketball

AQUATICS LESSON—DAY 4

Performance Objectives (Student Outcomes)

Students will work cooperatively in a physical activity setting.

Students will demonstrate an ability to tread water.

Students will work on their cardiorespiratory fitness by learning backstroke skills.

Introductory Activity: Partner Resistance Kicking

Students are introduced to the flutter kick while they lie on their backs, working outside the pool on the deck. Students work with a partner and take turns practicing a flutter kick. They perform a flutter kick, while a partner applies gentle resistance by holding their ankles.

Note: You may want to have students do this individually, sitting on the side of the pool kicking upward with their toes just breaking the surface of the water. This method gives students the realistic feeling of resistance. This will not meet your objective of having students work cooperatively for kicking, although they do work together in the skills section.

Fitness: Treading Water

Students perform treading-water intervals in chest-high water. Begin by having students attempt 15 seconds of treading water with 10-second rest intervals. Increase the treading time to 20 seconds with a 15-second rest interval. Music may be played during the treading portion, and mild stretching can be added to the rest intervals.

FIGURE 19.17 *(continued)*

Lesson: Backstroke Skills

Have students work with partners. They begin with a back float, keeping the head back with the water line at the tip of the chin and the middle of the top of the head and the ears in the water, while staying relaxed.

Add a slow flutter kick to glide the body. Kicking movement originates from the hip, and power comes from the upward motion. At the end of the upbeat kick, the toes should reach the surface. Students may use kickboards for flotation assistance or keep their arms to their sides to help with body position.

Add arm movements, which alternately use a power phase and a recovery phase. In the power phase, the pinkie finger enters the water first and the hand sweeps outward and downward as the elbow bends; the hand sweeps the water past the thigh. In the recovery phase, the shoulder lifts from the water as the arm is lifted straight and relaxed from the water, thumb first. Rolling the body makes the recovery phase easier.

Activity: Five Passes

Divide students into two teams. Scatter players across the shallow end of pool. The object of the game is for one team to make five consecutive passes to five different players using a flotation ball, without losing possession of the ball. Players may not hold the ball longer than three seconds. If a team successfully makes five consecutive passes, they score a point, and possession goes to the other team. If defense takes possession of the ball, they begin their five passing attempts.

Materials needed:

- Kickboards
- Flotation ball

AQUATICS LESSON—DAY 5

Performance Objectives (Student Outcomes)

Students will work toward improving their fitness by participating in cardiorespiratory water activities.

Students will demonstrate their knowledge of basic swimming skills.

Students will work cooperatively in a partner task assessment.

Introductory Activity: Lazy River

Students walk slowly in the shallow end of the pool, as if they are wading through a river. Students walk in their own personal space. The teacher calls out new directions every 30 to 60 seconds. Examples of student walking directions include normal steps, short steps, long steps, backward steps, sidesteps, and leg crossovers (carioca movements).

Fitness: Racetrack Fitness in Water

Task cards are in six posted locations spaced at equal distance around pool. Students are divided into six teams, and one team starts at each station. On the whistle, students swim to the next station and start their new task.

Stations include the following activities: jog in place; front crawl stroke, using arms only and keeping legs stationary; flutter kick with both hands on the pool edge; breast stroke using arms only and keeping legs stationary; frog kick with both hands on the edge of the pool; treading water.

Lesson: Partner Task Assessment Sheet

Have students work with partners to demonstrate learned aquatics skills. One partner performs tasks, while the other partner observes and uses a checklist to note whether each task is performed. After all tasks are attempted and assessed, partners switch positions.

Activity: Water Disc Game

Divide the class into two equal teams. Create a boundary in the shallow end of the pool, where students can

FIGURE 19.17 *(continued)*

19

play comfortably. Teams attempt to maintain possession of the disc by making five consecutive passes. Players may hold onto the disc no longer than five seconds. If a team makes five consecutive passes to five different teammates, they score a point and turn over possession to the other team. If the defense intercepts the disc, they become the offense and start their attempt to make five consecutive passes.

Materials needed:

- Racetrack fitness signs and cones
- Partner task assessment sheets, clipboards, and pens
- Discs

FIGURE 19.17 *(continued)*

AQUATICS SKILLS

Name _____ Partner or scorer name _____

Student is a _____ nonswimmer _____ beginning swimmer _____ experienced swimmer

Pool Entry and Exit

____ Enters shallow end using feet first

____ Ensures that no students are in path

____ Exits shallow end using two hands

Floating on Back

____ Holds head back and comfortably maintains a floating position

____ Is able to limit arm and leg movement while floating

Level of Participation During Fitness Component

____ Participates fully

____ Participates with reservations

Front Crawl Skills

____ Flutter kick movement starts from hips

____ Arms alternate using power phase and recovery

Emergency Action Plan Response

____ Exits pool and goes to bleachers quickly

____ Sits in bleachers quietly

____ Remains calm and follows directions

Breathing Technique for Front Crawl Stroke

____ With face in water, can exhale, blowing bubbles

____ Turns head to side to take a breath, keeping side of head in water

Treading Water

____ Is able to tread water comfortably for 30 seconds

____ Keeps body upright while treading

Backstroke Skills

____ Flutter kick movement from hips

____ Brings thumb out of the water first and submerges pinkie first

FIGURE 19.18 Aquatics skills partner task assessment.

neck, or back injuries; chlorine or chemical leakage; or other situations that are an immediate threat to human life or serious bodily injury. In such an emergency, the teacher must immediately activate the facility's EAP.

All school personnel and students in the aquatics facility should be familiar with the EAP and trained to activate the EAP in response to any emergency. When activated, student readiness is critical for a safe and timely response. The EAP should clearly outline specific actions and realistic expectations of teachers, staff, and students. Although the teacher fully directs the plan, students may be designated for specific actions, such as contacting administrators and emergency services. Therefore, EAP practice drills should be conducted regularly with staff and students so that response actions are automatic and calmly executed.

The EAP should detail the activation of emergency sounds, immediate exit of all people from the pool, a designated location for students, the notification of school administration and emergency services, retrieval or use of lifesaving equipment, and escort of emergency personnel to and from the facility. The EAP should contain emergency telephone numbers, dialing instructions, directions to and from the facility, and a diagram of an evacuation route.

Although every emergency is unique, successful response actions in emergency situations require training readiness, student awareness, teamwork, and communication. Every staff member must strictly adhere to safety responsibilities, which include identifying potential hazards and enforcing pool rules at all times.

Tennis

Developing from a crude handball game played in 14th-century France, the game of tennis became one of the most popular sports of the 1980s. Part of its popularity stems from the fact that it is truly a game for a lifetime. Children as young as 6 years old can learn to play. In fact, most of today's superstars began playing at very early ages. Those in older age groups can also play tennis well. The United States Tennis Association (USTA), the governing body for tennis in the United States, conducts national championships and has established national rankings for age groups beginning with the 12-years-old-and-under group and continuing through the 70-years-old-and-older group. Another reason for the popularity of tennis is that men and women can compete on the same court at the same time (mixed doubles). Few other serious sports offer this possibility. The popularity of tennis is evident by the

thousands of tennis courts across the country, usually with people waiting in line to play. The huge audiences at classic tournaments such as Wimbledon and the U.S. Open also attest to the game's popularity.

Although some tennis is played on grass courts (as at Wimbledon), and some is played on clay courts, most American tennis is played on hard surfaces such as asphalt or concrete. The court is separated by a net, which is 3 feet (90 cm) high at the center and 3.5 feet (1.05 m) high at the net posts.

In singles, one player is on each side of the net. In doubles, two players are on each side of the net. All players have a racket. The ball is put into play with a serve. After the return of the serve, players may hit the ball before it bounces or may allow the ball to bounce once before hitting it. The object of the game is to hit the ball legally over the net into the opponent's court. Most coaches of the sport say that to win, all you have to do is to hit the ball over the net one more time than the opponent does.

Sequence of Skills

Tennis skills fall into five basic categories. Some skills may not fit exactly into any one category, but for organizational purposes, these five will suffice: volley, ground strokes, lob, overhead, and serve.

Volley

The volley should be the first stroke learned because it is the simplest stroke. The eye–hand coordination involved is similar to that involved in catching a thrown ball, a skill that most students have mastered by high school. The volley requires no backswing, and the ball does not bounce, so timing is simplified.

Ground Strokes

The forehand and backhand ground strokes are considered the foundation of a solid game. The forehand is the easier of the two for most people and should be learned first. The backhand is more difficult but not too challenging to learn with proper instruction.

Lob

After learning the ground strokes, learning the lob is relatively easy. The lob is basically a ground stroke hit at a different angle. Backswing and body position are identical to those of the ground stroke.

Overhead

The overhead and serve are different from the other strokes and require learning new patterns. The overhead,

19

or smash, should be taught first because this stroke resembles a simplified service motion. When students master the skill of hitting an overhead, they will find it easier to learn to hit a serve.

Serve

The serve is a complicated stroke, and some tennis coaches prefer to introduce it as soon as possible to give students the maximum amount of time to master it. If the serve is the last skill taught, however, students are by then more familiar with the equipment, have a better feel for the game, and may be more successful with this skill.

Ideas for Effective Instruction

This section highlights numerous ideas to allow for more effective instruction.

The Court

The game of tennis is played on a court as diagrammed in figure 19.19. A working knowledge of the court areas is vital to the student, not only for its importance in playing the game but also for the following instructions.

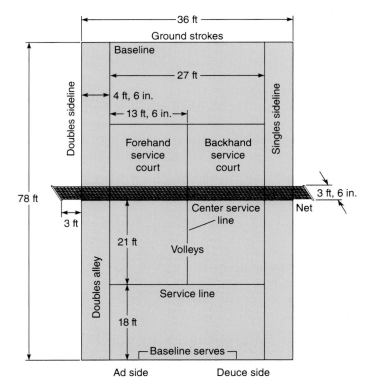

FIGURE 19.19 Tennis court markings.

Singles Sideline

The singles sideline delineates the playing court for singles. A ball landing on the sideline is in play.

Doubles Sideline

The doubles sideline delineates the playing court for doubles. A ball landing on the doubles sideline is in play in doubles.

Doubles Alley

The doubles alley is the area of the court in play in doubles after the serve. It includes the doubles sideline.

Baseline

The baseline delineates the length of the court for both singles and doubles. When hitting a serve, the player must stand behind the baseline and may not touch it or step over it onto the court until the ball has left the racket. A ball landing on the baseline is in play.

Service Line

The service line delineates the length of the service court. A serve must land between the net and the service line or on the service line to be in play.

Center Service Line

The center service line divides the service court into deuce and ad sides. A serve hitting the center service line is in play.

Ad Court

The ad court is the service court to the receiver's left. Any time an odd number of points has been played, the serve is made to this court (that is, 15–0, 30–40, ad in, or ad out).

Deuce Court

The deuce court is the service court to the receiver's right. Any time an even number of points has been played, the serve is made to this court (that is, 0–0, 15–15, 40–15, deuce).

The Match

Most people play tennis to try to win the match. To win a match, a player must win a predetermined number of sets (usually two out of three). To win a set, a player must win six games with at least a two-game margin. If a set ties at six games each, a tie breaker is played to determine the winner of the set. To win a game, a player must be the first to win four points. Each of these terms is explained in the following discussion.

Points and Games

A player wins a point if the opponent fails to return the ball legally or if the opponent, while serving, fails to put the ball into play legally. The opponent is awarded a point in any of these situations: The ball bounces more than once before it is returned, the ball is returned so that it does not cross the net or land within the playing court, the ball is hit twice while it is being returned, the ball touches the player while it is in play, or the player touches the net while the ball is in play.

Two methods are currently used for scoring games. The conventional scoring progression is love (0), 15, 30, 40, game. Both players start at love, and a player must win four points to win the game. The one exception is that a player must win by a two-point margin. If the server leads 40–30 and the receiver wins the next point, the score is deuce. The next player who wins two consecutive points wins the game. At deuce, if the server wins the following point, the score is advantage in (ad in). If the receiver wins the point, the score is advantage out (ad out). When a player with the advantage wins the next point, that player also wins the game.

Another scoring system, called no-ad, or VASS, simplifies this process, speeds the game along, and is better suited for physical education classes in which time limits are a factor. In this system, points are counted 0, 1, 2, 3, game. A two-point lead is not required because the first player to win a fourth point wins the game. Using this system, there is no ad or deuce.

Sets

The first player or doubles team to win six games wins the set if they have a two-game lead. A set might therefore last only six games (6–0), or it might go to 10 or more games (6–4). If a set is tied at 5–all, the winner of the next game would go up 6–5 and would not have the necessary two-game margin to win the set. Should the leader win the next game, that player would also win the set, 7–5. If a set ties at six games each, however, a tiebreaker is used. The winner of the tiebreaker is the winner of the set, and the score is recorded at 7–6.

Tiebreaker

The USTA has established that the 12-point tiebreaker be used at 6–all. This occurs in the following manner:

1. The player who served the first game of the set serves the first point.
2. The receiver of point one serves points two and three, and the serve changes after every 2 points from that time.

3. Players change sides of the net at every six points (6–0, 3–3, 6–6).
4. The first player to reach 7 points with at least a 2-point margin wins the tiebreaker. If the first player to reach seven does not have a 2-point margin, play continues until one player establishes a two-point lead.

In women's tennis and in almost all of men's tennis, the winner of a match is determined by the first player or team to win two sets. Some men's tennis is played to the best three of five sets. Therefore, if Smith defeated Jones (6–4, 3–6, 7–6, [9–7]), Smith won the first set 6–4, lost the second set 3–6, and won the third set in a tie breaker, the score of which was 9–7.

General Rules

The match usually begins with players spinning a racket to determine who serves the first game. The winner of the toss can choose to serve or to receive and can also choose which side of the net to begin from, or he or she can elect to have the opponent decide. After the initial choices are made, the opponent makes all other choices.

One player serves for a whole game. The first serve is hit from the right side of the court into the diagonal service area. The server has two chances to put the ball into play. If the serve is a fault, the second ball is served. If this serve is also a fault, the server loses the point. Any serve that touches the net but still lands in the proper service court is a "let," and the serve is hit again. After the first point of the game, the following serve takes place from the left side of the court. The serve alternates back and forth on each successive point throughout the game.

An exception to this rule applies to no-ad scoring. At 3–3 in a no-ad game, the receiver chooses the side into which the serve will be made. The serve is not automatically made to the deuce side, as might be expected, but the receiver may choose to receive from either side. The opponent then serves the next game in the same manner. The serve alternates after each successive game for the entire match. In doubles, each team may choose which player serves first for that team, and the players alternate each time their team serves.

At the conclusion of every odd-numbered game, players change sides of the net. Therefore, after the first, third, and fifth game, and so forth, players change courts.

Tennis is governed by a strict set of rules, which cover every imaginable situation. A thorough knowledge of these rules is important for the tennis instructor. A copy of the rules of tennis can be ordered from the USTA (see References and Suggested Readings at the end of this chapter).

19

Etiquette

Rules of etiquette are a vital part of tennis. Except for large tournaments and professional matches, referees and ball retrievers are seldom present at tennis matches. Players must follow rules of etiquette for the game of tennis to be enjoyable.

Most rules of etiquette can be summed up in this motto: "Do unto others as you would have them do unto you." For instance, if a player does not clearly see whether a ball was out or in, play it over. When the point is over, a player should try to return the balls to the opponent, not merely in the general direction.

Players should never enter a court (or walk behind one) while a rally is in progress. A player who must walk through a court should wait until there is a court change.

A rule of tennis states that any interference during play shall cause a "let." The point is then replayed. If the opponent claims distraction during play, do not hesitate to play the point over.

Minimize verbal outbursts on the court. Such behavior is distracting not only to the opponent but also to players on other courts. Never throw rackets or slam balls around in anger. These actions are dangerous and unsportsmanlike.

Organization and Skill Work

Most tennis classes are organized along traditional lines—that is, the instructor shows groups of students proper grips, stances, backswings, and so forth, at the same time. Another method of organizing the class is to allow students to progress at their own rate. This approach can be accomplished by using a unit with performance objectives. Each student knows exactly what is expected and moves from one task to the next when able.

Prepare a unit for each student in the class. As the students come to class, give them a unit, give them access to balls and rackets, and encourage them to get started.

When the entire class has arrived, call the students together for an organizational meeting. These meetings might include a tennis tip for the day, some comment about the unit, or some skill analysis. The meeting should be short so that most of the class time can be devoted to practicing and mastering skills.

If stations are used, each court can be designated for a particular skill (e.g., one court for volleys, one for ground strokes, and one for serving). Provide plenty of balls (beginners will fare as well with older balls as with newer ones) and rackets. Post the suggested skill tasks on the net or fence and let students progress at a personalized rate. Be available for questions and feedback. Do not hesitate to intervene when a student is having difficulty.

Skill Work

The strength of the system is that it allows the teacher to help specific students with particular problems. After the class has started, the teacher is free to roam the courts and to help students who are having problems. Key points to remember in teaching basic skills include the following:

Volley

1. Watch the ball hit the racket.
2. Focus on footwork. Step across to hit the volley (a volley to the right should have a final step with the left foot).
3. Minimize backswing. Swing no farther back than the shoulder.
4. Punch the ball and follow through.
5. Never drop the racket head below the wrist. Bend the knees instead.
6. Squeeze the racket grip when contacting the ball.

Ground Strokes

1. Change grips for the backhand and forehand.
2. Prepare for an early backswing by getting the racket back as soon as possible.
3. Set up with the side of the body facing the net.
4. Contact the ball even with the front foot; do not wait until the ball gets into the body.
5. Contact the ball with the racket perpendicular to the ground.
6. Follow through.
7. Keep the knees bent throughout the stroke.

Lobs

1. Set up exactly as you do for ground strokes.
2. Open the racket face (approximately 45 degrees).
3. Lift up through the swing and finish with a high follow-through.

Overheads

1. Get the racket in "back-scratcher" position early.
2. Turn the side of the body toward the net.
3. Contact the ball in front of the body. Do not let it float overhead.

Serves

1. First and foremost, control the toss.
2. Use the continental or backhand grip (this grip will cause a slice serve, which is the most consistent).
3. "Throw" the racket at the ball; use plenty of wrist and elbow.
4. Follow through; the back foot (from the stance) should end up on the court.

Safety

Tennis is a safe sport. Most injuries that occur are self-inflicted, such as ankle sprains, muscle sprains, or blisters. A few precautions can help prevent unnecessary injuries.

1. Warm up properly before beginning play.
2. Never leave loose balls lying around the court.
3. Never hit balls (especially serves) when your opponent is not ready.
4. Communicate. Both players on a doubles team going for an overhead can cost the team a point and cause an injury.
5. Wear appropriate footwear.

Lead-Up and Modified Games and Rainy Day Activities

Practice is often enhanced, especially for advanced players, when stroke practice is conducted under gamelike conditions. Many students enjoy competing. The following drills can be done competitively.

Twenty-One

In the game of 21, both players must remain behind the baseline. The ball is put into play when either player drops the ball and hits a ground stroke. From that point on, the game uses the same rules as tennis, except that neither player may volley.

Advanced players can include the rule that any ball landing in front of the service line is out, or the ball may be approached from behind and volleyed. The first player to accrue 21 points wins.

Approach Game

To practice approaching the net, players use half of the court, from the doubles sideline to the center service line. After starting with a ground stroke, the first player moves halfway to the service line. After returning the first ball, the second player moves halfway to the service line. After their next shots, players move to the service line

and then continue to close in as far as possible, hitting volleys and half volleys. The game may be played to any total, usually 10 or 15.

Lob–Smash

Begin with one player at the net and the other at the baseline. Baseline players hit a lob, which is returned with an overhead. They play out the point and begin again. After 10 points, players change positions. The winner is the player with the most points after these 20 points have been played. Lob–smash can also be played with doubles.

Short Game

Players begin at the service lines and hit soft ground strokes. The ball may not land behind the service line. Regular tennis scoring can be used, or a point total can be set.

Return Drill

The return drill can be used to improve a player's return. One player practices returns, and three to five players alternate serves. The receiver returns the serves from the court (either ad or deuce) for the entire time. Servers get two serves, just like the real game, and play the point. Only the server gets a point when a rally is won. When a server gets a designated number of points (usually 4 or 5), the receiver and server exchange places, and all servers' scores return to 0. Each receiver thus gets at least 12 to 15 returns before rotating. The next time this player becomes the receiver, she or he makes returns from the opposite court. A variation is to have all servers serve and volley.

Half-Court Volleys

Divide the court into halves (as in the Approach Game). One player begins at the net, and the other begins at the baseline. The volleyer puts the ball into play, and the player at the baseline must hit a passing shot (ground stroke). The ball must be kept in the half-court. They play to 10 points, switch places, and continue for 10 more points. As a variation, after the initial shot, the ground stroker may hit lobs and may approach the net if the opportunity arises.

Backboard Practice

If wall space is available in the gymnasium, ground strokes or volleys can be hit against the gym wall.

Service Practice

The gymnasium is an excellent place for beginners to practice the toss. Any line on the gym floor can be sub-

19

stituted for the baseline. Soft foam-rubber tennis balls are excellent for practice of the entire service motion in the gym.

Volleys

Without a net, players can practice volleys indoors. Have them stand 10 to 20 feet (3 to 6 m) apart and hit soft volleys to each other.

Suggested Performance Objectives

Students should work with a partner. When a student has mastered an objective to specification, have a partner (or instructor, where indicated) initial the task. The tasks are designed to be progressively more difficult. A student should therefore not proceed to a new task until she or he has completed all preliminary tasks. The court markings in figure 19.19 will aid in the comprehension of many of the tasks. Students should refer to the diagram as needed until they learn the markings.

Volley

1. Without a racket, assume a ready position (feet shoulder-width apart, knees bent, weight forward, hands in front of the body). Have a partner toss tennis balls to the dominant side. Stepping with the opposite foot, reach forward and catch five consecutive balls thrown from a distance of 15 feet (5 m).

2. From the ready position, gripping the racket at its head and using proper footwork (instructor will demonstrate), hit five consecutive forehand volleys to your partner, who feeds the balls from a distance of 15 feet (5 m). (Balls may not bounce.)

3. Perform task 2 but grip the racket just above the grip (five consecutive times).

4. Demonstrate to the instructor the continental grip—the grip with which volleys are hit.

5. Perform task 2 but use the continental grip, and grip the racket on the grip (five consecutive times).

6. Perform task 2 but use the backhand side of racket (five consecutive times).

7. Perform task 2 but grip the racket just above the grip and use the backhand (five consecutive times).

8. Perform task 5 but use backhand (five consecutive times).

9. Stand halfway between the net and the service line. The partner or instructor stands across the net at the baseline and drops and hits balls at

you. Volley 8 of 10 forehands across the net into the singles court.

10. Perform task 9 but use the backhand 8 of 10 times.

11. Standing as in task 9, your partner randomly hits to your forehand and backhand side. Volley 8 of 10 balls into the singles court.

12. Perform task 11 but place balls in the singles court behind the service line 8 of 10 times.

13. From a distance of at least 6 feet (1.8 m) from a wall, hit 15 consecutive volleys above a 3-foot (90 cm) mark. The ball may not touch the ground.

Ground Strokes

1. Demonstrate to the instructor the eastern forehand and backhand grips.

2. Without a ball, practice 20 consecutive alternate forehand and backhand ground strokes, alternating the grip each time.

3. Standing behind the baseline, drop and hit 10 consecutive forehands across the net into the singles court.

4. Perform task 3 but use the backhand 10 consecutive times.

5. Stand behind the baseline. Your partner stands 20 feet (6 m) away and bounces balls to your forehand. Hit five of seven forehands across the net into the singles court.

6. Perform task 5 but use the backhand five of seven times.

7. Standing behind the baseline with a partner across the net, have your partner hit or toss balls to your forehand. Hit 8 of 10 forehands across the net into the singles court.

8. Perform task 7 but use the backhand 8 of 10 times.

9. Perform tasks 7 and 8 but have your partner randomly toss balls to your forehand and backhand 8 of 10 times.

10. Standing behind a line 27 feet (8.2 m) from the backboard, hit 10 consecutive ground strokes that strike the backboard on or above the white line, which is 3 feet (90 cm) above the ground.

11. Perform task 10 but hit 20 consecutive ground strokes.

12. With a partner (or instructor) at the opposite baseline, rally 20 consecutive ground strokes (ball may bounce more than once on each side of the net).

Lobs

1. From the baseline, drop and hit five consecutive forehand lobs into the opposite singles court behind the service line. Hit the balls high enough that your partner, from volley position, cannot touch them with the racket.

2. Perform task 1 but hit backhand lobs five consecutive times.

3. With a partner tossing or hitting balls from the other side of the net, hit five consecutive forehand lobs into the opposite singles court behind the service line.

4. Perform task 3 but hit backhand lobs five consecutive times.

Serves

1. Demonstrate to the teacher the proper service stance and grip for serving.

2. Using an overhead throwing motion, throw 5 consecutive balls into the service court from the baseline on both the deuce and ad sides (10 total).

3. Demonstrate the proper toss technique to the instructor.

4. Lay the racket on the ground with the face 6 inches (15 cm) in front of your front foot. Using the nonracket hand, toss balls approximately 2 feet (60 cm) higher than your head; three of five must hit the racket face or frame.

5. Make your normal toss into the air and using the racket hand without a racket, come through the service motion and hit five consecutive balls with the palm of your hand.

6. With a racket in the "back-scratcher" position, hit five of seven serves into the proper service court.

7. Demonstrate to the instructor an acceptable full backswing for the service.

8. Perform task 6 but use the full backswing to hit five of seven serves into the forehand service court.

9. Place four empty tennis ball cans in the outside corner of the forehand service box. Serve until you have knocked over one can.

10. Perform task 9 but place cans in the inside corner.

11. Perform task 9 but place cans in the backhand court.

12. Perform task 9 but place cans in the inside corner of the backhand court.

Overheads

1. Using the service grip and standing in the service area (at the net), have a partner hit short lobs. Allow the ball to bounce. Hit three of five forehand overheads into the singles court.

2. Repeat task 1 but hit the ball before it bounces (three of five times).

3. Repeat task 1 but stand behind the baseline three of five times.

4. Perform task 1 but hit six consecutive balls.

5. Perform task 2 but hit six consecutive balls.

6. Perform task 3 but hit six consecutive balls.

LEARNING AIDS

WEBSITES

Bowling

www.bowlingindex.com
www.bowlersed.com
www.bowlingfoundation.org

Disc Games

www.discgolf.com
www.upa.org

Golf

www.golfonline.com
www.thefirsttee.org

19

Racquetball

www.usra.org

Strength Training

www.biggerfasterstronger.com

Tennis

www.tennisserver.com
www.usta.com

REFERENCES AND SUGGESTED READINGS

Bowling

Fronske, H. (2008). *Teaching cues for sport skills* (4th ed.). San Francisco, CA: Benjamin Cummings.

Martin, J.L., Tandy, R.E., & Agne-Traub, C. (1994). *Bowling* (7th ed.). Dubuque, IA: Brown & Benchmark.

National Association for Girls and Women in Sport. (1979–1981). *Bowling-golf.* Reston, VA: AAHPERD.

Schmottlach, N., & McManama, J. (2010). *Physical education activity handbook* (12th ed.). San Francisco, CA: Pearson Higher Education/ Benjamin Cummings.

Disc Games

Caporali, J.M. (1988). The ultimate alternative. *Journal of Physical Education, Recreation, and Dance, 59*(9), 98–101.

Demas, K. (2002). Ultimate. In N. Dougherty (Ed.), *Physical activity and sport for the secondary school student* (5th ed.). Reston, VA: NASPE and AAHPERD.

Fronske, H. (2008). *Teaching cues for sport skills* (4th ed.). San Francisco, CA: Pearson Higher Education/Benjamin Cummings.

Schmottlach, N., & McManama, J. (2010). *Physical education activity handbook* (12th ed.). San Francisco, CA: Pearson Higher Education/ Benjamin Cummings.

Golf

Fronske, H. (2008). *Teaching cues for sport skills* (4th ed.). San Francisco, CA: Pearson Higher Education/ Benjamin Cummings.

Mood, D.P., Musker, F.F., & Rink, J.E. (2007). *Sports and recreational activities* (14th ed.). Boston, MA: McGraw-Hill.

Nance, V.L., Davis, E.C., & McMahon, K.E. (1994). *Golf* (7th ed.). Dubuque, IA: Brown & Benchmark.

Owens, B.B. (1989). *Golf: Steps to success.* Champaign, IL: Human Kinetics.

Owens, B.B. (1992). *Advanced golf: Steps to success.* Champaign, IL: Human Kinetics.

Schmottlach, N., & McManama, J. (2010). *Physical education activity handbook* (12th ed.). San Francisco, CA: Pearson Higher Education/ Benjamin Cummings.

White, H. (2002). Golf. In N. Dougherty (Ed.), *Physical activity and sport for the secondary school student* (5th ed.). Reston, VA: NASPE and AAHPERD.

In-Line Skating

Fronske, H. (2008). *Teaching cues for sport skills* (4th ed.). San Francisco, CA: Pearson Higher Education/Benjamin Cummings.

Schmottlach, N., & McManama, J. (2010). *Physical education activity handbook* (12th ed.). San Francisco, CA: Pearson Higher Education/ Benjamin Cummings.

Jogging

Fronske, H. (2008). *Teaching cues for sport skills* (4th ed.). San Francisco, CA: Pearson Higher Education/Benjamin Cummings.

Mood, D.P., Musker, F.F., & Rink, J.E. (2007). *Sports and recreational activities* (14th ed.). Boston, MA: McGraw-Hill.

Schmottlach, N., & McManama, J. (2010). *Physical education activity handbook* (12th ed.). San Francisco, CA: Pearson Higher Education/Benjamin Cummings.

Racquetball

Allsen, P.E., & Witbeck, P. (1992). *Racquetball* (5th ed.). Dubuque, IA: Brown & Benchmark.

Fronske, H. (2008). *Teaching cues for sport skills* (4th ed.). San Francisco, CA: Pearson Higher Education/Benjamin Cummings.

Kittleson, S. (1993). *Teaching racquetball: Steps to success.* Champaign, IL: Human Kinetics.

Liles, L., & Neimeyer, R.A. (1993). *Winning racquetball.* Dubuque, IA: Brown & Benchmark.

Mood, D.P., Musker, F.F., & Rink, J.E. (2007). *Sports and recreational activities* (14th ed.). Boston, MA: McGraw-Hill.

Schmottlach, N., & McManama, J. (2010). *Physical education activity handbook* (12th ed.). San Francisco, CA: Pearson Higher Education/Benjamin Cummings.

Rhythmic Activity

Doan, R.J., MacDonald, L.C., & Chepko, S. (2017). *Lesson planning for middle school physical education.* Champaign, IL: Human Kinetics.

Durden, E.M. (2018). *Beginning hip-hop dance.* Champaign, IL: Human Kinetics.

Fey, J. (2011). *Dance units for middle school.* Champaign, IL: Human Kinetics.

Hernandez, B. (2002). Dance education. In N. Dougherty (Ed.), *Physical activity and sport for the secondary school student* (5th ed.). Reston, VA: NASPE and AAHPERD.

Kassing, G. (2020). *Dance teaching methods and curriculum design* (2nd ed.). Champaign, IL: Human Kinetics.

Laufman, D., & Laufman, J. (2009). *Traditional barn dances with calls & fiddling.* Champaign, IL: Human Kinetics.

Livingston, P., (1981). *The complete book of country swing and western dance.* Garden City, NY: Doubleday.

MacDonald, L.C., Doan, R.J., Chepko, S. (2017). *Lesson planning for high school physical education.* Champaign, IL: Human Kinetics.

Mood, D.P., Musker, F.F., & Rink, J.E. (2007). *Sports and recreational activities* (14th ed.). Boston. MA: McGraw-Hill.

Pittman, A.M., Waller, M.S., & Dark, C.L. (2009). *Dance a while: Handbook for folk, square, contra, and social dance* (10th ed.). San Francisco, CA: Pearson Higher Education/Benjamin Cummings.

Ray, O.M. (1992). *Encyclopedia of line dances: The steps that came and stayed.* Reston, VA: AAHPERD.

Rope Jumping

American Alliance for Health, Physical Education, Recreation and Dance. (1992). *Jump rope for heart.* Reston, VA: AAHPERD. (*Jump Rope for Heart* materials can be obtained by contacting the local affiliate of the American Heart Association or by calling the AAHPERD Special Events Office at 703-476-3489.)

American Heart Association. (1984a). *Jump for the health of it: Basic skills.* Dallas, TX: Author.

American Heart Association. (1984b). *Jump for the health of it: Intermediate single- and double-dutch skills.* Dallas, TX: Author.

Melson, B., & Worrell, V. (1986). *Rope skipping for fun and fitness.* Wichita, KS: Woodlawn.

Poppen, J.D. (1989). *Action packet on jumping rope.* Puyallup, WA: Action Productions.

Sutherland, M., & Carnes, C. (1987). *Awesome jump rope activities book.* Carmichael, CA: Education Co.

Strength Training

Baechle, T.R. (1992). *Weight training.* Champaign, IL: Human Kinetics.

Fronske, H. (2008). *Teaching cues for sport skills* (4th ed.). San Francisco, CA: Pearson Higher Education/Benjamin Cummings.

Groves, B. (2002). Weight training. In N. Dougherty (Ed.), *Physical activity and sport for the secondary school student* (5th ed.). Reston, VA: NASPE and AAHPERD.

Mood, D.P., Musker, F.F., & Rink, J.E. (2007). *Sports and recreational activities* (14th ed.). Boston, MA: McGraw-Hill.

Moran, G., & McGlynn, G. (1990). *Dynamics of strength training.* Dubuque, IA: Brown & Benchmark.

Rasch, P.J. (1990). *Weight training* (5th ed.). Dubuque, IA: Brown & Benchmark.

Schmottlach, N., & McManama, J. (2010). *Physical education activity handbook* (12th ed.). San Francisco, CA: Pearson Higher Education/Benjamin Cummings.

Westcott, W.L. (1995). *Strength fitness: Physiological principles and training techniques* (4th ed.). Dubuque, IA: Brown & Benchmark.

Swimming and Aquatics

American Red Cross. (1993). *Swimming and diving.* St. Louis. MO: Mosby.

Fronske, H. (2008). *Teaching cues for sport skills* (4th ed.). San Francisco, CA: Pearson Higher Education/Benjamin Cummings.

Hallett, B., & Clayton, R.D. (Eds.). (1980). *Course syllabus: Teacher of swimming.* Reston, VA: American Alliance for

19

Health, Physical Education, Recreation and Dance (AAHPERD).

Johnson, R. (2002). Swimming. In N. Dougherty (Ed.), *Physical activity and sport for the secondary school student* (5th ed.). Reston, VA: NASPE and AAHPERD.

Mood, D.P., Musker, F.F., & Rink, J.E. (2007). *Sports and recreational activities* (14th ed.). Boston, MA: McGraw-Hill.

Schmottlach, N., & McManama, J. (2010). *Physical education activity handbook* (12th ed.). San Francisco, CA: Pearson Higher Education/Benjamin Cummings.

Vickers, B.J., & Vincent, W. (1994). *Swimming* (6th ed.). Dubuque, IA: Brown & Benchmark.

Tennis

The following publications contain material pertaining to rules and regulations: *The Rules of Tennis, Rules of Tennis and Cases and Decisions, A Friend at Court (Rules, Cases, Decisions, Officials, and Officiating),* and *The Code (Unwritten Rules Players Should Follow in Unofficiated Matches).* All may be purchased from the United States Tennis Association, Education and Research Center, Publications Department, 729 Alexander Road, Princeton, NJ 08540.

Dusel, J. (2002). Tennis. In N. Dougherty (Ed.), *Physical activity and sport for the secondary school student* (5th ed.). Reston, VA: NASPE and AAHPERD.

Fronske, H. (2008). *Teaching cues for sport skills* (4th ed.). San Francisco, CA: Pearson Higher Education/Benjamin Cummings.

Johnson, J.D. (1993). *Tennis* (6th ed.). Dubuque, IA: Brown & Benchmark.

Mood, D.P., Musker, F.F., & Rink, J.E. (2007). *Sports and recreational activities* (14th ed.). Boston, MA: McGraw-Hill.

Schmottlach, N., & McManama, J. (2010). *Physical education activity handbook* (12th ed.). San Francisco. CA: Pearson Higher Education/ Benjamin Cummings.

Adventure Activities

Many physical education programs have added popular outdoor adventure activities to the secondary physical education curriculum. These pursuits have included rock climbing, caving, canoeing, fly-fishing, orienteering, outdoor initiative activities, and backpacking. Many students are interested in these activities, which are challenging and provide a sense of risk and adventure. The activities can be added to the curriculum as standalone units or as a combination unit that provides introductory information in many of these areas. In addition to the detailed information on ropes course activities, orienteering, and group initiative games, we have added resources and websites in many other areas to help physical education teachers add these lifetime activities to the curriculum. For many students, these pursuits will be their favorite physical activities. The activities have a lifetime focus that will draw in students and get them engaged quickly.

Learning Objectives

- ▶ Discuss and set up a wide variety of ropes course activities.
- ▶ Explain and organize group initiative games or activities that will engage secondary students.
- ▶ Discuss and set up orienteering activities with the sequence of skills to be taught, learning activities, possible competitive events, block plan possibilities, and suggested performance objectives.
- ▶ Discuss and set up traverse climbing-wall activities with safety rules, basic holds, individual challenges, and partner activities.

Group Initiative Activities

Group initiative activities are physical and mental challenges that require the cooperation and joint efforts of a group of students. They require the group to think, plan, and execute a strategy for solving the challenge. Teamwork and cooperation are necessary. These activities force students to work together. Some of the activities involve risk, excitement, and adventure, so proper safety and supervision strategies must be implemented. The activities can be completed indoors or outdoors. They can be conducted in conjunction with ropes course activities or as totally separate activities. Many of them require a few special props to be effective.

Electric Fence

The object is to get a group of students over the "electric fence" without touching it (see figure 20.1). A piece of rope is stretched between two trees. The rope should be 5 feet (1.5 m) off the ground. The students should be given a 4-by-4-inch (10 by 10 cm) beam that is about 8 feet (2.4 m) long to help them. Students are not allowed to use the support trees, nor are they allowed to reach under the rope. They can reach over the top of the rope.

FIGURE 20.1 Electric fence.

Many solutions are feasible. A good procedure is to have the group hold the beam on their shoulders and get a few stronger people over first. Then they can hold the beam on the opposite side for the others.

Boardwalk

This activity involves the use of four 2-by-4-inch (5 by 10 cm) boards that are 10 to 12 feet (3.0 to 3.7 m) long. Two sets of two boards are connected by ropes and eyebolts. About 10 students stand on two of the boards and then hold the other boards at about waist level (see figure 20.2). Working together, the students alternate lifting the boards and move forward as a group. All participants must keep their feet on the boards. The activity can be a race or just a challenge to work together.

FIGURE 20.2 Boardwalk.

Platforms

A group of six to eight students stands on the first of three platforms. The platforms are 14 feet (4.3 m) apart in a straight line. The students are given a 12-foot (3.7 m) board and a 4-foot (1.2 m) board. The challenge is to move the group from platform to platform without touching the ground with either the boards or any person in the group (see figure 20.3). The best solution is to extend the smaller board out from the platform about 2 feet (60 cm) and get the entire group to stand on this board. Then, a smaller person can walk out on the board and place the 12-foot board to the next platform and walk across. After three or four people have reached the second platform, the boards need to be switched so that the smaller one is now on the second platform. This process continues until all students are on the third platform.

Nitro Crossing

The object is to get each member of a group to swing across an area with a bucket of "nitro" (water) without spilling it. The swing rope must be attached to some type of tree limb or cross board that provides a good swinging area. Two trip boards need to be placed about 1 foot (30 cm) off the ground on either side of the swing area (see figure 20.4). The trip boards can be on top of cones or blocks of wood. Half of the group starts on one side, and half starts on the other side. They try to swing their group members to the opposite side without spilling the nitro.

The Beam and the Wall

The object of this activity is to move a group of students over a log beam (see figure 20.5) about 8 feet (2.5 m) above the ground or a solid wooden wall (see figure 20.6) 12 to 14 feet (3.5 to 4.0 m) above the ground. Group members cannot use the support trees or posts. They must work together to support each member up and over the obstacle. The wall can be built with a walkway on the back side where students can stand. After students get to the top, they can reach down and help others up.

FIGURE 20.3 Platforms.

FIGURE 20.4 Nitro crossing.

20

Faith Fall and Trust Dive

The individual falls backward into the arms of a group of students. The individual stands on a balance beam or similar elevated object. The group lines up shoulder to shoulder in two opposite and facing lines (see figures 20.7 and 20.8). Students extend their arms and alternate them with the arms of the person directly across from them. Do not allow students to lock wrists because the partners may bump heads. The person falls when the catching line is ready.

FIGURE 20.5   The beam.

FIGURE 20.7   Faith fall.

FIGURE 20.6   The wall.

FIGURE 20.8 Trust dive.

Human Circle Pass

The group forms a tight circle about 6 feet (1.8 m) in diameter, with the arms up in a catching position. One person is put in the middle and closes his or her eyes. When ready, the person falls backward, forward, or sideways into the hands of the group members. They support and pass the person around the circle. Everyone takes a turn being in the center of the circle.

Human Line Pass

Students sit in a line on the ground with legs straight out and feet touching the person in front of them. The first person in line stands and sits back into the hands of the sitting people, who pass the person backward over their heads. The process continues until all students have been passed. Spotters can be placed on each side of the line to ensure safety.

Sasquatch Race

Two groups are formed and instructed to make a moving object with a specified number of feet and hands on the ground. Everybody must be part of the group and joined to the others. After the sasquatch is built, the two groups race to a finish line.

Platform Stand

A platform with 20- to 24-inch (50 to 60 cm) sides can be used as the base of support. The object is to get as many people as possible standing on the platform simultaneously. The pose must be held for eight seconds.

Stream Crossing

Students must move from one side of the area to the other without touching the floor. They are given small carpet squares on which to move across an imaginary stream. Fewer than the necessary number of squares are handed out, however, so students have to pass the squares back and forth to get their team across. The first team to move all members across the stream is declared the winner.

Height Alignment

Members of the group keep their eyes closed and are instructed to align themselves in a single-file line from shortest person to tallest person. The students cannot talk and can use only their hands to figure out the arrangement.

Orienteering

Orienteering is a challenging outdoor adventure activity that combines cross country running and the ability to read a map and use a compass or GPS. It has been called the thinking sport because participants need to make quick decisions about which route to follow so that they minimize the time and energy used. Ideally, the orienteering competition should take place in a wilderness area that is not familiar to the participants. Orienteering events can be set up for beginners, novices, and experts, enabling people of all ages and abilities to take part and find success. The need for both physical and mental skills can result in an enjoyable experience for all students and members of a family.

Orienteering activities can be easily modified and adapted to secondary physical education programs. Many activities can be completed in a classroom or gymnasium or on the school grounds. Teachers can use compasses or GPS units and homemade maps of the school grounds to develop a challenging unit. A nearby park or a vacant lot can add variety to orienteering courses.

Sequence of Skills

The basic skills involved in orienteering are reading a topographical map, using a compass or GPS device, and

20

pacing various distances. Because many students have had little experience with these skills, teachers should introduce new information and terminology slowly. Students can perform many of the activities with a partner so that two heads will be working together on a problem. Teachers can include a variety of maps, a compass, and new pacing activities each day to keep the students challenged. Many types of activities and hands-on experiences should be incorporated in the unit. Competitive events can be added after students begin to understand basic map and compass skills. The block plan at the end of this unit provides some ideas for the sequencing of learning activities.

Learning Activities: Compass

Parts of the Compass

Make students aware of the basic parts of the compass and the way that the instrument works (see figure 20.9).

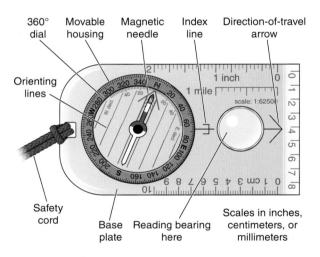

FIGURE 20.9 Parts of a compass.

Following a Bearing

Discuss how to hold the compass properly. Give students a bearing to find and follow. Have them stand in one line facing the instructor. Call out a bearing and have them rotate their bodies in place until they are facing the bearing direction.

Compass Bearings and Directions

Have the students complete the directions and degrees shown in figure 20.10.

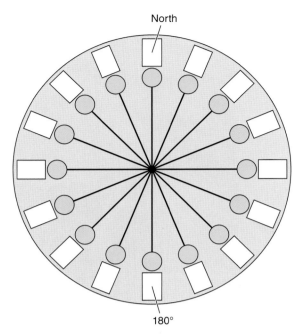

FIGURE 20.10 Compass bearings and directions.

Landmarks

Call out various visible landmarks and have students shoot a bearing from where they are standing to the landmark.

Forming a Triangle

Have students place a penny or other small object on the ground. They set any bearing less than 90 degrees and walk 10 paces on that bearing. They then add 120 degrees and walk another 10 paces. They repeat the procedure again and end up where they started. The drill can be repeated with another bearing and a different number of paces.

Forming a Square

Introduce the same basic game as forming a triangle except that 90-degree bearings are added each time, and four sides are formed. The distance must be the same each time.

Numbers and Numerals

Tape the numbers 1 to 10 on the floor in scattered positions around the gymnasium (see figure 20.11). Next, tape the roman numerals I to X in scattered positions on the gymnasium walls. The students begin by standing on any of the numbers on the floor and shooting a bearing to the corresponding numeral on the wall. This drill can be made competitive by trying for the fastest time and correct bearing.

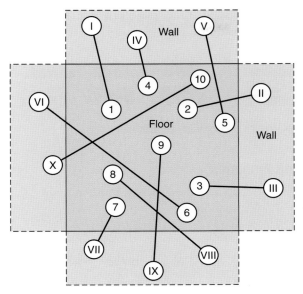

FIGURE 20.11 Numbers and numerals.

Bearing	Distance (cm)	Bearing	Distance (cm)
1. 269	2.2	9.136	6.3
2. 2	2.7	10.293	1.9
3. 266	4.9	11.141	5.2
4. 30	6.5	12.284	2.4
5. 246	2.6	13.125	5.2
6. 34	5.0	14.271	5.1
7. 244	2.0	15.179	2.7
8. 37	4.6		

FIGURE 20.12 Forming a Christmas tree.

Map Bearings

Teach students to determine the bearing between points on a map. The teacher puts several points on a map and tells the students to find the bearing and distance between the points. Ten numbered points might be shown, and students can find the bearing and distance from 1 to 2, from 2 to 3, and so forth. Advanced orienteering can include a discussion of magnetic declination and the addition or subtraction of declination.

Destination Unknown

Divide the class into four teams. Each team follows the bearings and paces shown in figure 20.13. All teams should end up at the same destination.

Forming a Christmas Tree

On a piece of graph paper, have students place a dot in the southeast quadrant of the paper. From this starting dot, have them draw a line for the distances shown in figure 20.12 and on the appropriate bearing.

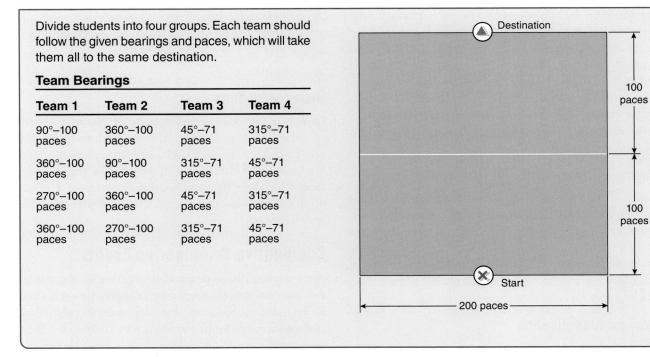

FIGURE 20.13 Destination unknown.

Schoolyard Compass Game and Competitive Compass Game

Consider arranging two challenging and inexpensive compass games that can be set up easily in a school setting. See the Websites section at the end of this chapter for contact information.

Learning Activities: Map

Mapping the School

Have students draw rough maps of the school grounds with all the various buildings, fields, and identification points. These maps can later be used in orienteering competitions.

Map Squares

Cut up several topographical maps of the local area into small squares. Students try to locate the cut squares on an uncut map. Have students identify points of interest, symbols, distances, contour lines, vegetation, roads, water, and so forth.

Map Symbol Relay

Draw a map symbol on one side of an index card and write the name of a different symbol on the back of the card. A duplicate set of cards is necessary for each team in the relay (four teams require four sets of cards). The game begins with the cards on one side of the gym and the teams on the opposite side. The teacher calls out the first symbol, such as a school. The first member of the team runs to the cards, finds the symbol, and then runs back to the team. The name of the next symbol to be found is on the back of the card with the school symbol. The game continues until all the cards are played. Students waiting in line can be reviewing symbols. Students who select the wrong symbol must run back and find the correct symbol.

Taking a Trip

Label 10 to 15 points on several topographical maps and have students calculate the actual distance between a certain number of points. They can calculate map distance and actual mileage. Next, have the students estimate how many days would be necessary to complete the trip. They should be able to describe what the terrain is like and where the water stops are located.

Contour Identification

Have students identify various mountainous and hilly areas from the way those areas look on a contour map.

Figure 20.14 shows four examples of contour representation of elevations.

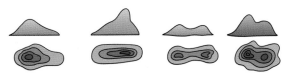

FIGURE 20.14 Contour identification.

Map Problems

Make up map activities, such as those in figure 20.15, for a local situation.

Dot-to-Dot Hike

Students start at the X in the northwest corner (see figure 20.16) and draw in the figure by following the directions. Students can develop their own dot-to-dot hike, making other figures.

Learning Activities: Pacing

Distance by Pace

Orienteers must be able to judge distance by their pace. One pace equals two steps. A good drill for determining the length of the pace is to set up a course that is 100 feet (30 m) long. Students walk, jog, or run the course and count the number of times that the right foot hits the ground. The length of the course (100 feet) is then divided by the number of paces to determine length of pace. Pace is usually rounded off to the nearest 6 inches (10 cm). Pace will vary with walking, jogging, and running.

Distance by Time

One-mile (1.5 km) courses can be set up in a variety of terrain, such as open road, open field, open woods, vegetated areas, dense woods, and mountainous areas. Students cover these areas by walking or jogging and recording their times. The ability to cover a given distance at a consistent pace can be used later for competitive meets.

Competitive Orienteering Events

After students have received instruction in the use of the compass, maps, and pacing, competitive events can be introduced. Students should understand that they can compete against the environment, themselves, their peers, and elapsed time. They do not have to win the event to be successful.

MAP PROBLEMS

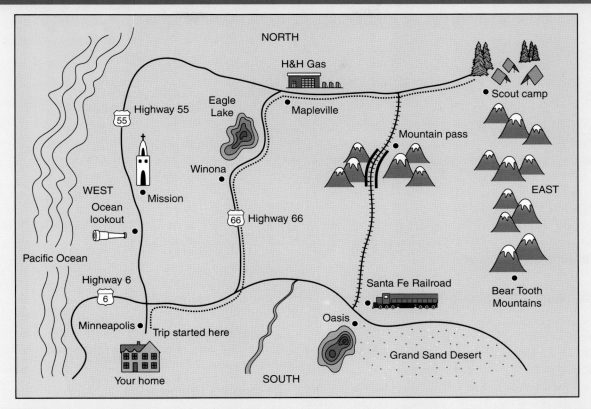

The dotted line on the map shows how you drove from your home to the Scout camp. The questions that follow are about the map. Circle the best answer on this sheet.

1. When you started your trip, in what direction did you go first?
   north   south   east   west

2. If you had walked west from Minneapolis, what would you have come to?
   Great Sand Desert   ocean lookout   Pacific Ocean

3. When you got to Highway 66, what town did you pass first?
   Mapleville   Winona   H & H Gas

4. The mission is _____ of the Pacific Ocean.
   north   south   east   west

5. The Santa Fe Railroad runs _____ and _____.
   north   south   east   west

6. The Scout camp is _____ of H & H Gas.
   north   south   east   west

7. The oasis is _____ of Highway 66.
   north   south   east   west

8. From ocean lookout, what direction is the Bear Tooth mountain range?
   north   south   east   west

9. The first town west of the Scout camp is _____.
   Winona   H & H Gas   Mapleville

10. In the winter the birds fly _____.
    north   south   east   west

FIGURE 20.15 Map problems.

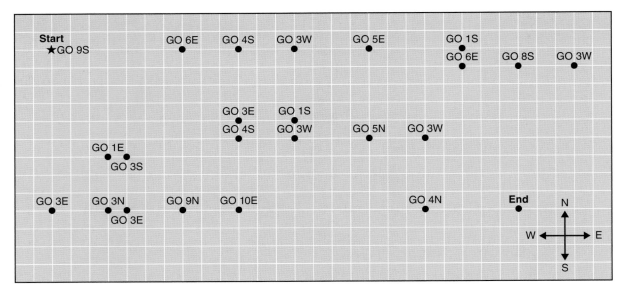

FIGURE 20.16 Dot-to-dot hike.

Cross-Country or Point-to-Point Orienteering

Ten checkpoints are set up over the entire school grounds or park area. Teachers develop a map of the area to be covered, and duplicate maps are made for all participants. Each participant uses a map and compass to find the checkpoints as quickly as possible. A compass is not necessary. As they begin, participants must quickly make decisions about the best route. Several master maps should be set out with the locations of the checkpoints. Participants copy the checkpoints from the master map onto their own maps. The time spent copying down the checkpoints can be included in the overall accumulated time.

Each checkpoint should have a secret letter, word, or name that students must record on some type of card to show that they actually visited the checkpoint. In regulation meets, a coded punch with a number or letter is used at each control site. These punches are available from the Silva Company, but they are not a necessity. Checkpoints can be a boundary cone, an index card, an envelope, or something similar.

Score Orienteering

In score orienteering, each checkpoint has a designated point value. The checkpoints that are hardest to find and farthest from the starting point are assigned the highest point totals. The object of the event is to accumulate the most points within a set time. Students are given a map of the area on which they copy the locations of the checkpoints from a master map. Students must visit as many sites as possible within the time limit and then return to the starting point. If they are late, they can be disqualified or assessed a penalty. Students use some type of standard card to record the clue at each checkpoint that they visit.

Descriptive Orienteering

This type of event requires a compass and pacing skills instead of a map. Students attempt to find the checkpoints as quickly as possible by following a bearing (90 degrees), a distance (50 yards [m]), and a descriptive clue (small tree). The descriptive clue can be eliminated for advanced participants. Students start at a designated master point and return to that point each time before starting toward the next point. In this way, teachers at the master point can monitor student progress throughout the meet. The checkpoints can all have letters, words, or team names. Each student is given a sheet similar to the one shown in figure 20.17. A more challenging variation is to give students only the bearing and distance to one checkpoint. When they find that checkpoint, they will find the bearing and distance posted for the next checkpoint. Students must find each checkpoint to get directions to the next point. Students can be started at different checkpoints.

Block Plan

Figure 20.18 is a sample block plan that offers a suggested 15-day unit for orienteering. This plan can be modified to fit a 5- or 10-day unit.

ORIENTEERING

Name _____ Date _____

In the answers column, fill in the keyword or letter that you find at each checkpoint.

Checkpoint	Bearing	Description	Distance	Answers
1	90°	Backstop	50 yd	
2	180°	Goalpost	35 yd	
3	230°	Cottonwood	75 m	
4	160°	Irrigation	100 m	
5	341°	Hoop	200 ft	
6	45°	Palo Verde	400 ft	
7	106°	Trash barrel	150 yd	
8	270°	Power pole	250 ft	
9	78°	Fence post	350 yd	
10	200°	Jumping pit	40 m	

FIGURE 20.17 Sample checkpoint handout.

Performance Objectives

These objectives could be used in a middle or high school unit on orienteering.

1. Identify the compass points.
2. Name the parts of a compass.
3. Find a compass bearing on a map.
4. Follow a compass bearing on the ground.
5. Shoot bearings on key points.
6. Identify map symbols.
7. Identify map distances.
8. Determine the pace for 100 yards (m).
9. Form a triangle using three bearings.
10. Form a square using four bearings.
11. Complete an orienteering course in a time designated by the teacher.

    Standard no. 1 = 5 points

    Standard no. 2 = 3 points

    Standard no. 3 = 1 point

12. Take a 10-question exam on orienteering.

    Score: 100% = 5 points

    90% = 4 points

    80% = 3 points

    70% = 2 points

    60% = 1 point

Traverse Climbing-Wall Activities

Climbing walls are an excellent way to develop strength and coordination while solving climbing challenges. Students can learn to cooperate with others, and accomplishment of a climbing task contributes to student self-esteem. A certain amount of risk taking is associated with climbing, but it is minimized by proper safety and minimal climbing heights. Most traverse walls in middle schools are about 10 feet (3 m) high and feature a red line that keeps climbers close to the floor. Additional safety mats are placed along the base of the wall. High school walls can be much higher and more sophisticated. A typical wall may be 40 feet (12 m) wide or wider and have 200 to 300 handholds. The handholds are often color-coded for level of difficulty (see figure 20.19).

Safety Rules

Climbing walls can be used safely in a physical education setting, but students must be made aware of and follow appropriate safety rules. Examples of rules include the following:

- Climbing walls are used only when a teacher is directly supervising the activity.
- Only soft-soled shoes are used during climbing activities.
- Climbers must have a spotter; climbing alone is not allowed.

1. Introduction	2. Review	3. Review	4. Review	5. Review
What is orienteering?	Directions and degrees	Maps, symbols, and so on	Compass and bearings	Map bearings
Brief history	**Teach**	**Teach**	**Teach**	Map symbols
Directions and degrees	Maps, symbols, scales, contours	Parts of compass	Landmark bearings	**Teach**
Dot-to-dot problems	**Activities**	How to hold	Map bearings	Pacing
Compass rose activity	Map the school	**Activities**	**Activities**	**Activities**
	Map squares	Taking a bearing	Scout map problem	Distance by pace
	Contour identification	Dial a bearing	Sea adventure	Triangle game
		Magnetic influence	Christmas tree	Square game
				Map symbol relay
6. Review	**7. Review**	**8. Teach**	**9. Review**	**10. Review**
Pacing	Orienteering	Magnetic declination	Pacing	Declination
Teach	**Activity**	**Activities**	Bearings	**Activities**
Orienteering	Descriptive meet—have students return to master table each time for the next bearing, clue, and distance	Declination problems	Orienteering	Descriptive meet (short)
Point-to-point activity		Meridian map and compass fun	**Activity**	Clues picked up at the next control
Score		Point-to-point activity	Point-to-point meet	Competitive compass game, or pacing by time and distance
Descriptive		Schoolyard compass game		
Relay				
Activities				
Taking a trip				
Numbers and numerals				
Destination unknown				
11. Review	**12. Activities**	**13.**	**14.**	**15.**
Materials for written exam	Relay orienteering meet	Written examination	Final score orienteering exam meet (off campus if possible)	Final point-to-point orienteering meet (off campus if possible)
Activities	Schoolyard compass game and competitive compass game for skill test	Pacing—distance by time		
Score orienteering meet (20 min)				
Landmark bearings for skill test				

FIGURE 20.18 Sample orienteering block plan.

FIGURE 20.19 Variety of handholds and footholds on a climbing wall.

- Climbing above the red line is not allowed. The climber's feet must stay below the red line at all times.
- Climbers are not to touch or interfere with another climber on the wall.
- Only climbers and spotters are allowed on the safety mats.
- Participants must climb down from the wall; jumping down is *not* allowed.

Basic Holds

Students need to learn the basic ways to climb on the wall. Explain and practice handholds and footholds on the wall at a low level before proceeding to climb. The following are basic holds:

- Pinch—This basic hold is performed by simply squeezing the hold between the thumb and fingers.
- Finger grip—Just the fingers are used to hold a rock while adjusting the legs to a stable rock position.
- Crimp—Grasp the hold with the fingers at the middle joint and wrap the thumb over the first joint of the index finger.
- Edge—This foothold uses the ball-to-toe part of the foot. Either side of the shoe can be used, that is, the front with the toe pointing or the outside edge of the shoe.
- Lock-off—A crimp grip is used on the hold, and the arm is bent at the elbow and held close to the climber's body. This hold is used to stabilize the body close to the wall so that the other arm can be used to reach for a new hold.

Individual Challenge Activities

A positive aspect of climbing walls is that students can use footholds to help them climb. This technique helps students who are overweight find success. Do not rush students who are challenged. Give them activities to do that are near the floor and let them determine when they are ready to challenge themselves. Climbing challenges are individual in nature; each student strives to improve his or her performance without concern for how others are climbing. The following are examples of climbing activities that can be used to motivate students to stay on the wall and practice their skills.

- Four-point hold—Climbers take a four-point rock position (each hand and foot on a separate rock) and move to four new rocks.
- Red-line climb—Students climb high enough to get footholds on rocks above the red line.
- Red line with challenges—Similar to the previous climb except that students are challenged to climb using only certain-colored rocks.
- Up and down—Students climb above the red line and then return to the floor using the same pathway (same rocks).
- Three-point hold—Students climb off the floor and below the red line. They balance themselves, lift a limb from a hold, and then try lifting a different limb.
- Catwalk—Climbers move without dragging their feet against the wall. The goal is to place the feet accurately on the next foothold.
- Rotation—Climbers establish a four-point hold and then try to rotate their bodies (left or right) until their backs are to the wall. If successful, they continue to rotate in the same direction until they face the wall.
- Move the treasure—Stationary climbers move a beanbag or similar object from one rock to another. Also, they can try picking up the treasure from the floor and placing it on a specified rock.
- Long traverse—Students start at one end of the wall and move to the other end. Allow climbers to move at a pace suited to them. If some students are faster climbers, they can descend to the floor, pass slower moving students, and continue their climb.

Partner Activities

Partner activities are motivating because they bring a social and cooperative aspect to climbing. Allow students to change partners regularly so that they learn to understand individual differences. Encourage students to be helpful but not to touch their partners while they are climbing.

- Point and move—One partner is on the floor, while the other partner assumes a four-point hold on the wall. The floor partner points to a handhold or foothold that is the next move the climber must make. The purpose is to challenge partners with reasonable moves, not impossible tasks. Change roles after five moves.
- Sightless climbing—The climbing partner puts on a blindfold, and the partner on the floor guides the climber. The partner on the floor describes the direction and distance of the move to the climber.
- Keep in touch—Partners are connected with a jump rope, each end of which a partner tucks into his or her pocket or waistband. No more than 6 inches (15 cm) of rope is tucked in so that this activity is challenging. Both partners begin climbing with the challenge of not losing contact (rope being pulled out).
- Obstacle course—The object is to climb through and over objects without touching them while climbing. Special holds for hoops and sticks are made so that these obstacles can be fastened to the wall.
- Gold and silver—Climbers work together to transport treasure from one point to another across the wall. After the climbers are on the wall, if they touch the floor, they must start over. Treasure can be an item such as a wand, hoop, or

20

racket. To increase the challenge, have students move two or three pieces of treasure.

- Climb and pass—The goal is for climbers to begin about 5 feet (1.5 m) apart on the wall and then pass their partners to the opposite side without touching the floor. They must pass each other and cannot go below the partner to pass.

Ropes Course Activities

Some schools may have a ropes course or access to one in the community. If so, the following are example activities. Ropes course activities involve obstacles that use ropes, cables, logs, trees, ladders, tires, swings, cargo nets, rings, and other equipment to present students with a challenge that usually has a degree of controlled risk. These obstacles require students to climb, swing, crawl, and balance themselves. Beneath many of the obstacles are water, mud, people, cargo nets, and trees. All the activities are completed with student spotters or a safety belay line of some type under the direct supervision of the teacher. The activities can be linked together in sequence, or they can be used as separate challenges. Certain activities require strength and endurance, whereas others require balance and coordination. The ropes course activities can function as lead-up activities for rock climbing, caving, rappelling, or other adventure activities.

Teachers need to be certain that students begin with activities containing little risk. Student safety is always the most important factor. Generally, the beginning ropes course activities are situated close to the ground with many spotters available, thereby assuring students that little danger is involved. As they gain knowledge, experience, physical skill, and confidence, students can move to higher and more challenging obstacles. Teachers need to be aware of varying ability levels of students and not require all students to attempt the same activities unless they are ready for the obstacle. Students who display fear of these types of activities should be encouraged rather than pushed.

Ropes course activities, like any other adventure activity, can be risky and have the potential for physical injury if safety factors are overlooked. We recommend that teachers seek the advice of experienced ropes course builders before constructing any of these activities (see References and Suggested Readings at the end of this chapter). Ropes course activities can be built into the existing environment, or posts and logs can be placed in the ground. The following are examples of ropes course activities that could be used in this type of program.

Commando Crawl

In this activity, the student crawls across the top of a 2-inch (5 cm) manila hawser rope by placing the chest on the rope and passing the rope under the body (see figure 20.20). One foot is hooked over the top of the rope and the other leg hangs down for balance. The student slowly pulls her or his way across the rope by using the arms and the top leg. The student should be spotted on both sides of the rope in case of a fall. If a fall does occur, the spotters should catch the student and slowly lower her or him to the ground. The rope should be secured to two trees, 4 to 5 feet (1.2 to 1.5 m) above the ground. A bowline knot can be used on one side of the rope, and the opposite side should be wrapped around the tree and tied off with two half hitches. Wooden blocks may be secured to the trees below the rope to prevent the rope from slipping.

FIGURE 20.20   Commando crawl.

Tire Swing

Students swing across a set of tires that are secured to a top rope or cable (see figure 20.21). The tires are set at varying heights above the ground, anywhere from 3 to 4 feet (90 to 120 cm) high. The tires should be 3 to 4 feet (90 to 120 cm) apart. The top cable should be 10 to 12 feet (3 to 4 m) above the ground. To prevent a fall, spotters should be placed on both sides of the students as they proceed.

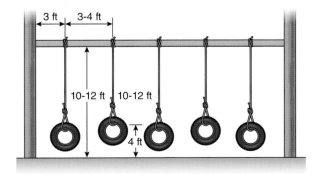

FIGURE 20.21   Tire swing.

Kitten Crawl

Students crawl along two parallel inclined ropes that are secured at 5 feet (1.5 m) high at one end and at 2 feet (60 cm) high at the other end. Students should be on all fours and can slowly crawl up or down the rope (see figure 20.22). Spotters should be aware that the participants can fall through the middle of the two ropes as well as over the sides. Wooden blocks can be used to prevent the rope from slipping down on the secured ends. The height of the ropes can be varied according to the ability levels of the participants.

FIGURE 20.22   Kitten crawl.

Two-Rope Bridge

Two parallel ropes about 5 to 6 feet (1.5 to 1.8 m) apart are secured to trees or posts. The students stand sideways on the bottom rope and hold on to the top rope with their hands. They slowly slide their way across the rope (see figure 20.23). The height of the bottom rope should be less than 5 to 6 feet (1.5 to 1.8 m) for beginners. If the height of the bottom rope is higher than 6 feet (1.8 m), then a belay (securing a rope by wrapping it on a pin, cleat, or other fixed object) or other safety system should be used. A 15-foot (5 m) swami belt (a simple harness worn around the waist, used to attach a person to a rope) or waist loop of 1-inch (2.5 cm) tubular nylon flat rope can be wrapped around the student's waist and attached with a carabiner to a belay line. The top of the belay line can be attached with a carabiner to the top rope of the bridge. Spotters can be used for lower bridges, and they should follow the participant across the rope and be ready for a fall.

FIGURE 20.23   Two-rope bridge.

Three-Rope Bridge

The three-rope bridge has been used in many areas for crossing various ravines, rivers, and mountain passes. It consists of two parallel ropes about waist high for handholds and a bottom rope to walk on (see figure 20.24). A number of V-shaped ropes should be placed about 2 feet (60 cm) apart along the bridge to support all three ropes. A rope or cable across the top of the bridge should be constructed for attaching a safety line. A swami belt can be attached to the student and then clipped to the top line with carabiners and a piece of nylon webbing. The height of the bridge can vary; it can be low or high depending on the local area. If possible, place the bridge over a natural obstacle to add to the excitement. Use wooden blocks to prevent the ropes from slipping and to ensure that the ropes are kept tight.

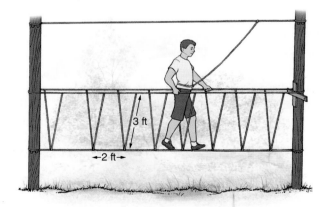

FIGURE 20.24   Three-rope bridge.

20

Tension Traverse

The student balances and moves across a rope suspended between two trees. A top support rope is attached to one tree, and the student applies tension on this rope for balance while sliding across the rope. The student should slide sideways across the rope. One hand should hold the support rope at the waist, and the other hand should hold the rope above the head (see figure 20.25). The bottom rope is 2 to 3 feet (60 to 90 cm) above the ground and should always be taut. Again, wooden blocks should be used to prevent the rope from slipping down. Spotters should be used for safety, and students should be instructed to let go of the support rope and jump off if they are going to fall. If they hold on to the top rope while falling, they will swing into the tree or post.

FIGURE 20.26 Triangle tension traverse.

FIGURE 20.25 Tension traverse.

Triangle Tension Traverse

This activity is similar to the tension traverse and adds two more sides to the activity. The bottom rope is placed in a triangle, and the student starts at one intersection of the triangle (see figure 20.26). The student balances and moves around the triangle with a top support rope similar to the straight tension traverse. Spotters should be used for safety as the students move around the triangle. The height of the bottom rope should be 4 to 5 feet (1.2 to 1.5 m), and it should be taut and blocked to prevent slipping.

Balance Beam

The balance beam is a log attached between two trees or posts, anywhere from 5 to 10 feet (1.5 to 3.0 m) high (see figure 20.27). This obstacle can be used as a bridge between two other rope activities. The students simply walk across the beam. If several beams are used in a course, they can be constructed at varying heights. If the beam is higher than 5 feet (1.5 m), a top safety belay line should be used. If the beam is lower than 5 feet (1.5 m), then student spotters are necessary for safety.

FIGURE 20.27 Balance beam.

Inclined Log

The inclined log is simply a balance beam placed at an angle (see figure 20.28). Beginners can more easily walk on an obstacle that moves from the ground to a higher level. Students can walk up the log, bear crawl on all fours, or hug the log as they move up, depending on their comfort level. A moving belay should be set up slightly off-center from the log so that students will not fall into the log. As students move up the height of the log, the belay person or spotters should move with them. The log should be notched to enhance the footing and nailed and lashed to the trees or posts for support.

FIGURE 20.29   Swinging log.

FIGURE 20.28   Inclined log.

Swinging Log

Students walk along a moving log that is suspended from trees by ropes (see figure 20.29). The log should never be more than 1 foot (30 cm) above the ground because falls will be frequent in this activity. All rocks, stumps, and objects should be cleared away from the area. The log should be notched where the ropes are attached to hold them in place. The upper attachment of the ropes should be blocked to prevent any slipping. Rubber tires can be nailed to the trees to prevent damage from the moving log. Participants need to move carefully to avoid falling on the log itself. Spotters can be used to help students keep their balance.

Cargo Net Jump

Students move up an inclined log to a jumping platform and then jump into a cargo net in the tucked position. The cargo net should be made of 1-inch (2.5 cm) manila rope with a small mesh (see figure 20.30). A rope ladder could be used to exit the net. The net can be secured 15 to 20 feet (5 to 6 m) above the ground or lower, and the jumping platform should be about 5 feet (1.5 m) higher than the net. The corners of the net should be secured and blocked to avoid slipping. These secured corners should be inspected regularly before each use. The instructor needs to be careful with students on a jumping platform. Students should be instructed to jump into the center of the net, and only one student should be allowed in the net at a time.

FIGURE 20.30   Cargo net jump.

Giant's Ladder

The students balance, jump, and swing up a giant ladder that is made of logs. The ladder encourages development of balance, strength, agility, and endurance. Students stand and balance on the first rung and then jump to the next rung and land on the chest or abdominal area (see figure 20.31). The feet swing free below the rung; students then pull upward onto the rung and get ready to move up to the next rung. The rungs become farther apart as the student moves higher on the ladder. The second rung is 4 to 5 feet (1.2 to 1.5 m) from the first, and the third rung is 5 to 6 feet (1.5 to 1.8 m) up the ladder. Students must be belayed throughout the climb. A top cable should be used to attach the belay rope. The instructor should keep a tight belay on students so that they do not swing into any of the logs.

FIGURE 20.31   Giant's ladder.

LEARNING AIDS

WEBSITES

Adventure Activities

www.adventurehardware.com
www.jmu.edu/kinesiology/hpainstitute/documents/CooperativeGames.pdf
www.pa.org

Hiking and Backpacking

https://us.humankinetics.com/products/hiking-and-backpacking

Everlast Climbing: Climbing Wall Activities

https://everlastclimbing.com/pages/climbing-wall-activities

Fly-Fishing

www.flyfishinginschools.org/
www.tu.org

Geocaching

www.geocaching.com
www.natureplaywa.org.au/library/1/file/Geocaching/Lesson1.pdf

Orienteering

www.orienteering.org
www.pecentral.org/lessonideas/ViewLesson.asp?ID=6510#.XKI-LaR7mUk

REFERENCES AND SUGGESTED READINGS

Casten, C. (2011). *Lesson plans for dynamic physical education for secondary school students* (7th ed.) San Francisco, CA: Pearson Higher Education/Benjamin Cummings.

Darst, P., & Armstrong, G. (1991). *Outdoor adventure activities for school and recreation programs.* Prospect Heights, IL: Waveland Press.

Doody, A.J. (2002). Climbing and challenge course. In N. Dougherty (Ed.), *Physical activity and sport for the secondary school student* (5th ed.). Reston, VA: NASPE and AAHPERD.

Geary, D. (1995). *Using a map and compass.* Mechanicsburg, PA: Stackpole Books.

Hammes, R. (2007, May/June). Orienteering with adventure education: New games for the 21st century. *Strategies,* 7–13.

Ibrahim, H. (1993). *Outdoor education.* Dubuque, IA: Brown & Benchmark.

Kjellstrom, B. (1994). *Be expert with map and compass* (5th ed.). New York, NY: Macmillan.

Mood, D.P., Musker, F.F., & Rink, J.E. (2007). *Sports and recreational activities* (14th ed.). Boston, MA: McGraw-Hill.

O'Brien, J. (2002). Orienteering. In N. Dougherty (Ed.), *Physical activity and sport for the secondary school student* (5th ed.). Reston, VA: NASPE and AAHPERD.

Orlick, T. (1982). *The second cooperative sports and games book.* New York, NY: Pantheon Books/Random House.

Renfrew, T. (1997). *Orienteering.* Champaign, IL: Human Kinetics.

Rohnke, K. (1984). *Silver bullets: A guide to initiative problems, adventure games, and trust activities.* Dubuque, IA: Kendall/Hunt.

Rohnke, K., Tait, C., Wall, J., & Rodgers, D. (2007). *The complete ropes course manual.* Dubuque, IA: Kendall/Hunt and Wall's Outdoor Associates.

Schmottlach, N., & McManama, J. (2010). *The physical education handbook* (12th ed.). San Francisco, CA: Pearson Higher Education/Benjamin Cummings.

Webster, S. (1989). *Ropes course safety manual: An instructor's guide to initiatives and low and high elements.* Dubuque, IA: Kendall/Hunt.

20

GLOSSARY

adapted physical education An individualized program designed to meet the unique needs of an individual student.

adapted sport Sport modified to meet the unique needs of people with disabilities.

agility The ability of the body to change position rapidly and accurately while moving.

assessment The measurement or collection of information regarding student performance of skills, knowledge, and attitudes taught in physical education classes.

authentic assessment A performance assessment that determines how successful a student is in the application of skills in a gamelike setting.

balance The body's ability to maintain a state of equilibrium while remaining stationary or moving.

ballistic stretches Stretches involving quick bouncing movements.

body composition The proportion of body fat to lean body mass.

cardiorespiratory endurance The ability of the heart, blood vessels, and respiratory system to deliver oxygen efficiently over an extended time.

chronological age The age of a person as measured from birth to a given date.

content standards Fixed goals for student learning that determine what students should know and be able to do when they complete their schooling.

cooperative learning A learning style in which students depend on others to achieve group goals.

coordination The ability of the body to perform more than one motor task smoothly and successfully at the same time.

developmental age The age at which a person functions emotionally, physically, cognitively, and socially.

direct instruction style A teacher-centered teaching style that is most effective for teaching beginning levels of physical skills and fitness activities such as aerobic routines and martial arts.

discipline Dealing with unacceptable behavior and behavior that disrupts the flow and continuity of teaching and learning.

dynamic stretches Stretching that involves moving parts of the body, gradually increasing range of motion or speed of movement or both.

Education for All Handicapped Children Act Legislation that introduced new requirements, vocabulary, and concepts into physical education programs across the United States, including individualized educational programs (IEPs), mainstreaming, least restrictive environments, zero reject, and progressive inclusion.

emotional characteristics A person's ability to deal with challenges and bounce back from them, not how they respond in any given moment.

evaluation The process of using the assessment information to make a judgment on student performance.

fitness activities Make up 23 to 27% of lesson, focused on the development of physical fitness.

flexibility The range of movement through which a joint or sequence of joints can move.

formal assessment Assessment with the intent to affect grading procedures.

fundamental motor skills Skills that are basic to full functioning and quality of life.

grading A composite score that incorporates the information and data gathered through the assessment and evaluation process.

guided discovery (convergent) style An inquiry style of instruction in which the teacher leads students to discover one planned solution to a given problem.

health-related physical fitness Exercises done to maintain or improve physical health, particularly in the categories of cardiorespiratory endurance, muscular strength and endurance, body composition, and flexibility.

inclusion The integration of students with disabilities into a regular class to receive physical education.

individualized educational program (IEP) Identifies the student's unique qualities and determines educationally relevant strengths and weaknesses. A plan is then devised based on the diagnosis.

individualized style An instructional approach that uses learning packets and resources centers that leads to self-paced learning.

Individuals with Disabilities Education Act (IDEA) of 2004 A United States law that mandates equity, accountability, and excellence in education for children with disabilities. It defines physical education as a necessary component of special education for student ages 3 to 21.

informal assessment Assessment conducted to obtain knowledge about student performance but not for use in the determination of grades.

inquiry style A learning style in which students are placed in situations where they must inquire, speculate, reflect, analyze, and discover.

instructional cues Words that quickly and efficiently communicate to the learner proper technique and performance of skills or movement tasks.

instructional feedback A practical strategy for monitoring student learning in response to instruction and providing prompts to students to confirm, refine, or clarify their misunderstandings.

intellectual characteristics Something related to or using the mind or intellect.

introductory (warm-up) activity First 6 to 10% of lesson, intended to prepare student for activity.

knowledge of performance Intrinsic or extrinsic feedback related to the process of a skill after it has been performed.

knowledge of results Extrinsic feedback related to the product or outcome of a skill after it has been performed.

least restrictive environment Refers to the idea that not all individuals can do all the same activities in the same environment. The focus should be on placing students into settings that offer the best opportunity for educational advancement.

lesson focus and game activity Makes up 50 to 66% of lesson; instructional portion of the lesson focusing on skill development, cognitive learning, and enhancement of affective domain.

locomotor skills Used to move the body from one pace to another or to project the body upward.

management Techniques and strategies for moving, organizing, and grouping students for instructional purposes and developing appropriate behavior during class

manipulative skills Skills needed for objective manipulation that help in games and lifetime activities.

mastery learning (outcomes-based) style An instructional approach that takes a terminal target skill and divides it into progressive subskills.

mental practice Thinking about the successful performance of a motor skill in a quiet, relaxed environment.

movement concepts The ideas needed to modify or improve skill; including body awareness, space awareness, qualities of movement, and relationships.

movement themes The movement experiences needed to develop fundamental skills.

muscular endurance The ability to exert force over an extended period.

muscular strength The ability of muscles to exert force.

nonlocomotor skills Stationary or static skills.

outcomes The knowledge and skills that students should attain in physical education, notably in physical activity and health.

physical characteristics Defining traits or features about the body. These aspects are visually apparent but provide no other knowledge about the person.

organizing center Common theme that drives curriculum development.

physical education A learning process that focuses on knowledge, attitudes, and behaviors relative to physical activity.

physical education curriculum A framework of student-centered physical activities that promotes physical activity and skill development. A curriculum is a delivery system that gives sequence and direction to the learning experiences of students. Curriculum is based on a theoretical framework in addition to local, state, and national standards already established.

Physical Education Curriculum Analysis Tool A tool developed to assist in the development and enhancement of programs for the purpose of influencing school-aged students' physical activity behaviors. It is designed to analyze curricula content and student assessment.

power The ability to transfer energy explosively into force.

problem-solving (divergent) style An inquiry style of learning in which students move to the discovery of multiple correct answers to a problem.

proximity A teacher's nearness to his or her students during a lesson.

reaction time The response time it takes to move after a person realizes the need to act.

reciprocal teaching style A form of cooperative learning in which several students are involved with different roles, such as a doer, retriever, and observer.

rhythmic movement Motion that possesses regularity and predictable pattern.

skill-related physical fitness Also known as performance fitness; the ability to perform during games and sports and includes categories of agility, balance, coordination, power, reaction time, and speed.

social characteristics The characteristics of the type of person you are in society.

specialized skills The skills needed to be successful in sport, games, adventure activities, tumbling, swimming, dance, etc.

speed The ability of the body to perform movement in a short time.

static stretches Low and sustained stretches in which the person reaches the point of mild discomfort.

student objectives Outcomes expected to demonstrate student learning. They are usually written in behavioral terms and contain four key characteristics: (1) actor, or student, (2) behavior that is observable and measurable, (3) conditions or environment in which the behavior should occur, and (4) degree or criterion for success that can be measured.

task (station) style An instructional approach that involves selecting and arranging tasks for students to practice in specific learning areas called stations.

Title IX of the Educational Amendments Act of 1972 The main purpose was to prohibit discrimination based on sex in any education program or activity that is federally funded.

transitions Periods when, under teacher direction, students move as a group or switch to a different task. Transitions include organizing students into groups, changing from one part of the lesson to another, and issuing and putting away equipment. Transitions are an integral part of effective instruction.

value orientations Reflect philosophical positions that can be operationally defined within educational settings. They describe educational belief systems that influence curricular decisions.

INDEX

Note: The italicized *f* and *t* following page numbers refer to figures and tables, respectively.

ABOUT THE AUTHORS

Timothy A. Brusseau, PhD, is an associate professor and director of health and kinesiology at the University of Utah. Tim is a national expert on school-based multicomponent interventions, particularly comprehensive school physical activity programs (CSPAPs). He has received numerous awards and recognition for his teaching and research. He has 128 peer-reviewed publications on the topics of physical education, physical activity, and health and has made more than 175 conference presentations on topics related to physical education and physical activity programs.

Courtesy of University of Kentucky.

Heather Erwin, PhD, is department chair and a professor in the department of kinesiology and health promotion at the University of Kentucky. She is widely published in journals devoted to physical education and activity and has made more than 100 presentations to state, national, and international audiences on quality physical education programs and related topics. Heather also has been recognized throughout her career for her scholarship and teaching, most recently as a Teacher Who Made a Difference at the University of Kentucky and as KAHPERD's University Physical Education Teacher of the Year in 2019.

Paul W. Darst is a professor emeritus at Arizona State University in the area of physical education teacher preparation. His research and teaching focus on secondary school physical education curriculum, methods of teaching in the secondary schools, and activity habits of middle and high school students. He has been active professionally at the state, district, and national levels of SHAPE America—formerly known as American Alliance for Health, Physical Education, Recreation and Dance (AAHPERD)—and has received numerous honors and speaking invitations. In addition to coauthoring multiple editions of *Dynamic Physical Education for Secondary School Students* with Bob Pangrazi, Darst also authored *Outdoor Adventure Activities for School and Recreation Programs* (Waveland Press), *Analyzing Physical Education and Sport Instruction* (Human Kinetics), and *Cycling* (Scott, Foresman and Company, Sport for Life Series). He has written many articles and made numerous presentations to teachers on new ideas in teaching and on working with students.

Robert P. Pangrazi, PhD, taught for 31 years at Arizona State University in the department of exercise science and physical education and is now a professor emeritus. An honor fellow of SHAPE America—formerly known as American Alliance for Health, Physical Education, Recreation and Dance (AAHPERD)—Dr. Pangrazi was also presented with that organization's Margie Hanson Distinguished Service Award. Dr. Pangrazi is also a fellow in the American Kinesiology Association, formerly known as the Academy of Kinesiology and Physical Education. He is a best-selling author of numerous books and texts over the years, including multiple editions of *Dynamic Physical Education for Elementary School Children* and *Dynamic Physical Education for Secondary School Children*. He and Chuck Corbin coedited *Toward a Better Understanding of Physical Fitness and Activity: Selected Topics* for the President's Council on Physical Fitness and Sports. In addition to numerous other books and texts, he has written many journal articles and scholarly papers for publication.

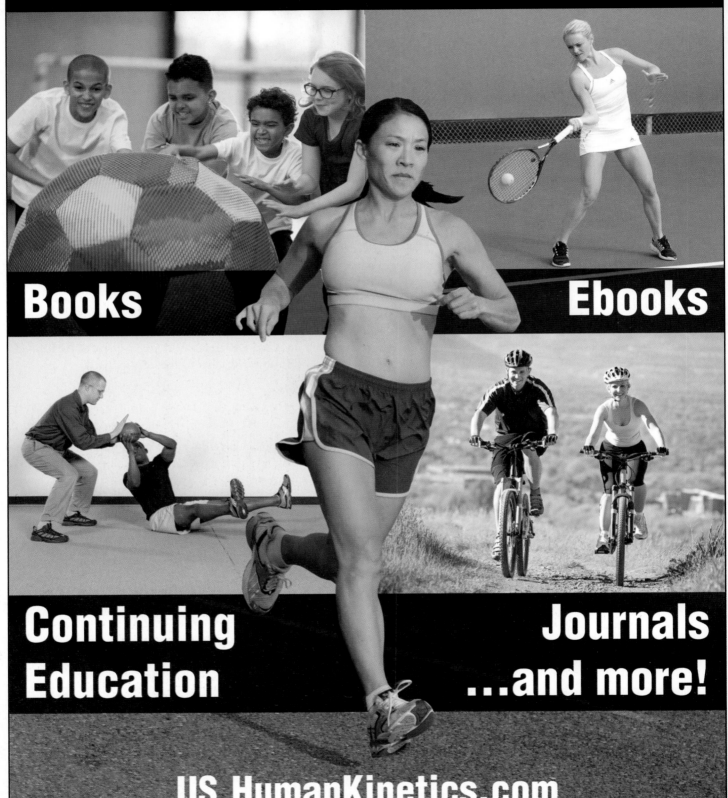